Revenue Statistics 2022

THE IMPACT OF COVID-19 ON OECD TAX REVENUES

1965-2021

OECD
BETTER POLICIES FOR BETTER LIVES

Please cite this publication as:
OECD (2022), *Revenue Statistics 2022: The Impact of COVID-19 on OECD Tax Revenues*, OECD Publishing, Paris, https://doi.org/10.1787/8a691b03-en.

ISBN 978-92-64-56018-5 (print)
ISBN 978-92-64-75818-6 (pdf)
ISBN 978-92-64-70452-7 (HTML)
ISBN 978-92-64-98266-6 (epub)

Revenue Statistics
ISSN 2522-7696 (print)
ISSN 2522-770X (online)

Photo credits: Cover © some of the graphic elements in the main cover illustration were adapted from Freepik.com.

Corrigenda to publications may be found on line at: www.oecd.org/about/publishing/corrigenda.htm.

Foreword

This annual publication provides internationally comparative data on tax levels and tax structures in member countries of the Organisation for Economic Cooperation and Development (OECD). The taxes imposed in each country are presented in a standardised framework based upon the OECD classification of taxes and its Interpretative Guide as contained in Annex A to this Report. The data for the Report has, for the most part, been provided by Delegates to Working Party No.2 (WP2) on Tax Policy Analysis and Tax Statistics of the Committee on Fiscal Affairs. The OECD acknowledges the co-operation of the International Monetary Fund, whose classification of tax revenues in the *Government Finance Statistics Manual 2014* is in many respects similar to that of the OECD. The most important of the other classifications currently in use is the System of National Accounts (henceforth referred to as SNA) and the European System of Integrated Economic Accounts of EU member states (henceforth referred to as ESA), which is primarily an elaboration of SNA, though differing from it in certain respects. Subject to a few exceptions, SNA/ESA figures can be reconciled with the figures in the present Report, since SNA criteria and definitions have been adopted unless the contrary is specifically indicated.

The material is organised in six chapters. Chapter 1 summarises tax trends over the past six decades, with a focus on tax-to-GDP ratios, tax structures and taxes by level of government. It also discusses the treatment of non-wastable tax credits and provides information on financing of social security-type benefits. This year's issue also carries in Chapter 2 a special feature on "The impact of COVID-19 on OECD tax revenues". Chapter 3 contains a set of comparative statistical tables for years 1965-2021. Chapter 4 provides country tables with tax revenue and tax-to-GDP ratios broken down by selected tax categories and by level of government for years between 1990 and 2020. Two memorandum tables show how countries finance their social benefits and report taxes and social security contributions paid by general government as a percentage of GDP. Chapter 5, only available online, provides statistical tables with a detailed breakdown of tax revenues by country between 1965 and 2020. Two memorandum tables show how countries finance their social benefits, and report taxes and social security contributions paid by general government in national currency. Chapter 6, which is also only available online, attributes tax revenues to general government by the following sub-sectors: central, state, local and social security funds. It contains tables that provide a detailed breakdown of tax revenues by country between 1975 and 2020. Because of space limitations, Chapters 4, 5 and 6 show data for selected years between 1965 and 2020; data for the years not shown are available online.

Revenue Statistics 2022 has been produced by the OECD's Centre Centre for Tax Policy and Administration (CTPA). The authors of this edition were Alexander Pick, Nicolás Miranda and Michael Sharratt. The special feature was written by Alexander Pick, Nicolás Miranda and Jingjing Xia. The authors would like to thank colleagues in the OECD for their invaluable comments and practical support in finalising the publication, including David Bradbury, Bert Brys, Richard Clarke, Kurt Van Dender, Karena Garnier, Natalie Lagorce and Violet Sochay in CTPA, and the Statistical Editors and Content Management Team in the Press and Communications Directorate. Stephanie Coic in the Development Co-operation Directorate designed the cover. The authors would also like to thank WP2 delegates and their colleagues working in national administrations for their input and comments.

Table of contents

Foreword 3

Executive summary 10

1 Tax revenue trends 1965-2021 12
Tax-to-GDP ratios 13
Tax structures 21
Taxes by level of government 25
Non-wastable tax credits 30
Financing of social security-type benefits in OECD countries 32

2 The impact of COVID-19 on OECD tax revenues 35
Introduction 36
Overview: changes to total tax revenues, GDP and the tax-to-GDP ratio 36
Tax policy reforms and revenue trends in 2021 40
Changes in revenue by tax type in 2020 and 2021 48
References 50
Annex 2.A. Changes in tax-to-GDP ratios by country and tax type 51

3 Tax levels and tax structures, 1965-2021 55

4 Country tables, 1990-2020 77
4.1. Tax revenue and % of GDP by selected tax category and by level of government 78
4.2. Memorandum tables 155

5 Detailed country tables, 1965-2020 158
5.1. Tax revenues 159
5.2. Memorandum tables 265

6 Tax revenues by subsectors of general government 280
6.1. Country tables 1975, 1985, 1995, 2005 and 2020 281

Annex A. The OECD classification of taxes and interpretative guide 320

FIGURES

Figure 1.1. Trends in tax-to-GDP ratios, 1965-2021p (as % of GDP) 14
Figure 1.2. Changes in tax-to-GDP ratios, p.p., 2020-21p and 2010-21p 16

Figure 1.3. Relative changes in nominal tax revenues and nominal GDP (%), 2020-21p 18
Figure 1.4. Tax to GDP ratios in 2020 and 2021p (as % of GDP) 19
Figure 1.5. Tax structures in 2020 (as % of total tax revenue) 21
Figure 1.6. Trends in tax structures (1965-2020, as % of total tax revenue) 22
Figure 1.7. Composition of social security contributions, as % of total social security contributions, 2020 23
Figure 1.8. Share of general consumption tax revenues (left panel) and specific consumption revenues (right panel) as % of total revenues, 1975-2020 24
Figure 1.9. Composition of revenues of federal or central government (left) and sub-national government (right), 2020 28
Figure 1.10. Composition of earmarked financing for social security-type benefits, 2020 32
Figure 1.11. Tax-to-GDP ratios and earmarked social security financing (% of GDP, 2020) 33
Figure 2.1. Changes in nominal tax and nominal GDP, 2020-2021 37
Figure 2.2. Changes in nominal tax and nominal GDP, all years 38
Figure 2.3. Unemployment rate: pre-crisis, peak, and most recent 41
Figure 2.4. Composition of GDP (expenditure approach), 2019-21 43
Figure 2.5. Changes in tax revenues by category as a share of GDP, 2020-21 44
Figure 2.6. Change between preliminary and final data for main tax types, 2020 46
Figure 2.7. Decomposition of change in OECD tax-to-GDP ratios by tax category, 2020-21 47
Figure 2.8. Distribution of changes in revenues by tax types 49

Annex Figure 2.A.1. Changes in tax-to-GDP ratios, 2019-2021, by tax type 53

TABLES

Table 1.1. Revenue Statistics: overview 15
Table 1.2. Tax structures in the OECD area, selected years (unweighted average as % of GDP) 20
Table 1.3. Attribution of tax revenues to sub-sectors of general government as % of total tax revenue, federal countries 26
Table 1.4. Attribution of tax revenues to sub-sectors of general government as % of total tax revenue, unitary countries 27
Table 1.5. Levies collected on behalf of the European Union, as % of GDP 29
Table 1.6. Effect of alternative treatments of non-wastable tax credits, 2020 31
Table 2.1. Individual tax types used in this chapter 39
Table 2.2. Comparison of changes in nominal tax revenues and nominal GDP, 2020-21 40
Table 2.3. Distribution of nominal revenue changes by tax category and of GDP 48
Table 3.1. Total tax revenue as % of GDP 57
Table 3.2. Total tax revenue in billions of US dollars at market exchange rates 58
Table 3.3. Tax revenue of main headings as % of GDP, 2020 59
Table 3.4. Tax revenue of main headings as % of total tax revenue, 2020 60
Table 3.5. Tax revenue of main headings as % of GDP, 2021p 61
Table 3.6. Tax revenue of main headings as % of total tax revenue, 2021p 62
Table 3.7. Taxes on income and profits (1000) as % of GDP and as % of total tax revenue 63
Table 3.8. Taxes on personal income (1100) as % of GDP and as % of total tax revenue 64
Table 3.9. Taxes on corporate income (1200) as % of GDP and as % of total tax revenue 65
Table 3.10. Social security contributions (2000) as % of GDP and as % of total tax revenue 66
Table 3.11. Taxes on payroll and workforce (3000) as % of GDP and as % of total tax revenue 67
Table 3.12. Taxes on property (4000) as % of GDP and as % of total tax revenue 68
Table 3.13. Taxes on goods and services (5000) as % of GDP and as % of total tax revenue 69
Table 3.14. Value added taxes (5111) as % of GDP and as % of total tax revenue 70
Table 3.15. Tax revenues of sub-sectors of general government as % of GDP 71
Table 3.16. Main central government taxes as % of total tax revenues of central government, 2020 72
Table 3.17. Main state government taxes as % of total tax revenues of state government, 2020 73
Table 3.18. Main local government taxes as % of total tax revenues of local government, 2020 74
Table 3.19. Gross domestic product for tax reporting years at market prices, in billions of national currency 75
Table 3.20. Exchange rates used, national currency per US dollar at market exchange rates 76
Table 4.1. Australia, tax revenue and % of GDP by selected tax category 79
Table 4.2. Australia, tax revenue and % of GDP by level of government and main taxes 80

Table 4.3. Austria, tax revenue and % of GDP by selected tax category 81
Table 4.4. Austria, tax revenue and % of GDP by level of government and main taxes 82
Table 4.5. Belgium, tax revenue and % of GDP by selected tax category 83
Table 4.6. Belgium, tax revenue and % of GDP by level of government and main taxes 84
Table 4.7. Canada, tax revenue and % of GDP by selected tax category 85
Table 4.8. Canada, tax revenue and % of GDP by level of government and main taxes 86
Table 4.9. Chile, tax revenue and % of GDP by selected tax category 87
Table 4.10. Chile, tax revenue and % of GDP by level of government and main taxes 88
Table 4.11. Colombia, tax revenue and % of GDP by selected tax category 89
Table 4.12. Colombia, tax revenue and % of GDP by level of government and main taxes 90
Table 4.13. Costa Rica, tax revenue and % of GDP by selected tax category 91
Table 4.14. Costa Rica, tax revenue and % of GDP by level of government and main taxes 92
Table 4.15. Czech Republic, tax revenue and % of GDP by selected tax category 93
Table 4.16. Czech Republic, tax revenue and % of GDP by level of government and main taxes 94
Table 4.17. Denmark, tax revenue and % of GDP by selected tax category 95
Table 4.18. Denmark, tax revenue and % of GDP by level of government and main taxes 96
Table 4.19. Estonia, tax revenue and % of GDP by selected tax category 97
Table 4.20. Estonia, tax revenue and % of GDP by level of government and main taxes 98
Table 4.21. Finland, tax revenue and % of GDP by selected tax category 99
Table 4.22. Finland, tax revenue and % of GDP by level of government and main taxes 100
Table 4.23. France, tax revenue and % of GDP by selected tax category 101
Table 4.24. France, tax revenue and % of GDP by level of government and main taxes 102
Table 4.25. Germany, tax revenue and % of GDP by selected tax category 103
Table 4.26. Germany, tax revenue and % of GDP by level of government and main taxes 104
Table 4.27. Greece, tax revenue and % of GDP by selected tax category 105
Table 4.28. Greece, tax revenue and % of GDP by level of government and main taxes 106
Table 4.29. Hungary, tax revenue and % of GDP by selected tax category 107
Table 4.30. Hungary, tax revenue and % of GDP by level of government and main taxes 108
Table 4.31. Iceland, tax revenue and % of GDP by selected tax category 109
Table 4.32. Iceland, tax revenue and % of GDP by level of government and main taxes 110
Table 4.33. Ireland, tax revenue and % of GDP by selected tax category 111
Table 4.34. Ireland, tax revenue and % of GDP by level of government and main taxes 112
Table 4.35. Israel, tax revenue and % of GDP by selected tax category 113
Table 4.36. Israel, tax revenue and % of GDP by level of government and main taxes 114
Table 4.37. Italy, tax revenue and % of GDP by selected tax category 115
Table 4.38. Italy, tax revenue and % of GDP by level of government and main taxes 116
Table 4.39. Japan, tax revenue and % of GDP by selected tax category 117
Table 4.40. Japan, tax revenue and % of GDP by level of government and main taxes 118
Table 4.41. Korea, tax revenue and % of GDP by selected tax category 119
Table 4.42. Korea, tax revenue and % of GDP by level of government and main taxes 120
Table 4.43. Latvia, tax revenue and % of GDP by selected tax category 121
Table 4.44. Latvia, tax revenue and % of GDP by level of government and main taxes 122
Table 4.45. Lithuania, tax revenue and % of GDP by selected tax category 123
Table 4.46. Lithuania, tax revenue and % of GDP by level of government and main taxes 124
Table 4.47. Luxembourg, tax revenue and % of GDP by selected tax category 125
Table 4.48. Luxembourg, tax revenue and % of GDP by level of government and main taxes 126
Table 4.49. Mexico, tax revenue and % of GDP by selected tax category 127
Table 4.50. Mexico, tax revenue and % of GDP by level of government and main taxes 128
Table 4.51. Netherlands, tax revenue and % of GDP by selected tax category 129
Table 4.52. Netherlands, tax revenue and % of GDP by level of government and main taxes 130
Table 4.53. New Zealand, tax revenue and % of GDP by selected tax category 131
Table 4.54. New Zealand, tax revenue and % of GDP by level of government and main taxes 132
Table 4.55. Norway, tax revenue and % of GDP by selected tax category 133
Table 4.56. Norway, tax revenue and % of GDP by level of government and main taxes 134
Table 4.57. Poland, tax revenue and % of GDP by selected tax category 135
Table 4.58. Poland, tax revenue and % of GDP by level of government and main taxes 136
Table 4.59. Portugal, tax revenue and % of GDP by selected tax category 137
Table 4.60. Portugal, tax revenue and % of GDP by level of government and main taxes 138
Table 4.61. Slovak Republic, tax revenue and % of GDP by selected tax category 139
Table 4.62. Slovak Republic, tax revenue and % of GDP by level of government and main taxes 140

Table 4.63. Slovenia, tax revenue and % of GDP by selected tax category 141
Table 4.64. Slovenia, tax revenue and % of GDP by level of government and main taxes 142
Table 4.65. Spain, tax revenue and % of GDP by selected tax category 143
Table 4.66. Spain, tax revenue and % of GDP by level of government and main taxes 144
Table 4.67. Sweden, tax revenue and % of GDP by selected tax category 145
Table 4.68. Sweden, tax revenue and % of GDP by level of government and main taxes 146
Table 4.69. Switzerland, tax revenue and % of GDP by selected tax category 147
Table 4.70. Switzerland, tax revenue and % of GDP by level of government and main taxes 148
Table 4.71. Türkiye, tax revenue and % of GDP by selected tax category 149
Table 4.72. Türkiye, tax revenue and % of GDP by level of government and main taxes 150
Table 4.73. United Kingdom, tax revenue and % of GDP by selected tax category 151
Table 4.74. United Kingdom, tax revenue and % of GDP by level of government and main taxes 152
Table 4.75. United States, tax revenue and % of GDP by selected tax category 153
Table 4.76. United States, tax revenue and % of GDP by level of government and main taxes 154
Table 4.77. Financing of social security benefits 156
Table 4.78. Social security contributions and payroll taxes paid by government, totals 157
Table 5.1. Australia: Details of tax revenue, 1965-2020 160
Table 5.2. Austria: Details of tax revenue, 1965-2020 162
Table 5.3. Belgium: Details of tax revenue, 1965-2020 166
Table 5.4. Canada: Details of tax revenue, 1965-2020 169
Table 5.5. Chile: Details of tax revenue, 1965-2020 172
Table 5.6. Colombia: Details of tax revenue, 1965-2020 174
Table 5.7. Costa Rica: Details of tax revenue, 1965-2020 176
Table 5.8. Czech Republic: Details of tax revenue, 1965-2020 178
Table 5.9. Denmark: Details of tax revenue, 1965-2020 181
Table 5.10. Estonia: Details of tax revenue, 1965-2020 185
Table 5.11. Finland: Details of tax revenue, 1965-2020 187
Table 5.12. France: Details of tax revenue, 1965-2020 190
Table 5.13. Germany: Details of tax revenue, 1965-2020 195
Table 5.14. Greece: Details of tax revenue, 1965-2020 198
Table 5.15. Hungary: Details of tax revenue, 1965-2020 200
Table 5.16. Iceland: Details of tax revenue, 1965-2020 204
Table 5.17. Ireland: Details of tax revenue, 1965-2020 206
Table 5.18. Israel: Details of tax revenue, 1965-2020 208
Table 5.19. Italy: Details of tax revenue, 1965-2020 210
Table 5.20. Japan: Details of tax revenue, 1965-2020 214
Table 5.21. Korea: Details of tax revenue, 1965-2020 217
Table 5.22. Latvia: Details of tax revenue, 1965-2020 220
Table 5.23. Lithuania: Details of tax revenue, 1965-2020 223
Table 5.24. Luxembourg: Details of tax revenue, 1965-2020 225
Table 5.25. Mexico: Details of tax revenue, 1965-2020 228
Table 5.26. Netherlands: Details of tax revenue, 1965-2020 230
Table 5.27. New Zealand: Details of tax revenue, 1965-2020 233
Table 5.28. Norway: Details of tax revenue, 1965-2020 236
Table 5.29. Poland: Details of tax revenue, 1965-2020 238
Table 5.30. Portugal: Details of tax revenue, 1965-2020 240
Table 5.31. Slovak Republic: Details of tax revenue, 1965-2020 243
Table 5.32. Slovenia: Details of tax revenue, 1965-2020 245
Table 5.33. Spain: Details of tax revenue, 1965-2020 248
Table 5.34. Sweden: Details of tax revenue, 1965-2020 251
Table 5.35. Switzerland: Details of tax revenue, 1965-2020 254
Table 5.36. Türkiye: Details of tax revenue, 1965-2020 257
Table 5.37. United Kingdom: Details of tax revenue, 1965-2020 259
Table 5.38. United States: Details of tax revenue, 1965-2020 262
Table 5.39. Financing social benefits 266
Table 5.40. Social security contributions and payroll taxes paid by government, details 270
Table 6.1. Australia, tax revenues by sub-sectors of government 282
Table 6.2. Austria, tax revenues by sub-sectors of government 283
Table 6.3. Belgium, tax revenues by sub-sectors of government 284
Table 6.4. Canada, tax revenues by sub-sectors of government 285

Table 6.5. Chile, tax revenues by sub-sectors of government 286
Table 6.6. Colombia, tax revenues by sub-sectors of government 287
Table 6.7. Costa Rica, tax revenues by sub-sectors of government 288
Table 6.8. Czech Republic, tax revenues by sub-sectors of government 289
Table 6.9. Denmark, tax revenues by sub-sectors of government 290
Table 6.10. Estonia, tax revenues by sub-sectors of government 291
Table 6.11. Finland, tax revenues by sub-sectors of government 292
Table 6.12. France, tax revenues by sub-sectors of government 293
Table 6.13. Germany, tax revenues by sub-sectors of government 294
Table 6.14. Greece, tax revenues by sub-sectors of government 295
Table 6.15. Hungary, tax revenues by sub-sectors of government 296
Table 6.16. Iceland, tax revenues by sub-sectors of government 297
Table 6.17. Ireland, tax revenues by sub-sectors of government 298
Table 6.18. Israel, tax revenues by sub-sectors of government 299
Table 6.19. Italy, tax revenues by sub-sectors of government 300
Table 6.20. Japan, tax revenues by sub-sectors of government 301
Table 6.21. Korea, tax revenues by sub-sectors of government 302
Table 6.22. Latvia, tax revenues by sub-sectors of government 303
Table 6.23. Lithuania, tax revenues by sub-sectors of government 304
Table 6.24. Luxembourg, tax revenues by sub-sectors of government 305
Table 6.25. Mexico, tax revenues by sub-sectors of government 306
Table 6.26. Netherlands, tax revenues by sub-sectors of government 307
Table 6.27. New Zealand, tax revenues by sub-sectors of government 308
Table 6.28. Norway, tax revenues by sub-sectors of government 309
Table 6.29. Poland, tax revenues by sub-sectors of government 310
Table 6.30. Portugal, tax revenues by sub-sectors of government 311
Table 6.31. Slovak Republic, tax revenues by sub-sectors of government 312
Table 6.32. Slovenia, tax revenues by sub-sectors of government 313
Table 6.33. Spain, tax revenues by sub-sectors of government 314
Table 6.34. Sweden, tax revenues by sub-sectors of government 315
Table 6.35. Switzerland, tax revenues by sub-sectors of government 316
Table 6.36. Türkiye, tax revenues by sub-sectors of government 317
Table 6.37. United Kingdom, tax revenues by sub-sectors of government 318
Table 6.38. United States, tax revenues by sub-sectors of government 319

Annex Table 2.A.1. Changes in tax-to-GDP ratios, 2020-2021, by tax type 51

Additional chapters

Two chapters are available on line only at: https://doi.org/10.1787/6e87f932-en

- Chapter 5. Detailed country tables
- Chapter 6. Tax revenues by subsectors of general government

Follow OECD Publications on:

https://twitter.com/OECD

https://www.facebook.com/theOECD

https://www.linkedin.com/company/organisation-eco-cooperation-development-organisation-cooperation-developpement-eco/

https://www.youtube.com/user/OECDiLibrary

https://www.oecd.org/newsletters/

This book has...

StatLinks

A service that delivers Excel® files from the printed page!

Look for the StatLink at the bottom of the tables or graphs in this book. To download the matching Excel® spreadsheet, just type the link into your Internet browser or click on the link from the digital version.

Executive summary

In 2021, the average OECD tax-to-GDP ratio rose by 0.6 percentage points (p.p.) to 34.1%, as countries recovered from the economic shock induced by the COVID-19 pandemic in 2020. Tax revenues increased by 12.8% in nominal terms on average across the OECD in 2021 according to preliminary data, while GDP rose by 10.5%. Although the OECD's tax-to-GDP ratio also increased in 2020 (by 0.2 p.p.), this was in the context of widespread declines in tax revenues and GDP in nominal terms.

In this publication, taxes are defined as compulsory, unrequited payments to the general government or to a supranational authority. They are unrequited in that the benefits provided by governments to taxpayers are not normally allocated in proportion to their payments. Taxes are classified by their base: income, profits and capital gains; payroll; property; goods and services; and other taxes. Compulsory social security contributions paid to general government are also treated as taxes. Revenues are analysed by level of government: federal or central; state; local; and social security funds. Detailed information on the classifications applied is set out in the Interpretative Guide in Annex A.

Tax levels in 2021

Across OECD countries, tax-to-GDP ratios in 2021 ranged from 16.7% in Mexico to 46.9% in Denmark. Between 2020 and 2021, the OECD average tax-to-GDP ratio increased from 33.6% to 34.1%.

- Tax-to-GDP ratios increased from the previous year in 24 of the 36 countries for which preliminary 2021 data is available, declined in 11 countries and remained unchanged in one.
- The largest increase in 2021 was observed in Norway, whose tax-to-GDP ratio rose by 3.4 p.p. due to an increase in corporate income tax (CIT) caused by higher revenues from petroleum extraction following exceptional declines the previous year. The second-largest increase was in Chile (2.8 p.p.), while increases in excess of 2 p.p. were also observed in Israel and Korea.
- Among the 11 countries where the tax-to-GDP ratio declined in 2021, the largest fall was seen in Hungary (2.1 p.p.). Canada, Iceland, Mexico and Türkiye also recorded a decline in their tax-to-GDP ratio of 1 p.p. or more. Decreases of less than one percentage point were observed in six countries.

Thirty-two OECD countries reported higher tax-to-GDP ratios in 2021 than in 2010, with the largest increases in the Slovak Republic, Korea and Spain (7.8 p.p., 7.5 p.p., and 7.1 p.p., respectively). Among the remaining six countries, tax levels in 2021 were more than 6 p.p. lower than in 2010 in Ireland and over 2 p.p. lower in Hungary.

Impact of COVID-19 on OECD tax revenues

A special feature in this publication looks at tax revenues during the second year of the COVID-19 pandemic, considering both the impact of the economic recovery and the evolution of tax policy on tax revenues in 2020 and 2021. It looks at changes in nominal taxes and nominal GDP, as well as changes in revenues from different tax types, to demonstrate which tax types contributed most to changes in the OECD average tax-to-GDP ratio in 2021.

Across the OECD, the priority for tax policy in 2021 was to support a recovery from the economic contraction observed in 2020. Measures introduced to support households and businesses in 2020 were withdrawn as economic activity picked up and the unemployment rate fell back to pre-pandemic levels in a majority of countries. Changes to labour taxation in 2021 were primarily intended to boost economic growth and promote equity, while CIT measures aimed to stimulate investment and innovation, especially in the green economy. In the area of value-added tax (VAT), e-invoicing and digital reporting requirements were widely adopted in 2021 as countries responded to the rapid growth of e-commerce during the pandemic. Towards the end of 2021, countries began to implement tax measures to shield households and firms from rising energy prices.

The special feature attributes the recovery in tax revenues across the OECD in 2021 to a rebound in revenues from CIT and VAT, which rose by 0.5 p.p. and 0.4 p.p. of GDP respectively in 2021. In 2020, CIT revenues recorded the largest decline of any major tax type, of 0.3 p.p., while VAT was unchanged as a share of GDP in the same year. Personal income tax (PIT) and social security contributions had underpinned the resilience of tax revenues in the OECD in 2020, both rising by 0.3 p.p.; in the second year of the pandemic, revenues from PIT remained unchanged as a share of GDP, while social security contributions declined by 0.2 p.p. Revenues from excises declined slightly in both years, while property taxes remained unchanged as a share of GDP in 2020 and 2021.

Tax structure in 2020

In 2020, the latest year in which final data is available for all OECD countries, social security contributions accounted for the largest share of tax revenues in the OECD, at just over one-quarter (26.6%), on average. Together with PIT (24.1%), these two tax types amounted to over half of tax revenues in OECD countries. VAT accounted for one-fifth of total revenues (20.2%), with other consumption taxes generating a further 11.9%. CIT accounted for 9.0% of total tax revenues in 2020, with property taxes (5.7%) and residual taxes accounting for the remainder.

Between 2019 and 2020, the average share of income taxes in total tax revenues declined by 0.2 p.p. to 33.7%, as declines in CIT offset increases in PIT. The average share of tax revenues from taxes on goods and services also decreased in 2020 (by 0.5 p.p.) while the share of social security contributions in the OECD average tax structure rose by 0.7 p.p.

Changes by level of government

On average, subnational governments received a higher share of tax revenues in 2020 than in 2019. The central government's average share of revenues in 2020 fell from 52.9% to 51.9% of general government revenue in federal countries and from 63.2% to 62.4% in unitary countries. In federal countries, 25.7% of tax revenues were received at subnational level on average (ranging from 5.3% in Austria to 49.4% in Canada), with approximately two-thirds of revenues received by state governments and one-third by local governments. In unitary countries, the share of local government revenues was 11.1% on average, ranging from less than 0.8% in Estonia to 36.8% in Sweden.

1 Tax revenue trends 1965-2021

Chapter 1 provides information on trends in tax revenues in OECD countries, including changes in tax-to-GDP ratios, tax structures, taxes by level of government, non-wastable tax credits and financing of social security-type benefits.

Revenue Statistics 2022 presents detailed internationally comparable data on tax revenues of OECD countries for all levels of government. The latest edition provides final data on tax revenues in 1965-2020. In addition, provisional estimates of tax revenues in 2021 are included for almost all OECD countries.[1]

Box 1.1. Revenue Statistics in OECD countries – definitions & classifications

In *Revenue Statistics 2022*, taxes are defined as compulsory, unrequited payments to the general government or to a supranational authority. Taxes are unrequited in the sense that benefits provided by government are not normally in proportion to their payments.

In the OECD classification, taxes are classified by the base of the tax:

- Income and profits (heading 1000)
- Compulsory social security contributions paid to general government that are treated as taxes (heading 2000)
- Payroll and workforce (heading 3000)
- Property (heading 4000)
- Goods and services (heading 5000)
- Other (heading 6000)

Much greater detail on the tax concepts, the classification of taxes and the accrual basis of reporting is set out in the OECD Interpretative Guide in Annex A of *Revenue Statistics 2022.*

All the averages presented in this summary are unweighted.

Tax-to-GDP ratios

Tax ratios for 2021 (provisional data)

New OECD data in the annual *Revenue Statistics 2022* publication show that, on average, tax revenues as a percentage of GDP (i.e. the tax-to-GDP ratio) were 34.1% in 2021, an increase of 0.6 percentage points (p.p.) of GDP relative to 2020. The increase in the OECD average tax-to-GDP ratio in 2021 occurred against the backdrop of a strong economic recovery following the contraction caused by the COVID-19 pandemic in 2020, which caused widespread falls in both nominal tax revenues and nominal GDP.

In 2021, GDP and nominal tax revenues both rebounded. The tax-to-GDP ratio increased in 24 of the countries for which full 2021 data are available, decreased in 11 and was unchanged in one; on average, the increases were larger than the decreases (1.2 p.p. versus 0.8 p.p.). Chapter 2 of this publication provides more information on the changes in tax revenues for each country, including for different types of taxes, and compares year-on-year changes in 2021 with those in 2020.

Figure 1.1. Trends in tax-to-GDP ratios, 1965-2021p (as % of GDP)

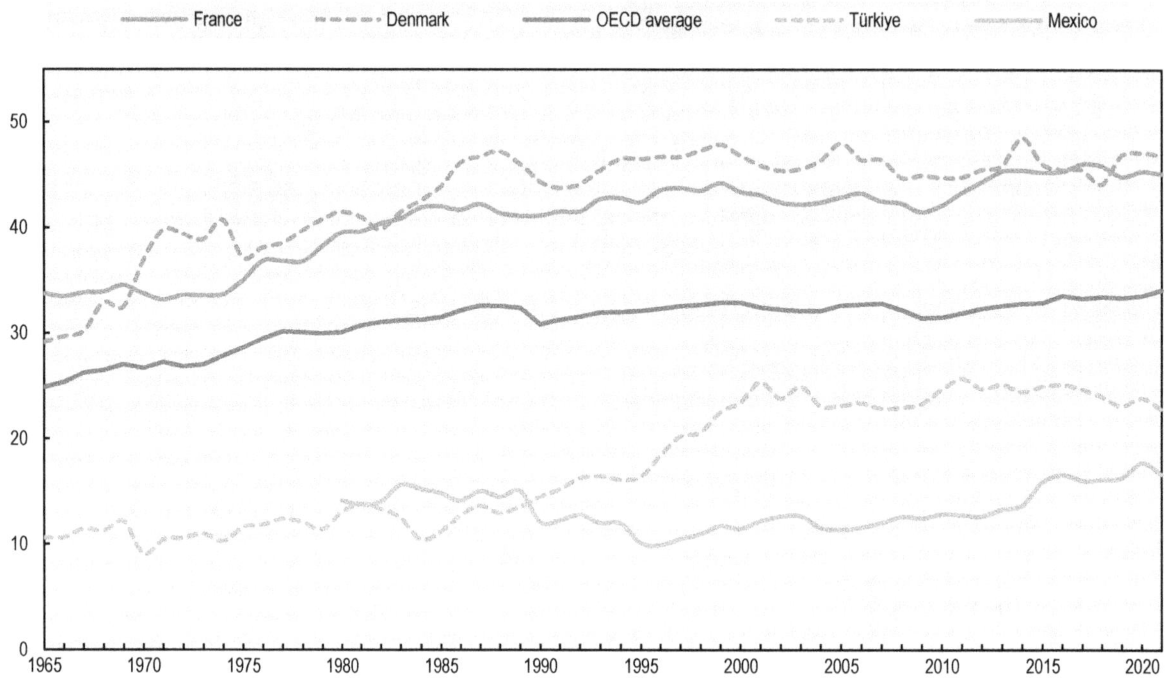

Notes: Data for 2021 are preliminary. The OECD average in 2021 is calculated by applying the unweighted average percentage change for 2021 in the 36 countries providing data for that year to the overall average tax-to-GDP ratio in 2020.
The 2016 OECD average tax-to-GDP ratio includes the one-off revenues from stability contributions in Iceland. Excluding these revenues, the OECD average tax-to-GDP ratio in 2016 would have been 33.6%.
Source: Table 3.1.

StatLink https://stat.link/w6m97e

Country tax-to-GDP ratios in 2021 varied considerably (Table 1.1), both across countries and from the level in 2020. Key observations include:

- Denmark had the highest tax-to-GDP ratio in 2021 (46.9%), and with the exceptions of 2017 and 2018, in which France was higher, has had the highest tax-to-GDP ratio of OECD countries since 2002. France had the second-highest tax-to-GDP ratio in 2021 (45.1%). Mexico had the lowest tax-to-GDP ratio (16.7%).
- Of the 36 countries for which data for 2021 are available, the ratio of tax revenues to GDP rose in 24 compared to 2020, remained unchanged in one and fell in 11.
- Between 2020 and 2021, the largest tax ratio increase was in Norway, at 3.4 p.p. This was largely due to an increase in revenues from corporate income tax (CIT) as a share of GDP (7.3 p.p.). The second largest increase was in Chile (2.8 p.p.), largely driven by an increase of 1.5 p.p. in revenues from value-added tax (VAT) (see Chapter 2 for more information). Israel and Korea were the other countries with an increase of over 2 p.p. (Figure 1.2).
- The largest fall in the tax-to-GDP ratio between 2020 and 2021 was in Hungary, at 2.1 p.p., due to falls in revenues from all major tax types as a share of GDP, in particular a decline of 1.0 p.p. in social security contributions[2]. Decreases larger than one percentage point were also seen in Iceland and Mexico (both 1.1 p.p.). In Iceland, this was largely due to a decline in revenues from personal income tax (PIT) and in Mexico to a decline in revenues from excises (1.1 p.p. and 0.4 p.p. respectively).

Table 1.1. Revenue Statistics: overview

	Tax revenue as % of GDP				Tax revenue as % of total tax revenue in 2020						
	2021p	2020	2019	2000	1100 Taxes on income, individuals (PIT)	1200 Taxes on income, corporates (CIT)	2000 Social security contributions (SSC)	4000 Taxes on property	5111 Value added taxes	Other consumption taxes[3]	All other taxes[4]
OECD Average[2]	**34.1**	**33.6**	**33.4**	**32.9**	**24.1**	**9.0**	**26.6**	**5.7**	**20.2**	**11.9**	**2.5**
Australia	..	28.5	27.7	30.4	40.1	18.8	0.0	10.1	12.4	14.1	4.5
Austria[1]	43.5	42.2	42.6	42.3	22.2	5.1	36.8	1.4	17.6	9.5	7.5
Belgium[1]	42.0	42.5	42.4	43.8	27.8	7.7	32.0	8.0	15.0	9.4	0.0
Canada	33.2	34.3	33.1	34.7	36.9	11.8	14.3	12.0	13.2	8.3	3.5
Chile	22.2	19.4	21.0	18.7	10.2	24.3	8.0	5.3	41.1	13.7	-2.7
Colombia	19.5	18.8	19.7	15.7	7.7	23.0	9.9	9.7	28.7	12.7	8.2
Costa Rica	24.2	22.7	23.4	21.1	6.8	8.4	36.1	2.0	19.7	13.6	13.4
Czech Republic	33.8	34.7	34.8	32.3	13.4	9.4	45.5	0.6	21.3	9.8	0.0
Denmark[1]	46.9	47.1	46.9	46.9	54.2	6.1	0.1	4.2	20.8	9.9	4.8
Estonia	33.5	33.3	33.5	31.1	18.1	4.9	36.5	0.6	26.7	13.2	0.0
Finland	43.0	41.8	42.3	45.8	30.0	5.1	27.4	3.6	22.1	11.7	0.1
France[1]	45.1	45.3	44.9	43.4	21.0	5.1	32.7	8.7	15.4	11.7	5.3
Germany	39.5	37.9	38.6	36.4	27.0	4.3	39.7	3.3	17.2	8.5	0.0
Greece	39.0	38.9	39.5	33.4	16.3	3.1	33.2	7.8	20.1	18.4	1.0
Hungary	34.0	36.1	36.4	38.5	14.6	3.6	30.8	2.9	27.1	18.1	3.0
Iceland	35.1	36.1	34.9	35.9	43.1	6.1	8.3	6.2	22.0	9.6	4.6
Ireland	21.1	19.9	21.9	30.8	32.9	16.1	16.6	5.0	17.2	11.1	1.0
Israel	32.2	29.6	30.0	34.1	21.9	9.2	17.4	10.3	23.9	11.5	5.9
Italy	43.3	42.7	42.3	40.5	26.8	4.8	31.8	5.7	14.1	12.8	3.9
Japan	..	33.2	31.5	25.3	18.7	11.7	40.4	8.1	14.9	6.0	0.3
Korea	29.9	27.7	27.2	20.9	18.8	12.1	28.0	14.2	15.1	9.3	2.4
Latvia	31.2	31.8	30.9	29.0	19.3	2.3	31.4	3.0	27.5	16.5	0.0
Lithuania[1]	32.8	30.8	30.3	30.8	23.0	5.1	33.2	1.0	25.6	12.1	0.0
Luxembourg[1]	38.6	38.1	39.6	37.0	25.5	12.5	29.2	10.0	14.9	7.9	0.1
Mexico	16.7	17.8	16.3	11.5	21.0	20.1	13.9	1.9	23.8	13.4	5.9
Netherlands	39.7	40.0	39.3	36.9	22.9	7.8	34.1	4.3	18.5	11.9	0.5
New Zealand	33.8	33.8	31.3	32.5	38.5	15.4	0.0	5.5	30.6	7.4	2.6
Norway	42.2	38.8	40.1	41.7	29.4	6.2	28.9	3.4	23.6	8.5	0.2
Poland[1]	36.8	35.5	35.1	32.9	14.8	6.4	37.9	3.6	22.4	13.8	1.0
Portugal	35.8	35.3	34.5	30.9	19.9	7.9	29.6	4.2	23.8	13.7	1.0
Slovak Republic	35.8	35.2	34.6	33.6	10.8	8.6	43.9	1.4	21.0	13.5	0.7
Slovenia[1]	37.4	37.2	37.0	37.7	14.1	5.2	45.2	1.7	20.2	13.5	0.1
Spain	38.4	36.7	34.7	33.0	23.7	5.3	37.4	6.7	17.1	9.6	0.0
Sweden	42.6	42.3	42.8	50.0	28.8	7.0	21.4	2.2	21.6	6.9	12.1
Switzerland[1]	28.0	27.5	27.3	27.0	32.1	11.0	25.2	8.1	11.3	8.7	3.7
Türkiye	22.8	23.9	23.1	23.5	13.2	8.7	29.7	4.4	19.2	23.8	1.0
United Kingdom	33.5	32.1	32.2	32.7	28.6	7.3	21.0	11.6	20.2	11.0	0.4
United States	26.6	25.8	25.2	28.3	40.6	4.9	24.8	12.4	0.0	17.2	0.1

.. Not available

1. The total tax revenue has been reduced by the amount of any capital transfer that represents uncollected taxes.
2. 2021 provisional average calculated by applying the unweighted average percentage change for 2021 in the 36 countries providing data for that year to the overall average tax to GDP ratio in 2020.
3. Calculated as 5000 Taxes on goods and services less 5111 Value added taxes.
4. Includes 1300 Unallocable between personal and corporate income tax, 3000 Taxes on payroll and workforce and 6000 Other taxes.

StatLink https://stat.link/xk1atw

The OECD average tax-to-GDP ratio was higher in 2021 than in 2010, when it was 31.5% of GDP on average. Across countries, the tax-to-GDP ratio was higher in 2021 than in 2010 in 32 countries. The largest increases were seen in the Slovak Republic (7.8 p.p.) and Korea (7.5 p.p.); increases of over 5 p.p. were also seen in Spain, Japan (2020 figure), Greece, Poland and Portugal. Decreases since 2010 were seen in the remaining six countries. The largest fall has been in Ireland, from 27.7% in 2010 to 21.1% in 2021, largely due to the exceptional increase in GDP in 2015. The next largest decrease was seen in Hungary (2.8 p.p.) (Figure 1.2).

Changes in the tax-to-GDP ratio are driven by the relative changes in nominal tax revenues and in nominal GDP. From one year to the next, if tax revenues rise more than GDP (or fall less than GDP) the tax-to-GDP ratio will increase. Conversely, if tax revenues rise less than GDP, or fall further, the tax-to-GDP ratio will go down. Therefore, a higher tax-to-GDP ratio does not necessarily mean that the amount of tax revenues has increased in nominal, or even real, terms.

In 2021, nominal tax revenues and GDP increased in all OECD countries from the previous year. Twenty-four countries experienced an increase in their tax-to-GDP ratio relative to 2020 as a result of the increase in revenues exceeding the growth in GDP. In 11 countries, tax revenues rose by less than GDP, resulting in a decline in the tax-to-GDP ratio (Figure 1.3)[3]. In Figure 1.3, changes between 2019 and 2020 are shown for Australia and Japan, where the tax-to-GDP ratio is not available in 2021. In both countries, the tax-to-GDP rose between 2019 and 2020: in Australia this was because nominal tax revenues increased by more than GDP, while in Japan nominal tax revenues increased but GDP declined.

Figure 1.2. Changes in tax-to-GDP ratios, p.p., 2020-21p and 2010-21p

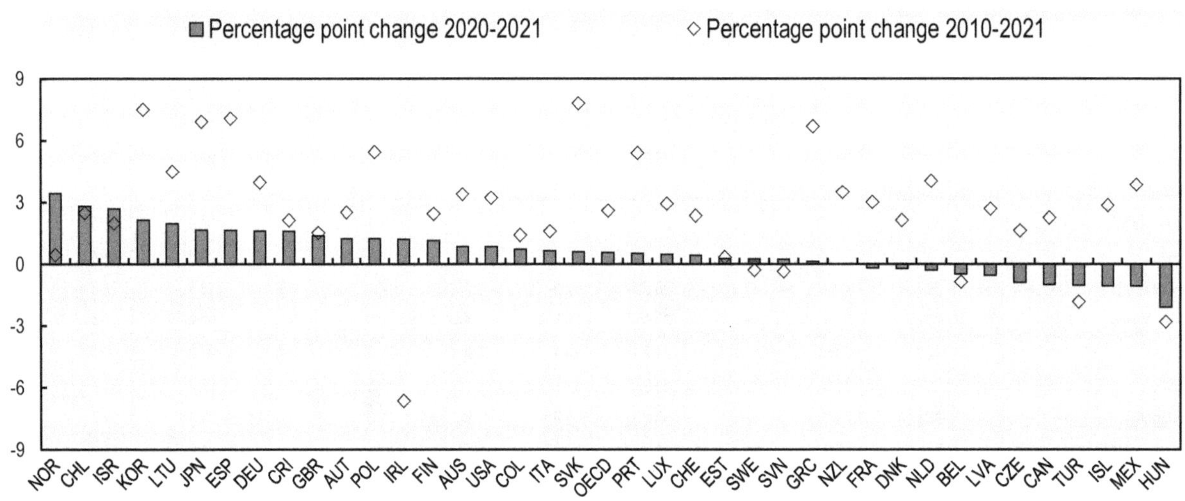

Note: Preliminary data for 2021 was not available for Australia and Japan. For these countries, the comparison shown is 2019-2020 and 2010-2020 data.
Source: Secretariat calculations based on Table 3.1.

StatLink https://stat.link/wu905r

Box 1.2. Methodology: the tax-to-GDP ratio

The tax-to-GDP ratios shown in *Revenue Statistics 2022* express aggregate tax revenues as a percentage of GDP. The value of this ratio depends on its denominator (GDP) as well as its numerator (tax revenue). The denominator – GDP – is subject to historical revision.

The numerator (tax revenue)

- For the numerator, the OECD Secretariat uses revenue figures that are submitted annually by correspondents from national Ministries of Finance, Tax Administrations or National Statistics Offices. Although provisional figures for most countries become available with a lag of about six months, finalised data become available with a lag of around one and a half years. Final revenue data for 2020 were received during the period May-August 2022.
- In 35 OECD countries the reporting year coincides with the calendar year. Three countries - Australia, Japan and New Zealand – have different reporting years. Reporting year 2019 includes Q2/2019 – Q1/2020 (Japan) and Q3/2019 – Q2/2020 (Australia and New Zealand) respectively (Q = quarter).

The denominator (GDP)

- For the denominator, the GDP figures used for *Revenue Statistics 2022* are the most recently available in October 2022. At that point, the 2020 and 2021 GDP figures were available for all OECD countries.
- Using these GDP figures ensures a maximum of consistency and international comparability for the reported tax-to-GDP ratios.
- The GDP figures are based on the OECD Annual National Accounts (ANA – SNA) for the 35 OECD countries where the reporting year is the actual calendar year.
- Where the reporting year differs from the calendar year, the annual GDP estimates are obtained by aggregating quarterly GDP estimates provided by the OECD Statistics Directorate for those quarters corresponding to each country's fiscal (tax) year.

The average shown in this publication is an unweighted average of all countries for which data is available. The 2021 provisional average is calculated by applying the unweighted average percentage change for 2021 in the 36 countries providing data for that year to the overall average tax-to-GDP ratio in 2020.

Figure 1.3. Relative changes in nominal tax revenues and nominal GDP (%), 2020-21p

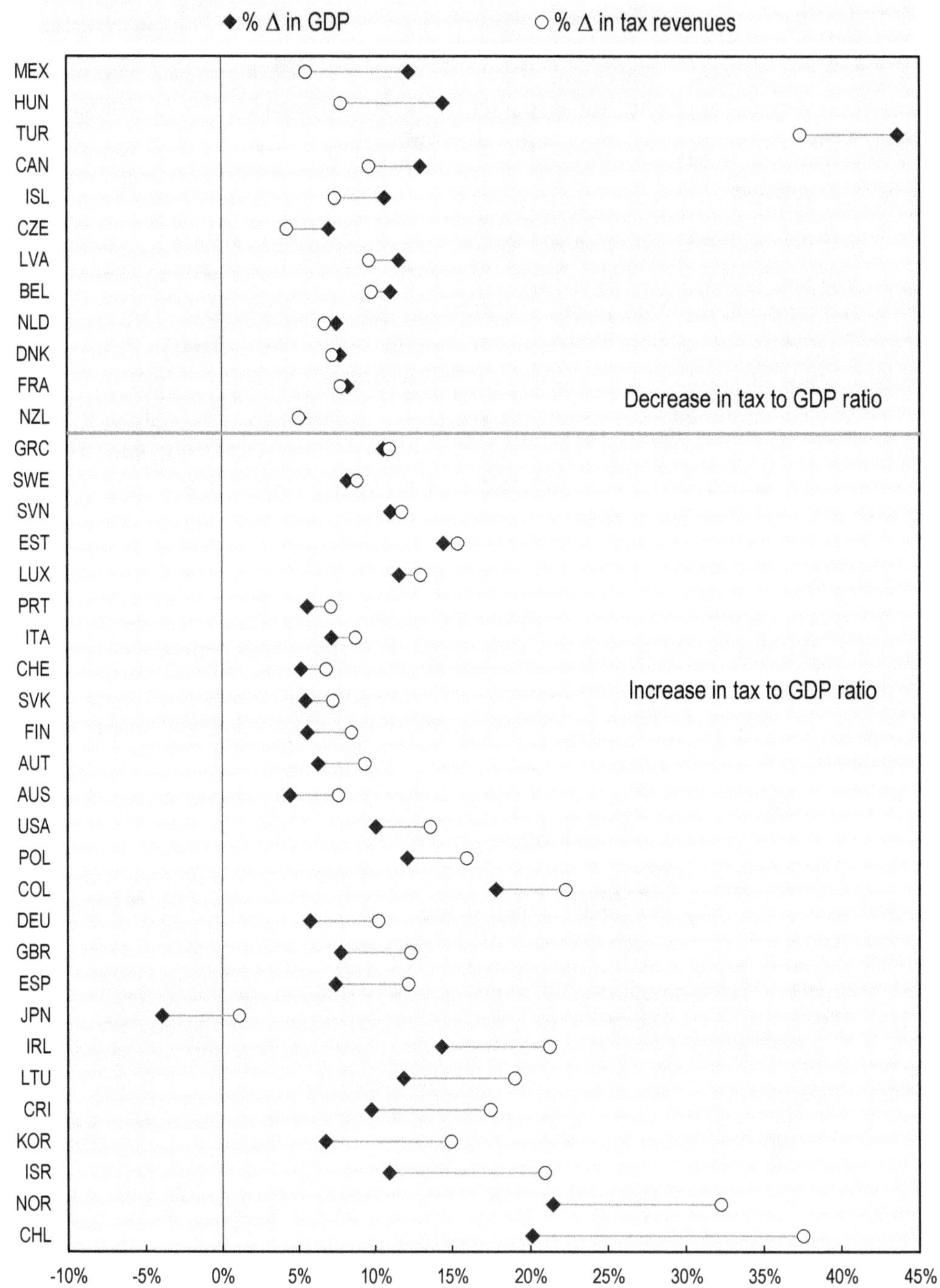

Note: Data for Australia and Japan show the change between 2019 and 2020, as preliminary data for 2021 was not available for Australia and Japan.

Source: Secretariat calculations based on Chapter 4 (tax revenues) and Table 3.19 (GDP).

StatLink https://stat.link/q813bf

Figure 1.4. Tax to GDP ratios in 2020 and 2021p (as % of GDP)

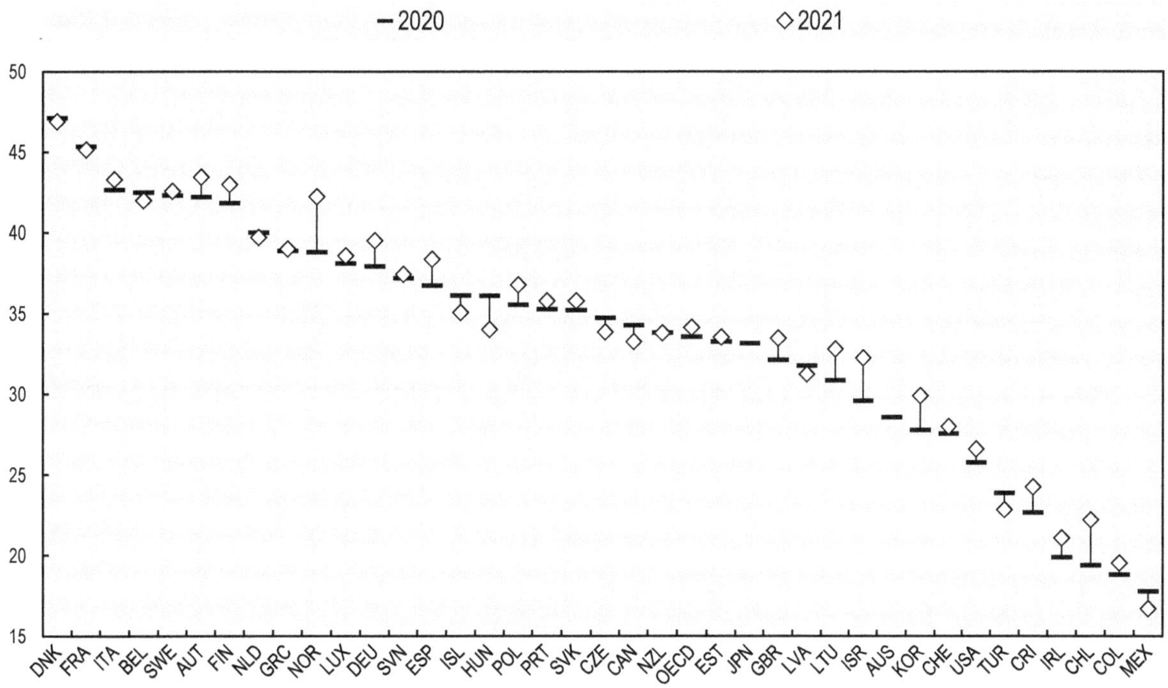

Note: Preliminary data for 2021 were not available for Australia and Japan.
Source: Secretariat calculations based on Table 3.1

StatLink https://stat.link/hp2i9v

Tax-to-GDP ratios for 2020 (final data)

The latest year for which tax-to-GDP ratios are based on final revenue data and available for all OECD countries is 2020 (Figure 1.4). These data show that tax ratios varied considerably across countries:

- In 2020, Denmark had the highest tax-to-GDP ratio (47.1%), followed by France (45.3%). Five other countries had tax-to-GDP ratios above 40% (Austria, Belgium, Finland, Italy and Sweden).
- Mexico had the lowest ratio at 17.8% followed by Colombia (18.8%), Chile (19.4%), Ireland (19.9%), Costa Rica (22.7%) and Türkiye (23.9%). No other countries had a tax-to-GDP ratio lower than 25% in 2020 and five other countries had ratios below 30% (Australia, Israel, Korea, Switzerland and the United States).
- The tax-to-GDP ratio in the OECD area as a whole (un-weighted average) was 33.6% in 2020. In 2019, it was 33.4%.
- Relative to 2019, overall tax ratios rose in 22 OECD member countries and fell in 16.
- The largest increases in the tax-to-GDP ratio were in New Zealand (2.5 p.p.) and Spain (2.0 p.p.). Canada, Iceland, Japan and Mexico all recorded increases in excess of 1.0 p.p.
- The largest declines were in Ireland (2.0 p.p.) and Chile (1.6 p.p.).

Between 2019 and 2020, the increase in the average tax-to-GDP ratio was driven by increases in revenues from PIT and social security contributions (0.3 p.p. each), which more than offset by a decline in CIT revenues (0.2 p.p.).

Table 1.2. Tax structures in the OECD area, selected years (unweighted average as % of GDP)
Per cent

	1965	1990	2000	2007	2010	2015	2018	2019	2020
Total tax revenue	24.9	30.8	32.9	32.8	31.5	32.9	33.5	33.4	33.6
1000 Taxes on income, profits and capital gains	8.7	11.5	11.4	11.7	10.2	10.9	11.3	11.3	11.3
of which:									
1100 Taxes on income, profits and capital gains of individuals	6.8	9.3	8.5	7.8	7.2	7.9	7.9	8.0	8.3
1200 Taxes on income, profits and capital gains of corporates	2.1	2.4	3.1	3.6	2.7	2.8	3.1	3.0	2.8
2000 Social security contributions (SSC)	4.5	7.1	8.4	8.2	8.6	8.8	8.9	8.9	9.2
3000 Taxes on payroll and workforce	0.3	0.4	0.4	0.4	0.4	0.4	0.4	0.5	0.5
4000 Taxes on property	1.9	1.7	1.7	1.7	1.6	1.8	1.8	1.8	1.9
5000 Taxes on goods and services	9.4	9.9	10.8	10.7	10.5	10.8	10.8	10.7	10.6
of which:									
5111 Value added taxes	0.7	5.1	6.3	6.5	6.4	6.6	6.7	6.7	6.7
5121 Excises	3.5	2.5	2.8	2.6	2.6	2.5	2.4	2.3	2.3
6000 Other Taxes	0.1	0.4	0.2	0.2	0.2	0.2	0.2	0.2	0.2

Note: Percentage share of major tax categories in GDP. Data are included from 1965 onwards for Australia, Austria, Belgium, Canada, Denmark, Finland, France, Germany, Greece, Iceland, Ireland, Italy, Japan, Luxembourg, the Netherlands, New Zealand, Norway, Portugal, Spain, Sweden, Switzerland, Türkiye, United Kingdom and United States; from 1972 for Korea; from 1980 for Mexico; from 1990 for Chile, Colombia and Costa Rica; from 1991 for Hungary and Poland; from 1993 for the Czech Republic and from 1995 for Estonia, Israel, Latvia, Lithuania, the Slovak Republic and Slovenia. The figures for the 2016 OECD average includes the one-off revenues from stability contributions in Iceland.
Source: OECD (2022), "Revenue Statistics: Comparative tables", *OECD Tax Statistics (database)*.

StatLink https://stat.link/abltj8

Tax ratio changes between 1965 and 2020

Between 1965 and 2020[4], the average tax-to-GDP ratio in the OECD area increased from 24.9% to 33.6%, an increase of 8.7 p.p. (Figure 1.1). Before the first oil shock (1973 to 1974), strong, almost uninterrupted income growth enabled tax levels to rise in all OECD countries. In part, tax levels rose automatically through the effect of fiscal drag on PIT schedules. From 1975 to 1985, the tax burden in the OECD area increased by 2.9 p.p. After the mid-1970s, the combination of slower real income growth and higher levels of unemployment apparently limited the revenue raising capacity of governments. But during and after the deep recession following the second oil shock (1980), countries in Europe saw tax levels rise further, to finance higher spending on social security and rein in budget deficits.

After the mid-1980s, most OECD countries substantially reduced the statutory rates of their personal and corporate income tax, but the negative revenue impact of widespread tax reforms was often offset by reducing or abolishing tax reliefs. By 1999, the average OECD tax-to-GDP ratio had risen to 33.0%, the highest recorded level at that time. It fell back slightly between 2001 and 2004, but then rose again between 2005 and 2007 before falling back during the global financial crisis in 2008 and 2009. Taking these changes together, the average tax level in the OECD area increased by 1.4 p.p. between 1995 and 2020 (Figure 1.1).

The OECD average conceals great variety in national tax-to-GDP ratios. In 1965, tax-to-GDP ratios in OECD countries ranged from 10.6% in Türkiye to 33.7% in France. By 2020, the corresponding range was from 17.8% in Mexico to 47.1% in Denmark. The trend towards higher tax levels over this period reflects the need to finance a significant increase of public sector outlays in almost all OECD countries.

Tax structures

Tax structures are measured by the share of major taxes in total tax revenue. In 2020, the tax structures of OECD countries varied. Seventeen countries raised the largest part of their revenues from income taxes (both corporate and personal), eleven countries raised the largest part of their revenues from social security contributions and 10 countries raised the largest part of their revenues from consumption taxes (including VAT). Taxes on property and payroll taxes played a smaller role in the revenue systems of OECD countries in 2020, both on average and within most countries (Figure 1.5).

Figure 1.5. Tax structures in 2020 (as % of total tax revenue)

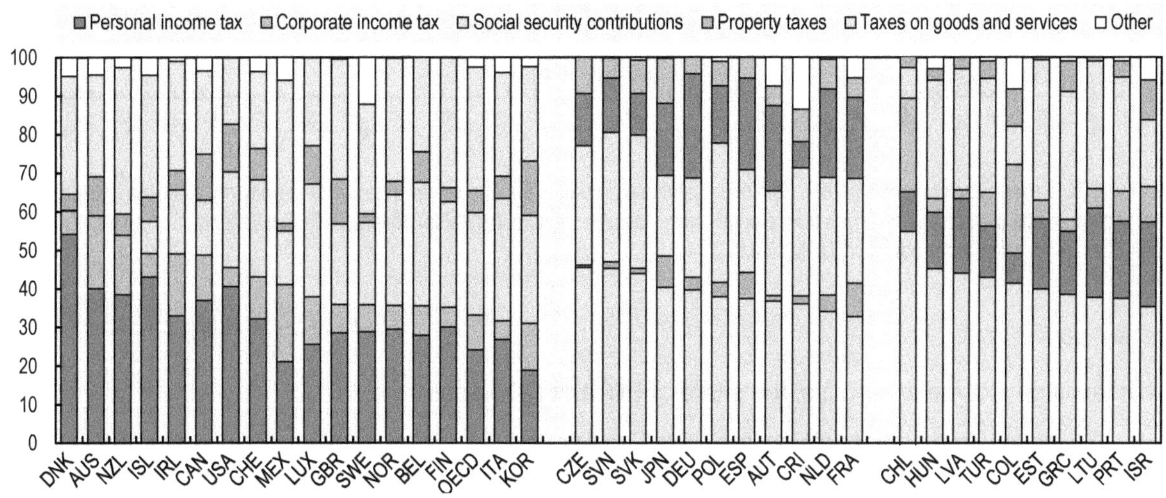

Note: Countries are grouped and ranked by those where income tax revenues (personal and corporate) form the highest share of total tax revenues, followed by those where social security contributions, or taxes on goods and services, form the highest share.
Source: Secretariat calculations based on data in Chapter 4.

StatLink https://stat.link/9sxy54

While tax levels have generally been rising on average, the tax structure or tax 'mix' has been remarkably stable over time. Nevertheless, several trends have emerged up to 2020 – the latest year for which data is available for all 38 OECD countries. These trends are discussed further below.

Taxes on income and profits

On average, in 2020, OECD countries collected 33.7% of their tax revenues through taxes on income and profits (personal and corporate income taxes taken together). Taxes on personal and corporate incomes remain the most important source of revenues used to finance public spending in 17 OECD countries, and in nine of them – Australia, Canada, Denmark, Iceland, Ireland, Mexico, New Zealand, Switzerland and the United States – the share of income taxes in the tax mix exceeded 40% in 2020.

Figure 1.6. Trends in tax structures (1965-2020, as % of total tax revenue)

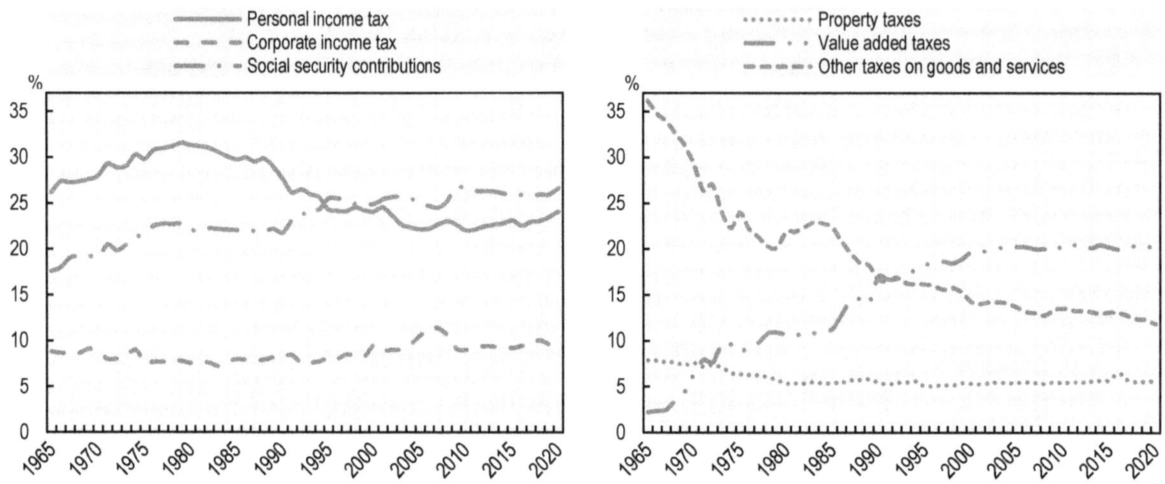

Note: The OECD average tax revenue in 2016 from main categories includes the one-off revenues from stability contributions in Iceland. This predominately affects the average revenues from property taxes, as a percentage of total tax revenues, in that year only.
Source: Secretariat calculations based on Tables 3.8 to 3.14.

StatLink https://stat.link/r9ui85

Within taxes on income and profits, the share of PIT and CIT varies:

- Revenues from personal income taxes generated 24.1% of total taxes on average in 2020 compared with around 30% in the 1980s. About two percentage points of this reduction can be attributed to the impact on the average of a number of relatively recent entrants to the OECD from Eastern Europe and Latin America for which tax revenue data is only available from the 1990s onwards. These countries tend to have relatively low personal income tax revenues and high revenues from social security contributions or corporate income taxes, but this impact is observed in the post-1990 data only.
- The variation in the share of PIT between countries is considerable. In 2020, it ranged from 6.8% in Costa Rica to 43.1% in Iceland and 54.2% in Denmark (Figure 1.5).
- CIT revenues represented between 8% and 9% of total tax revenues, on average, throughout the period 1965 to 2003. They then increased to a high of 11.3% in 2007, before dropping to 9.0% in 2010, directly after the global financial crisis. They remained at between 9.0% and 10.0% of total revenues thereafter, except in 2018, when they accounted for 10.1%. CIT generated 9.0% of revenues in 2020.
- The share of CIT in total tax revenues in 2020 varied considerably across countries from less than 5% (Estonia, Germany, Greece, Hungary, Italy, Latvia and the United States) to over 20% in Mexico (20.1%), Colombia (23.0%) and Chile (24.3%). Apart from the spread in statutory CIT rates, these differences are partly explained by institutional and country-specific factors, including:
    - the degree to which firms are incorporated,
    - the breadth of the CIT base; for example some narrowing may occur as a consequence of generous depreciation schemes and tax incentives,
    - the degree of cyclicality of the corporate tax system, for which one of the important elements is loss offset provisions,
    - the extent of reliance upon tax revenues from the exploitation of oil and/or mineral deposits, or
    - other instruments to postpone the taxation of earned profits.

Social security contributions

Social security contributions (SSCs) accounted for 26.6% of total tax revenues on average across the OECD in 2020. They were highest in the Czech Republic, Slovenia and the Slovak Republic (45.5%, 45.2% and 43.9%, respectively). In contrast, Australia and New Zealand do not levy social security contributions.

There was wide variation across OECD countries in the relative proportions of social security contributions paid by employees and employers in 2020 (Figure 1.7):

- Ten countries (Chile, Denmark, Greece, Hungary, Israel, Lithuania, Luxembourg, Poland, Slovenia and Switzerland) raise more revenues from employee SSCs, whereas the remainder raise more from employer SSCs.
- The highest share of employee SSC revenues is found in Lithuania, at 25.3% of total revenues. Germany, Greece, Hungary, Japan, Poland and Slovenia also have employee SSC revenues of over 15% of total tax revenues. Denmark had the lowest share, at 0.1% of total revenues. Apart from Denmark, only Estonia had revenues from employee SSCs of less than 5% of total revenues.
- The highest share of employer social security contribution revenues is found in Estonia, at 32.6% of total tax revenues. The Czech Republic (28.9%), Spain (27.3%) and the Slovak Republic (26.7%) also had employer SSC revenues of over 25% of total tax revenues. Denmark and Chile had the lowest shares, at 0.1% and 0.3% of total revenues respectively.
- The highest share of self-employed or non-employed SSC revenues are found in the Netherlands and Poland, at 7.6% and 7.7% of total revenues respectively.

Figure 1.7. Composition of social security contributions, as % of total social security contributions, 2020

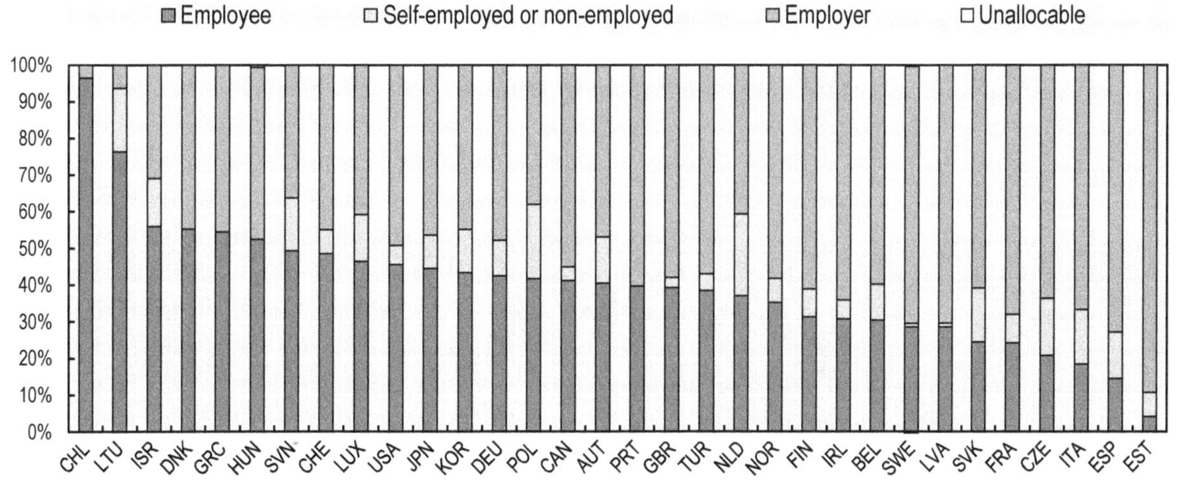

Note: Australia, Costa Rica, Colombia, Iceland, Mexico and New Zealand are not included within figure 1.7. Although Colombia, Costa Rica, Iceland and Mexico collect social security contributions, disaggregated data is not available. New Zealand and Australia do not levy social security contributions.
Source: Secretariat calculations based on data in Chapter 4.

StatLink https://stat.link/dgmfqt

Property taxes

Between 1965 and 2020, the share of taxes on property fell from 7.9% to 5.7% of total tax revenues on average across the OECD (Figure 1.6). In Australia, Canada, Israel, Korea, the United Kingdom and the United States, property tax revenues amounted to more than 10% of total revenues in 2020. By contrast, property taxes accounted for less than 1% of total revenues in the Czech Republic, Estonia and Lithuania.

Consumption taxes

- The share of taxes on consumption (general consumption taxes plus specific consumption taxes) fell from 38.4% to 32.1% between 1965 and 2020 (Figure 1.6).
- During this period, the composition of taxes on goods and services has fundamentally changed. A fast-growing revenue source has been general consumption taxes, especially VAT, which is imposed in 37 of 38 OECD countries.[5]
- General consumption taxes accounted for 20.9% of total tax revenue in 2020, compared with only 11.9% in the mid-1960s. In 2020, the vast majority of this was from VAT (20.2% of total tax revenues).
- The increased importance of VAT has served to counteract the diminishing share of specific consumption taxes, such as excises and custom duties.
- Between 1975 and 2020, the share of specific taxes on consumption (mostly on tobacco, alcoholic drinks and fuels, as well as some environment-related taxes) almost halved, from 17.7% to 9.1% of total revenues. In 2020, excises were the largest single category of total revenues under this heading, accounting for 6.9% of total revenues (Figure 1.8).
- Rates of taxes on imported goods were considerably reduced across all OECD countries, reflecting a global trend to remove trade barriers.
- Nevertheless, countries such as Greece, Hungary, Latvia, Lithuania, Mexico, Poland, Portugal and the Slovak Republic (between 11%-15%) and Türkiye (22.4%) still collected a relatively large proportion of their tax revenues through taxes on specific goods and services in 2020.

Figure 1.8. Share of general consumption tax revenues (left panel) and specific consumption revenues (right panel) as % of total revenues, 1975-2020

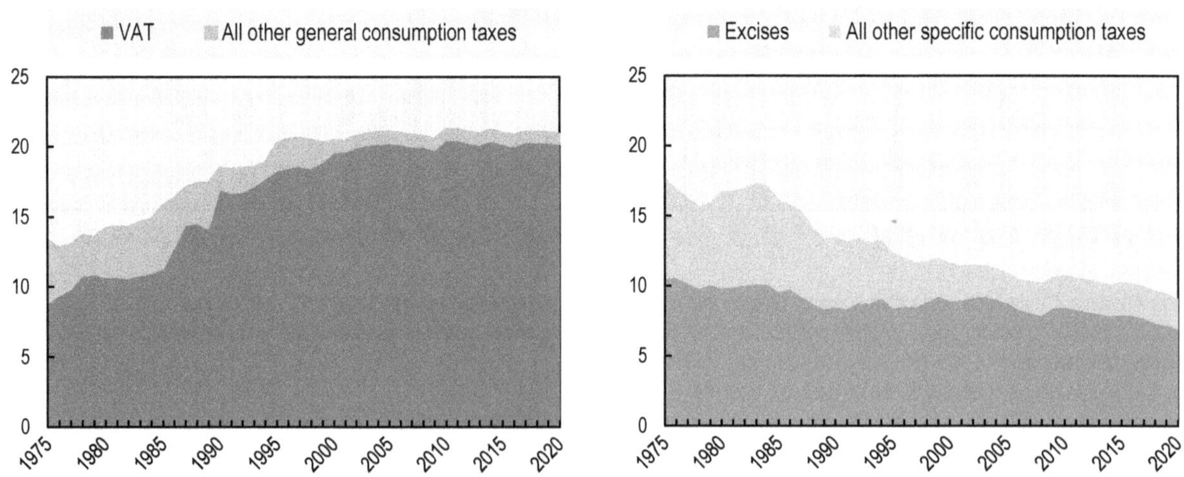

Note: The unweighted average for each year includes all countries which report revenue in the categories shown in that year. The OECD averages for 2016 include the one-off revenues from stability contributions in Iceland.
Source: Secretariat calculations based on Chapter 4.

StatLink https://stat.link/v4yf7j

Taxes by level of government

This section discusses the relative share of tax revenues attributed to the various sub-sectors of general government in 2020. The different sub-sectors are:

- Central government
- State government (federal and regional countries only)
- Local government
- Social security funds
- Supranational authorities (EU countries only)

The guidelines for attributing these revenue shares to the different levels of government are based on the final version of the 2008 System of National Accounts. These guidelines are discussed in the special feature S.1 in the 2011 edition of OECD *Revenue Statistics*.

Revenues of sub-national government in federal and unitary countries

Eight OECD countries have a federal structure. Among these countries, central government received 51.9% of total revenues in 2020 on average. The second-highest share of revenues on average was received by social security funds, which are a sub-sector of general government, at 22.2% of total revenues, followed by 17.8% at the state level and 7.9% at the local level (Table 1.3). However, within countries there was considerable variation around these means:

- In 2020, the share of central government receipts in the eight federal OECD countries varied from 27.5% in Germany to 80.9% in Australia.
- In 2020, the share of the states varied from 2.1% in Austria, 3.9% in Mexico and 11.1% in Belgium to 39.2% in Canada. The share of local government varied from 1.5% in Mexico to 15.5% in the United States and 15.7% in Switzerland.
- Between 1975 and 2020, the share of federal government revenues declined by over 15 p.p. in Belgium and by more than 6 p.p. in Canada and the United States.
- The share of federal government revenues increased in Austria by over 11 p.p. There was little change in Australia.
- Of the seven federal countries with social security funds, five increased the share of revenue between 1975 and 2020. The exceptions were Canada and Mexico, where the share declined between 1975 (1980 for Mexico due to data availability) and 2020.

Colombia and Spain, which are classified as regional rather than unitary countries because of their highly decentralised political structure, have very different compositions by level of government. In Colombia, the share of central government receipts was 71.9% in 2020, with regional governments receiving 4.8% of total revenues and local governments receiving 13.3%. In Spain, the share of central government receipts in 2020 was 37.4% compared with 16.6% for regional governments and 8.8% for local governments.

Table 1.3. Attribution of tax revenues to sub-sectors of general government as % of total tax revenue, federal countries

Per cent

	Supranational			Central government			State or Regional government			Local government			Social Security Funds		
	1975	1995	2020	1975	1995	2020	1975	1995	2020	1975	1995	2020	1975	1995	2020
Federal countries															
Australia	..	..	..	80.1	77.5	80.9	15.7	19.0	15.7	4.2	3.4	3.4	0.0	0.0	0.0
Austria[1]	..	0.4	0.4	51.7	64.7	63.1	10.6	1.8	2.1	12.4	4.1	3.2	25.3	29.0	31.1
Belgium[1]	1.4	1.0	0.9	65.3	60.1	49.5	..	1.8	11.1	4.4	4.8	5.1	28.8	32.2	33.4
Canada	..	..	..	47.6	39.1	41.1	32.5	37.1	39.2	9.9	9.8	10.2	10.0	14.0	9.5
Germany	1.2	0.6	0.5	33.5	31.4	27.5	22.3	21.6	24.0	9.0	7.4	8.2	34.0	39.0	39.7
Mexico	..	..	..	..	73.9	80.7	..	2.8	3.9	..	1.5	1.5	..	21.8	13.9
Switzerland[1]	..	..	..	30.7	31.7	33.5	27.0	24.0	25.6	20.3	17.5	15.7	22.0	26.8	25.2
United States	..	..	..	45.4	41.4	38.6	19.5	20.0	21.1	14.7	13.3	15.5	20.5	25.2	24.8
Unweighted average	1.3	0.7	0.6	50.6	52.5	51.9	21.3	16.0	17.8	10.7	7.7	7.9	20.1	23.5	22.2
Regional countries															
Colombia[2]	..	..	..	..	63.2	71.9	..	5.5	4.8	..	8.6	13.3	..	22.7	9.9
Spain[2]	..	0.8	0.6	48.2	51.1	37.4	..	5.0	16.6	4.3	8.6	8.8	47.5	34.6	36.6

.. Not available

1. The total tax revenue has been reduced by the amount of any capital transfer that represents uncollected taxes.

2. Colombia and Spain are not constitutionally federal countries, but both have a highly decentralised political structure, with high autonomy of their territorial entities.

StatLink https://stat.link/q8t6so

The remaining twenty-eight OECD countries have a unitary structure. In these countries, an average of 62.4% of revenues were derived at the central level in 2020, with 26.1% accounted for by social security funds. A further 11.1% were raised by local governments. Among unitary OECD countries:

- The share of central government receipts in 2020 varied from 32.1% in France to 93.9% in New Zealand.
- The local government share varied from 0.8% in Estonia to 36.8% in Sweden.
- Between 1975 and 2020, there were increases in the local government share in excess of 5 p.p. in six countries: France, Iceland, Italy, Korea, Portugal and Sweden. Decreases of 5 p.p. or more in the other direction occurred in three countries: Ireland, Norway and the United Kingdom.[6]
- Between 1975 and 2020, there were increases in the share of social security funds of 7 p.p. or more in four countries (Finland, France, Japan and Korea) and corresponding decreases in two countries (Italy and Norway).

Table 1.4. Attribution of tax revenues to sub-sectors of general government as % of total tax revenue, unitary countries

Per cent

	Supranational			Central government			State or Regional government			Local government			Social Security Funds		
	1975	1995	2020	1975	1995	2020	1975	1995	2020	1975	1995	2020	1975	1995	2020
Unitary countries															
Chile	..	..	..	..	89.9	84.6	..	..	..	..	6.5	8.7	..	3.6	6.7
Costa Rica	..	..	..	..	65.5	55.2	..	..	..	..	1.6	3.1	..	33.0	41.6
Czech Republic	..	..	0.4	..	57.7	53.1	..	..	..	..	0.9	1.0	..	41.4	45.5
Denmark[1]	1.0	0.5	0.3	69.1	68.2	72.8	..	..	..	29.8	31.3	26.9	0.1	0.0	0.1
Estonia	..	..	0.5	..	84.3	81.3	..	..	..	..	0.8	0.8	..	14.9	17.4
Finland	..	0.4	0.4	56.0	46.6	47.5	..	..	..	23.5	22.3	24.7	20.4	30.8	27.4
France[1]	0.7	0.7	0.5	51.2	42.5	32.1	..	..	..	7.6	11.0	13.5	40.6	45.8	53.9
Greece	..	0.6	0.5	67.1	66.3	63.6	..	..	..	3.4	2.0	2.5	29.5	31.0	33.3
Hungary	..	..	0.4	..	63.8	64.2	..	..	..	..	2.5	5.2	..	33.6	30.2
Iceland	..	..	..	81.3	79.2	70.2	..	..	..	18.7	20.8	29.8	0.0	0.0	0.0
Ireland	2.3	1.5	0.6	77.4	83.1	83.8	..	..	..	7.3	2.7	1.1	13.1	12.7	14.6
Israel	..	..	..	..	79.0	74.7	..	..	..	..	7.1	7.9	..	13.9	17.4
Italy	..	0.4	0.4	53.2	62.7	56.7	..	..	..	0.9	5.4	11.0	45.9	31.5	31.8
Japan	..	..	..	45.5	41.2	36.6	..	..	..	25.6	25.2	23.0	29.0	33.6	40.4
Korea	..	..	..	89.0	69.2	53.0	..	..	..	10.1	18.7	19.0	0.9	12.1	28.0
Latvia	..	..	0.6	..	43.5	51.1	..	..	..	..	19.5	17.9	..	36.9	30.4
Lithuania[1]	..	..	0.9	..	71.7	64.9	..	..	..	..	2.3	1.1	..	26.1	33.2
Luxembourg[1]	0.8	0.4	0.8	63.6	66.4	66.6	..	..	..	6.7	6.5	4.2	29.0	26.6	28.4
Netherlands	1.5	1.3	1.1	58.9	56.0	61.3	..	..	..	1.2	3.1	3.5	38.4	39.5	34.1
New Zealand	..	..	..	92.3	94.7	93.9	..	..	..	7.7	5.3	6.1	0.0	0.0	0.0
Norway	..	..	..	50.6	57.6	83.1	..	..	..	22.4	20.0	16.9	27.0	22.4	0.0
Poland[1]	..	..	0.5	..	61.2	49.2	..	..	..	..	8.5	12.4	..	30.3	37.9
Portugal	..	0.8	0.5	65.4	72.3	64.1	..	..	..	0.0	5.4	7.2	34.6	21.5	28.2
Slovak Republic	..	..	0.4	..	62.6	54.9	..	..	..	..	1.3	2.1	..	36.1	42.6
Slovenia[1]	..	..	0.4	..	50.6	45.1	..	..	..	..	6.2	9.7	..	43.2	44.8
Sweden	..	0.4	0.3	51.3	46.9	50.3	..	..	..	29.2	30.9	36.8	19.5	21.8	12.6
Türkiye	..	..	..	..	75.1	60.9	..	..	..	..	12.8	9.4	..	12.1	29.7
United Kingdom	1.0	1.0	0.4	70.5	77.5	73.0	..	..	..	11.1	3.7	5.6	17.5	17.8	21.0
Unweighted average	1.2	0.7	0.5	65.2	65.6	62.4	..	..	..	12.8	10.2	11.1	21.6	24.0	26.1

.. Not available

1. The total tax revenue has been reduced by the amount of any capital transfer that represents uncollected taxes.

StatLink https://stat.link/6nzj8t

Composition of central and sub-central government revenues

Figure 1.9 shows revenues from each major category of tax revenue for central and sub-central governments. For federal and regional countries, the sub-central level includes revenues received by both state and local governments. Figure 1.9 demonstrates that:

- Central government revenues in almost all OECD countries are predominantly derived from taxes on income and on goods and services, with a negligible share from property taxes.
- At the subnational level, property taxes provide a much larger share of revenues than at the central level, and account for over 90% of revenues in four countries (Israel, Ireland, Greece and the United Kingdom).

- By contrast, the share of income taxes and taxes on goods and services is lower at the sub-central level, the exceptions being Finland, Luxembourg and Sweden, where over 90% of sub-central revenues are derived from income taxes.

Figure 1.9. Composition of revenues of federal or central government (left) and sub-national government (right), 2020

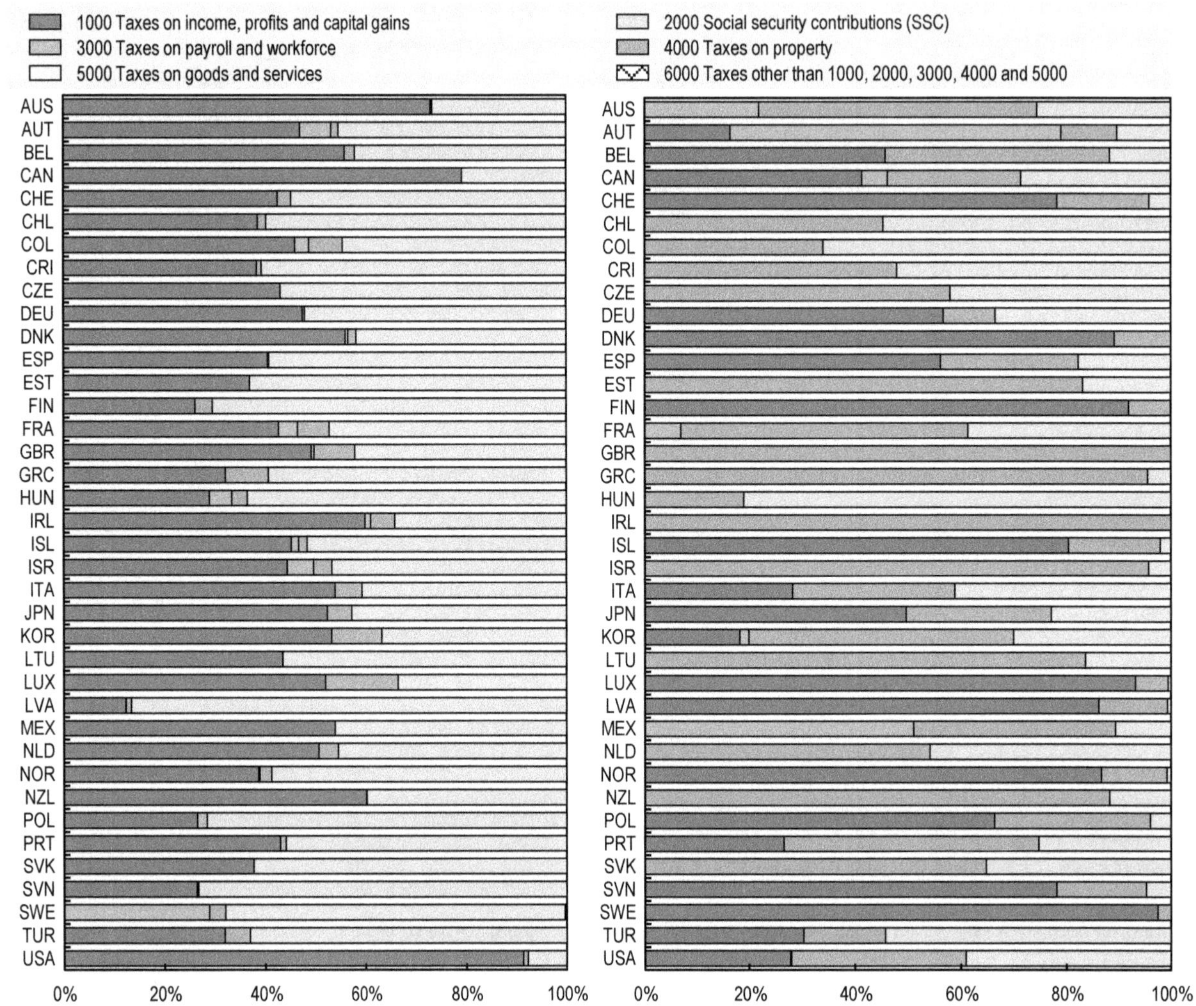

Note: The left-hand panel (a) refers to only those taxes which are classified as central government taxes. Social security contributions paid to social security funds are excluded. The right-hand panel (b) refers only to those taxes which are classified as sub-central taxes (local and (where relevant) state taxes). Social security contributions paid to social security funds are excluded.
Source: Secretariat calculations based on tables 3.16 to 3.18.

StatLink https://stat.link/q2nutd

Revenues paid to a supranational authority

The 22 member states of the European Union (EU) that are also members of the OECD collect taxes on behalf of the EU, as did the United Kingdom prior to 2020. These taxes primarily consist of customs duties and Single Resolution Fund (SRF) contributions.[7] Both taxes are collected on behalf of the EU by national tax administrations and are included in the total tax figures under headings 5123 and 5126 at the SUPRA level of government. In addition, they are shown as a memorandum item separately from the main figures since they represent a tax imposed by the EU and collected by national administrations.[8]

Table 1.5 shows the level of taxes collected on behalf of supranational governments in EU countries that are also OECD members, divided into those countries in the Euro area and other EU member countries.

Table 1.5. Levies collected on behalf of the European Union, as % of GDP

Per cent

	2000	2005	2010	2015	2016	2017	2018	2019	2020	2021p
Euro area										
Austria, total supranational	0.2	0.1	0.1	0.2	0.2	0.2	0.2	0.2	0.2	0.2
of which: Customs duties	0.2	0.1	0.1	0.1	0.1	0.1	0.1	0.1	0.1	0.1
of which: SRF contributions	..	..	..	0.1	0.1	0.1	0.1	0.0	0.1	0.1
Belgium, total supranational	0.4	0.4	0.4	0.4	0.4	0.4	0.4	0.4	0.4	0.4
of which: Customs duties	0.4	0.4	0.3	0.3	0.4	0.4	0.4	0.4	0.3	0.3
of which: SRF contributions	..	..	..	0.1	0.1	0.1	0.1	0.1	0.1	0.1
Estonia, total supranational	..	0.2	0.2	0.2	0.2	0.2	0.2	0.2	0.2	0.2
of which: Customs duties	..	0.2	0.2	0.2	0.2	0.2	0.2	0.2	0.2	0.2
of which: SRF contributions	..	..	..	..	0.0	0.0	0.0	0.0	0.0	0.0
Finland, total supranational	0.1	0.1	0.1	0.1	0.1	0.1	0.1	0.2	0.2	0.2
of which: Customs duties	0.1	0.1	0.1	0.1	0.1	0.1	0.1	0.1	0.1	0.1
of which: SRF contributions	..	..	..	0.0	0.1	0.1	0.0	0.1	0.1	0.1
France, total supranational	0.1	0.1	0.1	0.1	0.2	0.2	0.2	0.2	0.2	0.2
of which: Customs duties	0.1	0.1	0.1	0.1	0.1	0.1	0.1	0.1	0.1	0.1
of which: SRF contributions	..	..	..	0.0	0.1	0.1	0.1	0.1	0.1	0.1
Germany, total supranational	0.2	0.2	0.2	0.2	0.2	0.2	0.2	0.2	0.2	0.2
of which: Customs duties	0.2	0.2	0.2	0.2	0.2	0.2	0.1	0.1	0.1	0.1
of which: SRF contributions	..	..	..	0.1	0.1	0.1	0.1	0.1	0.1	0.1
Greece, total supranational	0.2	0.1	0.1	0.2	0.2	0.2	0.2	0.2	0.2	0.2
of which: Customs duties	0.1	0.1	0.1	0.1	0.1	0.2	0.1	0.2	0.2	0.2
of which: SRF contributions	..	..	..	0.1	0.1	0.1	0.1	0.0	0.1	0.0
Ireland, total supranational	0.2	0.1	0.1	0.1	0.2	0.1	0.1	0.1	0.1	0.2
of which: Customs duties	0.2	0.1	0.1	0.1	0.1	0.1	0.1	0.1	0.1	0.1
of which: SRF contributions[1]	..	..	..	..	0.1	0.0	0.0	0.0	0.0	0.1
Italy, total supranational	0.1	0.1	0.1	0.3	0.2	0.3	0.2	0.2	0.2	0.2
of which: Customs duties	0.1	0.1	0.1	0.1	0.1	0.1	0.1	0.1	0.1	0.1
of which: SRF contributions[2]	..	..	..	0.1	0.0	0.1	0.1	0.0	0.1	0.1
Lithuania, total supranational	..	0.2	0.2	0.3	0.3	0.3	0.3	0.3	0.3	0.3
of which: Customs duties	..	0.2	0.2	0.3	0.2	0.2	0.3	0.3	0.3	0.3
of which: SRF contributions	..	..	..	0.0	0.0	0.0	0.0	0.0	0.0	0.0
Latvia, total supranational	..	0.2	0.1	0.2	0.2	0.2	0.2	0.2	0.2	0.2
of which: Customs duties	..	0.2	0.1	0.2	0.2	0.2	0.2	0.2	0.2	0.2
of which: SRF contributions	..	..	..	0.0	0.0	0.0	0.0	0.0	0.0	0.0
Luxembourg, total supranational	0.1	0.1	0.0	0.1	0.2	0.2	0.3	0.3	0.3	0.4
of which: Customs duties	0.1	0.1	0.0	0.0	0.0	0.0	0.0	0.0	0.0	0.0
of which: SRF contributions	..	..	..	0.1	0.1	0.2	0.2	0.2	0.3	0.3
Netherlands, total supranational	0.4	0.3	0.3	0.4	0.4	0.4	0.4	0.4	0.4	0.5
of which: Customs duties	0.3	0.2	0.3	0.3	0.3	0.3	0.3	0.3	0.3	0.3
of which: SRF contributions	..	..	..	0.1	0.1	0.1	0.1	0.1	0.1	0.1
Portugal, total supranational	0.2	0.1	0.1	0.1	0.2	0.2	0.2	0.2	0.2	0.2
of which: Customs duties	0.1	0.1	0.1	0.1	0.1	0.1	0.1	0.1	0.1	0.1
of which: SRF contributions	..	..	..	..	0.1	0.1	0.1	0.1	0.1	0.1
Slovak Republic, total supranational	..	0.1	0.2	0.1	0.2	0.2	0.2	0.2	0.2	0.1
of which: Customs duties	..	0.1	0.2	0.1	0.2	0.2	0.2	0.1	0.1	0.1

	2000	2005	2010	2015	2016	2017	2018	2019	2020	2021p
of which: SRF contributions	..	..	..	..	0.0	0.0	0.0	0.0	0.0	0.0
Slovenia, total supranational	..	0.1	0.2	0.2	0.2	0.2	0.1	0.1	0.2	0.2
of which: Customs duties	..	0.1	0.2	0.1	0.1	0.1	0.1	0.1	0.1	0.2
of which: SRF contributions	..	..	..	0.0	0.0	0.0	0.0	0.0	0.0	0.0
Spain, total supranational	0.2	0.2	0.1	0.2	0.2	0.2	0.2	0.2	0.2	0.2
of which: Customs duties	0.1	0.2	0.1	0.2	0.2	0.2	0.2	0.2	0.1	0.2
of which: SRF contributions	..	..	..	0.1	0.1	0.1	0.1	0.1	0.1	0.1
Non-euro area										
Czech Republic, total supranational	..	0.2	0.2	0.2	0.2	0.2	0.2	0.2	0.1	0.2
of which: Customs duties	..	0.2	0.2	0.2	0.2	0.2	0.2	0.2	0.1	0.2
Denmark, total supranational	0.2	0.2	0.2	0.2	0.1	0.1	0.1	0.1	0.1	0.1
of which: Customs duties	0.2	0.2	0.2	0.2	0.1	0.1	0.1	0.1	0.1	0.1
Hungary, total supranational	..	0.1	0.1	0.1	0.1	0.1	0.1	0.1	0.1	0.1
of which: Customs duties	..	0.1	0.1	0.1	0.1	0.1	0.1	0.1	0.1	0.1
Poland, total supranational	..	0.1	0.1	0.2	0.2	0.2	0.2	0.2	0.2	0.2
of which: Customs duties	..	0.1	0.1	0.2	0.2	0.2	0.2	0.2	0.2	0.2
Sweden, total supranational	0.2	0.2	0.2	0.1	0.1	0.1	0.1	0.1	0.1	0.1
of which: Customs duties	0.1	0.1	0.2	0.1	0.1	0.1	0.1	0.1	0.1	0.1
United Kingdom, total supranational[3]	0.2	0.2	0.2	0.2	0.2	0.2	0.2	0.1	0.1	..
of which: Customs duties	0.2	0.1	0.2	0.2	0.2	0.2	0.2	0.1	0.1	..

.. Not available
Note: SRF figures may differ slightly from those published on the SRB website. These differences are primarily due to timing. Details on these revenues for each country can be found in Chapters 4 and 5.
1. In 2016, the figure includes the 2016 payment of 99.12 and also a payment of 75.89 which was due in Quarter 4 of 2015 but was paid in Quarter 1 of 2016. The figures in this table were reported by the Central Statistics Office and are gross amounts and therefore due to adjustments will differ from the figures reported on the SRB website, which are net figures.
2. The "Bank contribution to the unique European Resolution Fund" amount includes not only the European but also the National Resolution Fund, as required by Eurostat classification.
3. Supranational taxes reported by the United Kingdom are reported until 2020 in Revenue Statistics. From 2021, at the end of the Brexit transition period, this came to an end and taxes subsequently introduced by the United Kingdom are reflected in the appropriate tax category at the national or subnational levels of government, as appropriate.
Source: *Revenue Statistics 2022*, supplemented by discussions with delegates.

StatLink https://stat.link/6xf3ol

In 2020, the combined total of payments collected for the EU was highest in Belgium and the Netherlands, at 0.4% of GDP. Levels above 0.2% of GDP were also seen in France, Germany, Greece, Lithuania, Luxembourg and Spain. All other EU countries that are also members of the OECD collected revenues on behalf of the EU equivalent to between 0.1% and 0.2% of GDP. In all countries except Finland, France and Luxembourg, customs duties were the majority source of these revenues.

Non-wastable tax credits

OECD countries apply two kinds of tax credits to income taxes (both personal and corporate):

- Non-payable or wastable tax credits are those that can only ever be used to reduce or eliminate a tax liability. They cannot be paid out to either taxpayers or non-taxpayers as a benefit. They are, therefore, the same as a tax allowance or relief.
- In contrast, payable or non-wastable tax credits can be partitioned into two parts. One part is used to reduce or eliminate a tax liability in the same way as a wastable tax credit. The other part can be paid directly to recipients as a benefit payment when the benefit exceeds the tax liability.

The OECD methodology for classifying non-wastable tax credits is set out in paragraphs 25 and 26 of the *Interpretative Guide*. These state that only the part of a non-wastable tax credit that is used to reduce or eliminate a taxpayer's tax liability should be subtracted in the reporting of tax revenues. This is referred to as the 'tax expenditure component' of the credit. In contrast, the part of the tax credit that exceeds the taxpayer's tax liability and is paid to that taxpayer is treated as an expenditure item and not subtracted in the reporting of tax revenues. This part is referred to as the 'transfer component'.

Table 1.6. Effect of alternative treatments of non-wastable tax credits, 2020

	Non-wastable tax credits in billions of national currency			Total tax revenue in billions of national currency			Total tax revenue as a percentage of GDP		
	Total value	Transfer component	Tax expenditure component	Net basis	Split basis (per current guidance)	Gross basis	Net basis	Split basis (per current guidance)	Gross basis
Australia	10.1	6.6	3.5	584.2	590.7	594.2	28.2	28.5	28.7
Austria[1, 2]	0.3	0.1	0.2	160.1	160.2	160.4	42.2	42.2	42.3
Belgium[2]	1.1	0.3	0.9	193.8	194.1	194.9	42.4	42.5	42.7
Canada[3]	18.3	13.6	4.7	742.4	756.0	760.7	33.6	34.3	34.5
Chile[4]	298.0	223.0	74.9	38 817.2	39 040.3	39 115.2	19.4	19.5	19.5
Czech Republic	38.9	7.9	31.1	1 974.7	1 982.6	2 013.6	34.6	34.7	35.3
Denmark[2]	3.0	0.2	2.9	1 094.7	1 094.8	1 097.7	47.1	47.1	47.2
France[2]	26.1	14.3	11.7	1 033.2	1 047.6	1 059.3	44.7	45.3	45.8
Germany	51.9	20.3	31.5	1 270.7	1 291.0	1 322.6	37.3	37.9	38.8
Iceland	4.4	4.4	0.8	1 056.7	1 061.1	1 061.9	36.0	36.1	36.1
Ireland	0.4	0.0	0.4	..	74.0	74.4	..	19.9	20.0
Israel	1.3	0.0	1.3	420.6	420.6	421.9	29.6	29.6	29.7
Italy	12.1	1.8	10.4	705.0	706.7	717.1	42.5	42.7	43.3
Luxembourg[2, 5]	0.2	..	..	..	..	24.7	..	..	38.1
Mexico	50.5	0.5	50.0	4 148.2	4 148.7	4 198.7	17.8	17.8	18.0
New Zealand	3.0	1.4	1.5	114.2	115.6	117.1	33.4	33.8	34.2
Norway	4.0	3.2	0.8	1 319.9	1 323.1	1 323.9	38.7	38.8	38.8
Slovak Republic[5]	0.4	..	..	..	..	32.4	..	..	35.2
Spain	3.0	1.7	1.2	410.2	412.0	413.2	36.6	36.7	36.8
United Kingdom[6]	23.9	19.9	4.0	670.6	690.5	694.5	31.2	32.1	32.3
United States	526.6	433.7	93.0	4 946.6	5 380.2	5 473.2	23.7	25.8	26.2

.. Not available

Note: In *Revenue Statistics 2022* the tax revenue data are reported on a split basis, unless indicated otherwise.

1. The children's tax credit is not regarded as a tax credit in *Revenue Statistics* and is treated entirely as an expenditure provision.
2. The total tax revenue has been reduced by the amount of any capital transfer that represents uncollected taxes.
3. Some non-wastable tax credits cannot be split into the transfer and tax expenditure components. Their total values have been added to the transfer component.
4. In *Revenue Statistics 2022*, the tax revenue data for Chile are reported on a net basis.
5. In *Revenue Statistics 2022*, the tax revenue data for Luxembourg and Slovak Republic are reported on a gross basis.
6. Please note that the non-wastable tax credit data for the United Kingdom is on a cash basis and includes estimates in some years. Please see the footnotes in the table for the United Kingdom in Chapter 5 for more information.

StatLink https://stat.link/blxmjz

Table 1.6 provides information on the non-wastable tax credits in 2020 for those countries reporting them in *Revenue Statistics 2022* (although it may be that some countries with non-wastable tax credits do not appear in the table). It shows the amount of the non-wastable tax credits and their two components together with the results of using the figures to calculate tax revenue values and the associated tax-to-GDP ratios. Table 1.6 also shows two alternative treatments:

- The 'net basis', which treats non-wastable tax credits entirely as tax provisions, so that the full value of the tax credit reduces reported tax revenues, as shown in columns 4 and 7.
- The 'gross basis' is the opposite, treating non-wastable tax credits entirely as expenditure provisions, with neither the transfer component nor the tax expenditure component deducted from tax revenues, as shown in columns 6 and 9. This is the approach followed by the GFSM and the SNA.

Table 1.6 shows that, with some exceptions, the choice of method for reporting non-wastable tax credits has only a small impact on the ratio of total tax revenue to GDP. For the countries with available data, the difference between the ratios on a net basis and on a gross basis is one percentage point or more in only France, Germany, the United Kingdom and the United States, and between half a percentage point and one percentage point in Canada, the Czech Republic, Italy and New Zealand.

Financing of social security-type benefits in OECD countries

A memorandum item[9] in *Revenue Statistics 2022* describes the financing of social security-type benefits in OECD countries. Unlike social assistance benefits, which are funded from general government revenues, social security-type benefits are funded via contributions to social security or to private insurance schemes, or by other earmarked sources of funding. These sources of financing include:

- Earmarked financing from tax revenues:
  1. Social security contributions (category 2000 in the OECD classification)
  2. Other taxes earmarked for social security-type benefits
- Earmarked financing from non-tax revenues:
  3. Voluntary contributions to the government (VCG)
  4. Compulsory contributions to the private sector (CCPS)

Figure 1.10 shows the relative contribution of each of these sources to financing for social security-type benefits in OECD countries, based on data provided by countries for inclusion in the memorandum item in *Revenue Statistics 2022.*

Figure 1.10. Composition of earmarked financing for social security-type benefits, 2020

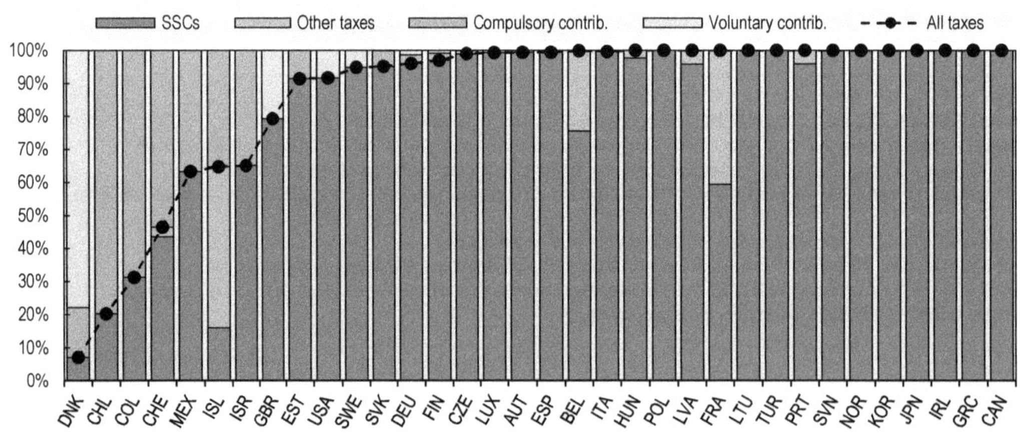

Note: Two countries (Australia and New Zealand) provide social benefits via social assistance rather than via social security, so are not included in the table. In addition, Costa Rica and the Netherlands are also not included in the figure as complete data on contributions were not available in Revenue Statistics. The figures for Denmark should be interpreted with care as the level of social security-type benefits is very small compared to the level of social assistance benefits. Further, there may be borderline issues in some countries when distinguishing between quasi-compulsory and voluntary schemes.

Source: Secretariat calculations based on Chapter 4

StatLink https://stat.link/f5ydem

Taxes represent the largest source of earmarked financing for social security-type benefits, predominantly via social security contributions. Together, social security contributions and other earmarked taxes account for over 90% of the financing of social security-type benefits in 26 OECD countries and 100% in 11 countries. In the remaining nine OECD countries that provide this data, compulsory contributions to the private sector play a larger role, at 79.7% in Chile, 68.7% in Colombia and 53.5% in Switzerland, with smaller shares in Iceland, Mexico and Israel. Few countries received significant shares of voluntary contributions: only in the United Kingdom and Denmark do these exceed 10% of financing.

Figure 1.11 shows tax-to-GDP ratios (as in Table 1.1 and Figure 1.4) both *exclusive* of earmarked funding for social security-type benefits (i.e. tax-to-GDP ratios *less* social security contributions and other earmarked taxes) and *inclusive* of all non-tax earmarked financing for social security-type benefits (i.e. tax-to-GDP ratios - including social security contributions and other earmarked taxes - *plus* compulsory contributions to the private sector and voluntary contributions to government).

The countries with the largest share of social security-type schemes financed by non-tax earmarked contributions are Switzerland (8.5% of GDP), Iceland and Chile (6.6% and 6.1% respectively), which materially affects their rankings:

- Switzerland has a relatively low tax-to-GDP ratio among OECD countries, at 27.5%, but its combined ratio is above halfway in the OECD distribution.
- Iceland has a tax-to-GDP ratio of 36.1%, in the top-third of OECD countries, and a combined ratio of 42.7%, which is the fourth-highest in the OECD.
- Chile has the third-lowest tax-to-GDP ratio and the fifth-lowest combined ratio.

Figure 1.11. Tax-to-GDP ratios and earmarked social security financing (% of GDP, 2020)

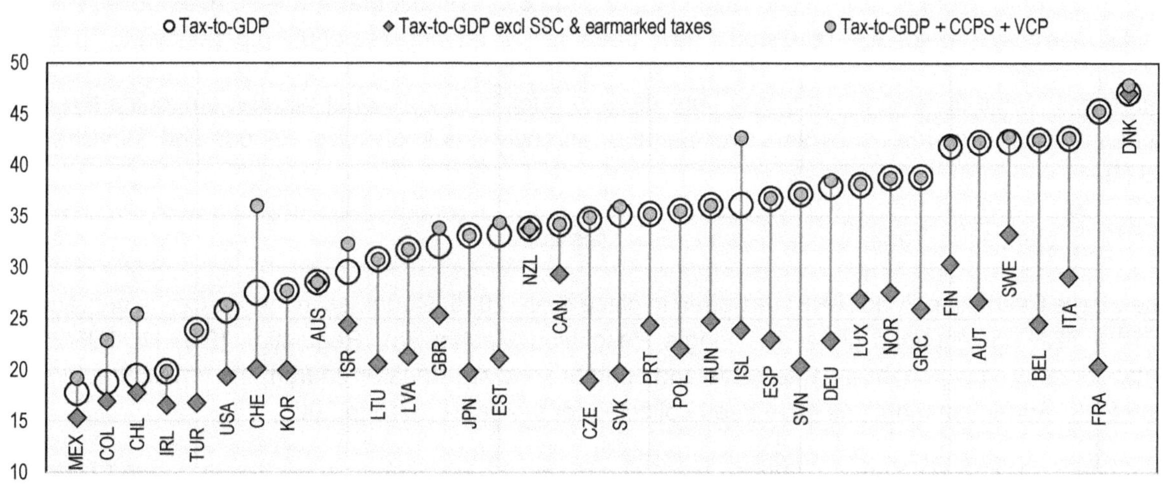

Note: Costa Rica and the Netherlands are not included in the figure as complete data on social security financing in both countries were not available.
Source: Secretariat calculations based on data in Chapter 4.

StatLink https://stat.link/l34zfq

Excluding earmarked financing for social security benefits from the tax-to-GDP ratio does not affect Australia, Denmark and New Zealand, where benefits are funded out of general taxation. Figure 1.11 highlights that the largest share of earmarked funding for social security-type benefits is seen in France, at 25.0% of GDP, as indicated by the difference between the highest and lowest points on the figure. Belgium, Iceland, the Slovak Republic and Slovenia have the next highest shares, at between 16% and 19% of GDP.

Notes

[1] Provisional 2021 figures are not available for Australia and provisional figures on social security contributions in Japan are also not available as at the time *Revenue Statistics 2022* was published.

[2] As Hungary reports revenues on a cash basis for the preliminary year, data for 2021 in this edition of *Revenue Statistics* may change in future editions of the publication once accrual data are available.

[3] The difference between the increase in nominal tax revenues (5.06%) and nominal GDP (5.12%) in New Zealand is only visible on the second decimal place, such that the chapter refers to the tax-to-GDP ratio being unchanged between 2020 and 2021 even though nominal GDP rose by slightly more than nominal tax revenues.

[4] In 2016, Iceland received revenues from one-off stability contributions from entities that previously operated as commercial or savings banks and were concluding operations. The revenue from these contributions led to unusually high tax revenues for a single year and consequently, Iceland's tax-to-GDP ratio rose from 35.1% in 2015 to 50.3% in 2016, before dropping to 37.1% in 2017. This led to an artificial high in the OECD average tax-to-GDP ratio in 2016 of 33.6%. Without these one-off revenues in Iceland, the OECD average tax-to-GDP ratio would have been 33.1%, an increase of 0.2 p.p. relative to 2015.

[5] The terms "value-added tax" and "VAT" are used to refer to any national tax that embodies the basic features of a value-added tax by whatever name or acronym it is known e.g. "Goods and Services Tax" ("GST").

[6] For 1975, please see Table 1.4 of *Revenue Statistics 2022*.

[7] The Single Resolution Fund (SRF) has been in place since 2015. Countries in the Eurozone are required to make SRF contributions under the Single Resolution Mechanism (Regulation (EU) No 806/2014). Contributions are paid on an ex-ante basis and contributions are transferred from the national authorities to the SRF. So far, contributions have been collected for the years 2015 to 2021.

[8] In addition, EU civil servants pay income taxes and social security contributions directly to the EU. These revenues are not included in the data for total tax revenues in this publication as they are not paid to or collected by a national government. However, for the four countries with the highest number of EU civil servants (Belgium, Luxembourg, Italy and Germany), a memorandum account at the end of the respective country table in Chapter 5 provides information on the scale of these payments.

[9] The financing of social security-type benefits is shown in Table 4.77 on a comparable basis (percentage of GDP) and in Table 5.39 on a national currency basis.

2 The impact of COVID-19 on OECD tax revenues

Chapter 2 examines the impact of COVID-19 on tax revenues in OECD countries in 2021, the second year of the pandemic. In 2021, tax policies supported a rebound in economic activity, employment and revenues across the OECD following the widespread declines in gross domestic product (GDP) and tax revenues experienced in 2020. The chapter uses preliminary data on revenues by tax type to analyse the ongoing impact of the pandemic on personal and corporate income taxes, social security contributions, property taxes, VAT and excises, considering changes in nominal terms and as a share of GDP. It compares revenue changes from different tax types in 2020 and 2021.

Introduction

Although the COVID-19 pandemic continued in 2021, economies across the OECD recovered strongly from the shock experienced in 2020. On average, gross domestic product (GDP) grew by 5.5% in the OECD, following a contraction of 4.6% in 2020, bringing output close to pre-pandemic levels in most countries (OECD, 2022[1]). The development and roll-out of COVID-19 vaccines combined with continued policy support for households and businesses and favourable financial conditions underpinned this recovery, which was accompanied by a recovery in labour markets in many parts of the OECD. The unemployment rate in the OECD in 2021 was lower than the pre-pandemic average.

As discussed in Chapter 1, the economic recovery was accompanied by an upturn in tax revenues. Nominal tax revenues increased in all 38 countries between 2020 and 2021, with the year-on-year increase in tax revenues exceeding GDP growth in a majority of cases. Fiscal positions recovered as a result. On average, the fiscal deficit for OECD countries declined from 10.4% of GDP in 2020 to 7.4% in 2021, but stayed significantly above pre-pandemic levels. At USD 15.1 trillion, central government borrowing also remained well above pre-pandemic levels in 2021, despite declining slightly from USD 16.4 trillion in 2020 (OECD, 2022[2]). However, inflationary pressures emerged over the course of the year: the average inflation rate was 5.2% in the fourth quarter of 2021, versus 1.5% in 2020 and a long-term average of 1.7% (OECD, 2022[1]).

This chapter uses preliminary data for 2021 to analyse changes in tax revenues across the OECD during the second year of the pandemic. It identifies major trends in tax policy in OECD countries in 2021 in the context of a strong recovery from the initial impact of the COVID-19 pandemic. It explores how revenues from different tax types performed in 2021, tracking their changes both in nominal terms and as a share of GDP. It then compares these changes with those observed in 2020, and it analyses the relationship between changes in tax levels and in GDP for the main tax types in both years, thereby showing which taxes have been most affected over the course of the pandemic.

Overview: changes to total tax revenues, GDP and the tax-to-GDP ratio

Impact of COVID-19: changes in 2021 relative to 2020

As highlighted in Chapter 1, the average OECD tax-to-GDP ratio increased by 0.6 percentage points (p.p.) in 2021 relative to 2020 to 34.4% of GDP. Increases in the tax-to-GDP ratio were observed in 26 out of 37 OECD countries for which data is available over the same period[1], while 11 countries recorded a decline in their tax-to-GDP ratio.

Figure 2.1 shows the increases in nominal taxes and nominal GDP across the OECD between 2020 and 2021. In all 37 countries for which data is available, both tax revenues and GDP increased in nominal terms. In the 26 countries where the tax-to-GDP ratio increased, the relative increases in nominal tax revenues were larger than the relative increases in GDP; in the other 11 countries, the opposite occurred.

In 2021, nominal tax revenues increased by 13.4% from the previous year on average across the OECD. Nineteen countries observed an increase in nominal tax revenues larger than 10%, with largest increases in Chile (37.5%), Türkiye (37.4%) and Norway (32.2%). The increase in tax revenues was larger than the increase in GDP in all 19 countries except Türkiye, where nominal GDP increased by 43.6% in 2021, resulting in a fall of 1.0 percentage point (p.p.) in the country's tax-to-GDP ratio.

In the 11 countries where the tax-to-GDP ratio declined between 2020 and 2021, revenues grew by less than 10% in nominal terms, with the exception of Türkiye. Among the countries where the tax-to-GDP ratio decreased in 2021, Hungary[2] and the Czech Republic also recorded a decline in their tax-to-GDP ratio in 2020.

Figure 2.1. Changes in nominal tax and nominal GDP, 2020-2021

Year-on-year % change

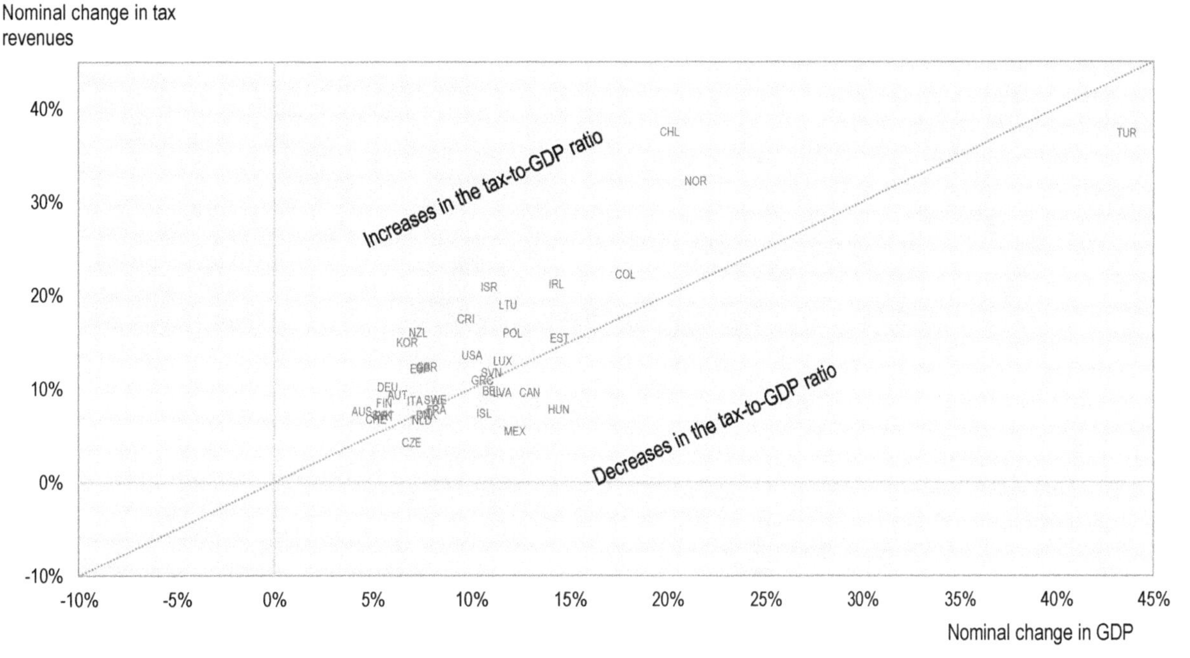

Note: Data for 2021 are preliminary and should be interpreted with caution; please see Box 2.2 for more details. Data for Australia and New Zealand show the change between the fiscal years 2019 and 2020, as both countries report tax revenues on a fiscal year basis that includes the first two quarters of 2021 in the 2020 fiscal year. Data for Japan are not included as data on SSC revenues are not available. See Box 2.1 for more information. The diagonal line across the graph represents the point at which the change in tax revenues and in GDP were of the same magnitude and therefore the point at which the tax-to-GDP ratio remained unchanged. Countries above the diagonal line had increases in their tax to GDP ratios; countries below it had falls.
Source: *Revenue Statistics 2022* and authors' calculations.

StatLink https://stat.link/u5vb0y

During the first year of the pandemic in 2020, tax-to-GDP ratios increased from the previous year in 20 out of 38 OECD countries and the average tax-to-GDP ratio remained unchanged. However, the increases in 2020 occurred in a context of declining nominal revenues and declining GDP, whereas both rebounded strongly in 2021. This is shown by Figure 2.2, which shows changes in tax revenues and GDP in individual OECD countries in 2020 (the orange dots) and in 2021 (the blue dots).[3]

Figure 2.2. Changes in nominal tax and nominal GDP, all years

Year-on-year % change

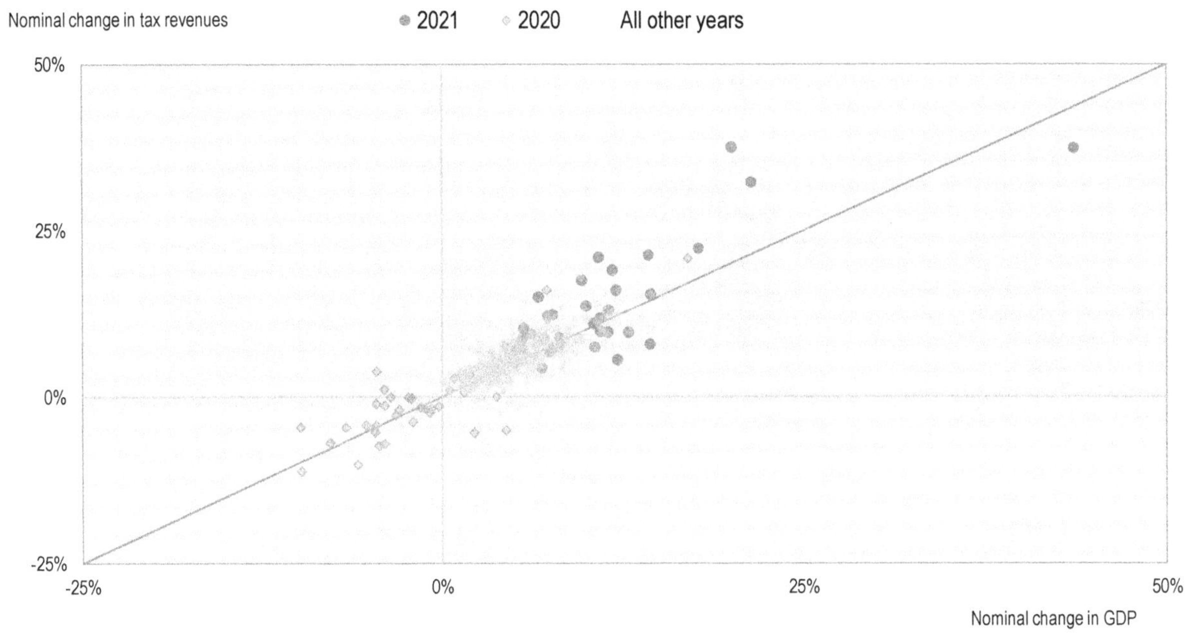

Note: Data for 2021 are preliminary and should be interpreted with caution; please see Box 2.2 for more details. Outliers have been excluded to improve the readability of the figure. The grey dots show nominal changes in tax revenues and GDP in OECD countries since 1995.
Source: *Revenue Statistics 2022* and authors' calculations.

StatLink https://stat.link/e85oub

As the orange dots in Figure 2.2 demonstrate, tax revenues and GDP declined in nominal terms in 2020 in most OECD countries. In total, 25 countries recorded a decline in GDP and tax revenues in 2020, two countries recorded an increase in tax revenues but a decline in GDP, three recorded a decline in tax revenues but an increase in GDP, and eight recorded an increase in both indicators. Where tax-to-GDP ratios increased in 2020, this tended to be because GDP (the denominator in the tax-to-GDP ratio) in most countries shrunk by more than tax revenues (the numerator) during the first year of the COVID-19 crisis.

In 2021, on the other hand, nominal tax revenues and nominal GDP both rose in all countries in the OECD for which data are available. In general, the increases in tax revenues and GDP recorded in 2021 (as shown by the blue dots in Figure 2.2) were larger than the declines in 2020, suggesting a strong economic rebound and recovery in tax revenues, at least in nominal terms. However, it is important to note that inflation rose sharply over the course of 2021.

Box 2.1. Tax types considered and country coverage

Tax types considered in the analysis

This chapter considers changes in both total tax revenues and several individual categories of tax revenues of particular size or policy significance. These taxes include:

Table 2.1. Individual tax types used in this chapter

Detailed tax types	Acronym	Corresponding *Revenue Statistics 2022* codes
Personal income tax	PIT	1100 Personal income tax
Corporate income tax	CIT	1200 Corporate income tax
Social security contributions & payroll taxes	SSC	2000 Social security contributions; 3000 Payroll taxes
Property taxes	Prop.	4000 Taxes on property
Value-added taxes	VAT	5111 Value-added taxes
Excises	Exc.	5121 Excises
Other consumption taxes	OCT	All other taxes under 5000 (5112, 5113, 5122, 5123, 5124, 5125, 5126, 5127, 5128, 5200, 5300)
Residual	Res.	1300 Unallocable between 1100 and 1200; 6000 Other taxes

Information is presented for two different indicators: tax revenues in nominal currency and tax revenues as a share of GDP. The GDP data that is used for each country is the same as shown in Table 3.19 of the publication, except for adjustments related to the assumptions about fiscal years noted below. The averages shown in this chapter are unweighted. For the reasons detailed below, they may differ from the other averages for 2021 presented elsewhere in the report.

Caveats for individual countries

All OECD countries other than Australia, Japan and New Zealand provide data on a calendar year basis. In Australia and New Zealand, the fiscal year runs from 1 July of the current year to 30 June of the following year, whereas in Japan the fiscal year runs from 1 April in the current year to 31 March the following year. Japan's fiscal year 2020 included the first quarter of 2021, while the first two quarters of 2021 occurred in fiscal year 2020 for Australia and New Zealand. In this chapter, the changes shown for Australia and New Zealand are from the 2019 to 2020 fiscal years for consistency between the two countries.

In a few countries, preliminary data for the year 2021 was only partially available at the time this publication was prepared. Data that was unavailable include:

- Social security contributions in Japan: This chapter does not present data for SSCs or for total tax revenues for Japan, and Japan is not included in the averages for these two items. Data for Japan is included in the averages for all other tax types.
- A breakdown of income tax revenues (between personal income tax [PIT, category 1100] and corporate income tax [CIT, category 1200] and of taxes on goods and services (including VAT [category 5111] and excises [category 5121]) in Greece: In this chapter, data is shown for total income taxes (category 1000) and total taxes on goods and services (category 5000). Greece is not included in the averages for PIT, CIT, VAT or excises.

Tax revenue data are available for most OECD countries on an accrual basis, except for Chile, Colombia, Costa Rica, Israel, Korea, Mexico and Türkiye, which report on a cash basis. Information on PIT in Canada is also reported on a cash basis. In addition, preliminary 2021 data for Hungary are on a cash basis, while the final data for years up to and including 2020 are on an accrual basis.

It is worth noting that tax revenues in the OECD proved more resilient than elsewhere in 2020. In the Asia-Pacific region, tax revenues declined by 8.8% in nominal terms and the average tax-to-GDP ratio fell by 1.2 p.p. between 2019 and 2020 to 19.1%. In Latin America and the Caribbean, tax revenues declined by 8.0% in nominal terms and the average tax-to-GDP ratio fell by 0.8 p.p. between 2019 and 2020 to 21.9%. In Africa, tax revenues declined by 0.5% in nominal terms and the average tax-to-GDP ratio fell by 0.3 p.p. to 16.0%.

Table 2.2 shows the different dynamics of nominal GDP and nominal tax revenues in OECD countries over the first two years of the pandemic. Tax revenues grew more strongly than GDP in 2021 and did not decline as sharply as GDP in 2020, leading to an increase in the tax-to-GDP ratio in 2021, while 2020 remained unchanged. The table also confirms that the mean increase in tax revenues in 2021, of 13.4% in nominal terms, was far larger than the decline in tax revenues in 2020, of 1.8% in nominal terms. Similarly, mean GDP growth across the OECD in 2021, of 10.7% in nominal terms, far exceeded the fall in 2020, of 1.8%.

Table 2.2. Comparison of changes in nominal tax revenues and nominal GDP, 2020-21

Year-on-year % change

		Mean	Lower quartile	Median	Upper quartile
Tax	2020	-1.8	-4.6	-1.7	-0.1
	2021	13.4	7.8	10.2	16.0
GDP	2020	-1.8	-4.5	-2.2	0.8
	2021	10.7	7.0	9.9	12.0
Tax/GDP	2020	0.0	-0.6	0.1	0.6
	2021	0.6	-0.2	0.6	1.3

Note: Data for 2021 are preliminary and should be interpreted with caution; please see Box 2.2 for more details. The mean tax-to-GDP ratio in 2021 in this table differs from that shown in the other chapters in the report due to the use of the 2020 fiscal years for Australia and New Zealand in this chapter, for the reasons explained in Box 2.1.
Source: *Revenue Statistics 2022* and authors' calculations.

StatLink https://stat.link/z0vyx3

Tax policy reforms and revenue trends in 2021

The differing trends in tax revenues and GDP between 2020 and 2021 discussed in the previous section attest to the strong recovery by OECD countries following the initial shock of the COVID-19 pandemic. Tax policy played an important role in this recovery, as it did in supporting businesses and households during the downturn. This section begins by examining the evolution of tax policy in the second year of the pandemic in the context of this recovery. It then analyses revenues from different tax types in 2021, comparing changes in 2021 with those recorded in 2020 in nominal terms and as a share of GDP.

Tax policy reforms in 2021

Tax policy has been a critical tool in governments' response to COVID-19 across the OECD. Over the course of the pandemic, the objectives of tax policy have evolved in line with the evolution of the pandemic itself and governments' broader policy goals. In general, tax policy in 2020 was characterised by measures to protect workers and businesses from the disruptions caused by the pandemic, while there has been greater focus on policies to promote investment and accelerate the post-pandemic recovery in 2021. Some tax policy measures have evolved over the course of the pandemic to become more targeted, while others were eliminated altogether. While a majority of the measures were temporary, most of these temporary measures were extended beyond their initial duration. Other measures became permanent.

Labour markets rebounded in many parts of the OECD in 2021, with total employment and the unemployment rate returning to pre-pandemic levels by the end of the year on average, as shown in Figure 2.3 (OECD, 2022[3]). However, the recovery in employment has been uneven, with labour force participation and employment rates still below pre-crisis levels in some countries (OECD, 2022[3]). Employment growth has been stronger in high-pay service industries than in low-pay contact-intensive industries. Many young, low-paid and low-skilled workers, who were particularly vulnerable to the pandemic's initial impact, have benefited relatively little from the recovery in the labour market; the youth employment rate is still below pre-crisis levels in over half of OECD countries. Long-term unemployment remained above pre-pandemic levels in 20 out of 32 countries for which data was available (OECD, 2022[3]).

Figure 2.3. Unemployment rate: pre-crisis, peak, and most recent

Percent of labour force, seasonally adjusted

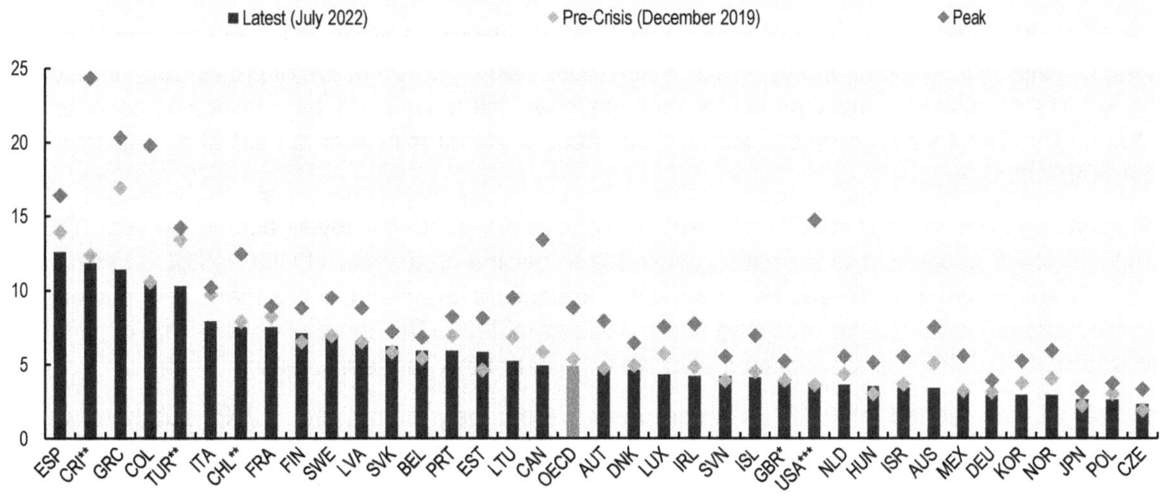

Note: For countries marked with *, the latest data refer to May 2022; for those marked with **, the latest data refer to June 2022; and for those marked with ***, the latest data refer to August 2022.
Source: OECD Short-term Labour Market Statistics.

StatLink https://stat.link/myt5dv

Nonetheless, labour shortages emerged in many countries during the second half of 2021, with vacancy rates reaching historic highs in a number of OECD countries. Labour supply did not keep up with a surge in demand driven by the economic recovery and large-scale recovery plans, leading to shortages across many sectors. However, shortages also reflect workers' reticence to take jobs in certain sectors due to tough working conditions and/or low pay. It is notable that, unlike the current situation, vacancies remained depressed two years after the Global Financial Crisis of 2008-09 (OECD, 2022[3]).

Changes to labour taxation in 2021 were primarily intended to boost economic growth and promote equity (OECD, 2022[4]). The most common measures were to narrow the base for personal income tax (PIT) in order to raise employment, provide in work-benefits, and support low-income families with children. A small number of countries reduced PIT rates, particularly for low- and middle-income households. Some countries introduced measures to narrow the social security contributions (SSC) base, while a smaller number lowered rates for SSCs, typically on a temporary basis. While many of the measures introduced in 2020 to help workers and households deal with the pandemic were withdrawn or scaled back in 2021, a number of countries introduced new measures in 2021.

The tax burden on labour in OECD countries decreased slightly for most household types on average in 2021, following sharp declines in 2020. However, for most household types in a majority of OECD countries, the tax wedge increased between 2020 and 2021 due to a combination of increases in average wages and the withdrawal of policies introduced in the first year of the pandemic. In most countries, increases to the tax wedge in 2021 more than offset the declines recorded in 2020 and the tax wedge has rebounded to higher levels than in 2019, before the pandemic (OECD, 2022[5]).

In 2021, the policy priority for corporate income tax (CIT) reforms was to stimulate investment and innovation (OECD, 2022[4]). To this end, a number of OECD countries introduced more generous corporate tax incentives, particularly for capital expenditure and research and development to promote environmental sustainability. This tendency contrasts with 2020, when CIT revenues were affected by widespread use of tax measures to support business liquidity and cash flow during the economic shock caused by the pandemic. Measures adopted in 2020 included deferrals of tax payments, filing extensions and flexible tax payment plans, applied in over 70% of OECD countries. Several OECD countries suspended or reduced prepayments of CIT, many of which were targeted at SMEs, and refunds of advance payments and CIT credits were accelerated in many jurisdictions (OECD, 2022[4]).

Also in 2021, 137 jurisdictions agreed to the Two-Pillar Solution to Address the Tax Challenges Arising from the Digitalisation of the Economy, under which more than USD 125 billion of profits from around 100 of the world's largest and most profitable multi-national enterprises will be reallocated to countries worldwide. The Two-Pillar agreement will also introduce a global minimum tax set at an effective rate of 15% (OECD, 2022[6]).

Retail spending grew strongly in 2021 and was well above pre-pandemic levels across the year (OECD, 2022[1]). However, household consumption continued to decline as a share of GDP in 2021, having also fallen in 2020 (Figure 2.4). Measured under the expenditure approach, investment and net exports rebounded strongly in 2021 after recording sharp declines in 2020. The share of government expenditure declined slightly in 2021 after increasing during the first year of the pandemic.

In the area of value-added tax (VAT), standard rates were largely maintained in 2021 but there were a large number of changes to the base. The majority of temporary changes to VAT rates that were introduced in 2020 to address the pandemic were withdrawn in 2021, except those related to medical supplies used to respond to the pandemic (OECD, 2022[4]). At the same time, some countries applied reduced VAT rates to a wider range of goods and services on a permanent basis in 2021 to address equity concerns. There was strong growth in e-invoicing and digital reporting requirements in 2021 as countries implemented reforms to e-commerce, whose expansion accelerated significantly as a result of the pandemic. Meanwhile, there were further increases in excise duties in 2021, especially on tobacco products (OECD, 2022[4]).

In the final quarter of 2021, a number of countries applied reduced VAT rates and lowered import duties and excise taxes on energy sources in order to shield households and firms from rising prices, a trend that continued into 2022 (OECD, 2022[4]). High energy prices have also prompted policy makers to impose changes to environmentally-related taxes. In 2021, progress on environmentally related taxation continued but at a slower pace than prior to the pandemic. Carbon taxes on fuels were expanded in 2021, and a selection of countries in the European Union introduced a tax on plastic (OECD, 2022[4]).

In 2021, there were fewer reforms to property taxes than in previous years. The majority of measures in this tax category involved increases in tax rates or a broadening of the tax base. These measures were mostly targeted at high net worth individuals or entities that use properties primarily as an investment vehicle. Reforms have increasingly focused on promoting the efficient use of the existing housing stock as well as the fairness of property taxation more generally (OECD, 2022[4]).

Figure 2.4. Composition of GDP (expenditure approach), 2019-21

Average shares across OECD countries

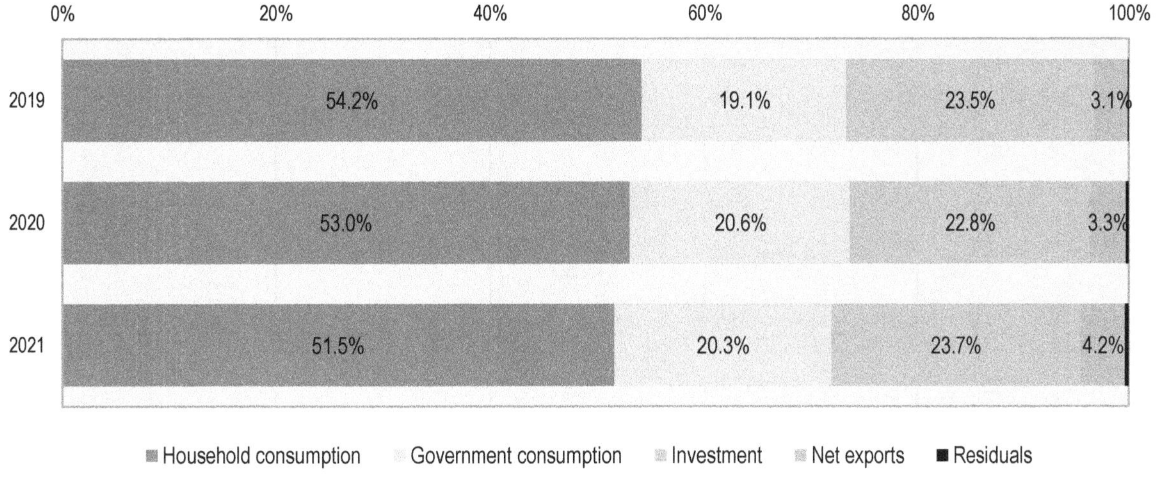

Note: Data for 2021 are the average of 33 OECD countries for which these data were available.
Source: OECD National Accounts and authors' calculations (accessed on 18/10/2022).

StatLink https://stat.link/0n31kj

Changes in revenues from different tax types, 2020-2021

Against the backdrop of evolving tax policies and economic recovery described above, the revenue dynamics of different tax types varied between 2020 and 2021. This section analyses changes in revenues from the main tax categories between 2020 and 2021, both as a share of GDP and in nominal terms. Box 2.1 provides more information on the tax types considered.

Changes in revenues by tax type as a share of GDP

On average, the 0.6 p.p. increase in tax revenues as a percentage of GDP in OECD countries between 2020 and 2021 was driven by higher revenues from CIT and VAT (Figure 2.5).[4] CIT revenues rose by 0.5 p.p. on average between 2020 and 2021, having recorded the largest decline of any major tax type between 2019 and 2020 (0.3 p.p.). VAT revenues rose by 0.4 p.p. in the second year of the pandemic, having remained unchanged as a proportion of GDP in 2020.[5]

Revenues from SSCs, on the other hand, declined by 0.2 p.p. on average in 2021, having risen by 0.3 p.p. in 2020. Revenues from excises also declined by 0.1 p.p., having fallen by the same amount in 2020. PIT revenues, which rose by 0.3 p.p. in 2020, remained unchanged as a share of GDP in 2021, while revenues from property taxes remained unchanged as a share of GDP in both years.

CIT revenues increased as a share of GDP in 24 of the 37 countries for which preliminary data are available in 2021, declined in nine and were unchanged in four. The largest increase was observed in Norway, where CIT revenues rebounded from a 3.6 p.p. decline in 2020 to rise by 7.3 p.p. in 2021 due to an increase in revenues from petroleum extraction following an exceptional decline the previous year. Eleven other countries observed increases in CIT revenues larger than 0.5 p.p. while only Chile observed a decline in CIT revenues in excess of 0.5 p.p. (0.9 p.p.), which was a result of the pandemic's impact on the economy and policies to mitigate this impact on small firms.

Figure 2.5. Changes in tax revenues by category as a share of GDP, 2020-21

Year-on-year change, p.p.

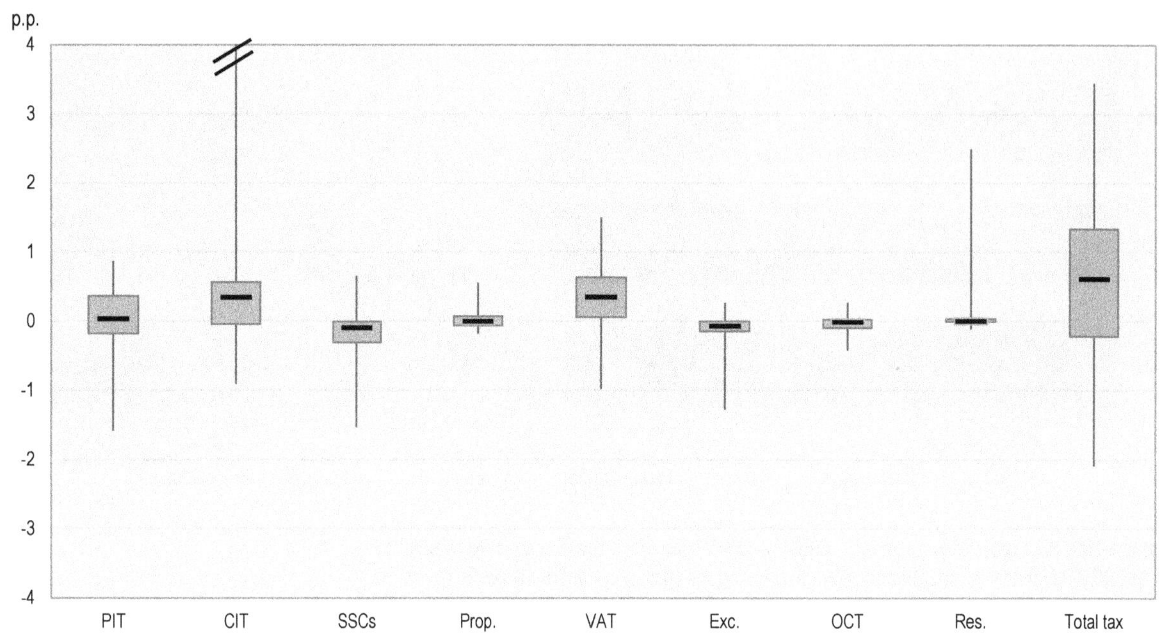

Note: Data for 2021 are preliminary and should be interpreted with caution; please see Box 2.2 for more details. In the figure, the lowest point represents the minimum country change for the tax type between 2020-2021; the box represents the changes for countries between the lower and upper quartiles (i.e. 50% of OECD countries had changes within the range shown by each box); and the upper point for each tax type represents the maximum country change. The line in each box represents the median country change (i.e. half of OECD countries were both above and below this line).
Source: *Revenue Statistics 2022* and authors' calculations.

StatLink https://stat.link/ygazvw

Revenues from VAT increased as a share of GDP in 30 countries in 2021, remained unchanged in three and declined as a share of GDP in three. The increase in VAT revenues exceeded 0.5 p.p. in 13 countries, with the largest increase observed in Chile (1.5 p.p.). The largest decline occurred in Norway, where VAT revenues declined by 1.0 p.p., although in nominal terms revenues from VAT increased by 8.5% in Norway.

Excise revenues declined as a share of GDP in 21 countries, increased in six and were unchanged in ten. The largest decline, of 1.3 p.p., was recorded in Türkiye, and was caused by an automatic adjustment of taxes on fuel to compensate for higher prices. With the exception of the decreases in Norway (0.5 p.p.) and Mexico (0.4 p.p.), the changes in the other countries did not exceed 0.3 p.p.

PIT revenues increased as a share of GDP in 17 countries in 2021, declined in 14 and remained unchanged in seven. Increases exceeded 0.5 p.p. in seven countries, with the largest increases observed in Korea (0.9 p.p.), attributable to higher wages and employment as well as increases in revenues from capital gains, notably from real estate transactions. Estonia, the United Kingdom and Israel all recorded increases of 0.8 p.p. in PIT revenues; in the case of Estonia, this was partly driven by a pension reform in 2021. The decreases in PIT exceeded 0.5 p.p. in six countries, with the largest declines recorded in the Czech Republic (1.6 p.p.), Iceland (1.1 p.p.) and Denmark (1.0 p.p.). The fall in the Czech Republic was a result of a reduction of the employee tax base and an increase in tax credits.

SSCs increased as a share of GDP in eight countries, declined in 22 and were unchanged in six. The decreases were larger than 0.5 p.p. in five countries, with the largest falls recorded in Norway (1.5 p.p.), Hungary (1.0 p.p.) and Luxembourg (0.8 p.p.). Hungary reduced the SSC rate from 17.5% to 15.5% in July

2020. There was only one country – the Czech Republic – where the increase exceeded 0.5 p.p.; this was caused by an increase in minimum wages and also reflects the fact that SSCs fell sharply in 2020 as a result of a COVID-19 measure.

Property taxes increased as a share of GDP in 11 countries, declined in 13 and were unchanged in 13. None of the changes exceeded 0.3 p.p. except in Korea and Israel, where revenues from property taxes increased by 0.6 p.p. and 0.5 p.p. respectively. The increase in Korea was partly a consequence of higher real estate prices.

Box 2.2. The accuracy of preliminary data during the COVID-19 pandemic

The indicators shown in this chapter are based on preliminary data provided for the year 2021 as part of the data collection round for this year's edition of *Revenue Statistics*. Normally, the publication does not place emphasis on these preliminary data as they are subject to revisions in future years. However, due to interest in the impacts of the COVID-19 pandemic on tax revenues, the special features for the 2021 and 2022 editions of *Revenue Statistics* use preliminary data to provide an initial snapshot of tax revenues during the first two years of the pandemic. While the data should be treated with caution, they nonetheless permit insights into the impact of COVID-19 on tax revenues across OECD countries.

Many macroeconomic indicators, including gross domestic product (GDP), are subject to revisions. Initial estimates are usually released one to two months after the reference period, aiming to strike a balance between the accuracy and timeliness of the results, in order to support economic analysis and decision-making. In most countries, more complete data become available over time and National Statistical Offices progressively revise their estimates to further improve their accuracy. The OECD frequently conducts studies into the size and direction of revisions across OECD countries, the most recent of which occurred in 2018 and provides a benchmark for analysing the scale of revisions for 2020 data.

Last year's edition of *Revenue Statistics* advised that 'initial estimates released during the pandemic may be subject to larger and more frequent revisions than normal', reflecting unprecedented 'collection, compilation and methodological challenges', although it highlighted steps taken by the international statistical community to mitigate these challenges, including alternative or proxy data sources to assist in overcoming specific data gaps (OECD, 2021[7]). It also stated that preliminary data for 2020 might be subject to larger than normal revisions 'due to the support measures introduced by governments to support households and businesses in the crisis, including the widespread use of tax deferrals, extension of filing deadlines and increased flexibility with the treatment of tax losses'.

A comparison between the preliminary data for 2020 reported in the special feature of last year's *Revenue Statistics* and final data for 2020 shown in Chapter 1 of this year's edition reveals that a few OECD member states reported large adjustments to data for the first year of the COVID-19 pandemic, but the majority of data revisions were not significant. Figure 2.6 provides a snapshot of the change between preliminary and final data for the main tax types in 38 OECD countries. The shading in blue represents the difference in the share of each tax in GDP between the two datasets, with darker blue indicating larger variations.

Figure 2.6. Change between preliminary and final data for main tax types, 2020

Percentage change in the tax-to-GDP ratio

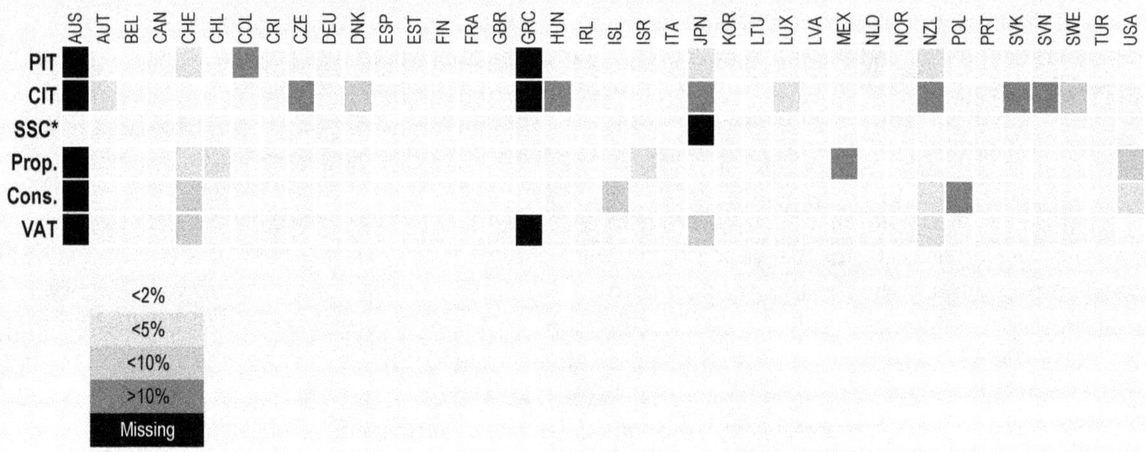

Note: 'Cons' includes all consumption taxes (5000) except VAT. No shading indicates that the tax category did not exist in the country while black shading indicates that data was not available.

* 'SSC' in the graph refers to category 2000 only, unlike the rest of this chapter, which combines revenues from category 2000 and 3000. Please see Box 2.1 for more details.

Source: *Revenue Statistics 2022* and authors' calculations.

StatLink https://stat.link/axto8u

The percentage change in the share of each tax revenue type to GDP was below 2% in all but 27 of the 216 tax categories across all OECD countries. In only nine individual taxes of the 216 categories shown did the change from preliminary to final taxes result in a change greater than 10% of that tax's share of GDP. Most of these larger changes were recorded in CIT revenues.

Preliminary and final data were also compared to examine whether differences between the two data sets would have significantly changed conclusions about changes in the tax-to-GDP ratios for all tax types between 2019 and 2020. In 137 (63%) of the 216 tax categories, there was little change in the level reported in the publication. Among the remaining 79 categories, there was a change in sign in 22 cases (i.e. one dataset indicated a positive change while the other showed a negative change).

By comparison, when preliminary data for 2018 was compared with final data for that year, five individual taxes out of 216 categories reported a change larger than 10% of that tax category's share of GDP. When looking at changes in revenues from individual taxes as a share of GDP, revisions between preliminary and final data for 2018 resulted in a change of sign in eight cases.

Source: OECD Statistics and Data Directorate, country inputs and authors' contributions.

Figure 2.7 shows the decomposition of changes to the tax-to-GDP ratio in 37 OECD countries included in this analysis. In 18 of the 25 countries where the tax-to-GDP ratio increased between 2020 and 2021 (not including Greece for reasons of data aggregation), an increase in either CIT or VAT revenues was the main driver of the rise. However, it is notable that PIT increased as a share of GDP in 17 of these 25 countries – two fewer than was the case for CIT. PIT revenues declined as a share of GDP in all but two of the 11 countries whose tax-to-GDP decreased in 2021, underlining the importance of variations in this tax type to overall revenue levels.

Sixteen of the 26 countries whose tax-to-GDP ratio increased overall in 2021 experienced a decline in SSCs, while all but three of the countries whose tax-to-GDP ratio decreased overall experienced a decline in SSCs. Korea was the only country to record an increase across all the main tax types as a share of GDP between 2020 and 2021, while Canada and Hungary were the only countries not to record an increase in revenues from any of the main tax types as a share of GDP over the same period.

Figure 2.7. Decomposition of change in OECD tax-to-GDP ratios by tax category, 2020-21

Year-on-year change, p.p.

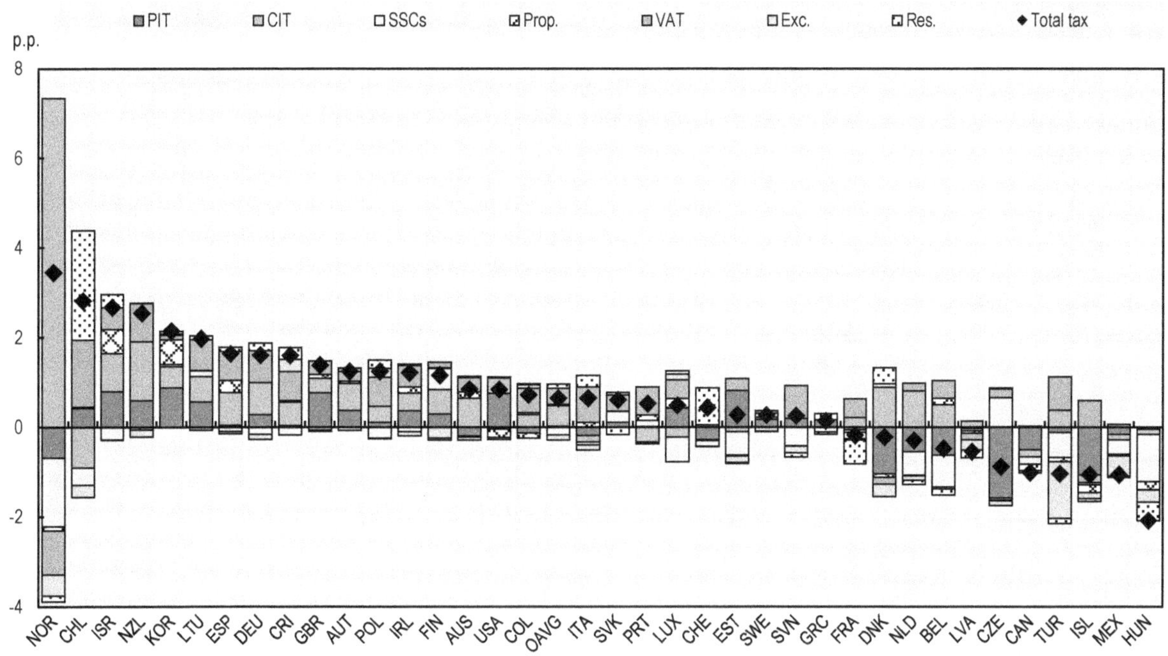

Note: Data for 2021 are preliminary and should be interpreted with caution; please see Box 2.2 for more details. This graph includes the change between years 2019 and 2020 for Australia and New Zealand, as both countries report tax revenues on a fiscal year basis that includes the first and second quarters of 2021 in the 2020 fiscal year. Due to data availability, the average excludes Japan; it also excludes Greece for PIT (category 1100), CIT (category 1200), VAT (category 5111) and excises (category 5121) due to disaggregated data for these categories not being available. Greece's PIT data in the graph refers to its total income tax revenue.
Source: *Revenue Statistics 2022* and authors' calculations.

StatLink https://stat.link/2ql31u

Changes in nominal tax revenues by tax type

Revenues from all tax types increased in nominal terms between 2020 and 2021. In total, mean tax revenues increased by 13.4%, while the median increase was 10.2%. Nominal GDP registered a mean increase of 10.7% and a median increase of 9.9% over the same period. Table 2.3 compares the distribution of changes in revenues from different tax types in nominal terms between 2020 and 2021 with the changes observed between 2019 and 2020, the first year of the pandemic.

In 2021, the largest increase in mean tax revenues was observed for CIT, which rose by 23.1% in nominal terms in 2021. This contrasts with results for 2020, when CIT revenues fell by 9.8%, the largest decline of any tax type in that year. CIT revenues increased in nominal terms in 34 out of the 37 countries for which data are available in 2021, with eight countries observing increases in excess of 40%.

Mean VAT revenues increased by 17.3% in nominal terms between 2020 and 2021. Revenues from VAT rose in all countries, with the increase exceeding 20% in nine. VAT revenues declined by 2.4% in nominal terms in 2020. Meanwhile, excise revenues registered the weakest mean growth in 2021, of 5.5% (versus a 5.4% decline in 2020). Excise revenues rose in nominal terms in 29 countries and declined in eight. The increase exceeded 10% in six countries while the decline exceeded this threshold in two countries.

Mean nominal revenues from PIT increased by 11.7% in 2021 while SSCs rose by 9.0%. PIT revenues rose in every country except one, with the increase exceeding 20% in seven countries. SSCs rose in every country that levies SSCs except one; the increase exceeded 10% in eight countries. In 2020, PIT was the only main tax category to record an increase in revenues in 2020 in nominal terms (of 1.9%); SSCs declined by 0.3% in nominal terms between 2019 and 2020. Revenues from property taxes, which rose by 0.1% in nominal terms in 2020, registered mean growth of 10.6% in 2021, rising in all but two countries. The increase in nominal revenues from property taxes was larger than 20% in five countries.

Changes in total tax revenues were closely correlated with changes in GDP in 2020 and 2021. However, there are some notable differences in the correlation of changes in different tax types with GDP between 2020 and 2021. In both 2020 and 2021, changes in VAT revenues were closely correlated with fluctuations in GDP. However, the correlation of changes in PIT revenues with GDP was significantly stronger in 2021 than in 2020, while the correlation between changes in GDP and revenues from CIT and excises became weaker over the same period, turning negative in the case of excises. Revenues from property taxes and SSCs were more closely correlated with GDP in 2021 than was the case in 2020.

Table 2.3. Distribution of nominal revenue changes by tax category and of GDP

	2020-2021					2019-2020				
	Mean	Lower quartile	Median	Upper quartile	Correlation with GDP	Mean	Lower quartile	Median	Upper quartile	Correlation with GDP
PIT	11.7	6.1	10.0	16.0	58.4	1.9	-1.1	1.0	4.7	22.1
CIT	23.1	6.9	22.1	36.9	29.5	-9.8	-17.1	-8.6	-1.4	51.3
SSC	9.0	5.2	7.5	9.7	31.9	-0.3	-2.9	0.4	2.2	30.1
Prop.	10.6	4.5	9.1	15.4	42.8	0.1	-4.5	0.3	3.3	37.2
VAT	17.3	9.7	14.4	19.7	80.4	-2.4	-8.1	-1.7	1.4	66.4
Exc.	5.5	2.6	5.1	8.4	-3.8	-5.4	-11.0	-5.3	-1.7	70.8
Total Tax	13.4	7.8	10.2	16.0	78.5	-1.8	-4.6	-1.7	-0.1	76.4
GDP	10.7	7.0	9.9	12.0	..	-1.8	-4.5	-2.2	0.8	..

Note: Data for 2021 are preliminary and should be interpreted with caution; please see Box 2.2 for more details.
The correlation for CIT revenues and GDP in 2020 excludes Latvia, which saw a significant increase in CIT revenues in nominal terms (346.4%) due to the correction following abnormally high repayments in 2019, see the discussion above for more information) and the relatively low share of CIT to GDP in Latvia (0.2% in 2019 and 0.7% in 2020). If Latvia were included in the correlation for nominal CIT revenues in 2020, it would be 4.7%. Norway's growth in CIT revenues in 2021 (of 394.6% in nominal terms) is excluded from calculations.
Source: *Revenue Statistics 2022* and authors' calculations.

StatLink https://stat.link/y5igex

Changes in revenue by tax type in 2020 and 2021

Figure 2.8 shows the distribution of changes in revenues from different taxes as a percentage of GDP in 2020 and 2021 respectively. The changes in overall tax revenues were more widely distributed in 2021 than in 2020; the largest change (positive or negative) observed in 2021 exceeded the largest change observed in 2020, while there was much greater variation among the middle 50% of the distribution. The graph underlines the different trends among different tax types across OECD countries during the first two years of the pandemic. In 2020, PIT and SSCs were most resilient, increasing on average and in a majority of OECD countries as a share of GDP. In the same year, there was a clear fall in CIT revenues as a share of GDP across the OECD while VAT revenues remained steady on average and varied within a relatively narrow range across OECD countries

In 2021, a strong rebound in CIT revenues as a percentage of GDP was observed across the OECD, along with widespread increases in VAT revenues. PIT remained unchanged as a percentage of GDP in 2021, with only slightly more countries experiencing increases than declines, and there were widespread declines in SSCs, leading to a fall in SSCs as a percentage of GDP on average. For the other tax types, the graph shows that changes in revenues from property taxes across the OECD were very similar in both years while declines in revenues from excises were more widespread in 2021, although the average fall was only marginally larger than that observed in 2020.

Figure 2.8. Distribution of changes in revenues by tax types

Changes as p.p. of GDP, from lowest to highest: minimum, lower quartile, median, upper quartile, maximum

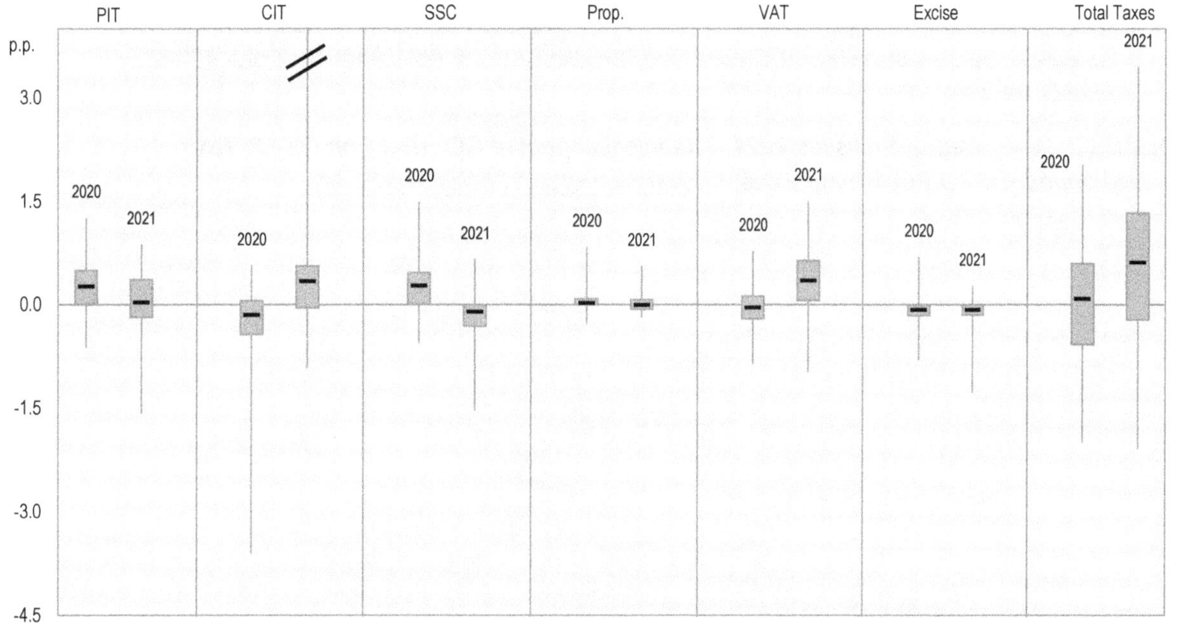

Note: Data for 2021 are preliminary and should be interpreted with caution; please see Box 2.2 for more details. In the figure, the lowest point represents the minimum country change for the tax type; the box represents the changes for countries between the lower and upper quartiles (i.e. 50% of OECD countries had changes within the range shown by each box); and the upper point for each tax type represents the maximum country change. The line in each box represents the median country change (i.e. half of OECD countries were both above and below this line).
Source: *Revenue Statistics 2022* and authors' calculations.

StatLink https://stat.link/jeuzyk

References

OECD (2022), *OECD Economic Outlook, Volume 2022 Issue 1*, OECD Publishing, Paris, https://doi.org/10.1787/62d0ca31-en. [1]

OECD (2022), *OECD Employment Outlook 2022: Building Back More Inclusive Labour Markets*, OECD Publishing, Paris, https://doi.org/10.1787/1bb305a6-en. [3]

OECD (2022), *OECD Sovereign Borrowing Outlook 2022*, OECD Publishing, Paris,, https://doi.org/10.1787/b2d85ea7-en. [2]

OECD (2022), *Tax Policy Reforms 2022: OECD and Selected Partner Economies*, OECD Publishing, Paris, https://doi.org/10.1787/067c593d-en. [4]

OECD (2022), *Taxing Wages 2022: Impact of COVID-19 on the Tax Wedge in OECD Countries*, OECD Publishing, Paris, https://doi.org/10.1787/f7f1e68a-en. [5]

OECD (2022), *Two-Pillar Solution to Address the Tax Challenges Arising from the Digitalisation of the Economy (FAQs)*, OECD Publishing, Paris, https://www.oecd.org/tax/beps/faqs-two-pillar-solution-to-address-the-tax-challenges-arising-from-the-digitalisation-of-the-economy-july-2022.pdf. [6]

OECD (2021), *Revenue Statistics 2021: The Initial Impact of COVID-19 on OECD Tax Revenues*, OECD Publishing, Paris, https://doi.org/10.1787/6e87f932-en. [7]

Annex 2.A. Changes in tax-to-GDP ratios by country and tax type

Annex Table 2.A.1. Changes in tax-to-GDP ratios, 2020-2021, by tax type

Year-on-year change, percentage points

	PIT	CIT	SSCs	Prop.	VAT	Excises	OCT	Res.	Total Taxes	Basis of reporting*
Australia	-0.2	0.6	0.0	0.2	0.3	0.0	-0.1	0.0	0.8	Accrual (1998)
Austria	0.4	0.6	-0.1	0.1	0.2	0.1	-0.1	0.1	1.2	Accrual
Belgium	-0.6	0.5	-0.7	0.1	0.4	0.0	-0.1	0.0	-0.5	Accrual
Canada	-0.5	-0.2	-0.2	-0.1	0.0	-0.1	0.0	0.0	-1.0	Accrual (1999)*
Chile	0.4	-0.9	-0.4	0.0	1.5	-0.3	-0.1	2.5	2.8	Cash
Colombia	-0.1	0.3	0.0	-0.1	0.5	0.1	0.0	0.0	0.7	Cash
Costa Rica	0.0	0.5	-0.2	0.0	0.6	0.3	0.3	0.0	1.6	Cash
Czech Republic	-1.6	0.0	0.7	0.0	0.2	-0.1	0.0	0.0	-0.9	Accrual
Denmark	-1.0	0.9	0.1	-0.1	-0.1	-0.3	-0.1	0.4	-0.2	Accrual
Estonia	0.8	-0.1	-0.5	0.0	0.3	-0.1	0.0	0.0	0.3	Accrual
Finland	0.3	0.5	0.5	0.0	0.1	-0.2	-0.1	0.0	1.1	Accrual
France	-0.1	0.2	-0.1	-0.1	0.4	0.0	-0.4	-0.1	-0.2	Accrual
Germany	0.3	0.7	-0.2	0.0	0.7	-0.1	0.2	0.0	1.6	Accrual (2002)
Greece	0.2		-0.1	-0.1			0.1	0.0	0.1	Accrual (1998)
Hungary	0.0	-0.1	-1.0	-0.2	0.0	-0.3	-0.4	0.0	-2.1	Accrual (2002)*
Iceland	-1.1	-0.2	0.0	-0.2	0.6	-0.1	-0.1	0.1	-1.1	Accrual (1998)
Ireland	0.4	0.4	-0.1	0.1	0.5	-0.1	0.0	0.0	1.2	Accrual (1998)
Israel	0.8	0.8	-0.3	0.5	0.5	0.0	0.0	0.2	2.7	Cash
Italy	-0.2	-0.1	-0.1	0.1	0.8	-0.1	0.0	0.3	0.6	Accrual (2000)
Japan	0.0	0.4		0.0	0.1	0.0	0.0			Accrual
Korea	0.9	0.5	0.1	0.6	0.1	0.0	0.0	0.0	2.1	Cash
Latvia	0.0	0.1	-0.1	-0.1	-0.1	-0.2	-0.2	0.0	-0.5	Accrual
Lithuania	0.6	0.6	0.1	0.0	0.7	-0.1	0.1	0.0	2.0	Accrual
Luxembourg	0.4	-0.2	-0.5	0.2	0.4	0.1	0.1	0.0	0.5	Accrual
Mexico	-0.2	-0.1	-0.3	0.0	0.1	-0.4	0.0	0.0	-1.1	Cash
Netherlands	-0.6	0.8	-0.5	0.0	0.2	-0.1	0.0	-0.1	-0.3	Accrual (1999)
New Zealand	0.6	1.3	0.0	-0.1	0.9	-0.2	0.0	0.0	2.5	Accrual
Norway	-0.7	7.3	-1.5	-0.1	-1.0	-0.5	-0.1	0.0	3.4	Accrual (2000)
Poland	0.1	0.4	-0.2	0.0	0.6	0.2	0.2	0.0	1.2	Accrual (2002)
Portugal	0.0	-0.3	0.1	0.1	0.6	0.0	0.0	0.0	0.5	Accrual
Slovak Republic	0.1	0.0	0.2	0.0	0.4	0.1	-0.2	0.0	0.6	Accrual
Slovenia	0.2	0.0	-0.4	0.0	0.7	-0.1	-0.1	0.0	0.2	Accrual
Spain	0.0	0.7	-0.1	0.3	0.6	-0.1	0.1	0.0	1.6	Accrual (2000)
Sweden	0.2	0.1	0.1	0.0	0.1	-0.1	0.0	0.0	0.3	Accrual (2000)
Switzerland	-0.3	0.0	-0.1	0.0	0.0	0.0	-0.1	0.9	0.4	Accrual
Türkiye	-0.1	0.4	-0.6	-0.1	0.7	-1.3	-0.1	0.0	-1.0	Cash*
United Kingdom	0.8	0.3	-0.1	0.1	0.3	0.0	0.0	0.0	1.4	Accrual
United States	0.7	0.3	0.0	-0.2	0.0	0.0	0.0	0.0	0.8	Accrual
Average	**0.0**	**0.5**	**-0.2**	**0.0**	**0.4**	**-0.1**	**0.0**	**0.1**	**0.6**	

Note: Data for 2021 are preliminary and should be interpreted with caution; please see Box 2.2 for more details. This graph includes the change between years 2019 and 2020 for Australia and New Zealand, as both countries report tax revenues on a fiscal year basis that includes the first two quarters of 2021 in the 2020 fiscal year. Due to data availability, the average excludes Japan for SSCs (category 2000) and for total tax revenues; it also excludes Greece for PIT (category 1100), CIT (category 1200), VAT (category 5111) and excises (5111) due to disaggregated data for these categories not being available.
* The basis of reporting reported here is as indicated in Chapter 5 under each country table. The year indicated in brackets is the year from data on an accrual basis are available if this was later than 1995. Please also note: CAN: data are on accrual basis except that personal income taxes are on a modified cash basis; HUN: preliminary data for 2021 are on a cash basis; TUR: SSCs are reported on an assessment basis.
Source: *Revenue Statistics 2022* and authors' calculations.

StatLink https://stat.link/8abche

Annex Figure 2.A.1. Changes in tax-to-GDP ratios, 2019-2021, by tax type

Year-on-year percentage change

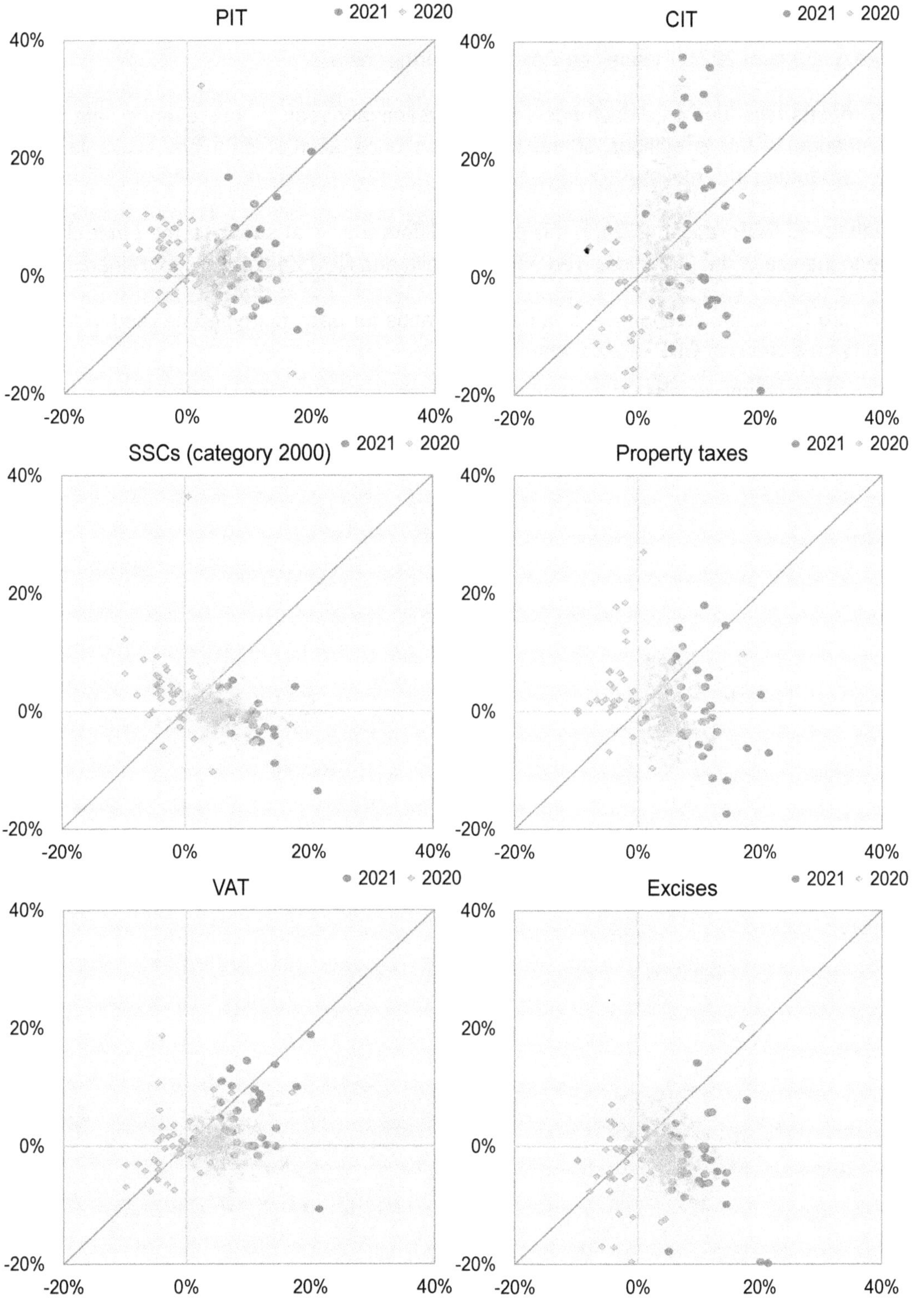

Note: Data for 2021 are preliminary and should be interpreted with caution; please see Box 2.2 for more details.

Source: *Revenue Statistics 2022* and authors' calculations.

StatLink https://stat.link/zikrdm

Notes

[1] Japan is not included in this sample because it was unable to provide preliminary data on all major tax types for 2021. Data for the 2020 fiscal year is used for Australia and New Zealand, as this period covers the first two quarters of 2021. Please see Box 2.1 for further details.

[2] Hungary reports revenues on a cash basis for the preliminary year. Its tax revenue data for 2021 may therefore change in future editions of the publication once accrual data are available. Please see Table 2.A.1 for further information.

[3] The mean tax-to-GDP ratio in 2021 in this chapter differs from that shown in the other chapters in the report due to the use of the 2020 fiscal years for Australia and New Zealand, as explained in Box 2.1

[4] Annex Figure 2.A.1. shows changes in tax-to-GDP ratios for each tax type analysed in this section for each country as a share of GDP in 2020 and 2021.

[5] In addition to the countries missing for reasons explained in Box 2.1, the United States is not included in this sample because it does not impose a VAT.

3 Tax levels and tax structures, 1965-2021

Chapter 3 provides an overview of tax levels and tax structures in OECD countries.

In all the following tables, the symbol (..) indicates not available or not applicable. The main series in this chapter cover a selection of years between 1990 and 2020. A complete series is available online. Data for 1955 and 1960 (for nineteen OECD countries) are provided in Part V of the 1998 edition of this Report.

The Gross Domestic Product (GDP) figures are based on the 2008 System of National Accounts (SNA) for all OECD countries.

Box 3.1. Treatment of capital transfers

Footnotes to Tables 3.1 to 3.18 refer to the treatment of the capital transfers that some countries make to account for taxes that have been assessed but not collected. The capital transfer has been subtracted directly from the specific taxes to which they relate, except for France, where the capital transfer has been allocated between tax headings in proportion to their tax revenues at the level of government against which these transfers were recorded.

Countries reporting capital transfers include:

- Austria from 2020
- Belgium from 1995
- Denmark from 1971
- France from 1992
- Lithuania from 1999
- Luxembourg from 2013
- Poland from 1995
- Slovenia from 1995
- Switzerland from 1990

Table 3.1. Total tax revenue as % of GDP

	1965	1990	2000	2007	2010	2015	2018	2019	2020	2021p
Australia	20.6	28.1	30.4	29.4	25.2	27.8	28.6	27.7	28.5	..
Austria[1]	33.5	39.3	42.3	40.5	41.0	43.1	42.2	42.6	42.2	43.5
Belgium[1]	30.8	41.4	43.8	42.9	42.9	44.1	43.8	42.4	42.5	42.0
Canada	25.0	35.1	34.7	32.5	31.0	32.8	33.5	33.1	34.3	33.2
Chile	..	16.8	18.7	22.8	19.7	20.5	21.3	21.0	19.4	22.2
Colombia	..	11.3	15.7	19.3	18.1	19.9	19.3	19.7	18.8	19.5
Costa Rica	..	22.4	21.1	23.1	22.1	22.9	23.2	23.4	22.7	24.2
Czech Republic	..	..	32.3	34.1	32.2	33.1	35.0	34.8	34.7	33.8
Denmark[1]	29.1	44.4	46.9	46.4	44.8	46.1	44.2	46.9	47.1	46.9
Estonia	..	..	31.1	31.0	33.2	33.3	32.9	33.5	33.3	33.5
Finland	30.0	42.9	45.8	41.4	40.6	43.5	42.4	42.3	41.8	43.0
France[1]	33.7	41.2	43.4	42.5	42.1	45.3	45.9	44.9	45.3	45.1
Germany	31.7	34.8	36.4	35.4	35.5	37.3	38.5	38.6	37.9	39.5
Greece	17.1	25.2	33.4	31.8	32.3	36.6	40.0	39.5	38.9	39.0
Hungary	..	..	38.5	39.2	36.8	38.7	36.8	36.4	36.1	34.0
Iceland	25.7	30.5	35.9	38.4	32.2	35.1	36.5	34.9	36.1	35.1
Ireland	24.5	32.4	30.8	30.8	27.7	23.2	22.3	21.9	19.9	21.1
Israel	..	..	34.1	33.3	30.3	31.0	30.7	30.0	29.6	32.2
Italy	24.6	36.3	40.5	41.6	41.7	43.0	41.7	42.3	42.7	43.3
Japan	17.3	27.7	25.3	27.2	26.2	30.2	31.5	31.5	33.2	..
Korea	..	18.6	20.9	23.7	22.4	23.7	26.7	27.2	27.7	29.9
Latvia	..	..	29.0	28.2	28.5	29.8	31.1	30.9	31.8	31.2
Lithuania[1]	..	..	30.8	30.1	28.3	28.9	30.2	30.3	30.8	32.8
Luxembourg[1]	27.3	34.7	37.0	35.7	35.7	34.8	39.4	39.6	38.1	38.6
Mexico	..	12.1	11.5	12.0	12.8	15.9	16.1	16.3	17.8	16.7
Netherlands	30.5	39.7	36.9	35.7	35.7	37.0	38.8	39.3	40.0	39.7
New Zealand	24.5	36.2	32.5	33.9	30.3	31.5	32.2	31.3	33.8	33.8
Norway	29.4	40.2	41.7	42.0	41.8	38.4	39.4	40.1	38.8	42.2
Poland[1]	..	..	32.9	34.6	31.3	32.4	35.1	35.1	35.5	36.8
Portugal	15.7	26.5	30.9	31.8	30.4	34.4	34.7	34.5	35.3	35.8
Slovak Republic	..	..	33.6	29.2	28.0	32.6	34.2	34.6	35.2	35.8
Slovenia[1]	..	..	37.7	38.0	37.8	37.3	37.2	37.0	37.2	37.4
Spain	14.3	31.5	33.0	36.4	31.3	33.8	34.7	34.7	36.7	38.4
Sweden	30.9	48.8	50.0	44.9	42.9	42.6	43.8	42.8	42.3	42.6
Switzerland[1]	16.0	23.1	27.0	25.4	25.6	26.6	26.8	27.3	27.5	28.0
Türkiye	10.6	14.5	23.5	22.9	24.7	25.0	24.0	23.1	23.9	22.8
United Kingdom	30.1	32.9	32.7	32.8	32.0	31.6	32.4	32.2	32.1	33.5
United States	23.6	26.0	28.3	26.7	23.4	26.2	24.9	25.2	25.8	26.6
Unweighted average										
OECD Average[2]	**24.9**	**30.8**	**32.9**	**32.8**	**31.5**	**32.9**	**33.5**	**33.4**	**33.6**	**34.1**

.. Not available

Note: Full time series can be accessed at http://oe.cd/full-time-series.

1. The capital transfers were subtracted directly from the specific taxes to which they relate, except for France, where the capital transfers have been allocated between tax headings in proportion to the reported tax revenue.

2. 2021: calculated by applying the unweighted average percentage change for 2021 in the 36 countries providing data for that year to the overall average tax to GDP ratio in 2020.

StatLink https://stat.link/oqmhlv

Table 3.2. Total tax revenue in billions of US dollars at market exchange rates

	1965	1990	2000	2007	2010	2015	2018	2019	2020	2021p
Australia	5.6	90.8	117.3	289.9	346.5	344.3	401.2	379.6	424.2	..
Austria[1]	..	68.6	83.2	157.6	160.5	164.7	192.2	189.5	182.5	207.2
Belgium[1]	..	89.4	103.6	201.9	206.2	203.9	237.9	227.0	221.2	252.0
Canada	14.2	210.1	260.0	477.2	501.4	511.1	576.6	576.0	563.7	661.3
Chile	..	5.8	14.6	39.4	42.8	49.7	62.8	58.3	49.0	70.3
Colombia	..	5.1	14.7	39.8	51.8	58.4	64.4	63.7	50.8	61.3
Costa Rica	..	1.3	3.2	6.2	8.4	13.0	14.4	15.1	14.1	15.6
Czech Republic	..	..	20.0	64.9	67.4	62.3	87.1	87.8	85.4	95.3
Denmark[1]	3.0	61.4	76.9	148.3	144.2	139.5	157.7	162.5	167.4	186.7
Estonia	..	..	1.8	7.0	6.5	7.6	10.1	10.4	10.4	12.5
Finland	..	49.6	57.5	106.0	101.1	102.1	116.8	113.5	113.5	127.8
France[1]	..	550.7	591.8	1 130.7	1 113.7	1 104.3	1 279.6	1 224.8	1 193.8	1 335.3
Germany	..	577.4	706.9	1 210.4	1 206.8	1 252.2	1 527.5	1 501.5	1 471.2	1 683.1
Greece	..	14.6	43.5	101.3	95.9	71.6	84.8	81.0	73.2	84.3
Hungary	..	..	18.2	55.0	48.7	48.4	59.1	59.6	56.6	62.0
Iceland	0.1	2.0	3.2	8.3	4.4	6.2	9.6	8.7	7.8	9.0
Ireland	0.7	15.6	30.7	83.2	61.5	67.6	86.0	87.3	84.4	106.2
Israel	..	..	46.4	61.3	72.3	94.2	115.6	120.8	122.2	157.4
Italy	..	336.6	463.6	918.8	889.9	788.9	872.4	850.1	805.4	908.9
Japan	17.1	920.0	1 224.6	1 281.0	1 545.1	1 386.4	1 594.7	1 616.8	1 649.2	..
Korea	..	52.6	120.5	278.2	256.2	347.9	460.4	449.7	456.3	540.9
Latvia	..	..	1.8	8.8	6.8	8.1	10.7	10.6	10.7	12.1
Lithuania[1]	..	..	3.8	11.9	10.5	12.0	16.2	16.6	17.4	21.5
Luxembourg[1]	..	4.7	7.8	18.4	20.0	20.9	27.9	27.6	28.1	33.0
Mexico	..	35.9	81.2	126.5	135.9	186.1	198.0	207.9	193.9	216.4
Netherlands	..	132.6	153.7	302.5	301.9	283.3	354.4	357.3	363.1	402.1
New Zealand	1.4	16.1	17.3	46.0	47.0	56.8	67.4	65.1	78.2	85.9
Norway	2.4	48.2	71.4	168.5	179.3	148.2	172.0	162.3	140.6	203.6
Poland[1]	..	..	56.6	148.7	150.4	154.9	206.5	209.7	213.2	249.7
Portugal	..	18.8	36.6	76.5	72.2	68.5	83.9	82.8	80.4	89.4
Slovak Republic	..	..	9.8	25.3	25.4	28.9	36.1	36.4	36.9	41.1
Slovenia[1]	..	..	6.6	18.3	18.2	16.1	20.2	20.1	19.9	23.1
Spain	..	131.6	197.3	536.1	444.4	404.6	492.2	483.3	469.5	546.6
Sweden	7.8	127.7	131.5	220.7	212.7	215.5	243.2	228.7	231.5	270.6
Switzerland[1]	2.6	61.6	75.5	125.4	154.6	187.1	197.2	199.5	207.1	227.2
Türkiye	1.3	30.2	64.5	156.2	192.0	215.5	186.3	175.7	171.7	186.7
United Kingdom	30.6	359.4	544.5	1 019.1	795.8	934.1	940.0	927.4	885.5	1 067.0
United States	167.0	1 552.4	2 900.5	3 868.6	3 517.1	4 773.7	5 116.0	5 385.0	5 380.2	6 112.3
Unweighted average										
OECD Average	**19.5**	**192.1**	**220.1**	**356.4**	**347.8**	**382.6**	**431.0**	**433.7**	**429.7**	..

.. Not available

Note: Full time series can be accessed at http://oe.cd/full-time-series.

1. The capital transfers were subtracted directly from the specific taxes to which they relate, except for France, where the capital transfers have been allocated between tax headings in proportion to the reported tax revenue.

StatLink https://stat.link/pc7uoj

Table 3.3. Tax revenue of main headings as % of GDP, 2020

	1000 Income & profits	2000 Social security	3000 Payroll	4000 Property	5000 Goods and services[3]	6000 Others	Memorandum item: supranational revenues
Australia	16.8	0.0	1.3	2.9	7.6	0.0	..
Austria[1]	11.7	15.5	2.8	0.6	11.5	0.2	0.2
Belgium[1]	15.1	13.6	0.0	3.4	10.4	0.0	0.4
Canada	17.1	4.9	0.8	4.1	7.4	0.0	..
Chile	6.3	1.5	0.0	1.0	10.6	-0.1	..
Colombia	6.2	1.9	0.4	1.8	7.8	0.8	..
Costa Rica	4.5	8.2	1.5	0.4	7.6	0.5	..
Czech Republic	7.9	15.8	0.0	0.2	10.8	0.0	0.1
Denmark[1]	30.5	0.1	0.2	2.0	14.4	0.0	0.1
Estonia	7.7	12.1	0.0	0.2	13.3	0.0	0.2
Finland	14.7	11.5	0.0	1.5	14.1	0.0	0.2
France[1]	11.9	14.8	1.9	4.0	12.3	0.5	0.2
Germany	11.9	15.0	0.0	1.2	9.7	0.0	0.2
Greece	7.9	12.9	0.0	3.0	15.0	0.0	0.2
Hungary	6.6	11.1	1.0	1.1	16.3	0.0	0.1
Iceland	18.4	3.0	0.3	2.3	11.4	0.7	..
Ireland	9.7	3.3	0.2	1.0	5.6	0.0	0.1
Israel	9.8	5.1	1.1	3.1	10.4	0.0	..
Italy	14.0	13.6	0.0	2.4	11.5	1.2	0.2
Japan	10.1	13.4	0.0	2.7	6.9	0.1	..
Korea	8.6	7.8	0.1	3.9	6.8	0.6	..
Latvia	6.9	10.0	0.0	1.0	14.0	0.0	0.2
Lithuania[1]	8.7	10.2	0.0	0.3	11.6	0.0	0.3
Luxembourg[1]	14.5	11.1	0.0	3.8	8.7	0.0	0.3
Mexico	7.6	2.5	0.5	0.3	6.6	0.3	..
Netherlands	12.3	13.6	0.0	1.7	12.2	0.2	0.4
New Zealand	19.1	0.0	0.0	1.9	12.8	0.0	..
Norway	13.8	11.2	0.1	1.3	12.4	0.0	..
Poland[1]	7.5	13.5	0.3	1.3	12.9	0.0	0.2
Portugal	9.8	10.5	0.0	1.5	13.2	0.3	0.2
Slovak Republic	7.1	15.5	0.0	0.5	12.2	0.0	0.2
Slovenia[1]	7.2	16.8	0.0	0.6	12.5	0.0	0.2
Spain	10.7	13.8	0.0	2.5	9.8	0.0	0.2
Sweden	15.1	9.0	5.1	1.0	12.1	0.0	0.1
Switzerland[1]	12.7	6.9	0.0	2.2	5.5	0.1	..
Türkiye	5.2	7.1	0.0	1.1	10.2	0.2	..
United Kingdom[2]	11.5	6.7	0.1	3.7	10.0	0.0	0.1
United States	11.7	6.4	0.0	3.2	4.4	0.0	..
Unweighted average							
OECD Average	**11.3**	**9.2**	**0.5**	**1.9**	**10.6**	**0.2**	**0.2**

.. Not available

1. The capital transfers were subtracted directly from the specific taxes to which they relate, except for France, where the capital transfers have been allocated between tax headings in proportion to the reported tax revenue.
2. Supranational taxes reported by the United Kingdom are reported until 2020 in Revenue Statistics. From 2021, at the end of the Brexit transition period, this came to an end and taxes subsequently introduced by the United Kingdom are reflected in the appropriate tax category at the national or subnational levels of government, as appropriate.
3. The figures in category 5000 include supranational revenues, which are also presented separately under the Supranational heading.

StatLink https://stat.link/4ghfmb

Table 3.4. Tax revenue of main headings as % of total tax revenue, 2020

	1000 Income & profits	2000 Social security	3000 Payroll	4000 Property	5000 Goods and services[3]	6000 Others	Memorandum item: supranational revenues
Australia	59.0	0.0	4.5	10.1	26.5	0.0	..
Austria[1]	27.8	36.8	6.5	1.4	27.1	0.4	0.4
Belgium[1]	35.6	32.0	0.0	8.0	24.4	0.0	0.9
Canada	49.8	14.3	2.3	12.0	21.5	0.1	..
Chile	32.3	8.0	0.0	5.3	54.8	-0.5	..
Colombia	32.9	9.9	2.0	9.7	41.4	4.1	..
Costa Rica	20.1	36.1	6.5	2.0	33.3	2.0	..
Czech Republic	22.9	45.5	0.0	0.6	31.1	0.0	0.4
Denmark[1]	64.7	0.1	0.4	4.2	30.6	0.0	0.3
Estonia	23.0	36.5	0.0	0.6	39.9	0.0	0.5
Finland	35.1	27.4	0.0	3.6	33.8	0.1	0.4
France[1]	26.2	32.7	4.1	8.7	27.1	1.2	0.5
Germany	31.3	39.7	0.0	3.3	25.7	0.0	0.5
Greece	20.4	33.2	0.0	7.8	38.5	0.0	0.5
Hungary	18.2	30.8	2.9	2.9	45.1	0.1	0.4
Iceland	51.1	8.3	0.9	6.2	31.7	1.8	..
Ireland	49.1	16.6	1.0	5.0	28.4	0.0	0.6
Israel	33.1	17.4	3.8	10.3	35.3	0.0	..
Italy	32.8	31.8	0.0	5.7	26.9	2.7	0.4
Japan	30.4	40.4	0.0	8.1	20.9	0.3	..
Korea	30.9	28.0	0.3	14.2	24.4	2.1	..
Latvia	21.6	31.4	0.0	3.0	44.0	0.0	0.6
Lithuania[1]	28.2	33.2	0.0	1.0	37.7	0.0	0.9
Luxembourg[1]	38.0	29.2	0.0	10.0	22.8	0.1	0.8
Mexico	42.6	13.9	2.5	1.9	37.2	1.8	..
Netherlands	30.7	34.1	0.0	4.3	30.5	0.5	1.1
New Zealand	56.5	0.0	0.0	5.5	38.0	0.0	..
Norway	35.6	28.9	0.2	3.4	32.0	0.0	..
Poland[1]	21.2	37.9	0.9	3.6	36.2	0.1	0.5
Portugal	27.7	29.6	0.0	4.2	37.5	1.0	0.5
Slovak Republic	20.2	43.9	0.0	1.4	34.6	0.0	0.4
Slovenia[1]	19.4	45.2	0.1	1.7	33.6	0.0	0.4
Spain	29.1	37.4	0.0	6.7	26.7	0.0	0.6
Sweden	35.8	21.4	12.0	2.2	28.5	0.1	0.3
Switzerland[1]	46.2	25.2	0.0	8.1	20.0	0.5	..
Türkiye	21.9	29.7	0.0	4.4	42.9	1.0	..
United Kingdom[2]	35.8	21.0	0.4	11.6	31.2	0.0	0.4
United States	45.5	24.8	0.1	12.4	17.2	0.0	..
Unweighted average							
OECD Average	**33.7**	**26.6**	**1.4**	**5.7**	**32.1**	**0.5**	**0.5**

.. Not available

1. The capital transfers were subtracted directly from the specific taxes to which they relate, except for France, where the capital transfers have been allocated between tax headings in proportion to the reported tax revenue.
2. Supranational taxes reported by the United Kingdom are reported until 2020 in Revenue Statistics. From 2021, at the end of the Brexit transition period, this came to an end and taxes subsequently introduced by the United Kingdom are reflected in the appropriate tax category at the national or subnational levels of government, as appropriate.
3. The figures in category 5000 include supranational revenues, which are also presented separately under the Supranational heading.

StatLink https://stat.link/br3ca7

Table 3.5. Tax revenue of main headings as % of GDP, 2021p

	1000 Income & profits	2000 Social security	3000 Payroll	4000 Property	5000 Goods and services[3]	6000 Others	Memorandum item: supranational revenues
Australia	..	..	..	..	..	..	..
Austria[1]	12.8	15.4	2.8	0.6	11.6	0.2	0.2
Belgium[1]	15.0	12.9	0.0	3.6	10.6	0.0	0.4
Canada	16.4	4.8	0.8	4.0	7.3	0.0	..
Chile	8.5	1.2	0.0	1.1	11.8	-0.3	..
Colombia	6.2	1.9	0.3	1.7	8.4	0.9	..
Costa Rica	5.2	8.1	1.4	0.5	8.7	0.4	..
Czech Republic	6.3	16.4	0.0	0.2	10.9	0.0	0.2
Denmark[1]	30.7	0.1	0.3	1.9	13.9	0.0	0.1
Estonia	8.4	11.6	0.0	0.2	13.4	0.0	0.2
Finland	15.5	12.0	0.0	1.5	14.0	0.0	0.2
France[1]	12.0	14.8	1.8	3.8	12.2	0.4	0.2
Germany	12.9	14.9	0.0	1.2	10.5	0.0	0.2
Greece	8.1	12.8	0.0	3.0	15.1	0.0	0.2
Hungary	6.4	10.1	1.0	0.9	15.6	0.0	0.1
Iceland	17.5	3.0	0.3	2.1	11.8	0.4	..
Ireland	10.5	3.2	0.2	1.1	6.0	0.0	0.2
Israel	11.7	5.0	0.9	3.6	11.0	0.0	..
Italy	13.8	13.5	0.0	2.5	12.2	1.3	0.2
Japan	10.5	..	0.0	2.6	7.0	0.1	..
Korea	9.9	7.8	0.1	4.5	6.9	0.6	..
Latvia	7.0	9.9	0.0	0.9	13.4	0.0	0.2
Lithuania[1]	9.8	10.3	0.0	0.3	12.3	0.0	0.3
Luxembourg[1]	14.6	10.6	0.0	4.0	9.3	0.0	0.4
Mexico	7.3	2.3	0.3	0.3	6.2	0.3	..
Netherlands	12.5	13.1	0.0	1.7	12.2	0.1	0.5
New Zealand	19.3	0.0	0.0	1.9	12.6	0.0	..
Norway	20.4	9.7	0.1	1.2	10.9	0.0	..
Poland[1]	8.0	13.0	0.6	1.3	13.9	0.0	0.2
Portugal	9.4	10.6	0.0	1.6	13.8	0.3	0.2
Slovak Republic	7.2	15.7	0.0	0.5	12.4	0.0	0.1
Slovenia[1]	7.4	16.4	0.0	0.6	13.0	0.0	0.2
Spain	11.4	13.7	0.0	2.7	10.5	0.0	0.2
Sweden	15.4	9.0	5.2	1.0	12.0	0.0	0.1
Switzerland[1]	13.3	6.8	0.0	2.2	5.5	0.1	..
Türkiye	5.5	6.5	0.0	1.0	9.6	0.2	..
United Kingdom[2]	12.6	6.7	0.1	3.8	10.3	0.0	..
United States	12.8	6.3	0.0	3.0	4.4	0.0	..

.. Not available

1. The capital transfers were subtracted directly from the specific taxes to which they relate, except for France, where the capital transfers have been allocated between tax headings in proportion to the reported tax revenue.
2. Supranational taxes reported by the United Kingdom are reported until 2020 in Revenue Statistics. From 2021, at the end of the Brexit transition period, this came to an end and taxes subsequently introduced by the United Kingdom are reflected in the appropriate tax category at the national or subnational levels of government, as appropriate.
3. The figures in category 5000 include supranational revenues, which are also presented separately under the Supranational heading.

StatLink https://stat.link/kx3lna

Table 3.6. Tax revenue of main headings as % of total tax revenue, 2021p

	1000 Income & profits	2000 Social security	3000 Payroll	4000 Property	5000 Goods and services[3]	6000 Others	Memorandum item: supranational revenues
Australia	..	..	..	..	..	..	..
Austria[1]	29.5	35.5	6.4	1.5	26.7	0.4	0.4
Belgium[1]	35.7	30.6	0.0	8.5	25.2	0.0	0.9
Canada	49.4	14.3	2.3	11.9	22.0	0.1	..
Chile	38.3	5.3	0.0	4.8	53.1	-1.5	..
Colombia	31.9	10.0	1.7	8.7	43.3	4.4	..
Costa Rica	21.4	33.2	5.8	2.0	36.0	1.6	..
Czech Republic	18.6	48.6	0.0	0.6	32.2	0.0	0.5
Denmark[1]	65.6	0.1	0.6	4.0	29.7	0.0	0.3
Estonia	24.9	34.6	0.0	0.6	39.9	0.0	0.7
Finland	36.1	27.8	0.0	3.5	32.5	0.1	0.4
France[1]	26.6	32.8	4.1	8.5	27.1	1.0	0.5
Germany	32.6	37.7	0.0	3.1	26.6	0.0	0.5
Greece	20.7	32.8	0.0	7.7	38.7	0.0	0.5
Hungary	18.8	29.8	2.9	2.6	45.9	0.0	0.4
Iceland	50.0	8.5	0.8	5.9	33.6	1.2	..
Ireland	49.8	15.2	0.9	5.4	28.7	0.0	0.8
Israel	36.2	15.7	2.9	11.2	34.1	0.0	..
Italy	31.9	31.2	0.0	5.9	28.1	2.9	0.5
Japan	..	..	..	..	..	..	..
Korea	33.2	26.2	0.3	15.1	23.1	2.1	..
Latvia	22.3	31.8	0.0	2.9	43.0	0.0	0.7
Lithuania[1]	29.9	31.6	0.0	0.9	37.6	0.0	1.0
Luxembourg[1]	38.0	27.4	0.0	10.4	24.1	0.1	1.0
Mexico	43.5	14.0	1.6	1.8	37.3	1.8	..
Netherlands	31.6	33.1	0.0	4.3	30.8	0.3	1.2
New Zealand	57.0	0.0	0.0	5.7	37.3	0.0	..
Norway	48.4	22.9	0.1	2.9	25.7	0.0	..
Poland[1]	21.7	35.4	1.5	3.5	37.8	0.1	0.6
Portugal	26.4	29.6	0.0	4.4	38.7	0.9	0.5
Slovak Republic	20.2	43.9	0.0	1.3	34.6	0.0	0.4
Slovenia[1]	19.7	43.8	0.1	1.6	34.7	0.0	0.5
Spain	29.9	35.6	0.0	7.1	27.4	0.0	0.7
Sweden	36.1	21.2	12.2	2.3	28.2	0.1	0.3
Switzerland[1]	47.6	24.3	0.0	8.0	19.6	0.5	..
Türkiye	24.0	28.6	0.0	4.2	42.1	1.0	..
United Kingdom[2]	37.6	19.9	0.4	11.4	30.7	0.0	..
United States	48.2	23.8	0.1	11.4	16.6	0.0	..

.. Not available

1. The capital transfers were subtracted directly from the specific taxes to which they relate, except for France, where the capital transfers have been allocated between tax headings in proportion to the reported tax revenue.
2. Supranational taxes reported by the United Kingdom are reported until 2020 in Revenue Statistics. From 2021, at the end of the Brexit transition period, this came to an end and taxes subsequently introduced by the United Kingdom are reflected in the appropriate tax category at the national or subnational levels of government, as appropriate.
3. The figures in category 5000 include supranational revenues, which are also presented separately under the Supranational heading.

StatLink https://stat.link/harypb

Table 3.7. Taxes on income and profits (1000) as % of GDP and as % of total tax revenue

	% of GDP					% of total tax revenue				
	1990	2000	2010	2019	2020	1990	2000	2010	2019	2020
Australia	16.0	17.6	14.3	16.4	16.8	57.1	57.9	56.7	59.2	59.0
Austria[1]	10.0	12.0	11.5	12.5	11.7	25.5	28.3	28.1	29.5	27.8
Belgium[1]	15.3	16.9	14.7	15.0	15.1	36.9	38.6	34.2	35.4	35.6
Canada	17.0	17.4	14.5	16.1	17.1	48.6	50.1	46.6	48.7	49.8
Chile	3.9	4.4	7.5	7.3	6.3	23.2	23.3	38.1	34.8	32.3
Colombia	3.4	3.6	4.8	6.4	6.2	29.9	23.2	26.6	32.3	32.9
Costa Rica	2.3	2.8	3.8	4.9	4.5	10.0	13.2	17.1	20.9	20.1
Czech Republic	..	7.4	6.5	7.9	7.9	..	22.8	20.2	22.8	22.9
Denmark[1]	27.2	28.8	27.5	30.4	30.5	61.2	61.4	61.5	64.8	64.7
Estonia	..	7.7	6.6	7.3	7.7	..	24.8	19.8	21.9	23.0
Finland	16.8	19.7	14.4	14.8	14.7	39.2	43.1	35.5	35.0	35.1
France[1]	6.6	10.8	9.5	11.5	11.9	16.1	24.8	22.6	25.7	26.2
Germany	11.3	11.0	10.1	12.6	11.9	32.4	30.1	28.3	32.6	31.3
Greece	5.0	9.0	7.1	8.5	7.9	19.9	26.8	22.0	21.6	20.4
Hungary	..	9.4	7.6	6.4	6.6	..	24.3	20.7	17.6	18.2
Iceland	9.0	14.3	14.3	17.4	18.4	29.7	39.9	44.3	49.9	51.1
Ireland	12.3	13.4	11.1	10.0	9.7	38.0	43.6	40.1	45.6	49.1
Israel	..	13.4	8.8	9.8	9.8	..	39.4	29.0	32.6	33.1
Italy	13.2	13.4	13.6	13.4	14.0	36.5	33.2	32.7	31.6	32.8
Japan	13.9	8.8	7.9	9.7	10.1	50.2	34.8	30.2	30.8	30.4
Korea	6.1	6.0	6.3	9.0	8.6	32.8	28.8	28.0	33.2	30.9
Latvia	..	7.0	7.1	6.6	6.9	..	24.1	25.0	21.4	21.6
Lithuania[1]	..	8.3	4.6	8.8	8.7	..	27.0	16.2	29.0	28.2
Luxembourg[1]	13.9	13.5	12.9	15.5	14.5	40.2	36.5	36.2	39.2	38.0
Mexico	4.1	4.1	5.1	6.9	7.6	34.0	36.0	39.8	42.4	42.6
Netherlands	12.8	9.6	9.9	12.2	12.3	32.3	25.9	27.9	31.0	30.7
New Zealand	21.6	19.5	16.3	17.2	19.1	59.6	60.0	53.8	55.1	56.5
Norway	14.2	18.9	19.8	16.4	13.8	35.2	45.3	47.3	40.9	35.6
Poland[1]	..	6.7	6.3	7.5	7.5	..	20.4	20.1	21.4	21.2
Portugal	6.8	9.1	8.1	9.5	9.8	25.7	29.4	26.7	27.4	27.7
Slovak Republic	..	6.9	5.3	7.1	7.1	..	20.5	18.8	20.5	20.2
Slovenia[1]	..	6.8	7.4	7.2	7.2	..	18.0	19.6	19.5	19.4
Spain	9.7	9.3	8.7	9.9	10.7	30.6	28.1	28.0	28.6	29.1
Sweden	20.3	21.4	15.3	15.3	15.1	41.6	42.7	35.7	35.7	35.8
Switzerland[1]	10.8	11.8	11.7	13.1	12.7	46.8	43.8	45.7	48.2	46.2
Türkiye	4.9	6.9	5.3	5.6	5.2	33.5	29.5	21.3	24.2	21.9
United Kingdom	12.9	12.9	12.0	11.2	11.5	39.3	39.5	37.4	34.6	35.8
United States	11.8	14.2	9.9	11.6	11.7	45.2	50.1	42.3	46.1	45.5
Unweighted average										
OECD Average	**11.5**	**11.4**	**10.2**	**11.3**	**11.3**	**36.2**	**33.9**	**32.2**	**34.0**	**33.7**

.. Not available

Note: Full time series can be accessed at http://oe.cd/full-time-series.

1. The capital transfers were subtracted directly from the specific taxes to which they relate, except for France, where the capital transfers have been allocated between tax headings in proportion to the reported tax revenue.

StatLink https://stat.link/evzfwx

Table 3.8. Taxes on personal income (1100) as % of GDP and as % of total tax revenue

	% of GDP					% of total tax revenue				
	1990	2000	2010	2019	2020	1990	2000	2010	2019	2020
Australia	12.1	11.5	9.7	11.7	11.5	43.0	37.7	38.7	42.0	40.1
Austria[1]	8.2	9.3	9.2	9.6	9.4	21.0	22.0	22.4	22.6	22.2
Belgium[1]	13.2	13.8	12.1	11.3	11.8	32.0	31.4	28.2	26.6	27.8
Canada	14.3	12.8	10.9	11.9	12.6	40.8	36.8	35.0	36.1	36.9
Chile	0.9	1.4	1.3	1.5	2.0	5.6	7.6	6.8	7.2	10.2
Colombia	0.2	0.8	1.0	1.3	1.4	1.8	4.9	5.3	6.8	7.7
Costa Rica	..	..	1.0	1.4	1.5	..	..	4.6	6.1	6.8
Czech Republic	..	4.2	3.3	4.4	4.7	..	12.9	10.2	12.7	13.4
Denmark[1]	24.0	24.7	23.3	24.5	25.5	54.0	52.6	52.0	52.2	54.2
Estonia	..	6.8	5.3	5.5	6.0	..	22.0	15.9	16.5	18.1
Finland	14.9	14.0	12.0	12.3	12.5	34.7	30.6	29.5	29.0	30.0
France[1]	4.4	7.8	7.2	9.3	9.5	10.7	17.9	17.0	20.7	21.0
Germany	9.6	9.2	8.6	10.6	10.2	27.6	25.3	24.1	27.4	27.0
Greece	3.6	4.3	4.0	6.0	6.3	14.1	13.0	12.4	15.2	16.3
Hungary	..	7.2	6.4	5.2	5.3	..	18.6	17.4	14.2	14.6
Iceland	8.2	12.5	11.7	14.3	15.6	26.9	34.8	36.4	41.0	43.1
Ireland	10.7	9.8	8.8	6.9	6.5	33.1	31.9	31.6	31.6	32.9
Israel	..	9.9	5.4	6.2	6.5	..	28.9	17.9	20.8	21.9
Italy	9.5	10.1	11.2	10.9	11.4	26.3	24.8	26.9	25.8	26.8
Japan	7.7	5.3	4.9	5.9	6.2	27.8	21.0	18.6	18.8	18.7
Korea	3.7	3.1	3.2	4.8	5.2	20.0	14.6	14.2	17.5	18.8
Latvia	..	5.5	6.2	6.5	6.1	..	18.8	21.6	20.9	19.3
Lithuania[1]	..	7.6	3.6	7.2	7.1	..	24.8	12.7	23.9	23.0
Luxembourg[1]	8.3	6.8	7.4	9.5	9.7	24.1	18.5	20.9	24.0	25.5
Mexico	..	..	2.3	3.4	3.7	..	..	18.3	20.8	21.0
Netherlands	9.8	5.6	7.7	8.5	9.2	24.7	15.1	21.5	21.6	22.9
New Zealand	17.4	14.0	11.4	12.4	13.0	48.0	43.1	37.7	39.7	38.5
Norway	10.5	10.1	9.9	10.4	11.4	26.2	24.2	23.7	25.9	29.4
Poland[1]	..	4.3	4.3	5.3	5.3	..	13.2	13.9	15.1	14.8
Portugal	4.2	5.3	5.4	6.3	7.0	15.9	17.0	17.7	18.4	19.9
Slovak Republic	..	3.3	2.6	3.8	3.8	..	9.9	9.3	10.9	10.8
Slovenia[1]	..	5.5	5.6	5.3	5.2	..	14.6	14.7	14.2	14.1
Spain	6.9	6.4	6.9	7.9	8.7	21.7	19.3	22.1	22.7	23.7
Sweden	18.8	17.7	12.1	12.3	12.2	38.5	35.4	28.1	28.7	28.8
Switzerland[1]	7.5	7.9	8.1	8.4	8.8	32.3	29.4	31.8	30.7	32.1
Türkiye	3.9	5.2	3.5	3.8	3.1	26.8	22.2	14.0	16.3	13.2
United Kingdom	9.7	9.5	9.1	8.9	9.2	29.4	29.0	28.5	27.6	28.6
United States	9.8	11.9	8.1	10.3	10.4	37.7	42.2	34.8	40.7	40.6
Unweighted average										
OECD Average	**9.3**	**8.5**	**7.2**	**8.0**	**8.3**	**27.6**	**24.1**	**22.0**	**23.5**	**24.1**

.. Not available

Note: Full time series can be accessed at http://oe.cd/full-time-series.

1. The capital transfers were subtracted directly from the specific taxes to which they relate, except for France, where the capital transfers have been allocated between tax headings in proportion to the reported tax revenue.

StatLink https://stat.link/tsz70j

Table 3.9. Taxes on corporate income (1200) as % of GDP and as % of total tax revenue

	% of GDP					% of total tax revenue				
	1990	2000	2010	2019	2020	1990	2000	2010	2019	2020
Australia	4.0	6.1	4.5	4.7	5.4	14.1	20.2	17.9	17.1	18.8
Austria[1]	1.4	1.9	1.9	2.7	2.2	3.6	4.6	4.6	6.4	5.1
Belgium[1]	2.0	3.1	2.5	3.7	3.3	4.8	7.2	5.9	8.7	7.7
Canada	2.5	4.2	3.2	3.7	4.1	7.0	12.2	10.5	11.3	11.8
Chile	2.1	2.1	4.0	4.9	4.7	12.4	11.2	20.4	23.4	24.3
Colombia	1.6	2.6	3.8	4.7	4.3	13.9	16.7	20.7	24.1	23.0
Costa Rica	..	..	2.3	2.8	1.9	..	..	10.3	11.9	8.4
Czech Republic	..	3.2	3.2	3.5	3.3	..	9.9	10.0	10.1	9.4
Denmark[1]	1.7	3.2	2.3	3.2	2.9	3.9	6.8	5.1	6.7	6.1
Estonia	..	0.9	1.3	1.8	1.6	..	2.8	4.0	5.5	4.9
Finland	1.9	5.7	2.4	2.5	2.1	4.5	12.5	6.0	6.0	5.1
France[1]	2.2	3.0	2.3	2.2	2.3	5.3	6.9	5.5	4.9	5.1
Germany	1.7	1.8	1.5	2.0	1.6	4.8	4.8	4.2	5.2	4.3
Greece	1.4	4.0	2.6	2.2	1.2	5.5	11.9	7.9	5.6	3.1
Hungary	..	2.2	1.2	1.2	1.3	..	5.7	3.3	3.4	3.6
Iceland	0.8	1.2	0.9	2.1	2.2	2.8	3.3	2.7	5.9	6.1
Ireland	1.6	3.6	2.4	3.1	3.2	4.9	11.7	8.5	14.0	16.1
Israel	..	3.2	2.6	3.0	2.7	..	9.5	8.6	10.1	9.2
Italy	3.6	2.8	2.3	2.0	2.1	10.0	6.9	5.5	4.6	4.8
Japan	6.2	3.5	3.0	3.8	3.9	22.4	13.7	11.6	12.0	11.7
Korea	2.4	3.0	3.1	4.3	3.4	12.8	14.1	13.8	15.7	12.1
Latvia	..	1.5	1.0	0.2	0.7	..	5.3	3.4	0.5	2.3
Lithuania[1]	..	0.7	1.0	1.6	1.6	..	2.2	3.5	5.1	5.1
Luxembourg[1]	5.6	6.7	5.4	6.0	4.8	16.1	18.0	15.3	15.2	12.5
Mexico	..	..	1.8	3.3	3.6	..	..	14.4	20.1	20.1
Netherlands	3.0	4.0	2.3	3.7	3.1	7.5	10.9	6.4	9.4	7.8
New Zealand	2.3	4.0	3.7	3.9	5.2	6.5	12.4	12.2	12.5	15.4
Norway	3.6	8.8	9.9	6.0	2.4	9.0	21.0	23.6	15.0	6.2
Poland[1]	..	2.4	1.9	2.2	2.3	..	7.3	6.2	6.3	6.4
Portugal	2.1	3.7	2.7	3.1	2.8	8.0	11.9	9.0	9.0	7.9
Slovak Republic	..	2.6	2.4	3.1	3.0	..	7.6	8.7	8.9	8.6
Slovenia[1]	..	1.1	1.8	2.0	1.9	..	3.0	4.9	5.3	5.2
Spain	2.8	2.9	1.8	2.1	2.0	8.8	8.8	5.9	5.9	5.3
Sweden	1.5	3.6	3.2	3.0	3.0	3.1	7.3	7.6	7.0	7.0
Switzerland[1]	1.7	2.4	2.6	3.1	3.0	7.3	8.8	10.1	11.2	11.0
Türkiye	1.0	1.7	1.8	1.8	2.1	6.7	7.3	7.3	7.9	8.7
United Kingdom	3.3	3.5	2.8	2.3	2.3	9.9	10.6	8.9	7.1	7.3
United States	2.0	2.2	1.8	1.4	1.3	7.5	7.9	7.5	5.4	4.9
Unweighted average										
OECD Average	**2.4**	**3.1**	**2.7**	**3.0**	**2.8**	**8.3**	**9.5**	**9.0**	**9.6**	**9.0**

.. Not available

Note: Full time series can be accessed at http://oe.cd/full-time-series.

1. The capital transfers were subtracted directly from the specific taxes to which they relate, except for France, where the capital transfers have been allocated between tax headings in proportion to the reported tax revenue.

StatLink https://stat.link/ujafz3

Table 3.10. Social security contributions (2000) as % of GDP and as % of total tax revenue

	% of GDP					% of total tax revenue				
	1990	2000	2010	2019	2020	1990	2000	2010	2019	2020
Australia	0.0	0.0	0.0	0.0	0.0	0.0	0.0	0.0	0.0	0.0
Austria[1]	12.9	14.3	14.0	14.9	15.5	32.9	33.8	34.2	34.9	36.8
Belgium[1]	13.7	13.5	13.9	13.2	13.6	33.2	30.8	32.4	31.1	32.0
Canada	4.3	4.7	4.6	4.7	4.9	12.1	13.6	14.9	14.2	14.3
Chile	1.5	1.4	1.3	1.5	1.5	9.0	7.3	6.8	7.3	8.0
Colombia	0.9	2.6	2.1	1.9	1.9	7.9	16.3	11.7	9.5	9.9
Costa Rica	6.5	6.4	7.3	8.0	8.2	28.9	30.4	33.1	34.2	36.1
Czech Republic	..	14.3	14.4	15.4	15.8	..	44.3	44.8	44.1	45.5
Denmark[1]	0.0	0.6	0.1	0.0	0.1	0.0	1.4	0.2	0.1	0.1
Estonia	..	10.9	12.7	11.7	12.1	..	35.1	38.4	35.0	36.5
Finland	11.0	11.5	12.0	11.8	11.5	25.6	25.2	29.7	27.9	27.4
France[1]	18.1	15.6	16.1	14.8	14.8	44.1	35.8	38.2	33.0	32.7
Germany	13.0	14.2	13.8	14.6	15.0	37.5	39.0	38.9	37.9	39.7
Greece	7.6	10.1	11.0	12.1	12.9	30.2	30.3	34.2	30.8	33.2
Hungary	..	11.3	11.6	11.7	11.1	..	29.4	31.4	32.0	30.8
Iceland	1.0	2.8	3.8	3.2	3.0	3.1	7.7	11.7	9.2	8.3
Ireland	4.6	3.7	5.1	3.7	3.3	14.1	11.9	18.2	16.8	16.6
Israel	..	5.0	5.1	5.2	5.1	..	14.6	16.8	17.3	17.4
Italy	11.9	11.6	13.0	13.2	13.6	32.9	28.5	31.1	31.2	31.8
Japan	7.3	8.9	10.8	12.9	13.4	26.5	35.2	41.1	41.1	40.4
Korea	1.9	3.5	5.2	7.3	7.8	10.1	16.7	23.3	26.7	28.0
Latvia	..	9.7	8.6	9.5	10.0	..	33.5	30.1	30.7	31.4
Lithuania[1]	..	9.9	11.6	9.7	10.2	..	32.2	41.1	31.9	33.2
Luxembourg[1]	9.6	9.7	10.3	11.0	11.1	27.5	26.1	29.0	27.8	29.2
Mexico	2.0	2.1	2.1	2.3	2.5	16.8	18.0	16.2	13.8	13.9
Netherlands	14.9	14.3	12.9	13.4	13.6	37.4	38.7	36.3	34.2	34.1
New Zealand	0.0	0.0	0.0	0.0	0.0	0.0	0.0	0.0	0.0	0.0
Norway	10.6	8.8	9.4	10.6	11.2	26.3	21.0	22.4	26.4	28.9
Poland[1]	..	12.9	10.8	13.2	13.5	..	39.2	34.4	37.6	37.9
Portugal	7.2	7.9	8.6	9.6	10.5	27.2	25.6	28.4	27.9	29.6
Slovak Republic	..	13.9	11.9	15.0	15.5	..	41.4	42.6	43.3	43.9
Slovenia[1]	..	14.9	15.8	15.6	16.8	..	39.6	41.8	42.2	45.2
Spain	11.2	11.5	11.9	12.3	13.8	35.4	34.9	37.9	35.3	37.4
Sweden	13.3	12.7	10.8	9.2	9.0	27.2	25.5	25.1	21.4	21.4
Switzerland[1]	5.4	6.5	6.1	6.5	6.9	23.3	24.2	23.7	23.7	25.2
Türkiye	2.9	4.4	6.1	7.3	7.1	19.7	18.7	24.9	31.4	29.7
United Kingdom	5.6	5.5	6.0	6.4	6.7	17.0	16.8	18.9	19.7	21.0
United States	6.7	6.7	6.1	6.1	6.4	25.6	23.6	26.1	24.3	24.8
Unweighted average										
OECD Average	**7.1**	**8.4**	**8.6**	**8.9**	**9.2**	**21.8**	**24.9**	**26.6**	**25.9**	**26.6**

.. Not available

Note: Full time series can be accessed at http://oe.cd/full-time-series.

1. The capital transfers were subtracted directly from the specific taxes to which they relate, except for France, where the capital transfers have been allocated between tax headings in proportion to the reported tax revenue.

StatLink https://stat.link/jpd627

Table 3.11. Taxes on payroll and workforce (3000) as % of GDP and as % of total tax revenue

	% of GDP					% of total tax revenue				
	1990	2000	2010	2019	2020	1990	2000	2010	2019	2020
Australia	1.7	1.4	1.3	1.3	1.3	6.1	4.5	5.2	4.7	4.5
Austria[1]	2.4	2.7	2.8	2.7	2.8	6.0	6.4	6.9	6.4	6.5
Belgium[1]	0.0	0.0	0.0	0.0	0.0	0.0	0.0	0.0	0.0	0.0
Canada	0.8	0.7	0.6	0.8	0.8	2.3	2.1	2.1	2.3	2.3
Chile	0.0	0.0	0.0	0.0	0.0	0.0	0.0	0.0	0.0	0.0
Colombia	0.0	0.7	0.7	0.3	0.4	0.0	4.2	4.1	1.7	2.0
Costa Rica	1.4	1.3	1.3	1.4	1.5	6.4	6.3	5.9	5.9	6.5
Czech Republic	..	0.0	0.0	0.0	0.0	..	0.0	0.0	0.0	0.0
Denmark[1]	0.3	0.2	0.2	0.3	0.2	0.7	0.4	0.5	0.6	0.4
Estonia	..	0.0	0.0	0.0	0.0	..	0.0	0.0	0.0	0.0
Finland	0.0	0.0	0.0	0.0	0.0	0.0	0.0	0.0	0.0	0.0
France[1]	0.8	1.0	1.3	1.8	1.9	1.9	2.3	3.2	4.0	4.1
Germany	0.0	0.0	0.0	0.0	0.0	0.0	0.0	0.0	0.0	0.0
Greece	0.2	0.0	0.0	0.0	0.0	0.7	0.0	0.0	0.0	0.0
Hungary	..	1.4	0.4	1.0	1.0	..	3.6	1.1	2.9	2.9
Iceland	1.1	0.0	0.2	0.3	0.3	3.5	0.1	0.5	0.9	0.9
Ireland	0.4	0.0	0.2	0.2	0.2	1.3	0.0	0.7	1.0	1.0
Israel	..	1.2	1.2	1.1	1.1	..	3.6	3.8	3.8	3.8
Italy	0.1	0.0	0.0	0.0	0.0	0.3	0.0	0.0	0.0	0.0
Japan	0.0	0.0	0.0	0.0	0.0	0.0	0.0	0.0	0.0	0.0
Korea	0.1	0.0	0.1	0.1	0.1	0.4	0.2	0.2	0.3	0.3
Latvia	..	0.0	0.0	0.0	0.0	..	0.0	0.1	0.0	0.0
Lithuania[1]	..	0.0	0.0	0.0	0.0	..	0.0	0.0	0.0	0.0
Luxembourg[1]	0.0	0.0	0.0	0.0	0.0	0.0	0.0	0.0	0.0	0.0
Mexico	0.2	0.2	0.3	0.4	0.5	1.8	1.5	2.2	2.5	2.5
Netherlands	0.0	0.0	0.0	0.0	0.0	0.0	0.0	0.0	0.0	0.0
New Zealand	0.0	0.0	0.0	0.0	0.0	0.0	0.0	0.0	0.0	0.0
Norway	0.0	0.0	0.0	0.1	0.1	0.0	0.0	0.0	0.1	0.2
Poland[1]	..	0.2	0.3	0.3	0.3	..	0.7	0.8	0.7	0.9
Portugal	0.0	0.0	0.0	0.0	0.0	0.0	0.0	0.0	0.0	0.0
Slovak Republic	..	0.0	0.0	0.0	0.0	..	0.0	0.0	0.0	0.0
Slovenia[1]	..	1.5	0.1	0.0	0.0	..	4.1	0.2	0.1	0.1
Spain	0.0	0.0	0.0	0.0	0.0	0.0	0.0	0.0	0.0	0.0
Sweden	1.2	2.1	3.0	5.3	5.1	2.5	4.2	7.0	12.4	12.0
Switzerland[1]	0.0	0.0	0.0	0.0	0.0	0.0	0.0	0.0	0.0	0.0
Türkiye	0.0	0.0	0.0	0.0	0.0	0.0	0.0	0.0	0.0	0.0
United Kingdom	0.0	0.0	0.0	0.1	0.1	0.0	0.0	0.0	0.4	0.4
United States	0.0	0.0	0.0	0.0	0.0	0.0	0.0	0.1	0.0	0.1
Unweighted average										
OECD Average	**0.4**	**0.4**	**0.4**	**0.5**	**0.5**	**1.2**	**1.2**	**1.2**	**1.3**	**1.4**

.. Not available

Note: Full time series can be accessed at http://oe.cd/full-time-series.

1. The capital transfers were subtracted directly from the specific taxes to which they relate, except for France, where the capital transfers have been allocated between tax headings in proportion to the reported tax revenue.

StatLink https://stat.link/kip7um

Table 3.12. Taxes on property (4000) as % of GDP and as % of total tax revenue

	% of GDP					% of total tax revenue				
	1990	2000	2010	2019	2020	1990	2000	2010	2019	2020
Australia	2.5	2.7	2.4	2.7	2.9	9.0	8.8	9.4	9.8	10.1
Austria[1]	1.1	0.6	0.5	0.5	0.6	2.7	1.3	1.3	1.3	1.4
Belgium[1]	1.6	2.1	3.1	3.4	3.4	3.8	4.7	7.2	8.1	8.0
Canada	3.5	3.3	3.8	3.8	4.1	10.0	9.5	12.3	11.6	12.0
Chile	1.0	1.3	0.8	1.1	1.0	6.2	7.0	4.1	5.5	5.3
Colombia	0.2	1.0	1.6	1.8	1.8	2.2	6.6	8.7	9.1	9.7
Costa Rica	0.3	0.2	0.3	0.4	0.4	1.3	0.9	1.5	1.9	2.0
Czech Republic	..	0.5	0.4	0.4	0.2	..	1.4	1.3	1.2	0.6
Denmark[1]	1.9	1.6	1.9	2.0	2.0	4.3	3.3	4.1	4.3	4.2
Estonia	..	0.4	0.3	0.2	0.2	..	1.2	1.0	0.6	0.6
Finland	1.1	1.1	1.1	1.4	1.5	2.4	2.4	2.7	3.4	3.6
France[1]	2.6	3.0	3.5	3.9	4.0	6.3	6.9	8.4	8.7	8.7
Germany	1.2	0.8	0.8	1.1	1.2	3.4	2.3	2.3	2.9	3.3
Greece	1.2	2.6	1.7	3.1	3.0	4.6	7.7	5.2	7.7	7.8
Hungary	..	0.7	1.1	0.9	1.1	..	1.7	3.1	2.6	2.9
Iceland	2.6	2.4	2.1	1.9	2.3	8.4	6.6	6.5	5.5	6.2
Ireland	1.5	1.8	1.4	1.2	1.0	4.6	5.7	5.1	5.7	5.0
Israel	..	3.2	3.4	3.2	3.1	..	9.5	11.1	10.6	10.3
Italy	0.8	1.9	2.0	2.4	2.4	2.3	4.6	4.8	5.7	5.7
Japan	2.6	2.7	2.6	2.6	2.7	9.4	10.5	9.7	8.2	8.1
Korea	2.2	2.6	2.5	3.1	3.9	11.8	12.4	11.3	11.4	14.2
Latvia	..	1.1	0.9	0.9	1.0	..	3.8	3.0	3.0	3.0
Lithuania[1]	..	0.5	0.4	0.3	0.3	..	1.5	1.3	1.0	1.0
Luxembourg[1]	2.9	4.0	2.5	3.9	3.8	8.4	10.7	7.0	9.8	10.0
Mexico	0.2	0.2	0.3	0.3	0.3	1.9	1.8	2.3	2.0	1.9
Netherlands	1.5	1.9	1.4	1.5	1.7	3.7	5.3	3.8	3.8	4.3
New Zealand	2.5	1.7	2.0	1.9	1.9	6.8	5.3	6.6	6.2	5.5
Norway	1.2	1.0	1.1	1.3	1.3	2.9	2.3	2.6	3.2	3.4
Poland[1]	..	1.4	1.3	1.3	1.3	..	4.3	4.2	3.6	3.6
Portugal	0.7	1.1	1.1	1.4	1.5	2.7	3.7	3.7	4.2	4.2
Slovak Republic	..	0.6	0.4	0.4	0.5	..	1.8	1.4	1.2	1.4
Slovenia[1]	..	0.6	0.6	0.6	0.6	..	1.7	1.6	1.7	1.7
Spain	1.7	2.1	2.1	2.5	2.5	5.5	6.5	6.6	7.1	6.7
Sweden	1.7	1.7	1.0	0.9	1.0	3.5	3.3	2.4	2.2	2.2
Switzerland[1]	2.1	2.6	2.0	2.1	2.2	8.9	9.7	7.7	7.7	8.1
Türkiye	0.3	0.7	1.0	1.0	1.1	2.3	3.2	4.1	4.2	4.4
United Kingdom	2.7	3.7	3.8	4.0	3.7	8.2	11.4	12.0	12.4	11.6
United States	3.1	2.9	3.1	3.0	3.2	11.7	10.3	13.5	12.1	12.4
Unweighted average										
OECD Average	**1.7**	**1.7**	**1.6**	**1.8**	**1.9**	**5.5**	**5.3**	**5.4**	**5.6**	**5.7**

.. Not available

Note: Full time series can be accessed at http://oe.cd/full-time-series.

1. The capital transfers were subtracted directly from the specific taxes to which they relate, except for France, where the capital transfers have been allocated between tax headings in proportion to the reported tax revenue.

StatLink https://stat.link/2lqr16

Table 3.13. Taxes on goods and services (5000) as % of GDP and as % of total tax revenue

	% of GDP					% of total tax revenue				
	1990	2000	2010	2019	2020	1990	2000	2010	2019	2020
Australia	7.8	8.8	7.2	7.3	7.6	27.8	28.8	28.8	26.3	26.5
Austria[1]	12.4	12.4	11.7	11.7	11.5	31.5	29.3	28.7	27.5	27.1
Belgium[1]	10.8	11.3	11.2	10.8	10.4	26.1	25.9	26.1	25.4	24.4
Canada	9.1	8.4	7.4	7.6	7.4	25.8	24.2	24.0	23.1	21.5
Chile	10.6	11.9	10.1	11.1	10.6	62.9	63.8	51.2	53.0	54.8
Colombia	6.1	7.3	8.2	8.5	7.8	53.8	46.3	45.1	43.0	41.4
Costa Rica	10.2	9.9	8.9	8.1	7.6	45.5	46.7	40.3	34.8	33.3
Czech Republic	..	10.2	10.9	11.1	10.8	..	31.5	33.8	31.9	31.1
Denmark[1]	15.0	15.7	15.0	14.2	14.4	33.9	33.5	33.6	30.2	30.6
Estonia	..	12.1	13.5	14.2	13.3	..	38.8	40.7	42.4	39.9
Finland	14.0	13.4	13.0	14.2	14.1	32.5	29.2	32.0	33.7	33.8
France[1]	11.7	11.5	11.2	12.4	12.3	28.4	26.4	26.6	27.6	27.1
Germany	9.3	10.4	10.8	10.3	9.7	26.7	28.5	30.5	26.6	25.7
Greece	11.2	11.8	12.5	15.8	15.0	44.5	35.2	38.6	39.9	38.5
Hungary	..	15.6	15.9	16.3	16.3	..	40.6	43.3	44.7	45.1
Iceland	15.6	16.3	11.5	11.4	11.4	51.3	45.3	35.8	32.8	31.7
Ireland	13.6	11.9	9.9	6.8	5.6	41.9	38.8	35.8	30.9	28.4
Israel	..	11.2	11.9	10.7	10.4	..	32.9	39.2	35.7	35.3
Italy	10.2	11.4	11.1	12.0	11.5	28.0	28.2	26.6	28.3	26.9
Japan	3.8	4.9	4.9	6.2	6.9	13.7	19.3	18.7	19.7	20.9
Korea	8.2	8.0	7.5	7.0	6.8	44.3	38.4	33.7	25.8	24.4
Latvia	..	11.2	11.9	13.9	14.0	..	38.6	41.8	44.9	44.0
Lithuania[1]	..	12.1	11.7	11.5	11.6	..	39.4	41.4	38.1	37.7
Luxembourg[1]	8.2	9.8	9.9	9.2	8.7	23.6	26.6	27.6	23.1	22.8
Mexico	5.3	4.8	4.9	6.2	6.6	44.0	41.7	38.0	37.6	37.2
Netherlands	10.5	10.9	11.2	12.1	12.2	26.4	29.7	31.5	30.7	30.5
New Zealand	12.1	11.3	12.0	12.1	12.8	33.6	34.7	39.6	38.7	38.0
Norway	14.3	13.1	11.6	11.8	12.4	35.5	31.4	27.7	29.3	32.0
Poland[1]	..	11.6	12.6	12.8	12.9	..	35.3	40.3	36.5	36.2
Portugal	11.7	12.6	12.3	13.7	13.2	44.2	40.7	40.4	39.8	37.5
Slovak Republic	..	12.2	10.4	12.1	12.2	..	36.3	37.2	35.0	34.6
Slovenia[1]	..	13.8	13.9	13.5	12.5	..	36.6	36.8	36.5	33.6
Spain	9.0	10.1	8.6	10.0	9.8	28.4	30.6	27.5	28.9	26.7
Sweden	12.2	12.1	12.7	12.1	12.1	25.0	24.2	29.7	28.2	28.5
Switzerland[1]	4.8	6.0	5.8	5.4	5.5	20.9	22.2	22.5	19.9	20.0
Türkiye	4.1	9.9	11.8	9.0	10.2	27.9	42.0	47.7	39.0	42.9
United Kingdom	10.2	10.6	10.1	10.6	10.0	31.0	32.3	31.7	32.8	31.2
United States	4.5	4.5	4.2	4.4	4.4	17.5	16.0	18.1	17.5	17.2
Unweighted average										
OECD Average	**9.9**	**10.8**	**10.5**	**10.7**	**10.6**	**33.7**	**33.9**	**34.0**	**32.6**	**32.1**

.. Not available

Note: Full time series can be accessed at http://oe.cd/full-time-series.

1. The capital transfers were subtracted directly from the specific taxes to which they relate, except for France, where the capital transfers have been allocated between tax headings in proportion to the reported tax revenue.

StatLink https://stat.link/dzc8e1

Table 3.14. Value added taxes (5111) as % of GDP and as % of total tax revenue

	% of GDP					% of total tax revenue				
	1990	2000	2010	2019	2020	1990	2000	2010	2019	2020
Australia	0.0	3.4	3.3	3.2	3.5	0.0	11.1	13.1	11.7	12.4
Austria[1]	8.2	7.9	7.7	7.7	7.4	20.8	18.7	18.7	18.0	17.6
Belgium[1]	6.8	7.1	7.0	6.6	6.4	16.4	16.1	16.2	15.6	15.0
Canada	0.0	3.2	4.2	4.5	4.5	0.0	9.2	13.7	13.5	13.2
Chile	6.3	7.8	7.6	8.3	8.0	37.4	41.8	38.5	39.9	41.1
Colombia	2.6	4.3	5.3	5.8	5.4	22.6	27.6	29.3	29.6	28.7
Costa Rica	4.1	4.8	4.6	4.3	4.5	18.1	22.8	21.0	18.5	19.7
Czech Republic	..	5.9	6.6	7.5	7.4	..	18.3	20.5	21.6	21.3
Denmark[1]	8.3	9.1	9.4	9.4	9.8	18.7	19.5	20.9	20.0	20.8
Estonia	..	8.4	8.5	8.9	8.9	..	27.1	25.7	26.7	26.7
Finland	8.3	8.0	8.3	9.2	9.2	19.3	17.4	20.4	21.7	22.1
France[1]	7.6	7.2	6.8	7.1	7.0	18.4	16.7	16.1	15.9	15.4
Germany	5.8	6.7	7.0	7.0	6.5	16.6	18.4	19.8	18.2	17.2
Greece	6.2	6.3	7.1	8.4	7.8	24.6	18.9	22.0	21.3	20.1
Hungary	..	8.7	8.5	9.5	9.8	..	22.5	23.0	26.2	27.1
Iceland	8.7	10.2	7.4	8.0	8.0	28.4	28.5	22.8	22.9	22.0
Ireland	6.6	7.0	6.0	4.3	3.4	20.4	22.9	21.7	19.6	17.2
Israel	..	7.2	7.4	7.1	7.1	..	21.0	24.3	23.8	23.9
Italy	5.3	6.2	6.1	6.2	6.0	14.7	15.4	14.5	14.7	14.1
Japan	1.2	2.3	2.5	4.2	4.9	4.4	9.1	9.6	13.2	14.9
Korea	3.5	3.6	3.9	4.3	4.2	18.7	17.0	17.5	15.7	15.1
Latvia	..	6.9	6.6	8.6	8.7	..	23.9	23.3	27.8	27.5
Lithuania[1]	..	7.5	7.8	7.9	7.9	..	24.4	27.5	26.0	25.6
Luxembourg[1]	4.2	4.9	6.2	5.8	5.7	12.1	13.2	17.3	14.7	14.9
Mexico	3.2	2.8	3.8	3.8	4.2	26.1	24.7	29.4	23.4	23.8
Netherlands	6.5	6.4	6.7	7.1	7.4	16.5	17.3	18.7	18.2	18.5
New Zealand	8.1	8.1	9.3	9.5	10.4	22.4	24.9	30.7	30.4	30.6
Norway	7.6	8.2	7.8	8.6	9.1	18.8	19.8	18.6	21.5	23.6
Poland[1]	..	6.9	7.6	7.9	8.0	..	21.0	24.2	22.6	22.4
Portugal	5.2	7.6	7.5	8.8	8.4	19.6	24.5	24.8	25.4	23.8
Slovak Republic	..	6.8	6.1	7.3	7.4	..	20.4	21.8	21.0	21.0
Slovenia[1]	..	8.5	8.1	8.0	7.5	..	22.7	21.3	21.6	20.2
Spain	5.0	5.8	5.2	6.5	6.3	15.7	17.6	16.5	18.7	17.1
Sweden	7.3	8.2	9.0	9.1	9.2	14.9	16.4	21.1	21.3	21.6
Switzerland[1]	2.7	3.5	3.3	3.1	3.1	11.5	13.0	12.7	11.3	11.3
Türkiye	2.7	5.7	5.4	4.2	4.6	18.3	24.2	21.7	18.1	19.2
United Kingdom	5.5	5.9	6.1	6.9	6.5	16.9	18.1	19.0	21.3	20.2
United States	0.0	0.0	0.0	0.0	0.0	0.0	0.0	0.0	0.0	0.0
Unweighted average										
OECD Average	**5.1**	**6.3**	**6.4**	**6.7**	**6.7**	**17.0**	**19.6**	**20.5**	**20.3**	**20.2**

.. Not available

Note: Full time series can be accessed at http://oe.cd/full-time-series.

1. The capital transfers were subtracted directly from the specific taxes to which they relate, except for France, where the capital transfers have been allocated between tax headings in proportion to the reported tax revenue.

StatLink https://stat.link/nmrfg9

Table 3.15. Tax revenues of sub-sectors of general government as % of GDP

	Supranational			Central government			State or Regional government			Local government			Social Security Funds		
	1975	1995	2020	1975	1995	2020	1975	1995	2020	1975	1995	2020	1975	1995	2020
Federal countries															
Australia	..	..	..	20.3	21.9	23.1	4.0	5.4	4.5	1.1	1.0	1.0	0.0	0.0	0.0
Austria[1]	..	0.2	0.2	18.8	26.7	26.7	3.9	0.7	0.9	4.5	1.7	1.3	9.2	12.0	13.1
Belgium[1]	0.6	0.4	0.4	25.4	25.8	21.0	..	0.8	4.7	1.7	2.0	2.2	11.2	13.8	14.2
Canada	..	..	..	14.8	13.5	14.1	10.1	12.8	13.4	3.1	3.4	3.5	3.1	4.8	3.2
Germany	0.4	0.2	0.2	11.5	11.4	10.4	7.6	7.9	9.1	3.1	2.7	3.1	11.7	14.1	15.0
Mexico	..	..	..	..	7.5	14.3	..	0.3	0.7	..	0.2	0.3	..	2.2	2.5
Switzerland[1]	..	..	..	6.7	7.9	9.2	5.9	6.0	7.1	4.4	4.4	4.3	4.8	6.7	6.9
United States	..	..	..	11.2	11.0	9.9	4.8	5.3	5.4	3.6	3.5	4.0	5.0	6.7	6.4
Unweighted average	0.5	0.3	0.3	15.5	15.7	16.1	6.0	4.9	5.7	3.1	2.4	2.5	6.4	7.5	7.7
Regional countries															
Colombia[2]	..	..	..	..	10.1	13.5	..	0.9	0.9	..	1.4	2.5	..	3.6	1.9
Spain[2]	..	0.2	0.2	8.6	16.0	13.7	..	1.6	6.1	0.8	2.7	3.2	8.5	10.8	13.4
Unitary countries															
Chile	..	..	..	..	16.3	16.4	..	..	..	..	1.2	1.7	..	0.7	1.3
Costa Rica	..	..	..	..	12.4	12.5	..	..	..	..	0.3	0.7	..	6.2	9.4
Czech Republic	..	..	0.1	..	19.9	18.4	..	..	..	..	0.3	0.3	..	14.3	15.8
Denmark[1]	0.4	0.2	0.1	25.6	31.7	34.3	..	..	..	11.0	14.6	12.7	0.0	0.0	0.0
Estonia	..	..	0.2	..	29.5	27.0	..	..	..	..	0.3	0.3	..	5.2	5.8
Finland	..	0.2	0.2	20.3	20.7	19.9	..	..	..	8.5	9.9	10.3	7.4	13.7	11.5
France[1]	0.2	0.3	0.2	17.9	18.0	14.6	..	..	..	2.6	4.7	6.1	14.2	19.4	24.4
Greece	..	0.2	0.2	12.5	18.8	24.7	..	..	..	0.6	0.6	1.0	5.5	8.8	13.0
Hungary	..	..	0.1	..	26.0	23.2	..	..	..	..	1.0	1.9	..	13.7	10.9
Iceland	..	..	..	24.0	24.3	25.3	..	..	..	5.5	6.4	10.8	0.0	0.0	0.0
Ireland	0.6	0.5	0.1	21.6	26.4	16.6	..	..	..	2.0	0.8	0.2	3.6	4.0	2.9
Israel	..	..	..	..	27.0	22.1	..	..	..	..	2.4	2.3	..	4.7	5.1
Italy	..	0.1	0.2	13.0	24.1	24.2	..	..	..	0.2	2.1	4.7	11.2	12.1	13.6
Japan	..	..	..	9.0	10.5	12.1	..	..	..	5.1	6.4	7.6	5.7	8.5	13.4
Korea	..	..	..	13.2	13.0	14.7	..	..	..	1.5	3.5	5.3	0.1	2.3	7.8
Latvia	..	..	0.2	..	12.9	16.2	..	..	..	..	5.8	5.7	..	11.0	9.7
Lithuania[1]	..	..	0.3	..	19.8	20.0	..	..	..	..	0.6	0.3	..	7.2	10.2
Luxembourg[1]	0.2	0.2	0.3	20.7	23.9	25.4	..	..	..	2.2	2.3	1.6	9.4	9.6	10.8
Netherlands	0.6	0.5	0.4	22.2	20.9	24.5	..	..	..	0.4	1.2	1.4	14.5	14.7	13.6
New Zealand	..	..	..	27.7	33.7	31.7	..	..	..	2.3	1.9	2.1	0.0	0.0	0.0
Norway	..	..	..	19.7	22.7	32.3	..	..	..	8.7	7.9	6.5	10.5	8.8	0.0
Poland[1]	..	..	0.2	..	22.4	17.5	..	..	..	..	3.1	4.4	..	11.1	13.5
Portugal	..	0.2	0.2	12.3	21.2	22.6	..	..	..	0.0	1.6	2.5	6.5	6.3	9.9
Slovak Republic	..	..	0.2	..	24.7	19.3	..	..	..	..	0.5	0.7	..	14.2	15.0
Slovenia[1]	..	..	0.2	..	19.8	16.8	..	..	..	..	2.4	3.6	..	16.9	16.6
Sweden	..	0.2	0.1	19.7	21.1	21.3	..	..	..	11.2	13.9	15.6	7.5	9.8	5.3
Türkiye	..	..	..	..	12.3	14.5	..	..	..	..	2.1	2.2	..	2.0	7.1
United Kingdom	0.3	0.3	0.1	24.1	22.7	23.4	..	..	..	3.8	1.1	1.8	6.0	5.2	6.7
Unweighted average	0.4	0.3	0.2	19.0	21.3	21.1	..	..	..	4.1	3.5	4.1	6.4	8.2	9.1

.. Not available

1. The capital transfers were subtracted directly from the specific taxes to which they relate, except for France, where the capital transfers have been allocated between tax headings in proportion to the reported tax revenue.

2. Colombia and Spain are not constitutionally federal countries, but both have a highly decentralised political structure, with high autonomy of their territorial entities.

StatLink https://stat.link/jov5ur

Table 3.16. Main central government taxes as % of total tax revenues of central government, 2020

	1000 Income & profits	2000 Social security[3]	3000 Payroll	4000 Property	5000 Goods and services	6000 Others
Federal countries						
Australia	72.9	0.0	0.4	0.0	26.7	0.0
Austria[1]	42.8	8.3	5.6	1.4	41.5	0.5
Belgium[1]	55.8	0.1	0.0	2.1	42.0	0.0
Canada	73.4	7.3	0.0	0.0	19.3	0.0
Germany	47.4	0.0	0.0	0.4	52.2	0.0
Mexico	52.8	0.0	0.0	0.0	45.5	1.7
Switzerland[1]	42.5	0.0	0.0	2.6	54.8	0.1
United States	91.5	0.0	0.0	0.9	7.6	0.0
Unweighted average	59.9	1.9	0.7	0.9	36.2	0.3
Regional countries						
Colombia[2]	45.8	0.0	2.7	6.7	44.5	0.2
Spain[2]	39.6	2.2	0.0	0.2	57.9	0.0
Unitary countries						
Chile	38.2	1.6	0.0	1.6	59.2	-0.5
Costa Rica	36.3	1.7	0.0	0.9	57.4	3.7
Czech Republic	43.0	0.0	0.0	0.0	56.9	0.0
Denmark[1]	55.9	0.1	0.5	1.8	41.7	0.0
Estonia	28.3	23.5	0.0	0.0	48.2	0.0
Finland	26.1	0.0	0.0	3.4	70.4	0.2
France[1]	41.5	2.4	3.6	6.0	46.1	0.3
Greece	32.1	0.1	0.0	8.5	59.3	0.0
Hungary	28.3	2.0	4.4	3.0	62.1	0.1
Iceland	38.6	11.9	1.2	1.4	44.3	2.6
Ireland	58.6	2.3	1.2	4.8	33.2	0.0
Israel	44.3	0.0	5.2	3.6	46.9	0.0
Italy	53.7	0.0	0.0	5.6	40.7	0.0
Japan	52.2	0.0	0.0	5.0	42.8	0.0
Korea	52.3	0.0	0.0	10.2	36.0	1.5
Latvia	12.1	2.0	0.1	1.0	84.8	0.0
Lithuania[1]	43.4	0.0	0.0	0.1	56.5	0.0
Luxembourg[1]	51.1	1.2	0.0	14.6	32.9	0.1
Netherlands	50.1	0.0	0.0	3.9	45.3	0.8
New Zealand	60.2	0.0	0.0	0.1	39.7	0.0
Norway	25.2	34.7	0.2	1.5	38.4	0.0
Poland[1]	26.5	0.0	1.9	0.0	71.6	0.0
Portugal	40.2	4.7	0.0	1.1	52.5	1.5
Slovak Republic	36.8	2.4	0.0	0.0	60.9	0.0
Slovenia[1]	26.1	1.0	0.3	0.0	72.6	0.0
Sweden	-0.3	17.4	23.9	2.7	56.2	0.2
Türkiye	31.6	0.0	0.0	5.1	62.6	0.7
United Kingdom	49.1	0.0	0.6	8.2	42.1	0.0
Unweighted average	38.6	3.9	1.5	3.4	52.2	0.4

Note: Excluding social security contributions accruing to social security funds.
1. The capital transfers were subtracted directly from the specific taxes to which they relate, except for France, where the capital transfers have been allocated between tax headings in proportion to the reported tax revenue.
2. Colombia and Spain are not constitutionally federal countries, but both have a highly decentralised political structure, with high autonomy of their territorial entities.
3. These comprise only social security contributions accruing to central government.

StatLink https://stat.link/7gzjpx

Table 3.17. Main state government taxes as % of total tax revenues of state government, 2020

	1000 Income & profits	2000 Social security	3000 Payroll	4000 Property	5000 Goods and services	6000 Others
Federal countries						
Australia	0.0	0.0	26.6	42.4	31.1	0.0
Austria[1, 2]	37.5	13.4	32.2	1.5	12.7	2.7
Belgium[1, 2]	49.2	1.2	0.0	35.6	14.0	0.0
Canada	50.0	4.6	5.9	5.2	34.3	0.0
Germany[2]	49.5	0.0	0.0	9.0	41.6	0.0
Mexico	0.0	0.0	65.4	16.4	13.2	5.0
Switzerland[1]	75.4	0.0	0.0	17.8	6.1	0.7
United States	44.0	0.0	0.3	3.3	52.4	0.0
Unweighted average	38.2	2.4	16.3	16.4	25.6	1.1
Regional countries						
Colombia[3]	0.0	0.0	0.0	0.0	72.3	27.7
Spain[2, 3]	76.2	0.0	0.0	16.1	7.7	0.0
Unitary countries						
Chile	..	..	..	..	..	..
Costa Rica	..	..	..	..	..	..
Czech Republic	..	..	..	..	..	..
Denmark	..	..	..	..	..	..
Estonia	..	..	..	..	..	..
Finland	..	..	..	..	..	..
France	..	..	..	..	..	..
Greece	..	..	..	..	..	..
Hungary	..	..	..	..	..	..
Iceland	..	..	..	..	..	..
Ireland	..	..	..	..	..	..
Israel	..	..	..	..	..	..
Italy	..	..	..	..	..	..
Japan	..	..	..	..	..	..
Korea	..	..	..	..	..	..
Latvia	..	..	..	..	..	..
Lithuania	..	..	..	..	..	..
Luxembourg	..	..	..	..	..	..
Netherlands	..	..	..	..	..	..
New Zealand	..	..	..	..	..	..
Norway	..	..	..	..	..	..
Poland	..	..	..	..	..	..
Portugal	..	..	..	..	..	..
Slovak Republic	..	..	..	..	..	..
Slovenia	..	..	..	..	..	..
Sweden	..	..	..	..	..	..
Türkiye	..	..	..	..	..	..
United Kingdom	..	..	..	..	..	..
Unweighted average	..	..	..	..	..	..

.. Not available

1. The capital transfers were subtracted directly from the specific taxes to which they relate.
2. Payments to the European Union are excluded from these comparisons.
3. Colombia and Spain are not constitutionally federal countries, but both have a highly decentralised political structure, with high autonomy of their territorial entities.

StatLink https://stat.link/6siuc8

Table 3.18. Main local government taxes as % of total tax revenues of local government, 2020

	1000 Income & profits	2000 Social security	3000 Payroll	4000 Property	5000 Goods and services	6000 Others
Federal countries						
Australia	0.0	0.0	0.0	100.0	0.0	0.0
Austria[1, 2]	0.0	4.7	72.0	15.0	6.9	1.4
Belgium[1, 2]	36.8	0.2	0.0	56.5	6.4	0.0
Canada	0.0	0.0	0.0	97.3	1.6	1.1
Germany[2]	77.7	0.0	0.0	12.4	9.7	0.2
Mexico	0.0	0.0	0.0	82.4	1.0	16.6
Switzerland[1]	80.5	0.0	0.0	17.0	0.6	2.0
United States	5.8	0.0	0.0	73.2	21.0	0.0
Unweighted average	25.1	0.6	9.0	56.7	5.9	2.7
Regional countries						
Colombia[3]	0.0	0.0	0.0	36.4	44.2	19.3
Spain[2, 3]	18.6	0.0	0.0	44.7	36.5	0.1
Unitary countries						
Chile	0.0	0.0	0.0	45.3	54.7	0.0
Costa Rica	0.0	0.0	0.0	47.9	52.1	0.0
Czech Republic[2]	0.0	0.0	0.0	58.0	42.0	0.0
Denmark[1, 2]	89.3	0.0	0.0	10.7	0.0	0.0
Estonia[2]	0.0	0.0	0.0	83.1	16.9	0.0
Finland[2]	92.1	0.0	0.0	7.9	0.0	0.0
France[1, 2]	0.0	0.0	6.5	50.3	35.7	7.5
Greece[2]	0.0	0.0	0.0	95.6	4.4	0.0
Hungary[2]	0.0	0.0	0.0	19.0	81.0	0.0
Iceland	80.4	0.0	0.0	17.6	2.0	0.0
Ireland[2]	0.0	10.2	0.0	89.8	0.0	0.0
Israel	0.0	0.0	0.0	95.8	4.2	0.0
Italy[2]	21.2	0.0	0.0	23.0	30.9	24.9
Japan	49.1	0.0	0.0	27.2	22.7	1.1
Korea	16.9	0.0	1.6	46.4	27.9	7.2
Latvia[2]	86.1	0.0	0.0	13.2	0.6	0.0
Lithuania[1]	0.0	0.0	0.0	83.6	16.4	0.0
Luxembourg[1, 2]	93.2	0.0	0.0	6.2	0.5	0.1
Netherlands[2]	0.0	0.0	0.0	54.1	45.9	0.0
New Zealand	0.0	0.0	0.0	88.2	11.8	0.0
Norway	86.6	0.0	0.0	12.6	0.7	0.0
Poland[1, 2]	65.7	0.0	0.0	29.4	3.8	1.0
Portugal[2]	26.5	0.0	0.0	48.0	25.3	0.2
Slovak Republic[2]	0.0	0.0	0.0	64.7	35.3	0.0
Slovenia[1, 2]	78.1	0.0	0.0	17.2	4.6	0.0
Sweden[2]	97.5	0.0	0.0	2.5	0.0	0.0
Türkiye	28.4	0.0	0.0	14.4	50.9	6.3
United Kingdom[2]	0.0	0.0	0.0	100.0	0.0	0.0
Unweighted average	32.5	0.4	0.3	44.7	20.4	1.7

1. The capital transfers were subtracted directly from the specific taxes to which they relate, except for France, where the capital transfers have been allocated between tax headings in proportion to the reported tax revenue.
2. Payments to the European Union are excluded from these comparisons.
3. Colombia and Spain are not constitutionally federal countries, but both have a highly decentralised political structure, with high autonomy of their territorial entities.

StatLink https://stat.link/omf694

Table 3.19. Gross domestic product for tax reporting years at market prices, in billions of national currency

		1965	1990	2000	2007	2010	2015	2018	2019	2020	2021p
Australia[1]	AUD	24.4	415.0	706.4	1 178.6	1 417.9	1 657.7	1 946.2	1 980.9	2 069.2	2 296.6
Austria	EUR	18.5	137.5	213.6	284.0	295.9	344.3	385.4	397.5	379.3	403.1
Belgium	EUR	20.9	170.1	256.4	343.6	363.1	416.7	460.1	478.2	456.7	507.2
Canada	CAD	61.3	696.1	1 125.5	1 577.7	1 666.0	1 990.4	2 231.2	2 310.7	2 206.8	2 493.1
Chile	CLP	..	10 594.8	42 215.0	90 159.5	110 777.9	158 622.9	189 434.9	195 816.5	200 343.7	240 633.3
Colombia	COP	..	22 731.4	195 108.6	428 506.0	544 060.0	804 692.0	987 791.0	1 060 068.0	998 719.0	1 176 694.3
Costa Rica[2]	CRC	..	525.3	4 627.1	13 889.1	19 802.0	30 171.9	36 014.7	37 832.1	36 356.3	39 905.6
Czech Republic	CZK	..	731.2	2 386.3	3 859.5	3 992.9	4 625.4	5 410.8	5 791.5	5 709.1	6 108.4
Denmark	DKK	71.5	855.6	1 326.9	1 738.8	1 810.9	2 036.4	2 253.3	2 311.0	2 323.9	2 504.2
Estonia	EUR	..	..	6.2	16.4	14.7	20.6	25.9	27.8	27.5	31.4
Finland	EUR	4.5	91.0	136.4	187.1	188.1	211.4	233.5	239.9	238.0	251.4
France	EUR	76.4	1 053.5	1 478.6	1 941.4	1 995.3	2 198.4	2 363.3	2 437.6	2 310.5	2 500.9
Germany	EUR	234.8	1 306.7	2 109.1	2 499.6	2 564.4	3 026.2	3 365.5	3 473.3	3 405.4	3 601.8
Greece	EUR	0.7	45.5	141.2	232.7	224.1	176.4	179.6	183.3	165.3	182.8
Hungary	HUF	..	..	13 324.1	25 749.4	27 496.7	34 975.3	43 392.4	47 530.6	48 276.4	55 256.7
Iceland	ISK	0.2	377.0	709.6	1 387.0	1 681.0	2 310.8	2 844.4	3 043.8	2 937.9	3 251.2
Ireland	EUR	1.3	37.9	108.5	197.1	167.4	263.0	326.6	356.7	372.8	426.3
Israel	ILS	..	124.3	554.7	756.1	891.2	1 179.3	1 352.5	1 434.6	1 422.6	1 578.0
Italy	EUR	22.4	730.9	1 241.5	1 614.8	1 611.3	1 655.4	1 771.4	1 796.6	1 657.0	1 775.4
Japan[1]	JPY	35 750.7	472 519.8	537 616.3	538 483.9	504 872.1	540 739.3	556 650.0	556 557.6	534 730.0	541 580.8
Korea[3]	KRW	831.4	200 556.2	651 634.4	1 089 660.2	1 322 611.2	1 658 020.4	1 898 192.6	1 924 498.1	1 940 726.2	2 071 658.0
Latvia	EUR	..	..	6.9	22.7	18.1	24.6	29.2	30.6	29.5	32.9
Lithuania	EUR	..	..	13.4	29.0	28.0	37.3	45.5	48.9	49.5	55.4
Luxembourg	EUR	1.0	10.6	23.0	37.6	42.4	54.1	60.1	62.4	64.8	72.3
Mexico	MXN	..	843.6	6 693.7	11 504.1	13 366.4	18 572.1	23 524.4	24 453.3	23 357.4	26 213.0
Netherlands	EUR	35.6	263.0	452.0	619.2	639.2	690.0	774.0	813.1	796.5	856.4
New Zealand[1]	NZD	4.1	75.9	122.2	188.8	205.7	258.8	310.2	318.6	342.0	359.5
Norway	NOK	57.2	749.9	1 507.3	2 350.2	2 591.5	3 111.2	3 553.9	3 563.5	3 410.4	4 141.9
Poland	PLN	..	62.7	748.5	1 187.5	1 446.8	1 801.1	2 121.6	2 293.2	2 339.0	2 622.2
Portugal	EUR	0.6	56.0	128.4	175.5	179.6	179.7	205.2	214.4	200.1	211.3
Slovak Republic	EUR	..	10.0	31.7	63.2	68.5	79.9	89.4	94.0	92.1	97.1
Slovenia	EUR	..	0.9	18.9	35.1	36.4	38.9	45.9	48.5	47.0	52.2
Spain	EUR	8.7	328.7	647.9	1 075.5	1 072.7	1 077.6	1 203.3	1 244.4	1 121.9	1 205.1
Sweden	SEK	129.3	1 549.8	2 408.2	3 320.3	3 573.6	4 260.5	4 828.3	5 049.6	5 038.5	5 451.8
Switzerland	CHF	70.1	369.5	472.6	592.4	629.3	675.7	719.3	727.2	706.2	742.8
Türkiye	TRY	0.0	0.5	171.5	887.7	1 167.7	2 350.9	3 758.8	4 311.7	5 048.2	7 248.8
United Kingdom	GBP	36.4	615.7	1 098.5	1 552.5	1 612.2	1 935.2	2 174.4	2 255.3	2 150.4	2 317.1
United States	USD	709.0	5 963.1	10 251.0	14 474.2	15 049.0	18 206.0	20 527.2	21 372.6	20 893.7	22 996.1

.. Not available

1. GDP is fiscal year. The year Y is calculated as the sum of: Q2(Y) to Q1(Y+1) for Japan; and Q3(Y) to Q2(Y+1) for Australia and New Zealand.
2. The GDP shown for 1990 in Costa Rica is taken from the IMF (World Economic Outlook Database, accessed in October 2022). The GDP for all other years is taken from the OECD National Accounts.
3. The GDP shown for 2021 in Korea is taken from the OECD National Accounts, accessed in October 2022, and is an estimated value.

Source: OECD National Accounts, accessed in October 2022.

StatLink https://stat.link/ovua06

Table 3.20. Exchange rates used, national currency per US dollar at market exchange rates

		1965	1990	2000	2007	2010	2015	2018	2019	2020	2021p
Australia	AUD	0.9	1.3	1.8	1.2	1.0	1.3	1.4	1.4	1.4	1.3
Austria	EUR	..	0.8	1.1	0.7	0.8	0.9	0.8	0.9	0.9	0.8
Belgium	EUR	..	0.8	1.1	0.7	0.8	0.9	0.8	0.9	0.9	0.8
Canada	CAD	1.1	1.2	1.5	1.1	1.0	1.3	1.3	1.3	1.3	1.3
Chile	CLP	0.0	304.9	539.4	522.2	510.0	654.3	641.9	703.3	791.7	759.8
Colombia	COP	10.5	502.3	2 087.6	2 077.7	1 899.8	2 744.5	2 956.9	3 281.1	3 695.6	3 744.3
Costa Rica	CRC	6.6	91.6	307.4	517.2	521.9	534.6	577.2	587.0	584.7	621.4
Czech Republic	CZK	..	..	38.6	20.3	19.1	24.6	21.7	22.9	23.2	21.7
Denmark	DKK	6.9	6.2	8.1	5.4	5.6	6.7	6.3	6.7	6.5	6.3
Estonia	EUR	..	0.8	1.1	0.7	0.8	0.9	0.8	0.9	0.9	0.8
Finland	EUR	..	0.8	1.1	0.7	0.8	0.9	0.8	0.9	0.9	0.8
France	EUR	..	0.8	1.1	0.7	0.8	0.9	0.8	0.9	0.9	0.8
Germany	EUR	..	0.8	1.1	0.7	0.8	0.9	0.8	0.9	0.9	0.8
Greece	EUR	..	0.8	1.1	0.7	0.8	0.9	0.8	0.9	0.9	0.8
Hungary	HUF	..	63.2	282.3	183.6	207.8	279.2	270.2	290.6	308.0	303.2
Iceland	ISK	0.4	58.4	78.8	64.1	122.2	131.9	108.3	122.6	135.4	127.0
Ireland	EUR	0.5	0.8	1.1	0.7	0.8	0.9	0.8	0.9	0.9	0.8
Israel	ILS	0.0	2.0	4.1	4.1	3.7	3.9	3.6	3.6	3.4	3.2
Italy	EUR	..	0.8	1.1	0.7	0.8	0.9	0.8	0.9	0.9	0.8
Japan	JPY	361.7	142.2	111.2	114.2	85.7	118.0	110.1	108.5	107.5	109.8
Korea	KRW	266.3	708.0	1 130.6	929.5	1 155.4	1 131.3	1 100.2	1 165.3	1 180.1	1 144.5
Latvia	EUR	..	0.8	1.1	0.7	0.8	0.9	0.8	0.9	0.9	0.8
Lithuania	EUR	..	0.8	1.1	0.7	0.8	0.9	0.8	0.9	0.9	0.8
Luxembourg	EUR	..	0.8	1.1	0.7	0.8	0.9	0.8	0.9	0.9	0.8
Mexico	MXN	0.0	2.8	9.5	10.9	12.6	15.9	19.2	19.2	21.4	20.2
Netherlands	EUR	..	0.8	1.1	0.7	0.8	0.9	0.8	0.9	0.9	0.8
New Zealand	NZD	0.7	1.7	2.3	1.4	1.3	1.4	1.5	1.5	1.5	1.4
Norway	NOK	7.2	6.3	8.8	5.9	6.0	8.1	8.1	8.8	9.4	8.6
Poland	PLN	0.0	1.0	4.3	2.8	3.0	3.8	3.6	3.8	3.9	3.9
Portugal	EUR	..	0.8	1.1	0.7	0.8	0.9	0.8	0.9	0.9	0.8
Slovak Republic	EUR	..	0.8	1.1	0.7	0.8	0.9	0.8	0.9	0.9	0.8
Slovenia	EUR	..	0.8	1.1	0.7	0.8	0.9	0.8	0.9	0.9	0.8
Spain	EUR	..	0.8	1.1	0.7	0.8	0.9	0.8	0.9	0.9	0.8
Sweden	SEK	5.2	5.9	9.2	6.8	7.2	8.4	8.7	9.5	9.2	8.6
Switzerland	CHF	4.3	1.4	1.7	1.2	1.0	1.0	1.0	1.0	0.9	0.9
Türkiye	TRY	0.0	0.0	0.6	1.3	1.5	2.7	4.8	5.7	7.0	8.9
United Kingdom	GBP	0.4	0.6	0.7	0.5	0.6	0.7	0.7	0.8	0.8	0.7
United States	USD	1.0	1.0	1.0	1.0	1.0	1.0	1.0	1.0	1.0	1.0

.. Not available
Source: OECD Financial indicators data.

StatLink https://stat.link/8xi73y

4 Country tables, 1990-2020

Chapter 4 provides a summary of tax revenues by category and by level of government for each OECD country.

4.1. Tax revenue and % of GDP by selected tax category and by level of government

In all the following tables, the symbol (..) indicates not available or not applicable. The main series in this chapter cover a selection of years between 1990 and 2020. A complete series is available online. Data for 1955 and 1960 (for nineteen OECD countries) are provided in Part V of the 1998 edition of this Report.

Gross Domestic Product (GDP) figures are based on the 2008 System of National Accounts (SNA) for all OECD countries.

Box 4.1. Treatment of capital transfers

Some tables refer to the treatment of the capital transfers that some countries make to account for taxes that have been assessed but not collected. The capital transfer has been subtracted directly from the specific taxes to which they relate, except for France, where the capital transfer has been allocated between tax headings in proportion to their tax revenues at the level of government against which these transfers were recorded.

Countries reporting capital transfers include:

- Austria from 2020
- Belgium from 1995
- Denmark from 1971
- France from 1992
- Lithuania from 1999
- Luxembourg from 2013
- Poland from 1995
- Slovenia from 1995
- Switzerland from 1990

Table 4.1. Australia, tax revenue and % of GDP by selected tax category

	Billion AUD					% of GDP				
	1990	2000	2010	2019	2020	1990	2000	2010	2019	2020
Total tax revenue	**116.5**	**214.8**	**356.7**	**548.9**	**590.7**	**28.1**	**30.4**	**25.2**	**27.7**	**28.5**
1000 Taxes on income, profits and capital gains	**66.5**	**124.4**	**202.2**	**324.8**	**348.3**	**16.0**	**17.6**	**14.3**	**16.4**	**16.8**
1100 Of individuals	50.1	81.0	138.2	230.8	236.9	12.1	11.5	9.7	11.7	11.5
1200 Corporate	16.5	43.4	64.0	94.0	111.3	4.0	6.1	4.5	4.7	5.4
1300 Unallocable between 1100 and 1200	0.0	0.0	0.0	0.0	0.0	0.0	0.0	0.0	0.0	0.0
2000 Social security contributions	**0.0**	**0.0**	**0.0**	**0.0**	**0.0**	**0.0**	**0.0**	**0.0**	**0.0**	**0.0**
2100 Employees	0.0	0.0	0.0	0.0	0.0	0.0	0.0	0.0	0.0	0.0
2200 Employers	0.0	0.0	0.0	0.0	0.0	0.0	0.0	0.0	0.0	0.0
2300 Self-employed or non-employed	0.0	0.0	0.0	0.0	0.0	0.0	0.0	0.0	0.0	0.0
2400 Unallocable between 2100, 2200 and 2300	0.0	0.0	0.0	0.0	0.0	0.0	0.0	0.0	0.0	0.0
3000 Taxes on payroll and workforce	**7.1**	**9.6**	**18.5**	**25.7**	**26.4**	**1.7**	**1.4**	**1.3**	**1.3**	**1.3**
4000 Taxes on property	**10.4**	**18.8**	**33.5**	**54.0**	**59.5**	**2.5**	**2.7**	**2.4**	**2.7**	**2.9**
4100 Recurrent taxes on immovable property	6.1	9.1	19.9	33.8	34.5	1.5	1.3	1.4	1.7	1.7
4200 Recurrent taxes on net wealth	0.0	0.0	0.0	0.0	0.0	0.0	0.0	0.0	0.0	0.0
4300 Estate, inheritance and gift taxes	0.0	0.0	0.0	0.0	0.0	0.0	0.0	0.0	0.0	0.0
4400 Taxes on financial and capital transactions	4.3	9.8	13.6	20.2	25.0	1.0	1.4	1.0	1.0	1.2
4500 Non-recurrent taxes	0.0	0.0	0.0	0.0	0.0	0.0	0.0	0.0	0.0	0.0
4600 Other recurrent taxes on property	0.0	0.0	0.0	0.0	0.0	0.0	0.0	0.0	0.0	0.0
5000 Taxes on goods and services	**32.4**	**61.9**	**102.6**	**144.4**	**156.6**	**7.8**	**8.8**	**7.2**	**7.3**	**7.6**
5100 Taxes on production, sale, transfer, etc	27.2	56.2	90.8	123.6	135.1	6.6	8.0	6.4	6.2	6.5
5110 General taxes	9.4	25.8	48.1	65.7	75.3	2.3	3.7	3.4	3.3	3.6
5111 Value added taxes	0.0	23.9	46.9	64.0	73.3	0.0	3.4	3.3	3.2	3.5
5120 Taxes on specific goods and services	17.8	30.3	42.7	57.9	59.8	4.3	4.3	3.0	2.9	2.9
5121 Excises	12.0	19.8	26.7	24.1	25.9	2.9	2.8	1.9	1.2	1.2
5200 Taxes on use of goods and perform activities	5.2	5.7	11.7	20.8	21.5	1.3	0.8	0.8	1.0	1.0
5300 Unallocable between 5100 and 5200	0.0	0.0	0.0	0.0	0.0	0.0	0.0	0.0	0.0	0.0
6000 Other taxes	**0.0**	**0.0**	**0.0**	**0.0**	**0.0**	**0.0**	**0.0**	**0.0**	**0.0**	**0.0**
Non-wastable tax credits										
Non-wastable tax credits against 1000	..	0.2	6.7	10.6	10.1	..	0.0	0.5	0.5	0.5
Transfer component	..	0.0	4.4	6.8	6.6	..	0.0	0.3	0.3	0.3
Tax expenditure component	..	0.2	2.4	3.8	3.5	..	0.0	0.2	0.2	0.2

.. Not available

Note: More detailed country data and country notes are available in Chapter 5 "Detailed country tables". Full time series can be accessed at http://oe.cd/full-time-series.

Source: Australian Bureau of Statistics.

StatLink https://stat.link/ulx746

Table 4.2. Australia, tax revenue and % of GDP by level of government and main taxes

	Billion AUD					% of GDP				
	1990	2000	2010	2019	2020	1990	2000	2010	2019	2020
Federal or Central government										
Total tax revenue	**92.6**	**175.7**	**285.9**	**443.8**	**477.7**	**22.3**	**24.9**	**20.2**	**22.4**	**23.1**
1000 Taxes on income, profits and capital gains	66.5	124.4	202.2	324.8	348.3	16.0	17.6	14.3	16.4	16.8
2000 Social security contributions	0.0	0.0	0.0	0.0	0.0	0.0	0.0	0.0	0.0	0.0
3000 Taxes on payroll and workforce	1.3	0.1	0.5	1.0	1.7	0.3	0.0	0.0	0.1	0.1
4000 Taxes on property	0.2	0.0	0.0	0.0	0.0	0.1	0.0	0.0	0.0	0.0
5000 Taxes on goods and services	24.5	51.1	83.2	118.0	127.7	5.9	7.2	5.9	6.0	6.2
6000 Other taxes	0.0	0.0	0.0	0.0	0.0	0.0	0.0	0.0	0.0	0.0
State/Regional										
Total tax revenue	**19.7**	**32.7**	**58.4**	**85.5**	**93.0**	**4.7**	**4.6**	**4.1**	**4.3**	**4.5**
1000 Taxes on income, profits and capital gains	0.0	0.0	0.0	0.0	0.0	0.0	0.0	0.0	0.0	0.0
2000 Social security contributions	0.0	0.0	0.0	0.0	0.0	0.0	0.0	0.0	0.0	0.0
3000 Taxes on payroll and workforce	5.8	9.5	18.0	24.7	24.7	1.4	1.3	1.3	1.2	1.2
4000 Taxes on property	6.0	12.4	21.0	34.4	39.4	1.4	1.8	1.5	1.7	1.9
5000 Taxes on goods and services	7.9	10.8	19.3	26.4	28.9	1.9	1.5	1.4	1.3	1.4
6000 Other taxes	0.0	0.0	0.0	0.0	0.0	0.0	0.0	0.0	0.0	0.0
Local government										
Total tax revenue	**4.2**	**6.4**	**12.4**	**19.6**	**20.1**	**1.0**	**0.9**	**0.9**	**1.0**	**1.0**
1000 Taxes on income, profits and capital gains	0.0	0.0	0.0	0.0	0.0	0.0	0.0	0.0	0.0	0.0
2000 Social security contributions	0.0	0.0	0.0	0.0	0.0	0.0	0.0	0.0	0.0	0.0
3000 Taxes on payroll and workforce	0.0	0.0	0.0	0.0	0.0	0.0	0.0	0.0	0.0	0.0
4000 Taxes on property	4.2	6.4	12.4	19.6	20.1	1.0	0.9	0.9	1.0	1.0
5000 Taxes on goods and services	0.0	0.0	0.0	0.0	0.0	0.0	0.0	0.0	0.0	0.0
6000 Other taxes	0.0	0.0	0.0	0.0	0.0	0.0	0.0	0.0	0.0	0.0
Social Security Funds										
Total tax revenue	**0.0**	**0.0**	**0.0**	**0.0**	**0.0**	**0.0**	**0.0**	**0.0**	**0.0**	**0.0**
1000 Taxes on income, profits and capital gains	0.0	0.0	0.0	0.0	0.0	0.0	0.0	0.0	0.0	0.0
2000 Social security contributions	0.0	0.0	0.0	0.0	0.0	0.0	0.0	0.0	0.0	0.0
3000 Taxes on payroll and workforce	0.0	0.0	0.0	0.0	0.0	0.0	0.0	0.0	0.0	0.0
4000 Taxes on property	0.0	0.0	0.0	0.0	0.0	0.0	0.0	0.0	0.0	0.0
5000 Taxes on goods and services	0.0	0.0	0.0	0.0	0.0	0.0	0.0	0.0	0.0	0.0
6000 Other taxes	0.0	0.0	0.0	0.0	0.0	0.0	0.0	0.0	0.0	0.0

Note: More detailed country data and country notes are available in Chapter 6 "Tax revenues by sub-sectors of general government". Full time series can be accessed at http://oe.cd/full-time-series.
Source: Australian Bureau of Statistics.

StatLink https://stat.link/jwpcy4

Table 4.3. Austria, tax revenue and % of GDP by selected tax category

	Billion EUR					% of GDP				
	1990	2000	2010	2019	2020	1990	2000	2010	2019	2020
Total tax revenue	**54.0**	**90.3**	**121.2**	**169.3**	**160.2**	**39.3**	**42.3**	**41.0**	**42.6**	**42.2**
1000 Taxes on income, profits and capital gains	**13.8**	**25.6**	**34.0**	**49.9**	**44.5**	**10.0**	**12.0**	**11.5**	**12.5**	**11.7**
1100 Of individuals	11.3	19.9	27.1	38.3	35.5	8.2	9.3	9.2	9.6	9.4
1200 Corporate	1.9	4.2	5.5	10.8	8.2	1.4	1.9	1.9	2.7	2.2
1300 Unallocable between 1100 and 1200	0.5	1.5	1.4	0.8	0.8	0.4	0.7	0.5	0.2	0.2
2000 Social security contributions	**17.8**	**30.5**	**41.4**	**59.1**	**58.9**	**12.9**	**14.3**	**14.0**	**14.9**	**15.5**
2100 Employees	7.5	12.5	16.8	23.8	23.8	5.5	5.8	5.7	6.0	6.3
2200 Employers	8.8	14.7	19.4	27.8	27.7	6.4	6.9	6.6	7.0	7.3
2300 Self-employed or non-employed	1.5	3.4	5.2	7.5	7.5	1.1	1.6	1.7	1.9	2.0
2400 Unallocable between 2100, 2200 and 2300	0.0	0.0	0.0	0.0	0.0	0.0	0.0	0.0	0.0	0.0
3000 Taxes on payroll and workforce	**3.3**	**5.8**	**8.4**	**10.8**	**10.4**	**2.4**	**2.7**	**2.8**	**2.7**	**2.8**
4000 Taxes on property	**1.5**	**1.2**	**1.6**	**2.2**	**2.2**	**1.1**	**0.6**	**0.5**	**0.5**	**0.6**
4100 Recurrent taxes on immovable property	0.4	0.5	0.7	0.8	0.9	0.3	0.2	0.2	0.2	0.2
4200 Recurrent taxes on net wealth	0.6	0.0	0.0	0.0	0.0	0.5	0.0	0.0	0.0	0.0
4300 Estate, inheritance and gift taxes	0.1	0.1	0.0	0.0	0.0	0.1	0.1	0.0	0.0	0.0
4400 Taxes on financial and capital transactions	0.4	0.6	0.8	1.3	1.3	0.3	0.3	0.3	0.3	0.3
4500 Non-recurrent taxes	0.0	0.0	0.0	0.0	0.0	0.0	0.0	0.0	0.0	0.0
4600 Other recurrent taxes on property	0.0	0.0	0.0	0.0	0.0	0.0	0.0	0.0	0.0	0.0
5000 Taxes on goods and services	**17.0**	**26.5**	**34.7**	**46.5**	**43.4**	**12.4**	**12.4**	**11.7**	**11.7**	**11.5**
5100 Taxes on production, sale, transfer, etc	16.2	24.6	32.1	42.5	39.4	11.8	11.5	10.9	10.7	10.4
5110 General taxes	11.2	16.9	22.7	30.4	28.2	8.2	7.9	7.7	7.7	7.4
5111 Value added taxes	11.2	16.9	22.7	30.4	28.2	8.2	7.9	7.7	7.7	7.4
5120 Taxes on specific goods and services	4.9	7.7	9.4	12.1	11.2	3.5	3.6	3.2	3.0	2.9
5121 Excises	3.3	5.5	6.9	8.2	7.2	2.4	2.6	2.3	2.1	1.9
5200 Taxes on use of goods and perform activities	0.9	1.9	2.6	4.0	4.1	0.6	0.9	0.9	1.0	1.1
5300 Unallocable between 5100 and 5200	0.0	0.0	0.0	0.0	0.0	0.0	0.0	0.0	0.0	0.0
6000 Other taxes	**0.7**	**0.8**	**1.1**	**0.8**	**0.7**	**0.5**	**0.4**	**0.4**	**0.2**	**0.2**
Non-wastable tax credits										
Non-wastable tax credits against 1000	..	0.7	0.7	0.3	0.3	..	0.3	0.2	0.1	0.1
Transfer component	..	0.1	0.2	0.1	0.1	..	0.0	0.1	0.0	0.0
Tax expenditure component	..	0.6	0.4	0.2	0.2	..	0.3	0.1	0.1	0.1
Revenues collected on behalf of the EU										
Revenues collected on behalf of the EU, total	..	0.4	0.3	0.7	0.7	..	0.2	0.1	0.2	0.2
Customs duties	..	0.4	0.3	0.5	0.5	..	0.2	0.1	0.1	0.1
SRF contributions	..	..	..	0.2	0.2	..	..	..	0.0	0.1

.. Not available

Note: The total tax revenue has been reduced by the amount of any capital transfer that represents uncollected taxes. The capital transfers were subtracted directly from the specific taxes to which they relate. Therefore, the tax revenue amounts are different to those reported in the detailed country data available in Chapter 5 "Detailed country tables".

More detailed country data and country notes are available in Chapter 5 "Detailed country tables". Full time series can be accessed at http://oe.cd/full-time-series.

Source: Statistics Austria.

StatLink https://stat.link/5mfbo0

Table 4.4. Austria, tax revenue and % of GDP by level of government and main taxes

	Billion EUR					% of GDP				
	1990	2000	2010	2019	2020	1990	2000	2010	2019	2020
Federal or Central government										
Total tax revenue	**27.2**	**60.5**	**80.7**	**109.9**	**101.2**	**19.8**	**28.3**	**27.3**	**27.7**	**26.7**
1000 Taxes on income, profits and capital gains	8.6	24.9	33.1	48.6	43.2	6.2	11.7	11.2	12.2	11.4
2000 Social security contributions	2.4	5.1	6.3	8.5	8.4	1.7	2.4	2.1	2.1	2.2
3000 Taxes on payroll and workforce	2.6	3.9	5.8	5.8	5.7	1.9	1.8	1.9	1.5	1.5
4000 Taxes on property	0.9	0.7	0.9	1.4	1.4	0.6	0.3	0.3	0.3	0.4
5000 Taxes on goods and services	12.3	25.3	33.7	45.0	41.9	8.9	11.8	11.4	11.3	11.1
6000 Other taxes	0.5	0.6	0.9	0.6	0.5	0.4	0.3	0.3	0.1	0.1
State/Regional										
Total tax revenue	**5.8**	**1.4**	**2.0**	**3.5**	**3.3**	**4.2**	**0.7**	**0.7**	**0.9**	**0.9**
1000 Taxes on income, profits and capital gains	2.8	0.6	0.9	1.3	1.3	2.0	0.3	0.3	0.3	0.3
2000 Social security contributions	0.2	0.4	0.5	0.5	0.4	0.2	0.2	0.2	0.1	0.1
3000 Taxes on payroll and workforce	0.0	0.1	0.2	1.1	1.1	0.0	0.1	0.1	0.3	0.3
4000 Taxes on property	0.1	0.0	0.0	0.1	0.0	0.0	0.0	0.0	0.0	0.0
5000 Taxes on goods and services	2.7	0.2	0.3	0.5	0.4	2.0	0.1	0.1	0.1	0.1
6000 Other taxes	0.0	0.1	0.1	0.1	0.1	0.0	0.0	0.0	0.0	0.0
Local government										
Total tax revenue	**6.1**	**3.2**	**3.8**	**5.3**	**5.1**	**4.4**	**1.5**	**1.3**	**1.3**	**1.3**
1000 Taxes on income, profits and capital gains	2.4	0.0	0.0	0.0	0.0	1.8	0.0	0.0	0.0	0.0
2000 Social security contributions	0.2	0.3	0.3	0.2	0.2	0.1	0.1	0.1	0.1	0.1
3000 Taxes on payroll and workforce	0.7	1.8	2.4	3.8	3.7	0.5	0.8	0.8	1.0	1.0
4000 Taxes on property	0.5	0.5	0.6	0.7	0.8	0.4	0.2	0.2	0.2	0.2
5000 Taxes on goods and services	2.1	0.6	0.4	0.4	0.4	1.5	0.3	0.1	0.1	0.1
6000 Other taxes	0.2	0.1	0.1	0.2	0.1	0.1	0.0	0.0	0.0	0.0
Social Security Funds										
Total tax revenue	**15.0**	**24.8**	**34.4**	**49.8**	**49.9**	**10.9**	**11.6**	**11.6**	**12.5**	**13.1**
1000 Taxes on income, profits and capital gains	0.0	0.0	0.0	0.0	0.0	0.0	0.0	0.0	0.0	0.0
2000 Social security contributions	15.0	24.8	34.4	49.8	49.9	10.9	11.6	11.6	12.5	13.1
3000 Taxes on payroll and workforce	0.0	0.0	0.0	0.0	0.0	0.0	0.0	0.0	0.0	0.0
4000 Taxes on property	0.0	0.0	0.0	0.0	0.0	0.0	0.0	0.0	0.0	0.0
5000 Taxes on goods and services	0.0	0.0	0.0	0.0	0.0	0.0	0.0	0.0	0.0	0.0
6000 Other taxes	0.0	0.0	0.0	0.0	0.0	0.0	0.0	0.0	0.0	0.0

Note: The total tax revenue has been reduced by the amount of any capital transfer that represents uncollected taxes. The capital transfers were subtracted directly from the specific taxes to which they relate. Therefore, the tax revenue amounts are different to those reported in the detailed country data available in Chapter 6 "Tax revenues by sub-sectors of general government".
More detailed country data and country notes are available in Chapter 6 "Tax revenues by sub-sectors of general government". Full time series can be accessed at http://oe.cd/full-time-series.
Source: Statistics Austria.

StatLink https://stat.link/e69db2

Table 4.5. Belgium, tax revenue and % of GDP by selected tax category

	Billion EUR					% of GDP				
	1990	2000	2010	2019	2020	1990	2000	2010	2019	2020
Total tax revenue	**70.4**	**112.4**	**155.7**	**202.8**	**194.1**	**41.4**	**43.8**	**42.9**	**42.4**	**42.5**
1000 Taxes on income, profits and capital gains	**26.0**	**43.4**	**53.2**	**71.8**	**69.0**	**15.3**	**16.9**	**14.7**	**15.0**	**15.1**
1100 Of individuals	22.5	35.3	44.0	54.0	54.0	13.2	13.8	12.1	11.3	11.8
1200 Corporate	3.4	8.1	9.2	17.7	14.9	2.0	3.1	2.5	3.7	3.3
1300 Unallocable between 1100 and 1200	0.0	0.1	0.0	0.1	0.1	0.0	0.0	0.0	0.0	0.0
2000 Social security contributions	**23.4**	**34.6**	**50.5**	**63.1**	**62.1**	**13.7**	**13.5**	**13.9**	**13.2**	**13.6**
2100 Employees	7.2	10.9	15.0	19.1	18.8	4.2	4.3	4.1	4.0	4.1
2200 Employers	14.7	20.8	30.9	37.8	37.1	8.6	8.1	8.5	7.9	8.1
2300 Self-employed or non-employed	1.5	2.9	4.6	6.2	6.1	0.9	1.1	1.3	1.3	1.3
2400 Unallocable between 2100, 2200 and 2300	0.0	0.0	0.0	0.0	0.0	0.0	0.0	0.0	0.0	0.0
3000 Taxes on payroll and workforce	**0.0**	**0.0**	**0.0**	**0.0**	**0.0**	**0.0**	**0.0**	**0.0**	**0.0**	**0.0**
4000 Taxes on property	**2.7**	**5.3**	**11.3**	**16.4**	**15.6**	**1.6**	**2.1**	**3.1**	**3.4**	**3.4**
4100 Recurrent taxes on immovable property	0.6	1.2	4.6	6.1	6.1	0.4	0.5	1.3	1.3	1.3
4200 Recurrent taxes on net wealth	0.0	0.1	0.2	0.9	1.0	0.0	0.0	0.1	0.2	0.2
4300 Estate, inheritance and gift taxes	0.5	1.1	2.3	2.9	3.0	0.3	0.4	0.6	0.6	0.6
4400 Taxes on financial and capital transactions	1.5	2.7	3.5	5.4	5.0	0.9	1.0	1.0	1.1	1.1
4500 Non-recurrent taxes	0.0	0.1	0.3	0.5	0.3	0.0	0.0	0.1	0.1	0.1
4600 Other recurrent taxes on property	0.1	0.2	0.3	0.5	0.3	0.1	0.1	0.1	0.1	0.1
5000 Taxes on goods and services	**18.4**	**29.1**	**40.7**	**51.6**	**47.3**	**10.8**	**11.3**	**11.2**	**10.8**	**10.4**
5100 Taxes on production, sale, transfer, etc	17.4	27.0	38.3	48.7	44.6	10.2	10.5	10.5	10.2	9.8
5110 General taxes	11.6	18.2	25.5	32.1	29.3	6.8	7.1	7.0	6.7	6.4
5111 Value added taxes	11.5	18.1	25.3	31.7	29.1	6.8	7.1	7.0	6.6	6.4
5120 Taxes on specific goods and services	5.8	8.7	12.8	16.6	15.3	3.4	3.4	3.5	3.5	3.3
5121 Excises	3.5	5.7	7.8	10.0	9.0	2.0	2.2	2.1	2.1	2.0
5200 Taxes on use of goods and perform activities	1.0	2.1	2.4	2.9	2.7	0.6	0.8	0.7	0.6	0.6
5300 Unallocable between 5100 and 5200	0.0	0.0	0.0	0.0	0.0	0.0	0.0	0.0	0.0	0.0
6000 Other taxes	**0.0**	**0.0**	**0.0**	**0.0**	**0.0**	**0.0**	**0.0**	**0.0**	**0.0**	**0.0**
Non-wastable tax credits										
Non-wastable tax credits against 1000	..	..	1.0	1.1	1.1	..	..	0.3	0.2	0.2
Transfer component	..	..	0.4	0.3	0.3	..	..	0.1	0.1	0.1
Tax expenditure component	..	..	0.6	0.9	0.9	..	..	0.2	0.2	0.2
Revenues collected on behalf of the EU										
Revenues collected on behalf of the EU, total	0.9	1.0	1.3	2.0	1.7	0.6	0.4	0.4	0.4	0.4
Customs duties	..	1.0	1.2	1.7	1.4	..	0.4	0.3	0.4	0.3
SRF contributions	..	..	..	0.3	0.3	..	..	..	0.1	0.1

.. Not available

Note: The total tax revenue has been reduced by the amount of any capital transfer that represents uncollected taxes. The capital transfers were subtracted directly from the specific taxes to which they relate. Therefore, the tax revenue amounts are different to those reported in the detailed country data available in Chapter 5 "Detailed country tables".

More detailed country data and country notes are available in Chapter 5 "Detailed country tables". Full time series can be accessed at http://oe.cd/full-time-series.

Source: Institute for National Accounts; Federal Ministry of Finance.

StatLink https://stat.link/p0fi5t

Table 4.6. Belgium, tax revenue and % of GDP by level of government and main taxes

	Billion EUR					% of GDP				
	1990	2000	2010	2019	2020	1990	2000	2010	2019	2020
Federal or Central government										
Total tax revenue	**42.5**	**69.4**	**87.8**	**103.3**	**96.1**	**25.0**	**27.1**	**24.2**	**21.6**	**21.0**
1000 Taxes on income, profits and capital gains	23.9	39.6	49.3	57.0	53.6	14.0	15.4	13.6	11.9	11.7
2000 Social security contributions	0.9	1.3	2.5	0.1	0.1	0.5	0.5	0.7	0.0	0.0
3000 Taxes on payroll and workforce	0.0	0.0	0.0	0.0	0.0	0.0	0.0	0.0	0.0	0.0
4000 Taxes on property	1.1	2.3	0.9	2.2	2.1	0.6	0.9	0.3	0.5	0.5
5000 Taxes on goods and services	16.7	26.3	35.0	44.0	40.4	9.8	10.2	9.7	9.2	8.8
6000 Other taxes	0.0	0.0	0.0	0.0	0.0	0.0	0.0	0.0	0.0	0.0
State/Regional										
Total tax revenue	**1.2**	**2.4**	**8.1**	**21.5**	**21.5**	**0.7**	**1.0**	**2.2**	**4.5**	**4.7**
1000 Taxes on income, profits and capital gains	0.0	0.1	0.0	10.0	10.6	0.0	0.0	0.0	2.1	2.3
2000 Social security contributions	0.0	0.0	0.0	0.3	0.3	0.0	0.0	0.0	0.1	0.1
3000 Taxes on payroll and workforce	0.0	0.0	0.0	0.0	0.0	0.0	0.0	0.0	0.0	0.0
4000 Taxes on property	0.9	1.9	5.6	8.1	7.6	0.5	0.7	1.5	1.7	1.7
5000 Taxes on goods and services	0.2	0.5	2.4	3.2	3.0	0.1	0.2	0.7	0.7	0.7
6000 Other taxes	0.0	0.0	0.0	0.0	0.0	0.0	0.0	0.0	0.0	0.0
Local government										
Total tax revenue	**3.1**	**4.6**	**7.9**	**10.0**	**9.9**	**1.8**	**1.8**	**2.2**	**2.1**	**2.2**
1000 Taxes on income, profits and capital gains	2.1	3.1	2.9	3.5	3.7	1.2	1.2	0.8	0.7	0.8
2000 Social security contributions	0.1	0.0	0.0	0.0	0.0	0.1	0.0	0.0	0.0	0.0
3000 Taxes on payroll and workforce	0.0	0.0	0.0	0.0	0.0	0.0	0.0	0.0	0.0	0.0
4000 Taxes on property	0.6	1.0	4.4	5.7	5.6	0.3	0.4	1.2	1.2	1.2
5000 Taxes on goods and services	0.3	0.4	0.6	0.7	0.6	0.2	0.2	0.2	0.2	0.1
6000 Other taxes	0.0	0.0	0.0	0.0	0.0	0.0	0.0	0.0	0.0	0.0
Social Security Funds										
Total tax revenue	**22.7**	**34.9**	**50.7**	**66.1**	**64.9**	**13.4**	**13.6**	**14.0**	**13.8**	**14.2**
1000 Taxes on income, profits and capital gains	0.0	0.6	1.0	1.3	1.2	0.0	0.2	0.3	0.3	0.3
2000 Social security contributions	22.4	33.3	48.0	62.8	61.7	13.2	13.0	13.2	13.1	13.5
3000 Taxes on payroll and workforce	0.0	0.0	0.0	0.0	0.0	0.0	0.0	0.0	0.0	0.0
4000 Taxes on property	0.1	0.2	0.3	0.3	0.3	0.1	0.1	0.1	0.1	0.1
5000 Taxes on goods and services	0.2	0.8	1.3	1.7	1.6	0.1	0.3	0.4	0.4	0.4
6000 Other taxes	0.0	0.0	0.0	0.0	0.0	0.0	0.0	0.0	0.0	0.0

Note: The total tax revenue has been reduced by the amount of any capital transfer that represents uncollected taxes. The capital transfers were subtracted directly from the specific taxes to which they relate. Therefore, the tax revenue amounts are different to those reported in the detailed country data available in Chapter 6 "Tax revenues by sub-sectors of general government".

More detailed country data and country notes are available in Chapter 6 "Tax revenues by sub-sectors of general government". Full time series can be accessed at http://oe.cd/full-time-series.

Source: Institute for National Accounts; Federal Ministry of Finance.

StatLink https://stat.link/ca5te6

Table 4.7. Canada, tax revenue and % of GDP by selected tax category

	Billion CAD					% of GDP				
	1990	2000	2010	2019	2020	1990	2000	2010	2019	2020
Total tax revenue	**244.2**	**390.2**	**516.6**	**764.4**	**756.0**	**35.1**	**34.7**	**31.0**	**33.1**	**34.3**
1000 Taxes on income, profits and capital gains	**118.6**	**195.3**	**241.0**	**372.2**	**376.5**	**17.0**	**17.4**	**14.5**	**16.1**	**17.1**
1100 Of individuals	99.7	143.7	180.9	275.6	278.9	14.3	12.8	10.9	11.9	12.6
1200 Corporate	17.2	47.6	54.1	86.6	89.5	2.5	4.2	3.2	3.7	4.1
1300 Unallocable between 1100 and 1200	1.7	4.0	6.0	10.0	8.2	0.2	0.4	0.4	0.4	0.4
2000 Social security contributions	**29.7**	**53.1**	**76.8**	**108.4**	**107.9**	**4.3**	**4.7**	**4.6**	**4.7**	**4.9**
2100 Employees	10.6	21.4	30.6	44.2	44.5	1.5	1.9	1.8	1.9	2.0
2200 Employers	18.4	30.3	43.5	60.2	59.4	2.7	2.7	2.6	2.6	2.7
2300 Self-employed or non-employed	0.6	1.4	2.6	3.9	4.0	0.1	0.1	0.2	0.2	0.2
2400 Unallocable between 2100, 2200 and 2300	0.0	0.0	0.0	0.0	0.0	0.0	0.0	0.0	0.0	0.0
3000 Taxes on payroll and workforce	**5.5**	**8.0**	**10.8**	**17.4**	**17.4**	**0.8**	**0.7**	**0.6**	**0.8**	**0.8**
4000 Taxes on property	**24.5**	**37.2**	**63.7**	**88.8**	**90.6**	**3.5**	**3.3**	**3.8**	**3.8**	**4.1**
4100 Recurrent taxes on immovable property	20.2	30.2	51.7	70.8	72.2	2.9	2.7	3.1	3.1	3.3
4200 Recurrent taxes on net wealth	1.9	4.2	1.5	0.5	0.5	0.3	0.4	0.1	0.0	0.0
4300 Estate, inheritance and gift taxes	0.0	0.0	0.2	0.3	0.3	0.0	0.0	0.0	0.0	0.0
4400 Taxes on financial and capital transactions	0.0	0.0	3.1	6.7	7.9	0.0	0.0	0.2	0.3	0.4
4500 Non-recurrent taxes	2.4	2.7	7.3	10.5	9.7	0.3	0.2	0.4	0.5	0.4
4600 Other recurrent taxes on property	0.0	0.0	0.0	0.0	0.0	0.0	0.0	0.0	0.0	0.0
5000 Taxes on goods and services	**63.1**	**94.5**	**123.8**	**176.6**	**162.8**	**9.1**	**8.4**	**7.4**	**7.6**	**7.4**
5100 Taxes on production, sale, transfer, etc	59.6	88.9	116.2	165.7	152.4	8.6	7.9	7.0	7.2	6.9
5110 General taxes	34.5	55.3	72.1	108.8	102.7	5.0	4.9	4.3	4.7	4.7
5111 Value added taxes	0.0	35.9	70.7	103.4	99.7	0.0	3.2	4.2	4.5	4.5
5120 Taxes on specific goods and services	25.2	33.6	44.0	56.9	49.6	3.6	3.0	2.6	2.5	2.2
5121 Excises	14.5	18.4	23.3	28.9	27.9	2.1	1.6	1.4	1.2	1.3
5200 Taxes on use of goods and perform activities	3.5	5.6	7.6	10.9	10.4	0.5	0.5	0.5	0.5	0.5
5300 Unallocable between 5100 and 5200	0.0	0.0	0.0	0.0	0.0	0.0	0.0	0.0	0.0	0.0
6000 Other taxes	**2.9**	**2.2**	**0.6**	**1.0**	**0.9**	**0.4**	**0.2**	**0.0**	**0.0**	**0.0**
Non-wastable tax credits										
Non-wastable tax credits against 1000	..	3.4	11.1	18.3	18.3	..	0.3	0.7	0.8	0.8
Transfer component	..	3.1	10.2	14.4	13.6	..	0.3	0.6	0.6	0.6
Tax expenditure component	..	0.3	0.9	4.0	4.7	..	0.0	0.1	0.2	0.2

.. Not available

Note: More detailed country data and country notes are available in Chapter 5 "Detailed country tables". Full time series can be accessed at http://oe.cd/full-time-series.

Source: Statistics Canada.

StatLink https://stat.link/kyienm

Table 4.8. Canada, tax revenue and % of GDP by level of government and main taxes

	Billion CAD					% of GDP				
	1990	2000	2010	2019	2020	1990	2000	2010	2019	2020
Federal or Central government										
Total tax revenue	**101.7**	**184.4**	**212.8**	**314.2**	**310.8**	**14.6**	**16.4**	**12.8**	**13.6**	**14.1**
1000 Taxes on income, profits and capital gains	73.6	126.3	148.7	227.5	228.3	10.6	11.2	8.9	9.8	10.3
2000 Social security contributions	0.0	18.8	17.9	23.4	22.6	0.0	1.7	1.1	1.0	1.0
3000 Taxes on payroll and workforce	0.0	0.0	0.0	0.0	0.0	0.0	0.0	0.0	0.0	0.0
4000 Taxes on property	0.0	0.0	0.0	0.0	0.0	0.0	0.0	0.0	0.0	0.0
5000 Taxes on goods and services	28.1	39.4	46.2	63.3	60.0	4.0	3.5	2.8	2.7	2.7
6000 Other taxes	0.0	0.0	0.0	0.0	0.0	0.0	0.0	0.0	0.0	0.0
State/Regional										
Total tax revenue	**89.3**	**148.2**	**201.1**	**303.6**	**296.2**	**12.8**	**13.2**	**12.1**	**13.1**	**13.4**
1000 Taxes on income, profits and capital gains	44.9	69.0	92.2	144.7	148.2	6.5	6.1	5.5	6.3	6.7
2000 Social security contributions	0.0	8.3	11.7	14.6	13.7	0.0	0.7	0.7	0.6	0.6
3000 Taxes on payroll and workforce	5.5	8.0	10.8	17.4	17.4	0.8	0.7	0.6	0.8	0.8
4000 Taxes on property	4.2	8.4	9.8	14.9	15.4	0.6	0.7	0.6	0.6	0.7
5000 Taxes on goods and services	34.6	54.5	76.7	112.0	101.6	5.0	4.8	4.6	4.8	4.6
6000 Other taxes	0.0	0.0	0.0	0.0	0.0	0.0	0.0	0.0	0.0	0.0
Local government										
Total tax revenue	**23.5**	**31.5**	**55.4**	**76.2**	**77.3**	**3.4**	**2.8**	**3.3**	**3.3**	**3.5**
1000 Taxes on income, profits and capital gains	0.0	0.0	0.0	0.0	0.0	0.0	0.0	0.0	0.0	0.0
2000 Social security contributions	0.0	0.0	0.0	0.0	0.0	0.0	0.0	0.0	0.0	0.0
3000 Taxes on payroll and workforce	0.0	0.0	0.0	0.0	0.0	0.0	0.0	0.0	0.0	0.0
4000 Taxes on property	20.3	28.8	53.9	73.9	75.2	2.9	2.6	3.2	3.2	3.4
5000 Taxes on goods and services	0.4	0.6	0.9	1.4	1.2	0.1	0.1	0.1	0.1	0.1
6000 Other taxes	2.9	2.2	0.6	1.0	0.9	0.4	0.2	0.0	0.0	0.0
Social Security Funds										
Total tax revenue	**29.7**	**26.0**	**47.2**	**70.4**	**71.6**	**4.3**	**2.3**	**2.8**	**3.0**	**3.2**
1000 Taxes on income, profits and capital gains	0.0	0.0	0.0	0.0	0.0	0.0	0.0	0.0	0.0	0.0
2000 Social security contributions	29.7	26.0	47.2	70.4	71.6	4.3	2.3	2.8	3.0	3.2
3000 Taxes on payroll and workforce	0.0	0.0	0.0	0.0	0.0	0.0	0.0	0.0	0.0	0.0
4000 Taxes on property	0.0	0.0	0.0	0.0	0.0	0.0	0.0	0.0	0.0	0.0
5000 Taxes on goods and services	0.0	0.0	0.0	0.0	0.0	0.0	0.0	0.0	0.0	0.0
6000 Other taxes	0.0	0.0	0.0	0.0	0.0	0.0	0.0	0.0	0.0	0.0

Note: More detailed country data and country notes are available in Chapter 6 "Tax revenues by sub-sectors of general government". Full time series can be accessed at http://oe.cd/full-time-series.
Source: Statistics Canada.

StatLink https://stat.link/8n7xsd

Table 4.9. Chile, tax revenue and % of GDP by selected tax category

	Billion CLP					% of GDP				
	1990	2000	2010	2019	2020	1990	2000	2010	2019	2020
Total tax revenue	**1 777.2**	**7 902.0**	**21 845.7**	**41 025.5**	**38 817.2**	**16.8**	**18.7**	**19.7**	**21.0**	**19.4**
1000 Taxes on income, profits and capital gains	**413.0**	**1 841.6**	**8 329.1**	**14 283.2**	**12 540.3**	**3.9**	**4.4**	**7.5**	**7.3**	**6.3**
1100 Of individuals	99.2	604.1	1 492.8	2 937.5	3 976.0	0.9	1.4	1.3	1.5	2.0
1200 Corporate	219.6	882.9	4 448.7	9 597.5	9 429.8	2.1	2.1	4.0	4.9	4.7
1300 Unallocable between 1100 and 1200	94.2	354.6	2 387.5	1 748.2	-865.5	0.9	0.8	2.2	0.9	-0.4
2000 Social security contributions	**159.6**	**576.8**	**1 494.0**	**2 994.9**	**3 104.9**	**1.5**	**1.4**	**1.3**	**1.5**	**1.5**
2100 Employees	154.0	553.9	1 433.2	2 894.7	2 994.0	1.5	1.3	1.3	1.5	1.5
2200 Employers	5.5	22.8	60.8	100.2	110.8	0.1	0.1	0.1	0.1	0.1
2300 Self-employed or non-employed	0.0	0.0	0.0	0.0	0.0	0.0	0.0	0.0	0.0	0.0
2400 Unallocable between 2100, 2200 and 2300	0.0	0.0	0.0	0.0	0.0	0.0	0.0	0.0	0.0	0.0
3000 Taxes on payroll and workforce	**0.0**	**0.0**	**0.0**	**0.0**	**0.0**	**0.0**	**0.0**	**0.0**	**0.0**	**0.0**
4000 Taxes on property	**109.3**	**554.0**	**898.6**	**2 242.6**	**2 071.9**	**1.0**	**1.3**	**0.8**	**1.1**	**1.0**
4100 Recurrent taxes on immovable property	60.0	302.2	662.4	1 507.2	1 562.3	0.6	0.7	0.6	0.8	0.8
4200 Recurrent taxes on net wealth	0.0	0.0	0.0	0.0	0.0	0.0	0.0	0.0	0.0	0.0
4300 Estate, inheritance and gift taxes	3.4	10.9	39.3	62.8	155.4	0.0	0.0	0.0	0.0	0.1
4400 Taxes on financial and capital transactions	45.9	240.9	196.9	672.6	354.2	0.4	0.6	0.2	0.3	0.2
4500 Non-recurrent taxes	0.0	0.0	0.0	0.0	0.0	0.0	0.0	0.0	0.0	0.0
4600 Other recurrent taxes on property	0.0	0.0	0.0	0.0	0.0	0.0	0.0	0.0	0.0	0.0
5000 Taxes on goods and services	**1 118.7**	**5 041.8**	**11 185.2**	**21 755.4**	**21 275.1**	**10.6**	**11.9**	**10.1**	**11.1**	**10.6**
5100 Taxes on production, sale, transfer, etc	1 074.0	4 789.8	10 532.9	20 167.0	19 614.2	10.1	11.3	9.5	10.3	9.8
5110 General taxes	664.4	3 306.4	8 399.9	16 348.9	15 963.0	6.3	7.8	7.6	8.3	8.0
5111 Value added taxes	664.4	3 306.4	8 399.9	16 348.9	15 963.0	6.3	7.8	7.6	8.3	8.0
5120 Taxes on specific goods and services	409.6	1 483.5	2 133.0	3 818.1	3 651.2	3.9	3.5	1.9	1.9	1.8
5121 Excises	166.0	816.2	1 561.2	2 862.3	2 900.2	1.6	1.9	1.4	1.5	1.4
5200 Taxes on use of goods and perform activities	44.7	251.9	652.3	1 588.4	1 660.9	0.4	0.6	0.6	0.8	0.8
5300 Unallocable between 5100 and 5200	0.0	0.0	0.0	0.0	0.0	0.0	0.0	0.0	0.0	0.0
6000 Other taxes	**-23.4**	**-112.2**	**-61.1**	**-250.5**	**-175.0**	**-0.2**	**-0.3**	**-0.1**	**-0.1**	**-0.1**
Non-wastable tax credits										
Non-wastable tax credits against 1000	0.0	0.0	0.0	278.8	298.0	0.0	0.0	0.0	0.1	0.1
Transfer component	..	..	..	200.6	223.0	..	..	..	0.1	0.1
Tax expenditure component	..	..	..	78.2	74.9	..	..	..	0.0	0.0

.. Not available

Note: More detailed country data and country notes are available in Chapter 5 "Detailed country tables". Full time series can be accessed at http://oe.cd/full-time-series.

Source: *Servicio de Impuestos internos* (Chile's Tax Service).

StatLink https://stat.link/cp9i57

Table 4.10. Chile, tax revenue and % of GDP by level of government and main taxes

	Billion CLP					% of GDP				
	1990	2000	2010	2019	2020	1990	2000	2010	2019	2020
Federal or Central government										
Total tax revenue	**1 579.7**	**6 936.8**	**19 214.8**	**35 124.7**	**32 833.3**	**14.9**	**16.4**	**17.3**	**17.9**	**16.4**
1000 Taxes on income, profits and capital gains	413.0	1 841.6	8 329.1	14 283.2	12 540.3	3.9	4.4	7.5	7.3	6.3
2000 Social security contributions	66.7	232.7	371.4	495.1	510.8	0.6	0.6	0.3	0.3	0.3
3000 Taxes on payroll and workforce	0.0	0.0	0.0	0.0	0.0	0.0	0.0	0.0	0.0	0.0
4000 Taxes on property	59.7	255.4	245.0	759.3	535.0	0.6	0.6	0.2	0.4	0.3
5000 Taxes on goods and services	1 063.7	4 719.3	10 330.4	19 837.6	19 422.1	10.0	11.2	9.3	10.1	9.7
6000 Other taxes	-23.4	-112.2	-61.1	-250.5	-175.0	-0.2	-0.3	-0.1	-0.1	-0.1
State/Regional										
Total tax revenue	**..**	**..**	**..**	**..**	**..**	**..**	**..**	**..**	**..**	**..**
1000 Taxes on income, profits and capital gains	..	..	..	..	..	..	..	..	..	..
2000 Social security contributions	..	..	..	..	..	..	..	..	..	..
3000 Taxes on payroll and workforce	..	..	..	..	..	..	..	..	..	..
4000 Taxes on property	..	..	..	..	..	..	..	..	..	..
5000 Taxes on goods and services	..	..	..	..	..	..	..	..	..	..
6000 Other taxes	..	..	..	..	..	..	..	..	..	..
Local government										
Total tax revenue	**104.7**	**621.2**	**1 508.3**	**3 401.0**	**3 389.9**	**1.0**	**1.5**	**1.4**	**1.7**	**1.7**
1000 Taxes on income, profits and capital gains	0.0	0.0	0.0	0.0	0.0	0.0	0.0	0.0	0.0	0.0
2000 Social security contributions	0.0	0.0	0.0	0.0	0.0	0.0	0.0	0.0	0.0	0.0
3000 Taxes on payroll and workforce	0.0	0.0	0.0	0.0	0.0	0.0	0.0	0.0	0.0	0.0
4000 Taxes on property	49.6	298.7	653.6	1 483.3	1 537.0	0.5	0.7	0.6	0.8	0.8
5000 Taxes on goods and services	55.0	322.5	854.8	1 917.8	1 853.0	0.5	0.8	0.8	1.0	0.9
6000 Other taxes	0.0	0.0	0.0	0.0	0.0	0.0	0.0	0.0	0.0	0.0
Social Security Funds										
Total tax revenue	**92.8**	**344.0**	**1 122.6**	**2 499.8**	**2 594.0**	**0.9**	**0.8**	**1.0**	**1.3**	**1.3**
1000 Taxes on income, profits and capital gains	0.0	0.0	0.0	0.0	0.0	0.0	0.0	0.0	0.0	0.0
2000 Social security contributions	92.8	344.0	1 122.6	2 499.8	2 594.0	0.9	0.8	1.0	1.3	1.3
3000 Taxes on payroll and workforce	0.0	0.0	0.0	0.0	0.0	0.0	0.0	0.0	0.0	0.0
4000 Taxes on property	0.0	0.0	0.0	0.0	0.0	0.0	0.0	0.0	0.0	0.0
5000 Taxes on goods and services	0.0	0.0	0.0	0.0	0.0	0.0	0.0	0.0	0.0	0.0
6000 Other taxes	0.0	0.0	0.0	0.0	0.0	0.0	0.0	0.0	0.0	0.0

.. Not available

Note: More detailed country data and country notes are available in Chapter 6 "Tax revenues by sub-sectors of general government". Full time series can be accessed at http://oe.cd/full-time-series.

Source: *Servicio de Impuestos internos* (Chile's Tax Service).

StatLink https://stat.link/opxgcd

Table 4.11. Colombia, tax revenue and % of GDP by selected tax category

	Billion COP					% of GDP				
	1990	2000	2010	2019	2020	1990	2000	2010	2019	2020
Total tax revenue	**2 579.4**	**30 598.6**	**98 455.3**	**209 071.3**	**187 664.6**	**11.3**	**15.7**	**18.1**	**19.7**	**18.8**
1000 Taxes on income, profits and capital gains	**771.7**	**7 103.5**	**26 218.9**	**67 519.6**	**61 812.5**	**3.4**	**3.6**	**4.8**	**6.4**	**6.2**
1100 Of individuals	47.2	1 499.3	5 192.4	14 233.7	14 469.9	0.2	0.8	1.0	1.3	1.4
1200 Corporate	359.8	5 119.8	20 405.2	50 287.1	43 240.2	1.6	2.6	3.8	4.7	4.3
1300 Unallocable between 1100 and 1200	364.7	484.4	621.3	2 998.8	4 102.5	1.6	0.2	0.1	0.3	0.4
2000 Social security contributions	**203.6**	**4 989.0**	**11 478.1**	**19 875.4**	**18 615.4**	**0.9**	**2.6**	**2.1**	**1.9**	**1.9**
2100 Employees	..	..	..	..	..	..	..	..	..	..
2200 Employers	..	..	..	..	..	..	..	..	..	..
2300 Self-employed or non-employed	..	..	..	..	..	..	..	..	..	..
2400 Unallocable between 2100, 2200 and 2300	203.6	4 989.0	11 478.1	19 875.4	18 615.4	0.9	2.6	2.1	1.9	1.9
3000 Taxes on payroll and workforce	**0.0**	**1 286.8**	**4 022.5**	**3 604.1**	**3 670.5**	**0.0**	**0.7**	**0.7**	**0.3**	**0.4**
4000 Taxes on property	**56.2**	**2 027.7**	**8 535.2**	**18 984.4**	**18 167.4**	**0.2**	**1.0**	**1.6**	**1.8**	**1.8**
4100 Recurrent taxes on immovable property	56.2	991.1	3 338.9	8 743.1	9 109.6	0.2	0.5	0.6	0.8	0.9
4200 Recurrent taxes on net wealth	0.0	0.0	1 970.5	923.3	957.1	0.0	0.0	0.4	0.1	0.1
4300 Estate, inheritance and gift taxes	0.0	0.0	0.0	0.0	0.0	0.0	0.0	0.0	0.0	0.0
4400 Taxes on financial and capital transactions	0.0	1 036.6	3 225.8	8 190.5	7 476.3	0.0	0.5	0.6	0.8	0.7
4500 Non-recurrent taxes	0.0	0.0	0.0	1 127.5	624.3	0.0	0.0	0.0	0.1	0.1
4600 Other recurrent taxes on property	0.0	0.0	0.0	0.0	0.0	0.0	0.0	0.0	0.0	0.0
5000 Taxes on goods and services	**1 388.7**	**14 180.5**	**44 411.6**	**89 797.9**	**77 752.5**	**6.1**	**7.3**	**8.2**	**8.5**	**7.8**
5100 Taxes on production, sale, transfer, etc	1 388.7	14 048.7	44 038.1	88 064.1	75 960.4	6.1	7.2	8.1	8.3	7.6
5110 General taxes	672.4	9 585.9	33 333.8	71 235.1	62 866.7	3.0	4.9	6.1	6.7	6.3
5111 Value added taxes	583.1	8 445.8	28 811.7	61 936.3	53 912.6	2.6	4.3	5.3	5.8	5.4
5120 Taxes on specific goods and services	716.3	4 462.8	10 704.3	16 828.9	13 093.7	3.2	2.3	2.0	1.6	1.3
5121 Excises	404.7	2 718.7	6 052.3	12 996.0	10 159.9	1.8	1.4	1.1	1.2	1.0
5200 Taxes on use of goods and perform activities	0.0	131.8	373.6	1 733.8	1 792.2	0.0	0.1	0.1	0.2	0.2
5300 Unallocable between 5100 and 5200	0.0	0.0	0.0	0.0	0.0	0.0	0.0	0.0	0.0	0.0
6000 Other taxes	**159.3**	**1 011.2**	**3 789.0**	**9 289.9**	**7 646.3**	**0.7**	**0.5**	**0.7**	**0.9**	**0.8**
Non-wastable tax credits										
Non-wastable tax credits against 1000	..	..	..	..	..	..	..	..	..	..
Transfer component	..	..	..	..	..	..	..	..	..	..
Tax expenditure component	..	..	..	..	..	..	..	..	..	..

.. Not available

Note: More detailed country data and country notes are available in Chapter 5 "Detailed country tables". Full time series can be accessed at http://oe.cd/full-time-series.

Source: Dirección de Impuestos y Aduanas Nacionales de Colombia, Ministerio de Hacienda y Crédito Público y Banco Central de Colombia. (National Tax and Customs Administration, Ministry of Finance and Public Credit and Central Bank of Colombia).

StatLink https://stat.link/0he4qx

Table 4.12. Colombia, tax revenue and % of GDP by level of government and main taxes

	Billion COP					% of GDP				
	1990	2000	2010	2019	2020	1990	2000	2010	2019	2020
Federal or Central government										
Total tax revenue	**1 885.9**	**21 016.3**	**71 304.3**	**152 621.7**	**134 938.4**	**8.3**	**10.8**	**13.1**	**14.4**	**13.5**
1000 Taxes on income, profits and capital gains	771.7	7 103.5	26 218.9	67 519.6	61 812.5	3.4	3.6	4.8	6.4	6.2
2000 Social security contributions	0.0	0.0	0.0	0.0	0.0	0.0	0.0	0.0	0.0	0.0
3000 Taxes on payroll and workforce	0.0	1 286.8	4 022.5	3 604.1	3 670.5	0.0	0.7	0.7	0.3	0.4
4000 Taxes on property	0.0	1 036.6	5 196.3	10 241.3	9 057.8	0.0	0.5	1.0	1.0	0.9
5000 Taxes on goods and services	1 035.9	11 108.6	35 382.9	70 637.1	60 110.7	4.6	5.7	6.5	6.7	6.0
6000 Other taxes	78.3	480.8	483.8	619.7	286.9	0.3	0.2	0.1	0.1	0.0
State/Regional										
Total tax revenue	**263.4**	**1 723.2**	**4 781.3**	**10 472.5**	**9 095.0**	**1.2**	**0.9**	**0.9**	**1.0**	**0.9**
1000 Taxes on income, profits and capital gains	0.0	0.0	0.0	0.0	0.0	0.0	0.0	0.0	0.0	0.0
2000 Social security contributions	0.0	0.0	0.0	0.0	0.0	0.0	0.0	0.0	0.0	0.0
3000 Taxes on payroll and workforce	0.0	0.0	0.0	0.0	0.0	0.0	0.0	0.0	0.0	0.0
4000 Taxes on property	0.0	0.0	0.0	0.0	0.0	0.0	0.0	0.0	0.0	0.0
5000 Taxes on goods and services	263.4	1 481.7	3 406.3	7 496.6	6 575.4	1.2	0.8	0.6	0.7	0.7
6000 Other taxes	0.0	241.5	1 375.0	2 975.9	2 519.6	0.0	0.1	0.3	0.3	0.3
Local government										
Total tax revenue	**226.5**	**2 870.1**	**10 891.7**	**26 101.8**	**25 015.8**	**1.0**	**1.5**	**2.0**	**2.5**	**2.5**
1000 Taxes on income, profits and capital gains	0.0	0.0	0.0	0.0	0.0	0.0	0.0	0.0	0.0	0.0
2000 Social security contributions	0.0	0.0	0.0	0.0	0.0	0.0	0.0	0.0	0.0	0.0
3000 Taxes on payroll and workforce	0.0	0.0	0.0	0.0	0.0	0.0	0.0	0.0	0.0	0.0
4000 Taxes on property	56.2	991.1	3 338.9	8 743.1	9 109.6	0.2	0.5	0.6	0.8	0.9
5000 Taxes on goods and services	89.3	1 590.1	5 622.5	11 664.3	11 066.4	0.4	0.8	1.0	1.1	1.1
6000 Other taxes	81.0	288.9	1 930.3	5 694.4	4 839.8	0.4	0.1	0.4	0.5	0.5
Social Security Funds										
Total tax revenue	**203.6**	**4 989.0**	**11 478.1**	**19 875.4**	**18 615.4**	**0.9**	**2.6**	**2.1**	**1.9**	**1.9**
1000 Taxes on income, profits and capital gains	0.0	0.0	0.0	0.0	0.0	0.0	0.0	0.0	0.0	0.0
2000 Social security contributions	203.6	4 989.0	11 478.1	19 875.4	18 615.4	0.9	2.6	2.1	1.9	1.9
3000 Taxes on payroll and workforce	0.0	0.0	0.0	0.0	0.0	0.0	0.0	0.0	0.0	0.0
4000 Taxes on property	0.0	0.0	0.0	0.0	0.0	0.0	0.0	0.0	0.0	0.0
5000 Taxes on goods and services	0.0	0.0	0.0	0.0	0.0	0.0	0.0	0.0	0.0	0.0
6000 Other taxes	0.0	0.0	0.0	0.0	0.0	0.0	0.0	0.0	0.0	0.0

Note: More detailed country data and country notes are available in Chapter 6 "Tax revenues by sub-sectors of general government". Full time series can be accessed at http://oe.cd/full-time-series.
Source: Dirección de Impuestos y Aduanas Nacionales de Colombia, Ministerio de Hacienda y Crédito Público y Banco Central de Colombia. (National Tax and Customs Administration, Ministry of Finance and Public Credit and Central Bank of Colombia).

StatLink https://stat.link/f497he

Table 4.13. Costa Rica, tax revenue and % of GDP by selected tax category

	Billion CRC					% of GDP				
	1990	2000	2010	2019	2020	1990	2000	2010	2019	2020
Total tax revenue	**117.7**	**978.1**	**4 382.4**	**8 855.9**	**8 235.5**	**22.4**	**21.1**	**22.1**	**23.4**	**22.7**
1000 Taxes on income, profits and capital gains	**11.8**	**128.8**	**748.1**	**1 854.9**	**1 651.2**	**2.3**	**2.8**	**3.8**	**4.9**	**4.5**
1100 Of individuals	..	..	202.8	541.0	556.1	..	..	1.0	1.4	1.5
1200 Corporate	..	..	450.3	1 058.1	692.6	..	..	2.3	2.8	1.9
1300 Unallocable between 1100 and 1200	11.8	128.8	94.9	255.8	402.6	2.3	2.8	0.5	0.7	1.1
2000 Social security contributions	**34.0**	**297.1**	**1 450.5**	**3 026.7**	**2 971.6**	**6.5**	**6.4**	**7.3**	**8.0**	**8.2**
2100 Employees	..	..	..	..	..	..	..	..	..	..
2200 Employers	3.4	37.3	207.2	381.9	387.8	0.7	0.8	1.0	1.0	1.1
2300 Self-employed or non-employed	..	..	..	..	..	..	..	..	..	..
2400 Unallocable between 2100, 2200 and 2300	30.5	259.8	1 243.3	2 644.8	2 583.7	5.8	5.6	6.3	7.0	7.1
3000 Taxes on payroll and workforce	**7.6**	**61.8**	**260.7**	**522.5**	**537.7**	**1.4**	**1.3**	**1.3**	**1.4**	**1.5**
4000 Taxes on property	**1.6**	**8.4**	**63.7**	**168.0**	**162.9**	**0.3**	**0.2**	**0.3**	**0.4**	**0.4**
4100 Recurrent taxes on immovable property	1.2	5.4	49.0	125.4	127.6	0.2	0.1	0.2	0.3	0.4
4200 Recurrent taxes on net wealth	0.0	0.0	0.0	0.0	0.0	0.0	0.0	0.0	0.0	0.0
4300 Estate, inheritance and gift taxes	0.0	0.0	0.0	0.0	0.0	0.0	0.0	0.0	0.0	0.0
4400 Taxes on financial and capital transactions	0.4	3.0	14.7	42.6	35.3	0.1	0.1	0.1	0.1	0.1
4500 Non-recurrent taxes	0.0	0.0	0.0	0.0	0.0	0.0	0.0	0.0	0.0	0.0
4600 Other recurrent taxes on property	0.0	0.0	0.0	0.0	0.0	0.0	0.0	0.0	0.0	0.0
5000 Taxes on goods and services	**53.5**	**456.9**	**1 766.9**	**3 081.9**	**2 745.1**	**10.2**	**9.9**	**8.9**	**8.1**	**7.6**
5100 Taxes on production, sale, transfer, etc	49.9	425.7	1 600.3	2 756.8	2 500.5	9.5	9.2	8.1	7.3	6.9
5110 General taxes	21.3	222.8	920.3	1 662.5	1 649.5	4.1	4.8	4.6	4.4	4.5
5111 Value added taxes	21.3	222.8	920.3	1 635.0	1 623.7	4.1	4.8	4.6	4.3	4.5
5120 Taxes on specific goods and services	28.5	202.9	680.0	1 094.3	851.0	5.4	4.4	3.4	2.9	2.3
5121 Excises	11.1	157.2	523.6	865.0	688.8	2.1	3.4	2.6	2.3	1.9
5200 Taxes on use of goods and perform activities	3.6	31.1	166.6	325.2	244.6	0.7	0.7	0.8	0.9	0.7
5300 Unallocable between 5100 and 5200	0.0	0.0	0.0	0.0	0.0	0.0	0.0	0.0	0.0	0.0
6000 Other taxes	**9.3**	**25.2**	**92.5**	**201.9**	**167.0**	**1.8**	**0.5**	**0.5**	**0.5**	**0.5**
Non-wastable tax credits										
Non-wastable tax credits against 1000	..	..	..	..	..	..	..	..	..	..
Transfer component	..	..	..	..	..	..	..	..	..	..
Tax expenditure component	..	..	..	..	..	..	..	..	..	..

.. Not available

Note: More detailed country data and country notes are available in Chapter 5 "Detailed country tables". Full time series can be accessed at http://oe.cd/full-time-series.

Source: *Secretaría Técnica de la Autoridad Presupuestaria, Ministerio de Finanzas y Contraloría General de la República* (Technical Secretary of the Budgeting Authority, Ministry of Finance and National General Comptroller).

StatLink https://stat.link/bm0h1y

Table 4.14. Costa Rica, tax revenue and % of GDP by level of government and main taxes

	Billion CRC					% of GDP				
	1990	2000	2010	2019	2020	1990	2000	2010	2019	2020
Federal or Central government										
Total tax revenue	**75.0**	**619.3**	**2 616.6**	**5 121.6**	**4 549.0**	**14.3**	**13.4**	**13.2**	**13.5**	**12.5**
1000 Taxes on income, profits and capital gains	11.8	128.8	748.1	1 854.9	1 651.2	2.3	2.8	3.8	4.9	4.5
2000 Social security contributions	1.3	18.7	61.2	77.5	79.4	0.3	0.4	0.3	0.2	0.2
3000 Taxes on payroll and workforce	0.0	0.0	0.0	0.0	0.0	0.0	0.0	0.0	0.0	0.0
4000 Taxes on property	0.4	3.0	18.3	47.3	40.0	0.1	0.1	0.1	0.1	0.1
5000 Taxes on goods and services	52.2	444.9	1 696.6	2 940.1	2 611.5	9.9	9.6	8.6	7.8	7.2
6000 Other taxes	9.3	24.0	92.5	201.8	166.9	1.8	0.5	0.5	0.5	0.5
State/Regional										
Total tax revenue	..	..	..	..	..	..	..	..	..	..
1000 Taxes on income, profits and capital gains	..	..	..	..	..	..	..	..	..	..
2000 Social security contributions	..	..	..	..	..	..	..	..	..	..
3000 Taxes on payroll and workforce	..	..	..	..	..	..	..	..	..	..
4000 Taxes on property	..	..	..	..	..	..	..	..	..	..
5000 Taxes on goods and services	..	..	..	..	..	..	..	..	..	..
6000 Other taxes	..	..	..	..	..	..	..	..	..	..
Local government										
Total tax revenue	**2.5**	**18.6**	**115.8**	**262.6**	**256.7**	**0.5**	**0.4**	**0.6**	**0.7**	**0.7**
1000 Taxes on income, profits and capital gains	0.0	0.0	0.0	0.0	0.0	0.0	0.0	0.0	0.0	0.0
2000 Social security contributions	0.0	0.0	0.0	0.0	0.0	0.0	0.0	0.0	0.0	0.0
3000 Taxes on payroll and workforce	0.0	0.0	0.0	0.0	0.0	0.0	0.0	0.0	0.0	0.0
4000 Taxes on property	1.2	5.4	45.4	120.7	123.0	0.2	0.1	0.2	0.3	0.3
5000 Taxes on goods and services	1.3	12.0	70.3	141.8	133.6	0.2	0.3	0.4	0.4	0.4
6000 Other taxes	0.0	1.2	0.0	0.1	0.1	0.0	0.0	0.0	0.0	0.0
Social Security Funds										
Total tax revenue	**40.2**	**340.2**	**1 650.0**	**3 471.7**	**3 429.8**	**7.7**	**7.4**	**8.3**	**9.2**	**9.4**
1000 Taxes on income, profits and capital gains	0.0	0.0	0.0	0.0	0.0	0.0	0.0	0.0	0.0	0.0
2000 Social security contributions	32.6	278.4	1 389.3	2 949.2	2 892.2	6.2	6.0	7.0	7.8	8.0
3000 Taxes on payroll and workforce	7.6	61.8	260.7	522.5	537.7	1.4	1.3	1.3	1.4	1.5
4000 Taxes on property	0.0	0.0	0.0	0.0	0.0	0.0	0.0	0.0	0.0	0.0
5000 Taxes on goods and services	0.0	0.0	0.0	0.0	0.0	0.0	0.0	0.0	0.0	0.0
6000 Other taxes	0.0	0.0	0.0	0.0	0.0	0.0	0.0	0.0	0.0	0.0

.. Not available

Note: More detailed country data and country notes are available in Chapter 6 "Tax revenues by sub-sectors of general government". Full time series can be accessed at http://oe.cd/full-time-series.

Source: *Secretaría Técnica de la Autoridad Presupuestaria, Ministerio de Finanzas y Contraloría General de la República* (Technical Secretary of the Budgeting Authority, Ministry of Finance and National General Comptroller).

StatLink https://stat.link/rc32pb

Table 4.15. Czech Republic, tax revenue and % of GDP by selected tax category

	Billion CZK					% of GDP				
	1990	2000	2010	2019	2020	1990	2000	2010	2019	2020
Total tax revenue	..	**771.6**	**1 286.9**	**2 014.2**	**1 982.6**	..	**32.3**	**32.2**	**34.8**	**34.7**
1000 Taxes on income, profits and capital gains	..	**175.8**	**259.9**	**458.8**	**453.2**	..	**7.4**	**6.5**	**7.9**	**7.9**
1100 Of individuals	..	99.7	131.7	255.7	266.6	..	4.2	3.3	4.4	4.7
1200 Corporate	..	76.2	128.2	203.1	186.6	..	3.2	3.2	3.5	3.3
1300 Unallocable between 1100 and 1200	..	0.0	0.0	0.0	0.0	..	0.0	0.0	0.0	0.0
2000 Social security contributions	..	**341.5**	**576.0**	**889.2**	**901.7**	..	**14.3**	**14.4**	**15.4**	**15.8**
2100 Employees	..	77.3	116.8	184.6	187.7	..	3.2	2.9	3.2	3.3
2200 Employers	..	220.2	363.1	569.5	573.8	..	9.2	9.1	9.8	10.0
2300 Self-employed or non-employed	..	44.1	96.1	135.2	140.2	..	1.8	2.4	2.3	2.5
2400 Unallocable between 2100, 2200 and 2300	..	0.0	0.0	0.0	0.0	..	0.0	0.0	0.0	0.0
3000 Taxes on payroll and workforce	..	**0.0**	**0.0**	**0.0**	**0.0**	..	**0.0**	**0.0**	**0.0**	**0.0**
4000 Taxes on property	..	**10.9**	**16.4**	**24.1**	**11.6**	..	**0.5**	**0.4**	**0.4**	**0.2**
4100 Recurrent taxes on immovable property	..	4.5	8.8	11.0	11.6	..	0.2	0.2	0.2	0.2
4200 Recurrent taxes on net wealth	..	0.0	0.0	0.0	0.0	..	0.0	0.0	0.0	0.0
4300 Estate, inheritance and gift taxes	..	0.6	0.2	0.0	0.0	..	0.0	0.0	0.0	0.0
4400 Taxes on financial and capital transactions	..	5.8	7.4	13.1	0.0	..	0.2	0.2	0.2	0.0
4500 Non-recurrent taxes	..	0.0	0.0	0.0	0.0	..	0.0	0.0	0.0	0.0
4600 Other recurrent taxes on property	..	0.0	0.0	0.0	0.0	..	0.0	0.0	0.0	0.0
5000 Taxes on goods and services	..	**243.0**	**434.4**	**641.9**	**615.9**	..	**10.2**	**10.9**	**11.1**	**10.8**
5100 Taxes on production, sale, transfer, etc	..	226.4	408.6	613.0	588.3	..	9.5	10.2	10.6	10.3
5110 General taxes	..	141.2	263.5	435.5	422.5	..	5.9	6.6	7.5	7.4
5111 Value added taxes	..	141.2	263.5	435.5	422.5	..	5.9	6.6	7.5	7.4
5120 Taxes on specific goods and services	..	85.1	145.2	177.5	165.9	..	3.6	3.6	3.1	2.9
5121 Excises	..	71.4	138.4	168.2	157.4	..	3.0	3.5	2.9	2.8
5200 Taxes on use of goods and perform activities	..	16.6	25.7	28.9	27.5	..	0.7	0.6	0.5	0.5
5300 Unallocable between 5100 and 5200	..	0.0	0.0	0.0	0.0	..	0.0	0.0	0.0	0.0
6000 Other taxes	..	**0.4**	**0.1**	**0.2**	**0.2**	..	**0.0**	**0.0**	**0.0**	**0.0**
Non-wastable tax credits										
Non-wastable tax credits against 1000	..	0.0	25.7	39.9	38.9	..	0.0	0.6	0.7	0.7
Transfer component	..	..	7.8	8.3	7.9	..	..	0.2	0.1	0.1
Tax expenditure component	..	..	17.9	31.6	31.1	..	..	0.4	0.5	0.5
Revenues collected on behalf of the EU										
Revenues collected on behalf of the EU, total	..	..	6.6	8.8	8.1	..	..	0.2	0.2	0.1
Customs duties	..	..	6.6	8.8	8.1	..	..	0.2	0.2	0.1

.. Not available

Note: More detailed country data and country notes are available in Chapter 5 "Detailed country tables". Full time series can be accessed at http://oe.cd/full-time-series.

Source: Ministry of Finance, Tax Analyses Department.

StatLink https://stat.link/1vlp60

Table 4.16. Czech Republic, tax revenue and % of GDP by level of government and main taxes

	Billion CZK					% of GDP				
	1990	2000	2010	2019	2020	1990	2000	2010	2019	2020
Federal or Central government										
Total tax revenue	**..**	**423.4**	**687.3**	**1 096.7**	**1 052.9**	**..**	**17.7**	**17.2**	**18.9**	**18.4**
1000 Taxes on income, profits and capital gains	..	175.8	259.9	458.8	453.2	..	7.4	6.5	7.9	7.9
2000 Social security contributions	..	0.0	0.0	0.0	0.0	..	0.0	0.0	0.0	0.0
3000 Taxes on payroll and workforce	..	0.0	0.0	0.0	0.0	..	0.0	0.0	0.0	0.0
4000 Taxes on property	..	6.4	7.6	13.1	0.0	..	0.3	0.2	0.2	0.0
5000 Taxes on goods and services	..	241.0	419.6	624.5	599.4	..	10.1	10.5	10.8	10.5
6000 Other taxes	..	0.1	0.1	0.2	0.2	..	0.0	0.0	0.0	0.0
State/Regional										
Total tax revenue	**..**	**..**	**..**	**..**	**..**	**..**	**..**	**..**	**..**	**..**
1000 Taxes on income, profits and capital gains	..	..	..	..	..	..	..	..	..	..
2000 Social security contributions	..	..	..	..	..	..	..	..	..	..
3000 Taxes on payroll and workforce	..	..	..	..	..	..	..	..	..	..
4000 Taxes on property	..	..	..	..	..	..	..	..	..	..
5000 Taxes on goods and services	..	..	..	..	..	..	..	..	..	..
6000 Other taxes	..	..	..	..	..	..	..	..	..	..
Local government										
Total tax revenue	**..**	**6.7**	**17.0**	**19.5**	**19.9**	**..**	**0.3**	**0.4**	**0.3**	**0.3**
1000 Taxes on income, profits and capital gains	..	0.0	0.0	0.0	0.0	..	0.0	0.0	0.0	0.0
2000 Social security contributions	..	0.0	0.0	0.0	0.0	..	0.0	0.0	0.0	0.0
3000 Taxes on payroll and workforce	..	0.0	0.0	0.0	0.0	..	0.0	0.0	0.0	0.0
4000 Taxes on property	..	4.5	8.7	10.9	11.6	..	0.2	0.2	0.2	0.2
5000 Taxes on goods and services	..	2.0	8.2	8.6	8.4	..	0.1	0.2	0.1	0.1
6000 Other taxes	..	0.3	0.0	0.0	0.0	..	0.0	0.0	0.0	0.0
Social Security Funds										
Total tax revenue	**..**	**341.5**	**576.0**	**889.2**	**901.7**	**..**	**14.3**	**14.4**	**15.4**	**15.8**
1000 Taxes on income, profits and capital gains	..	0.0	0.0	0.0	0.0	..	0.0	0.0	0.0	0.0
2000 Social security contributions	..	341.5	576.0	889.2	901.7	..	14.3	14.4	15.4	15.8
3000 Taxes on payroll and workforce	..	0.0	0.0	0.0	0.0	..	0.0	0.0	0.0	0.0
4000 Taxes on property	..	0.0	0.0	0.0	0.0	..	0.0	0.0	0.0	0.0
5000 Taxes on goods and services	..	0.0	0.0	0.0	0.0	..	0.0	0.0	0.0	0.0
6000 Other taxes	..	0.0	0.0	0.0	0.0	..	0.0	0.0	0.0	0.0

.. Not available

Note: More detailed country data and country notes are available in Chapter 6 "Tax revenues by sub-sectors of general government". Full time series can be accessed at http://oe.cd/full-time-series.

Source: Ministry of Finance, Tax Analyses Department.

StatLink https://stat.link/4qw07e

Table 4.17. Denmark, tax revenue and % of GDP by selected tax category

	Billion DKK					% of GDP				
	1990	2000	2010	2019	2020	1990	2000	2010	2019	2020
Total tax revenue	**379.8**	**622.0**	**810.5**	**1 083.7**	**1 094.8**	**44.4**	**46.9**	**44.8**	**46.9**	**47.1**
1000 Taxes on income, profits and capital gains	**232.3**	**382.0**	**498.8**	**701.8**	**708.0**	**27.2**	**28.8**	**27.5**	**30.4**	**30.5**
1100 Of individuals	205.1	327.3	421.3	565.6	593.2	24.0	24.7	23.3	24.5	25.5
1200 Corporate	14.7	42.3	41.1	72.8	66.6	1.7	3.2	2.3	3.2	2.9
1300 Unallocable between 1100 and 1200	12.6	12.4	36.5	63.4	48.2	1.5	0.9	2.0	2.7	2.1
2000 Social security contributions	**0.1**	**8.5**	**1.8**	**1.0**	**1.4**	**0.0**	**0.6**	**0.1**	**0.0**	**0.1**
2100 Employees	0.1	8.2	0.9	0.7	0.8	0.0	0.6	0.0	0.0	0.0
2200 Employers	0.0	0.2	0.9	0.3	0.6	0.0	0.0	0.1	0.0	0.0
2300 Self-employed or non-employed	0.0	0.0	0.0	0.0	0.0	0.0	0.0	0.0	0.0	0.0
2400 Unallocable between 2100, 2200 and 2300	0.0	0.0	0.0	0.0	0.0	0.0	0.0	0.0	0.0	0.0
3000 Taxes on payroll and workforce	**2.5**	**2.3**	**4.2**	**6.5**	**4.2**	**0.3**	**0.2**	**0.2**	**0.3**	**0.2**
4000 Taxes on property	**16.3**	**20.7**	**33.5**	**46.3**	**45.6**	**1.9**	**1.6**	**1.9**	**2.0**	**2.0**
4100 Recurrent taxes on immovable property	8.9	13.6	24.2	30.6	31.6	1.0	1.0	1.3	1.3	1.4
4200 Recurrent taxes on net wealth	0.9	0.0	0.0	0.0	0.0	0.1	0.0	0.0	0.0	0.0
4300 Estate, inheritance and gift taxes	2.2	2.9	3.6	8.5	6.7	0.3	0.2	0.2	0.4	0.3
4400 Taxes on financial and capital transactions	4.2	4.2	5.7	7.2	7.4	0.5	0.3	0.3	0.3	0.3
4500 Non-recurrent taxes	0.1	0.1	0.0	0.0	0.0	0.0	0.0	0.0	0.0	0.0
4600 Other recurrent taxes on property	0.0	0.0	0.0	0.0	0.0	0.0	0.0	0.0	0.0	0.0
5000 Taxes on goods and services	**128.7**	**208.1**	**271.9**	**327.8**	**335.4**	**15.0**	**15.7**	**15.0**	**14.2**	**14.4**
5100 Taxes on production, sale, transfer, etc	122.7	197.3	252.3	302.3	310.8	14.3	14.9	13.9	13.1	13.4
5110 General taxes	79.7	121.2	169.6	217.1	227.5	9.3	9.1	9.4	9.4	9.8
5111 Value added taxes	71.2	121.2	169.6	217.1	227.5	8.3	9.1	9.4	9.4	9.8
5120 Taxes on specific goods and services	43.0	76.0	82.7	85.2	83.2	5.0	5.7	4.6	3.7	3.6
5121 Excises	38.3	69.0	74.0	76.8	75.5	4.5	5.2	4.1	3.3	3.2
5200 Taxes on use of goods and perform activities	4.4	7.5	14.7	16.1	15.0	0.5	0.6	0.8	0.7	0.6
5300 Unallocable between 5100 and 5200	1.6	3.4	4.9	9.3	9.6	0.2	0.3	0.3	0.4	0.4
6000 Other taxes	**0.0**	**0.4**	**0.2**	**0.3**	**0.3**	**0.0**	**0.0**	**0.0**	**0.0**	**0.0**
Non-wastable tax credits										
Non-wastable tax credits against 1000	..	..	5.0	3.1	3.0	..	..	0.3	0.1	0.1
Transfer component	..	..	0.2	0.2	0.2	..	..	0.0	0.0	0.0
Tax expenditure component	..	..	4.7	2.9	2.9	..	..	0.3	0.1	0.1
Revenues collected on behalf of the EU										
Revenues collected on behalf of the EU, total	2.7	2.6	3.3	3.1	3.1	0.3	0.2	0.2	0.1	0.1
Customs duties	1.8	2.3	3.2	3.1	3.1	0.2	0.2	0.2	0.1	0.1

.. Not available

Note: More detailed country data and country notes are available in Chapter 5 "Detailed country tables". Full time series can be accessed at http://oe.cd/full-time-series.

The total tax revenue has been reduced by the amount of any capital transfer that represents uncollected taxes. The capital transfers were subtracted directly from the specific taxes to which they relate. Therefore, the tax revenue amounts are different to those reported in the detailed country data available in Chapter 5 "Detailed country tables".

Source: Statistics Denmark.

StatLink https://stat.link/us05q8

Table 4.18. Denmark, tax revenue and % of GDP by level of government and main taxes

	Billion DKK					% of GDP				
	1990	2000	2010	2019	2020	1990	2000	2010	2019	2020
Federal or Central government										
Total tax revenue	**259.5**	**420.6**	**589.0**	**802.0**	**796.5**	**30.3**	**31.7**	**32.5**	**34.7**	**34.3**
1000 Taxes on income, profits and capital gains	123.4	203.9	305.7	454.1	445.0	14.4	15.4	16.9	19.7	19.1
2000 Social security contributions	0.1	1.4	0.9	0.7	0.8	0.0	0.1	0.1	0.0	0.0
3000 Taxes on payroll and workforce	2.5	2.3	4.2	6.5	4.2	0.3	0.2	0.2	0.3	0.2
4000 Taxes on property	7.6	7.2	9.4	15.8	14.1	0.9	0.5	0.5	0.7	0.6
5000 Taxes on goods and services	126.0	205.5	268.7	324.6	332.3	14.7	15.5	14.8	14.0	14.3
6000 Other taxes	0.0	0.4	0.2	0.3	0.3	0.0	0.0	0.0	0.0	0.0
State/Regional										
Total tax revenue	..	..	..	..	..	..	..	..	..	..
1000 Taxes on income, profits and capital gains	..	..	..	..	..	..	..	..	..	..
2000 Social security contributions	..	..	..	..	..	..	..	..	..	..
3000 Taxes on payroll and workforce	..	..	..	..	..	..	..	..	..	..
4000 Taxes on property	..	..	..	..	..	..	..	..	..	..
5000 Taxes on goods and services	..	..	..	..	..	..	..	..	..	..
6000 Other taxes	..	..	..	..	..	..	..	..	..	..
Local government										
Total tax revenue	**117.6**	**191.7**	**217.3**	**278.3**	**294.6**	**13.8**	**14.4**	**12.0**	**12.0**	**12.7**
1000 Taxes on income, profits and capital gains	108.9	178.1	193.1	247.7	263.0	12.7	13.4	10.7	10.7	11.3
2000 Social security contributions	0.0	0.0	0.0	0.0	0.0	0.0	0.0	0.0	0.0	0.0
3000 Taxes on payroll and workforce	0.0	0.0	0.0	0.0	0.0	0.0	0.0	0.0	0.0	0.0
4000 Taxes on property	8.7	13.6	24.2	30.6	31.6	1.0	1.0	1.3	1.3	1.4
5000 Taxes on goods and services	0.0	0.0	0.0	0.0	0.0	0.0	0.0	0.0	0.0	0.0
6000 Other taxes	0.0	0.0	0.0	0.0	0.0	0.0	0.0	0.0	0.0	0.0
Social Security Funds										
Total tax revenue	**0.0**	**7.1**	**0.9**	**0.3**	**0.6**	**0.0**	**0.5**	**0.1**	**0.0**	**0.0**
1000 Taxes on income, profits and capital gains	0.0	0.0	0.0	0.0	0.0	0.0	0.0	0.0	0.0	0.0
2000 Social security contributions	0.0	7.1	0.9	0.3	0.6	0.0	0.5	0.1	0.0	0.0
3000 Taxes on payroll and workforce	0.0	0.0	0.0	0.0	0.0	0.0	0.0	0.0	0.0	0.0
4000 Taxes on property	0.0	0.0	0.0	0.0	0.0	0.0	0.0	0.0	0.0	0.0
5000 Taxes on goods and services	0.0	0.0	0.0	0.0	0.0	0.0	0.0	0.0	0.0	0.0
6000 Other taxes	0.0	0.0	0.0	0.0	0.0	0.0	0.0	0.0	0.0	0.0

.. Not available

Note: More detailed country data and country notes are available in Chapter 6 "Tax revenues by sub-sectors of general government". Full time series can be accessed at http://oe.cd/full-time-series.

The total tax revenue has been reduced by the amount of any capital transfer that represents uncollected taxes. The capital transfers were subtracted directly from the specific taxes to which they relate. Therefore, the tax revenue amounts are different to those reported in the detailed country data available in Chapter 6 "Tax revenues by sub-sectors of general government".

Source: Statistics Denmark.

StatLink https://stat.link/t08imp

Table 4.19. Estonia, tax revenue and % of GDP by selected tax category

	Billion EUR					% of GDP				
	1990	2000	2010	2019	2020	1990	2000	2010	2019	2020
Total tax revenue	..	**1.9**	**4.9**	**9.3**	**9.1**	..	**31.1**	**33.2**	**33.5**	**33.3**
1000 Taxes on income, profits and capital gains	..	**0.5**	**1.0**	**2.0**	**2.1**	..	**7.7**	**6.6**	**7.3**	**7.7**
1100 Of individuals	..	0.4	0.8	1.5	1.7	..	6.8	5.3	5.5	6.0
1200 Corporate	..	0.1	0.2	0.5	0.4	..	0.9	1.3	1.8	1.6
1300 Unallocable between 1100 and 1200	..	0.0	0.0	0.0	0.0	..	0.0	0.0	0.0	0.0
2000 Social security contributions	..	**0.7**	**1.9**	**3.3**	**3.3**	..	**10.9**	**12.7**	**11.7**	**12.1**
2100 Employees	..	0.0	0.1	0.1	0.1	..	0.0	0.8	0.5	0.5
2200 Employers	..	0.7	1.7	3.1	3.0	..	10.7	11.8	11.2	10.8
2300 Self-employed or non-employed	..	0.0	0.0	0.0	0.2	..	0.2	0.1	0.1	0.8
2400 Unallocable between 2100, 2200 and 2300	..	0.0	0.0	0.0	0.0	..	0.0	0.0	0.0	0.0
3000 Taxes on payroll and workforce	..	**0.0**	**0.0**	**0.0**	**0.0**	..	**0.0**	**0.0**	**0.0**	**0.0**
4000 Taxes on property	..	**0.0**	**0.1**	**0.1**	**0.1**	..	**0.4**	**0.3**	**0.2**	**0.2**
4100 Recurrent taxes on immovable property	..	0.0	0.1	0.1	0.1	..	0.4	0.3	0.2	0.2
4200 Recurrent taxes on net wealth	..	0.0	0.0	0.0	0.0	..	0.0	0.0	0.0	0.0
4300 Estate, inheritance and gift taxes	..	0.0	0.0	0.0	0.0	..	0.0	0.0	0.0	0.0
4400 Taxes on financial and capital transactions	..	0.0	0.0	0.0	0.0	..	0.0	0.0	0.0	0.0
4500 Non-recurrent taxes	..	0.0	0.0	0.0	0.0	..	0.0	0.0	0.0	0.0
4600 Other recurrent taxes on property	..	0.0	0.0	0.0	0.0	..	0.0	0.0	0.0	0.0
5000 Taxes on goods and services	..	**0.7**	**2.0**	**3.9**	**3.6**	..	**12.1**	**13.5**	**14.2**	**13.3**
5100 Taxes on production, sale, transfer, etc	..	0.7	1.9	3.7	3.4	..	11.7	13.1	13.4	12.5
5110 General taxes	..	0.5	1.3	2.5	2.4	..	8.4	8.6	8.9	8.9
5111 Value added taxes	..	0.5	1.3	2.5	2.4	..	8.4	8.5	8.9	8.9
5120 Taxes on specific goods and services	..	0.2	0.7	1.2	1.0	..	3.3	4.6	4.5	3.6
5121 Excises	..	0.2	0.6	1.1	0.9	..	3.0	4.2	4.1	3.3
5200 Taxes on use of goods and perform activities	..	0.0	0.1	0.2	0.2	..	0.4	0.4	0.8	0.7
5300 Unallocable between 5100 and 5200	..	0.0	0.0	0.0	0.0	..	0.0	0.0	0.0	0.0
6000 Other taxes	..	**0.0**	**0.0**	**0.0**	**0.0**	..	**0.0**	**0.0**	**0.0**	**0.0**
Non-wastable tax credits										
Non-wastable tax credits against 1000	..	..	..	..	..	..	..	..	..	..
Transfer component	..	..	..	..	..	..	..	..	..	..
Tax expenditure component	..	..	..	..	..	..	..	..	..	..
Revenues collected on behalf of the EU										
Revenues collected on behalf of the EU, total	..	..	0.0	0.1	0.1	..	..	0.2	0.2	0.2
Customs duties	..	..	0.0	0.1	0.0	..	..	0.2	0.2	0.2
SRF contributions	..	..	..	0.0	0.0	..	..	..	0.0	0.0

.. Not available

Note: More detailed country data and country notes are available in Chapter 5 "Detailed country tables". Full time series can be accessed at http://oe.cd/full-time-series.

Source: Statistics Estonia.

StatLink https://stat.link/u7x4bi

Table 4.20. Estonia, tax revenue and % of GDP by level of government and main taxes

	Billion EUR					% of GDP				
	1990	2000	2010	2019	2020	1990	2000	2010	2019	2020
Federal or Central government										
Total tax revenue	**..**	**1.6**	**3.9**	**7.6**	**7.4**	**..**	**26.3**	**26.7**	**27.5**	**27.0**
1000 Taxes on income, profits and capital gains	..	0.5	1.0	2.0	2.1	..	7.7	6.6	7.3	7.7
2000 Social security contributions	..	0.4	1.0	1.7	1.7	..	6.6	6.8	6.2	6.4
3000 Taxes on payroll and workforce	..	0.0	0.0	0.0	0.0	..	0.0	0.0	0.0	0.0
4000 Taxes on property	..	0.0	0.0	0.0	0.0	..	0.0	0.0	0.0	0.0
5000 Taxes on goods and services	..	0.7	2.0	3.9	3.6	..	12.0	13.2	13.9	13.0
6000 Other taxes	..	0.0	0.0	0.0	0.0	..	0.0	0.0	0.0	0.0
State/Regional										
Total tax revenue	**..**	**..**	**..**	**..**	**..**	**..**	**..**	**..**	**..**	**..**
1000 Taxes on income, profits and capital gains	..	..	..	..	..	..	..	..	..	..
2000 Social security contributions	..	..	..	..	..	..	..	..	..	..
3000 Taxes on payroll and workforce	..	..	..	..	..	..	..	..	..	..
4000 Taxes on property	..	..	..	..	..	..	..	..	..	..
5000 Taxes on goods and services	..	..	..	..	..	..	..	..	..	..
6000 Other taxes	..	..	..	..	..	..	..	..	..	..
Local government										
Total tax revenue	**..**	**0.0**	**0.1**	**0.1**	**0.1**	**..**	**0.5**	**0.5**	**0.3**	**0.3**
1000 Taxes on income, profits and capital gains	..	0.0	0.0	0.0	0.0	..	0.0	0.0	0.0	0.0
2000 Social security contributions	..	0.0	0.0	0.0	0.0	..	0.0	0.0	0.0	0.0
3000 Taxes on payroll and workforce	..	0.0	0.0	0.0	0.0	..	0.0	0.0	0.0	0.0
4000 Taxes on property	..	0.0	0.1	0.1	0.1	..	0.4	0.3	0.2	0.2
5000 Taxes on goods and services	..	0.0	0.0	0.0	0.0	..	0.1	0.1	0.0	0.0
6000 Other taxes	..	0.0	0.0	0.0	0.0	..	0.0	0.0	0.0	0.0
Social Security Funds										
Total tax revenue	**..**	**0.3**	**0.9**	**1.5**	**1.6**	**..**	**4.3**	**5.9**	**5.5**	**5.8**
1000 Taxes on income, profits and capital gains	..	0.0	0.0	0.0	0.0	..	0.0	0.0	0.0	0.0
2000 Social security contributions	..	0.3	0.9	1.5	1.6	..	4.3	5.9	5.5	5.8
3000 Taxes on payroll and workforce	..	0.0	0.0	0.0	0.0	..	0.0	0.0	0.0	0.0
4000 Taxes on property	..	0.0	0.0	0.0	0.0	..	0.0	0.0	0.0	0.0
5000 Taxes on goods and services	..	0.0	0.0	0.0	0.0	..	0.0	0.0	0.0	0.0
6000 Other taxes	..	0.0	0.0	0.0	0.0	..	0.0	0.0	0.0	0.0

.. Not available

Note: More detailed country data and country notes are available in Chapter 6 "Tax revenues by sub-sectors of general government". Full time series can be accessed at http://oe.cd/full-time-series.

Source: Statistics Estonia.

StatLink https://stat.link/6vlqwk

Table 4.21. Finland, tax revenue and % of GDP by selected tax category

	Billion EUR					% of GDP				
	1990	2000	2010	2019	2020	1990	2000	2010	2019	2020
Total tax revenue	**39.1**	**62.4**	**76.3**	**101.4**	**99.6**	**42.9**	**45.8**	**40.6**	**42.3**	**41.8**
1000 Taxes on income, profits and capital gains	**15.3**	**26.9**	**27.1**	**35.5**	**35.0**	**16.8**	**19.7**	**14.4**	**14.8**	**14.7**
1100 Of individuals	13.6	19.1	22.5	29.4	29.9	14.9	14.0	12.0	12.3	12.5
1200 Corporate	1.8	7.8	4.6	6.1	5.1	1.9	5.7	2.4	2.5	2.1
1300 Unallocable between 1100 and 1200	0.0	0.0	0.0	0.0	0.0	0.0	0.0	0.0	0.0	0.0
2000 Social security contributions	**10.0**	**15.8**	**22.6**	**28.3**	**27.3**	**11.0**	**11.5**	**12.0**	**11.8**	**11.5**
2100 Employees	1.2	2.9	4.7	8.5	8.6	1.3	2.1	2.5	3.6	3.6
2200 Employers	8.1	11.6	16.0	17.8	16.7	8.9	8.5	8.5	7.4	7.0
2300 Self-employed or non-employed	0.7	1.3	1.9	2.0	2.1	0.8	0.9	1.0	0.8	0.9
2400 Unallocable between 2100, 2200 and 2300	0.0	0.0	0.0	0.0	0.0	0.0	0.0	0.0	0.0	0.0
3000 Taxes on payroll and workforce	**0.0**	**0.0**	**0.0**	**0.0**	**0.0**	**0.0**	**0.0**	**0.0**	**0.0**	**0.0**
4000 Taxes on property	**1.0**	**1.5**	**2.1**	**3.5**	**3.6**	**1.1**	**1.1**	**1.1**	**1.4**	**1.5**
4100 Recurrent taxes on immovable property	0.1	0.6	1.2	1.9	2.0	0.1	0.4	0.6	0.8	0.8
4200 Recurrent taxes on net wealth	0.0	0.2	0.0	0.0	0.0	0.0	0.1	0.0	0.0	0.0
4300 Estate, inheritance and gift taxes	0.1	0.4	0.4	0.7	0.8	0.2	0.3	0.2	0.3	0.3
4400 Taxes on financial and capital transactions	0.7	0.4	0.5	0.9	0.8	0.8	0.3	0.3	0.4	0.3
4500 Non-recurrent taxes	0.0	0.0	0.0	0.0	0.0	0.0	0.0	0.0	0.0	0.0
4600 Other recurrent taxes on property	0.0	0.0	0.0	0.0	0.0	0.0	0.0	0.0	0.0	0.0
5000 Taxes on goods and services	**12.7**	**18.2**	**24.4**	**34.1**	**33.7**	**14.0**	**13.4**	**13.0**	**14.2**	**14.1**
5100 Taxes on production, sale, transfer, etc	12.6	17.8	23.6	32.7	32.2	13.8	13.0	12.6	13.6	13.5
5110 General taxes	7.5	10.9	15.5	22.0	22.0	8.3	8.0	8.3	9.2	9.2
5111 Value added taxes	7.5	10.9	15.5	22.0	22.0	8.3	8.0	8.3	9.2	9.2
5120 Taxes on specific goods and services	5.0	6.9	8.1	10.7	10.2	5.5	5.1	4.3	4.5	4.3
5121 Excises	3.8	5.6	6.3	8.1	8.0	4.2	4.1	3.3	3.4	3.4
5200 Taxes on use of goods and perform activities	0.2	0.4	0.8	1.5	1.5	0.2	0.3	0.4	0.6	0.6
5300 Unallocable between 5100 and 5200	0.0	0.0	0.0	0.0	0.0	0.0	0.0	0.0	0.0	0.0
6000 Other taxes	**0.1**	**0.0**	**0.1**	**0.1**	**0.1**	**0.1**	**0.0**	**0.0**	**0.0**	**0.0**
Non-wastable tax credits										
Non-wastable tax credits against 1000	..	..	..	..	..	..	..	..	..	..
Transfer component	..	..	..	..	..	..	..	..	..	..
Tax expenditure component	..	..	..	..	..	..	..	..	..	..
Revenues collected on behalf of the EU										
Revenues collected on behalf of the EU, total	..	0.1	0.2	0.4	0.4	..	0.1	0.1	0.2	0.2
Customs duties	..	0.1	0.2	0.2	0.2	..	0.1	0.1	0.1	0.1
SRF contributions	..	..	..	0.2	0.2	..	..	..	0.1	0.1

.. Not available

Note: More detailed country data and country notes are available in Chapter 5 "Detailed country tables". Full time series can be accessed at http://oe.cd/full-time-series.

Source: Statistics Finland, basing on data from State Treasury, Tax Administration, Finnish Customs, Finnish Transport and Communication Agency, Financial Stability Authority and Financial Supervisory Authority. Supplementary information from unpublished sources.

StatLink https://stat.link/50vnus

Table 4.22. Finland, tax revenue and % of GDP by level of government and main taxes

	Billion EUR					% of GDP				
	1990	2000	2010	2019	2020	1990	2000	2010	2019	2020
Federal or Central government										
Total tax revenue	**20.7**	**33.1**	**35.0**	**49.6**	**47.3**	**22.7**	**24.2**	**18.6**	**20.7**	**19.9**
1000 Taxes on income, profits and capital gains	7.0	14.0	9.8	14.2	12.3	7.7	10.3	5.2	5.9	5.2
2000 Social security contributions	0.0	0.0	0.0	0.0	0.0	0.0	0.0	0.0	0.0	0.0
3000 Taxes on payroll and workforce	0.0	0.0	0.0	0.0	0.0	0.0	0.0	0.0	0.0	0.0
4000 Taxes on property	0.9	0.9	0.9	1.6	1.6	1.0	0.7	0.5	0.7	0.7
5000 Taxes on goods and services	12.7	18.1	24.3	33.7	33.3	14.0	13.2	12.9	14.1	14.0
6000 Other taxes	0.1	0.0	0.1	0.1	0.1	0.1	0.0	0.0	0.0	0.0
State/Regional										
Total tax revenue	**..**	**..**	**..**	**..**	**..**	**..**	**..**	**..**	**..**	**..**
1000 Taxes on income, profits and capital gains	..	..	..	..	..	..	..	..	..	..
2000 Social security contributions	..	..	..	..	..	..	..	..	..	..
3000 Taxes on payroll and workforce	..	..	..	..	..	..	..	..	..	..
4000 Taxes on property	..	..	..	..	..	..	..	..	..	..
5000 Taxes on goods and services	..	..	..	..	..	..	..	..	..	..
6000 Other taxes	..	..	..	..	..	..	..	..	..	..
Local government										
Total tax revenue	**8.4**	**13.5**	**18.5**	**23.2**	**24.6**	**9.2**	**9.9**	**9.8**	**9.7**	**10.3**
1000 Taxes on income, profits and capital gains	8.3	12.9	17.3	21.3	22.6	9.1	9.4	9.2	8.9	9.5
2000 Social security contributions	0.0	0.0	0.0	0.0	0.0	0.0	0.0	0.0	0.0	0.0
3000 Taxes on payroll and workforce	0.0	0.0	0.0	0.0	0.0	0.0	0.0	0.0	0.0	0.0
4000 Taxes on property	0.1	0.6	1.2	1.9	2.0	0.1	0.4	0.6	0.8	0.8
5000 Taxes on goods and services	0.0	0.0	0.0	0.0	0.0	0.0	0.0	0.0	0.0	0.0
6000 Other taxes	0.0	0.0	0.0	0.0	0.0	0.0	0.0	0.0	0.0	0.0
Social Security Funds										
Total tax revenue	**10.0**	**15.8**	**22.6**	**28.3**	**27.3**	**11.0**	**11.5**	**12.0**	**11.8**	**11.5**
1000 Taxes on income, profits and capital gains	0.0	0.0	0.0	0.0	0.0	0.0	0.0	0.0	0.0	0.0
2000 Social security contributions	10.0	15.8	22.6	28.3	27.3	11.0	11.5	12.0	11.8	11.5
3000 Taxes on payroll and workforce	0.0	0.0	0.0	0.0	0.0	0.0	0.0	0.0	0.0	0.0
4000 Taxes on property	0.0	0.0	0.0	0.0	0.0	0.0	0.0	0.0	0.0	0.0
5000 Taxes on goods and services	0.0	0.0	0.0	0.0	0.0	0.0	0.0	0.0	0.0	0.0
6000 Other taxes	0.0	0.0	0.0	0.0	0.0	0.0	0.0	0.0	0.0	0.0

.. Not available

Note: More detailed country data and country notes are available in Chapter 6 "Tax revenues by sub-sectors of general government". Full time series can be accessed at http://oe.cd/full-time-series.

Source: Statistics Finland, basing on data from State Treasury, Tax Administration, Finnish Customs, Finnish Transport and Communication Agency, Financial Stability Authority and Financial Supervisory Authority. Supplementary information from unpublished sources.

StatLink https://stat.link/ti6gm1

Table 4.23. France, tax revenue and % of GDP by selected tax category

	Billion EUR					% of GDP				
	1990	2000	2010	2019	2020	1990	2000	2010	2019	2020
Total tax revenue	**433.8**	**642.2**	**840.9**	**1 094.1**	**1 047.6**	**41.2**	**43.4**	**42.1**	**44.9**	**45.3**
1000 Taxes on income, profits and capital gains	**69.6**	**159.5**	**189.7**	**280.8**	**273.9**	**6.6**	**10.8**	**9.5**	**11.5**	**11.9**
1100 Of individuals	46.3	115.2	143.1	226.7	220.3	4.4	7.8	7.2	9.3	9.5
1200 Corporate	23.1	44.3	46.6	54.2	53.6	2.2	3.0	2.3	2.2	2.3
1300 Unallocable between 1100 and 1200	0.3	0.0	0.0	0.0	0.0	0.0	0.0	0.0	0.0	0.0
2000 Social security contributions	**191.1**	**230.2**	**321.3**	**361.4**	**342.6**	**18.1**	**15.6**	**16.1**	**14.8**	**14.8**
2100 Employees	57.3	57.3	77.7	87.4	82.9	5.4	3.9	3.9	3.6	3.6
2200 Employers	118.1	158.3	218.0	245.8	232.9	11.2	10.7	10.9	10.1	10.1
2300 Self-employed or non-employed	15.7	14.6	25.7	28.3	26.7	1.5	1.0	1.3	1.2	1.2
2400 Unallocable between 2100, 2200 and 2300	0.0	0.0	0.0	0.0	0.0	0.0	0.0	0.0	0.0	0.0
3000 Taxes on payroll and workforce	**8.3**	**14.9**	**26.8**	**43.4**	**43.2**	**0.8**	**1.0**	**1.3**	**1.8**	**1.9**
4000 Taxes on property	**27.4**	**44.0**	**70.5**	**94.8**	**91.6**	**2.6**	**3.0**	**3.5**	**3.9**	**4.0**
4100 Recurrent taxes on immovable property	14.8	27.3	47.6	57.6	54.8	1.4	1.8	2.4	2.4	2.4
4200 Recurrent taxes on net wealth	2.6	2.4	4.4	2.0	2.0	0.2	0.2	0.2	0.1	0.1
4300 Estate, inheritance and gift taxes	4.1	6.9	7.7	15.2	15.0	0.4	0.5	0.4	0.6	0.6
4400 Taxes on financial and capital transactions	5.9	7.4	10.8	19.9	19.8	0.6	0.5	0.5	0.8	0.9
4500 Non-recurrent taxes	0.0	0.0	0.0	0.0	0.0	0.0	0.0	0.0	0.0	0.0
4600 Other recurrent taxes on property	0.0	0.0	0.0	0.0	0.0	0.0	0.0	0.0	0.0	0.0
5000 Taxes on goods and services	**123.2**	**169.5**	**223.3**	**301.5**	**283.7**	**11.7**	**11.5**	**11.2**	**12.4**	**12.3**
5100 Taxes on production, sale, transfer, etc	119.2	162.8	214.6	289.6	272.6	11.3	11.0	10.8	11.9	11.8
5110 General taxes	81.3	109.8	150.6	193.6	180.8	7.7	7.4	7.5	7.9	7.8
5111 Value added taxes	80.0	107.1	135.2	174.3	161.4	7.6	7.2	6.8	7.1	7.0
5120 Taxes on specific goods and services	37.9	53.0	64.0	96.0	91.8	3.6	3.6	3.2	3.9	4.0
5121 Excises	26.8	39.7	45.6	64.6	60.9	2.5	2.7	2.3	2.7	2.6
5200 Taxes on use of goods and perform activities	4.0	6.7	8.8	11.9	11.1	0.4	0.5	0.4	0.5	0.5
5300 Unallocable between 5100 and 5200	0.0	0.0	0.0	0.0	0.0	0.0	0.0	0.0	0.0	0.0
6000 Other taxes	**14.1**	**24.1**	**9.2**	**12.2**	**12.5**	**1.3**	**1.6**	**0.5**	**0.5**	**0.5**
Non-wastable tax credits										
Non-wastable tax credits against 1000	..	0.5	17.4	35.4	26.1	..	0.0	0.9	1.5	1.1
Transfer component	..	..	7.9	18.5	14.3	..	..	0.4	0.8	0.6
Tax expenditure component	..	..	9.5	16.9	11.7	..	..	0.5	0.7	0.5
Revenues collected on behalf of the EU										
Revenues collected on behalf of the EU, total	2.6	1.9	2.0	4.6	5.1	0.2	0.1	0.1	0.2	0.2
Customs duties	..	1.5	1.8	2.0	2.1	..	0.1	0.1	0.1	0.1
SRF contributions	..	..	..	2.4	3.0	..	..	..	0.1	0.1

.. Not available

Note: More detailed country data and country notes are available in Chapter 5 "Detailed country tables". Full time series can be accessed at http://oe.cd/full-time-series.

The total tax revenue has been reduced by the amount of any capital transfer that represents uncollected taxes. The capital transfer has been allocated between tax headings in proportion to the reported tax revenue. Therefore, the tax revenue amounts are different to those reported in the detailed country data available in Chapter 5 "Detailed country tables".

Source: National accounts for France, Insee.

StatLink https://stat.link/5bdszm

Table 4.24. France, tax revenue and % of GDP by level of government and main taxes

	Billion EUR					% of GDP				
	1990	2000	2010	2019	2020	1990	2000	2010	2019	2020
Federal or Central government										
Total tax revenue	**200.1**	**270.3**	**299.6**	**356.6**	**336.3**	**19.0**	**18.3**	**15.0**	**14.6**	**14.6**
1000 Taxes on income, profits and capital gains	69.6	94.4	97.0	143.7	139.6	6.6	6.4	4.9	5.9	6.0
2000 Social security contributions	3.2	5.4	7.6	8.1	8.2	0.3	0.4	0.4	0.3	0.4
3000 Taxes on payroll and workforce	6.2	10.6	4.2	11.2	12.2	0.6	0.7	0.2	0.5	0.5
4000 Taxes on property	8.6	11.4	13.4	20.5	20.3	0.8	0.8	0.7	0.8	0.9
5000 Taxes on goods and services	112.1	145.5	170.0	172.0	155.0	10.6	9.8	8.5	7.1	6.7
6000 Other taxes	0.4	3.1	7.4	1.1	1.1	0.0	0.2	0.4	0.0	0.0
State/Regional										
Total tax revenue	..	..	..	..	..	..	..	..	..	..
1000 Taxes on income, profits and capital gains	..	..	..	..	..	..	..	..	..	..
2000 Social security contributions	..	..	..	..	..	..	..	..	..	..
3000 Taxes on payroll and workforce	..	..	..	..	..	..	..	..	..	..
4000 Taxes on property	..	..	..	..	..	..	..	..	..	..
5000 Taxes on goods and services	..	..	..	..	..	..	..	..	..	..
6000 Other taxes	..	..	..	..	..	..	..	..	..	..
Local government										
Total tax revenue	**40.2**	**64.7**	**89.3**	**148.4**	**141.7**	**3.8**	**4.4**	**4.5**	**6.1**	**6.1**
1000 Taxes on income, profits and capital gains	0.0	0.0	0.1	0.0	0.0	0.0	0.0	0.0	0.0	0.0
2000 Social security contributions	0.0	0.0	0.0	0.0	0.0	0.0	0.0	0.0	0.0	0.0
3000 Taxes on payroll and workforce	1.7	3.9	7.5	11.1	9.2	0.2	0.3	0.4	0.5	0.4
4000 Taxes on property	18.8	32.7	57.1	74.3	71.3	1.8	2.2	2.9	3.0	3.1
5000 Taxes on goods and services	6.0	7.3	23.0	52.5	50.6	0.6	0.5	1.2	2.2	2.2
6000 Other taxes	13.7	20.9	1.6	10.5	10.6	1.3	1.4	0.1	0.4	0.5
Social Security Funds										
Total tax revenue	**190.9**	**305.3**	**450.1**	**584.5**	**564.5**	**18.1**	**20.6**	**22.6**	**24.0**	**24.4**
1000 Taxes on income, profits and capital gains	0.0	65.0	92.7	137.1	134.3	0.0	4.4	4.6	5.6	5.8
2000 Social security contributions	187.9	224.8	313.7	353.4	334.4	17.8	15.2	15.7	14.5	14.5
3000 Taxes on payroll and workforce	0.4	0.4	15.1	21.0	21.9	0.0	0.0	0.8	0.9	0.9
4000 Taxes on property	0.0	0.0	0.0	0.0	0.0	0.0	0.0	0.0	0.0	0.0
5000 Taxes on goods and services	2.5	14.9	28.4	72.4	73.1	0.2	1.0	1.4	3.0	3.2
6000 Other taxes	0.0	0.1	0.2	0.6	0.8	0.0	0.0	0.0	0.0	0.0

.. Not available

Note: More detailed country data and country notes are available in Chapter 6 "Tax revenues by sub-sectors of general government". Full time series can be accessed at http://oe.cd/full-time-series.

The total tax revenue has been reduced by the amount of any capital transfer that represents uncollected taxes. The capital transfer has been allocated between tax headings in proportion to the reported tax revenue. Therefore, the tax revenue amounts are different to those reported in the detailed country data available in Chapter 6 "Tax revenues by sub-sectors of general government".

Source: National accounts for France, Insee.

StatLink https://stat.link/okhnez

Table 4.25. Germany, tax revenue and % of GDP by selected tax category

	Billion EUR					% of GDP				
	1990	2000	2010	2019	2020	1990	2000	2010	2019	2020
Total tax revenue	**454.8**	**767.0**	**911.2**	**1 341.3**	**1 291.0**	**34.8**	**36.4**	**35.5**	**38.6**	**37.9**
1000 Taxes on income, profits and capital gains	**147.3**	**231.2**	**257.8**	**436.8**	**404.6**	**11.3**	**11.0**	**10.1**	**12.6**	**11.9**
1100 Of individuals	125.3	194.2	219.4	367.2	348.9	9.6	9.2	8.6	10.6	10.2
1200 Corporate	22.0	37.1	38.4	69.5	55.6	1.7	1.8	1.5	2.0	1.6
1300 Unallocable between 1100 and 1200	0.0	0.0	0.0	0.0	0.0	0.0	0.0	0.0	0.0	0.0
2000 Social security contributions	**170.4**	**299.4**	**354.3**	**508.1**	**512.1**	**13.0**	**14.2**	**13.8**	**14.6**	**15.0**
2100 Employees	73.6	131.6	152.8	220.2	217.2	5.6	6.2	6.0	6.3	6.4
2200 Employers	86.7	147.4	165.5	238.4	244.7	6.6	7.0	6.5	6.9	7.2
2300 Self-employed or non-employed	10.2	20.4	36.0	49.6	50.2	0.8	1.0	1.4	1.4	1.5
2400 Unallocable between 2100, 2200 and 2300	0.0	0.0	0.0	0.0	0.0	0.0	0.0	0.0	0.0	0.0
3000 Taxes on payroll and workforce	**0.0**	**0.0**	**0.0**	**0.0**	**0.0**	**0.0**	**0.0**	**0.0**	**0.0**	**0.0**
4000 Taxes on property	**15.3**	**17.5**	**21.0**	**38.7**	**42.4**	**1.2**	**0.8**	**0.8**	**1.1**	**1.2**
4100 Recurrent taxes on immovable property	4.5	8.8	11.3	14.4	14.7	0.3	0.4	0.4	0.4	0.4
4200 Recurrent taxes on net wealth	6.2	0.4	0.0	1.5	1.5	0.5	0.0	0.0	0.0	0.0
4300 Estate, inheritance and gift taxes	1.5	3.0	4.4	7.0	8.7	0.1	0.1	0.2	0.2	0.3
4400 Taxes on financial and capital transactions	3.1	5.2	5.3	15.8	17.6	0.2	0.2	0.2	0.5	0.5
4500 Non-recurrent taxes	0.0	0.0	0.0	0.0	0.0	0.0	0.0	0.0	0.0	0.0
4600 Other recurrent taxes on property	0.0	0.0	0.0	0.0	0.0	0.0	0.0	0.0	0.0	0.0
5000 Taxes on goods and services	**121.6**	**218.7**	**277.9**	**357.4**	**331.7**	**9.3**	**10.4**	**10.8**	**10.3**	**9.7**
5100 Taxes on production, sale, transfer, etc	117.2	211.4	261.2	337.1	310.7	9.0	10.0	10.2	9.7	9.1
5110 General taxes	75.5	140.9	180.5	244.4	221.9	5.8	6.7	7.0	7.0	6.5
5111 Value added taxes	75.5	140.9	180.5	244.4	221.9	5.8	6.7	7.0	7.0	6.5
5120 Taxes on specific goods and services	41.7	70.6	80.3	92.4	88.5	3.2	3.3	3.1	2.7	2.6
5121 Excises	31.2	57.2	63.4	66.2	63.2	2.4	2.7	2.5	1.9	1.9
5200 Taxes on use of goods and perform activities	4.4	7.2	16.8	20.3	21.0	0.3	0.3	0.7	0.6	0.6
5300 Unallocable between 5100 and 5200	0.0	0.0	0.0	0.0	0.0	0.0	0.0	0.0	0.0	0.0
6000 Other taxes	**0.2**	**0.2**	**0.1**	**0.3**	**0.2**	**0.0**	**0.0**	**0.0**	**0.0**	**0.0**
Non-wastable tax credits										
Non-wastable tax credits against 1000	..	39.3	46.3	45.2	51.9	..	1.9	1.8	1.3	1.5
Transfer component	..	..	17.7	15.9	20.3	..	..	0.7	0.5	0.6
Tax expenditure component	..	..	28.6	29.3	31.5	..	..	1.1	0.8	0.9
Revenues collected on behalf of the EU										
Revenues collected on behalf of the EU, total	4.1	3.7	4.3	7.1	6.9	0.3	0.2	0.2	0.2	0.2
Customs duties	3.7	3.4	4.2	5.1	4.7	0.3	0.2	0.2	0.1	0.1
SRF contributions	..	..	..	2.0	2.2	..	..	..	0.1	0.1

.. Not available

Note: More detailed country data and country notes are available in Chapter 5 "Detailed country tables". Full time series can be accessed at http://oe.cd/full-time-series.

Source: *Finanzbericht*, Bonn; Tax Statistics. Unpublished estimates by the Ministry of Finance.

StatLink https://stat.link/57d8oz

Table 4.26. Germany, tax revenue and % of GDP by level of government and main taxes

	Billion EUR					% of GDP				
	1990	2000	2010	2019	2020	1990	2000	2010	2019	2020
Federal or Central government										
Total tax revenue	**143.9**	**234.8**	**283.2**	**393.6**	**355.6**	**11.0**	**11.1**	**11.0**	**11.3**	**10.4**
1000 Taxes on income, profits and capital gains	58.2	97.9	104.5	179.6	168.5	4.5	4.6	4.1	5.2	4.9
2000 Social security contributions	0.0	0.0	0.0	0.0	0.0	0.0	0.0	0.0	0.0	0.0
3000 Taxes on payroll and workforce	0.0	0.0	0.0	0.0	0.0	0.0	0.0	0.0	0.0	0.0
4000 Taxes on property	1.2	0.0	0.0	1.5	1.5	0.1	0.0	0.0	0.0	0.0
5000 Taxes on goods and services	84.6	136.9	178.6	212.5	185.5	6.5	6.5	7.0	6.1	5.4
6000 Other taxes	0.0	0.0	0.0	0.0	0.0	0.0	0.0	0.0	0.0	0.0
State/Regional										
Total tax revenue	**97.8**	**172.1**	**198.1**	**319.1**	**309.9**	**7.5**	**8.2**	**7.7**	**9.2**	**9.1**
1000 Taxes on income, profits and capital gains	58.2	88.9	97.6	166.7	153.3	4.5	4.2	3.8	4.8	4.5
2000 Social security contributions	0.0	0.0	0.0	0.0	0.0	0.0	0.0	0.0	0.0	0.0
3000 Taxes on payroll and workforce	0.0	0.0	0.0	0.0	0.0	0.0	0.0	0.0	0.0	0.0
4000 Taxes on property	7.0	8.5	9.7	24.3	27.8	0.5	0.4	0.4	0.7	0.8
5000 Taxes on goods and services	32.6	74.6	90.8	128.1	128.9	2.5	3.5	3.5	3.7	3.8
6000 Other taxes	0.0	0.0	0.0	0.0	0.0	0.0	0.0	0.0	0.0	0.0
Local government										
Total tax revenue	**38.4**	**57.0**	**71.4**	**113.4**	**106.5**	**2.9**	**2.7**	**2.8**	**3.3**	**3.1**
1000 Taxes on income, profits and capital gains	30.9	44.4	55.7	90.5	82.8	2.4	2.1	2.2	2.6	2.4
2000 Social security contributions	0.0	0.0	0.0	0.0	0.0	0.0	0.0	0.0	0.0	0.0
3000 Taxes on payroll and workforce	0.0	0.0	0.0	0.0	0.0	0.0	0.0	0.0	0.0	0.0
4000 Taxes on property	7.2	9.0	11.3	12.9	13.2	0.5	0.4	0.4	0.4	0.4
5000 Taxes on goods and services	0.3	3.4	4.3	9.7	10.3	0.0	0.2	0.2	0.3	0.3
6000 Other taxes	0.2	0.1	0.1	0.3	0.2	0.0	0.0	0.0	0.0	0.0
Social Security Funds										
Total tax revenue	**170.4**	**299.4**	**354.3**	**508.1**	**512.1**	**13.0**	**14.2**	**13.8**	**14.6**	**15.0**
1000 Taxes on income, profits and capital gains	0.0	0.0	0.0	0.0	0.0	0.0	0.0	0.0	0.0	0.0
2000 Social security contributions	170.4	299.4	354.3	508.1	512.1	13.0	14.2	13.8	14.6	15.0
3000 Taxes on payroll and workforce	0.0	0.0	0.0	0.0	0.0	0.0	0.0	0.0	0.0	0.0
4000 Taxes on property	0.0	0.0	0.0	0.0	0.0	0.0	0.0	0.0	0.0	0.0
5000 Taxes on goods and services	0.0	0.0	0.0	0.0	0.0	0.0	0.0	0.0	0.0	0.0
6000 Other taxes	0.0	0.0	0.0	0.0	0.0	0.0	0.0	0.0	0.0	0.0

Note: More detailed country data and country notes are available in Chapter 6 "Tax revenues by sub-sectors of general government". Full time series can be accessed at http://oe.cd/full-time-series.
Source: *Finanzbericht*, Bonn; Tax Statistics. Unpublished estimates by the Ministry of Finance.

StatLink https://stat.link/90pr1h

Table 4.27. Greece, tax revenue and % of GDP by selected tax category

	Billion EUR					% of GDP				
	1990	2000	2010	2019	2020	1990	2000	2010	2019	2020
Total tax revenue	**11.5**	**47.2**	**72.4**	**72.4**	**64.2**	**25.2**	**33.4**	**32.3**	**39.5**	**38.9**
1000 Taxes on income, profits and capital gains	**2.3**	**12.7**	**16.0**	**15.6**	**13.1**	**5.0**	**9.0**	**7.1**	**8.5**	**7.9**
1100 Of individuals	1.6	6.1	9.0	11.0	10.4	3.6	4.3	4.0	6.0	6.3
1200 Corporate	0.6	5.6	5.7	4.1	2.0	1.4	4.0	2.6	2.2	1.2
1300 Unallocable between 1100 and 1200	0.0	0.9	1.2	0.6	0.7	0.1	0.6	0.5	0.3	0.4
2000 Social security contributions	**3.5**	**14.3**	**24.7**	**22.3**	**21.4**	**7.6**	**10.1**	**11.0**	**12.1**	**12.9**
2100 Employees	1.7	7.6	13.3	12.1	11.6	3.8	5.4	5.9	6.6	7.0
2200 Employers	1.7	6.7	11.5	10.2	9.7	3.8	4.7	5.1	5.6	5.9
2300 Self-employed or non-employed	0.0	0.0	0.0	0.0	0.0	0.0	0.0	0.0	0.0	0.0
2400 Unallocable between 2100, 2200 and 2300	0.0	0.0	0.0	0.0	0.0	0.0	0.0	0.0	0.0	0.0
3000 Taxes on payroll and workforce	**0.1**	**0.0**	**0.0**	**0.0**	**0.0**	**0.2**	**0.0**	**0.0**	**0.0**	**0.0**
4000 Taxes on property	**0.5**	**3.6**	**3.7**	**5.6**	**5.0**	**1.2**	**2.6**	**1.7**	**3.1**	**3.0**
4100 Recurrent taxes on immovable property	0.0	0.4	0.6	3.3	3.1	0.0	0.3	0.2	1.8	1.9
4200 Recurrent taxes on net wealth	0.0	0.7	1.3	1.2	1.2	0.0	0.5	0.6	0.7	0.7
4300 Estate, inheritance and gift taxes	0.1	0.4	0.2	0.2	0.2	0.3	0.3	0.1	0.1	0.1
4400 Taxes on financial and capital transactions	0.4	2.0	1.1	0.9	0.6	0.8	1.4	0.5	0.5	0.4
4500 Non-recurrent taxes	0.0	0.0	0.0	0.0	0.0	0.0	0.0	0.0	0.0	0.0
4600 Other recurrent taxes on property	0.0	0.1	0.6	0.0	0.0	0.0	0.1	0.3	0.0	0.0
5000 Taxes on goods and services	**5.1**	**16.6**	**28.0**	**28.9**	**24.7**	**11.2**	**11.8**	**12.5**	**15.8**	**15.0**
5100 Taxes on production, sale, transfer, etc	4.9	14.8	25.5	24.9	21.1	10.7	10.5	11.4	13.6	12.8
5110 General taxes	3.0	9.2	16.5	15.5	13.0	6.7	6.5	7.4	8.4	7.9
5111 Value added taxes	2.8	8.9	16.0	15.4	12.9	6.2	6.3	7.1	8.4	7.8
5120 Taxes on specific goods and services	1.8	5.5	8.9	9.4	8.1	3.9	3.9	4.0	5.1	4.9
5121 Excises	1.4	4.1	7.6	7.2	6.3	3.0	2.9	3.4	3.9	3.8
5200 Taxes on use of goods and perform activities	0.2	1.3	1.7	3.3	2.9	0.5	0.9	0.8	1.8	1.8
5300 Unallocable between 5100 and 5200	0.0	0.5	0.8	0.7	0.7	0.0	0.4	0.4	0.4	0.4
6000 Other taxes	**0.0**	**0.0**	**0.0**	**0.0**	**0.0**	**0.0**	**0.0**	**0.0**	**0.0**	**0.0**
Non-wastable tax credits										
Non-wastable tax credits against 1000	..	..	..	..	..	..	..	..	..	..
Transfer component	..	..	..	..	..	..	..	..	..	..
Tax expenditure component	..	..	..	..	..	..	..	..	..	..
Revenues collected on behalf of the EU										
Revenues collected on behalf of the EU, total	0.1	0.2	0.3	0.4	0.3	0.2	0.2	0.1	0.2	0.2
Customs duties	0.1	0.2	0.3	0.3	0.3	0.2	0.1	0.1	0.2	0.2
SRF contributions	..	..	..	0.1	0.1	..	..	..	0.0	0.1

.. Not available

Note: More detailed country data and country notes are available in Chapter 5 "Detailed country tables". Full time series can be accessed at http://oe.cd/full-time-series.

Source: Ministry of Finance, General Accounting Office, Directorate of General Government Budget in collaboration with the National Statistical Authority (ELSTAT).

StatLink https://stat.link/za2qnp

Table 4.28. Greece, tax revenue and % of GDP by level of government and main taxes

	Billion EUR					% of GDP				
	1990	2000	2010	2019	2020	1990	2000	2010	2019	2020
Federal or Central government										
Total tax revenue	**7.8**	**31.9**	**46.5**	**47.9**	**40.9**	**17.1**	**22.6**	**20.7**	**26.2**	**24.7**
1000 Taxes on income, profits and capital gains	2.3	12.7	15.9	15.6	13.1	5.0	9.0	7.1	8.5	7.9
2000 Social security contributions	0.0	0.7	1.3	0.1	0.1	0.1	0.5	0.6	0.0	0.0
3000 Taxes on payroll and workforce	0.0	0.0	0.0	0.0	0.0	0.0	0.0	0.0	0.0	0.0
4000 Taxes on property	0.5	2.6	2.1	4.0	3.5	1.2	1.8	0.9	2.2	2.1
5000 Taxes on goods and services	4.9	16.0	27.1	28.3	24.2	10.9	11.3	12.1	15.4	14.7
6000 Other taxes	0.0	0.0	0.0	0.0	0.0	0.0	0.0	0.0	0.0	0.0
State/Regional										
Total tax revenue	..	..	..	..	..	..	..	..	..	..
1000 Taxes on income, profits and capital gains	..	..	..	..	..	..	..	..	..	..
2000 Social security contributions	..	..	..	..	..	..	..	..	..	..
3000 Taxes on payroll and workforce	..	..	..	..	..	..	..	..	..	..
4000 Taxes on property	..	..	..	..	..	..	..	..	..	..
5000 Taxes on goods and services	..	..	..	..	..	..	..	..	..	..
6000 Other taxes	..	..	..	..	..	..	..	..	..	..
Local government										
Total tax revenue	**0.1**	**1.0**	**1.7**	**1.7**	**1.6**	**0.3**	**0.7**	**0.8**	**1.0**	**1.0**
1000 Taxes on income, profits and capital gains	0.0	0.0	0.0	0.0	0.0	0.0	0.0	0.0	0.0	0.0
2000 Social security contributions	0.0	0.0	0.0	0.0	0.0	0.0	0.0	0.0	0.0	0.0
3000 Taxes on payroll and workforce	0.1	0.0	0.0	0.0	0.0	0.2	0.0	0.0	0.0	0.0
4000 Taxes on property	0.0	0.8	1.5	1.6	1.6	0.0	0.6	0.7	0.9	0.9
5000 Taxes on goods and services	0.1	0.2	0.2	0.1	0.1	0.1	0.1	0.1	0.1	0.0
6000 Other taxes	0.0	0.0	0.0	0.0	0.0	0.0	0.0	0.0	0.0	0.0
Social Security Funds										
Total tax revenue	**3.4**	**14.1**	**24.0**	**22.3**	**21.4**	**7.5**	**10.0**	**10.7**	**12.2**	**13.0**
1000 Taxes on income, profits and capital gains	0.0	0.0	0.0	0.0	0.0	0.0	0.0	0.0	0.0	0.0
2000 Social security contributions	3.4	13.6	23.4	22.2	21.3	7.5	9.6	10.5	12.1	12.9
3000 Taxes on payroll and workforce	0.0	0.0	0.0	0.0	0.0	0.0	0.0	0.0	0.0	0.0
4000 Taxes on property	0.0	0.2	0.1	0.0	0.0	0.0	0.1	0.1	0.0	0.0
5000 Taxes on goods and services	0.0	0.3	0.4	0.1	0.1	0.0	0.2	0.2	0.1	0.1
6000 Other taxes	0.0	0.0	0.0	0.0	0.0	0.0	0.0	0.0	0.0	0.0

.. Not available

Note: More detailed country data and country notes are available in Chapter 6 "Tax revenues by sub-sectors of general government". Full time series can be accessed at http://oe.cd/full-time-series.

Source: Ministry of Finance, General Accounting Office, Directorate of General Government Budget in collaboration with the National Statistical Authority (ELSTAT).

StatLink https://stat.link/z72pvy

Table 4.29. Hungary, tax revenue and % of GDP by selected tax category

	Billion HUF					% of GDP				
	1990	2000	2010	2019	2020	1990	2000	2010	2019	2020
Total tax revenue	..	**5 132.6**	**10 121.7**	**17 308.7**	**17 425.6**	..	**38.5**	**36.8**	**36.4**	**36.1**
1000 Taxes on income, profits and capital gains	..	**1 247.4**	**2 093.8**	**3 045.9**	**3 165.9**	..	**9.4**	**7.6**	**6.4**	**6.6**
1100 Of individuals	..	954.7	1 764.1	2 457.6	2 543.6	..	7.2	6.4	5.2	5.3
1200 Corporate	..	292.7	329.7	588.3	622.3	..	2.2	1.2	1.2	1.3
1300 Unallocable between 1100 and 1200	..	0.0	0.0	0.0	0.0	..	0.0	0.0	0.0	0.0
2000 Social security contributions	..	**1 506.8**	**3 179.5**	**5 545.5**	**5 364.8**	..	**11.3**	**11.6**	**11.7**	**11.1**
2100 Employees	..	275.3	1 112.6	2 771.6	2 813.8	..	2.1	4.0	5.8	5.8
2200 Employers	..	1 213.2	2 043.8	2 746.0	2 521.7	..	9.1	7.4	5.8	5.2
2300 Self-employed or non-employed	..	0.9	0.0	0.0	0.0	..	0.0	0.0	0.0	0.0
2400 Unallocable between 2100, 2200 and 2300	..	17.4	23.2	28.0	29.3	..	0.1	0.1	0.1	0.1
3000 Taxes on payroll and workforce	..	**183.4**	**113.7**	**494.9**	**501.3**	..	**1.4**	**0.4**	**1.0**	**1.0**
4000 Taxes on property	..	**89.0**	**312.1**	**446.5**	**507.4**	..	**0.7**	**1.1**	**0.9**	**1.1**
4100 Recurrent taxes on immovable property	..	30.8	92.5	221.4	224.6	..	0.2	0.3	0.5	0.5
4200 Recurrent taxes on net wealth	..	0.0	135.7	44.9	108.1	..	0.0	0.5	0.1	0.2
4300 Estate, inheritance and gift taxes	..	5.5	6.3	11.4	9.5	..	0.0	0.0	0.0	0.0
4400 Taxes on financial and capital transactions	..	52.8	77.6	168.7	165.2	..	0.4	0.3	0.4	0.3
4500 Non-recurrent taxes	..	0.0	0.0	0.0	0.0	..	0.0	0.0	0.0	0.0
4600 Other recurrent taxes on property	..	0.0	0.0	0.0	0.0	..	0.0	0.0	0.0	0.0
5000 Taxes on goods and services	..	**2 081.4**	**4 383.9**	**7 742.1**	**7 863.9**	..	**15.6**	**15.9**	**16.3**	**16.3**
5100 Taxes on production, sale, transfer, etc	..	2 052.7	4 272.3	7 524.7	7 645.0	..	15.4	15.5	15.8	15.8
5110 General taxes	..	1 340.6	3 010.8	5 527.5	5 632.9	..	10.1	10.9	11.6	11.7
5111 Value added taxes	..	1 153.7	2 325.6	4 526.8	4 717.0	..	8.7	8.5	9.5	9.8
5120 Taxes on specific goods and services	..	712.1	1 261.5	1 997.3	2 012.1	..	5.3	4.6	4.2	4.2
5121 Excises	..	533.5	929.9	1 303.9	1 318.4	..	4.0	3.4	2.7	2.7
5200 Taxes on use of goods and perform activities	..	28.7	111.6	217.3	218.9	..	0.2	0.4	0.5	0.5
5300 Unallocable between 5100 and 5200	..	0.0	0.0	0.0	0.0	..	0.0	0.0	0.0	0.0
6000 Other taxes	..	**24.5**	**38.7**	**33.9**	**22.3**	..	**0.2**	**0.1**	**0.1**	**0.0**
Non-wastable tax credits										
Non-wastable tax credits against 1000	..	..	..	..	..	..	..	..	..	..
Transfer component	..	..	..	..	..	..	..	..	..	..
Tax expenditure component	..	..	..	..	..	..	..	..	..	..
Revenues collected on behalf of the EU										
Revenues collected on behalf of the EU, total	..	..	25.7	64.3	63.5	..	..	0.1	0.1	0.1
Customs duties	..	..	25.0	64.3	63.5	..	..	0.1	0.1	0.1

.. Not available

Note: More detailed country data and country notes are available in Chapter 5 "Detailed country tables". Full time series can be accessed at http://oe.cd/full-time-series.

Source: Ministry of Finance, Economic Department.

StatLink https://stat.link/hex7v6

Table 4.30. Hungary, tax revenue and % of GDP by level of government and main taxes

	Billion HUF					% of GDP				
	1990	2000	2010	2019	2020	1990	2000	2010	2019	2020
Federal or Central government										
Total tax revenue	..	**3 308.0**	**6 379.4**	**10 838.5**	**11 191.8**	..	**24.8**	**23.2**	**22.8**	**23.2**
1000 Taxes on income, profits and capital gains	..	1 230.8	2 064.3	3 033.9	3 165.6	..	9.2	7.5	6.4	6.6
2000 Social security contributions	..	136.6	182.0	287.4	228.6	..	1.0	0.7	0.6	0.5
3000 Taxes on payroll and workforce	..	15.4	103.1	484.7	491.8	..	0.1	0.4	1.0	1.0
4000 Taxes on property	..	29.1	182.8	279.5	335.3	..	0.2	0.7	0.6	0.7
5000 Taxes on goods and services	..	1 878.6	3 808.5	6 727.2	6 955.6	..	14.1	13.9	14.2	14.4
6000 Other taxes	..	17.5	38.7	25.8	14.9	..	0.1	0.1	0.1	0.0
State/Regional										
Total tax revenue	..	..	..	..	..	..	..	..	..	..
1000 Taxes on income, profits and capital gains	..	..	..	..	..	..	..	..	..	..
2000 Social security contributions	..	..	..	..	..	..	..	..	..	..
3000 Taxes on payroll and workforce	..	..	..	..	..	..	..	..	..	..
4000 Taxes on property	..	..	..	..	..	..	..	..	..	..
5000 Taxes on goods and services	..	..	..	..	..	..	..	..	..	..
6000 Other taxes	..	..	..	..	..	..	..	..	..	..
Local government										
Total tax revenue	..	**266.0**	**652.2**	**1 006.2**	**906.2**	..	**2.0**	**2.4**	**2.1**	**1.9**
1000 Taxes on income, profits and capital gains	..	2.2	0.1	0.0	0.0	..	0.0	0.0	0.0	0.0
2000 Social security contributions	..	0.0	0.0	0.0	0.0	..	0.0	0.0	0.0	0.0
3000 Taxes on payroll and workforce	..	1.2	1.2	0.0	0.0	..	0.0	0.0	0.0	0.0
4000 Taxes on property	..	59.9	129.3	166.9	172.1	..	0.4	0.5	0.4	0.4
5000 Taxes on goods and services	..	202.8	521.6	839.2	734.1	..	1.5	1.9	1.8	1.5
6000 Other taxes	..	0.0	0.0	0.0	0.0	..	0.0	0.0	0.0	0.0
Social Security Funds										
Total tax revenue	..	**1 558.6**	**3 064.5**	**5 399.7**	**5 264.1**	..	**11.7**	**11.1**	**11.4**	**10.9**
1000 Taxes on income, profits and capital gains	..	14.5	29.4	12.0	0.3	..	0.1	0.1	0.0	0.0
2000 Social security contributions	..	1 370.2	2 997.5	5 258.1	5 136.1	..	10.3	10.9	11.1	10.6
3000 Taxes on payroll and workforce	..	166.9	9.4	10.2	9.5	..	1.3	0.0	0.0	0.0
4000 Taxes on property	..	0.0	0.0	0.0	0.0	..	0.0	0.0	0.0	0.0
5000 Taxes on goods and services	..	0.0	28.1	111.4	110.7	..	0.0	0.1	0.2	0.2
6000 Other taxes	..	7.0	0.0	8.1	7.4	..	0.1	0.0	0.0	0.0

.. Not available

Note: More detailed country data and country notes are available in Chapter 6 "Tax revenues by sub-sectors of general government". Full time series can be accessed at http://oe.cd/full-time-series.

Source: Ministry of Finance, Economic Department.

StatLink https://stat.link/i29d8z

Table 4.31. Iceland, tax revenue and % of GDP by selected tax category

	Billion ISK					% of GDP				
	1990	2000	2010	2019	2020	1990	2000	2010	2019	2020
Total tax revenue	**114.9**	**254.6**	**541.6**	**1 062.0**	**1 061.1**	**30.5**	**35.9**	**32.2**	**34.9**	**36.1**
1000 Taxes on income, profits and capital gains	**34.1**	**101.5**	**239.7**	**530.2**	**542.0**	**9.0**	**14.3**	**14.3**	**17.4**	**18.4**
1100 Of individuals	30.9	88.5	197.3	435.4	457.3	8.2	12.5	11.7	14.3	15.6
1200 Corporate	3.2	8.4	14.6	63.0	64.4	0.8	1.2	0.9	2.1	2.2
1300 Unallocable between 1100 and 1200	0.0	4.6	27.7	31.9	20.3	0.0	0.7	1.7	1.0	0.7
2000 Social security contributions	**3.6**	**19.7**	**63.6**	**97.4**	**88.4**	**1.0**	**2.8**	**3.8**	**3.2**	**3.0**
2100 Employees	0.3	..	..	..	..	0.1	..	..	..	..
2200 Employers	3.3	..	..	..	..	0.9	..	..	..	..
2300 Self-employed or non-employed	0.0	..	..	..	..	0.0	..	..	..	..
2400 Unallocable between 2100, 2200 and 2300	0.0	19.7	63.6	97.4	88.4	0.0	2.8	3.8	3.2	3.0
3000 Taxes on payroll and workforce	**4.1**	**0.2**	**2.8**	**9.1**	**9.2**	**1.1**	**0.0**	**0.2**	**0.3**	**0.3**
4000 Taxes on property	**9.7**	**16.8**	**35.4**	**58.4**	**66.3**	**2.6**	**2.4**	**2.1**	**1.9**	**2.3**
4100 Recurrent taxes on immovable property	4.1	10.1	28.5	52.5	56.0	1.1	1.4	1.7	1.7	1.9
4200 Recurrent taxes on net wealth	2.4	5.2	3.8	0.0	0.0	0.6	0.7	0.2	0.0	0.0
4300 Estate, inheritance and gift taxes	0.2	0.8	2.6	4.7	9.1	0.1	0.1	0.2	0.2	0.3
4400 Taxes on financial and capital transactions	2.9	0.0	0.0	0.0	0.0	0.8	0.0	0.0	0.0	0.0
4500 Non-recurrent taxes	0.0	0.1	0.1	0.6	0.6	0.0	0.0	0.0	0.0	0.0
4600 Other recurrent taxes on property	0.0	0.7	0.3	0.5	0.6	0.0	0.1	0.0	0.0	0.0
5000 Taxes on goods and services	**58.9**	**115.4**	**194.1**	**348.3**	**336.0**	**15.6**	**16.3**	**11.5**	**11.4**	**11.4**
5100 Taxes on production, sale, transfer, etc	56.6	103.8	183.0	325.8	312.8	15.0	14.6	10.9	10.7	10.6
5110 General taxes	37.1	75.8	126.4	248.6	239.8	9.8	10.7	7.5	8.2	8.2
5111 Value added taxes	32.7	72.7	123.7	243.3	233.7	8.7	10.2	7.4	8.0	8.0
5120 Taxes on specific goods and services	19.5	28.0	56.6	77.2	73.0	5.2	3.9	3.4	2.5	2.5
5121 Excises	2.3	23.6	46.7	66.8	64.3	0.6	3.3	2.8	2.2	2.2
5200 Taxes on use of goods and perform activities	2.4	11.6	11.1	22.5	23.1	0.6	1.6	0.7	0.7	0.8
5300 Unallocable between 5100 and 5200	0.0	0.0	0.0	0.0	0.0	0.0	0.0	0.0	0.0	0.0
6000 Other taxes	**4.5**	**1.0**	**6.0**	**18.6**	**19.2**	**1.2**	**0.1**	**0.4**	**0.6**	**0.7**
Non-wastable tax credits										
Non-wastable tax credits against 1000	..	..	..	3.6	4.4	..	..	..	0.1	0.1
Transfer component	..	..	..	3.0	4.4	..	..	..	0.1	0.1
Tax expenditure component	..	..	..	0.6	0.8	..	..	..	0.0	0.0

.. Not available

Note: More detailed country data and country notes are available in Chapter 5 "Detailed country tables". Full time series can be accessed at http://oe.cd/full-time-series.

Source: Statistics Iceland.

StatLink https://stat.link/pwzj9e

Table 4.32. Iceland, tax revenue and % of GDP by level of government and main taxes

	Billion ISK					% of GDP				
	1990	2000	2010	2019	2020	1990	2000	2010	2019	2020
Federal or Central government										
Total tax revenue	**91.6**	**195.1**	**403.6**	**761.1**	**744.5**	**24.3**	**27.5**	**24.0**	**25.0**	**25.3**
1000 Taxes on income, profits and capital gains	19.9	55.5	132.9	288.8	287.5	5.3	7.8	7.9	9.5	9.8
2000 Social security contributions	3.6	19.7	63.6	97.4	88.4	1.0	2.8	3.8	3.2	3.0
3000 Taxes on payroll and workforce	4.1	0.2	2.8	9.1	9.2	1.1	0.0	0.2	0.3	0.3
4000 Taxes on property	6.0	6.7	7.0	6.1	10.5	1.6	0.9	0.4	0.2	0.4
5000 Taxes on goods and services	57.7	112.0	191.3	341.1	329.8	15.3	15.8	11.4	11.2	11.2
6000 Other taxes	0.4	1.0	6.0	18.6	19.2	0.1	0.1	0.4	0.6	0.7
State/Regional										
Total tax revenue	**..**	**..**	**..**	**..**	**..**	**..**	**..**	**..**	**..**	**..**
1000 Taxes on income, profits and capital gains	..	..	..	..	..	..	..	..	..	..
2000 Social security contributions	..	..	..	..	..	..	..	..	..	..
3000 Taxes on payroll and workforce	..	..	..	..	..	..	..	..	..	..
4000 Taxes on property	..	..	..	..	..	..	..	..	..	..
5000 Taxes on goods and services	..	..	..	..	..	..	..	..	..	..
6000 Other taxes	..	..	..	..	..	..	..	..	..	..
Local government										
Total tax revenue	**23.3**	**59.4**	**138.0**	**300.9**	**316.5**	**6.2**	**8.4**	**8.2**	**9.9**	**10.8**
1000 Taxes on income, profits and capital gains	14.2	46.0	106.8	241.4	254.6	3.8	6.5	6.4	7.9	8.7
2000 Social security contributions	0.0	0.0	0.0	0.0	0.0	0.0	0.0	0.0	0.0	0.0
3000 Taxes on payroll and workforce	0.0	0.0	0.0	0.0	0.0	0.0	0.0	0.0	0.0	0.0
4000 Taxes on property	3.7	10.1	28.4	52.3	55.8	1.0	1.4	1.7	1.7	1.9
5000 Taxes on goods and services	1.2	3.3	2.8	7.2	6.2	0.3	0.5	0.2	0.2	0.2
6000 Other taxes	4.1	0.0	0.0	0.0	0.0	1.1	0.0	0.0	0.0	0.0
Social Security Funds										
Total tax revenue	**0.0**	**0.0**	**0.0**	**0.0**	**0.0**	**0.0**	**0.0**	**0.0**	**0.0**	**0.0**
1000 Taxes on income, profits and capital gains	0.0	0.0	0.0	0.0	0.0	0.0	0.0	0.0	0.0	0.0
2000 Social security contributions	0.0	0.0	0.0	0.0	0.0	0.0	0.0	0.0	0.0	0.0
3000 Taxes on payroll and workforce	0.0	0.0	0.0	0.0	0.0	0.0	0.0	0.0	0.0	0.0
4000 Taxes on property	0.0	0.0	0.0	0.0	0.0	0.0	0.0	0.0	0.0	0.0
5000 Taxes on goods and services	0.0	0.0	0.0	0.0	0.0	0.0	0.0	0.0	0.0	0.0
6000 Other taxes	0.0	0.0	0.0	0.0	0.0	0.0	0.0	0.0	0.0	0.0

.. Not available

Note: More detailed country data and country notes are available in Chapter 5 "Detailed country tables". Full time series can be accessed at http://oe.cd/full-time-series.

Source: Statistics Iceland.

StatLink https://stat.link/3a47ie

Table 4.33. Ireland, tax revenue and % of GDP by selected tax category

	Billion EUR					% of GDP				
	1990	2000	2010	2019	2020	1990	2000	2010	2019	2020
Total tax revenue	**12.3**	**33.4**	**46.4**	**78.0**	**74.0**	**32.4**	**30.8**	**27.7**	**21.9**	**19.9**
1000 Taxes on income, profits and capital gains	**4.7**	**14.6**	**18.6**	**35.6**	**36.3**	**12.3**	**13.4**	**11.1**	**10.0**	**9.7**
1100 Of individuals	4.1	10.6	14.7	24.7	24.4	10.7	9.8	8.8	6.9	6.5
1200 Corporate	0.6	3.9	3.9	10.9	12.0	1.6	3.6	2.4	3.1	3.2
1300 Unallocable between 1100 and 1200	0.0	0.0	0.0	0.0	0.0	0.0	0.0	0.0	0.0	0.0
2000 Social security contributions	**1.7**	**4.0**	**8.5**	**13.1**	**12.3**	**4.6**	**3.7**	**5.1**	**3.7**	**3.3**
2100 Employees	0.6	1.0	3.2	4.0	3.8	1.5	0.9	1.9	1.1	1.0
2200 Employers	1.1	2.8	4.9	8.5	7.9	2.9	2.6	2.9	2.4	2.1
2300 Self-employed or non-employed	0.1	0.2	0.3	0.6	0.6	0.2	0.2	0.2	0.2	0.2
2400 Unallocable between 2100, 2200 and 2300	0.0	0.0	0.0	0.0	0.0	0.0	0.0	0.0	0.0	0.0
3000 Taxes on payroll and workforce	**0.2**	**0.0**	**0.3**	**0.8**	**0.7**	**0.4**	**0.0**	**0.2**	**0.2**	**0.2**
4000 Taxes on property	**0.6**	**1.9**	**2.4**	**4.4**	**3.7**	**1.5**	**1.8**	**1.4**	**1.2**	**1.0**
4100 Recurrent taxes on immovable property	0.3	0.6	1.3	1.9	1.2	0.8	0.5	0.8	0.5	0.3
4200 Recurrent taxes on net wealth	0.0	0.0	0.0	0.0	0.0	0.0	0.0	0.0	0.0	0.0
4300 Estate, inheritance and gift taxes	0.0	0.2	0.2	0.5	0.5	0.1	0.2	0.1	0.1	0.1
4400 Taxes on financial and capital transactions	0.2	1.1	0.8	2.0	2.0	0.6	1.0	0.5	0.6	0.5
4500 Non-recurrent taxes	0.0	0.0	0.0	0.0	0.0	0.0	0.0	0.0	0.0	0.0
4600 Other recurrent taxes on property	0.0	0.0	0.0	0.0	0.0	0.0	0.0	0.0	0.0	0.0
5000 Taxes on goods and services	**5.1**	**12.9**	**16.6**	**24.1**	**21.0**	**13.6**	**11.9**	**9.9**	**6.8**	**5.6**
5100 Taxes on production, sale, transfer, etc	4.9	12.4	15.3	22.3	19.2	13.0	11.4	9.2	6.2	5.1
5110 General taxes	2.5	7.6	10.1	15.3	12.8	6.6	7.0	6.0	4.3	3.4
5111 Value added taxes	2.5	7.6	10.1	15.3	12.8	6.6	7.0	6.0	4.3	3.4
5120 Taxes on specific goods and services	2.4	4.7	5.3	7.0	6.4	6.4	4.4	3.1	2.0	1.7
5121 Excises	2.1	4.4	4.9	6.0	5.5	5.5	4.1	2.9	1.7	1.5
5200 Taxes on use of goods and perform activities	0.2	0.6	1.3	1.8	1.8	0.5	0.5	0.8	0.5	0.5
5300 Unallocable between 5100 and 5200	0.0	0.0	0.0	0.0	0.0	0.0	0.0	0.0	0.0	0.0
6000 Other taxes	**0.0**	**0.0**	**0.0**	**0.0**	**0.0**	**0.0**	**0.0**	**0.0**	**0.0**	**0.0**
Non-wastable tax credits										
Non-wastable tax credits against 1000	..	..	1.1	0.4	0.4	..	..	0.6	0.1	0.1
Transfer component	..	..	0.0	0.0	0.0	..	..	0.0	0.0	0.0
Tax expenditure component	..	..	1.1	0.4	0.4	..	..	0.6	0.1	0.1
Revenues collected on behalf of the EU										
Revenues collected on behalf of the EU, total	0.2	0.2	0.2	0.5	0.4	0.5	0.2	0.1	0.1	0.1
Customs duties	0.1	0.2	0.2	0.3	0.3	0.4	0.2	0.1	0.1	0.1
SRF contributions	..	..	..	0.1	0.1	..	..	..	0.0	0.0

.. Not available

Note: More detailed country data and country notes are available in Chapter 5 "Detailed country tables". Full time series can be accessed at http://oe.cd/full-time-series.

Source: Annual Report of the Revenue Commissioners, Financial Accounts and National Income and Expenditure Accounts.

StatLink https://stat.link/4av3mq

Table 4.34. Ireland, tax revenue and % of GDP by level of government and main taxes

	Billion EUR					% of GDP				
	1990	2000	2010	2019	2020	1990	2000	2010	2019	2020
Federal or Central government										
Total tax revenue	**10.1**	**28.7**	**37.9**	**64.3**	**62.0**	**26.7**	**26.5**	**22.7**	**18.0**	**16.6**
1000 Taxes on income, profits and capital gains	4.7	14.6	18.6	35.6	36.3	12.3	13.4	11.1	10.0	9.7
2000 Social security contributions	0.1	0.1	1.5	1.4	1.4	0.2	0.1	0.9	0.4	0.4
3000 Taxes on payroll and workforce	0.2	0.0	0.3	0.8	0.7	0.4	0.0	0.2	0.2	0.2
4000 Taxes on property	0.3	1.3	1.1	3.0	3.0	0.7	1.2	0.6	0.8	0.8
5000 Taxes on goods and services	5.0	12.7	16.4	23.6	20.6	13.1	11.7	9.8	6.6	5.5
6000 Other taxes	0.0	0.0	0.0	0.0	0.0	0.0	0.0	0.0	0.0	0.0
State/Regional										
Total tax revenue	..	..	..	..	..	..	..	..	..	..
1000 Taxes on income, profits and capital gains	..	..	..	..	..	..	..	..	..	..
2000 Social security contributions	..	..	..	..	..	..	..	..	..	..
3000 Taxes on payroll and workforce	..	..	..	..	..	..	..	..	..	..
4000 Taxes on property	..	..	..	..	..	..	..	..	..	..
5000 Taxes on goods and services	..	..	..	..	..	..	..	..	..	..
6000 Other taxes	..	..	..	..	..	..	..	..	..	..
Local government										
Total tax revenue	**0.3**	**0.7**	**1.5**	**1.5**	**0.8**	**0.9**	**0.6**	**0.9**	**0.4**	**0.2**
1000 Taxes on income, profits and capital gains	0.0	0.0	0.0	0.0	0.0	0.0	0.0	0.0	0.0	0.0
2000 Social security contributions	0.0	0.1	0.2	0.1	0.1	0.1	0.1	0.1	0.0	0.0
3000 Taxes on payroll and workforce	0.0	0.0	0.0	0.0	0.0	0.0	0.0	0.0	0.0	0.0
4000 Taxes on property	0.3	0.6	1.3	1.5	0.7	0.8	0.5	0.8	0.4	0.2
5000 Taxes on goods and services	0.0	0.0	0.0	0.0	0.0	0.0	0.0	0.0	0.0	0.0
6000 Other taxes	0.0	0.0	0.0	0.0	0.0	0.0	0.0	0.0	0.0	0.0
Social Security Funds										
Total tax revenue	**1.6**	**3.8**	**6.7**	**11.7**	**10.8**	**4.3**	**3.5**	**4.0**	**3.3**	**2.9**
1000 Taxes on income, profits and capital gains	0.0	0.0	0.0	0.0	0.0	0.0	0.0	0.0	0.0	0.0
2000 Social security contributions	1.6	3.8	6.7	11.7	10.8	4.3	3.5	4.0	3.3	2.9
3000 Taxes on payroll and workforce	0.0	0.0	0.0	0.0	0.0	0.0	0.0	0.0	0.0	0.0
4000 Taxes on property	0.0	0.0	0.0	0.0	0.0	0.0	0.0	0.0	0.0	0.0
5000 Taxes on goods and services	0.0	0.0	0.0	0.0	0.0	0.0	0.0	0.0	0.0	0.0
6000 Other taxes	0.0	0.0	0.0	0.0	0.0	0.0	0.0	0.0	0.0	0.0

.. Not available

Note: More detailed country data and country notes are available in Chapter 6 "Tax revenues by sub-sectors of general government". Full time series can be accessed at http://oe.cd/full-time-series.

Source: Annual Report of the Revenue Commissioners, Financial Accounts and National Income and Expenditure Accounts.

StatLink https://stat.link/xa5gz2

Table 4.35. Israel, tax revenue and % of GDP by selected tax category

	Billion ILS					% of GDP				
	1990	2000	2010	2019	2020	1990	2000	2010	2019	2020
Total tax revenue	..	**189.3**	**269.7**	**430.5**	**420.6**	..	**34.1**	**30.3**	**30.0**	**29.6**
1000 Taxes on income, profits and capital gains	..	**74.6**	**78.3**	**140.5**	**139.3**	..	**13.4**	**8.8**	**9.8**	**9.8**
1100 Of individuals	..	54.8	48.2	89.5	91.9	..	9.9	5.4	6.2	6.5
1200 Corporate	..	18.0	23.1	43.3	38.8	..	3.2	2.6	3.0	2.7
1300 Unallocable between 1100 and 1200	..	1.8	6.9	7.7	8.6	..	0.3	0.8	0.5	0.6
2000 Social security contributions	..	**27.6**	**45.3**	**74.4**	**73.0**	..	**5.0**	**5.1**	**5.2**	**5.1**
2100 Employees	..	15.8	27.8	41.9	40.8	..	2.8	3.1	2.9	2.9
2200 Employers	..	8.2	11.4	23.1	22.6	..	1.5	1.3	1.6	1.6
2300 Self-employed or non-employed	..	3.6	6.1	9.5	9.7	..	0.7	0.7	0.7	0.7
2400 Unallocable between 2100, 2200 and 2300	..	0.0	0.0	0.0	0.0	..	0.0	0.0	0.0	0.0
3000 Taxes on payroll and workforce	..	**6.8**	**10.3**	**16.2**	**16.2**	..	**1.2**	**1.2**	**1.1**	**1.1**
4000 Taxes on property	..	**18.0**	**30.0**	**45.8**	**43.4**	..	**3.2**	**3.4**	**3.2**	**3.1**
4100 Recurrent taxes on immovable property	..	11.3	18.8	27.1	25.0	..	2.0	2.1	1.9	1.8
4200 Recurrent taxes on net wealth	..	0.0	0.0	0.0	0.0	..	0.0	0.0	0.0	0.0
4300 Estate, inheritance and gift taxes	..	0.0	0.0	0.0	0.0	..	0.0	0.0	0.0	0.0
4400 Taxes on financial and capital transactions	..	3.2	4.1	6.9	6.9	..	0.6	0.5	0.5	0.5
4500 Non-recurrent taxes	..	3.5	7.2	11.8	11.5	..	0.6	0.8	0.8	0.8
4600 Other recurrent taxes on property	..	0.0	0.0	0.0	0.0	..	0.0	0.0	0.0	0.0
5000 Taxes on goods and services	..	**62.3**	**105.8**	**153.6**	**148.6**	..	**11.2**	**11.9**	**10.7**	**10.4**
5100 Taxes on production, sale, transfer, etc	..	57.9	98.1	143.1	138.7	..	10.4	11.0	10.0	9.8
5110 General taxes	..	49.9	79.9	120.5	118.9	..	9.0	9.0	8.4	8.4
5111 Value added taxes	..	39.8	65.5	102.5	100.4	..	7.2	7.4	7.1	7.1
5120 Taxes on specific goods and services	..	8.0	18.1	22.5	19.9	..	1.4	2.0	1.6	1.4
5121 Excises	..	6.6	15.5	19.5	17.0	..	1.2	1.7	1.4	1.2
5200 Taxes on use of goods and perform activities	..	4.5	7.7	10.6	9.9	..	0.8	0.9	0.7	0.7
5300 Unallocable between 5100 and 5200	..	0.0	0.0	0.0	0.0	..	0.0	0.0	0.0	0.0
6000 Other taxes	..	**0.0**	**0.0**	**0.0**	**0.0**	..	**0.0**	**0.0**	**0.0**	**0.0**
Non-wastable tax credits										
Non-wastable tax credits against 1000	..	..	0.1	1.3	1.3	..	..	0.0	0.1	0.1
Transfer component	..	..	0.0	0.0	0.0	..	..	0.0	0.0	0.0
Tax expenditure component	..	..	0.1	1.3	1.3	..	..	0.0	0.1	0.1

.. Not available

Note: More detailed country data and country notes are available in Chapter 5 "Detailed country tables". Full time series can be accessed at http://oe.cd/full-time-series.

Source: Israel Central Bureau of Statistics and Israel Ministry of Finance.

StatLink https://stat.link/2w8vci

Table 4.36. Israel, tax revenue and % of GDP by level of government and main taxes

	Billion ILS					% of GDP				
	1990	2000	2010	2019	2020	1990	2000	2010	2019	2020
Federal or Central government										
Total tax revenue	..	**148.0**	**199.9**	**320.2**	**314.2**	..	**26.7**	**22.4**	**22.3**	**22.1**
1000 Taxes on income, profits and capital gains	..	74.6	78.3	140.5	139.3	..	13.4	8.8	9.8	9.8
2000 Social security contributions	..	0.0	0.0	0.0	0.0	..	0.0	0.0	0.0	0.0
3000 Taxes on payroll and workforce	..	6.8	10.3	16.2	16.2	..	1.2	1.2	1.1	1.1
4000 Taxes on property	..	4.8	6.6	11.4	11.4	..	0.9	0.7	0.8	0.8
5000 Taxes on goods and services	..	61.8	104.7	152.1	147.2	..	11.1	11.8	10.6	10.3
6000 Other taxes	..	0.0	0.0	0.0	0.0	..	0.0	0.0	0.0	0.0
State/Regional										
Total tax revenue	..	..	..	..	..	..	..	..	..	..
1000 Taxes on income, profits and capital gains	..	..	..	..	..	..	..	..	..	..
2000 Social security contributions	..	..	..	..	..	..	..	..	..	..
3000 Taxes on payroll and workforce	..	..	..	..	..	..	..	..	..	..
4000 Taxes on property	..	..	..	..	..	..	..	..	..	..
5000 Taxes on goods and services	..	..	..	..	..	..	..	..	..	..
6000 Other taxes	..	..	..	..	..	..	..	..	..	..
Local government										
Total tax revenue	..	**13.7**	**24.5**	**35.9**	**33.4**	..	**2.5**	**2.7**	**2.5**	**2.3**
1000 Taxes on income, profits and capital gains	..	0.0	0.0	0.0	0.0	..	0.0	0.0	0.0	0.0
2000 Social security contributions	..	0.0	0.0	0.0	0.0	..	0.0	0.0	0.0	0.0
3000 Taxes on payroll and workforce	..	0.0	0.0	0.0	0.0	..	0.0	0.0	0.0	0.0
4000 Taxes on property	..	13.2	23.5	34.4	32.0	..	2.4	2.6	2.4	2.2
5000 Taxes on goods and services	..	0.6	1.0	1.5	1.4	..	0.1	0.1	0.1	0.1
6000 Other taxes	..	0.0	0.0	0.0	0.0	..	0.0	0.0	0.0	0.0
Social Security Funds										
Total tax revenue	..	**27.6**	**45.3**	**74.4**	**73.0**	..	**5.0**	**5.1**	**5.2**	**5.1**
1000 Taxes on income, profits and capital gains	..	0.0	0.0	0.0	0.0	..	0.0	0.0	0.0	0.0
2000 Social security contributions	..	27.6	45.3	74.4	73.0	..	5.0	5.1	5.2	5.1
3000 Taxes on payroll and workforce	..	0.0	0.0	0.0	0.0	..	0.0	0.0	0.0	0.0
4000 Taxes on property	..	0.0	0.0	0.0	0.0	..	0.0	0.0	0.0	0.0
5000 Taxes on goods and services	..	0.0	0.0	0.0	0.0	..	0.0	0.0	0.0	0.0
6000 Other taxes	..	0.0	0.0	0.0	0.0	..	0.0	0.0	0.0	0.0

.. Not available

Note: More detailed country data and country notes are available in Chapter 6 "Tax revenues by sub-sectors of general government". Full time series can be accessed at http://oe.cd/full-time-series.

Source: Israel Central Bureau of Statistics and Israel Ministry of Finance.

StatLink https://stat.link/rlhft7

Table 4.37. Italy, tax revenue and % of GDP by selected tax category

	Billion EUR					% of GDP				
	1990	2000	2010	2019	2020	1990	2000	2010	2019	2020
Total tax revenue	**265.1**	**503.1**	**671.9**	**759.4**	**706.7**	**36.3**	**40.5**	**41.7**	**42.3**	**42.7**
1000 Taxes on income, profits and capital gains	**96.7**	**166.9**	**219.5**	**239.9**	**231.9**	**13.2**	**13.4**	**13.6**	**13.4**	**14.0**
1100 Of individuals	69.7	124.9	180.5	196.3	189.2	9.5	10.1	11.2	10.9	11.4
1200 Corporate	26.6	34.7	36.7	35.2	34.2	3.6	2.8	2.3	2.0	2.1
1300 Unallocable between 1100 and 1200	0.4	7.3	2.3	8.4	8.5	0.1	0.6	0.1	0.5	0.5
2000 Social security contributions	**87.3**	**143.6**	**209.1**	**237.3**	**224.8**	**11.9**	**11.6**	**13.0**	**13.2**	**13.6**
2100 Employees	16.8	27.3	37.6	44.5	41.4	2.3	2.2	2.3	2.5	2.5
2200 Employers	62.5	99.9	144.3	158.6	149.8	8.6	8.0	9.0	8.8	9.0
2300 Self-employed or non-employed	8.0	16.4	27.2	34.2	33.6	1.1	1.3	1.7	1.9	2.0
2400 Unallocable between 2100, 2200 and 2300	0.0	0.0	0.0	0.0	0.0	0.0	0.0	0.0	0.0	0.0
3000 Taxes on payroll and workforce	**0.9**	**0.0**	**0.0**	**0.0**	**0.0**	**0.1**	**0.0**	**0.0**	**0.0**	**0.0**
4000 Taxes on property	**6.0**	**23.4**	**32.4**	**43.2**	**40.4**	**0.8**	**1.9**	**2.0**	**2.4**	**2.4**
4100 Recurrent taxes on immovable property	0.0	9.4	9.7	22.0	21.3	0.0	0.8	0.6	1.2	1.3
4200 Recurrent taxes on net wealth	0.0	0.0	2.1	0.2	0.4	0.0	0.0	0.1	0.0	0.0
4300 Estate, inheritance and gift taxes	0.4	1.0	0.5	0.8	0.4	0.1	0.1	0.0	0.0	0.0
4400 Taxes on financial and capital transactions	5.6	12.3	17.4	18.8	17.3	0.8	1.0	1.1	1.0	1.0
4500 Non-recurrent taxes	0.0	0.1	0.9	0.2	0.1	0.0	0.0	0.1	0.0	0.0
4600 Other recurrent taxes on property	0.0	0.6	1.9	1.2	1.0	0.0	0.0	0.1	0.1	0.1
5000 Taxes on goods and services	**74.3**	**141.9**	**178.9**	**214.8**	**190.2**	**10.2**	**11.4**	**11.1**	**12.0**	**11.5**
5100 Taxes on production, sale, transfer, etc	67.1	127.3	160.8	187.7	164.8	9.2	10.3	10.0	10.4	9.9
5110 General taxes	38.9	77.5	97.6	111.5	99.9	5.3	6.2	6.1	6.2	6.0
5111 Value added taxes	38.9	77.5	97.6	111.5	99.7	5.3	6.2	6.1	6.2	6.0
5120 Taxes on specific goods and services	28.0	49.8	63.2	76.2	64.9	3.8	4.0	3.9	4.2	3.9
5121 Excises	20.3	31.5	36.4	47.1	40.1	2.8	2.5	2.3	2.6	2.4
5200 Taxes on use of goods and perform activities	4.5	8.5	10.5	14.0	12.8	0.6	0.7	0.7	0.8	0.8
5300 Unallocable between 5100 and 5200	2.7	6.1	7.6	13.1	12.7	0.4	0.5	0.5	0.7	0.8
6000 Other taxes	**0.0**	**27.3**	**31.9**	**24.3**	**19.4**	**0.0**	**2.2**	**2.0**	**1.4**	**1.2**
Non-wastable tax credits										
Non-wastable tax credits against 1000	..	..	0.0	10.4	12.1	..	..	0.0	0.6	0.7
Transfer component	..	..	0.1	1.5	1.8	..	..	0.0	0.1	0.1
Tax expenditure component	..	..	-0.1	8.9	10.4	..	..	0.0	0.5	0.6
Revenues collected on behalf of the EU										
Revenues collected on behalf of the EU, total	1.3	1.5	2.2	3.2	3.0	0.2	0.1	0.1	0.2	0.2
Customs duties	0.8	1.5	2.2	2.3	2.0	0.1	0.1	0.1	0.1	0.1
SRF contributions	..	..	..	0.8	1.0	..	..	..	0.0	0.1

.. Not available

Note: More detailed country data and country notes are available in Chapter 5 "Detailed country tables". Full time series can be accessed at http://oe.cd/full-time-series.

Source: *Ministero dell'economia e delle finanze; Istituto nazionale di statistica.*

StatLink https://stat.link/kyaep3

Table 4.38. Italy, tax revenue and % of GDP by level of government and main taxes

	Billion EUR					% of GDP				
	1990	2000	2010	2019	2020	1990	2000	2010	2019	2020
Federal or Central government										
Total tax revenue	**168.9**	**280.8**	**357.3**	**432.6**	**400.9**	**23.1**	**22.6**	**22.2**	**24.1**	**24.2**
1000 Taxes on income, profits and capital gains	92.7	154.2	193.9	223.0	215.3	12.7	12.4	12.0	12.4	13.0
2000 Social security contributions	0.0	0.0	0.0	0.0	0.0	0.0	0.0	0.0	0.0	0.0
3000 Taxes on payroll and workforce	0.9	0.0	0.0	0.0	0.0	0.1	0.0	0.0	0.0	0.0
4000 Taxes on property	6.0	12.9	21.0	24.5	22.5	0.8	1.0	1.3	1.4	1.4
5000 Taxes on goods and services	69.3	113.6	142.5	185.1	163.2	9.5	9.2	8.8	10.3	9.8
6000 Other taxes	0.0	0.0	0.0	0.0	0.0	0.0	0.0	0.0	0.0	0.0
State/Regional										
Total tax revenue	**..**	**..**	**..**	**..**	**..**	**..**	**..**	**..**	**..**	**..**
1000 Taxes on income, profits and capital gains	..	..	..	..	..	..	..	..	..	..
2000 Social security contributions	..	..	..	..	..	..	..	..	..	..
3000 Taxes on payroll and workforce	..	..	..	..	..	..	..	..	..	..
4000 Taxes on property	..	..	..	..	..	..	..	..	..	..
5000 Taxes on goods and services	..	..	..	..	..	..	..	..	..	..
6000 Other taxes	..	..	..	..	..	..	..	..	..	..
Local government										
Total tax revenue	**7.7**	**77.2**	**103.2**	**86.4**	**78.1**	**1.1**	**6.2**	**6.4**	**4.8**	**4.7**
1000 Taxes on income, profits and capital gains	4.0	12.7	25.6	16.8	16.5	0.6	1.0	1.6	0.9	1.0
2000 Social security contributions	0.0	0.0	0.0	0.0	0.0	0.0	0.0	0.0	0.0	0.0
3000 Taxes on payroll and workforce	0.0	0.0	0.0	0.0	0.0	0.0	0.0	0.0	0.0	0.0
4000 Taxes on property	0.0	10.5	11.5	18.7	18.0	0.0	0.8	0.7	1.0	1.1
5000 Taxes on goods and services	3.7	26.7	34.2	26.5	24.1	0.5	2.1	2.1	1.5	1.5
6000 Other taxes	0.0	27.3	31.9	24.3	19.4	0.0	2.2	2.0	1.4	1.2
Social Security Funds										
Total tax revenue	**87.3**	**143.6**	**209.1**	**237.3**	**224.8**	**11.9**	**11.6**	**13.0**	**13.2**	**13.6**
1000 Taxes on income, profits and capital gains	0.0	0.0	0.0	0.0	0.0	0.0	0.0	0.0	0.0	0.0
2000 Social security contributions	87.3	143.6	209.1	237.3	224.8	11.9	11.6	13.0	13.2	13.6
3000 Taxes on payroll and workforce	0.0	0.0	0.0	0.0	0.0	0.0	0.0	0.0	0.0	0.0
4000 Taxes on property	0.0	0.0	0.0	0.0	0.0	0.0	0.0	0.0	0.0	0.0
5000 Taxes on goods and services	0.0	0.0	0.0	0.0	0.0	0.0	0.0	0.0	0.0	0.0
6000 Other taxes	0.0	0.0	0.0	0.0	0.0	0.0	0.0	0.0	0.0	0.0

.. Not available

Note: More detailed country data and country notes are available in Chapter 6 "Tax revenues by sub-sectors of general government". Full time series can be accessed at http://oe.cd/full-time-series.

Source: *Ministero dell'economia e delle finanze; Istituto nazionale di statistica*.

StatLink https://stat.link/8zfm04

Table 4.39. Japan, tax revenue and % of GDP by selected tax category

	Billion JPY					% of GDP				
	1990	2000	2010	2019	2020	1990	2000	2010	2019	2020
Total tax revenue	**130 842.7**	**136 235.8**	**132 484.3**	**175 379.7**	**177 308.3**	**27.7**	**25.3**	**26.2**	**31.5**	**33.2**
1000 Taxes on income, profits and capital gains	**65 681.6**	**47 398.2**	**40 034.3**	**53 993.6**	**53 933.8**	**13.9**	**8.8**	**7.9**	**9.7**	**10.1**
1100 Of individuals	36 393.6	28 677.3	24 662.7	32 947.2	33 188.6	7.7	5.3	4.9	5.9	6.2
1200 Corporate	29 288.0	18 720.9	15 371.6	21 046.4	20 745.2	6.2	3.5	3.0	3.8	3.9
1300 Unallocable between 1100 and 1200	0.0	0.0	0.0	0.0	0.0	0.0	0.0	0.0	0.0	0.0
2000 Social security contributions	**34 612.6**	**47 968.3**	**54 460.6**	**71 993.4**	**71 549.5**	**7.3**	**8.9**	**10.8**	**12.9**	**13.4**
2100 Employees	13 895.0	19 829.9	23 592.6	31 954.0	31 839.3	2.9	3.7	4.7	5.7	6.0
2200 Employers	16 648.8	22 455.5	24 674.2	33 487.9	33 244.8	3.5	4.2	4.9	6.0	6.2
2300 Self-employed or non-employed	4 068.8	5 682.9	6 193.8	6 551.5	6 465.4	0.9	1.1	1.2	1.2	1.2
2400 Unallocable between 2100, 2200 and 2300	0.0	0.0	0.0	0.0	0.0	0.0	0.0	0.0	0.0	0.0
3000 Taxes on payroll and workforce	**0.0**	**0.0**	**0.0**	**0.0**	**0.0**	**0.0**	**0.0**	**0.0**	**0.0**	**0.0**
4000 Taxes on property	**12 296.3**	**14 294.4**	**12 878.3**	**14 339.8**	**14 327.5**	**2.6**	**2.7**	**2.6**	**2.6**	**2.7**
4100 Recurrent taxes on immovable property	7 098.5	10 413.7	10 225.0	10 611.9	10 719.2	1.5	1.9	2.0	1.9	2.0
4200 Recurrent taxes on net wealth	0.0	0.0	0.0	0.0	0.0	0.0	0.0	0.0	0.0	0.0
4300 Estate, inheritance and gift taxes	1 918.0	1 782.2	1 250.4	2 300.5	2 314.5	0.4	0.3	0.2	0.4	0.4
4400 Taxes on financial and capital transactions	3 279.8	2 098.5	1 402.9	1 427.4	1 293.8	0.7	0.4	0.3	0.3	0.2
4500 Non-recurrent taxes	0.0	0.0	0.0	0.0	0.0	0.0	0.0	0.0	0.0	0.0
4600 Other recurrent taxes on property	0.0	0.0	0.0	0.0	0.0	0.0	0.0	0.0	0.0	0.0
5000 Taxes on goods and services	**17 916.8**	**26 227.2**	**24 730.2**	**34 598.6**	**37 053.1**	**3.8**	**4.9**	**4.9**	**6.2**	**6.9**
5100 Taxes on production, sale, transfer, etc	15 646.5	23 180.2	22 160.4	32 045.9	34 433.1	3.3	4.3	4.4	5.8	6.4
5110 General taxes	5 778.3	12 350.3	12 675.2	23 148.2	26 395.2	1.2	2.3	2.5	4.2	4.9
5111 Value added taxes	5 778.3	12 350.3	12 675.2	23 148.2	26 395.2	1.2	2.3	2.5	4.2	4.9
5120 Taxes on specific goods and services	9 868.2	10 829.9	9 485.2	8 897.7	8 037.9	2.1	2.0	1.9	1.6	1.5
5121 Excises	8 637.2	9 837.0	8 622.4	7 890.9	7 166.6	1.8	1.8	1.7	1.4	1.3
5200 Taxes on use of goods and perform activities	2 270.3	3 047.0	2 569.8	2 552.7	2 620.0	0.5	0.6	0.5	0.5	0.5
5300 Unallocable between 5100 and 5200	0.0	0.0	0.0	0.0	0.0	0.0	0.0	0.0	0.0	0.0
6000 Other taxes	**335.4**	**347.7**	**381.1**	**454.3**	**444.4**	**0.1**	**0.1**	**0.1**	**0.1**	**0.1**
Non-wastable tax credits										
Non-wastable tax credits against 1000	..	..	..	..	..	..	..	..	..	..
Transfer component	..	..	..	..	..	..	..	..	..	..
Tax expenditure component	..	..	..	..	..	..	..	..	..	..

.. Not available
Note: More detailed country data and country notes are available in Chapter 5 "Detailed country tables". Full time series can be accessed at http://oe.cd/full-time-series.
Source: Tax Bureau, Ministry of Finance.

StatLink https://stat.link/y0ax8u

Table 4.40. Japan, tax revenue and % of GDP by level of government and main taxes

	Billion JPY					% of GDP				
	1990	2000	2010	2019	2020	1990	2000	2010	2019	2020
Federal or Central government										
Total tax revenue	**62 779.7**	**52 720.8**	**43 707.4**	**62 175.1**	**64 933.1**	**13.3**	**9.8**	**8.7**	**11.2**	**12.1**
1000 Taxes on income, profits and capital gains	44 379.1	30 536.2	23 372.1	33 015.7	33 893.7	9.4	5.7	4.6	5.9	6.3
2000 Social security contributions	0.0	0.0	0.0	0.0	0.0	0.0	0.0	0.0	0.0	0.0
3000 Taxes on payroll and workforce	0.0	0.0	0.0	0.0	0.0	0.0	0.0	0.0	0.0	0.0
4000 Taxes on property	4 601.6	3 314.9	2 274.5	3 323.7	3 234.0	1.0	0.6	0.5	0.6	0.6
5000 Taxes on goods and services	13 799.0	18 869.7	18 060.9	25 835.1	27 805.2	2.9	3.5	3.6	4.6	5.2
6000 Other taxes	0.0	0.0	0.0	0.6	0.2	0.0	0.0	0.0	0.0	0.0
State/Regional										
Total tax revenue	**..**	**..**	**..**	**..**	**..**	**..**	**..**	**..**	**..**	**..**
1000 Taxes on income, profits and capital gains	..	..	..	..	..	..	..	..	..	..
2000 Social security contributions	..	..	..	..	..	..	..	..	..	..
3000 Taxes on payroll and workforce	..	..	..	..	..	..	..	..	..	..
4000 Taxes on property	..	..	..	..	..	..	..	..	..	..
5000 Taxes on goods and services	..	..	..	..	..	..	..	..	..	..
6000 Other taxes	..	..	..	..	..	..	..	..	..	..
Local government										
Total tax revenue	**33 450.4**	**35 546.7**	**34 316.3**	**41 211.2**	**40 825.7**	**7.1**	**6.6**	**6.8**	**7.4**	**7.6**
1000 Taxes on income, profits and capital gains	21 302.5	16 862.0	16 662.2	20 977.9	20 040.1	4.5	3.1	3.3	3.8	3.7
2000 Social security contributions	0.0	0.0	0.0	0.0	0.0	0.0	0.0	0.0	0.0	0.0
3000 Taxes on payroll and workforce	0.0	0.0	0.0	0.0	0.0	0.0	0.0	0.0	0.0	0.0
4000 Taxes on property	7 694.7	10 979.5	10 603.8	11 016.1	11 093.5	1.6	2.0	2.1	2.0	2.1
5000 Taxes on goods and services	4 117.8	7 357.5	6 669.3	8 763.5	9 247.9	0.9	1.4	1.3	1.6	1.7
6000 Other taxes	335.4	347.7	381.1	453.7	444.2	0.1	0.1	0.1	0.1	0.1
Social Security Funds										
Total tax revenue	**34 612.6**	**47 968.3**	**54 460.6**	**71 993.4**	**71 549.5**	**7.3**	**8.9**	**10.8**	**12.9**	**13.4**
1000 Taxes on income, profits and capital gains	0.0	0.0	0.0	0.0	0.0	0.0	0.0	0.0	0.0	0.0
2000 Social security contributions	34 612.6	47 968.3	54 460.6	71 993.4	71 549.5	7.3	8.9	10.8	12.9	13.4
3000 Taxes on payroll and workforce	0.0	0.0	0.0	0.0	0.0	0.0	0.0	0.0	0.0	0.0
4000 Taxes on property	0.0	0.0	0.0	0.0	0.0	0.0	0.0	0.0	0.0	0.0
5000 Taxes on goods and services	0.0	0.0	0.0	0.0	0.0	0.0	0.0	0.0	0.0	0.0
6000 Other taxes	0.0	0.0	0.0	0.0	0.0	0.0	0.0	0.0	0.0	0.0

.. Not available

Note: More detailed country data and country notes are available in Chapter 6 "Tax revenues by sub-sectors of general government". Full time series can be accessed at http://oe.cd/full-time-series.

Source: Tax Bureau, Ministry of Finance.

StatLink https://stat.link/jnbyot

Table 4.41. Korea, tax revenue and % of GDP by selected tax category

	Billion KRW					% of GDP				
	1990	2000	2010	2019	2020	1990	2000	2010	2019	2020
Total tax revenue	**37 261.7**	**136 295.0**	**295 968.0**	**523 985.0**	**538 450.0**	**18.6**	**20.9**	**22.4**	**27.2**	**27.7**
1000 Taxes on income, profits and capital gains	**12 203.5**	**39 254.0**	**82 905.0**	**174 040.0**	**166 564.0**	**6.1**	**6.0**	**6.3**	**9.0**	**8.6**
1100 Of individuals	7 440.4	19 950.0	42 098.0	91 714.0	101 286.0	3.7	3.1	3.2	4.8	5.2
1200 Corporate	4 756.6	19 271.0	40 807.0	82 326.0	65 278.0	2.4	3.0	3.1	4.3	3.4
1300 Unallocable between 1100 and 1200	6.5	33.0	0.0	0.0	0.0	0.0	0.0	0.0	0.0	0.0
2000 Social security contributions	**3 760.0**	**22 759.0**	**69 090.0**	**140 071.0**	**150 854.0**	**1.9**	**3.5**	**5.2**	**7.3**	**7.8**
2100 Employees	1 464.0	8 578.0	28 213.0	60 682.0	65 384.0	0.7	1.3	2.1	3.2	3.4
2200 Employers	1 694.0	9 409.0	30 856.0	63 780.0	67 676.0	0.8	1.4	2.3	3.3	3.5
2300 Self-employed or non-employed	602.0	4 772.0	10 021.0	15 609.0	17 794.0	0.3	0.7	0.8	0.8	0.9
2400 Unallocable between 2100, 2200 and 2300	0.0	0.0	0.0	0.0	0.0	0.0	0.0	0.0	0.0	0.0
3000 Taxes on payroll and workforce	**152.8**	**258.0**	**714.0**	**1 597.0**	**1 607.0**	**0.1**	**0.0**	**0.1**	**0.1**	**0.1**
4000 Taxes on property	**4 388.9**	**16 846.0**	**33 516.0**	**59 732.0**	**76 512.0**	**2.2**	**2.6**	**2.5**	**3.1**	**3.9**
4100 Recurrent taxes on immovable property	980.0	3 385.0	9 270.0	17 750.0	20 044.0	0.5	0.5	0.7	0.9	1.0
4200 Recurrent taxes on net wealth	0.0	0.0	0.0	0.0	0.0	0.0	0.0	0.0	0.0	0.0
4300 Estate, inheritance and gift taxes	353.9	989.0	3 076.0	8 329.0	10 375.0	0.2	0.2	0.2	0.4	0.5
4400 Taxes on financial and capital transactions	2 959.7	11 935.0	21 170.0	33 653.0	46 093.0	1.5	1.8	1.6	1.7	2.4
4500 Non-recurrent taxes	95.3	537.0	0.0	0.0	0.0	0.0	0.1	0.0	0.0	0.0
4600 Other recurrent taxes on property	0.0	0.0	0.0	0.0	0.0	0.0	0.0	0.0	0.0	0.0
5000 Taxes on goods and services	**16 497.5**	**52 271.0**	**99 769.0**	**135 276.0**	**131 353.0**	**8.2**	**8.0**	**7.5**	**7.0**	**6.8**
5100 Taxes on production, sale, transfer, etc	16 023.5	50 023.0	96 573.0	127 551.0	123 219.0	8.0	7.7	7.3	6.6	6.3
5110 General taxes	6 964.4	23 212.0	51 800.0	82 174.0	81 452.0	3.5	3.6	3.9	4.3	4.2
5111 Value added taxes	6 964.4	23 212.0	51 800.0	82 174.0	81 452.0	3.5	3.6	3.9	4.3	4.2
5120 Taxes on specific goods and services	9 059.1	26 811.0	44 773.0	45 377.0	41 767.0	4.5	4.1	3.4	2.4	2.2
5121 Excises	4 923.7	18 155.0	31 340.0	34 691.0	33 013.0	2.5	2.8	2.4	1.8	1.7
5200 Taxes on use of goods and perform activities	473.9	2 248.0	3 196.0	7 725.0	8 134.0	0.2	0.3	0.2	0.4	0.4
5300 Unallocable between 5100 and 5200	0.0	0.0	0.0	0.0	0.0	0.0	0.0	0.0	0.0	0.0
6000 Other taxes	**259.1**	**4 907.0**	**9 974.0**	**13 269.0**	**11 560.0**	**0.1**	**0.8**	**0.8**	**0.7**	**0.6**
Non-wastable tax credits										
Non-wastable tax credits against 1000	..	..	..	..	..	..	..	..	..	..
Transfer component	..	..	..	..	..	..	..	..	..	..
Tax expenditure component	..	..	..	..	..	..	..	..	..	..

.. Not available

Note: More detailed country data and country notes are available in Chapter 5 "Detailed country tables". Full time series can be accessed at http://oe.cd/full-time-series.

Source: Ministry of Finance and Economy, Ministry of Home Affairs.

StatLink https://stat.link/2u7301

Table 4.42. Korea, tax revenue and % of GDP by level of government and main taxes

	Billion KRW					% of GDP				
	1990	2000	2010	2019	2020	1990	2000	2010	2019	2020
Federal or Central government										
Total tax revenue	**27 140.8**	**92 935.0**	**177 718.0**	**293 454.0**	**285 547.0**	**13.5**	**14.3**	**13.4**	**15.2**	**14.7**
1000 Taxes on income, profits and capital gains	11 655.2	35 824.0	75 352.0	156 298.0	149 319.0	5.8	5.5	5.7	8.1	7.7
2000 Social security contributions	0.0	0.0	0.0	0.0	0.0	0.0	0.0	0.0	0.0	0.0
3000 Taxes on payroll and workforce	29.3	0.0	0.0	0.0	0.0	0.0	0.0	0.0	0.0	0.0
4000 Taxes on property	866.3	5 866.0	11 288.0	19 406.0	29 160.0	0.4	0.9	0.9	1.0	1.5
5000 Taxes on goods and services	14 377.5	46 812.0	86 629.0	111 877.0	102 903.0	7.2	7.2	6.5	5.8	5.3
6000 Other taxes	212.5	4 433.0	4 449.0	5 873.0	4 165.0	0.1	0.7	0.3	0.3	0.2
State/Regional										
Total tax revenue	**..**	**..**	**..**	**..**	**..**	**..**	**..**	**..**	**..**	**..**
1000 Taxes on income, profits and capital gains	..	..	..	..	..	..	..	..	..	..
2000 Social security contributions	..	..	..	..	..	..	..	..	..	..
3000 Taxes on payroll and workforce	..	..	..	..	..	..	..	..	..	..
4000 Taxes on property	..	..	..	..	..	..	..	..	..	..
5000 Taxes on goods and services	..	..	..	..	..	..	..	..	..	..
6000 Other taxes	..	..	..	..	..	..	..	..	..	..
Local government										
Total tax revenue	**6 360.9**	**20 601.0**	**49 160.0**	**90 460.0**	**102 049.0**	**3.2**	**3.2**	**3.7**	**4.7**	**5.3**
1000 Taxes on income, profits and capital gains	548.3	3 430.0	7 553.0	17 742.0	17 245.0	0.3	0.5	0.6	0.9	0.9
2000 Social security contributions	0.0	0.0	0.0	0.0	0.0	0.0	0.0	0.0	0.0	0.0
3000 Taxes on payroll and workforce	123.5	258.0	714.0	1 597.0	1 607.0	0.1	0.0	0.1	0.1	0.1
4000 Taxes on property	3 522.6	10 980.0	22 228.0	40 326.0	47 352.0	1.8	1.7	1.7	2.1	2.4
5000 Taxes on goods and services	2 120.0	5 459.0	13 140.0	23 399.0	28 450.0	1.1	0.8	1.0	1.2	1.5
6000 Other taxes	46.6	474.0	5 525.0	7 396.0	7 395.0	0.0	0.1	0.4	0.4	0.4
Social Security Funds										
Total tax revenue	**3 760.0**	**22 759.0**	**69 090.0**	**140 071.0**	**150 854.0**	**1.9**	**3.5**	**5.2**	**7.3**	**7.8**
1000 Taxes on income, profits and capital gains	0.0	0.0	0.0	0.0	0.0	0.0	0.0	0.0	0.0	0.0
2000 Social security contributions	3 760.0	22 759.0	69 090.0	140 071.0	150 854.0	1.9	3.5	5.2	7.3	7.8
3000 Taxes on payroll and workforce	0.0	0.0	0.0	0.0	0.0	0.0	0.0	0.0	0.0	0.0
4000 Taxes on property	0.0	0.0	0.0	0.0	0.0	0.0	0.0	0.0	0.0	0.0
5000 Taxes on goods and services	0.0	0.0	0.0	0.0	0.0	0.0	0.0	0.0	0.0	0.0
6000 Other taxes	0.0	0.0	0.0	0.0	0.0	0.0	0.0	0.0	0.0	0.0

.. Not available

Note: More detailed country data and country notes are available in Chapter 6 "Tax revenues by sub-sectors of general government". Full time series can be accessed at http://oe.cd/full-time-series.

Source: Ministry of Finance and Economy, Ministry of Home Affairs.

StatLink https://stat.link/6whdx7

Table 4.43. Latvia, tax revenue and % of GDP by selected tax category

	Billion EUR					% of GDP				
	1990	2000	2010	2019	2020	1990	2000	2010	2019	2020
Total tax revenue	..	**2.0**	**5.2**	**9.5**	**9.4**	..	**29.0**	**28.5**	**30.9**	**31.8**
1000 Taxes on income, profits and capital gains	..	**0.5**	**1.3**	**2.0**	**2.0**	..	**7.0**	**7.1**	**6.6**	**6.9**
1100 Of individuals	..	0.4	1.1	2.0	1.8	..	5.5	6.2	6.5	6.1
1200 Corporate	..	0.1	0.2	0.0	0.2	..	1.5	1.0	0.2	0.7
1300 Unallocable between 1100 and 1200	..	0.0	0.0	0.0	0.0	..	0.0	0.0	0.0	0.0
2000 Social security contributions	..	**0.7**	**1.6**	**2.9**	**2.9**	..	**9.7**	**8.6**	**9.5**	**10.0**
2100 Employees	..	0.2	0.4	0.8	0.8	..	2.4	2.2	2.8	2.9
2200 Employers	..	0.5	1.2	2.0	2.1	..	7.3	6.4	6.6	7.0
2300 Self-employed or non-employed	..	0.0	0.0	0.0	0.0	..	0.0	0.1	0.1	0.1
2400 Unallocable between 2100, 2200 and 2300	..	0.0	0.0	0.0	0.0	..	0.0	0.0	0.0	0.0
3000 Taxes on payroll and workforce	..	**0.0**	**0.0**	**0.0**	**0.0**	..	**0.0**	**0.0**	**0.0**	**0.0**
4000 Taxes on property	..	**0.1**	**0.2**	**0.3**	**0.3**	..	**1.1**	**0.9**	**0.9**	**1.0**
4100 Recurrent taxes on immovable property	..	0.1	0.1	0.2	0.2	..	0.9	0.7	0.7	0.8
4200 Recurrent taxes on net wealth	..	0.0	0.0	0.0	0.0	..	0.0	0.0	0.0	0.0
4300 Estate, inheritance and gift taxes	..	0.0	0.0	0.0	0.0	..	0.0	0.0	0.0	0.0
4400 Taxes on financial and capital transactions	..	0.0	0.0	0.0	0.0	..	0.2	0.1	0.1	0.1
4500 Non-recurrent taxes	..	0.0	0.0	0.0	0.0	..	0.0	0.0	0.0	0.0
4600 Other recurrent taxes on property	..	0.0	0.0	0.0	0.0	..	0.0	0.0	0.0	0.0
5000 Taxes on goods and services	..	**0.8**	**2.2**	**4.3**	**4.1**	..	**11.2**	**11.9**	**13.9**	**14.0**
5100 Taxes on production, sale, transfer, etc	..	0.7	2.0	4.0	3.9	..	10.8	11.2	13.0	13.2
5110 General taxes	..	0.5	1.3	2.8	2.7	..	6.9	7.2	9.1	9.2
5111 Value added taxes	..	0.5	1.2	2.6	2.6	..	6.9	6.6	8.6	8.7
5120 Taxes on specific goods and services	..	0.3	0.7	1.2	1.2	..	3.8	4.0	3.9	4.0
5121 Excises	..	0.2	0.6	1.1	1.1	..	3.4	3.6	3.5	3.6
5200 Taxes on use of goods and perform activities	..	0.0	0.1	0.3	0.2	..	0.5	0.7	0.9	0.7
5300 Unallocable between 5100 and 5200	..	0.0	0.0	0.0	0.0	..	0.0	0.0	0.0	0.0
6000 Other taxes	..	**0.0**	**0.0**	**0.0**	**0.0**	..	**0.0**	**0.0**	**0.0**	**0.0**
Non-wastable tax credits										
Non-wastable tax credits against 1000	..	..	..	..	..	..	..	..	..	..
Transfer component	..	..	..	..	..	..	..	..	..	..
Tax expenditure component	..	..	..	..	..	..	..	..	..	..
Revenues collected on behalf of the EU										
Revenues collected on behalf of the EU, total	..	..	0.0	0.1	0.1	..	..	0.1	0.2	0.2
Customs duties	..	..	0.0	0.0	0.0	..	..	0.1	0.2	0.2
SRF contributions	..	..	..	0.0	0.0	..	..	..	0.0	0.0

.. Not available
Note: More detailed country data and country notes are available in Chapter 5 "Detailed country tables". Full time series can be accessed at http://oe.cd/full-time-series.
Source: Ministry of Finance.

StatLink https://stat.link/k5t8vw

Table 4.44. Latvia, tax revenue and % of GDP by level of government and main taxes

	Billion EUR					% of GDP				
	1990	2000	2010	2019	2020	1990	2000	2010	2019	2020
Federal or Central government										
Total tax revenue	**..**	**1.0**	**2.5**	**4.8**	**4.8**	**..**	**14.4**	**14.1**	**15.6**	**16.2**
1000 Taxes on income, profits and capital gains	..	0.2	0.4	0.4	0.6	..	3.1	2.2	1.4	2.0
2000 Social security contributions	..	0.0	0.0	0.1	0.1	..	0.0	0.0	0.3	0.3
3000 Taxes on payroll and workforce	..	0.0	0.0	0.0	0.0	..	0.0	0.0	0.0	0.0
4000 Taxes on property	..	0.0	0.0	0.1	0.0	..	0.2	0.2	0.2	0.2
5000 Taxes on goods and services	..	0.8	2.1	4.2	4.1	..	11.1	11.7	13.6	13.8
6000 Other taxes	..	0.0	0.0	0.0	0.0	..	0.0	0.0	0.0	0.0
State/Regional										
Total tax revenue	**..**	**..**	**..**	**..**	**..**	**..**	**..**	**..**	**..**	**..**
1000 Taxes on income, profits and capital gains	..	..	..	..	..	..	..	..	..	..
2000 Social security contributions	..	..	..	..	..	..	..	..	..	..
3000 Taxes on payroll and workforce	..	..	..	..	..	..	..	..	..	..
4000 Taxes on property	..	..	..	..	..	..	..	..	..	..
5000 Taxes on goods and services	..	..	..	..	..	..	..	..	..	..
6000 Other taxes	..	..	..	..	..	..	..	..	..	..
Local government										
Total tax revenue	**..**	**0.3**	**1.0**	**1.8**	**1.7**	**..**	**4.9**	**5.7**	**6.0**	**5.7**
1000 Taxes on income, profits and capital gains	..	0.3	0.9	1.6	1.4	..	3.9	4.9	5.2	4.9
2000 Social security contributions	..	0.0	0.0	0.0	0.0	..	0.0	0.0	0.0	0.0
3000 Taxes on payroll and workforce	..	0.0	0.0	0.0	0.0	..	0.0	0.0	0.0	0.0
4000 Taxes on property	..	0.1	0.1	0.2	0.2	..	0.9	0.7	0.7	0.8
5000 Taxes on goods and services	..	0.0	0.0	0.0	0.0	..	0.1	0.1	0.1	0.0
6000 Other taxes	..	0.0	0.0	0.0	0.0	..	0.0	0.0	0.0	0.0
Social Security Funds										
Total tax revenue	**..**	**0.7**	**1.6**	**2.8**	**2.8**	**..**	**9.7**	**8.6**	**9.2**	**9.7**
1000 Taxes on income, profits and capital gains	..	0.0	0.0	0.0	0.0	..	0.0	0.0	0.0	0.0
2000 Social security contributions	..	0.7	1.6	2.8	2.8	..	9.7	8.6	9.2	9.6
3000 Taxes on payroll and workforce	..	0.0	0.0	0.0	0.0	..	0.0	0.0	0.0	0.0
4000 Taxes on property	..	0.0	0.0	0.0	0.0	..	0.0	0.0	0.0	0.0
5000 Taxes on goods and services	..	0.0	0.0	0.0	0.0	..	0.0	0.0	0.0	0.0
6000 Other taxes	..	0.0	0.0	0.0	0.0	..	0.0	0.0	0.0	0.0

.. Not available

Note: More detailed country data and country notes are available in Chapter 6 "Tax revenues by sub-sectors of general government". Full time series can be accessed at http://oe.cd/full-time-series.

Source: Ministry of Finance.

StatLink https://stat.link/e4rl38

Table 4.45. Lithuania, tax revenue and % of GDP by selected tax category

	Billion EUR					% of GDP				
	1990	2000	2010	2019	2020	1990	2000	2010	2019	2020
Total tax revenue	..	**4.1**	**7.9**	**14.8**	**15.3**	..	**30.8**	**28.3**	**30.3**	**30.8**
1000 Taxes on income, profits and capital gains	..	**1.1**	**1.3**	**4.3**	**4.3**	..	**8.3**	**4.6**	**8.8**	**8.7**
1100 Of individuals	..	1.0	1.0	3.5	3.5	..	7.6	3.6	7.2	7.1
1200 Corporate	..	0.1	0.3	0.8	0.8	..	0.7	1.0	1.6	1.6
1300 Unallocable between 1100 and 1200	..	0.0	0.0	0.0	0.0	..	0.0	0.0	0.0	0.0
2000 Social security contributions	..	**1.3**	**3.3**	**4.7**	**5.1**	..	**9.9**	**11.6**	**9.7**	**10.2**
2100 Employees	..	0.1	0.6	3.6	3.9	..	0.8	2.3	7.4	7.8
2200 Employers	..	1.1	2.1	0.3	0.3	..	8.1	7.4	0.7	0.7
2300 Self-employed or non-employed	..	0.1	0.5	0.8	0.9	..	1.0	1.9	1.6	1.8
2400 Unallocable between 2100, 2200 and 2300	..	0.0	0.0	0.0	0.0	..	0.0	0.0	0.0	0.0
3000 Taxes on payroll and workforce	..	**0.0**	**0.0**	**0.0**	**0.0**	..	**0.0**	**0.0**	**0.0**	**0.0**
4000 Taxes on property	..	**0.1**	**0.1**	**0.1**	**0.1**	..	**0.5**	**0.4**	**0.3**	**0.3**
4100 Recurrent taxes on immovable property	..	0.1	0.1	0.1	0.1	..	0.5	0.4	0.3	0.3
4200 Recurrent taxes on net wealth	..	0.0	0.0	0.0	0.0	..	0.0	0.0	0.0	0.0
4300 Estate, inheritance and gift taxes	..	0.0	0.0	0.0	0.0	..	0.0	0.0	0.0	0.0
4400 Taxes on financial and capital transactions	..	0.0	0.0	0.0	0.0	..	0.0	0.0	0.0	0.0
4500 Non-recurrent taxes	..	0.0	0.0	0.0	0.0	..	0.0	0.0	0.0	0.0
4600 Other recurrent taxes on property	..	0.0	0.0	0.0	0.0	..	0.0	0.0	0.0	0.0
5000 Taxes on goods and services	..	**1.6**	**3.3**	**5.6**	**5.8**	..	**12.1**	**11.7**	**11.5**	**11.6**
5100 Taxes on production, sale, transfer, etc	..	1.6	3.2	5.5	5.6	..	11.7	11.4	11.3	11.4
5110 General taxes	..	1.1	2.2	3.9	3.9	..	8.1	7.8	7.9	7.9
5111 Value added taxes	..	1.0	2.2	3.9	3.9	..	7.5	7.8	7.9	7.9
5120 Taxes on specific goods and services	..	0.5	1.0	1.7	1.7	..	3.5	3.6	3.4	3.5
5121 Excises	..	0.4	0.9	1.5	1.5	..	3.2	3.2	3.1	3.1
5200 Taxes on use of goods and perform activities	..	0.1	0.1	0.1	0.1	..	0.5	0.3	0.2	0.2
5300 Unallocable between 5100 and 5200	..	0.0	0.0	0.0	0.0	..	0.0	0.0	0.0	0.0
6000 Other taxes	..	**0.0**	**0.0**	**0.0**	**0.0**	..	**0.0**	**0.0**	**0.0**	**0.0**
Non-wastable tax credits										
Non-wastable tax credits against 1000	..	..	..	..	..	..	..	..	..	..
Transfer component	..	..	..	..	..	..	..	..	..	..
Tax expenditure component	..	..	..	..	..	..	..	..	..	..
Revenues collected on behalf of the EU										
Revenues collected on behalf of the EU, total	..	..	0.1	0.1	0.1	..	..	0.2	0.3	0.3
Customs duties	..	..	0.1	0.1	0.1	..	..	0.2	0.3	0.3
SRF contributions	..	..	..	0.0	0.0	..	..	..	0.0	0.0

.. Not available

Note: More detailed country data and country notes are available in Chapter 5 "Detailed country tables". Full time series can be accessed at http://oe.cd/full-time-series.

The total tax revenue has been reduced by the amount of any capital transfer that represents uncollected taxes. The capital transfers were subtracted directly from the specific taxes to which they relate. Therefore, the tax revenue amounts are different to those reported in the detailed country data available in Chapter 5 "Detailed country tables".

Source: Ministry of Finance.

StatLink https://stat.link/boe2ug

Table 4.46. Lithuania, tax revenue and % of GDP by level of government and main taxes

	Billion EUR					% of GDP				
	1990	2000	2010	2019	2020	1990	2000	2010	2019	2020
Federal or Central government										
Total tax revenue	..	**2.7**	**4.5**	**9.8**	**9.9**	..	**20.3**	**16.0**	**20.0**	**20.0**
1000 Taxes on income, profits and capital gains	..	1.1	1.3	4.3	4.3	..	8.3	4.6	8.8	8.7
2000 Social security contributions	..	0.0	0.0	0.0	0.0	..	0.0	0.0	0.0	0.0
3000 Taxes on payroll and workforce	..	0.0	0.0	0.0	0.0	..	0.0	0.0	0.0	0.0
4000 Taxes on property	..	0.0	0.0	0.0	0.0	..	0.0	0.0	0.0	0.0
5000 Taxes on goods and services	..	1.6	3.2	5.5	5.6	..	12.0	11.4	11.2	11.3
6000 Other taxes	..	0.0	0.0	0.0	0.0	..	0.0	0.0	0.0	0.0
State/Regional										
Total tax revenue	..	..	..	..	..	..	..	..	..	..
1000 Taxes on income, profits and capital gains	..	..	..	..	..	..	..	..	..	..
2000 Social security contributions	..	..	..	..	..	..	..	..	..	..
3000 Taxes on payroll and workforce	..	..	..	..	..	..	..	..	..	..
4000 Taxes on property	..	..	..	..	..	..	..	..	..	..
5000 Taxes on goods and services	..	..	..	..	..	..	..	..	..	..
6000 Other taxes	..	..	..	..	..	..	..	..	..	..
Local government										
Total tax revenue	..	**0.1**	**0.1**	**0.2**	**0.2**	..	**0.6**	**0.5**	**0.3**	**0.3**
1000 Taxes on income, profits and capital gains	..	0.0	0.0	0.0	0.0	..	0.0	0.0	0.0	0.0
2000 Social security contributions	..	0.0	0.0	0.0	0.0	..	0.0	0.0	0.0	0.0
3000 Taxes on payroll and workforce	..	0.0	0.0	0.0	0.0	..	0.0	0.0	0.0	0.0
4000 Taxes on property	..	0.1	0.1	0.1	0.1	..	0.5	0.4	0.3	0.3
5000 Taxes on goods and services	..	0.0	0.0	0.0	0.0	..	0.1	0.1	0.1	0.1
6000 Other taxes	..	0.0	0.0	0.0	0.0	..	0.0	0.0	0.0	0.0
Social Security Funds										
Total tax revenue	..	**1.3**	**3.3**	**4.7**	**5.1**	..	**9.9**	**11.6**	**9.7**	**10.2**
1000 Taxes on income, profits and capital gains	..	0.0	0.0	0.0	0.0	..	0.0	0.0	0.0	0.0
2000 Social security contributions	..	1.3	3.3	4.7	5.1	..	9.9	11.6	9.7	10.2
3000 Taxes on payroll and workforce	..	0.0	0.0	0.0	0.0	..	0.0	0.0	0.0	0.0
4000 Taxes on property	..	0.0	0.0	0.0	0.0	..	0.0	0.0	0.0	0.0
5000 Taxes on goods and services	..	0.0	0.0	0.0	0.0	..	0.0	0.0	0.0	0.0
6000 Other taxes	..	0.0	0.0	0.0	0.0	..	0.0	0.0	0.0	0.0

.. Not available

Note: More detailed country data and country notes are available in Chapter 6 "Tax revenues by sub-sectors of general government". Full time series can be accessed at http://oe.cd/full-time-series.

The total tax revenue has been reduced by the amount of any capital transfer that represents uncollected taxes. The capital transfers were subtracted directly from the specific taxes to which they relate. Therefore, the tax revenue amounts are different to those reported in the detailed country data available in Chapter 6 "Tax revenues by sub-sectors of general government".

Source: Ministry of Finance.

StatLink https://stat.link/dnpq8t

Table 4.47. Luxembourg, tax revenue and % of GDP by selected tax category

	Billion EUR					% of GDP				
	1990	2000	2010	2019	2020	1990	2000	2010	2019	2020
Total tax revenue	**3.7**	**8.5**	**15.1**	**24.7**	**24.7**	**34.7**	**37.0**	**35.7**	**39.6**	**38.1**
1000 Taxes on income, profits and capital gains	**1.5**	**3.1**	**5.5**	**9.7**	**9.4**	**13.9**	**13.5**	**12.9**	**15.5**	**14.5**
1100 Of individuals	0.9	1.6	3.2	5.9	6.3	8.3	6.8	7.4	9.5	9.7
1200 Corporate	0.6	1.5	2.3	3.8	3.1	5.6	6.7	5.4	6.0	4.8
1300 Unallocable between 1100 and 1200	0.0	0.0	0.0	0.0	0.0	0.0	0.0	0.0	0.0	0.0
2000 Social security contributions	**1.0**	**2.2**	**4.4**	**6.9**	**7.2**	**9.6**	**9.7**	**10.3**	**11.0**	**11.1**
2100 Employees	0.4	1.0	2.0	3.2	3.3	3.7	4.3	4.8	5.1	5.2
2200 Employers	0.5	1.0	1.9	2.8	2.9	4.7	4.2	4.5	4.6	4.5
2300 Self-employed or non-employed	0.1	0.3	0.5	0.8	0.9	1.2	1.2	1.1	1.4	1.4
2400 Unallocable between 2100, 2200 and 2300	0.0	0.0	0.0	0.0	0.0	0.0	0.0	0.0	0.0	0.0
3000 Taxes on payroll and workforce	**0.0**	**0.0**	**0.0**	**0.0**	**0.0**	**0.0**	**0.0**	**0.0**	**0.0**	**0.0**
4000 Taxes on property	**0.3**	**0.9**	**1.1**	**2.4**	**2.5**	**2.9**	**4.0**	**2.5**	**3.9**	**3.8**
4100 Recurrent taxes on immovable property	0.0	0.0	0.0	0.0	0.0	0.1	0.1	0.1	0.1	0.1
4200 Recurrent taxes on net wealth	0.2	0.6	0.8	1.8	1.9	1.6	2.8	2.0	3.0	2.9
4300 Estate, inheritance and gift taxes	0.0	0.0	0.1	0.1	0.1	0.1	0.1	0.1	0.2	0.1
4400 Taxes on financial and capital transactions	0.1	0.2	0.2	0.4	0.5	1.1	1.0	0.4	0.7	0.8
4500 Non-recurrent taxes	0.0	0.0	0.0	0.0	0.0	0.0	0.0	0.0	0.0	0.0
4600 Other recurrent taxes on property	0.0	0.0	0.0	0.0	0.0	0.0	0.0	0.0	0.0	0.0
5000 Taxes on goods and services	**0.9**	**2.3**	**4.2**	**5.7**	**5.6**	**8.2**	**9.8**	**9.9**	**9.2**	**8.7**
5100 Taxes on production, sale, transfer, etc	0.8	2.2	4.1	5.6	5.5	8.0	9.7	9.7	9.0	8.5
5110 General taxes	0.4	1.1	2.6	3.6	3.7	4.2	4.9	6.2	5.8	5.7
5111 Value added taxes	0.4	1.1	2.6	3.6	3.7	4.2	4.9	6.2	5.8	5.7
5120 Taxes on specific goods and services	0.4	1.1	1.5	2.0	1.9	3.8	4.8	3.5	3.2	2.9
5121 Excises	0.4	1.0	1.4	1.7	1.5	3.4	4.5	3.3	2.7	2.3
5200 Taxes on use of goods and perform activities	0.0	0.0	0.1	0.1	0.1	0.2	0.1	0.2	0.2	0.1
5300 Unallocable between 5100 and 5200	0.0	0.0	0.0	0.0	0.0	0.0	0.0	0.0	0.0	0.0
6000 Other taxes	**0.0**	**0.0**	**0.0**	**0.0**	**0.0**	**0.1**	**0.0**	**0.1**	**0.0**	**0.0**
Non-wastable tax credits										
Non-wastable tax credits against 1000	..	..	..	0.2	0.2	..	..	..	0.3	0.3
Transfer component	..	..	..	..	..	..	..	..	..	..
Tax expenditure component	..	..	..	..	..	..	..	..	..	..
Revenues collected on behalf of the EU										
Revenues collected on behalf of the EU, total	0.0	0.0	0.0	0.2	0.2	0.2	0.1	0.0	0.3	0.3
Customs duties	0.0	0.0	0.0	0.0	0.0	0.1	0.1	0.0	0.0	0.0
SRF contributions	..	..	..	0.1	0.2	..	..	..	0.2	0.3

.. Not available

Note: The total tax revenue has been reduced by the amount of any capital transfer that represents uncollected taxes. The capital transfers were subtracted directly from the specific taxes to which they relate. Therefore, the tax revenue amounts are different to those reported in the detailed country data available in Chapter 5 "Detailed country tables".

More detailed country data and country notes are available in Chapter 5 "Detailed country tables". Full time series can be accessed at http://oe.cd/full-time-series.

Source: General account of the State.

StatLink https://stat.link/ye2z5u

Table 4.48. Luxembourg, tax revenue and % of GDP by level of government and main taxes

	Billion EUR					% of GDP				
	1990	2000	2010	2019	2020	1990	2000	2010	2019	2020
Federal or Central government										
Total tax revenue	**2.4**	**5.8**	**10.2**	**16.7**	**16.4**	**22.9**	**25.4**	**24.0**	**26.7**	**25.4**
1000 Taxes on income, profits and capital gains	1.3	2.6	4.9	8.6	8.4	12.0	11.5	11.5	13.7	13.0
2000 Social security contributions	0.0	0.1	0.1	0.2	0.2	0.2	0.3	0.3	0.3	0.3
3000 Taxes on payroll and workforce	0.0	0.0	0.0	0.0	0.0	0.0	0.0	0.0	0.0	0.0
4000 Taxes on property	0.3	0.9	1.0	2.4	2.4	2.7	3.8	2.4	3.8	3.7
5000 Taxes on goods and services	0.8	2.2	4.2	5.5	5.4	8.0	9.7	9.8	8.9	8.4
6000 Other taxes	0.0	0.0	0.0	0.0	0.0	0.1	0.0	0.0	0.0	0.0
State/Regional										
Total tax revenue	**..**	**..**	**..**	**..**	**..**	**..**	**..**	**..**	**..**	**..**
1000 Taxes on income, profits and capital gains	..	..	..	..	..	..	..	..	..	..
2000 Social security contributions	..	..	..	..	..	..	..	..	..	..
3000 Taxes on payroll and workforce	..	..	..	..	..	..	..	..	..	..
4000 Taxes on property	..	..	..	..	..	..	..	..	..	..
5000 Taxes on goods and services	..	..	..	..	..	..	..	..	..	..
6000 Other taxes	..	..	..	..	..	..	..	..	..	..
Local government										
Total tax revenue	**0.2**	**0.5**	**0.7**	**1.2**	**1.0**	**2.2**	**2.2**	**1.5**	**1.9**	**1.6**
1000 Taxes on income, profits and capital gains	0.2	0.5	0.6	1.1	1.0	2.0	2.0	1.4	1.8	1.5
2000 Social security contributions	0.0	0.0	0.0	0.0	0.0	0.0	0.0	0.0	0.0	0.0
3000 Taxes on payroll and workforce	0.0	0.0	0.0	0.0	0.0	0.0	0.0	0.0	0.0	0.0
4000 Taxes on property	0.0	0.0	0.0	0.1	0.1	0.2	0.1	0.1	0.1	0.1
5000 Taxes on goods and services	0.0	0.0	0.0	0.0	0.0	0.0	0.0	0.0	0.0	0.0
6000 Other taxes	0.0	0.0	0.0	0.0	0.0	0.0	0.0	0.0	0.0	0.0
Social Security Funds										
Total tax revenue	**1.0**	**2.2**	**4.3**	**6.7**	**7.0**	**9.4**	**9.4**	**10.1**	**10.7**	**10.8**
1000 Taxes on income, profits and capital gains	0.0	0.0	0.0	0.0	0.0	0.0	0.0	0.0	0.0	0.0
2000 Social security contributions	1.0	2.2	4.3	6.7	7.0	9.4	9.4	10.1	10.7	10.8
3000 Taxes on payroll and workforce	0.0	0.0	0.0	0.0	0.0	0.0	0.0	0.0	0.0	0.0
4000 Taxes on property	0.0	0.0	0.0	0.0	0.0	0.0	0.0	0.0	0.0	0.0
5000 Taxes on goods and services	0.0	0.0	0.0	0.0	0.0	0.0	0.0	0.0	0.0	0.0
6000 Other taxes	0.0	0.0	0.0	0.0	0.0	0.0	0.0	0.0	0.0	0.0

.. Not available

Note: The total tax revenue has been reduced by the amount of any capital transfer that represents uncollected taxes. The capital transfers were subtracted directly from the specific taxes to which they relate. Therefore, the tax revenue amounts are different to those reported in the detailed country data available in Chapter 6 "Tax revenues by sub-sectors of general government".

More detailed country data and country notes are available in Chapter 6 "Tax revenues by sub-sectors of general government". Full time series can be accessed at http://oe.cd/full-time-series.

Source: General account of the State.

StatLink https://stat.link/g6lzhy

Table 4.49. Mexico, tax revenue and % of GDP by selected tax category

	Billion MXN					% of GDP				
	1990	2000	2010	2019	2020	1990	2000	2010	2019	2020
Total tax revenue	**102.0**	**767.2**	**1 716.2**	**3 995.7**	**4 148.7**	**12.1**	**11.5**	**12.8**	**16.3**	**17.8**
1000 Taxes on income, profits and capital gains	**34.7**	**276.5**	**683.6**	**1 694.1**	**1 768.2**	**4.1**	**4.1**	**5.1**	**6.9**	**7.6**
1100 Of individuals	..	..	313.5	829.5	872.6	..	..	2.3	3.4	3.7
1200 Corporate	..	..	246.7	803.6	832.1	..	..	1.8	3.3	3.6
1300 Unallocable between 1100 and 1200	34.7	276.5	123.4	61.0	63.4	4.1	4.1	0.9	0.2	0.3
2000 Social security contributions	**17.2**	**138.2**	**277.5**	**552.1**	**576.0**	**2.0**	**2.1**	**2.1**	**2.3**	**2.5**
2100 Employees	..	..	..	..	..	..	..	..	..	..
2200 Employers	..	..	..	..	..	..	..	..	..	..
2300 Self-employed or non-employed	..	..	..	..	..	..	..	..	..	..
2400 Unallocable between 2100, 2200 and 2300	17.2	138.2	277.5	552.1	576.0	2.0	2.1	2.1	2.3	2.5
3000 Taxes on payroll and workforce	**1.8**	**11.2**	**36.9**	**101.3**	**105.5**	**0.2**	**0.2**	**0.3**	**0.4**	**0.5**
4000 Taxes on property	**1.9**	**14.0**	**39.0**	**79.3**	**79.2**	**0.2**	**0.2**	**0.3**	**0.3**	**0.3**
4100 Recurrent taxes on immovable property	1.0	9.9	25.7	50.5	52.7	0.1	0.1	0.2	0.2	0.2
4200 Recurrent taxes on net wealth	0.0	0.0	0.0	0.0	0.0	0.0	0.0	0.0	0.0	0.0
4300 Estate, inheritance and gift taxes	0.0	0.0	0.0	0.0	0.0	0.0	0.0	0.0	0.0	0.0
4400 Taxes on financial and capital transactions	0.9	4.0	13.2	28.7	26.5	0.1	0.1	0.1	0.1	0.1
4500 Non-recurrent taxes	0.0	0.0	0.0	0.0	0.0	0.0	0.0	0.0	0.0	0.0
4600 Other recurrent taxes on property	0.0	0.0	0.0	0.0	0.0	0.0	0.0	0.0	0.0	0.0
5000 Taxes on goods and services	**44.8**	**319.6**	**651.9**	**1 504.3**	**1 544.2**	**5.3**	**4.8**	**4.9**	**6.2**	**6.6**
5100 Taxes on production, sale, transfer, etc	44.2	310.3	630.1	1 486.8	1 527.7	5.2	4.6	4.7	6.1	6.5
5110 General taxes	26.6	189.6	504.5	933.3	987.5	3.2	2.8	3.8	3.8	4.2
5111 Value added taxes	26.6	189.6	504.5	933.3	987.5	3.2	2.8	3.8	3.8	4.2
5120 Taxes on specific goods and services	17.5	120.7	125.6	553.4	540.1	2.1	1.8	0.9	2.3	2.3
5121 Excises	10.1	86.2	86.1	471.0	469.0	1.2	1.3	0.6	1.9	2.0
5200 Taxes on use of goods and perform activities	0.7	9.3	21.8	17.5	16.5	0.1	0.1	0.2	0.1	0.1
5300 Unallocable between 5100 and 5200	0.0	0.0	0.0	0.0	0.0	0.0	0.0	0.0	0.0	0.0
6000 Other taxes	**1.6**	**7.7**	**27.4**	**64.7**	**75.7**	**0.2**	**0.1**	**0.2**	**0.3**	**0.3**
Non-wastable tax credits										
Non-wastable tax credits against 1000	..	..	40.3	50.6	50.5	..	..	0.3	0.2	0.2
Transfer component	..	..	9.7	1.3	0.5	..	..	0.1	0.0	0.0
Tax expenditure component	..	..	30.6	49.4	50.0	..	..	0.2	0.2	0.2

.. Not available

Note: More detailed country data and country notes are available in Chapter 5 "Detailed country tables". Full time series can be accessed at http://oe.cd/full-time-series.

Source: Ministry of Finance, Economic Department.

StatLink https://stat.link/j38m2r

Table 4.50. Mexico, tax revenue and % of GDP by level of government and main taxes

	Billion MXN					% of GDP				
	1990	2000	2010	2019	2020	1990	2000	2010	2019	2020
Federal or Central government										
Total tax revenue	**81.4**	**600.5**	**1 351.5**	**3 213.2**	**3 347.5**	**9.7**	**9.0**	**10.1**	**13.1**	**14.3**
1000 Taxes on income, profits and capital gains	34.7	276.5	683.6	1 694.1	1 768.2	4.1	4.1	5.1	6.9	7.6
2000 Social security contributions	0.0	0.0	0.0	0.0	0.0	0.0	0.0	0.0	0.0	0.0
3000 Taxes on payroll and workforce	0.8	0.0	0.0	0.0	0.0	0.1	0.0	0.0	0.0	0.0
4000 Taxes on property	0.0	0.0	0.0	0.0	0.0	0.0	0.0	0.0	0.0	0.0
5000 Taxes on goods and services	44.6	318.1	645.6	1 477.9	1 522.3	5.3	4.8	4.8	6.0	6.5
6000 Other taxes	1.3	5.9	22.2	41.1	57.0	0.2	0.1	0.2	0.2	0.2
State/Regional										
Total tax revenue	**2.2**	**20.5**	**58.3**	**163.7**	**161.2**	**0.3**	**0.3**	**0.4**	**0.7**	**0.7**
1000 Taxes on income, profits and capital gains	0.0	0.0	0.0	0.0	0.0	0.0	0.0	0.0	0.0	0.0
2000 Social security contributions	0.0	0.0	0.0	0.0	0.0	0.0	0.0	0.0	0.0	0.0
3000 Taxes on payroll and workforce	1.0	11.2	36.8	101.3	105.5	0.1	0.2	0.3	0.4	0.5
4000 Taxes on property	0.9	7.0	13.1	29.2	26.4	0.1	0.1	0.1	0.1	0.1
5000 Taxes on goods and services	0.1	1.3	5.8	25.2	21.2	0.0	0.0	0.0	0.1	0.1
6000 Other taxes	0.2	0.9	2.5	8.1	8.0	0.0	0.0	0.0	0.0	0.0
Local government										
Total tax revenue	**1.3**	**8.0**	**29.0**	**66.7**	**64.1**	**0.1**	**0.1**	**0.2**	**0.3**	**0.3**
1000 Taxes on income, profits and capital gains	0.0	0.0	0.0	0.0	0.0	0.0	0.0	0.0	0.0	0.0
2000 Social security contributions	0.0	0.0	0.0	0.0	0.0	0.0	0.0	0.0	0.0	0.0
3000 Taxes on payroll and workforce	0.0	0.0	0.1	0.0	0.0	0.0	0.0	0.0	0.0	0.0
4000 Taxes on property	1.0	6.9	25.8	50.1	52.8	0.1	0.1	0.2	0.2	0.2
5000 Taxes on goods and services	0.1	0.2	0.5	1.2	0.7	0.0	0.0	0.0	0.0	0.0
6000 Other taxes	0.1	0.9	2.6	15.5	10.6	0.0	0.0	0.0	0.1	0.0
Social Security Funds										
Total tax revenue	**17.2**	**138.2**	**277.5**	**552.1**	**576.0**	**2.0**	**2.1**	**2.1**	**2.3**	**2.5**
1000 Taxes on income, profits and capital gains	0.0	0.0	0.0	0.0	0.0	0.0	0.0	0.0	0.0	0.0
2000 Social security contributions	17.2	138.2	277.5	552.1	576.0	2.0	2.1	2.1	2.3	2.5
3000 Taxes on payroll and workforce	0.0	0.0	0.0	0.0	0.0	0.0	0.0	0.0	0.0	0.0
4000 Taxes on property	0.0	0.0	0.0	0.0	0.0	0.0	0.0	0.0	0.0	0.0
5000 Taxes on goods and services	0.0	0.0	0.0	0.0	0.0	0.0	0.0	0.0	0.0	0.0
6000 Other taxes	0.0	0.0	0.0	0.0	0.0	0.0	0.0	0.0	0.0	0.0

Note: More detailed country data and country notes are available in Chapter 6 "Tax revenues by sub-sectors of general government". Full time series can be accessed at http://oe.cd/full-time-series.
Source: Ministry of Finance, Economic Department.

StatLink https://stat.link/qmabf6

Table 4.51. Netherlands, tax revenue and % of GDP by selected tax category

	Billion EUR					% of GDP				
	1990	2000	2010	2019	2020	1990	2000	2010	2019	2020
Total tax revenue	**104.4**	**166.8**	**227.9**	**319.2**	**318.6**	**39.7**	**36.9**	**35.7**	**39.3**	**40.0**
1000 Taxes on income, profits and capital gains	**33.7**	**43.3**	**63.6**	**99.0**	**97.8**	**12.8**	**9.6**	**9.9**	**12.2**	**12.3**
1100 Of individuals	25.8	25.1	49.0	69.0	73.1	9.8	5.6	7.7	8.5	9.2
1200 Corporate	7.9	18.1	14.6	30.0	24.7	3.0	4.0	2.3	3.7	3.1
1300 Unallocable between 1100 and 1200	0.0	0.0	0.0	0.0	0.0	0.0	0.0	0.0	0.0	0.0
2000 Social security contributions	**39.1**	**64.5**	**82.7**	**109.3**	**108.7**	**14.9**	**14.3**	**12.9**	**13.4**	**13.6**
2100 Employees	24.1	35.3	41.6	40.7	40.3	9.2	7.8	6.5	5.0	5.1
2200 Employers	7.8	18.7	29.4	43.7	44.1	3.0	4.1	4.6	5.4	5.5
2300 Self-employed or non-employed	7.1	10.5	11.7	24.9	24.3	2.7	2.3	1.8	3.1	3.0
2400 Unallocable between 2100, 2200 and 2300	0.0	0.0	0.0	0.0	0.0	0.0	0.0	0.0	0.0	0.0
3000 Taxes on payroll and workforce	**0.0**	**0.0**	**0.0**	**0.0**	**0.0**	**0.0**	**0.0**	**0.0**	**0.0**	**0.0**
4000 Taxes on property	**3.8**	**8.8**	**8.8**	**12.2**	**13.5**	**1.5**	**1.9**	**1.4**	**1.5**	**1.7**
4100 Recurrent taxes on immovable property	1.7	3.1	4.2	7.4	7.9	0.7	0.7	0.7	0.9	1.0
4200 Recurrent taxes on net wealth	0.6	0.8	0.0	0.0	0.0	0.2	0.2	0.0	0.0	0.0
4300 Estate, inheritance and gift taxes	0.5	1.5	1.7	1.8	2.1	0.2	0.3	0.3	0.2	0.3
4400 Taxes on financial and capital transactions	1.0	3.4	2.8	3.0	3.6	0.4	0.8	0.4	0.4	0.4
4500 Non-recurrent taxes	0.0	0.0	0.0	0.0	0.0	0.0	0.0	0.0	0.0	0.0
4600 Other recurrent taxes on property	0.0	0.0	0.0	0.0	0.0	0.0	0.0	0.0	0.0	0.0
5000 Taxes on goods and services	**27.6**	**49.5**	**71.9**	**98.0**	**97.0**	**10.5**	**10.9**	**11.2**	**12.1**	**12.2**
5100 Taxes on production, sale, transfer, etc	25.1	44.9	64.2	88.5	87.5	9.5	9.9	10.1	10.9	11.0
5110 General taxes	17.2	28.9	42.7	58.2	59.0	6.5	6.4	6.7	7.2	7.4
5111 Value added taxes	17.2	28.8	42.7	58.1	59.0	6.5	6.4	6.7	7.1	7.4
5120 Taxes on specific goods and services	7.9	16.0	21.6	30.3	28.5	3.0	3.5	3.4	3.7	3.6
5121 Excises	6.0	13.8	18.4	22.0	20.4	2.3	3.0	2.9	2.7	2.6
5200 Taxes on use of goods and perform activities	2.5	4.6	7.6	9.5	9.5	1.0	1.0	1.2	1.2	1.2
5300 Unallocable between 5100 and 5200	0.0	0.0	0.0	0.0	0.0	0.0	0.0	0.0	0.0	0.0
6000 Other taxes	**0.3**	**0.8**	**1.0**	**0.8**	**1.5**	**0.1**	**0.2**	**0.2**	**0.1**	**0.2**
Non-wastable tax credits										
Non-wastable tax credits against 1000	..	..	..	..	..	..	..	..	..	..
Transfer component	..	..	..	..	..	..	..	..	..	..
Tax expenditure component	..	..	..	..	..	..	..	..	..	..
Revenues collected on behalf of the EU										
Revenues collected on behalf of the EU, total	1.5	1.6	2.0	3.6	3.5	0.6	0.4	0.3	0.4	0.4
Customs duties	..	1.3	1.7	2.7	2.5	..	0.3	0.3	0.3	0.3
SRF contributions	..	..	..	0.6	0.7	..	..	..	0.1	0.1

.. Not available

Note: More detailed country data and country notes are available in Chapter 5 "Detailed country tables". Full time series can be accessed at http://oe.cd/full-time-series.

Source: Social security contributions and local taxes: Central Bureau of Statistics. Other taxes: Ministry of Finance.

StatLink https://stat.link/fy8wgq

Table 4.52. Netherlands, tax revenue and % of GDP by level of government and main taxes

	Billion EUR					% of GDP				
	1990	2000	2010	2019	2020	1990	2000	2010	2019	2020
Federal or Central government										
Total tax revenue	**61.4**	**95.1**	**135.1**	**195.5**	**195.3**	**23.3**	**21.0**	**21.1**	**24.0**	**24.5**
1000 Taxes on income, profits and capital gains	33.7	43.3	63.6	99.0	97.8	12.8	9.6	9.9	12.2	12.3
2000 Social security contributions	0.0	0.0	0.0	0.0	0.0	0.0	0.0	0.0	0.0	0.0
3000 Taxes on payroll and workforce	0.0	0.0	0.0	0.0	0.0	0.0	0.0	0.0	0.0	0.0
4000 Taxes on property	2.1	5.7	4.6	6.5	7.5	0.8	1.3	0.7	0.8	0.9
5000 Taxes on goods and services	25.3	45.4	66.2	89.2	88.4	9.6	10.0	10.3	11.0	11.1
6000 Other taxes	0.3	0.8	0.8	0.8	1.5	0.1	0.2	0.1	0.1	0.2
State/Regional										
Total tax revenue	..	..	..	..	..	..	..	..	..	..
1000 Taxes on income, profits and capital gains	..	..	..	..	..	..	..	..	..	..
2000 Social security contributions	..	..	..	..	..	..	..	..	..	..
3000 Taxes on payroll and workforce	..	..	..	..	..	..	..	..	..	..
4000 Taxes on property	..	..	..	..	..	..	..	..	..	..
5000 Taxes on goods and services	..	..	..	..	..	..	..	..	..	..
6000 Other taxes	..	..	..	..	..	..	..	..	..	..
Local government										
Total tax revenue	**2.5**	**5.6**	**8.1**	**10.9**	**11.1**	**0.9**	**1.2**	**1.3**	**1.3**	**1.4**
1000 Taxes on income, profits and capital gains	0.0	0.0	0.0	0.0	0.0	0.0	0.0	0.0	0.0	0.0
2000 Social security contributions	0.0	0.0	0.0	0.0	0.0	0.0	0.0	0.0	0.0	0.0
3000 Taxes on payroll and workforce	0.0	0.0	0.0	0.0	0.0	0.0	0.0	0.0	0.0	0.0
4000 Taxes on property	1.7	3.1	4.2	5.7	6.0	0.7	0.7	0.7	0.7	0.8
5000 Taxes on goods and services	0.8	2.5	3.7	5.2	5.1	0.3	0.6	0.6	0.6	0.6
6000 Other taxes	0.0	0.0	0.2	0.0	0.0	0.0	0.0	0.0	0.0	0.0
Social Security Funds										
Total tax revenue	**39.1**	**64.5**	**82.7**	**109.3**	**108.7**	**14.9**	**14.3**	**12.9**	**13.4**	**13.6**
1000 Taxes on income, profits and capital gains	0.0	0.0	0.0	0.0	0.0	0.0	0.0	0.0	0.0	0.0
2000 Social security contributions	39.1	64.5	82.7	109.3	108.7	14.9	14.3	12.9	13.4	13.6
3000 Taxes on payroll and workforce	0.0	0.0	0.0	0.0	0.0	0.0	0.0	0.0	0.0	0.0
4000 Taxes on property	0.0	0.0	0.0	0.0	0.0	0.0	0.0	0.0	0.0	0.0
5000 Taxes on goods and services	0.0	0.0	0.0	0.0	0.0	0.0	0.0	0.0	0.0	0.0
6000 Other taxes	0.0	0.0	0.0	0.0	0.0	0.0	0.0	0.0	0.0	0.0

.. Not available

Note: More detailed country data and country notes are available in Chapter 6 "Tax revenues by sub-sectors of general government". Full time series can be accessed at http://oe.cd/full-time-series.

Source: Social security contributions and local taxes: Central Bureau of Statistics. Other taxes: Ministry of Finance.

StatLink https://stat.link/s43v90

Table 4.53. New Zealand, tax revenue and % of GDP by selected tax category

	Billion NZD					% of GDP				
	1990	2000	2010	2019	2020	1990	2000	2010	2019	2020
Total tax revenue	**27.5**	**39.8**	**62.3**	**99.6**	**115.6**	**36.2**	**32.5**	**30.3**	**31.3**	**33.8**
1000 Taxes on income, profits and capital gains	**16.4**	**23.9**	**33.5**	**54.9**	**65.3**	**21.6**	**19.5**	**16.3**	**17.2**	**19.1**
1100 Of individuals	13.2	17.1	23.5	39.6	44.5	17.4	14.0	11.4	12.4	13.0
1200 Corporate	1.8	4.9	7.6	12.4	17.8	2.3	4.0	3.7	3.9	5.2
1300 Unallocable between 1100 and 1200	1.4	1.8	2.4	2.9	3.0	1.9	1.5	1.2	0.9	0.9
2000 Social security contributions	**0.0**	**0.0**	**0.0**	**0.0**	**0.0**	**0.0**	**0.0**	**0.0**	**0.0**	**0.0**
2100 Employees	0.0	0.0	0.0	0.0	0.0	0.0	0.0	0.0	0.0	0.0
2200 Employers	0.0	0.0	0.0	0.0	0.0	0.0	0.0	0.0	0.0	0.0
2300 Self-employed or non-employed	0.0	0.0	0.0	0.0	0.0	0.0	0.0	0.0	0.0	0.0
2400 Unallocable between 2100, 2200 and 2300	0.0	0.0	0.0	0.0	0.0	0.0	0.0	0.0	0.0	0.0
3000 Taxes on payroll and workforce	**0.0**	**0.0**	**0.0**	**0.0**	**0.0**	**0.0**	**0.0**	**0.0**	**0.0**	**0.0**
4000 Taxes on property	**1.9**	**2.1**	**4.1**	**6.1**	**6.4**	**2.5**	**1.7**	**2.0**	**1.9**	**1.9**
4100 Recurrent taxes on immovable property	1.7	2.0	4.0	6.0	6.3	2.3	1.7	2.0	1.9	1.8
4200 Recurrent taxes on net wealth	0.0	0.0	0.0	0.0	0.0	0.0	0.0	0.0	0.0	0.0
4300 Estate, inheritance and gift taxes	0.1	0.0	0.0	0.0	0.0	0.1	0.0	0.0	0.0	0.0
4400 Taxes on financial and capital transactions	0.1	0.1	0.1	0.1	0.1	0.1	0.0	0.0	0.0	0.0
4500 Non-recurrent taxes	0.0	0.0	0.0	0.0	0.0	0.0	0.0	0.0	0.0	0.0
4600 Other recurrent taxes on property	0.0	0.0	0.0	0.0	0.0	0.0	0.0	0.0	0.0	0.0
5000 Taxes on goods and services	**9.2**	**13.8**	**24.7**	**38.6**	**43.9**	**12.1**	**11.3**	**12.0**	**12.1**	**12.8**
5100 Taxes on production, sale, transfer, etc	8.7	12.9	23.1	36.0	41.1	11.4	10.5	11.2	11.3	12.0
5110 General taxes	6.2	9.9	19.1	30.3	35.4	8.1	8.1	9.3	9.5	10.4
5111 Value added taxes	6.2	9.9	19.1	30.3	35.4	8.1	8.1	9.3	9.5	10.4
5120 Taxes on specific goods and services	2.5	3.0	4.0	5.7	5.7	3.3	2.5	1.9	1.8	1.7
5121 Excises	1.9	2.1	1.8	2.5	2.1	2.5	1.8	0.9	0.8	0.6
5200 Taxes on use of goods and perform activities	0.5	0.9	1.6	2.6	2.8	0.7	0.7	0.8	0.8	0.8
5300 Unallocable between 5100 and 5200	0.0	0.0	0.0	0.0	0.0	0.0	0.0	0.0	0.0	0.0
6000 Other taxes	**0.0**	**0.0**	**0.0**	**0.0**	**0.0**	**0.0**	**0.0**	**0.0**	**0.0**	**0.0**
Non-wastable tax credits										
Non-wastable tax credits against 1000	..	1.1	2.8	3.0	3.0	..	0.9	1.4	0.9	0.9
Transfer component	..	0.7	1.8	1.5	1.4	..	0.6	0.9	0.5	0.4
Tax expenditure component	..	0.3	1.0	1.5	1.5	..	0.3	0.5	0.5	0.4

.. Not available

Note: More detailed country data and country notes are available in Chapter 5 "Detailed country tables". Full time series can be accessed at http://oe.cd/full-time-series.

Source: Statistics New Zealand.

StatLink https://stat.link/pq0k2a

Table 4.54. New Zealand, tax revenue and % of GDP by level of government and main taxes

	Billion NZD					% of GDP				
	1990	2000	2010	2019	2020	1990	2000	2010	2019	2020
Federal or Central government										
Total tax revenue	**25.8**	**37.5**	**57.9**	**92.8**	**108.5**	**34.0**	**30.7**	**28.1**	**29.1**	**31.7**
1000 Taxes on income, profits and capital gains	16.4	23.9	33.5	54.9	65.3	21.6	19.5	16.3	17.2	19.1
2000 Social security contributions	0.0	0.0	0.0	0.0	0.0	0.0	0.0	0.0	0.0	0.0
3000 Taxes on payroll and workforce	0.0	0.0	0.0	0.0	0.0	0.0	0.0	0.0	0.0	0.0
4000 Taxes on property	0.3	0.1	0.1	0.1	0.1	0.4	0.1	0.0	0.0	0.0
5000 Taxes on goods and services	9.1	13.6	24.3	37.8	43.1	12.0	11.1	11.8	11.9	12.6
6000 Other taxes	0.0	0.0	0.0	0.0	0.0	0.0	0.0	0.0	0.0	0.0
State/Regional										
Total tax revenue	**..**	**..**	**..**	**..**	**..**	**..**	**..**	**..**	**..**	**..**
1000 Taxes on income, profits and capital gains	..	..	..	..	..	..	..	..	..	..
2000 Social security contributions	..	..	..	..	..	..	..	..	..	..
3000 Taxes on payroll and workforce	..	..	..	..	..	..	..	..	..	..
4000 Taxes on property	..	..	..	..	..	..	..	..	..	..
5000 Taxes on goods and services	..	..	..	..	..	..	..	..	..	..
6000 Other taxes	..	..	..	..	..	..	..	..	..	..
Local government										
Total tax revenue	**1.7**	**2.3**	**4.5**	**6.8**	**7.1**	**2.2**	**1.9**	**2.2**	**2.1**	**2.1**
1000 Taxes on income, profits and capital gains	0.0	0.0	0.0	0.0	0.0	0.0	0.0	0.0	0.0	0.0
2000 Social security contributions	0.0	0.0	0.0	0.0	0.0	0.0	0.0	0.0	0.0	0.0
3000 Taxes on payroll and workforce	0.0	0.0	0.0	0.0	0.0	0.0	0.0	0.0	0.0	0.0
4000 Taxes on property	1.6	2.0	4.0	6.0	6.3	2.0	1.7	2.0	1.9	1.8
5000 Taxes on goods and services	0.1	0.2	0.4	0.8	0.8	0.2	0.2	0.2	0.2	0.2
6000 Other taxes	0.0	0.0	0.0	0.0	0.0	0.0	0.0	0.0	0.0	0.0
Social Security Funds										
Total tax revenue	**0.0**	**0.0**	**0.0**	**0.0**	**0.0**	**0.0**	**0.0**	**0.0**	**0.0**	**0.0**
1000 Taxes on income, profits and capital gains	0.0	0.0	0.0	0.0	0.0	0.0	0.0	0.0	0.0	0.0
2000 Social security contributions	0.0	0.0	0.0	0.0	0.0	0.0	0.0	0.0	0.0	0.0
3000 Taxes on payroll and workforce	0.0	0.0	0.0	0.0	0.0	0.0	0.0	0.0	0.0	0.0
4000 Taxes on property	0.0	0.0	0.0	0.0	0.0	0.0	0.0	0.0	0.0	0.0
5000 Taxes on goods and services	0.0	0.0	0.0	0.0	0.0	0.0	0.0	0.0	0.0	0.0
6000 Other taxes	0.0	0.0	0.0	0.0	0.0	0.0	0.0	0.0	0.0	0.0

.. Not available

Note: More detailed country data and country notes are available in Chapter 6 "Tax revenues by sub-sectors of general government". Full time series can be accessed at http://oe.cd/full-time-series.

Source: Statistics New Zealand.

StatLink https://stat.link/s0prkq

Table 4.55. Norway, tax revenue and % of GDP by selected tax category

	Billion NOK					% of GDP				
	1990	2000	2010	2019	2020	1990	2000	2010	2019	2020
Total tax revenue	**301.8**	**628.0**	**1 083.3**	**1 427.8**	**1 323.1**	**40.2**	**41.7**	**41.8**	**40.1**	**38.8**
1000 Taxes on income, profits and capital gains	**106.3**	**284.2**	**512.2**	**583.6**	**470.5**	**14.2**	**18.9**	**19.8**	**16.4**	**13.8**
1100 Of individuals	79.1	152.0	256.5	369.8	389.1	10.5	10.1	9.9	10.4	11.4
1200 Corporate	27.2	132.2	255.7	213.8	81.4	3.6	8.8	9.9	6.0	2.4
1300 Unallocable between 1100 and 1200	0.0	0.0	0.0	0.0	0.0	0.0	0.0	0.0	0.0	0.0
2000 Social security contributions	**79.4**	**132.2**	**243.0**	**377.1**	**381.8**	**10.6**	**8.8**	**9.4**	**10.6**	**11.2**
2100 Employees	25.3	45.2	81.0	130.9	134.5	3.4	3.0	3.1	3.7	3.9
2200 Employers	50.1	79.2	148.0	221.0	222.2	6.7	5.3	5.7	6.2	6.5
2300 Self-employed or non-employed	3.9	7.8	13.9	25.2	25.2	0.5	0.5	0.5	0.7	0.7
2400 Unallocable between 2100, 2200 and 2300	0.0	0.0	0.0	0.0	0.0	0.0	0.0	0.0	0.0	0.0
3000 Taxes on payroll and workforce	**0.0**	**0.0**	**0.0**	**2.0**	**2.1**	**0.0**	**0.0**	**0.0**	**0.1**	**0.1**
4000 Taxes on property	**8.9**	**14.4**	**28.5**	**46.3**	**44.7**	**1.2**	**1.0**	**1.1**	**1.3**	**1.3**
4100 Recurrent taxes on immovable property	2.2	2.7	7.1	14.7	14.8	0.3	0.2	0.3	0.4	0.4
4200 Recurrent taxes on net wealth	5.1	7.7	13.2	21.2	18.5	0.7	0.5	0.5	0.6	0.5
4300 Estate, inheritance and gift taxes	0.4	1.3	2.4	0.0	0.1	0.1	0.1	0.1	0.0	0.0
4400 Taxes on financial and capital transactions	1.1	2.7	5.9	10.3	11.4	0.1	0.2	0.2	0.3	0.3
4500 Non-recurrent taxes	0.0	0.0	0.0	0.0	0.0	0.0	0.0	0.0	0.0	0.0
4600 Other recurrent taxes on property	0.0	0.0	0.0	0.0	0.0	0.0	0.0	0.0	0.0	0.0
5000 Taxes on goods and services	**107.3**	**197.2**	**299.5**	**418.8**	**424.0**	**14.3**	**13.1**	**11.6**	**11.8**	**12.4**
5100 Taxes on production, sale, transfer, etc	102.9	185.9	284.6	398.9	403.9	13.7	12.3	11.0	11.2	11.8
5110 General taxes	56.7	125.0	201.8	308.3	312.9	7.6	8.3	7.8	8.7	9.2
5111 Value added taxes	56.7	124.2	201.2	307.0	311.6	7.6	8.2	7.8	8.6	9.1
5120 Taxes on specific goods and services	46.2	60.9	82.8	90.7	91.0	6.2	4.0	3.2	2.5	2.7
5121 Excises	37.5	54.9	76.3	79.7	81.7	5.0	3.6	2.9	2.2	2.4
5200 Taxes on use of goods and perform activities	4.4	11.3	14.9	19.9	20.1	0.6	0.7	0.6	0.6	0.6
5300 Unallocable between 5100 and 5200	0.0	0.0	0.0	0.0	0.0	0.0	0.0	0.0	0.0	0.0
6000 Other taxes	**0.0**	**0.0**	**0.0**	**0.0**	**0.0**	**0.0**	**0.0**	**0.0**	**0.0**	**0.0**
Non-wastable tax credits										
Non-wastable tax credits against 1000	..	..	1.2	4.2	4.0	..	..	0.0	0.1	0.1
Transfer component	..	..	1.2	3.4	3.2	..	..	0.0	0.1	0.1
Tax expenditure component	..	..	0.1	0.8	0.8	..	..	0.0	0.0	0.0

.. Not available

Note: More detailed country data and country notes are available in Chapter 5 "Detailed country tables". Full time series can be accessed at http://oe.cd/full-time-series.

Source: Statistics Norway; National Accounts.

StatLink https://stat.link/kyo4pv

Table 4.56. Norway, tax revenue and % of GDP by level of government and main taxes

	Billion NOK					% of GDP				
	1990	2000	2010	2019	2020	1990	2000	2010	2019	2020
Federal or Central government										
Total tax revenue	**165.4**	**532.5**	**935.7**	**1 208.0**	**1 100.1**	**22.1**	**35.3**	**36.1**	**33.9**	**32.3**
1000 Taxes on income, profits and capital gains	50.6	198.4	381.0	393.9	277.3	6.8	13.2	14.7	11.1	8.1
2000 Social security contributions	4.7	132.2	243.0	377.1	381.8	0.6	8.8	9.4	10.6	11.2
3000 Taxes on payroll and workforce	0.0	0.0	0.0	2.0	2.1	0.0	0.0	0.0	0.1	0.1
4000 Taxes on property	3.4	6.8	13.7	17.9	16.5	0.5	0.5	0.5	0.5	0.5
5000 Taxes on goods and services	106.7	195.1	298.0	417.2	422.4	14.2	12.9	11.5	11.7	12.4
6000 Other taxes	0.0	0.0	0.0	0.0	0.0	0.0	0.0	0.0	0.0	0.0
State/Regional										
Total tax revenue	..	..	..	..	..	..	..	..	..	..
1000 Taxes on income, profits and capital gains	..	..	..	..	..	..	..	..	..	..
2000 Social security contributions	..	..	..	..	..	..	..	..	..	..
3000 Taxes on payroll and workforce	..	..	..	..	..	..	..	..	..	..
4000 Taxes on property	..	..	..	..	..	..	..	..	..	..
5000 Taxes on goods and services	..	..	..	..	..	..	..	..	..	..
6000 Other taxes	..	..	..	..	..	..	..	..	..	..
Local government										
Total tax revenue	**61.6**	**95.5**	**147.7**	**219.8**	**223.0**	**8.2**	**6.3**	**5.7**	**6.2**	**6.5**
1000 Taxes on income, profits and capital gains	55.7	85.8	131.2	189.8	193.2	7.4	5.7	5.1	5.3	5.7
2000 Social security contributions	0.0	0.0	0.0	0.0	0.0	0.0	0.0	0.0	0.0	0.0
3000 Taxes on payroll and workforce	0.0	0.0	0.0	0.0	0.0	0.0	0.0	0.0	0.0	0.0
4000 Taxes on property	5.5	7.6	14.9	28.4	28.2	0.7	0.5	0.6	0.8	0.8
5000 Taxes on goods and services	0.4	2.1	1.6	1.6	1.6	0.1	0.1	0.1	0.0	0.0
6000 Other taxes	0.0	0.0	0.0	0.0	0.0	0.0	0.0	0.0	0.0	0.0
Social Security Funds										
Total tax revenue	**74.8**	**0.0**	**0.0**	**0.0**	**0.0**	**10.0**	**0.0**	**0.0**	**0.0**	**0.0**
1000 Taxes on income, profits and capital gains	0.0	0.0	0.0	0.0	0.0	0.0	0.0	0.0	0.0	0.0
2000 Social security contributions	74.6	0.0	0.0	0.0	0.0	10.0	0.0	0.0	0.0	0.0
3000 Taxes on payroll and workforce	0.0	0.0	0.0	0.0	0.0	0.0	0.0	0.0	0.0	0.0
4000 Taxes on property	0.0	0.0	0.0	0.0	0.0	0.0	0.0	0.0	0.0	0.0
5000 Taxes on goods and services	0.2	0.0	0.0	0.0	0.0	0.0	0.0	0.0	0.0	0.0
6000 Other taxes	0.0	0.0	0.0	0.0	0.0	0.0	0.0	0.0	0.0	0.0

.. Not available

Note: More detailed country data and country notes are available in Chapter 6 "Tax revenues by sub-sectors of general government". Full time series can be accessed at http://oe.cd/full-time-series.

Source: Statistics Norway; National Accounts.

StatLink https://stat.link/0td2m5

Table 4.57. Poland, tax revenue and % of GDP by selected tax category

	Billion PLN					% of GDP				
	1990	2000	2010	2019	2020	1990	2000	2010	2019	2020
Total tax revenue	..	**246.0**	**453.3**	**805.0**	**831.3**	..	**32.9**	**31.3**	**35.1**	**35.5**
1000 Taxes on income, profits and capital gains	..	**50.3**	**91.0**	**172.5**	**175.8**	..	**6.7**	**6.3**	**7.5**	**7.5**
1100 Of individuals	..	32.4	62.9	121.9	123.0	..	4.3	4.3	5.3	5.3
1200 Corporate	..	17.9	28.1	50.6	52.9	..	2.4	1.9	2.2	2.3
1300 Unallocable between 1100 and 1200	..	0.0	0.0	0.0	0.0	..	0.0	0.0	0.0	0.0
2000 Social security contributions	..	**96.4**	**156.0**	**302.3**	**315.4**	..	**12.9**	**10.8**	**13.2**	**13.5**
2100 Employees	..	42.2	59.7	127.5	131.6	..	5.6	4.1	5.6	5.6
2200 Employers	..	41.4	66.1	115.7	119.9	..	5.5	4.6	5.0	5.1
2300 Self-employed or non-employed	..	12.8	30.2	59.1	63.9	..	1.7	2.1	2.6	2.7
2400 Unallocable between 2100, 2200 and 2300	..	0.0	0.0	0.0	0.0	..	0.0	0.0	0.0	0.0
3000 Taxes on payroll and workforce	..	**1.6**	**3.7**	**5.9**	**7.7**	..	**0.2**	**0.3**	**0.3**	**0.3**
4000 Taxes on property	..	**10.6**	**19.1**	**29.0**	**30.3**	..	**1.4**	**1.3**	**1.3**	**1.3**
4100 Recurrent taxes on immovable property	..	8.4	16.4	25.2	26.5	..	1.1	1.1	1.1	1.1
4200 Recurrent taxes on net wealth	..	0.0	0.0	0.0	0.0	..	0.0	0.0	0.0	0.0
4300 Estate, inheritance and gift taxes	..	0.2	0.3	0.3	0.3	..	0.0	0.0	0.0	0.0
4400 Taxes on financial and capital transactions	..	2.0	2.4	3.5	3.5	..	0.3	0.2	0.2	0.2
4500 Non-recurrent taxes	..	0.0	0.0	0.0	0.0	..	0.0	0.0	0.0	0.0
4600 Other recurrent taxes on property	..	0.0	0.0	0.0	0.0	..	0.0	0.0	0.0	0.0
5000 Taxes on goods and services	..	**86.9**	**182.8**	**294.1**	**301.0**	..	**11.6**	**12.6**	**12.8**	**12.9**
5100 Taxes on production, sale, transfer, etc	..	84.9	176.0	281.8	283.8	..	11.3	12.2	12.3	12.1
5110 General taxes	..	51.6	109.7	182.1	186.0	..	6.9	7.6	7.9	8.0
5111 Value added taxes	..	51.6	109.7	182.1	186.0	..	6.9	7.6	7.9	8.0
5120 Taxes on specific goods and services	..	33.3	66.3	99.6	97.9	..	4.4	4.6	4.3	4.2
5121 Excises	..	27.2	62.0	83.9	81.8	..	3.6	4.3	3.7	3.5
5200 Taxes on use of goods and perform activities	..	2.0	6.8	12.4	17.2	..	0.3	0.5	0.5	0.7
5300 Unallocable between 5100 and 5200	..	0.0	0.0	0.0	0.0	..	0.0	0.0	0.0	0.0
6000 Other taxes	..	**0.3**	**0.6**	**1.1**	**1.0**	..	**0.0**	**0.0**	**0.0**	**0.0**
Non-wastable tax credits										
Non-wastable tax credits against 1000	..	..	..	..	..	..	..	..	..	..
Transfer component	..	..	..	..	..	..	..	..	..	..
Tax expenditure component	..	..	..	..	..	..	..	..	..	..
Revenues collected on behalf of the EU										
Revenues collected on behalf of the EU, total	..	..	1.7	4.5	4.4	..	..	0.1	0.2	0.2
Customs duties	..	..	1.6	4.5	4.4	..	..	0.1	0.2	0.2

.. Not available

Note: The total tax revenue has been reduced by the amount of any capital transfer that represents uncollected taxes. The capital transfers were subtracted directly from the specific taxes to which they relate. Therefore, the tax revenue amounts are different to those reported in the detailed country data available in Chapter 5 "Detailed country tables".

More detailed country data and country notes are available in Chapter 5 "Detailed country tables". Full time series can be accessed at http://oe.cd/full-time-series.

Source: Ministry of Finance, Economic Department.

StatLink https://stat.link/gonptw

Table 4.58. Poland, tax revenue and % of GDP by level of government and main taxes

	Billion PLN					% of GDP				
	1990	2000	2010	2019	2020	1990	2000	2010	2019	2020
Federal or Central government										
Total tax revenue	..	**126.9**	**238.4**	**396.7**	**408.6**	..	**17.0**	**16.5**	**17.3**	**17.5**
1000 Taxes on income, profits and capital gains	..	40.0	57.7	105.1	108.2	..	5.3	4.0	4.6	4.6
2000 Social security contributions	..	0.0	0.0	0.0	0.0	..	0.0	0.0	0.0	0.0
3000 Taxes on payroll and workforce	..	1.6	3.7	5.9	7.7	..	0.2	0.3	0.3	0.3
4000 Taxes on property	..	0.0	0.0	0.0	0.0	..	0.0	0.0	0.0	0.0
5000 Taxes on goods and services	..	85.3	177.0	285.7	292.7	..	11.4	12.2	12.5	12.5
6000 Other taxes	..	0.0	0.0	0.0	0.0	..	0.0	0.0	0.0	0.0
State/Regional										
Total tax revenue	..	..	..	..	..	..	..	..	..	..
1000 Taxes on income, profits and capital gains	..	..	..	..	..	..	..	..	..	..
2000 Social security contributions	..	..	..	..	..	..	..	..	..	..
3000 Taxes on payroll and workforce	..	..	..	..	..	..	..	..	..	..
4000 Taxes on property	..	..	..	..	..	..	..	..	..	..
5000 Taxes on goods and services	..	..	..	..	..	..	..	..	..	..
6000 Other taxes	..	..	..	..	..	..	..	..	..	..
Local government										
Total tax revenue	..	**22.7**	**57.1**	**101.5**	**102.9**	..	**3.0**	**3.9**	**4.4**	**4.4**
1000 Taxes on income, profits and capital gains	..	10.3	33.3	67.4	67.6	..	1.4	2.3	2.9	2.9
2000 Social security contributions	..	0.0	0.0	0.0	0.0	..	0.0	0.0	0.0	0.0
3000 Taxes on payroll and workforce	..	0.0	0.0	0.0	0.0	..	0.0	0.0	0.0	0.0
4000 Taxes on property	..	10.6	19.1	29.0	30.3	..	1.4	1.3	1.3	1.3
5000 Taxes on goods and services	..	1.5	4.1	4.0	4.0	..	0.2	0.3	0.2	0.2
6000 Other taxes	..	0.3	0.6	1.1	1.0	..	0.0	0.0	0.0	0.0
Social Security Funds										
Total tax revenue	..	**96.4**	**156.0**	**302.3**	**315.4**	..	**12.9**	**10.8**	**13.2**	**13.5**
1000 Taxes on income, profits and capital gains	..	0.0	0.0	0.0	0.0	..	0.0	0.0	0.0	0.0
2000 Social security contributions	..	96.4	156.0	302.3	315.4	..	12.9	10.8	13.2	13.5
3000 Taxes on payroll and workforce	..	0.0	0.0	0.0	0.0	..	0.0	0.0	0.0	0.0
4000 Taxes on property	..	0.0	0.0	0.0	0.0	..	0.0	0.0	0.0	0.0
5000 Taxes on goods and services	..	0.0	0.0	0.0	0.0	..	0.0	0.0	0.0	0.0
6000 Other taxes	..	0.0	0.0	0.0	0.0	..	0.0	0.0	0.0	0.0

.. Not available

Note: The total tax revenue has been reduced by the amount of any capital transfer that represents uncollected taxes. The capital transfers were subtracted directly from the specific taxes to which they relate. Therefore, the tax revenue amounts are different to those reported in the detailed country data available in Chapter 6 "Tax revenues by sub-sectors of general government".

More detailed country data and country notes are available in Chapter 6 "Tax revenues by sub-sectors of general government". Full time series can be accessed at http://oe.cd/full-time-series.

Source: Ministry of Finance, Economic Department.

StatLink https://stat.link/mxqdi5

Table 4.59. Portugal, tax revenue and % of GDP by selected tax category

	Billion EUR					% of GDP				
	1990	2000	2010	2019	2020	1990	2000	2010	2019	2020
Total tax revenue	**14.8**	**39.7**	**54.5**	**74.0**	**70.5**	**26.5**	**30.9**	**30.4**	**34.5**	**35.3**
1000 Taxes on income, profits and capital gains	**3.8**	**11.7**	**14.6**	**20.3**	**19.5**	**6.8**	**9.1**	**8.1**	**9.5**	**9.8**
1100 Of individuals	2.4	6.8	9.6	13.6	14.0	4.2	5.3	5.4	6.3	7.0
1200 Corporate	1.2	4.7	4.9	6.7	5.5	2.1	3.7	2.7	3.1	2.8
1300 Unallocable between 1100 and 1200	0.3	0.2	0.0	0.0	0.0	0.5	0.1	0.0	0.0	0.0
2000 Social security contributions	**4.0**	**10.2**	**15.5**	**20.6**	**20.9**	**7.2**	**7.9**	**8.6**	**9.6**	**10.5**
2100 Employees	1.5	4.3	6.7	8.2	8.3	2.6	3.3	3.7	3.8	4.1
2200 Employers	2.4	5.9	8.8	12.4	12.6	4.3	4.6	4.9	5.8	6.3
2300 Self-employed or non-employed	0.1	0.0	0.0	0.0	0.0	0.3	0.0	0.0	0.0	0.0
2400 Unallocable between 2100, 2200 and 2300	0.0	0.0	0.0	0.0	0.0	0.0	0.0	0.0	0.0	0.0
3000 Taxes on payroll and workforce	**0.0**	**0.0**	**0.0**	**0.0**	**0.0**	**0.0**	**0.0**	**0.0**	**0.0**	**0.0**
4000 Taxes on property	**0.4**	**1.5**	**2.0**	**3.1**	**2.9**	**0.7**	**1.1**	**1.1**	**1.4**	**1.5**
4100 Recurrent taxes on immovable property	0.1	0.5	1.1	1.7	1.6	0.2	0.4	0.6	0.8	0.8
4200 Recurrent taxes on net wealth	0.0	0.0	0.0	0.0	0.0	0.0	0.0	0.0	0.0	0.0
4300 Estate, inheritance and gift taxes	0.1	0.1	0.1	0.0	0.0	0.1	0.1	0.0	0.0	0.0
4400 Taxes on financial and capital transactions	0.2	0.9	0.8	1.4	1.3	0.3	0.7	0.5	0.6	0.6
4500 Non-recurrent taxes	0.0	0.0	0.0	0.0	0.0	0.0	0.0	0.0	0.0	0.0
4600 Other recurrent taxes on property	0.0	0.0	0.0	0.0	0.0	0.0	0.0	0.0	0.0	0.0
5000 Taxes on goods and services	**6.6**	**16.2**	**22.0**	**29.4**	**26.5**	**11.7**	**12.6**	**12.3**	**13.7**	**13.2**
5100 Taxes on production, sale, transfer, etc	6.4	15.8	21.4	28.1	25.2	11.5	12.3	11.9	13.1	12.6
5110 General taxes	2.9	9.7	13.5	18.8	16.8	5.2	7.6	7.5	8.8	8.4
5111 Value added taxes	2.9	9.7	13.5	18.8	16.8	5.2	7.6	7.5	8.8	8.4
5120 Taxes on specific goods and services	3.5	6.1	7.9	9.3	8.4	6.3	4.8	4.4	4.3	4.2
5121 Excises	2.1	4.5	5.7	6.2	5.5	3.7	3.5	3.1	2.9	2.7
5200 Taxes on use of goods and perform activities	0.1	0.3	0.6	1.3	1.3	0.2	0.2	0.3	0.6	0.6
5300 Unallocable between 5100 and 5200	0.0	0.0	0.0	0.0	0.0	0.0	0.0	0.0	0.0	0.0
6000 Other taxes	**0.0**	**0.2**	**0.4**	**0.6**	**0.7**	**0.1**	**0.2**	**0.2**	**0.3**	**0.3**
Non-wastable tax credits										
Non-wastable tax credits against 1000	..	..	..	..	..	..	..	..	..	..
Transfer component	..	..	..	..	..	..	..	..	..	..
Tax expenditure component	..	..	..	..	..	..	..	..	..	..
Revenues collected on behalf of the EU										
Revenues collected on behalf of the EU, total	0.2	0.2	0.2	0.4	0.3	0.3	0.2	0.1	0.2	0.2
Customs duties	..	0.2	0.2	0.2	0.2	..	0.1	0.1	0.1	0.1
SRF contributions	..	..	..	0.1	0.1	..	..	..	0.1	0.1

.. Not available

Note: More detailed country data and country notes are available in Chapter 5 "Detailed country tables". Full time series can be accessed at http://oe.cd/full-time-series.

Source: Instituto Nacional de Estatística.

StatLink https://stat.link/d2gpy1

Table 4.60. Portugal, tax revenue and % of GDP by level of government and main taxes

	Billion EUR					% of GDP				
	1990	2000	2010	2019	2020	1990	2000	2010	2019	2020
Federal or Central government										
Total tax revenue	**9.8**	**27.6**	**36.4**	**48.6**	**45.2**	**17.6**	**21.5**	**20.2**	**22.7**	**22.6**
1000 Taxes on income, profits and capital gains	3.6	11.1	13.5	18.9	18.2	6.4	8.7	7.5	8.8	9.1
2000 Social security contributions	0.0	1.3	1.9	2.1	2.1	0.0	1.0	1.1	1.0	1.1
3000 Taxes on payroll and workforce	0.0	0.0	0.0	0.0	0.0	0.0	0.0	0.0	0.0	0.0
4000 Taxes on property	0.1	0.3	0.3	0.5	0.5	0.1	0.2	0.2	0.2	0.2
5000 Taxes on goods and services	6.1	14.7	20.2	26.5	23.7	10.9	11.4	11.2	12.4	11.9
6000 Other taxes	0.0	0.2	0.4	0.6	0.7	0.1	0.2	0.2	0.3	0.3
State/Regional										
Total tax revenue	**..**	**..**	**..**	**..**	**..**	**..**	**..**	**..**	**..**	**..**
1000 Taxes on income, profits and capital gains	..	..	..	..	..	..	..	..	..	..
2000 Social security contributions	..	..	..	..	..	..	..	..	..	..
3000 Taxes on payroll and workforce	..	..	..	..	..	..	..	..	..	..
4000 Taxes on property	..	..	..	..	..	..	..	..	..	..
5000 Taxes on goods and services	..	..	..	..	..	..	..	..	..	..
6000 Other taxes	..	..	..	..	..	..	..	..	..	..
Local government										
Total tax revenue	**0.8**	**2.5**	**3.6**	**5.4**	**5.1**	**1.5**	**2.0**	**2.0**	**2.5**	**2.5**
1000 Taxes on income, profits and capital gains	0.2	0.6	1.1	1.4	1.4	0.4	0.4	0.6	0.6	0.7
2000 Social security contributions	0.0	0.0	0.0	0.0	0.0	0.0	0.0	0.0	0.0	0.0
3000 Taxes on payroll and workforce	0.0	0.0	0.0	0.0	0.0	0.0	0.0	0.0	0.0	0.0
4000 Taxes on property	0.3	1.2	1.7	2.6	2.4	0.6	0.9	1.0	1.2	1.2
5000 Taxes on goods and services	0.3	0.7	0.8	1.4	1.3	0.5	0.6	0.4	0.7	0.6
6000 Other taxes	0.0	0.0	0.0	0.0	0.0	0.0	0.0	0.0	0.0	0.0
Social Security Funds										
Total tax revenue	**4.0**	**9.4**	**14.4**	**19.6**	**19.9**	**7.2**	**7.3**	**8.0**	**9.1**	**9.9**
1000 Taxes on income, profits and capital gains	0.0	0.0	0.0	0.0	0.0	0.0	0.0	0.0	0.0	0.0
2000 Social security contributions	4.0	8.8	13.5	18.5	18.8	7.2	6.9	7.5	8.6	9.4
3000 Taxes on payroll and workforce	0.0	0.0	0.0	0.0	0.0	0.0	0.0	0.0	0.0	0.0
4000 Taxes on property	0.0	0.0	0.0	0.0	0.0	0.0	0.0	0.0	0.0	0.0
5000 Taxes on goods and services	0.0	0.5	0.8	1.1	1.1	0.0	0.4	0.5	0.5	0.5
6000 Other taxes	0.0	0.0	0.0	0.0	0.0	0.0	0.0	0.0	0.0	0.0

.. Not available

Note: More detailed country data and country notes are available in Chapter 6 "Tax revenues by sub-sectors of general government". Full time series can be accessed at http://oe.cd/full-time-series.

Source: Instituto Nacional de Estatística.

StatLink https://stat.link/7dil1t

Table 4.61. Slovak Republic, tax revenue and % of GDP by selected tax category

	Billion EUR					% of GDP				
	1990	2000	2010	2019	2020	1990	2000	2010	2019	2020
Total tax revenue	..	**10.6**	**19.2**	**32.5**	**32.4**	..	**33.6**	**28.0**	**34.6**	**35.2**
1000 Taxes on income, profits and capital gains	..	**2.2**	**3.6**	**6.7**	**6.5**	..	**6.9**	**5.3**	**7.1**	**7.1**
1100 Of individuals	..	1.1	1.8	3.5	3.5	..	3.3	2.6	3.8	3.8
1200 Corporate	..	0.8	1.7	2.9	2.8	..	2.6	2.4	3.1	3.0
1300 Unallocable between 1100 and 1200	..	0.3	0.2	0.2	0.2	..	1.0	0.2	0.3	0.3
2000 Social security contributions	..	**4.4**	**8.2**	**14.1**	**14.2**	..	**13.9**	**11.9**	**15.0**	**15.5**
2100 Employees	..	0.9	2.1	3.4	3.5	..	2.8	3.0	3.7	3.8
2200 Employers	..	2.9	4.6	8.5	8.7	..	9.0	6.7	9.1	9.4
2300 Self-employed or non-employed	..	0.7	1.5	2.1	2.1	..	2.1	2.2	2.2	2.3
2400 Unallocable between 2100, 2200 and 2300	..	0.0	0.0	0.0	0.0	..	0.0	0.0	0.0	0.0
3000 Taxes on payroll and workforce	..	**0.0**	**0.0**	**0.0**	**0.0**	..	**0.0**	**0.0**	**0.0**	**0.0**
4000 Taxes on property	..	**0.2**	**0.3**	**0.4**	**0.4**	..	**0.6**	**0.4**	**0.4**	**0.5**
4100 Recurrent taxes on immovable property	..	0.1	0.3	0.4	0.4	..	0.5	0.4	0.4	0.5
4200 Recurrent taxes on net wealth	..	0.0	0.0	0.0	0.0	..	0.0	0.0	0.0	0.0
4300 Estate, inheritance and gift taxes	..	0.0	0.0	0.0	0.0	..	0.0	0.0	0.0	0.0
4400 Taxes on financial and capital transactions	..	0.0	0.0	0.0	0.0	..	0.1	0.0	0.0	0.0
4500 Non-recurrent taxes	..	0.0	0.0	0.0	0.0	..	0.0	0.0	0.0	0.0
4600 Other recurrent taxes on property	..	0.0	0.0	0.0	0.0	..	0.0	0.0	0.0	0.0
5000 Taxes on goods and services	..	**3.9**	**7.1**	**11.4**	**11.2**	..	**12.2**	**10.4**	**12.1**	**12.2**
5100 Taxes on production, sale, transfer, etc	..	3.6	6.6	10.5	10.4	..	11.5	9.6	11.2	11.3
5110 General taxes	..	2.2	4.2	6.8	6.8	..	6.8	6.1	7.3	7.4
5111 Value added taxes	..	2.2	4.2	6.8	6.8	..	6.8	6.1	7.3	7.4
5120 Taxes on specific goods and services	..	1.5	2.4	3.7	3.6	..	4.6	3.5	3.9	3.9
5121 Excises	..	1.0	2.1	2.8	2.8	..	3.1	3.0	3.0	3.0
5200 Taxes on use of goods and perform activities	..	0.2	0.4	0.7	0.6	..	0.7	0.6	0.7	0.7
5300 Unallocable between 5100 and 5200	..	0.0	0.1	0.2	0.2	..	0.0	0.2	0.2	0.2
6000 Other taxes	..	**0.0**	**0.0**	**0.0**	**0.0**	..	**0.0**	**0.0**	**0.0**	**0.0**
Non-wastable tax credits										
Non-wastable tax credits against 1000	..	..	0.3	0.3	0.4	..	..	0.4	0.4	0.4
Transfer component	..	..	..	..	..	..	..	..	..	..
Tax expenditure component	..	..	..	..	..	..	..	..	..	..
Revenues collected on behalf of the EU										
Revenues collected on behalf of the EU, total	..	..	0.1	0.1	0.1	..	..	0.2	0.2	0.2
Customs duties	..	..	0.1	0.1	0.1	..	..	0.2	0.1	0.1
SRF contributions	..	..	..	0.0	0.0	..	..	..	0.0	0.0

.. Not available

Note: More detailed country data and country notes are available in Chapter 5 "Detailed country tables". Full time series can be accessed at http://oe.cd/full-time-series.

Source: Ministry of Finance.

StatLink https://stat.link/thsb8y

Table 4.62. Slovak Republic, tax revenue and % of GDP by level of government and main taxes

	Billion EUR					% of GDP				
	1990	2000	2010	2019	2020	1990	2000	2010	2019	2020
Federal or Central government										
Total tax revenue	**..**	**6.2**	**10.5**	**18.0**	**17.8**	**..**	**19.5**	**15.4**	**19.2**	**19.3**
1000 Taxes on income, profits and capital gains	..	2.2	3.6	6.7	6.5	..	6.9	5.3	7.1	7.1
2000 Social security contributions	..	0.1	0.2	0.4	0.4	..	0.3	0.3	0.4	0.5
3000 Taxes on payroll and workforce	..	0.0	0.0	0.0	0.0	..	0.0	0.0	0.0	0.0
4000 Taxes on property	..	0.1	0.0	0.0	0.0	..	0.2	0.0	0.0	0.0
5000 Taxes on goods and services	..	3.9	6.7	11.0	10.8	..	12.2	9.8	11.7	11.7
6000 Other taxes	..	0.0	0.0	0.0	0.0	..	0.0	0.0	0.0	0.0
State/Regional										
Total tax revenue	**..**	**..**	**..**	**..**	**..**	**..**	**..**	**..**	**..**	**..**
1000 Taxes on income, profits and capital gains	..	..	..	..	..	..	..	..	..	..
2000 Social security contributions	..	..	..	..	..	..	..	..	..	..
3000 Taxes on payroll and workforce	..	..	..	..	..	..	..	..	..	..
4000 Taxes on property	..	..	..	..	..	..	..	..	..	..
5000 Taxes on goods and services	..	..	..	..	..	..	..	..	..	..
6000 Other taxes	..	..	..	..	..	..	..	..	..	..
Local government										
Total tax revenue	**..**	**0.1**	**0.5**	**0.6**	**0.7**	**..**	**0.5**	**0.8**	**0.6**	**0.7**
1000 Taxes on income, profits and capital gains	..	0.0	0.0	0.0	0.0	..	0.0	0.0	0.0	0.0
2000 Social security contributions	..	0.0	0.0	0.0	0.0	..	0.0	0.0	0.0	0.0
3000 Taxes on payroll and workforce	..	0.0	0.0	0.0	0.0	..	0.0	0.0	0.0	0.0
4000 Taxes on property	..	0.1	0.3	0.4	0.4	..	0.4	0.4	0.4	0.5
5000 Taxes on goods and services	..	0.0	0.3	0.2	0.2	..	0.0	0.4	0.2	0.3
6000 Other taxes	..	0.0	0.0	0.0	0.0	..	0.0	0.0	0.0	0.0
Social Security Funds										
Total tax revenue	**..**	**4.3**	**7.9**	**13.7**	**13.8**	**..**	**13.6**	**11.6**	**14.6**	**15.0**
1000 Taxes on income, profits and capital gains	..	0.0	0.0	0.0	0.0	..	0.0	0.0	0.0	0.0
2000 Social security contributions	..	4.3	7.9	13.7	13.8	..	13.6	11.6	14.6	15.0
3000 Taxes on payroll and workforce	..	0.0	0.0	0.0	0.0	..	0.0	0.0	0.0	0.0
4000 Taxes on property	..	0.0	0.0	0.0	0.0	..	0.0	0.0	0.0	0.0
5000 Taxes on goods and services	..	0.0	0.0	0.0	0.0	..	0.0	0.0	0.0	0.0
6000 Other taxes	..	0.0	0.0	0.0	0.0	..	0.0	0.0	0.0	0.0

.. Not available

Note: More detailed country data and country notes are available in Chapter 6 "Tax revenues by sub-sectors of general government". Full time series can be accessed at http://oe.cd/full-time-series.

Source: Ministry of Finance.

StatLink https://stat.link/w204id

Table 4.63. Slovenia, tax revenue and % of GDP by selected tax category

	Billion EUR					% of GDP				
	1990	2000	2010	2019	2020	1990	2000	2010	2019	2020
Total tax revenue	..	**7.1**	**13.7**	**18.0**	**17.5**	..	**37.7**	**37.8**	**37.0**	**37.2**
1000 Taxes on income, profits and capital gains	..	**1.3**	**2.7**	**3.5**	**3.4**	..	**6.8**	**7.4**	**7.2**	**7.2**
1100 Of individuals	..	1.0	2.0	2.5	2.5	..	5.5	5.6	5.3	5.2
1200 Corporate	..	0.2	0.7	1.0	0.9	..	1.1	1.8	2.0	1.9
1300 Unallocable between 1100 and 1200	..	0.0	0.0	0.0	0.0	..	0.1	0.0	0.0	0.0
2000 Social security contributions	..	**2.8**	**5.7**	**7.6**	**7.9**	..	**14.9**	**15.8**	**15.6**	**16.8**
2100 Employees	..	1.4	2.8	4.2	3.9	..	7.7	7.7	8.6	8.3
2200 Employers	..	1.0	2.1	2.8	2.9	..	5.3	5.7	5.7	6.1
2300 Self-employed or non-employed	..	0.4	0.9	0.6	1.1	..	1.9	2.5	1.3	2.4
2400 Unallocable between 2100, 2200 and 2300	..	0.0	0.0	0.0	0.0	..	0.0	0.0	0.0	0.0
3000 Taxes on payroll and workforce	..	**0.3**	**0.0**	**0.0**	**0.0**	..	**1.5**	**0.1**	**0.0**	**0.0**
4000 Taxes on property	..	**0.1**	**0.2**	**0.3**	**0.3**	..	**0.6**	**0.6**	**0.6**	**0.6**
4100 Recurrent taxes on immovable property	..	0.1	0.2	0.2	0.2	..	0.4	0.5	0.5	0.5
4200 Recurrent taxes on net wealth	..	0.0	0.0	0.0	0.0	..	0.0	0.0	0.0	0.0
4300 Estate, inheritance and gift taxes	..	0.0	0.0	0.0	0.0	..	0.0	0.0	0.0	0.0
4400 Taxes on financial and capital transactions	..	0.0	0.0	0.0	0.0	..	0.1	0.1	0.1	0.1
4500 Non-recurrent taxes	..	0.0	0.0	0.0	0.0	..	0.1	0.0	0.0	0.0
4600 Other recurrent taxes on property	..	0.0	0.0	0.0	0.0	..	0.0	0.0	0.0	0.0
5000 Taxes on goods and services	..	**2.6**	**5.1**	**6.6**	**5.9**	..	**13.8**	**13.9**	**13.5**	**12.5**
5100 Taxes on production, sale, transfer, etc	..	2.5	4.8	6.1	5.4	..	13.2	13.3	12.6	11.6
5110 General taxes	..	1.6	2.9	3.9	3.5	..	8.7	8.1	8.0	7.5
5111 Value added taxes	..	1.6	2.9	3.9	3.5	..	8.5	8.1	8.0	7.5
5120 Taxes on specific goods and services	..	0.8	1.9	2.2	1.9	..	4.5	5.3	4.6	4.1
5121 Excises	..	0.6	1.6	1.7	1.4	..	3.1	4.3	3.4	3.0
5200 Taxes on use of goods and perform activities	..	0.1	0.2	0.5	0.4	..	0.6	0.6	0.9	0.9
5300 Unallocable between 5100 and 5200	..	0.0	0.0	0.0	0.0	..	0.0	0.0	0.0	0.0
6000 Other taxes	..	**0.0**	**0.0**	**0.0**	**0.0**	..	**0.0**	**0.0**	**0.0**	**0.0**
Non-wastable tax credits										
Non-wastable tax credits against 1000	..	..	..	..	..	..	..	..	..	..
Transfer component	..	..	..	..	..	..	..	..	..	..
Tax expenditure component	..	..	..	..	..	..	..	..	..	..
Revenues collected on behalf of the EU										
Revenues collected on behalf of the EU, total	..	..	0.1	0.1	0.1	..	..	0.2	0.1	0.2
Customs duties	..	..	0.1	0.1	0.1	..	..	0.2	0.1	0.1
SRF contributions	..	..	..	0.0	0.0	..	..	..	0.0	0.0

.. Not available

Note: The total tax revenue has been reduced by the amount of any capital transfer that represents uncollected taxes. The capital transfers were subtracted directly from the specific taxes to which they relate. Therefore, the tax revenue amounts are different to those reported in the detailed country data available in Chapter 5 "Detailed country tables".

More detailed country data and country notes are available in Chapter 5 "Detailed country tables". Full time series can be accessed at http://oe.cd/full-time-series.

Source: Statistical Office of the Republic of Slovenia.

StatLink https://stat.link/bfg54s

Table 4.64. Slovenia, tax revenue and % of GDP by level of government and main taxes

	Billion EUR					% of GDP				
	1990	2000	2010	2019	2020	1990	2000	2010	2019	2020
Federal or Central government										
Total tax revenue	..	**3.8**	**6.5**	**8.8**	**7.9**	..	**20.2**	**18.0**	**18.1**	**16.8**
1000 Taxes on income, profits and capital gains	..	0.9	1.6	2.3	2.1	..	4.8	4.3	4.7	4.4
2000 Social security contributions	..	0.0	0.1	0.1	0.1	..	0.1	0.2	0.2	0.2
3000 Taxes on payroll and workforce	..	0.3	0.0	0.0	0.0	..	1.5	0.1	0.0	0.0
4000 Taxes on property	..	0.0	0.0	0.0	0.0	..	0.1	0.0	0.0	0.0
5000 Taxes on goods and services	..	2.6	4.9	6.4	5.7	..	13.7	13.5	13.2	12.2
6000 Other taxes	..	0.0	0.0	0.0	0.0	..	0.0	0.0	0.0	0.0
State/Regional										
Total tax revenue	..	..	..	..	..	..	..	..	..	..
1000 Taxes on income, profits and capital gains	..	..	..	..	..	..	..	..	..	..
2000 Social security contributions	..	..	..	..	..	..	..	..	..	..
3000 Taxes on payroll and workforce	..	..	..	..	..	..	..	..	..	..
4000 Taxes on property	..	..	..	..	..	..	..	..	..	..
5000 Taxes on goods and services	..	..	..	..	..	..	..	..	..	..
6000 Other taxes	..	..	..	..	..	..	..	..	..	..
Local government										
Total tax revenue	..	**0.5**	**1.5**	**1.6**	**1.7**	..	**2.7**	**4.0**	**3.3**	**3.6**
1000 Taxes on income, profits and capital gains	..	0.4	1.1	1.2	1.3	..	2.0	3.1	2.5	2.8
2000 Social security contributions	..	0.0	0.0	0.0	0.0	..	0.0	0.0	0.0	0.0
3000 Taxes on payroll and workforce	..	0.0	0.0	0.0	0.0	..	0.0	0.0	0.0	0.0
4000 Taxes on property	..	0.1	0.2	0.3	0.3	..	0.6	0.6	0.6	0.6
5000 Taxes on goods and services	..	0.0	0.1	0.1	0.1	..	0.1	0.3	0.2	0.2
6000 Other taxes	..	0.0	0.0	0.0	0.0	..	0.0	0.0	0.0	0.0
Social Security Funds										
Total tax revenue	..	**2.8**	**5.7**	**7.5**	**7.8**	..	**14.8**	**15.6**	**15.5**	**16.6**
1000 Taxes on income, profits and capital gains	..	0.0	0.0	0.0	0.0	..	0.0	0.0	0.0	0.0
2000 Social security contributions	..	2.8	5.7	7.5	7.8	..	14.8	15.6	15.5	16.6
3000 Taxes on payroll and workforce	..	0.0	0.0	0.0	0.0	..	0.0	0.0	0.0	0.0
4000 Taxes on property	..	0.0	0.0	0.0	0.0	..	0.0	0.0	0.0	0.0
5000 Taxes on goods and services	..	0.0	0.0	0.0	0.0	..	0.0	0.0	0.0	0.0
6000 Other taxes	..	0.0	0.0	0.0	0.0	..	0.0	0.0	0.0	0.0

.. Not available

Note: The total tax revenue has been reduced by the amount of any capital transfer that represents uncollected taxes. The capital transfers were subtracted directly from the specific taxes to which they relate. Therefore, the tax revenue amounts are different to those reported in the detailed country data available in Chapter 6 "Tax revenues by sub-sectors of general government".

More detailed country data and country notes are available in Chapter 6 "Tax revenues by sub-sectors of general government". Full time series can be accessed at http://oe.cd/full-time-series.

Source: Statistical Office of the Republic of Slovenia.

StatLink https://stat.link/dwg5rf

Table 4.65. Spain, tax revenue and % of GDP by selected tax category

	Billion EUR					% of GDP				
	1990	2000	2010	2019	2020	1990	2000	2010	2019	2020
Total tax revenue	**103.7**	**214.1**	**335.6**	**431.7**	**412.0**	**31.5**	**33.0**	**31.3**	**34.7**	**36.7**
1000 Taxes on income, profits and capital gains	**31.8**	**60.1**	**93.8**	**123.6**	**119.8**	**9.7**	**9.3**	**8.7**	**9.9**	**10.7**
1100 Of individuals	22.5	41.2	74.1	98.0	97.8	6.9	6.4	6.9	7.9	8.7
1200 Corporate	9.1	18.9	19.7	25.7	22.0	2.8	2.9	1.8	2.1	2.0
1300 Unallocable between 1100 and 1200	0.1	0.0	0.0	0.0	0.0	0.0	0.0	0.0	0.0	0.0
2000 Social security contributions	**36.7**	**74.7**	**127.2**	**152.5**	**154.3**	**11.2**	**11.5**	**11.9**	**12.3**	**13.8**
2100 Employees	6.0	11.7	19.4	23.3	22.2	1.8	1.8	1.8	1.9	2.0
2200 Employers	26.4	54.2	89.7	112.3	112.4	8.0	8.4	8.4	9.0	10.0
2300 Self-employed or non-employed	4.4	8.7	18.1	17.0	19.7	1.3	1.4	1.7	1.4	1.8
2400 Unallocable between 2100, 2200 and 2300	0.0	0.0	0.0	0.0	0.0	0.0	0.0	0.0	0.0	0.0
3000 Taxes on payroll and workforce	**0.0**	**0.0**	**0.0**	**0.0**	**0.0**	**0.0**	**0.0**	**0.0**	**0.0**	**0.0**
4000 Taxes on property	**5.7**	**13.8**	**22.2**	**30.6**	**27.6**	**1.7**	**2.1**	**2.1**	**2.5**	**2.5**
4100 Recurrent taxes on immovable property	1.5	4.0	9.7	13.5	13.2	0.4	0.6	0.9	1.1	1.2
4200 Recurrent taxes on net wealth	0.6	1.4	0.7	2.2	2.3	0.2	0.2	0.1	0.2	0.2
4300 Estate, inheritance and gift taxes	0.4	1.4	2.4	2.5	2.5	0.1	0.2	0.2	0.2	0.2
4400 Taxes on financial and capital transactions	2.5	5.9	7.6	9.3	7.5	0.8	0.9	0.7	0.7	0.7
4500 Non-recurrent taxes	0.6	1.1	1.8	3.0	2.1	0.2	0.2	0.2	0.2	0.2
4600 Other recurrent taxes on property	0.0	0.0	0.0	0.0	0.0	0.0	0.0	0.0	0.0	0.0
5000 Taxes on goods and services	**29.4**	**65.5**	**92.3**	**124.9**	**110.2**	**9.0**	**10.1**	**8.6**	**10.0**	**9.8**
5100 Taxes on production, sale, transfer, etc	26.7	59.4	85.0	115.1	100.9	8.1	9.2	7.9	9.3	9.0
5110 General taxes	16.6	37.8	55.6	81.1	70.8	5.1	5.8	5.2	6.5	6.3
5111 Value added taxes	16.3	37.8	55.3	80.9	70.6	5.0	5.8	5.2	6.5	6.3
5120 Taxes on specific goods and services	10.1	21.6	29.4	34.0	30.1	3.1	3.3	2.7	2.7	2.7
5121 Excises	6.0	18.0	24.4	26.3	23.2	1.8	2.8	2.3	2.1	2.1
5200 Taxes on use of goods and perform activities	2.6	6.1	7.4	9.7	9.3	0.8	0.9	0.7	0.8	0.8
5300 Unallocable between 5100 and 5200	0.1	0.0	0.0	0.0	0.0	0.0	0.0	0.0	0.0	0.0
6000 Other taxes	**0.0**	**0.0**	**0.0**	**0.2**	**0.1**	**0.0**	**0.0**	**0.0**	**0.0**	**0.0**
Non-wastable tax credits										
Non-wastable tax credits against 1000	..	..	1.9	2.5	3.0	..	..	0.2	0.2	0.3
Transfer component	..	..	1.2	1.4	1.7	..	..	0.1	0.1	0.2
Tax expenditure component	..	..	0.7	1.1	1.2	..	..	0.1	0.1	0.1
Revenues collected on behalf of the EU										
Revenues collected on behalf of the EU, total	0.5	1.0	1.5	2.7	2.5	0.2	0.2	0.1	0.2	0.2
Customs duties	..	1.0	1.5	2.0	1.7	..	0.1	0.1	0.2	0.1
SRF contributions	..	..	..	0.7	0.8	..	..	..	0.1	0.1

.. Not available

Note: More detailed country data and country notes are available in Chapter 5 "Detailed country tables". Full time series can be accessed at http://oe.cd/full-time-series.

Source: Information from the Ministry of Finance for taxes and from Social Security System for social security contributions up to 1994. Since 1995 (accrual basis), national account data (IGAE-Ministry of Finance).

StatLink https://stat.link/n7e5ms

Table 4.66. Spain, tax revenue and % of GDP by level of government and main taxes

	Billion EUR					% of GDP				
	1990	2000	2010	2019	2020	1990	2000	2010	2019	2020
Federal or Central government										
Total tax revenue	**53.7**	**104.7**	**135.9**	**173.6**	**154.0**	**16.3**	**16.2**	**12.7**	**14.0**	**13.7**
1000 Taxes on income, profits and capital gains	29.5	51.0	60.6	69.6	61.0	9.0	7.9	5.6	5.6	5.4
2000 Social security contributions	0.4	2.3	3.5	3.5	3.4	0.1	0.4	0.3	0.3	0.3
3000 Taxes on payroll and workforce	0.0	0.0	0.0	0.0	0.0	0.0	0.0	0.0	0.0	0.0
4000 Taxes on property	0.4	0.4	0.1	0.3	0.4	0.1	0.1	0.0	0.0	0.0
5000 Taxes on goods and services	23.4	51.1	71.7	100.2	89.1	7.1	7.9	6.7	8.0	7.9
6000 Other taxes	0.0	0.0	0.0	0.1	0.1	0.0	0.0	0.0	0.0	0.0
State/Regional										
Total tax revenue	**5.0**	**16.9**	**44.1**	**66.7**	**68.4**	**1.5**	**2.6**	**4.1**	**5.4**	**6.1**
1000 Taxes on income, profits and capital gains	0.4	5.6	28.1	47.0	52.1	0.1	0.9	2.6	3.8	4.6
2000 Social security contributions	0.0	0.0	0.0	0.0	0.0	0.0	0.0	0.0	0.0	0.0
3000 Taxes on payroll and workforce	0.0	0.0	0.0	0.0	0.0	0.0	0.0	0.0	0.0	0.0
4000 Taxes on property	3.0	7.7	9.7	12.8	11.0	0.9	1.2	0.9	1.0	1.0
5000 Taxes on goods and services	1.6	3.6	6.3	6.9	5.3	0.5	0.6	0.6	0.6	0.5
6000 Other taxes	0.0	0.0	0.0	0.0	0.0	0.0	0.0	0.0	0.0	0.0
Local government										
Total tax revenue	**8.1**	**19.0**	**30.3**	**39.7**	**36.3**	**2.5**	**2.9**	**2.8**	**3.2**	**3.2**
1000 Taxes on income, profits and capital gains	1.9	3.5	5.2	7.1	6.8	0.6	0.5	0.5	0.6	0.6
2000 Social security contributions	0.0	0.0	0.0	0.0	0.0	0.0	0.0	0.0	0.0	0.0
3000 Taxes on payroll and workforce	0.0	0.0	0.0	0.0	0.0	0.0	0.0	0.0	0.0	0.0
4000 Taxes on property	2.3	5.8	12.4	17.5	16.2	0.7	0.9	1.2	1.4	1.4
5000 Taxes on goods and services	3.9	9.7	12.8	15.1	13.3	1.2	1.5	1.2	1.2	1.2
6000 Other taxes	0.0	0.0	0.0	0.0	0.0	0.0	0.0	0.0	0.0	0.0
Social Security Funds										
Total tax revenue	**36.4**	**72.4**	**123.7**	**149.0**	**150.8**	**11.1**	**11.2**	**11.5**	**12.0**	**13.4**
1000 Taxes on income, profits and capital gains	0.0	0.0	0.0	0.0	0.0	0.0	0.0	0.0	0.0	0.0
2000 Social security contributions	36.4	72.4	123.7	149.0	150.8	11.1	11.2	11.5	12.0	13.4
3000 Taxes on payroll and workforce	0.0	0.0	0.0	0.0	0.0	0.0	0.0	0.0	0.0	0.0
4000 Taxes on property	0.0	0.0	0.0	0.0	0.0	0.0	0.0	0.0	0.0	0.0
5000 Taxes on goods and services	0.0	0.0	0.0	0.0	0.0	0.0	0.0	0.0	0.0	0.0
6000 Other taxes	0.0	0.0	0.0	0.0	0.0	0.0	0.0	0.0	0.0	0.0

Note: More detailed country data and country notes are available in Chapter 6 "Tax revenues by sub-sectors of general government". Full time series can be accessed at http://oe.cd/full-time-series.
Source: Information from the Ministry of Finance for taxes and from Social Security System for social security contributions up to 1994. Since 1995 (accrual basis), national account data (IGAE-Ministry of Finance).

StatLink https://stat.link/sfcjpr

Table 4.67. Sweden, tax revenue and % of GDP by selected tax category

	Billion SEK					% of GDP				
	1990	2000	2010	2019	2020	1990	2000	2010	2019	2020
Total tax revenue	**756.0**	**1 204.8**	**1 532.3**	**2 162.9**	**2 132.4**	**48.8**	**50.0**	**42.9**	**42.8**	**42.3**
1000 Taxes on income, profits and capital gains	**314.8**	**514.7**	**546.7**	**772.1**	**762.7**	**20.3**	**21.4**	**15.3**	**15.3**	**15.1**
1100 Of individuals	291.1	427.0	430.9	620.2	613.9	18.8	17.7	12.1	12.3	12.2
1200 Corporate	23.7	87.8	115.8	152.0	148.8	1.5	3.6	3.2	3.0	3.0
1300 Unallocable between 1100 and 1200	0.0	0.0	0.0	0.0	0.0	0.0	0.0	0.0	0.0	0.0
2000 Social security contributions	**205.9**	**307.0**	**384.7**	**462.9**	**455.4**	**13.3**	**12.7**	**10.8**	**9.2**	**9.0**
2100 Employees	0.8	63.1	89.2	128.2	131.0	0.1	2.6	2.5	2.5	2.6
2200 Employers	196.9	237.6	288.3	331.1	321.6	12.7	9.9	8.1	6.6	6.4
2300 Self-employed or non-employed	8.1	5.6	7.6	4.3	4.1	0.5	0.2	0.2	0.1	0.1
2400 Unallocable between 2100, 2200 and 2300	0.0	0.8	-0.4	-0.7	-1.4	0.0	0.0	0.0	0.0	0.0
3000 Taxes on payroll and workforce	**18.7**	**50.1**	**107.5**	**268.8**	**255.9**	**1.2**	**2.1**	**3.0**	**5.3**	**5.1**
4000 Taxes on property	**26.6**	**39.9**	**36.5**	**47.3**	**47.9**	**1.7**	**1.7**	**1.0**	**0.9**	**1.0**
4100 Recurrent taxes on immovable property	8.9	23.3	26.4	34.4	34.6	0.6	1.0	0.7	0.7	0.7
4200 Recurrent taxes on net wealth	3.2	8.2	0.0	0.0	0.0	0.2	0.3	0.0	0.0	0.0
4300 Estate, inheritance and gift taxes	1.4	2.5	0.0	0.0	0.0	0.1	0.1	0.0	0.0	0.0
4400 Taxes on financial and capital transactions	13.1	5.8	10.1	12.9	13.3	0.8	0.2	0.3	0.3	0.3
4500 Non-recurrent taxes	0.0	0.0	0.0	0.0	0.0	0.0	0.0	0.0	0.0	0.0
4600 Other recurrent taxes on property	0.0	0.0	0.0	0.0	0.0	0.0	0.0	0.0	0.0	0.0
5000 Taxes on goods and services	**188.7**	**291.6**	**455.4**	**610.2**	**608.2**	**12.2**	**12.1**	**12.7**	**12.1**	**12.1**
5100 Taxes on production, sale, transfer, etc	181.6	284.2	439.1	589.5	586.6	11.7	11.8	12.3	11.7	11.6
5110 General taxes	112.4	199.6	326.7	459.8	461.3	7.3	8.3	9.1	9.1	9.2
5111 Value added taxes	112.4	197.5	322.6	459.7	461.1	7.3	8.2	9.0	9.1	9.2
5120 Taxes on specific goods and services	69.2	84.6	112.4	129.7	125.3	4.5	3.5	3.1	2.6	2.5
5121 Excises	55.3	70.3	91.5	104.5	105.1	3.6	2.9	2.6	2.1	2.1
5200 Taxes on use of goods and perform activities	7.1	7.4	16.4	20.7	21.6	0.5	0.3	0.5	0.4	0.4
5300 Unallocable between 5100 and 5200	0.0	0.0	0.0	0.0	0.0	0.0	0.0	0.0	0.0	0.0
6000 Other taxes	**1.3**	**1.5**	**1.4**	**1.7**	**2.4**	**0.1**	**0.1**	**0.0**	**0.0**	**0.0**
Non-wastable tax credits										
Non-wastable tax credits against 1000	..	..	..	..	..	..	..	..	..	..
Transfer component	..	..	..	..	..	..	..	..	..	..
Tax expenditure component	..	..	..	..	..	..	..	..	..	..
Revenues collected on behalf of the EU										
Revenues collected on behalf of the EU, total	..	3.8	5.7	6.9	6.2	..	0.2	0.2	0.1	0.1
Customs duties	..	3.4	5.4	6.9	6.2	..	0.1	0.2	0.1	0.1

.. Not available

Note: More detailed country data and country notes are available in Chapter 5 "Detailed country tables". Full time series can be accessed at http://oe.cd/full-time-series.

Source: National Financial Management Authority, Stockholm.

StatLink https://stat.link/kr98jm

Table 4.68. Sweden, tax revenue and % of GDP by level of government and main taxes

	Billion SEK					% of GDP				
	1990	2000	2010	2019	2020	1990	2000	2010	2019	2020
Federal or Central government										
Total tax revenue	**383.9**	**737.9**	**806.2**	**1 122.7**	**1 071.7**	**24.8**	**30.6**	**22.6**	**22.2**	**21.3**
1000 Taxes on income, profits and capital gains	94.7	178.4	23.8	23.9	-3.4	6.1	7.4	0.7	0.5	-0.1
2000 Social security contributions	54.8	180.2	201.2	196.3	186.3	3.5	7.5	5.6	3.9	3.7
3000 Taxes on payroll and workforce	18.7	50.1	107.5	268.8	255.9	1.2	2.1	3.0	5.3	5.1
4000 Taxes on property	26.6	39.9	22.5	28.6	28.6	1.7	1.7	0.6	0.6	0.6
5000 Taxes on goods and services	187.8	287.8	449.8	603.3	602.0	12.1	12.0	12.6	11.9	11.9
6000 Other taxes	1.3	1.5	1.4	1.7	2.4	0.1	0.1	0.0	0.0	0.0
State/Regional										
Total tax revenue	..	..	..	..	..	..	..	..	..	..
1000 Taxes on income, profits and capital gains	..	..	..	..	..	..	..	..	..	..
2000 Social security contributions	..	..	..	..	..	..	..	..	..	..
3000 Taxes on payroll and workforce	..	..	..	..	..	..	..	..	..	..
4000 Taxes on property	..	..	..	..	..	..	..	..	..	..
5000 Taxes on goods and services	..	..	..	..	..	..	..	..	..	..
6000 Other taxes	..	..	..	..	..	..	..	..	..	..
Local government										
Total tax revenue	**221.0**	**336.3**	**536.9**	**766.8**	**785.4**	**14.3**	**14.0**	**15.0**	**15.2**	**15.6**
1000 Taxes on income, profits and capital gains	220.1	336.3	522.9	748.2	766.1	14.2	14.0	14.6	14.8	15.2
2000 Social security contributions	0.0	0.0	0.0	0.0	0.0	0.0	0.0	0.0	0.0	0.0
3000 Taxes on payroll and workforce	0.0	0.0	0.0	0.0	0.0	0.0	0.0	0.0	0.0	0.0
4000 Taxes on property	0.0	0.0	14.0	18.6	19.3	0.0	0.0	0.4	0.4	0.4
5000 Taxes on goods and services	0.9	0.0	0.0	0.0	0.0	0.1	0.0	0.0	0.0	0.0
6000 Other taxes	0.0	0.0	0.0	0.0	0.0	0.0	0.0	0.0	0.0	0.0
Social Security Funds										
Total tax revenue	**151.1**	**126.8**	**183.5**	**266.5**	**269.1**	**9.7**	**5.3**	**5.1**	**5.3**	**5.3**
1000 Taxes on income, profits and capital gains	0.0	0.0	0.0	0.0	0.0	0.0	0.0	0.0	0.0	0.0
2000 Social security contributions	151.1	126.8	183.5	266.5	269.1	9.7	5.3	5.1	5.3	5.3
3000 Taxes on payroll and workforce	0.0	0.0	0.0	0.0	0.0	0.0	0.0	0.0	0.0	0.0
4000 Taxes on property	0.0	0.0	0.0	0.0	0.0	0.0	0.0	0.0	0.0	0.0
5000 Taxes on goods and services	0.0	0.0	0.0	0.0	0.0	0.0	0.0	0.0	0.0	0.0
6000 Other taxes	0.0	0.0	0.0	0.0	0.0	0.0	0.0	0.0	0.0	0.0

.. Not available

Note: More detailed country data and country notes are available in Chapter 6 "Tax revenues by sub-sectors of general government". Full time series can be accessed at http://oe.cd/full-time-series.

Source: National Financial Management Authority, Stockholm.

StatLink https://stat.link/mt4rka

Table 4.69. Switzerland, tax revenue and % of GDP by selected tax category

	Billion CHF					% of GDP				
	1990	2000	2010	2019	2020	1990	2000	2010	2019	2020
Total tax revenue	**85.5**	**127.5**	**161.2**	**198.3**	**194.4**	**23.1**	**27.0**	**25.6**	**27.3**	**27.5**
1000 Taxes on income, profits and capital gains	**40.0**	**55.8**	**73.6**	**95.5**	**89.9**	**10.8**	**11.8**	**11.7**	**13.1**	**12.7**
1100 Of individuals	27.7	37.5	51.2	60.8	62.4	7.5	7.9	8.1	8.4	8.8
1200 Corporate	6.3	11.2	16.2	22.2	21.4	1.7	2.4	2.6	3.1	3.0
1300 Unallocable between 1100 and 1200	6.1	7.1	6.2	12.5	6.1	1.6	1.5	1.0	1.7	0.9
2000 Social security contributions	**19.9**	**30.8**	**38.3**	**47.1**	**48.9**	**5.4**	**6.5**	**6.1**	**6.5**	**6.9**
2100 Employees	9.3	14.5	17.5	22.0	23.7	2.5	3.1	2.8	3.0	3.4
2200 Employers	9.3	14.5	17.6	22.0	22.0	2.5	3.1	2.8	3.0	3.1
2300 Self-employed or non-employed	1.2	1.9	3.2	3.1	3.2	0.3	0.4	0.5	0.4	0.5
2400 Unallocable between 2100, 2200 and 2300	0.0	0.0	0.0	0.0	0.0	0.0	0.0	0.0	0.0	0.0
3000 Taxes on payroll and workforce	**0.0**	**0.0**	**0.0**	**0.0**	**0.0**	**0.0**	**0.0**	**0.0**	**0.0**	**0.0**
4000 Taxes on property	**7.6**	**12.3**	**12.4**	**15.2**	**15.7**	**2.1**	**2.6**	**2.0**	**2.1**	**2.2**
4100 Recurrent taxes on immovable property	0.4	0.7	1.0	1.3	1.3	0.1	0.2	0.2	0.2	0.2
4200 Recurrent taxes on net wealth	3.4	5.3	7.1	9.9	10.0	0.9	1.1	1.1	1.4	1.4
4300 Estate, inheritance and gift taxes	0.9	1.2	1.0	1.2	1.3	0.2	0.3	0.2	0.2	0.2
4400 Taxes on financial and capital transactions	2.2	4.3	2.4	1.7	2.0	0.6	0.9	0.4	0.2	0.3
4500 Non-recurrent taxes	0.0	0.0	0.0	0.0	0.0	0.0	0.0	0.0	0.0	0.0
4600 Other recurrent taxes on property	0.6	0.8	0.9	1.1	1.2	0.2	0.2	0.1	0.1	0.2
5000 Taxes on goods and services	**17.9**	**28.3**	**36.4**	**39.5**	**38.9**	**4.8**	**6.0**	**5.8**	**5.4**	**5.5**
5100 Taxes on production, sale, transfer, etc	16.0	25.3	32.1	34.2	33.5	4.3	5.4	5.1	4.7	4.7
5110 General taxes	9.9	16.9	20.9	22.7	22.4	2.7	3.6	3.3	3.1	3.2
5111 Value added taxes	9.9	16.6	20.5	22.3	22.0	2.7	3.5	3.3	3.1	3.1
5120 Taxes on specific goods and services	6.1	8.3	11.2	11.3	11.0	1.6	1.8	1.8	1.6	1.6
5121 Excises	4.6	6.8	8.3	8.4	8.0	1.2	1.4	1.3	1.1	1.1
5200 Taxes on use of goods and perform activities	1.9	3.0	4.2	5.3	5.4	0.5	0.6	0.7	0.7	0.8
5300 Unallocable between 5100 and 5200	0.0	0.0	0.0	0.0	0.0	0.0	0.0	0.0	0.0	0.0
6000 Other taxes	**0.1**	**0.2**	**0.6**	**1.0**	**1.0**	**0.0**	**0.0**	**0.1**	**0.1**	**0.1**
Non-wastable tax credits										
Non-wastable tax credits against 1000	..	..	..	..	..	..	..	..	..	..
Transfer component	..	..	..	..	..	..	..	..	..	..
Tax expenditure component	..	..	..	..	..	..	..	..	..	..

.. Not available

Note: More detailed country data and country notes are available in Chapter 5 "Detailed country tables". Full time series can be accessed at http://oe.cd/full-time-series.

The total tax revenue has been reduced by the amount of any capital transfer that represents uncollected taxes. The capital transfers were subtracted directly from the specific taxes to which they relate. Therefore, the tax revenue amounts are different to those reported in the detailed country data available in Chapter 5 "Detailed country tables".

Source: Financial Statistics, Federal Finance Administration.

StatLink https://stat.link/jsfulb

Table 4.70. Switzerland, tax revenue and % of GDP by level of government and main taxes

	Billion CHF					% of GDP				
	1990	2000	2010	2019	2020	1990	2000	2010	2019	2020
Federal or Central government										
Total tax revenue	**29.4**	**47.3**	**58.5**	**71.0**	**65.1**	**7.9**	**10.0**	**9.3**	**9.8**	**9.2**
1000 Taxes on income, profits and capital gains	10.9	17.0	22.7	33.3	27.6	2.9	3.6	3.6	4.6	3.9
2000 Social security contributions	0.0	0.0	0.0	0.0	0.0	0.0	0.0	0.0	0.0	0.0
3000 Taxes on payroll and workforce	0.0	0.0	0.0	0.0	0.0	0.0	0.0	0.0	0.0	0.0
4000 Taxes on property	2.1	4.1	2.2	1.4	1.7	0.6	0.9	0.3	0.2	0.2
5000 Taxes on goods and services	16.4	26.1	33.5	36.3	35.7	4.4	5.5	5.3	5.0	5.1
6000 Other taxes	0.0	0.0	0.0	0.1	0.1	0.0	0.0	0.0	0.0	0.0
State/Regional										
Total tax revenue	**21.3**	**28.9**	**39.9**	**49.6**	**49.8**	**5.8**	**6.1**	**6.3**	**6.8**	**7.1**
1000 Taxes on income, profits and capital gains	16.4	21.7	30.8	37.6	37.6	4.4	4.6	4.9	5.2	5.3
2000 Social security contributions	0.0	0.0	0.0	0.0	0.0	0.0	0.0	0.0	0.0	0.0
3000 Taxes on payroll and workforce	0.0	0.0	0.0	0.0	0.0	0.0	0.0	0.0	0.0	0.0
4000 Taxes on property	3.5	5.1	6.4	8.7	8.8	0.9	1.1	1.0	1.2	1.3
5000 Taxes on goods and services	1.4	2.1	2.7	3.0	3.0	0.4	0.4	0.4	0.4	0.4
6000 Other taxes	0.0	0.0	0.0	0.3	0.4	0.0	0.0	0.0	0.0	0.1
Local government										
Total tax revenue	**14.9**	**20.5**	**24.6**	**30.6**	**30.6**	**4.0**	**4.3**	**3.9**	**4.2**	**4.3**
1000 Taxes on income, profits and capital gains	12.7	17.1	20.1	24.6	24.6	3.4	3.6	3.2	3.4	3.5
2000 Social security contributions	0.0	0.0	0.0	0.0	0.0	0.0	0.0	0.0	0.0	0.0
3000 Taxes on payroll and workforce	0.0	0.0	0.0	0.0	0.0	0.0	0.0	0.0	0.0	0.0
4000 Taxes on property	2.0	3.1	3.8	5.1	5.2	0.5	0.7	0.6	0.7	0.7
5000 Taxes on goods and services	0.1	0.1	0.1	0.2	0.2	0.0	0.0	0.0	0.0	0.0
6000 Other taxes	0.1	0.2	0.6	0.6	0.6	0.0	0.0	0.1	0.1	0.1
Social Security Funds										
Total tax revenue	**19.9**	**30.8**	**38.3**	**47.1**	**48.9**	**5.4**	**6.5**	**6.1**	**6.5**	**6.9**
1000 Taxes on income, profits and capital gains	0.0	0.0	0.0	0.0	0.0	0.0	0.0	0.0	0.0	0.0
2000 Social security contributions	19.9	30.8	38.3	47.1	48.9	5.4	6.5	6.1	6.5	6.9
3000 Taxes on payroll and workforce	0.0	0.0	0.0	0.0	0.0	0.0	0.0	0.0	0.0	0.0
4000 Taxes on property	0.0	0.0	0.0	0.0	0.0	0.0	0.0	0.0	0.0	0.0
5000 Taxes on goods and services	0.0	0.0	0.0	0.0	0.0	0.0	0.0	0.0	0.0	0.0
6000 Other taxes	0.0	0.0	0.0	0.0	0.0	0.0	0.0	0.0	0.0	0.0

Note: More detailed country data and country notes are available in Chapter 6 "Tax revenues by sub-sectors of general government". Full time series can be accessed at http://oe.cd/full-time-series.
The total tax revenue has been reduced by the amount of any capital transfer that represents uncollected taxes. The capital transfers were subtracted directly from the specific taxes to which they relate. Therefore, the tax revenue amounts are different to those reported in the detailed country data available in Chapter 6 "Tax revenues by sub-sectors of general government".
Source: Financial Statistics, Federal Finance Administration.

StatLink https://stat.link/smc8za

Table 4.71. Türkiye, tax revenue and % of GDP by selected tax category

	Billion TRY					% of GDP				
	1990	2000	2010	2019	2020	1990	2000	2010	2019	2020
Total tax revenue	**0.1**	**40.3**	**287.9**	**997.6**	**1 204.6**	**14.5**	**23.5**	**24.7**	**23.1**	**23.9**
1000 Taxes on income, profits and capital gains	**0.0**	**11.9**	**61.3**	**241.5**	**263.9**	**4.9**	**6.9**	**5.3**	**5.6**	**5.2**
1100 Of individuals	0.0	9.0	40.4	162.7	158.8	3.9	5.2	3.5	3.8	3.1
1200 Corporate	0.0	2.9	20.9	78.8	105.1	1.0	1.7	1.8	1.8	2.1
1300 Unallocable between 1100 and 1200	0.0	0.0	0.0	0.0	0.0	0.0	0.0	0.0	0.0	0.0
2000 Social security contributions	**0.0**	**7.5**	**71.7**	**312.8**	**357.7**	**2.9**	**4.4**	**6.1**	**7.3**	**7.1**
2100 Employees	0.0	2.7	26.9	120.1	137.7	1.1	1.6	2.3	2.8	2.7
2200 Employers	0.0	3.6	39.4	178.3	204.0	1.6	2.1	3.4	4.1	4.0
2300 Self-employed or non-employed	0.0	1.2	5.4	14.4	15.9	0.2	0.7	0.5	0.3	0.3
2400 Unallocable between 2100, 2200 and 2300	0.0	0.0	0.0	0.0	0.0	0.0	0.0	0.0	0.0	0.0
3000 Taxes on payroll and workforce	**0.0**	**0.0**	**0.0**	**0.0**	**0.0**	**0.0**	**0.0**	**0.0**	**0.0**	**0.0**
4000 Taxes on property	**0.0**	**1.3**	**11.7**	**41.7**	**53.5**	**0.3**	**0.7**	**1.0**	**1.0**	**1.1**
4100 Recurrent taxes on immovable property	0.0	0.2	2.7	9.7	11.2	0.0	0.1	0.2	0.2	0.2
4200 Recurrent taxes on net wealth	0.0	0.0	0.0	0.0	0.0	0.0	0.0	0.0	0.0	0.0
4300 Estate, inheritance and gift taxes	0.0	0.0	0.2	1.1	1.3	0.0	0.0	0.0	0.0	0.0
4400 Taxes on financial and capital transactions	0.0	1.1	8.8	30.9	41.0	0.3	0.6	0.8	0.7	0.8
4500 Non-recurrent taxes	0.0	0.0	0.0	0.0	0.0	0.0	0.0	0.0	0.0	0.0
4600 Other recurrent taxes on property	0.0	0.0	0.0	0.0	0.0	0.0	0.0	0.0	0.0	0.0
5000 Taxes on goods and services	**0.0**	**16.9**	**137.3**	**389.1**	**517.3**	**4.1**	**9.9**	**11.8**	**9.0**	**10.2**
5100 Taxes on production, sale, transfer, etc	0.0	16.3	131.9	373.7	500.4	4.0	9.5	11.3	8.7	9.9
5110 General taxes	0.0	9.7	62.5	180.7	230.8	2.9	5.7	5.4	4.2	4.6
5111 Value added taxes	0.0	9.7	62.5	180.7	230.8	2.7	5.7	5.4	4.2	4.6
5120 Taxes on specific goods and services	0.0	6.6	69.3	193.0	269.6	1.1	3.8	5.9	4.5	5.3
5121 Excises	0.0	4.7	57.3	147.1	207.3	0.1	2.8	4.9	3.4	4.1
5200 Taxes on use of goods and perform activities	0.0	0.6	5.4	15.4	16.9	0.1	0.3	0.5	0.4	0.3
5300 Unallocable between 5100 and 5200	0.0	0.0	0.0	0.0	0.0	0.0	0.0	0.0	0.0	0.0
6000 Other taxes	**0.0**	**2.7**	**5.9**	**12.4**	**12.2**	**2.4**	**1.6**	**0.5**	**0.3**	**0.2**
Non-wastable tax credits										
Non-wastable tax credits against 1000	..	..	..	..	..	..	..	..	..	..
Transfer component	..	..	..	..	..	..	..	..	..	..
Tax expenditure component	..	..	..	..	..	..	..	..	..	..

.. Not available

Note: More detailed country data and country notes are available in Chapter 5 "Detailed country tables". Full time series can be accessed at http://oe.cd/full-time-series.

Source: Bulletin of national accounts and the Budget revenue Bulletin.

StatLink https://stat.link/mj9gr0

Table 4.72. Türkiye, tax revenue and % of GDP by level of government and main taxes

	Billion TRY					% of GDP				
	1990	2000	2010	2019	2020	1990	2000	2010	2019	2020
Federal or Central government										
Total tax revenue	**0.1**	**29.1**	**189.4**	**593.1**	**733.6**	**10.4**	**17.0**	**16.2**	**13.8**	**14.5**
1000 Taxes on income, profits and capital gains	0.0	10.5	54.6	212.3	231.8	4.3	6.1	4.7	4.9	4.6
2000 Social security contributions	0.0	0.0	0.0	0.0	0.0	0.0	0.0	0.0	0.0	0.0
3000 Taxes on payroll and workforce	0.0	0.0	0.0	0.0	0.0	0.0	0.0	0.0	0.0	0.0
4000 Taxes on property	0.0	0.9	8.1	28.3	37.2	0.3	0.5	0.7	0.7	0.7
5000 Taxes on goods and services	0.0	15.2	124.0	346.1	459.6	3.6	8.9	10.6	8.0	9.1
6000 Other taxes	0.0	2.5	2.7	6.4	5.1	2.2	1.4	0.2	0.1	0.1
State/Regional										
Total tax revenue	..	..	..	..	..	..	..	..	..	..
1000 Taxes on income, profits and capital gains	..	..	..	..	..	..	..	..	..	..
2000 Social security contributions	..	..	..	..	..	..	..	..	..	..
3000 Taxes on payroll and workforce	..	..	..	..	..	..	..	..	..	..
4000 Taxes on property	..	..	..	..	..	..	..	..	..	..
5000 Taxes on goods and services	..	..	..	..	..	..	..	..	..	..
6000 Other taxes	..	..	..	..	..	..	..	..	..	..
Local government										
Total tax revenue	**0.0**	**3.6**	**26.8**	**91.7**	**113.3**	**1.3**	**2.1**	**2.3**	**2.1**	**2.2**
1000 Taxes on income, profits and capital gains	0.0	1.4	6.7	29.2	32.1	0.6	0.8	0.6	0.7	0.6
2000 Social security contributions	0.0	0.0	0.0	0.0	0.0	0.0	0.0	0.0	0.0	0.0
3000 Taxes on payroll and workforce	0.0	0.0	0.0	0.0	0.0	0.0	0.0	0.0	0.0	0.0
4000 Taxes on property	0.0	0.3	3.6	13.4	16.4	0.0	0.2	0.3	0.3	0.3
5000 Taxes on goods and services	0.0	1.7	13.3	43.0	57.7	0.5	1.0	1.1	1.0	1.1
6000 Other taxes	0.0	0.2	3.2	6.0	7.1	0.2	0.1	0.3	0.1	0.1
Social Security Funds										
Total tax revenue	**0.0**	**7.5**	**71.7**	**312.8**	**357.7**	**2.9**	**4.4**	**6.1**	**7.3**	**7.1**
1000 Taxes on income, profits and capital gains	0.0	0.0	0.0	0.0	0.0	0.0	0.0	0.0	0.0	0.0
2000 Social security contributions	0.0	7.5	71.7	312.8	357.7	2.9	4.4	6.1	7.3	7.1
3000 Taxes on payroll and workforce	0.0	0.0	0.0	0.0	0.0	0.0	0.0	0.0	0.0	0.0
4000 Taxes on property	0.0	0.0	0.0	0.0	0.0	0.0	0.0	0.0	0.0	0.0
5000 Taxes on goods and services	0.0	0.0	0.0	0.0	0.0	0.0	0.0	0.0	0.0	0.0
6000 Other taxes	0.0	0.0	0.0	0.0	0.0	0.0	0.0	0.0	0.0	0.0

.. Not available

Note: More detailed country data and country notes are available in Chapter 6 "Tax revenues by sub-sectors of general government". Full time series can be accessed at http://oe.cd/full-time-series.

Source: Bulletin of national accounts and the Budget revenue Bulletin.

StatLink https://stat.link/8uo51z

Table 4.73. United Kingdom, tax revenue and % of GDP by selected tax category

	Billion GBP					% of GDP				
	1990	2000	2010	2019	2020	1990	2000	2010	2019	2020
Total tax revenue	**202.4**	**359.7**	**515.3**	**726.7**	**690.5**	**32.9**	**32.7**	**32.0**	**32.2**	**32.1**
1000 Taxes on income, profits and capital gains	**79.6**	**142.2**	**192.8**	**251.7**	**247.3**	**12.9**	**12.9**	**12.0**	**11.2**	**11.5**
1100 Of individuals	59.5	104.1	147.0	200.5	197.2	9.7	9.5	9.1	8.9	9.2
1200 Corporate	20.1	38.1	45.8	51.3	50.1	3.3	3.5	2.8	2.3	2.3
1300 Unallocable between 1100 and 1200	0.0	0.0	0.0	0.0	0.0	0.0	0.0	0.0	0.0	0.0
2000 Social security contributions	**34.5**	**60.3**	**97.3**	**143.3**	**145.0**	**5.6**	**5.5**	**6.0**	**6.4**	**6.7**
2100 Employees	13.3	24.2	38.7	56.2	56.8	2.2	2.2	2.4	2.5	2.6
2200 Employers	20.0	34.0	55.9	82.7	84.0	3.2	3.1	3.5	3.7	3.9
2300 Self-employed or non-employed	1.2	2.0	2.8	4.4	4.1	0.2	0.2	0.2	0.2	0.2
2400 Unallocable between 2100, 2200 and 2300	0.0	0.0	0.0	0.0	0.0	0.0	0.0	0.0	0.0	0.0
3000 Taxes on payroll and workforce	**0.0**	**0.0**	**0.0**	**2.8**	**2.9**	**0.0**	**0.0**	**0.0**	**0.1**	**0.1**
4000 Taxes on property	**16.5**	**41.1**	**61.8**	**90.3**	**80.1**	**2.7**	**3.7**	**3.8**	**4.0**	**3.7**
4100 Recurrent taxes on immovable property	13.5	30.6	50.0	68.8	61.3	2.2	2.8	3.1	3.0	2.9
4200 Recurrent taxes on net wealth	0.0	0.0	0.0	0.0	0.0	0.0	0.0	0.0	0.0	0.0
4300 Estate, inheritance and gift taxes	1.3	2.2	2.6	5.2	5.3	0.2	0.2	0.2	0.2	0.2
4400 Taxes on financial and capital transactions	1.8	8.4	9.1	16.0	13.2	0.3	0.8	0.6	0.7	0.6
4500 Non-recurrent taxes	0.0	0.0	0.0	0.5	0.4	0.0	0.0	0.0	0.0	0.0
4600 Other recurrent taxes on property	0.0	0.0	0.0	0.0	0.0	0.0	0.0	0.0	0.0	0.0
5000 Taxes on goods and services	**62.8**	**116.1**	**163.4**	**238.6**	**215.1**	**10.2**	**10.6**	**10.1**	**10.6**	**10.0**
5100 Taxes on production, sale, transfer, etc	59.4	110.8	155.5	229.6	206.1	9.6	10.1	9.6	10.2	9.6
5110 General taxes	34.1	65.0	97.6	155.0	139.5	5.5	5.9	6.1	6.9	6.5
5111 Value added taxes	34.1	65.0	97.6	155.0	139.5	5.5	5.9	6.1	6.9	6.5
5120 Taxes on specific goods and services	25.2	45.8	57.8	74.6	66.6	4.1	4.2	3.6	3.3	3.1
5121 Excises	19.7	37.3	45.5	49.3	44.9	3.2	3.4	2.8	2.2	2.1
5200 Taxes on use of goods and perform activities	3.4	5.3	7.9	9.0	9.1	0.6	0.5	0.5	0.4	0.4
5300 Unallocable between 5100 and 5200	0.0	0.0	0.0	0.0	0.0	0.0	0.0	0.0	0.0	0.0
6000 Other taxes	**9.0**	**0.0**	**0.0**	**0.0**	**0.0**	**1.5**	**0.0**	**0.0**	**0.0**	**0.0**
Non-wastable tax credits										
Non-wastable tax credits against 1000	7.5	4.7	30.2	25.3	23.9	1.2	0.4	1.9	1.1	1.1
Transfer component	0.5	3.4	23.7	21.4	19.9	0.1	0.3	1.5	0.9	0.9
Tax expenditure component	7.0	1.2	6.5	3.9	4.0	1.1	0.1	0.4	0.2	0.2
Revenues collected on behalf of the EU										
Revenues collected on behalf of the EU, total	1.8	2.1	2.9	3.3	2.9	0.3	0.2	0.2	0.1	0.1
Customs duties	..	1.8	2.9	3.3	2.9	..	0.2	0.2	0.1	0.1

.. Not available

Note: Please note that the non-wastable tax credit data for the United Kingdom is on a cash basis and includes estimates in some years. Please see the footnotes in the table for the United Kingdom in Chapter 5 for more information.

Supranational taxes reported by the United Kingdom are reported until 2020 in Revenue Statistics. From 2021, at the end of the Brexit transition period, this came to an end and taxes subsequently introduced by the United Kingdom are reflected in the appropriate tax category at the national or subnational levels of government, as appropriate.

More detailed country data and country notes are available in Chapter 5 "Detailed country tables". Full time series can be accessed at http://oe.cd/full-time-series.

Source: National Income and Expenditure; Central Statistical Office; Annual reports of His Majesty's Revenue and Customs.

StatLink https://stat.link/7oez01

Table 4.74. United Kingdom, tax revenue and % of GDP by level of government and main taxes

	Billion GBP					% of GDP				
	1990	2000	2010	2019	2020	1990	2000	2010	2019	2020
Federal or Central government										
Total tax revenue	**151.9**	**283.1**	**388.7**	**542.5**	**503.9**	**24.7**	**25.8**	**24.1**	**24.1**	**23.4**
1000 Taxes on income, profits and capital gains	79.6	142.2	192.8	251.7	247.3	12.9	12.9	12.0	11.2	11.5
2000 Social security contributions	0.0	0.0	0.0	0.0	0.0	0.0	0.0	0.0	0.0	0.0
3000 Taxes on payroll and workforce	0.0	0.0	0.0	2.8	2.9	0.0	0.0	0.0	0.1	0.1
4000 Taxes on property	11.4	26.9	35.5	52.7	41.4	1.9	2.5	2.2	2.3	1.9
5000 Taxes on goods and services	60.9	114.0	160.4	235.2	212.2	9.9	10.4	10.0	10.4	9.9
6000 Other taxes	0.0	0.0	0.0	0.0	0.0	0.0	0.0	0.0	0.0	0.0
State/Regional										
Total tax revenue	**..**	**..**	**..**	**..**	**..**	**..**	**..**	**..**	**..**	**..**
1000 Taxes on income, profits and capital gains	..	..	..	..	..	..	..	..	..	..
2000 Social security contributions	..	..	..	..	..	..	..	..	..	..
3000 Taxes on payroll and workforce	..	..	..	..	..	..	..	..	..	..
4000 Taxes on property	..	..	..	..	..	..	..	..	..	..
5000 Taxes on goods and services	..	..	..	..	..	..	..	..	..	..
6000 Other taxes	..	..	..	..	..	..	..	..	..	..
Local government										
Total tax revenue	**14.1**	**14.2**	**26.2**	**37.6**	**38.7**	**2.3**	**1.3**	**1.6**	**1.7**	**1.8**
1000 Taxes on income, profits and capital gains	0.0	0.0	0.0	0.0	0.0	0.0	0.0	0.0	0.0	0.0
2000 Social security contributions	0.0	0.0	0.0	0.0	0.0	0.0	0.0	0.0	0.0	0.0
3000 Taxes on payroll and workforce	0.0	0.0	0.0	0.0	0.0	0.0	0.0	0.0	0.0	0.0
4000 Taxes on property	5.1	14.2	26.2	37.6	38.7	0.8	1.3	1.6	1.7	1.8
5000 Taxes on goods and services	0.0	0.0	0.0	0.0	0.0	0.0	0.0	0.0	0.0	0.0
6000 Other taxes	9.0	0.0	0.0	0.0	0.0	1.5	0.0	0.0	0.0	0.0
Social Security Funds										
Total tax revenue	**34.5**	**60.3**	**97.3**	**143.3**	**145.0**	**5.6**	**5.5**	**6.0**	**6.4**	**6.7**
1000 Taxes on income, profits and capital gains	0.0	0.0	0.0	0.0	0.0	0.0	0.0	0.0	0.0	0.0
2000 Social security contributions	34.5	60.3	97.3	143.3	145.0	5.6	5.5	6.0	6.4	6.7
3000 Taxes on payroll and workforce	0.0	0.0	0.0	0.0	0.0	0.0	0.0	0.0	0.0	0.0
4000 Taxes on property	0.0	0.0	0.0	0.0	0.0	0.0	0.0	0.0	0.0	0.0
5000 Taxes on goods and services	0.0	0.0	0.0	0.0	0.0	0.0	0.0	0.0	0.0	0.0
6000 Other taxes	0.0	0.0	0.0	0.0	0.0	0.0	0.0	0.0	0.0	0.0

.. Not available

Note: More detailed country data and country notes are available in Chapter 6 "Tax revenues by sub-sectors of general government". Full time series can be accessed at http://oe.cd/full-time-series.

Source: National Income and Expenditure; Central Statistical Office; Annual reports of His Majesty's Revenue and Customs.

StatLink https://stat.link/ork9f7

Table 4.75. United States, tax revenue and % of GDP by selected tax category

	Billion USD					% of GDP				
	1990	2000	2010	2019	2020	1990	2000	2010	2019	2020
Total tax revenue	**1 552.4**	**2 900.5**	**3 517.1**	**5 385.0**	**5 380.2**	**26.0**	**28.3**	**23.4**	**25.2**	**25.8**
1000 Taxes on income, profits and capital gains	**701.7**	**1 453.9**	**1 488.7**	**2 482.9**	**2 446.9**	**11.8**	**14.2**	**9.9**	**11.6**	**11.7**
1100 Of individuals	584.7	1 224.5	1 223.2	2 193.0	2 183.2	9.8	11.9	8.1	10.3	10.4
1200 Corporate	117.0	229.3	265.5	289.9	263.8	2.0	2.2	1.8	1.4	1.3
1300 Unallocable between 1100 and 1200	0.0	0.0	0.0	0.0	0.0	0.0	0.0	0.0	0.0	0.0
2000 Social security contributions	**397.0**	**683.1**	**917.4**	**1 308.7**	**1 334.0**	**6.7**	**6.7**	**6.1**	**6.1**	**6.4**
2100 Employees	173.9	305.6	406.4	597.6	607.3	2.9	3.0	2.7	2.8	2.9
2200 Employers	204.1	343.2	461.7	642.8	656.6	3.4	3.3	3.1	3.0	3.1
2300 Self-employed or non-employed	19.0	34.4	49.3	68.3	70.1	0.3	0.3	0.3	0.3	0.3
2400 Unallocable between 2100, 2200 and 2300	0.0	0.0	0.0	0.0	0.0	0.0	0.0	0.0	0.0	0.0
3000 Taxes on payroll and workforce	**0.0**	**0.0**	**2.3**	**2.3**	**3.4**	**0.0**	**0.0**	**0.0**	**0.0**	**0.0**
4000 Taxes on property	**182.4**	**299.5**	**473.4**	**649.5**	**669.2**	**3.1**	**2.9**	**3.1**	**3.0**	**3.2**
4100 Recurrent taxes on immovable property	161.5	254.7	438.6	599.6	615.3	2.7	2.5	2.9	2.8	2.9
4200 Recurrent taxes on net wealth	0.0	0.0	0.0	0.0	0.0	0.0	0.0	0.0	0.0	0.0
4300 Estate, inheritance and gift taxes	15.8	35.6	19.7	21.7	24.8	0.3	0.3	0.1	0.1	0.1
4400 Taxes on financial and capital transactions	2.1	4.4	7.5	17.5	18.1	0.0	0.0	0.0	0.1	0.1
4500 Non-recurrent taxes	0.0	0.0	0.0	0.0	0.0	0.0	0.0	0.0	0.0	0.0
4600 Other recurrent taxes on property	3.0	4.8	7.7	10.6	10.9	0.0	0.0	0.1	0.0	0.1
5000 Taxes on goods and services	**271.3**	**464.0**	**635.3**	**941.7**	**926.7**	**4.5**	**4.5**	**4.2**	**4.4**	**4.4**
5100 Taxes on production, sale, transfer, etc	235.2	404.1	546.7	823.8	809.5	3.9	3.9	3.6	3.9	3.9
5110 General taxes	125.6	221.4	295.1	443.9	448.9	2.1	2.2	2.0	2.1	2.1
5111 Value added taxes	0.0	0.0	0.0	0.0	0.0	0.0	0.0	0.0	0.0	0.0
5120 Taxes on specific goods and services	109.7	182.7	251.6	379.9	360.7	1.8	1.8	1.7	1.8	1.7
5121 Excises	65.0	108.6	146.6	165.9	162.0	1.1	1.1	1.0	0.8	0.8
5200 Taxes on use of goods and perform activities	36.1	59.9	88.6	117.9	117.2	0.6	0.6	0.6	0.6	0.6
5300 Unallocable between 5100 and 5200	0.0	0.0	0.0	0.0	0.0	0.0	0.0	0.0	0.0	0.0
6000 Other taxes	**0.0**	**0.0**	**0.0**	**0.0**	**0.0**	**0.0**	**0.0**	**0.0**	**0.0**	**0.0**
Non-wastable tax credits										
Non-wastable tax credits against 1000	6.2	36.5	171.9	256.0	526.6	0.1	0.4	1.1	1.2	2.5
Transfer component	4.4	26.9	101.8	153.0	433.7	0.1	0.3	0.7	0.7	2.1
Tax expenditure component	1.8	9.6	70.1	103.0	93.0	0.0	0.1	0.5	0.5	0.4

Note: More detailed country data and country notes are available in Chapter 5 "Detailed country tables". Full time series can be accessed at http://oe.cd/full-time-series.

Source: Federal estimates are derived from the US Budget, the Final Monthly Treasury Statement and the Annual Report of the US Treasury Department. The State and Local estimates are derived from Government Finances, published by the Bureau of the Census.

StatLink https://stat.link/eohyqz

Table 4.76. United States, tax revenue and % of GDP by level of government and main taxes

	Billion USD					% of GDP				
	1990	2000	2010	2019	2020	1990	2000	2010	2019	2020
Federal or Central government										
Total tax revenue	**632.2**	**1 316.6**	**1 288.7**	**2 143.8**	**2 076.9**	**10.6**	**12.8**	**8.6**	**10.0**	**9.9**
1000 Taxes on income, profits and capital gains	569.7	1 201.3	1 176.8	1 952.9	1 899.8	9.6	11.7	7.8	9.1	9.1
2000 Social security contributions	0.0	0.0	0.0	0.0	0.0	0.0	0.0	0.0	0.0	0.0
3000 Taxes on payroll and workforce	0.0	0.0	0.0	0.0	0.0	0.0	0.0	0.0	0.0	0.0
4000 Taxes on property	11.6	28.1	15.1	16.2	19.1	0.2	0.3	0.1	0.1	0.1
5000 Taxes on goods and services	50.9	87.3	96.8	174.7	158.0	0.9	0.9	0.6	0.8	0.8
6000 Other taxes	0.0	0.0	0.0	0.0	0.0	0.0	0.0	0.0	0.0	0.0
State/Regional										
Total tax revenue	**309.7**	**547.6**	**723.9**	**1 118.2**	**1 133.1**	**5.2**	**5.3**	**4.8**	**5.2**	**5.4**
1000 Taxes on income, profits and capital gains	120.2	231.0	279.4	483.9	498.7	2.0	2.3	1.9	2.3	2.4
2000 Social security contributions	0.0	0.0	0.0	0.0	0.0	0.0	0.0	0.0	0.0	0.0
3000 Taxes on payroll and workforce	0.0	0.0	2.3	2.3	3.4	0.0	0.0	0.0	0.0	0.0
4000 Taxes on property	12.2	21.9	23.1	36.5	37.6	0.2	0.2	0.2	0.2	0.2
5000 Taxes on goods and services	177.3	294.7	419.1	595.5	593.5	3.0	2.9	2.8	2.8	2.8
6000 Other taxes	0.0	0.0	0.0	0.0	0.0	0.0	0.0	0.0	0.0	0.0
Local government										
Total tax revenue	**213.6**	**353.2**	**587.2**	**814.3**	**836.2**	**3.6**	**3.4**	**3.9**	**3.8**	**4.0**
1000 Taxes on income, profits and capital gains	11.9	21.6	32.5	46.0	48.5	0.2	0.2	0.2	0.2	0.2
2000 Social security contributions	0.0	0.0	0.0	0.0	0.0	0.0	0.0	0.0	0.0	0.0
3000 Taxes on payroll and workforce	0.0	0.0	0.0	0.0	0.0	0.0	0.0	0.0	0.0	0.0
4000 Taxes on property	158.6	249.5	435.3	596.8	612.5	2.7	2.4	2.9	2.8	2.9
5000 Taxes on goods and services	43.1	82.0	119.4	171.5	175.2	0.7	0.8	0.8	0.8	0.8
6000 Other taxes	0.0	0.0	0.0	0.0	0.0	0.0	0.0	0.0	0.0	0.0
Social Security Funds										
Total tax revenue	**397.0**	**683.1**	**917.4**	**1 308.7**	**1 334.0**	**6.7**	**6.7**	**6.1**	**6.1**	**6.4**
1000 Taxes on income, profits and capital gains	0.0	0.0	0.0	0.0	0.0	0.0	0.0	0.0	0.0	0.0
2000 Social security contributions	397.0	683.1	917.4	1 308.7	1 334.0	6.7	6.7	6.1	6.1	6.4
3000 Taxes on payroll and workforce	0.0	0.0	0.0	0.0	0.0	0.0	0.0	0.0	0.0	0.0
4000 Taxes on property	0.0	0.0	0.0	0.0	0.0	0.0	0.0	0.0	0.0	0.0
5000 Taxes on goods and services	0.0	0.0	0.0	0.0	0.0	0.0	0.0	0.0	0.0	0.0
6000 Other taxes	0.0	0.0	0.0	0.0	0.0	0.0	0.0	0.0	0.0	0.0

Note: More detailed country data and country notes are available in Chapter 6 "Tax revenues by sub-sectors of general government". Full time series can be accessed at http://oe.cd/full-time-series.
Source: Federal estimates are derived from the US Budget, the Final Monthly Treasury Statement and the Annual Report of the US Treasury Department. The State and Local estimates are derived from Government Finances, published by the Bureau of the Census.

StatLink https://stat.link/fdtek5

4.2. Memorandum tables

Table 4.77 shows different sources for financing social benefits, beyond compulsory social security contributions reported in section 4.1. In addition, this table shows also data on other taxes, on voluntary contributions to government and on compulsory contributions to private sector.

Table 4.78 shows social security contributions and payroll taxes paid by government. During the revision of the Interpretative Guide in 1984, the question arose of how to treat taxes paid by government. The two most prominent examples of such taxes are social security contributions and payroll taxes paid by government in respect of its employees. After a long discussion it was decided that the data shown in this publication should continue to include taxes paid by government (see §7 of the Interpretative Guide in Annex A).

Whilst it was recognised that for certain purposes (e.g. to show the cash flow to the government sector from the private sector) it would be appropriate to eliminate taxes paid by one sector of government to another or tax payments between different units of the same sector of government, the view was taken that to record tax flows in the context of the economy as a whole required that taxes paid by government should be included in the data. This treatment ensures that the different resource flows of an economy, including the calculation of the output of government, are measured consistently in after-tax units. Nevertheless, it was decided that data on identifiable taxes paid by government should be separately identified in a memorandum item and this is the purpose of the country tables which follow.

The data that are reproduced in the following tables refer to actual compulsory payments made by general government in respect of their employees. Fictive, voluntary and imputed contributions are excluded from these data. The definitions of social security contributions, payroll taxes and general government are those set out in §40 to §46, §47 and §3 to §4 of the Interpretative Guide. Information on the other taxes paid by government (namely property taxes and consumption taxes) is not available in most countries, although it is believed that in all countries taxes based upon payroll are the most important taxes paid by government. In many cases, the data are estimates and are not always constructed on a basis consistent with that used in the main tables.

Table 4.77. Financing of social security benefits

As % of GDP

	Total					2020				
	1990	2000	2010	2019	2020	Social security contributions	Other taxes	Voluntary contributions to government	Compulsory contributions to private sector	Total
Australia	0.0	0.0	0.0	0.0	0.0	..	..	..	..	0.0
Austria	13.0	14.4	14.1	14.9	15.6	15.5	0.0	0.1	0.0	15.6
Belgium	14.2	15.6	18.5	17.2	18.0	13.6	4.4	0.0	0.0	18.0
Canada	4.3	4.7	4.6	4.7	4.9	4.9	0.0	0.0	0.0	4.9
Chile	4.6	6.2	6.2	7.6	7.6	1.5	0.0	0.0	6.1	7.6
Colombia	0.9	2.6	7.1	6.0	6.0	1.9	0.0	0.0	4.1	6.0
Costa Rica	6.5	6.4	7.3	8.0	8.2	8.2	..	..	..	8.2
Czech Republic	..	14.5	14.6	15.5	16.0	15.8	0.0	0.0	0.2	16.0
Denmark	1.1	2.0	1.3	0.8	0.8	0.1	0.0	0.6	0.1	0.8
Estonia	..	10.9	13.0	12.8	13.3	12.1	0.0	0.0	1.1	13.3
Finland	12.2	12.4	12.5	12.2	11.8	11.5	0.0	0.1	0.3	11.8
France	18.4	21.0	23.0	24.4	25.0	14.8	10.1	0.0	0.0	25.0
Germany	14.2	15.6	14.4	15.2	15.7	15.0	0.0	0.2	0.4	15.7
Greece	7.6	10.1	11.0	12.1	12.9	12.9	0.0	0.0	0.0	12.9
Hungary	..	13.2	12.9	12.0	11.4	11.1	0.3	0.0	0.0	11.4
Iceland	10.0	13.4	14.1	15.5	18.8	3.0	9.2	0.0	6.6	18.8
Ireland	4.6	3.7	5.1	3.7	3.3	3.3	0.0	0.0	0.0	3.3
Israel	..	5.0	6.1	7.8	7.9	5.1	0.0	0.0	2.8	7.9
Italy	11.9	11.6	13.0	13.3	13.6	13.6	0.0	0.0	0.0	13.6
Japan	7.3	8.9	10.8	12.9	13.4	13.4	0.0	0.0	0.0	13.4
Korea	1.9	3.5	5.2	7.3	7.8	7.8	0.0	0.0	0.0	7.8
Latvia	..	9.9	8.8	10.0	10.4	10.0	0.4	0.0	0.0	10.4
Lithuania	..	9.9	12.0	9.7	10.2	10.2	0.0	0.0	0.0	10.2
Luxembourg	9.6	9.8	10.4	11.1	11.2	11.1	0.0	0.1	0.0	11.2
Mexico	2.5	3.1	3.2	3.5	3.9	2.5	0.0	0.0	1.4	3.9
Netherlands	17.1	22.5	12.9	13.4	13.6	13.6	0.0	0.0	..	13.6
New Zealand	0.0	0.0	0.0	0.0	0.0	..	..	..	..	0.0
Norway	10.6	8.8	9.4	10.6	11.2	11.2	0.0	0.0	0.0	11.2
Poland	..	12.9	10.8	13.2	13.5	13.5	0.0	0.0	0.0	13.5
Portugal	7.2	8.3	9.0	10.0	10.9	10.5	0.4	0.0	0.0	10.9
Slovak Republic	..	13.9	13.0	15.7	16.3	15.5	0.0	0.0	0.8	16.3
Slovenia	..	14.9	15.8	15.6	16.8	16.8	0.0	0.0	0.0	16.8
Spain	11.2	11.6	12.0	12.3	13.8	13.8	0.0	0.1	0.0	13.8
Sweden	13.3	13.1	11.1	9.7	9.5	9.0	0.0	0.5	0.0	9.5
Switzerland	11.3	13.7	14.4	15.5	15.9	6.9	0.5	0.0	8.5	15.9
Türkiye	2.9	4.4	6.1	7.3	7.1	7.1	0.0	0.0	0.0	7.1
United Kingdom	7.4	7.0	8.0	7.8	8.5	6.7	0.0	1.8	0.0	8.5
United States	6.9	6.9	6.5	6.6	7.0	6.4	0.0	0.6	0.0	7.0

.. Not available

StatLink https://stat.link/lai2ze

Table 4.78. Social security contributions and payroll taxes paid by government, totals

As % of GDP

	Total					2020				
	1990	2000	2010	2019	2020	Federal or Central government	State/Regional	Local government	Social security Funds	Total
Australia[1]	0.0	0.0	0.0	0.0	0.0	0.0	0.0	0.0	0.0	0.0
Austria	1.0	1.4	1.9	1.9	2.1	0.8	0.6	0.6	0.1	2.1
Belgium	1.0	1.2	1.5	1.8	1.9	0.2	0.6	1.0	0.1	1.9
Canada	..	0.6	0.6	0.6	0.7	0.1	0.3	0.2	0.0	0.7
Chile	..	0.1	0.2	0.2	0.2	0.1	..	0.1	0.0	0.2
Colombia	..	..	..	0.2	0.3	0.1	0.0	0.0	0.2	0.3
Costa Rica	0.7	0.9	1.1	1.1	1.1	1.1	0.0	0.1	0.0	1.1
Czech Republic	..	1.4	1.4	2.0	2.2	1.0	..	1.2	0.0	2.2
Denmark	0.0	0.0	0.0	0.0	0.0	..	..	..	..	0.0
Estonia	..	2.6	2.9	2.9	3.2	1.9	..	1.3	0.0	3.2
Finland	2.1	2.8	3.0	2.3	2.3	0.5	..	1.8	0.0	2.3
France	2.2	2.5	2.7	2.6	2.8	0.7	..	1.0	1.0	2.8
Germany	1.0	0.8	0.8	0.8	0.9	0.1	0.3	0.4	0.1	0.9
Greece	0.3	0.5	0.8	1.3	1.6	1.4	..	0.2	0.0	1.6
Hungary	..	2.8	2.4	1.5	1.4	1.1	..	0.3	0.0	1.4
Iceland	..	..	..	..	..	..	..	..	..	..
Ireland	0.4	0.4	0.7	0.5	0.5	0.2	..	0.3	0.0	0.5
Israel	..	0.7	0.8	0.8	0.8	0.7	..	0.2	0.0	0.8
Italy	..	3.0	3.1	2.9	3.2	0.0	..	0.0	3.2	3.2
Japan	0.4	0.5	0.6	0.6	0.7	0.2	0.0	0.5	0.0	0.7
Korea	..	..	..	..	..	..	..	..	..	..
Latvia	..	0.6	1.0	1.2	1.1	..	..	..	..	1.1
Lithuania	..	2.7	2.5	0.2	0.2	0.1	..	0.1	0.0	0.2
Luxembourg	2.5	1.3	1.2	1.3	1.3	1.3	..	0.0	0.0	1.3
Mexico	0.3	0.7	0.8	0.8	0.8	0.8	0.0	0.0	0.0	0.8
Netherlands	0.1	0.4	0.0	0.0	0.0	..	..	..	..	0.0
New Zealand	0.0	0.0	0.0	0.0	0.0	..	..	..	..	0.0
Norway	2.4	2.4	2.9	3.5	3.6	1.6	..	2.0	0.0	3.6
Poland	..	1.5	1.3	1.4	1.5	0.6	..	0.9	0.0	1.5
Portugal	0.1	0.2	0.0	0.0	0.0	..	..	..	..	0.0
Slovak Republic	..	2.0	2.0	2.5	2.7	1.5	..	1.1	0.1	2.7
Slovenia	..	1.9	1.7	1.5	1.8	1.2	..	0.6	0.0	1.8
Spain	1.2	1.5	1.7	1.8	2.1	0.3	1.3	0.5	0.0	2.1
Sweden	4.5	4.2	3.8	4.0	3.9	0.9	..	3.0	0.0	3.9
Switzerland	0.4	0.4	0.4	0.5	0.5	0.1	0.3	0.1	0.0	0.5
Türkiye	1.6	2.1	3.4	4.1	4.0	4.0	..	0.0	0.0	4.0
United Kingdom	0.7	0.6	0.7	0.7	0.8	0.5	..	0.2	0.0	0.8
United States	0.5	0.4	0.5	0.4	0.4	0.1	0.3	0.0	0.0	0.4

.. Not available

1. For Australia, the total differs from the sum of the four levels of government. The difference is due to a multi-jurisdictional (University) sector specific to this country. This sector contains units where jurisdiction is shared between two or more governments, or where classification of a unit to a jurisdiction is otherwise unclear. The main type of units currently falling into this category is public universities.

StatLink https://stat.link/qgom7f

5 Detailed country tables, 1965-2020

Chapter 5 provides detailed country information on tax revenues for each OECD country.

5.1. Tax revenues

In all the following tables, the symbol (..) indicates not available or not applicable. The main series in this chapter cover a selection of years between 1965 and 2020. A complete series is available online. Data for 1955 and 1960 (for nineteen OECD countries) are provided in Part V of the 1998 edition of this Report.

Table 5.1. Australia: Details of tax revenue, 1965-2020

Million AUD

	1965	1980	1990	2000	2007	2010	2013	2015	2019	2020
Total tax revenue	**5 024**	**39 878**	**116 500**	**214 753**	**346 772**	**356 747**	**431 200**	**460 729**	**548 914**	**590 730**
1000 Taxes on income, profits and capital gains	**2 547**	**22 383**	**66 542**	**124 427**	**206 134**	**202 184**	**246 073**	**261 345**	**324 826**	**348 274**
1100 Of individuals	1 729	17 532	50 062	80 991	127 587	138 163	169 972	191 720	230 798	236 926
1110 On income and profits	1 729	17 532	49 888	80 991	127 587	138 163	169 972	191 720	230 798	236 926
1120 On capital gains	0	0	174	0	0	0	0	0	0	0
1200 Corporate	818	4 851	16 480	43 436	78 547	64 021	76 101	69 625	94 028	111 348
1210 On profits	818	4 851	16 315	43 436	78 547	64 021	76 101	69 625	94 028	111 348
Income tax on companies	791	4 574	15 220	42 221	76 655	62 549	74 535	67 794	91 918	109 819
Dividend and interest taxes	17	161	899	846	1 892	1 472	1 566	1 831	2 110	1 529
Other withholding taxes	0	116	196	369	..	..	..	..	..	..
1220 On capital gains	0	0	165	0	0	0	0	0	0	0
1300 Unallocable between 1100 and 1200	0	0	0	0	0	0	0	0	0	0
2000 Social security contributions	**0**	**0**	**0**	**0**	**0**	**0**	**0**	**0**	**0**	**0**
2100 Employees	0	0	0	0	0	0	0	0	0	0
2110 On a payroll basis	..	..	..	..	..	..	..	..	..	..
2120 On an income tax basis	..	..	..	..	..	..	..	..	..	..
2200 Employers	0	0	0	0	0	0	0	0	0	0
2210 On a payroll basis	..	..	..	..	..	..	..	..	..	..
2220 On an income tax basis	..	..	..	..	..	..	..	..	..	..
2300 Self-employed or non-employed	0	0	0	0	0	0	0	0	0	0
2310 On a payroll basis	..	..	..	..	..	..	..	..	..	..
2320 On an income tax basis	..	..	..	..	..	..	..	..	..	..
2400 Unallocable between 2100, 2200 and 2300	0	0	0	0	0	0	0	0	0	0
2410 On a payroll basis	..	..	..	..	..	..	..	..	..	..
2420 On an income tax basis	..	..	..	..	..	..	..	..	..	..
3000 Taxes on payroll and workforce	**157**	**1 988**	**7 115**	**9 624**	**16 407**	**18 492**	**22 210**	**23 354**	**25 701**	**26 383**
4000 Taxes on property	**576**	**3 105**	**10 427**	**18 825**	**31 130**	**33 498**	**40 929**	**49 168**	**53 982**	**59 509**
4100 Recurrent taxes on immovable property	341	1 886	6 148	9 067	15 615	19 907	23 603	26 649	33 803	34 471
4110 Households	..	..	..	..	..	..	..	..	..	..
4120 Others	..	..	..	..	..	..	..	..	..	..
4200 Recurrent taxes on net wealth	0	0	0	0	0	0	0	0	0	0
4210 Individual	..	..	..	..	..	..	..	..	..	..
4220 Corporate	..	..	..	..	..	..	..	..	..	..
4300 Estate, inheritance and gift taxes	137	175	0	0	0	0	0	0	0	0
4310 Estate and inheritance taxes	131	174	..	..	..	..	..	..	..	..
Estate duty central government	36	17	..	..	..	..	..	..	..	..
St. and loc. estate probate and succession	95	157	..	..	..	..	..	..	..	..
4320 Gift taxes	7	1	..	..	..	..	..	..	..	..
4400 Taxes on financial and capital transactions	98	1 044	4 279	9 758	15 515	13 591	17 326	22 519	20 179	25 038
4500 Non-recurrent taxes	0	0	0	0	0	0	0	0	0	0
4510 On net wealth	..	..	..	..	..	..	..	..	..	..
4520 Other non-recurrent taxes	..	..	..	..	..	..	..	..	..	..
4600 Other recurrent taxes on property	0	0	0	0	0	0	0	0	0	0
5000 Taxes on goods and services	**1 744**	**12 402**	**32 416**	**61 877**	**93 101**	**102 573**	**121 988**	**126 862**	**144 405**	**156 564**
5100 Taxes on production, sale, transfer, etc.	1 508	11 097	27 213	56 179	84 104	90 824	101 312	109 050	123 639	135 100
5110 General taxes	370	2 102	9 365	25 830	44 739	48 146	54 711	60 680	65 720	75 298
5111 Value added taxes	0	0	0	23 854	43 634	46 910	53 409	59 177	64 048	73 297
5112 Sales tax	370	2 102	9 365	1 976	1 105	1 236	1 302	1 503	1 672	2 001
5113 Other	0	0	0	0	0	0	0	0	0	0
5120 Taxes on specific goods and services	1 138	8 995	17 848	30 349	39 365	42 678	46 601	48 370	57 919	59 802
5121 Excise duties	781	6 183	11 975	19 768	24 357	26 689	26 472	22 541	24 065	25 856
Excises central government	752	5 834	10 359	19 019	23 526	25 803	25 648	21 625	23 116	24 503
Statutory corporate payments	0	83	378	295	231	452	343	405	480	819
Primary production charges	29	266	1 238	454	600	434	481	511	469	534
5122 Profits of fiscal monopolies	0	0	0	0	0	0	0	0	0	0
5123 Customs and import duties	271	1 799	3 319	4 606	6 070	5 828	9 280	14 046	19 507	18 123
Customs duties central government	271	1 799	3 319	4 606	6 070	5 828	9 280	14 046	19 507	18 123
5124 Taxes on exports	1	117	57	0	10	11	10	11	0	0
Customs duties on coal exports	0	85	54	..	0	0	0	0	..	..
Other	1	32	3	..	10	11	10	11	..	..
5125 Taxes on investment goods	0	0	0	0	0	0	0	0	0	0
5126 Taxes on specific services	85	896	2 497	5 975	8 928	10 150	10 839	11 772	14 347	15 823
Taxes race meetings	31	240	651	301	359	373	326	265	596	795
Poker machines	16	140	295	2 074	3 009	3 125	3 238	3 684	3 202	3 935
Lotteries	7	122	325	890	1 118	1 141	1 250	1 362	1 676	1 813
Levies on fire insurance companies	16	157	363	574	937	1 232	740	786	932	1 115
Other	15	237	863	2 136	3 505	4 279	5 285	5 675	7 941	8 165
5127 Other taxes on internat. trade and transactions	0	0	0	0	0	0	0	0	0	0
5128 Other taxes	0	0	0	0	0	0	0	0	0	0

	1965	1980	1990	2000	2007	2010	2013	2015	2019	2020
5130 Unallocable between 5110 and 5120	0	0	0	0	0	0	0	0	0	0
5200 Taxes on use of goods and perform activities	236	1 305	5 203	5 698	8 997	11 749	20 676	17 812	20 766	21 464
5210 Recurrent taxes	197	1 260	5 109	5 698	8 997	11 749	20 676	15 898	18 609	19 831
5211 Paid by households: motor vehicles	65	448	1 373	2 748	4 381	5 064	6 533	7 253	8 128	8 479
5212 Paid by others: motor vehicles	65	351	937	1 285	2 005	2 397	2 357	2 649	3 174	3 653
Fees on motor vehicle registry	46	312	794	778	1 165	1 499	1 338	1 530	1 975	2 201
Drivers licences	12	30	111	0	0	0	0	0	0	0
Stamp duty on vehicle registry	6	9	32	506	839	898	1 019	1 119	1 199	1 452
5213 Paid in respect of other goods	67	461	2 799	1 665	2 611	4 288	11 786	5 996	7 307	7 699
Broadcasting tv licences	37	21	125	210	288	150	157	128	37	14
Business franchise lic. tobac. fuel	0	221	2 016	227	0	0	2	1	0	0
Other taxes	2	12	33	1 129	2 321	4 136	11 603	5 846	7 265	7 675
Liquor taxes	28	206	603	97	2	1	24	22	5	10
Dog licenses	0	1	22	0	0	0	0	0	0	0
5220 Non-recurrent taxes	39	45	94	0	0	0	0	1 914	2 157	1 633
5300 Unallocable between 5100 and 5200	0	0	0	0	0	0	0	0	0	0
6000 Other taxes	**0**	**0**	**0**	**0**	**0**	**0**	**0**	**0**	**0**	**0**
6100 Paid solely by business	..	..	..	..	..	..	..	..	..	..
6200 Other	..	..	..	..	..	..	..	..	..	..
Non-wastable tax credits										
Non-wastable tax credits against 1110	..	..	..	195	2 585	991	323	460	414	363
Tax expenditure component	..	..	..	175	178	110	215	334	292	252
Transfer component	..	..	..	20	2 407	881	108	126	122	111
Non-wastable tax credits against 1210	..	..	..	0	4 564	5 726	7 914	8 951	10 190	9 727
Tax expenditure component	..	..	..	..	1 922	2 253	2 147	3 438	3 471	3 258
Transfer component	..	..	..	..	2 642	3 473	5 767	5 513	6 719	6 469
Total tax revenue on cash basis	**5 024**	**39 878**	**116 500**	..	..	..	..	..	..	..
Total tax revenue on accrual basis	..	..	..	**214 753**	**346 772**	**356 747**	**431 200**	**460 729**	**548 914**	**590 730**
Conciliation with National Accounts										
Additional taxes included in National Accounts	..	..	..	0	0	0	0	0	0	0
Taxes excluded from National Accounts	..	..	..	0	0	0	0	0	0	0
Difference in treatment of tax credits	..	..	..	175	2 100	2 363	2 362	3 772	3 763	3 510
Capital transfer for uncollected revenue	..	..	..	0	0	0	0	0	0	0
Voluntary social security contributions	..	..	..	0	0	0	0	0	0	0
Miscellaneous differences	..	..	..	0	0	0	0	0	0	0
National Accounts: Taxes and actual social contributions	..	..	..	214 928	348 872	359 110	433 562	464 501	552 677	594 240
Imputed social contributions	..	..	..	0	0	0	0	0	0	0
National Accounts: Taxes and all social contributions	..	..	..	214 928	348 872	359 110	433 562	464 501	552 677	594 240

.. Not available

Note: Data are on a fiscal year basis beginning 1st July.

From 1998 taxes are recorded on an accrual basis; prior to that they were on a cash basis.

Direct taxes paid by public trading enterprises are excluded from receipts.

The figures for total tax revenue do not match the published totals in Taxation Revenue Australia. The latter is based on an accrual IMF GFS methodology and there are some differences between that and the OECD equivalent.

Heading 5213 includes radio and television licenses fees, though these are usually not regarded as a tax revenue in the OECD list.

Headings for non-wastable tax credits 1110 and 1210 include the private health insurance tax offset, family benefit, baby bonus tax offsets (paid during the 2003-04 budget year), film tax offset, and research and development tax offsets. The estimation of non-wastable credits into the expenditure and transfer components is in accordance with the OECD guidelines on the treatment and the data for this memorandum item has been provided by the Australian Taxation Office.

Source: Australian Bureau of Statistics.

StatLink https://stat.link/uk1ipy

Table 5.2. Austria: Details of tax revenue, 1965-2020

Million EUR

	1965	1980	1990	2000	2007	2010	2013	2015	2019	2020
Total tax revenue	**6 210**	**29 759**	**54 040**	**90 324**	**115 146**	**121 192**	**138 099**	**148 469**	**169 250**	**160 711**
Total tax revenue exclusive of taxes collected for the EU	..	..	**54 040**	**89 897**	**114 728**	**120 843**	**137 741**	**147 841**	**168 564**	**159 995**
1000 Taxes on income, profits and capital gains	**1 584**	**7 959**	**13 797**	**25 553**	**34 319**	**34 021**	**39 792**	**44 796**	**49 888**	**44 597**
1100 Of individuals	1 240	6 899	11 326	19 890	25 741	27 098	31 474	35 841	38 262	35 595
1110 On income and profits	1 240	6 899	11 326	19 890	25 741	27 098	31 474	35 841	38 262	35 595
Income tax	415	1 576	2 501	3 202	3 253	3 358	3 737	4 274	5 592	4 210
Special income tax	0	0	0	0	0	0	0	0	0	0
Wage tax	417	4 626	7 823	15 630	20 607	21 783	25 669	28 429	29 631	28 686
Tax on industry and trade	196	402	454	7	0	0	0	0	0	0
Tax on capital yields	2	14	46	354	970	938	981	1 979	1 683	1 342
Contribution to chambers	60	279	501	697	910	1 018	1 087	1 159	1 355	1 358
Water supply fund	151	0	0	0	0	0	0	0	0	0
Contribution emergency fund	0	0	0	0	0	0	0	0	0	0
1120 On capital gains	0	0	0	0	0	0	0	0	0	0
1200 Corporate	334	1 049	1 930	4 157	6 622	5 519	6 963	7 659	10 795	8 182
1210 On profits	334	1 049	1 930	4 157	6 622	5 519	6 963	7 659	10 795	8 182
Corporation tax	195	698	998	3 865	6 094	4 978	6 377	6 752	9 995	7 526
Tax on industry and trade	83	254	624	10	0	1	0	0	0	0
Special tax on income	0	0	0	0	0	0	0	0	0	0
Tax on capital yields	5	33	108	118	346	347	370	684	561	447
Water supply fund	35	0	0	0	0	0	0	0	0	0
Contribution emergency fund	0	0	0	0	0	0	0	0	0	0
Contribution to chambers	14	58	200	164	182	193	216	224	240	210
Directors tax	2	6	0	0	0	0	0	0	0	0
1220 On capital gains	0	0	0	0	0	0	0	0	0	0
1300 Unallocable between 1100 and 1200	10	12	540	1 506	1 956	1 405	1 354	1 295	830	819
Fines related to tax offences	10	12	18	33	77	99	73	70	85	28
Tax on interest	0	0	522	1 473	1 879	1 305	1 282	1 225	746	791
2000 Social security contributions	**1 548**	**9 200**	**17 763**	**30 510**	**38 453**	**41 423**	**46 845**	**49 867**	**59 083**	**59 094**
2100 Employees	686	3 792	7 512	12 477	15 612	16 846	18 931	20 115	23 778	23 857
2110 On a payroll basis	..	..	..	12 477	15 612	16 846	18 931	20 115	23 778	23 857
Health insurance contributions	..	..	..	2 606	3 326	3 675	4 082	4 347	5 206	5 249
Pension insurance contributions	..	..	..	6 410	8 274	8 986	10 183	10 896	13 216	13 350
Pension contributions, civil servants	..	..	..	1 489	1 579	1 625	1 672	1 629	1 553	1 504
Unemployment insurance contributions	..	..	..	1 854	2 284	2 385	2 803	3 040	3 567	3 504
Health insurance contributions, local government employees	..	..	..	100	130	156	169	181	206	222
Special unemployment insurance contributions	..	..	..	17	19	20	22	23	29	29
2120 On an income tax basis	..	..	..	0	0	0	0	0	0	0
2200 Employers	721	4 563	8 768	14 651	18 091	19 421	21 922	23 281	27 826	27 733
2210 On a payroll basis	..	..	..	14 651	18 091	19 421	21 922	23 281	27 826	27 733
Health insurance contributions	..	..	..	2 667	3 395	3 669	4 075	4 339	5 197	5 240
Pension insurance contributions	..	..	..	7 888	10 214	11 145	12 642	13 549	16 475	16 648
Pension contributions, civil servants	..	..	..	438	376	361	297	298	261	244
Accident insurance contributions	..	..	..	952	1 157	1 254	1 409	1 394	1 527	1 459
Unemployment insurance contributions	..	..	..	1 854	2 284	2 385	2 803	3 040	3 567	3 504
Health insurance contributions, local government employees	..	..	..	101	141	157	170	181	207	222
Contributions to sickness benefit fund	..	..	..	341	0	0	0	0	0	0
Special pension contributions, nightshift workers	..	..	..	11	18	15	31	38	44	46
Contributions to insolvency fund	..	..	..	381	488	416	473	419	394	234
Special unemployment insurance contributions construction workers	..	..	..	17	19	20	22	23	154	136
2220 On an income tax basis	..	..	..	0	0	0	0	0	0	0
2300 Self-employed or non-employed	141	845	1 482	3 382	4 750	5 155	5 993	6 470	7 479	7 504
2310 On a payroll basis	..	..	..	3 382	4 750	5 155	5 993	6 470	7 479	7 504
Health insurance contributions	..	..	..	1 971	2 724	3 090	3 441	3 664	4 142	4 219
Pension insurance contributions	..	..	..	1 117	1 527	1 524	1 973	2 210	2 712	2 574
Pension contributions, civil servants (retired)	..	..	..	116	274	297	315	317	308	311
Accident insurance contributions	..	..	..	77	85	88	95	98	110	178
Health insurance contributions, local government employees	..	..	..	101	140	156	169	181	206	222
2320 On an income tax basis	..	..	..	0	0	0	0	0	0	0
2400 Unallocable between 2100, 2200 and 2300	0	0	0	0	0	0	0	0	0	0
2410 On a payroll basis	..	..	..	..	..	..	..	..	..	..
2420 On an income tax basis	..	..	..	..	..	..	..	..	..	..

	1965	1980	1990	2000	2007	2010	2013	2015	2019	2020
3000 Taxes on payroll and workforce	**472**	**2 097**	**3 259**	**5 788**	**7 266**	**8 359**	**9 489**	**10 040**	**10 775**	**10 447**
Emplr. contr. equaliz. of family.burdens	318	1 397	2 147	3 140	3 915	4 762	5 319	5 623	5 548	5 389
Tax on sum of wages	82	375	669	1 735	2 238	2 402	2 742	2 911	3 471	3 326
Promotion residential buildings	44	217	389	595	754	811	915	965	1 157	1 149
Tax on employment (Vienna undergr.)	0	20	21	21	22	22	67	65	70	69
Special levy for households allowances	26	80	0	0	0	0	0	0	0	0
Disabled persons equalization levy	2	8	34	54	83	91	138	148	160	163
Contributions to chambers	0	0	0	242	253	271	308	327	369	352
4000 Taxes on property	**246**	**858**	**1 473**	**1 206**	**1 572**	**1 555**	**2 341**	**1 965**	**2 158**	**2 195**
4100 Recurrent taxes on immovable property	92	231	355	526	626	682	736	761	829	861
4110 Households	47	66	84	87	92	93	105	107	133	142
Duty on farms	9	15	20	20	20	20	29	30	40	32
Farm contr. equaliz. of family burdens	5	6	6	6	6	6	6	6	8	30
Farm contribution to chambers	14	23	32	32	39	40	43	44	51	49
Contr. residential buildings reconstruction	4	0	0	0	0	0	0	0	0	0
Land tax A	16	22	25	28	26	26	26	26	34	31
4120 Others	45	165	271	440	534	589	631	654	696	719
Tax on vacant plots	1	4	5	5	5	6	6	6	6	5
Land tax B	44	161	266	435	529	583	625	649	690	714
4200 Recurrent taxes on net wealth	103	401	642	1	0	0	0	0	0	0
4210 Individual	37	140	189	1	..	..	..	..	..	..
Capital tax	25	109	189	1	..	..	..	..	..	..
Contribution emergency fund	0	0	0	0	..	..	..	..	..	..
Tax on industry and trade	10	26	0	0	..	..	..	..	..	..
Contribution to chambers	2	6	0	0	..	..	..	..	..	..
4220 Corporate	66	260	453	0	..	..	..	..	..	..
Capital tax	24	139	322	0	..	..	..	..	..	..
Capital death duty	20	53	131	0	..	..	..	..	..	..
Contribution emergency fund	0	0	0	0	..	..	..	..	..	..
Tax on industry and trade	19	56	0	0	..	..	..	..	..	..
Contribution to chambers	3	13	0	0	..	..	..	..	..	..
4300 Estate, inheritance and gift taxes	16	50	77	111	155	35	19	12	0	0
4310 Estate and inheritance taxes	..	..	..	..	..	..	..	..	..	..
4320 Gift taxes	..	..	..	..	..	..	..	..	..	..
4400 Taxes on financial and capital transactions	35	176	399	568	791	828	858	1 116	1 318	1 320
Land transfer tax	30	150	251	452	644	727	790	1 014	1 317	1 319
Capital transfer tax	5	27	148	115	147	102	67	102	1	1
4500 Non-recurrent taxes	0	0	0	0	0	10	728	76	11	14
4510 On net wealth	..	..	..	..	..	0	717	4	0	0
Withholding tax	..	..	..	..	..	..	717	4	0	0
4520 Other non-recurrent taxes	..	..	..	..	..	10	11	72	11	14
Foundation tax	..	..	..	..	..	10	11	72	11	14
4600 Other recurrent taxes on property	0	0	0	0	0	0	0	0	0	0
5000 Taxes on goods and services	**2 321**	**9 379**	**17 034**	**26 497**	**32 609**	**34 740**	**38 701**	**41 064**	**46 533**	**43 690**
5100 Taxes on production, sale, transfer, etc.	2 275	9 006	16 169	24 616	30 180	32 114	35 721	37 633	42 488	39 625
5110 General taxes	1 160	5 984	11 229	16 857	20 941	22 711	24 920	26 282	30 426	28 437
5111 Value added taxes	0	5 984	11 229	16 857	20 941	22 711	24 920	26 282	30 426	28 437
5112 Sales tax	0	0	0	0	0	0	0	0	0	0
5113 Other	1 160	0	0	0	0	0	0	0	0	0
Turnover tax	664	..	..	..	..	..	..	..	..	..
Additional federal levy-turnover	332	..	..	..	..	..	..	..	..	..
Additional lieu invoice stp.	164	..	..	..	..	..	..	..	..	..
5120 Taxes on specific goods and services	1 115	2 996	4 873	7 721	9 236	9 400	10 800	11 348	12 057	11 186

	1965	1980	1990	2000	2007	2010	2013	2015	2019	2020
5121 Excise duties	610	2 219	3 290	5 484	6 760	6 921	7 598	7 749	8 217	7 246
Tax on beer	39	44	56	161	200	198	193	189	190	194
Tax on wine	7	0	0	0	0	0	0	0	0	0
Tax on sparkling wine	1	7	25	25	1	1	1	19	24	13
Tax on tobacco	188	519	820	1 197	1 446	1 502	1 664	1 782	1 891	1 983
Tax on mineral oils	50	136	1 426	2 726	3 689	3 854	4 173	4 218	4 480	3 579
Additional federal levy mineral oils	202	876	0	0	0	0	0	0	0	0
Special duty alcoholic drinks	0	142	193	0	0	0	0	0	0	0
Special duty vehicles	0	0	0	0	0	0	0	0	0	0
Duty on starch products	0	4	13	0	0	0	0	0	0	0
Beverage tax	46	216	364	178	3	-1	-1	0	0	0
Other receipts-Market Organisation Act	26	35	9	0	1	0	0	0	0	0
Transport equality levy	0	5	1	0	0	0	0	0	0	0
Market Organisation Act - milk	35	177	192	0	0	0	0	0	0	0
Market Organisation Act - livestock	0	0	0	0	0	0	0	0	0	0
Market Organisation Act - grain	16	23	142	0	0	0	0	0	0	0
Duty promotion milk distrib.	0	34	13	0	0	0	0	0	0	0
Special tax on mineral oils	0	0	37	0	0	0	0	0	0	0
Duty on vehicles (fuel consumption)	0	0	0	433	457	453	455	395	555	440
Agricultural fund	0	0	0	23	16	18	18	17	17	17
Tax on energy	0	0	0	562	764	726	886	931	866	836
Social contributions to the artists' fund	0	0	0	0	11	6	7	13	7	8
Duty on exceeding milk-quota	0	0	0	36	24	6	26	11	0	0
Car registration taxes	0	0	0	143	148	158	175	174	188	175
5122 Profits of fiscal monopolies	37	57	52	130	122	129	324	328	400	380
Duty on spirits	5	14	17	130	122	129	130	120	154	138
Federal monopolies salt	1	0	0	0	0	0	0	0	0	0
Federal monopolies spirits	30	43	35	0	0	0	0	0	0	0
Federal monopolies gambling	0	0	0	0	0	0	194	208	246	242
5123 Customs and import duties	332	354	677	351	390	340	328	415	488	474
Customs duties	310	237	418	352	390	339	328	415	488	474
Other import duties	0	21	61	0	0	0	0	0	0	0
Contribution promote foreign trade	10	63	171	0	0	0	0	0	0	0
Import equalization duties	12	33	27	0	0	0	0	0	0	0
5124 Taxes on exports	8	36	1	0	0	0	0	0	0	0
Contribution to promote foreign trade	8	36	1	..	..	..	..	..	..	..
5125 Taxes on investment goods	0	33	0	0	0	0	0	0	0	0
5126 Taxes on specific services	129	297	854	1 720	1 967	2 005	2 545	2 852	2 951	3 086
Insurance tax	25	135	384	745	993	1 017	1 056	1 122	1 215	1 240
Transport tax	63	0	0	0	0	0	0	0	0	0
Duty on casinos	2	28	64	105	71	55	45	70	114	80
Fire protection tax	5	24	50	45	54	56	57	61	67	67
Advertisement tax	7	31	65	62	0	0	0	0	0	0
Entertainment tax	2	2	2	5	8	9	21	18	0	0
Tax on tourism	8	43	71	103	142	171	182	186	261	235
Amusement tax	13	17	51	73	94	107	84	30	18	9
Announcement tax	3	18	40	81	0	1	0	0	0	0
Tax on interest yields	0	0	0	0	0	0	0	0	0	0
Tax on gambling stakes - licences	0	0	116	197	202	221	251	254	273	276
Tax on advertisement	0	0	0	33	108	110	110	107	106	88
Levy on dangerous waste	0	0	10	71	72	51	53	56	69	100
Duty for airways security	0	0	0	28	56	30	0	0	0	0
Tax on gambling stakes - gains	0	0	0	171	166	176	0	0	0	0
Flight Charge	0	0	0	0	0	0	98	109	72	23
Financial Institutions Stability Fees	0	0	0	0	0	0	588	640	558	724
SRF Contributions	..	..	0	0	0	0	0	198	198	242
5127 Other taxes on internat. trade and transactions	0	0	0	0	0	0	0	0	0	0
5128 Other taxes	0	0	0	34	-3	4	4	4	0	0
Levy on sugar	..	..	..	34	-3	4	4	4	..	..
5130 Unallocable between 5110 and 5120	0	26	66	38	3	4	2	4	5	2
Fines related to tax offenses	..	26	66	38	3	4	2	4	5	2
5200 Taxes on use of goods and perform activities	46	373	865	1 881	2 429	2 626	2 980	3 431	4 045	4 065
5210 Recurrent taxes	38	335	757	1 733	2 253	2 416	2 715	3 124	3 564	3 631
5211 Paid by households: motor vehicles	22	156	366	811	1 173	1 293	1 482	1 814	2 106	2 172
5212 Paid by others: motor vehicles	13	41	97	298	370	334	352	421	487	496
5213 Paid in respect of other goods	3	138	294	624	710	789	881	890	971	963
Hunting and fishing duties	1	4	7	10	10	10	19	22	25	15
Dog tax	1	4	6	8	10	11	17	18	21	21
Contribution to promotion of arts	1	3	8	71	120	132	147	143	163	162
Tax on radio and tv - licenses	0	15	46	450	571	636	698	708	763	765
Road transport duty	0	112	226	84	0	0	0	0	0	0

	1965	1980	1990	2000	2007	2010	2013	2015	2019	2020
5220 Non-recurrent taxes	8	38	108	147	175	210	265	307	481	434
Certain user fees; taxes on emission of noxious gases	8	38	108	147	175	210	265	307	481	434
5300 Unallocable between 5100 and 5200	0	0	0	0	0	0	0	0	0	0
6000 Other taxes	**38**	**266**	**714**	**770**	**928**	**1 095**	**931**	**737**	**814**	**688**
Tax on financial institutions	0	0	123	-3	0	0	0	0	0	0
Administration duties	4	17	32	278	366	521	517	302	341	352
Stamp fees	7	46	76	135	92	84	27	32	35	25
Contributions of interested persons	0	0	130	0	0	0	0	0	0	0
Parking duty	0	0	6	0	0	0	0	0	0	0
Contrbutions to students' associations	0	0	0	4	8	11	12	11	15	14
Duty on contribution to political parties	0	0	0	0	-1	1	0	0	0	0
Other fees, taxes on production n.e.c.	0	0	0	272	346	353	227	252	264	223
Embossing fee	0	0	0	0	1	1	1	1	1	0
Other taxes	28	202	347	82	115	124	145	137	153	70
Compensation levy according to the Vienna Tree Protection Act	..	..	0	1	1	2	1	2	5	3
6100 Paid solely by business	..	..	..	..	..	..	..	..	..	..
6200 Other	..	..	..	..	..	..	..	..	..	..
Memorandum items										
Customs duties collected on behalf of the EU	..	..	..	352	390	339	328	415	488	474
SRF contributions collected on behalf of the EU	..	..	..	..	..	..	..	198	198	242
Non-wastable tax credits										
Non-wastable tax credits against 1110	..	..	..	650	650	650	570	540	330	330
Tax expenditure component	..	..	..	590	450	422	341	295	210	210
Transfer component	..	..	..	60	200	228	229	245	120	120
Non-wastable tax credits against 1210	..	..	..	..	..	..	..	..	..	..
Tax expenditure component	..	..	..	..	..	..	..	..	..	..
Transfer component	..	..	..	..	..	..	..	..	..	..
Total tax revenue on cash basis	**6 210**	**29 759**	**54 040**	**90 299**	**115 045**	**120 735**	**137 970**	**148 036**	**168 681**	**158 726**
Total tax revenue on accrual basis	**..**	**..**	**..**	**90 324**	**115 146**	**121 192**	**138 099**	**148 469**	**169 250**	**160 711**
Conciliation with National Accounts										
Additional taxes included in National Accounts	..	..	..	..	..	..	..	..	..	..
Taxes excluded from National Accounts	..	..	..	..	..	..	..	..	..	..
Difference in treatment of tax credits	..	..	..	590	450	422	341	295	210	210
Capital transfer for uncollected revenue	..	..	..	..	..	..	..	..	..	-517
Voluntary social security contributions	..	..	..	206	256	339	299	321	336	344
Miscellaneous differences	..	..	..	0	0	0	0	0	0	0
National Accounts: Taxes and actual social contributions	..	..	..	91 120	115 853	121 953	138 739	149 085	169 796	160 748
Imputed social contributions	..	..	..	2 485	2 177	2 106	1 972	1 925	1 703	1 640
National Accounts: Taxes and all social contributions	..	..	..	93 605	118 030	124 060	140 711	151 010	171 499	162 388

.. Not available

Note: Year ending 31st December.

From 1995 data are on accrual basis.

The pre-1995 figures are not in all cases comparable with those from the following years (due to the switch to the new System of National Accounts implemented only from 1995 onwards).

Source: Statistics Austria.

StatLink https://stat.link/b0dgvi

Table 5.3. Belgium: Details of tax revenue, 1965-2020

Million EUR

	1965	1980	1990	2000	2007	2010	2013	2015	2019	2020
Total tax revenue	**6 421**	**37 443**	**70 408**	**112 710**	**147 861**	**156 317**	**177 657**	**184 374**	**203 451**	**195 051**
Total tax revenue exclusive of taxes collected for the EU	..	..	..	**111 675**	**146 411**	**155 042**	**176 479**	**182 758**	**201 498**	**193 310**
1000 Taxes on income, profits and capital gains	**1 774**	**15 379**	**25 983**	**43 461**	**52 854**	**53 313**	**62 762**	**65 572**	**71 827**	**69 113**
1100 Of individuals	1 317	13 626	22 538	35 318	41 020	44 027	50 518	51 877	54 027	54 104
1110 On income and profits	1 317	13 626	22 538	35 318	41 020	44 027	50 518	51 877	54 027	54 104
Immovable income withholding tax	148	532	1 053	1 857	0	0	0	0	0	0
Movable income withholding tax	119	1 062	3 014	1 755	2 351	2 426	4 314	4 104	3 700	3 120
Earned income withholding tax	740	9 119	15 422	27 778	36 022	39 829	44 686	45 658	47 635	48 443
Advance payments PIT	125	1 776	2 144	1 959	1 747	1 611	1 508	1 547	1 586	1 474
Non residents tax	0	-2	4	585	792	810	841	926	1 133	1 235
Assessments PIT	183	1 128	878	774	-915	-1 697	-1 988	-1 512	-1 337	-1 445
Special social contributions	0	0	19	602	957	1 032	1 117	1 106	1 267	1 223
Other income taxes	0	12	2	8	65	17	41	48	42	54
1120 On capital gains	0	0	0	0	0	0	0	0	0	0
1200 Corporate	397	1 744	3 405	8 065	11 749	9 249	12 192	13 644	17 730	14 941
1210 On profits	397	1 744	3 405	8 065	11 749	9 249	12 192	13 644	17 730	14 941
Immovable income withholding tax (corporate)	33	0	0	0	0	0	0	0	0	0
Movable income withholding tax (corporate)	41	367	1 206	527	686	315	477	466	354	200
Advance payments (corporate)	262	1 273	2 735	7 112	9 733	7 691	7 930	8 539	14 622	12 426
Assessments (corporate)	60	79	-553	404	1 270	1 196	3 662	4 466	2 571	2 246
Non residents tax (corporate)	0	-6	18	17	41	43	113	154	191	46
Other income taxes (corporate)	0	32	-2	5	19	4	10	19	-7	24
1220 On capital gains	0	0	0	0	0	0	0	0	0	0
1300 Unallocable between 1100 and 1200	61	9	40	77	85	38	52	51	71	68
Former income taxes	51	0	0	0	0	0	0	0	0	0
Penalties	3	0	0	0	0	0	0	0	0	0
Other	7	9	40	77	85	38	52	51	71	68
2000 Social security contributions	**2 018**	**10 798**	**23 386**	**34 865**	**45 929**	**50 674**	**56 527**	**58 812**	**63 203**	**62 276**
2100 Employees	569	3 130	7 152	10 932	13 847	14 996	16 476	17 036	19 071	18 846
2110 On a payroll basis	..	3 130	7 152	10 932	13 847	14 996	16 476	17 036	19 071	18 846
On gross wages	..	3 130	7 062	10 932	13 847	14 996	16 476	17 036	19 071	18 846
On social benefits	..	0	89	0	0	0	0	0	0	0
2120 On an income tax basis	..	0	0	0	0	0	0	0	0	0
2200 Employers	1 320	6 791	14 689	21 027	28 216	31 041	34 915	36 240	37 902	37 325
2210 On a payroll basis	..	6 791	14 689	21 027	28 216	31 041	34 915	36 240	37 902	37 325
Contributions by government	..	1 059	1 769	3 105	4 493	5 381	6 678	7 686	8 557	8 698
Contributions by other sectors	..	5 732	12 920	17 922	23 723	25 661	28 236	28 554	29 345	28 627
2220 On an income tax basis	..	0	0	0	0	0	0	0	0	0
2300 Self-employed or non-employed	129	877	1 546	2 906	3 866	4 637	5 136	5 537	6 230	6 104
Self-employed	..	803	1 230	2 053	2 678	3 342	3 703	3 975	4 327	4 088
Unemployed	..	0	0	0	0	0	0	0	0	0
Retired	..	29	198	709	1 012	1 134	1 324	1 449	1 778	1 890
Other	..	45	118	144	176	161	109	113	125	127
2310 On a payroll basis	..	877	1 546	2 906	3 866	4 637	5 136	5 537	6 230	6 104
2320 On an income tax basis	..	0	0	0	0	0	0	0	0	0
2400 Unallocable between 2100, 2200 and 2300	0	0	0	0	0	0	0	0	0	0
2410 On a payroll basis	..	..	..	..	..	..	..	..	..	..
2420 On an income tax basis	..	..	..	..	..	..	..	..	..	..
3000 Taxes on payroll and workforce	**0**	**0**	**0**	**0**	**6**	**7**	**8**	**8**	**9**	**5**
Levy on public mandates	..	..	..	..	6	7	8	8	9	5
4000 Taxes on property	**240**	**1 161**	**2 679**	**5 282**	**10 550**	**11 252**	**13 805**	**14 408**	**16 358**	**15 615**
4100 Recurrent taxes on immovable property	2	210	599	1 164	4 146	4 632	5 187	5 433	6 145	6 057
4110 Households	0	26	63	102	2 779	3 115	3 478	3 651	4 174	4 127
4120 Others	2	184	536	1 063	1 367	1 517	1 710	1 782	1 971	1 930
Tax on non profit institutions	2	7	17	41	32	33	38	41	47	50
Immovable income withholding tax (corporate)	0	177	519	929	1 269	1 416	1 584	1 651	1 830	1 794
Regional tax (Brussels)	0	0	0	94	66	68	88	90	94	86
4200 Recurrent taxes on net wealth	0	0	0	92	253	237	451	661	922	984
4210 Individual	..	..	..	0	0	0	0	0	0	0
4220 Corporate	..	..	..	92	253	237	451	661	922	984
4300 Estate, inheritance and gift taxes	75	309	504	1 101	2 053	2 269	3 096	2 996	2 936	2 967
4310 Estate and inheritance taxes	69	281	475	1 042	1 702	1 939	2 634	2 504	2 400	2 411
4320 Gift taxes	6	29	29	59	351	330	463	492	536	556

	1965	1980	1990	2000	2007	2010	2013	2015	2019	2020
4400 Taxes on financial and capital transactions	163	633	1 478	2 669	3 704	3 493	3 886	4 358	5 379	4 961
Registration duties	153	527	1 213	1 967	3 325	3 210	3 542	3 899	4 911	4 403
Mortgage duties	2	10	29	37	76	75	72	93	95	84
Court duties	2	8	29	38	31	34	37	41	32	19
Economic expansion fund	0	0	0	0	0	0	0	0	0	0
Tax on stock exchange transactions	4	31	92	386	234	134	193	287	298	413
Tax on stock exchange listings	2	4	21	0	0	0	0	0	0	0
Tax on bearer securities	0	0	0	79	3	0	6	0	0	0
Stamp duties	0	53	94	161	35	40	36	38	42	42
4500 Non-recurrent taxes	0	0	0	74	163	327	877	643	456	321
4510 On net wealth	..	..	..	0	0	0	0	0	0	0
4520 Other non-recurrent taxes	..	..	..	74	163	327	877	643	456	321
Tax on long term savings	..	..	..	74	163	194	207	413	342	203
Voluntary disclosure tax	..	..	..	0	0	0	0	0	0	0
Voluntary disclosure tax (Diamond)	..	..	..	0	0	0	0	0	0	0
Voluntary disclosure tax (bis)	..	..	..	0	0	133	614	152	28	26
Voluntary disclosure tax (ter)	..	..	..	0	0	0	54	78	85	92
Special contribution on credit associations	..	..	..	0	0	0	2	0	0	0
4600 Other recurrent taxes on property	0	8	99	182	232	294	309	318	522	325
Levy for fighting the non-use of an electric power production site by a producer	..	..	..	0	-16	0	0	0	0	0
Transfer to the Fund for Industrial Accidents of recognized private insurance corporations	..	..	..	182	249	294	309	318	305	297
Tax on securities accounts	..	..	..	0	0	0	0	0	217	27
5000 Taxes on goods and services	**2 386**	**10 105**	**18 360**	**29 103**	**38 462**	**41 035**	**44 509**	**45 535**	**52 054**	**48 043**
5100 Taxes on production, sale, transfer, etc.	2 187	9 606	17 387	27 000	36 091	38 646	42 079	43 043	49 165	45 293
5110 General taxes	1 355	6 321	11 570	18 258	24 411	25 882	27 979	28 170	32 563	30 008
5111 Value added taxes	0	6 321	11 547	18 132	24 140	25 628	27 738	27 952	32 181	29 761
VAT	..	6 293	11 491	18 132	24 140	25 628	27 738	27 952	32 181	29 761
Vehicle immatriculation tax	..	28	56	0	0	0	0	0	0	0
5112 Sales tax	0	0	23	126	271	253	241	219	381	247
5113 Other	1 355	0	0	0	0	0	0	0	0	0
Taxes assimilated to stamp duties	1 355	..	..	..	..	..	..	..	..	..
5120 Taxes on specific goods and services	832	3 285	5 818	8 742	11 680	12 764	14 100	14 873	16 602	15 285
5121 Excise duties	531	1 997	3 478	5 690	7 367	7 783	8 036	8 649	9 990	9 031
Mineral oil	278	1 109	2 017	3 392	3 891	4 148	4 072	4 556	5 426	4 401
Liquified gases and benzol	0	4	0	0	0	0	0	0	0	0
Tobacco	132	501	868	1 342	1 821	1 885	2 197	2 262	2 404	2 451
Spirits	23	123	191	206	225	235	272	318	311	344
Consumption tax on alcohol and spirits	26	54	0	0	0	0	0	0	0	0
Fermented sparkling beverages	1	7	11	24	39	57	77	92	104	90
Fermented fruit beverages	18	57	88	101	115	116	132	148	174	186
Beer	38	93	170	208	191	188	183	194	200	180
Non-alcoholic beverages	10	44	113	148	49	54	58	56	183	186
Coffee, sugar and syrup	5	5	22	13	12	13	15	14	15	15
Levy on energy	0	0	0	193	341	383	337	343	340	321
Intermediate alcoholic products	0	0	0	32	28	26	26	26	25	26
Inspection fee on domestic fuel oil	0	0	0	29	43	51	41	36	30	32
Ecotax	0	0	0	2	1	0	1	0	0	0
Levy on packaging	0	0	0	0	296	320	332	336	349	372
Federal contribution on electricity and natural gas	0	0	0	0	311	292	281	269	430	430
Environmental charge	0	0	0	0	5	15	14	1	0	0
5122 Profits of fiscal monopolies	0	0	0	0	0	0	0	0	0	0
5123 Customs and import duties	272	627	809	960	1 388	1 234	1 185	1 373	1 683	1 440
Import duties	206	0	0	0	0	0	0	0	0	0
Levies on agricultural products	63	0	0	0	0	0	0	0	0	0
ECSC levies	2	0	0	0	0	0	0	0	0	0
EU levies, import duties	0	383	716	932	1 365	1 210	1 149	1 368	1 683	1 440
EU levies on agricultural products	0	244	93	28	23	23	36	5	0	0
5124 Taxes on exports	0	1	0	0	0	0	0	0	0	0
5125 Taxes on investment goods	0	0	0	0	0	0	0	0	0	0
5126 Taxes on specific services	29	452	937	1 365	2 044	2 454	3 136	3 210	3 320	3 398
Gambling and betting tax	9	47	51	45	64	77	73	80	107	93
Insurance levy	19	404	885	1 282	1 930	2 123	2 285	2 307	2 512	2 566
Bill-posting tax	0	0	1	1	3	3	3	3	3	3
Deposit insurance	0	0	0	36	48	252	609	441	428	435
Resolution fund	..	..	..	0	0	0	167	380	270	301
5127 Other taxes on internat. trade and transactions	0	0	0	0	0	0	0	0	0	0
5128 Other taxes	0	208	593	726	881	1 294	1 743	1 640	1 609	1 416
5130 Unallocable between 5110 and 5120	0	0	0	0	0	0	0	0	0	0
5200 Taxes on use of goods and perform activities	199	496	966	2 096	2 363	2 384	2 420	2 482	2 877	2 738
5210 Recurrent taxes	199	496	966	1 887	2 032	2 005	2 023	2 032	1 973	1 934
Traffic tax	100	368	712	1 413	1 693	1 702	1 830	1 851	1 897	1 880

	1965	1980	1990	2000	2007	2010	2013	2015	2019	2020
5211 Paid by households: motor vehicles	0	204	458	889	1 051	1 054	1 148	1 163	1 270	1 260
5212 Paid by others: motor vehicles	0	164	254	525	642	648	683	689	626	620
5213 Paid in respect of other goods	99	127	254	474	338	303	193	181	76	54
Tax on entertainment devices	6	20	20	71	56	58	74	56	53	30
Tax on pubs	1	5	24	18	0	0	0	0	0	0
Hunting tax	2	0	0	0	0	0	0	0	0	0
Local taxes	90	15	19	38	99	112	10	22	23	24
Radio and television licence fees	0	87	191	347	184	133	108	103	0	0
5220 Non-recurrent taxes	0	0	0	209	332	379	397	451	904	804
Vehicle registration tax	..	..	..	209	332	379	360	349	497	455
Vehicle registration tax (households)	..	..	..	139	221	252	240	233	331	303
Vehicle registration tax (others)	..	..	..	70	111	126	120	116	166	152
Emission permits	..	..	..	0	0	0	36	101	407	349
5300 Unallocable between 5100 and 5200	0	3	7	7	7	6	10	9	13	12
6000 Other taxes	**2**	**0**	**0**	**0**	**61**	**36**	**46**	**40**	**0**	**0**
6100 Paid solely by business	0	..	..	..	0	0	0	0	..	..
6200 Other	2	..	..	..	61	36	46	40	..	..
Fines and interest	2	..	..	..	0	0	0	0	..	..
Memorandum items										
Customs duties collected on behalf of the EU	..	..	..	960	1 388	1 234	1 185	1 373	1 683	1 440
SRF contributions collected on behalf of the EU	..	..	..	..	..	..	167	380	270	301
Other taxes collected on behalf of the EU	..	..	..	75	62	42	-7	9	..	..
Taxes and compulsory social security contributions paid by EU civil servants	..	..	..	310	521	685	665	731	879	939
Taxes paid by EU civil servants: income taxes	..	..	..	174	270	345	336	370	446	477
Taxes paid by EU civil servants: compulsory social security contributions	..	..	..	136	250	340	330	360	433	462
Non-wastable tax credits										
Non-wastable tax credits against 1110	..	..	..	..	348	1 037	1 492	830	1 113	1 126
Tax expenditure component	..	..	..	..	78	588	1 077	537	863	868
Transfer component	..	..	..	..	270	449	415	293	250	258
Non-wastable tax credits against 1210	..	..	..	..	..	..	..	..	..	..
Tax expenditure component	..	..	..	..	..	..	..	..	..	..
Transfer component	..	..	..	..	..	..	..	..	..	..
Total tax revenue on cash basis	**6 421**	**37 438**	**70 268**	**..**	**..**	**..**	**..**	**..**	**..**	**..**
Total tax revenue on accrual basis	**..**	**37 443**	**70 408**	**112 710**	**147 861**	**156 317**	**177 657**	**184 374**	**203 451**	**195 051**
Conciliation with National Accounts										
Additional taxes included in National Accounts	..	107	447	1 300	1 740	2 458	3 362	3 670	4 898	5 219
National lottery profits	..	107	262	279	225	243	215	206	185	185
Water levies	..	0	66	378	119	137	122	104	142	135
Sanitel levy	..	0	0	14	13	15	14	6	8	12
Levy on industrial waste	..	0	27	74	68	54	46	55	81	76
Levy on manure	..	0	0	11	11	5	5	1	2	4
Levy on household waste	..	0	0	20	..	..	..	..	..	..
Earned income withholding tax (EU)	..	0	93	174	270	345	336	370	446	477
Social contributions (EU)	..	0	0	136	250	340	330	360	433	462
Imputed social contributions (EU)	..	0	0	213	431	508	511	554	663	703
Green certificates	..	..	..	..	354	812	1 777	1 959	2 333	2 433
Contracts art. 81 (Managed Entry Agreements)	..	..	..	..	..	..	8	55	605	733
Taxes excluded from National Accounts	..	0	0	0	0	0	0	0	0	0
Deposit insurance	..	..	..	..	..	..	..	..	..	..
Difference in treatment of tax credits	..	0	..	..	78	588	1 077	537	863	868
Capital transfer for uncollected revenue	..	0	0	-291	-381	-597	-730	-547	-632	-970
VAT on products assessed but unlikely to be collected	..	..	..	-18	-276	-367	-488	-357	-479	-700
Earned income withholding tax assessed but unlikely to be collected	..	..	..	-40	-53	-71	-47	-49	-45	-70
Employers' actual social contributions assessed but unlikely to be collected	..	..	..	-233	-52	-159	-194	-141	-107	-200
Voluntary social security contributions	..	41	52	58	57	59	77	70	84	82
Miscellaneous differences	..	0	0	0	0	0	0	0	0	0
Reallocation national levels of government	..	..	..	..	..	..	..	..	..	..
Reallocation EU	..	..	..	..	..	..	..	..	..	..
National Accounts: Taxes and actual social contributions	..	37 590	70 907	113 564	148 924	158 318	180 932	187 550	208 001	199 547
Imputed social contributions	..	1 497	2 886	5 377	7 568	8 713	10 071	9 812	11 051	11 416
National Accounts: Taxes and all social contributions	..	39 087	73 793	118 940	156 492	167 031	191 003	197 362	219 052	210 962

.. Not available

Note: Year ending 31st December. From 1970, data are on accrual basis

Source: Institute for National Accounts; Federal Ministry of Finance.

StatLink https://stat.link/uovpxr

Table 5.4. Canada: Details of tax revenue, 1965-2020

Million CAD

	1965	1980	1990	2000	2007	2010	2013	2015	2019	2020
Total tax revenue	**15 318**	**101 015**	**244 152**	**390 234**	**512 663**	**516 591**	**592 206**	**653 269**	**764 366**	**755 994**
1000 Taxes on income, profits and capital gains	**5 910**	**47 064**	**118 566**	**195 320**	**251 198**	**240 961**	**281 787**	**314 841**	**372 233**	**376 509**
1100 Of individuals	3 464	34 451	99 722	143 652	190 025	180 894	214 054	240 304	275 584	278 855
1110 On income and profits	3 464	34 451	99 722	143 652	190 025	180 894	214 054	240 304	275 584	278 855
Taxes federal government	2 635	21 231	60 252	90 694	116 395	109 341	127 655	143 315	164 485	164 902
Taxes on individuals - province	829	13 220	39 470	52 958	73 630	71 553	86 399	96 989	111 099	113 953
1120 On capital gains	0	0	0	0	0	0	0	0	0	0
1200 Corporate	2 276	11 741	17 190	47 643	54 272	54 101	62 359	67 894	86 615	89 503
1210 On profits	2 276	11 741	17 190	47 643	54 272	54 101	62 359	67 894	86 615	89 503
Taxes federal government	1 752	8 110	11 726	31 570	37 093	33 419	38 142	41 726	52 996	55 216
Taxes on corporations - province	524	3 631	5 464	16 073	17 179	20 682	24 217	26 168	33 619	34 287
1220 On capital gains	0	0	0	0	0	0	0	0	0	0
1300 Unallocable between 1100 and 1200	170	872	1 654	4 025	6 901	5 966	5 374	6 643	10 034	8 151
Non-resident withhold taxes - federal	170	872	1 654	4 025	6 901	5 966	5 374	6 643	10 034	8 151
2000 Social security contributions	**854**	**10 649**	**29 653**	**53 109**	**73 722**	**76 787**	**90 394**	**96 371**	**108 366**	**107 866**
2100 Employees	318	3 756	10 634	21 361	29 361	30 626	36 057	38 685	44 228	44 461
Canada pension plan	47	1 265	3 745	9 401	16 194	16 852	20 021	21 491	25 257	25 699
Quebec pension plan	15	431	1 108	2 897	4 124	5 450	5 815	6 293	7 963	8 105
Employment insurance	164	1 393	5 284	7 782	7 084	7 388	9 198	9 772	9 680	9 331
Hospital insurance premiums	92	667	496	1 281	1 959	937	1 023	1 128	1 327	1 325
2110 On a payroll basis	..	..	10 634	20 976	28 654	29 689	35 034	37 557	42 901	43 136
2120 On an income tax basis	..	..	0	385	707	937	1 023	1 128	1 327	1 325
2200 Employers	536	6 697	18 449	30 307	41 922	43 525	51 261	54 380	60 205	59 403
Canada pension plan	48	1 266	3 745	9 401	16 194	16 852	20 021	21 491	25 257	25 699
Quebec pension plan	15	432	1 108	2 897	4 124	5 450	5 815	6 293	7 963	8 105
Employment insurance	164	2 006	7 398	10 894	9 917	10 343	12 877	13 681	13 553	13 064
Hospital insurance premiums	92	1 270	496	897	1 252	0	0	0	0	0
Social insurance levies	217	1 723	5 702	6 218	10 434	10 881	12 548	12 914	13 432	12 535
2210 On a payroll basis	..	..	18 449	30 307	41 922	43 525	51 261	54 380	60 205	59 403
2220 On an income tax basis	..	..	0	0	0	0	0	0	0	0
2300 Self-employed or non-employed	0	196	570	1 442	2 440	2 636	3 076	3 307	3 933	4 002
Canada pension plan	..	153	478	1 200	2 096	2 181	2 591	2 781	3 268	3 326
Quebec pension plan	..	43	92	242	344	455	486	525	665	677
2310 On a payroll basis	..	196	570	1 442	2 440	2 636	3 076	3 307	3 933	4 002
2320 On an income tax basis	..	0	0	0	0	0	0	0	0	0
2400 Unallocable between 2100, 2200 and 2300	0	0	0	0	0	0	0	0	0	0
2410 On a payroll basis	..	..	..	..	..	..	..	..	..	..
2420 On an income tax basis	..	..	..	..	..	..	..	..	..	..
3000 Taxes on payroll and workforce	**0**	**0**	**5 499**	**8 013**	**10 038**	**10 760**	**12 482**	**13 256**	**17 390**	**17 360**
4000 Taxes on property	**2 186**	**9 195**	**24 467**	**37 157**	**54 507**	**63 735**	**70 451**	**77 778**	**88 812**	**90 611**
4100 Recurrent taxes on immovable property	1 830	8 315	20 189	30 242	44 567	51 702	57 769	62 651	70 781	72 198
On property provincial government	11	133	1 645	3 078	3 164	4 476	4 946	5 410	6 932	6 674
Personal property local government	17	0	18 544	27 165	41 403	47 226	52 823	57 241	63 849	65 524
Real property local government	1 802	8 182	0	0	0	0	0	0	0	0
4110 Households	..	..	..	..	..	..	..	..	..	..
4120 Others	..	..	..	..	..	..	..	..	..	..
4200 Recurrent taxes on net wealth	25	512	1 911	4 171	2 970	1 523	414	372	459	460
4210 Individual	0	0	0	0	0	0	0	0	0	0
4220 Corporate	25	512	1 911	4 171	2 970	1 523	414	372	459	460
4300 Estate, inheritance and gift taxes	223	75	3	2	0	178	221	268	344	339
4310 Estate and inheritance taxes	216	75	3	2	..	178	221	268	344	339
On inheritances federal government	108	0	0	0	..	0	0	0	0	0
Succession duties provincial government	108	75	3	2	..	178	221	268	344	339
4320 Gift taxes	7	0	0	0	..	0	0	0	0	0
On gifts federal government	7	..	..	..	..	..	..	..	..	..
4400 Taxes on financial and capital transactions	0	0	0	0	2 868	3 077	3 646	4 975	6 689	7 938
4500 Non-recurrent taxes	108	293	2 365	2 742	4 102	7 254	8 401	9 512	10 539	9 676
4510 On net wealth	0	0	0	0	0	0	0	0	0	0
4520 Other non-recurrent taxes	108	293	2 365	2 742	4 102	7 254	8 401	9 512	10 539	9 676
Special assessments and charges local govt.	108	293	2 365	2 742	4 102	7 254	8 401	9 512	10 539	9 676
4600 Other recurrent taxes on property	0	0	0	0	0	0	0	0	0	0
5000 Taxes on goods and services	**6 202**	**32 909**	**63 092**	**94 468**	**122 855**	**123 752**	**136 396**	**150 275**	**176 608**	**162 781**
5100 Taxes on production, sale, transfer, etc.	5 310	24 808	59 627	88 879	114 701	116 160	128 554	140 750	165 674	152 375
5110 General taxes	2 730	11 658	34 475	55 313	71 242	72 130	81 452	90 598	108 758	102 728
5111 Value added taxes	0	0	0	35 884	46 072	70 712	78 292	86 694	103 412	99 705
5112 Sales tax	2 730	11 658	34 475	19 429	25 170	1 418	3 160	3 904	5 346	3 023
Sales taxes federal government	813	5 429	16 866	0	0	0	0	0	0	0
Sales taxes provincial, local govt.	1 917	6 229	17 609	19 429	25 170	1 418	3 160	3 904	5 346	3 023
5113 Other	0	0	0	0	0	0	0	0	0	0

	1965	1980	1990	2000	2007	2010	2013	2015	2019	2020
5120 Taxes on specific goods and services	2 580	13 150	25 153	33 565	43 459	44 030	47 102	50 152	56 916	49 647
5121 Excise duties	1 499	6 805	14 473	18 417	22 759	23 281	24 470	25 284	28 859	27 901
Excises federal government	740	3 850	6 405	8 377	9 249	10 244	10 261	10 372	13 194	14 328
Liquor	..	..	926	1 103	1 224	1 554	1 488	1 521	1 881	2 023
Tobacco	..	..	2 247	2 176	2 466	3 025	3 019	2 875	3 024	3 024
Gasoline and motive fuel	..	..	2 472	4 807	5 272	5 306	5 460	5 678	5 795	5 055
Remitted gaming profits	..	..	45	0	0	0	0	0	0	0
Miscellaneous consumption taxes	..	..	715	291	287	358	294	297	2 494	4 226
Excises provincial government	759	2 955	8 067	10 039	13 510	13 037	14 209	14 912	15 665	13 573
Motor fuel	680	1 863	4 674	7 031	8 065	8 198	9 094	9 727	10 200	8 404
Tobacco	53	772	2 776	2 279	4 181	4 620	4 879	5 108	4 667	4 554
Other	26	320	617	730	1 264	219	236	77	798	615
5122 Profits of fiscal monopolies	294	1 406	3 758	8 756	11 565	11 565	12 059	13 016	14 316	10 562
Own enterprises contributions	294	1 406	3 758	8 756	11 565	11 565	12 059	13 016	14 316	10 562
5123 Customs and import duties	686	3 199	4 021	2 824	3 829	3 441	4 193	5 181	5 492	4 024
Customs and import duties federal govt.	686	3 199	4 021	2 824	3 829	3 441	4 193	5 181	5 492	4 024
5124 Taxes on exports	0	842	0	0	0	0	0	0	0	0
5125 Taxes on investment goods	0	0	0	0	0	0	0	0	0	0
5126 Taxes on specific services	84	575	2 385	2 524	4 088	4 489	5 087	5 213	6 613	5 927
Tax on insurance premiums, provincial govt.	45	261	1 141	1 740	2 796	3 305	3 901	3 962	5 118	5 399
Tax on insurance premiums, federal govt.	0	1	1	1	11	28	13	10	9	13
Amusement and admission taxes	4	25	126	538	537	322	280	291	314	86
Air transportation taxes	0	166	488	0	403	600	662	722	800	264
Racetrack betting	35	122	155	55	36	36	32	33	23	19
Tax on meals and hotels	0	0	473	191	305	198	199	195	349	146
5127 Other taxes on internat. trade and transactions	0	0	0	0	0	0	0	0	0	0
5128 Other taxes	17	323	517	1 045	1 217	1 255	1 292	1 458	1 636	1 233
Other taxes federal government	0	98	272	758	762	557	439	544	499	349
Other taxes provincial government	17	225	245	287	455	698	853	914	1 137	884
5130 Unallocable between 5110 and 5120	0	0	0	0	0	0	0	0	0	0
5200 Taxes on use of goods and perform activities	892	8 101	3 465	5 589	8 154	7 592	7 842	9 525	10 934	10 406
5210 Recurrent taxes	306	1 500	2 393	3 644	4 368	4 452	5 017	5 589	6 288	6 203
5211 Paid by households: motor vehicles	103	666	1 056	1 696	2 241	1 986	2 237	2 478	2 980	2 926
5212 Paid by others: motor vehicles	141	509	697	1 039	1 242	1 153	1 343	1 552	1 740	1 705
5213 Paid in respect of other goods	62	325	640	909	885	1 313	1 437	1 559	1 568	1 572
5220 Non-recurrent taxes	586	6 601	1 072	1 945	3 786	3 140	2 825	3 936	4 646	4 203
Licences and permits local govt.	36	132	317	499	889	807	952	1 023	1 143	1 094
Licences and permits provincial govt.	550	6 469	755	1 446	2 897	2 333	1 873	2 913	3 503	3 109
5300 Unallocable between 5100 and 5200	0	0	0	0	0	0	0	0	0	0
6000 Other taxes	**166**	**1 198**	**2 875**	**2 167**	**342**	**596**	**696**	**748**	**957**	**867**
6100 Paid solely by business	139	943	2 386	1 280	0	0	0	0	0	0
6200 Other	27	255	489	887	342	596	696	748	957	867
Poll tax local government	5	0	0	0	0	0	0	0	0	0
Miscellaneous local government	11	358	489	887	342	596	696	748	957	867
Other federal government	11	-103	0	0	0	0	0	0	0	0
Non-wastable tax credits										
Non-wastable tax credits against 1110	..	..	..	1 633	5 550	6 415	7 326	7 510	13 910	13 958
Tax expenditure component	..	..	..	276	824	875	965	968	3 943	4 681
Transfer component	..	..	..	1 357	4 726	5 540	6 361	6 542	9 967	9 277
Non-wastable tax credits against 1210	..	..	..	1 758	3 445	4 726	3 754	3 768	4 431	4 374
Tax expenditure component	..	..	..	20	12	19	17	15	25	23
Transfer component	..	..	..	1 738	3 433	4 707	3 737	3 753	4 406	4 351
Total tax revenue on cash basis	**15 318**	**101 015**	**244 152**	**388 833**	**527 734**	**..**	**..**	**..**	**..**	**..**
Total tax revenue on accrual basis	**..**	**..**	**..**	**390 234**	**512 663**	**516 591**	**592 206**	**653 269**	**764 366**	**755 994**
Conciliation with National Accounts										
Additional taxes included in National Accounts	..	..	..	0	0	0	0	0	0	0
Taxes excluded from National Accounts	..	..	..	0	0	0	0	0	0	0
Difference in treatment of tax credits	..	..	..	296	836	894	982	983	3 967	4 704
Capital transfer for uncollected revenue	..	..	..	0	0	0	0	0	0	0
Voluntary social security contributions	..	..	..	0	0	0	0	0	0	0
Miscellaneous differences	..	..	..	0	0	0	0	0	0	0
National Accounts: Taxes and actual social contributions	..	..	..	390 234	513 499	517 485	593 188	654 252	768 333	760 698
Imputed social contributions	..	..	..	0	0	0	0	0	0	0
National Accounts: Taxes and all social contributions	..	..	..	390 234	513 499	517 485	593 188	654 252	768 333	760 698

.. Not available

Note: From 2001, all data are for the year ending 31st December. For 2000 and earlier years, data for the Federal, Provincial and Territorial governments and Social security funds are on a fiscal year basis commencing 1st April. Data for local government are on a fiscal year basis commencing 1st January.
From 1999 data are on accrual basis.
There are some minor differences between the data for the years 1965 to 1978 and those for subsequent years. These mostly relate to the inclusion of fines and penalities or late payment of taxes and deductions for the child tax credits in the data for the years 1979 to 1983.
Heading 1210 - Taxes federal government: Federal corporate taxes include capital taxes.
Heading 2000: Includes receipts from the Canadian Pension Plan, Quebec Pension Plan, Unemployment Insurance Fund and Provincial Health Insurance. Premiums, Medicare Premiums and Social Insurance levies but excludes that part of the taxes on income and sales taxes earmarked for old age security. The practice of earmarking these taxes was discontinued in June 1975.
Heading 4400: From 2002 onward includes land transfer taxes of the provincial, territorial and local governments. Prior to 2002 land transfer taxes of the local government were included in line 6000 and those provincial and territorial governments were included in line 4520.
Heading 5121: The large increase in this heading between 1980 and 1981 is due to the introduction of a 'special petroleum compensation charge', a 'Canadian ownership special charge' and to an increase in the natural gas tax of C$ 2399 millions.
Heading 5122: From 1988, profits on fiscal monopolies include lottery profits.
Heading 5128: From 1988, other taxes of Federal Government does not include the annual fees for managing the spectrum (airwaves) allocation to the cellular industry.
Heading 5211: Some Québec motor vehicle licence administrative fees are included in sales of goods and services for the period 1988-89 to 1997-98.
From 1998-99 onward, these fees are included under other taxes - motor vehicle licences.
Source: Statistics Canada.

StatLink https://stat.link/iha1zo

Table 5.5. Chile: Details of tax revenue, 1965-2020

Million CLP

	1965	1980	1990	2000	2007	2010	2013	2015	2019	2020
Total tax revenue	..	..	**1 777 218**	**7 901 998**	**20 598 963**	**21 845 693**	**27 381 686**	**32 533 542**	**41 025 508**	**38 817 226**
1000 Taxes on income, profits and capital gains	..	..	**412 974**	**1 841 630**	**9 412 056**	**8 329 060**	**9 520 709**	**11 840 521**	**14 283 183**	**12 540 342**
1100 Of individuals	..	..	99 154	604 100	989 348	1 492 837	1 964 172	3 199 876	2 937 532	3 976 009
Second category tax	..	..	65 552	490 980	993 129	1 449 099	1 981 699	2 350 120	3 015 794	3 051 177
Global complementary tax	..	..	33 603	113 120	-3 781	43 738	-17 527	-36 757	-78 261	132 551
Other	..	..	0	0	0	0	0	886 513	0	792 281
1110 On income and profits	..	..	..	..	..	..	..	..	..	..
1120 On capital gains	..	..	..	..	..	..	..	..	..	..
1200 Corporate	..	..	219 586	882 896	6 054 487	4 448 745	6 041 089	6 839 133	9 597 472	9 429 787
First category tax	..	..	200 891	815 747	5 084 996	3 913 870	5 473 355	6 183 830	8 880 080	8 745 612
Surtax on state owned enterprises	..	..	16 074	47 634	113 334	194 203	124 220	132 352	122 054	203 416
Mining tax	..	..	0	0	835 452	298 558	324 577	323 507	277 861	267 544
Other	..	..	2 621	19 516	20 705	42 114	118 937	199 444	317 477	213 216
1210 On profits	..	..	..	..	..	..	..	..	..	..
1220 On capital gains	..	..	..	..	..	..	..	..	..	..
1300 Unallocable between 1100 and 1200	..	..	94 233	354 634	2 368 221	2 387 478	1 515 449	1 801 512	1 748 179	-865 454
Additional tax	..	..	59 082	350 301	1 462 715	1 414 057	1 337 721	1 429 758	1 902 585	2 063 149
Other	..	..	35 151	4 332	905 507	973 421	177 727	371 755	-154 406	-2 928 603
2000 Social security contributions	..	..	**159 559**	**576 758**	**1 148 647**	**1 493 987**	**1 968 973**	**2 252 490**	**2 994 906**	**3 104 866**
2100 Employees	..	..	154 021	553 937	1 098 620	1 433 159	1 906 340	2 188 576	2 894 725	2 994 036
2110 On a payroll basis	..	..	154 021	553 937	1 098 620	1 433 159	1 906 340	2 188 576	2 894 725	2 994 036
2120 On an income tax basis	..	..	0	0	0	0	0	0	0	0
2200 Employers	..	..	5 538	22 821	50 027	60 828	62 633	63 914	100 181	110 830
2210 On a payroll basis	..	..	5 538	22 821	50 027	60 828	62 633	63 914	100 181	110 830
2220 On an income tax basis	..	..	0	0	0	0	0	0	0	0
2300 Self-employed or non-employed	..	..	0	0	0	0	0	0	0	0
2310 On a payroll basis	..	..	..	..	..	..	..	..	..	..
2320 On an income tax basis	..	..	..	..	..	..	..	..	..	..
2400 Unallocable between 2100, 2200 and 2300	..	..	0	0	0	0	0	0	0	0
2410 On a payroll basis	..	..	..	..	..	..	..	..	..	..
2420 On an income tax basis	..	..	..	..	..	..	..	..	..	..
3000 Taxes on payroll and workforce	..	..	**0**	**0**	**0**	**0**	**0**	**0**	**0**	**0**
4000 Taxes on property	..	..	**109 319**	**554 037**	**1 013 571**	**898 607**	**1 133 765**	**1 421 274**	**2 242 561**	**2 071 921**
4100 Recurrent taxes on immovable property	..	..	59 968	302 244	496 311	662 368	840 842	1 056 920	1 507 182	1 562 317
4110 Households	..	..	..	..	..	..	..	..	..	..
4120 Others	..	..	..	..	..	..	..	..	..	..
4200 Recurrent taxes on net wealth	..	..	0	0	0	0	0	0	0	0
4210 Individual	..	..	..	..	..	..	..	..	..	..
4220 Corporate	..	..	..	..	..	..	..	..	..	..
4300 Estate, inheritance and gift taxes	..	..	3 444	10 906	28 501	39 338	45 550	92 236	62 824	155 433
4310 Estate and inheritance taxes	..	..	..	..	..	..	..	..	..	..
4320 Gift taxes	..	..	..	..	..	..	..	..	..	..
4400 Taxes on financial and capital transactions	..	..	45 907	240 886	488 759	196 901	247 373	272 118	672 555	354 171
4500 Non-recurrent taxes	..	..	0	0	0	0	0	0	0	0
4510 On net wealth	..	..	..	..	..	..	..	..	..	..
4520 Other non-recurrent taxes	..	..	..	..	..	..	..	..	..	..
4600 Other recurrent taxes on property	..	..	0	0	0	0	0	0	0	0
5000 Taxes on goods and services	..	..	**1 118 722**	**5 041 769**	**9 023 666**	**11 185 156**	**14 779 915**	**17 598 561**	**21 755 381**	**21 275 113**
5100 Taxes on production, sale, transfer, etc.	..	..	1 074 009	4 789 827	8 578 636	10 532 904	13 869 529	16 516 668	20 167 012	19 614 250
5110 General taxes	..	..	664 421	3 306 350	6 781 501	8 399 926	11 170 794	13 273 958	16 348 944	15 963 032
5111 Value added taxes	..	..	664 421	3 306 350	6 781 501	8 399 926	11 170 794	13 273 958	16 348 944	15 963 032
5112 Sales tax	..	..	0	0	0	0	0	0	0	0
5113 Other	..	..	0	0	0	0	0	0	0	0
5120 Taxes on specific goods and services	..	..	409 588	1 483 477	1 797 135	2 132 978	2 698 735	3 242 710	3 818 068	3 651 218
5121 Excise duties	..	..	166 050	816 160	1 299 844	1 561 205	1 987 475	2 413 957	2 862 327	2 900 245
Cigarettes and tobacco	..	..	60 604	283 275	455 595	647 637	815 991	982 609	973 335	1 021 917
Gasolene and diesel	..	..	105 445	532 885	844 249	913 568	1 171 483	1 388 218	1 811 132	1 799 846
Oil stabilisation fund	..	..	0	0	0	0	0	0	0	0
Fisheries Law Extraction Rights	..	..	0	0	0	0	0	8 558	17 662	33 104
Additional tax on new motor vehicles	..	..	0	0	0	0	0	34 571	60 197	45 379
5122 Profits of fiscal monopolies	..	..	0	0	0	0	0	0	0	0
5123 Customs and import duties	..	..	222 486	548 571	300 416	267 331	303 393	343 491	331 846	294 204
5124 Taxes on exports	..	..	0	0	0	0	0	0	0	0
5125 Taxes on investment goods	..	..	0	0	0	0	0	0	0	0
5126 Taxes on specific services	..	..	21 052	118 746	196 875	304 442	407 867	485 263	623 895	456 768
5127 Other taxes on internat. trade and transactions	..	..	0	0	0	0	0	0	0	0
5128 Other taxes	..	..	0	0	0	0	0	0	0	0
5130 Unallocable between 5110 and 5120	..	..	0	0	0	0	0	0	0	0
5200 Taxes on use of goods and perform activities	..	..	44 714	251 942	445 030	652 252	910 386	1 081 893	1 588 369	1 660 863

	1965	1980	1990	2000	2007	2010	2013	2015	2019	2020
5210 Recurrent taxes	..	..	44 714	251 942	445 030	652 252	910 386	1 081 893	1 461 686	1 503 269
Motor vehicles	..	..	24 469	93 880	155 158	218 219	330 754	397 608	592 327	585 116
5211 Paid by households: motor vehicles	..	..	0	0	0	0	0	0	0	0
5212 Paid by others: motor vehicles	..	..	0	0	0	0	0	0	0	0
5213 Paid in respect of other goods	..	..	20 245	158 062	289 872	434 033	579 632	684 285	869 359	918 153
Municipal permits	..	..	18 401	136 138	263 996	396 944	527 955	630 943	813 159	862 199
Mining patents	..	..	3 374	34 730	25 184	36 213	50 094	51 767	54 696	54 932
Other	..	..	-1 530	-12 806	692	876	1 583	1 575	1 504	1 023
5220 Non-recurrent taxes	..	..	0	0	0	0	0	0	126 683	157 594
Tax on Polluting Fixed Sources	..	..	..	..	..	..	..	..	126 683	157 594
5300 Unallocable between 5100 and 5200	..	..	0	0	0	0	0	0	0	0
6000 Other taxes	**..**	**..**	**-23 356**	**-112 195**	**1 023**	**-61 117**	**-21 676**	**-579 303**	**-250 523**	**-175 017**
6100 Paid solely by business	..	..	0	0	0	0	0	0	0	0
6200 Other	..	..	-23 356	-112 195	1 023	-61 117	-21 676	-579 303	-250 523	-175 017
Non-wastable tax credits										
Non-wastable tax credits against 1110	..	..	0	0	0	0	0	0	0	0
Tax expenditure component	..	..	..	..	..	..	..	..	..	..
Transfer component	..	..	..	..	..	..	..	..	..	..
Non-wastable tax credits against 1210	..	..	0	0	0	0	0	175 468	278 792	297 981
Tax expenditure component	..	..	..	..	..	..	..	45 774	78 226	74 949
Transfer component	..	..	..	..	..	..	..	129 694	200 566	223 032
Total tax revenue on cash basis	**..**	**..**	**1 777 218**	**7 901 998**	**20 598 963**	**21 845 693**	**27 381 686**	**32 533 542**	**41 025 508**	**38 817 226**
Total tax revenue on accrual basis	**..**	**..**	**..**	**..**	**..**	**..**	**..**	**..**	**..**	**..**
Conciliation with National Accounts										
Additional taxes included in National Accounts	..	..	..	..	..	..	..	..	..	..
Taxes excluded from National Accounts	..	..	..	..	..	..	..	..	..	..
Difference in treatment of tax credits	..	..	..	..	..	..	..	..	..	..
Capital transfer for uncollected revenue	..	..	..	..	..	..	..	..	..	..
Voluntary social security contributions	..	..	..	..	..	..	..	..	..	..
Miscellaneous differences	..	..	..	..	..	..	..	..	..	..
National Accounts: Taxes and actual social contributions	..	..	..	..	..	..	..	..	..	..
Imputed social contributions	..	..	..	..	..	..	..	..	..	..
National Accounts: Taxes and all social contributions	..	..	..	..	..	..	..	..	..	..

.. Not available

Note: Year ending 31st December.

The data are on a cash basis.

Source: *Servicio de Impuestos internos* (Chile's Tax Service).

StatLink https://stat.link/56gvsc

Table 5.6. Colombia: Details of tax revenue, 1965-2020

Million COP

	1965	1980	1990	2000	2007	2010	2013	2015	2019	2020
Total tax revenue	..	..	**2 579 426**	**30 598 630**	**82 697 457**	**98 455 335**	**142 976 023**	**160 157 693**	**209 071 314**	**187 664 589**
1000 Taxes on income, profits and capital gains	..	..	**771 694**	**7 103 525**	**24 010 404**	**26 218 852**	**47 743 096**	**52 656 876**	**67 519 599**	**61 812 525**
1100 Of individuals	..	..	47 210	1 499 345	4 751 580	5 192 384	7 797 962	9 219 350	14 233 704	14 469 873
1110 On income and profits	..	..	47 210	1 499 345	4 751 580	5 192 384	7 797 962	9 219 350	14 233 704	14 469 873
Income tax	..	..	47 210	1 499 345	4 751 580	5 192 384	7 797 962	9 219 350	14 227 156	14 434 275
Simple tax regime	..	..	0	0	0	0	0	0	6 549	35 598
1120 On capital gains	..	..	..	..	..	..	..	..	..	..
1200 Corporate	..	..	359 758	5 119 828	18 427 899	20 405 209	38 889 291	41 409 107	50 287 051	43 240 197
1210 On profits	..	..	359 758	5 119 828	18 427 899	20 405 209	38 889 291	41 409 107	50 287 051	43 240 197
Income tax	..	..	359 758	5 119 828	18 427 899	20 405 209	35 949 712	27 482 938	50 171 185	43 113 857
Pro Equity Income Tax - CREE	..	..	0	0	0	0	2 939 579	13 926 169	99 798	39 871
Simple tax regime	..	..	0	0	0	0	0	0	16 068	86 469
1220 On capital gains	..	..	..	..	..	..	..	..	..	..
1300 Unallocable between 1100 and 1200	..	..	364 726	484 352	830 925	621 258	1 055 842	2 028 420	2 998 844	4 102 455
Income tax	..	..	364 726	484 352	830 925	621 258	1 055 842	2 028 420	2 998 844	4 102 455
Pro Equity Income Tax - CREE	..	..	0	0	0	0	0	0	0	0
2000 Social security contributions	..	..	**203 596**	**4 989 000**	**9 694 000**	**11 478 085**	**16 644 445**	**13 585 138**	**19 875 398**	**18 615 408**
2100 Employees	..	..	..	..	..	..	..	..	..	..
2110 On a payroll basis	..	..	..	..	..	..	..	..	..	..
2120 On an income tax basis	..	..	..	..	..	..	..	..	..	..
2200 Employers	..	..	..	..	..	..	..	..	..	..
2210 On a payroll basis	..	..	..	..	..	..	..	..	..	..
2220 On an income tax basis	..	..	..	..	..	..	..	..	..	..
2300 Self-employed or non-employed	..	..	..	..	..	..	..	..	..	..
2310 On a payroll basis	..	..	..	..	..	..	..	..	..	..
2320 On an income tax basis	..	..	..	..	..	..	..	..	..	..
2400 Unallocable between 2100, 2200 and 2300	..	..	203 596	4 989 000	9 694 000	11 478 085	16 644 445	13 585 138	19 875 398	18 615 408
2410 On a payroll basis	..	..	203 596	4 989 000	9 694 000	11 478 085	16 644 445	13 585 138	19 875 398	18 615 408
2420 On an income tax basis	..	..	0	0	0	0	0	0	0	0
3000 Taxes on payroll and workforce	..	..	**0**	**1 286 803**	**2 798 906**	**4 022 503**	**3 527 459**	**2 797 308**	**3 604 071**	**3 670 490**
4000 Taxes on property	..	..	**56 160**	**2 027 654**	**6 459 259**	**8 535 238**	**14 907 909**	**18 156 105**	**18 984 414**	**18 167 358**
4100 Recurrent taxes on immovable property	..	..	56 160	991 070	2 298 829	3 338 935	4 735 321	6 061 965	8 743 115	9 109 598
4110 Households	..	..	0	0	0	0	0	0	0	0
4120 Others	..	..	56 160	991 070	2 298 829	3 338 935	4 735 321	6 061 965	8 743 115	9 109 598
4200 Recurrent taxes on net wealth	..	..	0	0	1 170 908	1 970 530	4 274 832	5 352 940	923 255	957 137
4210 Individual	..	..	..	..	1 170 908	1 970 530	4 274 832	5 352 940	923 255	957 137
4220 Corporate	..	..	..	..	0	0	0	0	0	0
4300 Estate, inheritance and gift taxes	..	..	0	0	0	0	0	0	0	0
4310 Estate and inheritance taxes	..	..	..	..	..	..	..	..	..	..
4320 Gift taxes	..	..	..	..	..	..	..	..	..	..
4400 Taxes on financial and capital transactions	..	..	0	1 036 584	2 989 522	3 225 773	5 897 755	6 741 200	8 190 516	7 476 295
4500 Non-recurrent taxes	..	..	0	0	0	0	0	0	1 127 528	624 327
4510 On net wealth	..	..	..	..	..	..	..	..	0	0
4520 Other non-recurrent taxes	..	..	..	..	..	..	..	..	1 127 528	624 327
4600 Other recurrent taxes on property	..	..	0	0	0	0	0	0	0	0
5000 Taxes on goods and services	..	..	**1 388 653**	**14 180 450**	**36 766 741**	**44 411 642**	**55 285 569**	**65 716 566**	**89 797 927**	**77 752 543**
5100 Taxes on production, sale, transfer, etc.	..	..	1 388 653	14 048 655	36 447 297	44 038 074	54 326 006	64 688 081	88 064 087	75 960 351
5110 General taxes	..	..	672 368	9 585 866	26 910 512	33 333 802	40 479 366	48 684 900	71 235 138	62 866 653
5111 Value added taxes	..	..	583 078	8 445 776	23 377 821	28 811 682	34 642 822	41 659 696	61 936 282	53 912 648
5112 Sales tax	..	..	89 290	1 140 090	3 532 691	4 522 121	5 836 544	7 025 204	9 298 856	8 954 004
Industry and commerce tax (State)	..	..	89 290	1 140 090	3 532 691	4 522 121	5 836 544	7 025 204	9 298 856	8 954 004
5113 Other	..	..	0	0	0	0	0	0	0	0
5120 Taxes on specific goods and services	..	..	716 285	4 462 789	9 536 785	10 704 271	13 846 640	16 003 181	16 828 948	13 093 698
5121 Excise duties	..	..	404 699	2 718 692	5 276 999	6 052 273	9 949 457	11 412 250	12 995 955	10 159 930
Petrol	..	..	141 270	833 004	1 211 511	1 418 766	2 883 410	3 297 392	1 585 141	1 205 806
Tobacco (State)	..	..	52 898	213 412	330 016	390 472	496 513	524 357	1 278 561	1 239 269
Beer (State)	..	..	85 722	471 135	1 203 838	1 432 453	2 031 349	2 305 895	2 611 466	2 243 811
Liquors (State)	..	..	124 808	520 394	834 390	929 328	1 292 743	1 253 466	2 146 818	1 675 472
Restaurant service, vehicle sale and mobile telephone service	..	..	0	0	0	0	1 181 998	1 684 179	2 208 669	1 226 863
Carbon	..	..	0	0	0	0	0	0	436 914	281 911
Plastic bags	..	..	0	0	0	0	0	0	37 331	43 777
Medicinal cannabis	..	..	0	0	0	0	0	0	145	972
Diesel surcharge	..	..	0	85 716	388 091	500 405	572 022	598 993	599 600	505 000
Petrol surcharge	..	..	0	595 031	1 309 154	1 380 848	1 491 423	1 747 969	2 091 310	1 737 050
5122 Profits of fiscal monopolies	..	..	0	0	0	0	0	0	0	0
5123 Customs and import duties	..	..	311 586	1 744 097	4 259 786	4 651 999	3 897 184	4 590 931	3 832 994	2 933 768
Custom duties	..	..	180 989	1 744 097	4 259 786	4 651 999	3 897 184	4 590 931	3 832 994	2 933 768
Imports surcharge	..	..	130 597	0	0	0	0	0	0	0

	1965	1980	1990	2000	2007	2010	2013	2015	2019	2020
5124 Taxes on exports	..	..	0	0	0	0	0	0	0	0
5125 Taxes on investment goods	..	..	0	0	0	0	0	0	0	0
5126 Taxes on specific services	..	..	0	0	0	0	0	0	0	0
5127 Other taxes on internat. trade and transactions	..	..	0	0	0	0	0	0	0	0
5128 Other taxes	..	..	0	0	0	0	0	0	0	0
5130 Unallocable between 5110 and 5120	..	..	0	0	0	0	0	0	0	0
5200 Taxes on use of goods and perform activities	..	..	0	131 795	319 444	373 568	959 563	1 028 485	1 733 840	1 792 192
5210 Recurrent taxes	..	..	..	131 795	319 444	373 568	959 563	1 028 485	1 733 840	1 792 192
5211 Paid by households: motor vehicles	..	..	..	131 795	319 444	373 568	959 563	1 028 485	1 733 840	1 792 192
Tax on motor vehicle ownership	..	..	..	131 795	319 444	373 568	959 563	1 028 485	1 733 840	1 792 192
5212 Paid by others: motor vehicles	..	..	..	..	..	..	..	..	..	..
5213 Paid in respect of other goods	..	..	..	..	..	..	..	..	..	..
5220 Non-recurrent taxes	..	..	..	..	..	..	..	..	..	..
5300 Unallocable between 5100 and 5200	..	..	0	0	0	0	0	0	0	0
6000 Other taxes	**..**	**..**	**159 323**	**1 011 197**	**2 968 147**	**3 789 014**	**4 867 545**	**7 245 701**	**9 289 906**	**7 646 264**
6100 Paid solely by business	..	..	0	0	0	0	0	0	0	0
6200 Other	..	..	159 323	1 011 197	2 968 147	3 789 014	4 867 545	7 245 701	9 289 906	7 646 264
Stamp tax	..	..	0	401 497	759 787	357 160	58 378	101 668	85 799	41 373
Other	..	..	78 306	79 287	86 297	126 602	200 465	318 271	533 852	245 541
Other (sub-national)	..	..	81 017	530 413	2 122 062	3 305 252	4 608 702	6 825 762	8 670 255	7 359 350
Total tax revenue on cash basis	**..**	**..**	**2 579 426**	**30 598 630**	**82 697 457**	**98 455 335**	**142 976 023**	**160 157 693**	**209 071 314**	**187 664 589**
Total tax revenue on accrual basis	**..**	**..**	**..**	**..**	**..**	**..**	**..**	**..**	**..**	**..**
Conciliation with National Accounts										
Additional taxes included in National Accounts	..	..	..	..	..	..	..	..	..	..
Taxes excluded from National Accounts	..	..	..	..	..	..	..	..	..	..
Difference in treatment of tax credits	..	..	..	..	..	..	..	..	..	..
Capital transfer for uncollected revenue	..	..	..	..	..	..	..	..	..	..
Voluntary social security contributions	..	..	..	..	..	..	..	..	..	..
Miscellaneous differences	..	..	..	..	..	..	..	..	..	..
National Accounts: Taxes and actual social contributions	..	..	..	..	..	..	..	..	..	..
Imputed social contributions	..	..	..	..	..	..	..	..	..	..
National Accounts: Taxes and all social contributions	..	..	..	..	..	..	..	..	..	..

.. Not available

Note: Year ending 31st December.

Data on an cash basis.

Includes the reported consolidated revenues of the territorial entities (departments and municipalities).

Heading 2000: Before 2013, social security contributions did not include all the contributions entering FOSYGA (Solidarity and Guarantee Fund). Only the portion of the contributions used to finance the subsidised regime (up to 1.5 pp of the 12.5% of the monthly wage paid by employers and employees as an obligatory health contribution) was included. The part of the contributions entering FOSYGA to finance the contributory regime was classified in the social security sector as "other incomes".

From 2013 onwards, all of the health contributions entering FOSYGA are classified as social security contributions. The portion of the contributions not entering FOSYGA that is both collected and spent by the health insurers – EPS - is not part of the fiscal accounts.

Headings 1100 and 1200: The data are estimated.

Source: *Dirección de Impuestos y Aduanas Nacionales de Colombia, Ministerio de Hacienda y Crédito Público y Banco Central de Colombia.*

(National Tax and Customs Administration, Ministry of Finance and Public Credit and Central Bank of Colombia).

StatLink https://stat.link/r5qxmo

Table 5.7. Costa Rica: Details of tax revenue, 1965-2020

Million CRC

	1965	1980	1990	2000	2007	2010	2013	2015	2019	2020
Total tax revenue	..	..	**117 711**	**978 114**	**3 213 401**	**4 382 367**	**5 851 096**	**6 923 575**	**8 855 885**	**8 235 528**
1000 Taxes on income, profits and capital gains	..	..	**11 820**	**128 805**	**531 552**	**748 093**	**1 014 440**	**1 247 308**	**1 854 866**	**1 651 249**
1100 Of individuals	..	..	..	..	123 194	202 849	316 894	386 241	540 954	556 084
1110 On income and profits	..	..	..	..	123 194	202 849	316 894	386 241	535 412	554 486
1120 On capital gains	..	..	..	..	0	0	0	0	5 542	1 598
1200 Corporate	..	..	..	..	348 826	450 312	545 183	659 951	1 058 086	692 551
1210 On profits	..	..	..	..	348 826	450 312	545 183	659 951	955 908	685 470
1220 On capital gains	..	..	..	..	0	0	0	0	102 177	7 081
1300 Unallocable between 1100 and 1200	..	..	11 820	128 805	59 531	94 932	152 363	201 116	255 827	402 613
2000 Social security contributions	..	..	**33 990**	**297 069**	**885 053**	**1 450 531**	**1 928 082**	**2 305 133**	**3 026 691**	**2 971 589**
2100 Employees	..	..	..	..	..	..	..	..	..	..
2110 On a payroll basis	..	..	..	..	..	..	..	..	..	..
2120 On an income tax basis	..	..	..	..	..	..	..	..	..	..
2200 Employers	..	..	3 447	37 313	107 398	207 206	272 706	318 652	381 940	387 840
Government contributions	..	..	3 447	37 313	107 398	207 206	272 706	318 652	381 940	387 840
2210 On a payroll basis	..	..	..	..	..	..	..	..	..	..
2220 On an income tax basis	..	..	..	..	..	..	..	..	..	..
2300 Self-employed or non-employed	..	..	..	..	..	..	..	..	..	..
2310 On a payroll basis	..	..	..	..	..	..	..	..	..	..
2320 On an income tax basis	..	..	..	..	..	..	..	..	..	..
2400 Unallocable between 2100, 2200 and 2300	..	..	30 543	259 756	777 654	1 243 325	1 655 376	1 986 481	2 644 751	2 583 749
Contributions by employees and non-government employers	..	..	30 543	249 182	727 844	1 139 265	1 511 383	1 785 522	2 274 644	2 212 249
Contributions for the special regimes	..	..	0	10 574	49 811	104 060	143 993	200 959	292 634	292 072
2410 On a payroll basis	..	..	..	..	..	..	..	..	..	..
2420 On an income tax basis	..	..	..	..	..	..	..	..	..	..
3000 Taxes on payroll and workforce	..	..	**7 575**	**61 796**	**170 996**	**260 664**	**352 755**	**423 616**	**522 529**	**537 654**
Contributions by non-government employers	..	..	7 484	59 129	165 677	248 259	337 696	406 296	501 734	515 624
Contributions by government employers	..	..	91	2 666	5 320	12 405	15 059	17 321	20 795	22 030
4000 Taxes on property	..	..	**1 566**	**8 396**	**42 658**	**63 706**	**99 030**	**123 261**	**167 952**	**162 950**
4100 Recurrent taxes on immovable property	..	..	1 200	5 390	23 293	48 963	70 785	90 003	125 398	127 625
Land tax	..	..	0	0	0	0	0	0	0	0
Additional land tax	..	..	0	0	0	0	0	0	0	0
Tax on sumptuary constructions	..	..	0	0	0	0	0	0	0	0
Immovable property tax	..	..	0	0	0	3 527	3 998	4 076	4 699	4 655
Municipal immovable property tax	..	..	1 200	5 390	23 293	45 436	66 787	85 927	120 698	122 970
4110 Households	..	..	..	..	..	..	..	..	..	..
4120 Others	..	..	..	..	..	..	..	..	..	..
4200 Recurrent taxes on net wealth	..	..	0	0	0	0	0	0	0	0
4210 Individual	..	..	..	..	..	..	..	..	..	..
4220 Corporate	..	..	..	..	..	..	..	..	..	..
4300 Estate, inheritance and gift taxes	..	..	0	0	0	0	0	0	0	0
4310 Estate and inheritance taxes	..	..	..	..	..	..	..	..	..	..
4320 Gift taxes	..	..	..	..	..	..	..	..	..	..
4400 Taxes on financial and capital transactions	..	..	366	3 007	19 366	14 743	28 246	33 258	42 554	35 300
4500 Non-recurrent taxes	..	..	0	0	0	0	0	0	0	24
4510 On net wealth	..	..	..	..	..	..	..	..	..	0
4520 Other non-recurrent taxes	..	..	..	..	..	..	..	..	..	24
4600 Other recurrent taxes on property	..	..	0	0	0	0	0	0	0	0
5000 Taxes on goods and services	..	..	**53 509**	**456 851**	**1 505 510**	**1 766 914**	**2 302 986**	**2 661 902**	**3 081 941**	**2 745 118**
5100 Taxes on production, sale, transfer, etc.	..	..	49 867	425 713	1 406 100	1 600 302	2 092 588	2 388 900	2 756 759	2 500 510
5110 General taxes	..	..	21 326	222 775	797 850	920 298	1 212 471	1 368 601	1 662 503	1 649 531
5111 Value added taxes	..	..	21 326	222 775	797 850	920 298	1 176 745	1 336 075	1 634 986	1 623 695
5112 Sales tax	..	..	0	0	0	0	0	0	0	0
5113 Other	..	..	0	0	0	0	35 726	32 526	27 517	25 836
5120 Taxes on specific goods and services	..	..	28 541	202 939	608 250	680 004	880 117	1 020 299	1 094 256	850 979
5121 Excise duties	..	..	11 096	157 204	447 168	523 617	689 528	798 412	864 985	688 784
Fuels and energy	..	..	0	0	250 577	320 638	404 210	457 827	552 017	436 384
Alcoholic beverages	..	..	0	8 229	23 802	28 035	35 254	43 095	43 849	44 373
Non alcoholic beverages	..	..	0	0	18 263	26 566	32 519	36 353	41 247	38 510
Soaps	..	..	0	0	883	1 317	1 989	2 562	3 020	3 052
Cement	..	..	0	0	0	227	291	304	216	123
Tobaco	..	..	0	0	0	0	38 860	33 681	27 185	23 896
Abolished specific taxes on production and consumption	..	..	0	0	0	0	0	0	0	0
Other specific taxes on consumption	..	..	11 096	148 975	153 643	146 834	176 405	224 590	197 452	142 447
5122 Profits of fiscal monopolies	..	..	0	0	0	0	0	0	0	0

	1965	1980	1990	2000	2007	2010	2013	2015	2019	2020
5123 Customs and import duties	..	..	15 052	40 485	134 576	126 134	154 576	174 568	164 224	133 733
Import duties	..	..	13 977	32 336	107 565	103 851	130 634	148 666	140 919	114 777
Custom duties	..	..	1 075	8 149	27 011	22 284	23 942	25 902	23 305	18 956
Import duties on animals	..	..	0	0	0	0	0	0	0	0
5124 Taxes on exports	..	..	2 113	2 238	2 432	3 973	4 877	4 468	5 412	5 471
Export duties	..	..	..	..	..	..	..	..	..	..
Export duties Law 133	..	..	..	..	..	..	..	..	..	..
Export duties Law 5519	..	..	..	..	..	..	..	..	..	..
Tax on banana exports	..	..	..	..	..	..	..	..	..	..
Export tax on ground transportation	..	..	..	..	..	..	..	..	..	..
5125 Taxes on investment goods	..	..	0	0	0	0	0	0	0	0
5126 Taxes on specific services	..	..	280	2 929	23 242	24 767	28 571	38 687	54 556	18 463
Casinos and gambling	..	..	0	225	442	445	1 019	1 455	1 241	378
Port cargo movements	..	..	0	6	0	0	0	0	0	0
Overseas departure tax	..	..	0	0	22 799	24 322	27 552	37 232	53 315	18 085
10% on public shows	..	..	0	0	0	0	0	0	0	0
Pro-national airports stamp tax	..	..	0	0	0	0	0	0	0	0
Stamp tax on the use of borders and ports	..	..	280	2 697	0	0	0	0	0	0
5127 Other taxes on internat. trade and transactions	..	..	0	83	832	1 513	2 565	3 093	3 841	3 304
5128 Other taxes	..	..	0	0	0	0	0	1 071	1 238	1 225
5130 Unallocable between 5110 and 5120	..	..	0	0	0	0	0	0	0	0
5200 Taxes on use of goods and perform activities	..	..	3 642	31 138	99 410	166 612	210 398	273 003	325 182	244 608
5210 Recurrent taxes	..	..	3 642	31 138	99 410	166 612	210 398	273 003	325 182	244 608
5211 Paid by households: motor vehicles	..	..	0	0	0	0	0	0	0	0
5212 Paid by others: motor vehicles	..	..	1 425	15 374	52 511	94 102	113 727	145 894	181 198	108 198
Property tax on vehicles, aircraft and boats	..	..	1 425	15 374	52 511	94 102	113 727	145 894	181 198	108 198
5213 Paid in respect of other goods	..	..	2 217	15 763	46 899	72 510	96 671	127 109	143 984	136 410
Local taxes	..	..	1 262	11 898	43 874	68 808	91 163	122 248	137 979	130 332
Hunting and fishing licences	..	..	0	0	0	0	0	0	0	0
Spirits license	..	..	0	0	0	0	0	0	0	0
Revenue stamps	..	..	955	3 866	3 025	3 702	5 508	4 861	6 004	6 078
Sport stamp tax	..	..	0	0	0	0	0	0	0	0
5220 Non-recurrent taxes	..	..	0	0	0	0	0	0	0	0
5300 Unallocable between 5100 and 5200	..	..	0	0	0	0	0	0	0	0
6000 Other taxes	**..**	**..**	**9 251**	**25 198**	**77 632**	**92 460**	**153 803**	**162 355**	**201 906**	**166 969**
6100 Paid solely by business	..	..	0	0	0	0	0	0	0	0
6200 Other	..	..	9 251	25 198	77 632	92 460	153 803	162 355	201 906	166 969
Transfers of vehicles, aircraft and boats	..	..	497	2 530	9 937	12 311	17 177	20 999	23 223	22 593
Tax revenue from decentralised units	..	..	2 764	15 048	22 257	29 969	45 700	49 334	67 968	60 054
Other taxes	..	..	5 990	7 620	45 438	50 180	90 926	92 022	110 654	84 266
Total tax revenue on cash basis	**..**	**..**	**..**	**..**	**..**	**..**	**..**	**..**	**..**	**..**
Total tax revenue on accrual basis	**..**	**..**	**..**	**..**	**..**	**..**	**..**	**..**	**..**	**..**
Conciliation with National Accounts										
Additional taxes included in National Accounts	..	..	..	..	..	..	..	..	..	..
Taxes excluded from National Accounts	..	..	..	..	..	..	..	..	..	..
Difference in treatment of tax credits	..	..	..	..	..	..	..	..	..	..
Capital transfer for uncollected revenue	..	..	..	..	..	..	..	..	..	..
Voluntary social security contributions	..	..	..	..	..	..	..	..	..	..
Miscellaneous differences	..	..	..	..	..	..	..	..	..	..
National Accounts: Taxes and actual social contributions	..	..	..	..	..	..	..	..	..	..
Imputed social contributions	..	..	..	..	..	..	..	..	..	..
National Accounts: Taxes and all social contributions	..	..	..	..	..	..	..	..	..	..

.. Not available

Note: Note: Year ending 31st December.

Data on an cash basis.

Heading 2000: The data include social security contributions paid by the governments for their employees as well as the contributions for special regimes (teachers and magistrates). In ECLAC data, social security contributions also include INA (National Institute of Apprenticeship), IMAS (Joint Social Aid Institute) and FODESAF (Social Development and Family Allowances Fund).

Heading 3000: In Costa Rica and for ECLAC, payments from decentralised institutions are classified under heading 2000.

Heading 5212: In ECLAC data, tax on ownership of vehicles, aircraft and boats is classified in category 4000.

In ECLAC data, the tax on the transfer of used vehicles Law No. 7088 of 30/11/87 is classified as a property tax.

Source: *Secretaría Técnica de la Autoridad Presupuestaria, Ministerio de Finanzas y Contraloría General de la República*.

(Technical Secretary of the Budgeting Authority, Ministry of Finance and National General Comptroller).

StatLink https://stat.link/synvda

Table 5.8. Czech Republic: Details of tax revenue, 1965-2020

Million CZK

	1965	1980	1990	2000	2007	2010	2013	2015	2019	2020
Total tax revenue	..	..	..	**771 596**	**1 316 197**	**1 286 861**	**1 396 555**	**1 532 565**	**2 014 190**	**1 982 587**
Total tax revenue exclusive of taxes collected for the EU	..	..	..	**771 596**	**1 309 754**	**1 280 288**	**1 390 999**	**1 524 653**	**2 005 418**	**1 974 510**
1000 Taxes on income, profits and capital gains	..	..	..	**175 846**	**327 771**	**259 934**	**290 263**	**329 768**	**458 786**	**453 244**
1100 Of individuals	..	..	..	99 668	155 817	131 706	149 831	164 678	255 670	266 628
1110 On income and profits	..	..	..	99 668	155 817	131 706	149 831	164 678	255 670	266 628
Wages and salaries withholding	..	..	..	73 474	127 524	115 755	129 793	139 888	221 720	233 421
Of unincorporated individuals	..	..	..	17 254	19 568	5 747	7 437	9 100	13 260	12 195
Withheld on interest and dividends paid to individuals	..	..	..	8 940	8 725	10 204	12 602	15 691	20 690	21 012
1120 On capital gains	..	..	..	0	0	0	0	0	0	0
1200 Corporate	..	..	..	76 178	171 954	128 228	140 432	165 090	203 116	186 617
1210 On profits	..	..	..	76 178	171 954	128 228	140 432	165 090	203 116	186 617
Profit tax	..	..	..	68 945	164 016	118 248	124 820	147 157	184 705	172 720
Withheld on interest and dividends paid to corporations	..	..	..	7 233	7 162	9 156	7 736	9 415	7 708	4 187
Levy on lottery revenue	..	..	..	0	776	824	7 876	8 518	10 703	9 709
1220 On capital gains	..	..	..	0	0	0	0	0	0	0
1300 Unallocable between 1100 and 1200	..	..	..	0	0	0	0	0	0	0
2000 Social security contributions	..	..	..	**341 544**	**573 417**	**576 029**	**603 072**	**659 743**	**889 237**	**901 670**
2100 Employees	..	..	..	77 272	127 662	116 818	123 353	133 878	184 563	187 733
2110 On a payroll basis	..	..	..	77 272	127 662	116 818	123 353	133 878	184 563	187 733
Retirement	..	..	..	40 489	66 644	69 272	71 871	78 120	108 137	107 988
State employment policy	..	..	..	2 492	4 101	0	0	0	0	0
Sick leave	..	..	..	6 852	11 279	0	0	0	0	0
Health insurance	..	..	..	27 439	45 638	47 546	51 482	55 758	76 426	79 745
2120 On an income tax basis	..	..	..	0	0	0	0	0	0	0
2200 Employers	..	..	..	220 207	359 493	363 074	382 498	417 778	569 522	573 753
2210 On a payroll basis	..	..	..	220 207	359 493	363 074	382 498	417 778	569 522	573 753
Retirement	..	..	..	121 547	220 591	229 450	239 248	261 786	358 382	357 887
State employment policy	..	..	..	19 933	12 303	12 756	13 345	14 604	19 989	19 961
Sick leave	..	..	..	20 555	33 834	24 332	25 454	27 851	36 427	34 687
Health insurance	..	..	..	54 879	91 275	95 095	102 964	111 517	152 853	159 493
Penalties	..	..	..	3 293	1 490	1 441	1 487	2 020	1 871	1 725
2220 On an income tax basis	..	..	..	0	0	0	0	0	0	0
2300 Self-employed or non-employed	..	..	..	44 065	86 262	96 137	97 221	108 088	135 153	140 184
2310 On a payroll basis	..	..	..	44 065	86 262	96 137	97 221	108 088	135 153	140 184
Retirement	..	..	..	7 819	19 508	20 510	21 262	22 472	30 441	20 882
State employment policy	..	..	..	1 082	1 114	1 173	911	962	1 305	896
Sick leave	..	..	..	0	0	0	0	0	0	0
Health insurance	..	..	..	34 992	65 483	74 299	74 908	84 460	103 232	118 288
Self-employed	..	..	..	7 328	15 921	17 603	18 732	20 748	27 925	17 846
Non-employed	..	..	..	200	2 103	3 996	2 500	2 768	3 458	3 180
Government	..	..	..	27 464	47 459	52 700	53 676	60 944	71 849	97 262
Penalties	..	..	..	172	157	155	140	193	175	118
2320 On an income tax basis	..	..	..	0	0	0	0	0	0	0
2400 Unallocable between 2100, 2200 and 2300	..	..	..	0	0	0	0	0	0	0
2410 On a payroll basis	..	..	..	..	..	..	..	..	..	..
2420 On an income tax basis	..	..	..	..	..	..	..	..	..	..
3000 Taxes on payroll and workforce	..	..	..	**0**	**0**	**0**	**0**	**0**	**0**	**0**
4000 Taxes on property	..	..	..	**10 890**	**15 495**	**16 364**	**19 210**	**21 920**	**24 080**	**11 615**
4100 Recurrent taxes on immovable property	..	..	..	4 469	5 126	8 752	9 852	10 333	10 967	11 606
4110 Households	..	..	..	1 452	2 228	4 302	5 387	5 433	5 828	6 079
Real property tax	..	..	..	1 452	2 228	4 302	5 387	5 433	5 828	6 079
4120 Others	..	..	..	3 017	2 898	4 450	4 465	4 900	5 138	5 526
Levy collected by Winery Fund	..	..	..	0	2	5	5	20	32	26
Real property tax	..	..	..	3 017	2 895	4 445	4 461	4 880	5 106	5 501
4200 Recurrent taxes on net wealth	..	..	..	0	0	0	0	0	0	0
4210 Individual	..	..	..	..	..	..	..	..	..	..
4220 Corporate	..	..	..	..	..	..	..	..	..	..
4300 Estate, inheritance and gift taxes	..	..	..	587	460	218	215	20	1	7
4310 Estate and inheritance taxes	..	..	..	112	115	78	76	10	0	8
Inheritance tax	..	..	..	112	115	78	76	10	0	8
4320 Gift taxes	..	..	..	475	345	140	139	10	0	-2
Gift tax	..	..	..	475	345	140	139	10	0	-2
4400 Taxes on financial and capital transactions	..	..	..	5 834	9 909	7 394	9 143	11 566	13 113	3
Real property transfer tax	..	..	..	5 834	9 909	7 394	9 143	11 566	13 113	3
4500 Non-recurrent taxes	..	..	..	0	0	0	0	0	0	0
4510 On net wealth	..	..	..	..	..	..	..	..	..	..
4520 Other non-recurrent taxes	..	..	..	..	..	..	..	..	..	..

	1965	1980	1990	2000	2007	2010	2013	2015	2019	2020
4600 Other recurrent taxes on property	..	..	..	0	0	0	0	0	0	0
5000 Taxes on goods and services	**..**	**..**	**..**	**242 960**	**399 484**	**434 386**	**483 943**	**520 747**	**641 867**	**615 888**
5100 Taxes on production, sale, transfer, etc.	..	..	..	226 354	372 441	408 645	459 419	495 291	613 003	588 343
5110 General taxes	..	..	..	141 235	232 288	263 457	303 822	333 274	435 463	422 479
5111 Value added taxes	..	..	..	141 235	232 288	263 457	303 822	333 274	435 463	422 479
5112 Sales tax	..	..	..	0	0	0	0	0	0	0
5113 Other	..	..	..	0	0	0	0	0	0	0
Previous turnover tax	..	..	..	..	..	..	..	..	..	..
5120 Taxes on specific goods and services	..	..	..	85 119	140 153	145 188	155 597	162 017	177 540	165 864
5121 Excise duties	..	..	..	71 404	133 492	138 401	149 760	153 785	168 195	157 444
On mineral oils	..	..	..	46 998	81 661	80 508	77 160	83 460	92 194	83 308
On alcohol and liquor	..	..	..	5 629	7 201	5 820	6 658	7 203	9 388	6 787
On beer	..	..	..	3 410	3 564	4 396	4 545	4 648	4 782	4 344
On wine	..	..	..	350	342	317	288	332	407	439
On tobacco products	..	..	..	14 984	40 713	44 062	52 193	53 380	55 967	57 148
Duty on CFC	..	..	..	33	0	0	0	0	0	0
Levy collected by Winery Fund	..	..	..	0	11	24	21	0	5	5
On electricity	..	..	..	0	0	1 433	1 305	1 229	1 575	1 497
On natural gas	..	..	..	0	0	1 347	1 256	1 146	1 360	1 434
On solid fuels	..	..	..	0	0	495	469	415	353	323
Fee on electricity from solar radiation	..	..	..	0	0	0	5 866	1 972	2 166	2 159
5122 Profits of fiscal monopolies	..	..	..	0	0	0	0	0	0	0
5123 Customs and import duties	..	..	..	13 572	6 443	6 573	5 556	7 912	8 772	8 077
Customs duties	..	..	..	13 572	6 443	6 573	5 556	7 912	8 772	8 077
Previous import surcharge	..	..	..	0	0	0	0	0	0	0
5124 Taxes on exports	..	..	..	0	0	0	0	0	0	0
5125 Taxes on investment goods	..	..	..	0	0	0	0	0	0	0
5126 Taxes on specific services	..	..	..	143	218	214	281	320	573	343
Fees on entry tickets	..	..	..	65	61	53	56	53	82	19
Fees on recreational units (based on capacity)	..	..	..	69	144	147	213	240	297	132
Fees on advertising facilities	..	..	..	0	0	0	0	0	0	0
Restaurant sale alcoh. beverages and tobac.products	..	..	..	0	0	0	0	0	0	0
Fees collected by the cinematography EBF	..	..	..	9	13	14	12	27	0	0
Fees on advertisement	..	..	..	0	0	0	126	191	194	191
5127 Other taxes on internat. trade and transactions	..	..	..	0	0	0	0	0	0	0
5128 Other taxes	..	..	..	0	0	0	0	0	0	0
5130 Unallocable between 5110 and 5120	..	..	..	0	0	0	0	0	0	0
5200 Taxes on use of goods and perform activities	..	..	..	16 606	27 043	25 740	24 523	25 456	28 864	27 545
5210 Recurrent taxes	..	..	..	10 788	18 100	18 461	18 176	19 023	21 627	20 999
Highway fee	..	..	..	1 753	2 429	3 061	3 803	4 397	5 384	4 930
5211 Paid by households: motor vehicles	..	..	..	0	0	0	0	0	0	0
5212 Paid by others: motor vehicles	..	..	..	5 456	5 882	5 138	5 323	5 868	6 501	5 933
Road tax (commercial)	..	..	..	5 456	5 882	5 138	5 323	5 868	6 501	5 933
5213 Paid in respect of other goods	..	..	..	3 579	9 790	10 262	9 050	8 758	9 743	10 137
Resort and recreation fees on visitors	..	..	..	232	312	284	301	327	435	322
Dog fees	..	..	..	191	277	281	281	277	275	287
Motor vehicle entry fees	..	..	..	32	25	23	14	13	19	14
Water pollution fee	..	..	..	520	404	202	208	173	22	228
Air pollution fee	..	..	..	685	525	399	268	283	457	451
Waste deposit fee	..	..	..	454	5 728	5 948	6 162	6 218	6 723	7 065
Levy on temp. withdrawal of land from agriculture	..	..	..	94	40	34	52	39	88	68
Radioactive waste fee	..	..	..	642	1 310	1 430	1 563	1 393	1 692	1 668
Fees on operated gambling machines	..	..	..	722	1 145	927	131	0	0	0
Fees on registration and recording of packaging	..	..	..	0	17	17	16	18	17	17
Levy on temp. withdrawal of land from forestry	..	..	..	7	6	6	6	7	7	11
Other environmental fees	..	..	..	0	0	710	47	11	7	5
5220 Non-recurrent taxes	..	..	..	5 818	8 943	7 280	6 348	6 433	7 237	6 546
Levy on withdrawal of land from agriculture	..	..	..	532	361	306	469	348	791	609
Levy on withdrawal of land from forestry	..	..	..	40	57	57	55	59	63	103
Tax on use of public space	..	..	..	645	639	626	629	632	739	506
Misc. licence and permit fees	..	..	..	4 601	7 881	6 279	5 187	5 382	5 631	5 293
Land betterment fee	..	..	..	0	4	11	7	11	12	35
Licence for lorry transport	..	..	..	0	1	1	0	1	0	0
5300 Unallocable between 5100 and 5200	..	..	..	0	0	0	0	0	0	0
6000 Other taxes	**..**	**..**	**..**	**356**	**29**	**149**	**67**	**387**	**220**	**170**
Unallocated previous taxes and levies	..	..	..	0	0	0	0	0	0	0
6100 Paid solely by business	..	..	..	0	0	0	0	0	0	0
6200 Other	..	..	..	356	29	149	67	387	220	170
Other taxes, fees and related payments	..	..	..	356	29	149	67	387	220	170
Memorandum item										
Customs duties collected on behalf of the EU	..	..	..	..	6 443	6 573	5 556	7 912	8 772	8 077

	1965	1980	1990	2000	2007	2010	2013	2015	2019	2020
Non-wastable tax credits										
Non-wastable tax credits against 1110	..	..	..	0	13 093	25 727	28 696	31 415	39 854	38 913
Tax expenditure component	..	..	..	..	10 487	17 922	20 203	22 532	31 554	31 057
Transfer component	..	..	..	..	2 606	7 805	8 493	8 883	8 301	7 856
Total tax revenue on cash basis	**..**	**..**	**..**	**772 272**	**1 310 618**	**1 273 676**	**1 353 469**	**1 478 758**	**1 982 448**	**1 937 606**
Total tax revenue on accrual basis	**..**	**..**	**..**	**771 596**	**1 316 197**	**1 286 861**	**1 396 555**	**1 532 565**	**2 014 190**	**1 982 587**
Conciliation with National Accounts										
Additional taxes included in National Accounts	..	..	..	2 837	5 757	6 094	6 424	0	0	0
Compulsory injury insurance	..	..	..	2 837	5 757	6 094	6 424	0	0	0
Driving licence fees	..	..	..	0	0	0	0	0	0	0
Taxes excluded from National Accounts	..	..	..	-9 488	-17 797	-20 096	-18 893	-20 314	-22 857	-21 838
Tax on use of public space	..	..	..	-645	-639	-632	-629	-632	-739	-506
Waste deposit fee	..	..	..	-454	-5 728	-5 948	-6 162	-6 218	-6 723	-7 065
Misc. licence and permit fees	..	..	..	-2 301	-3 940	-3 139	-2 593	-2 691	-2 816	-2 646
Radioactive waste fee	..	..	..	-642	-1 310	-1 430	-1 563	-1 393	-1 692	-1 668
Health insurance: non-employed	..	..	..	-200	-2 103	-3 996	-2 500	-2 768	-3 458	-3 180
Health insurance: government	..	..	..	0	0	0	0	0	0	0
Soc. Security contr. employers: Penalties	..	..	..	-3 293	-1 490	-1 441	-1 487	-2 020	-1 871	-1 725
Soc. Security contr. Self-employed or non-employed: Penalties	..	..	..	-200	-157	-155	-140	-193	-175	-118
Licence for lorry transport	..	..	..	0	-1	-1	0	-1	0	0
Highway fee	..	..	..	-1 753	-2 429	-3 061	-3 803	-4 397	-5 384	-4 930
Other environmental fees	..	..	..	0	0	-105	-14	0	0	0
Levy on loterry revenue	..	..	..	0	0	-187	0	0	0	0
Value added taxes	..	..	..	0	0	0	0	0	0	0
Difference in treatment of tax credits	..	..	..	0	-127	451	-778	118	272	0
Capital transfer for uncollected revenue	..	..	..	0	0	0	0	0	0	0
Voluntary social security contributions	..	..	..	1 099	974	661	337	386	578	537
Miscellaneous differences	..	..	..	2 162	0	0	0	0	0	0
National Accounts: Taxes and actual social contributions	..	..	..	768 206	1 305 004	1 273 971	1 383 645	1 512 755	1 992 183	1 961 286
Imputed social contributions	..	..	..	423	299	600	934	1 027	1 867	3 179
National Accounts: Taxes and all social contributions	..	..	..	768 629	1 305 303	1 274 571	1 384 579	1 513 782	1 994 050	1 964 465

.. Not available
Note: Year ending 31st December.
From 1995 data are on accrual basis.
Source: Ministry of Finance, Tax Analyses Department.

StatLink https://stat.link/6h0wx7

Table 5.9. Denmark: Details of tax revenue, 1965-2020

Million DKK

	1965	1980	1990	2000	2007	2010	2013	2015	2019	2020
Total tax revenue	**20 821**	**166 358**	**382 232**	**623 911**	**809 988**	**813 972**	**901 001**	**957 281**	**1 094 118**	**1 105 573**
Total tax revenue exclusive of taxes collected for the EU	..	..	**379 547**	**621 274**	**806 337**	**810 697**	**898 126**	**953 963**	**1 090 990**	**1 102 484**
1000 Taxes on income, profits and capital gains	**9 712**	**92 404**	**233 739**	**383 244**	**486 845**	**500 276**	**564 937**	**605 698**	**706 131**	**714 576**
1100 Of individuals	8 758	86 958	206 478	328 532	427 412	422 685	490 887	525 144	569 897	599 795
1110 On income and profits	8 758	86 909	206 335	328 305	427 070	422 364	490 627	524 856	569 673	599 528
Central government income tax	5 020	33 351	91 638	77 491	155 540	124 943	141 399	169 059	198 398	207 190
County income tax	0	10 742	31 361	56 135	0	0	0	0	0	0
Municipality income tax	2 948	33 555	77 571	121 975	173 114	193 111	209 303	220 815	247 730	263 001
Seaman's income tax	66	457	0	0	0	0	0	0	0	0
Old-age pension fund contributions	592	2 163	0	0	0	0	0	0	0	0
Social pension fund contributions	0	3 340	0	0	0	0	0	0	0	0
Sickness benefit fund contributions	0	1 804	0	0	0	0	0	0	0	0
Pension schemes and annuity insurance	22	355	2 627	6 923	8 948	9 842	42 974	22 842	5 555	5 705
Special income tax	101	1 054	2 810	0	0	0	0	0	0	0
Duty on canceled pension schemes	9	82	0	0	0	0	0	0	0	0
Duty on feed rent increases	0	8	5	0	0	0	0	0	0	0
Duty on employees' remuneration compens. fund releases	0	0	325	654	1 144	982	1 129	11 177	2 406	2 293
Duty on interest on consumer loans	0	0	0	0	0	0	0	0	0	0
Labour market contributions	0	0	0	56 729	76 609	80 863	82 599	87 359	100 814	106 263
Imputed income from owner-occupied dwelling	0	0	0	8 399	11 716	12 623	13 223	13 604	14 770	15 077
1120 On capital gains	0	49	144	226	343	321	260	289	224	267
Tax on winnings from lotteries, pools, etc.	..	49	144	226	343	321	260	289	224	267
1200 Corporate	954	5 446	14 660	42 279	54 871	41 057	54 066	57 723	72 820	66 551
1210 On profits	954	5 446	14 660	42 279	54 871	41 057	54 066	57 723	72 820	66 551
1220 On capital gains	0	0	0	0	0	0	0	0	0	0
1300 Unallocable between 1100 and 1200	0	0	12 601	12 434	4 562	36 535	19 984	22 832	63 414	48 230
2000 Social security contributions	**690**	**710**	**101**	**8 453**	**1 286**	**1 815**	**1 618**	**1 378**	**991**	**1 359**
2100 Employees	567	1	98	8 209	1 057	900	879	826	684	751
Sickness benefit fund contributions	30	0	0	0	0	0	0	0	0	0
Sickday benefit contributions, ordinary	534	0	0	0	0	0	0	0	0	0
Sickday benefit contributions, special	3	0	0	0	0	0	0	0	0	0
Contribution to merchant marine's welf. board	0	1	1	0	0	0	0	0	0	0
Special pension scheme savings	0	0	0	6 846	0	0	0	0	0	0
Contr. to pension funds from officials in companies	0	0	0	879	555	450	476	438	355	402
Contr. to pension funds from officials in non-profit institutions	0	0	96	485	502	450	403	388	328	349
2110 On a payroll basis	..	..	..	..	..	..	..	..	..	..
2120 On an income tax basis	..	..	..	..	..	..	..	..	..	..
2200 Employers	123	709	3	244	229	914	739	552	308	609
Unemployment insurance contributions	41	598	0	0	0	0	0	0	0	0
Disablement insurance contributions	21	58	0	0	0	0	0	0	0	0
Sickness benefit fund contributions	61	0	0	0	0	0	0	0	0	0
Contribution to employee's wage guarantee fund	0	50	0	241	227	908	731	542	305	601
Contribution to merchant marine's welf. board	0	1	1	0	0	0	0	0	0	0
Shipping owners contr. sickness assist. seamen	0	1	2	3	2	6	8	10	3	8
2210 On a payroll basis	..	..	..	..	..	..	..	..	..	..
2220 On an income tax basis	..	..	..	..	..	..	..	..	..	..
2300 Self-employed or non-employed	0	0	0	0	0	0	0	0	0	0
2310 On a payroll basis	..	..	..	..	..	..	..	..	..	..
2320 On an income tax basis	..	..	..	..	..	..	..	..	..	..
2400 Unallocable between 2100, 2200 and 2300	0	0	0	0	0	0	0	0	0	0
2410 On a payroll basis	..	..	..	..	..	..	..	..	..	..
2420 On an income tax basis	..	..	..	..	..	..	..	..	..	..
3000 Taxes on payroll and workforce	**0**	**0**	**2 494**	**2 258**	**3 975**	**4 160**	**6 130**	**5 894**	**6 534**	**4 203**
4000 Taxes on property	**1 691**	**9 806**	**16 269**	**20 738**	**31 556**	**33 533**	**34 995**	**39 169**	**46 352**	**45 629**
4100 Recurrent taxes on immovable property	1 029	5 676	8 891	13 565	18 996	24 161	26 370	28 085	30 567	31 581
Central government land tax	130	264	0	0	0	0	0	0	0	0
County land tax	169	2 315	2 915	4 070	0	0	0	0	0	0
Municipal land tax	408	2 257	4 123	7 049	15 601	19 645	22 580	24 707	27 433	28 440
Centr. Govt. fixed tax on real property	32	11	0	0	0	0	0	0	0	0
County fixed tax on real property	45	0	0	0	0	0	0	0	0	0
Municipal fixed tax on real property	190	91	0	0	0	0	0	0	0	0
County duty on land (public property)	4	22	22	25	0	0	0	0	0	0
County duty on buildings (public property)	0	53	88	97	0	0	0	0	0	0
Municipal duty on land (public property)	26	103	244	383	393	434	359	364	333	332
Municipal duty on buildings (residential)	0	195	335	381	757	814	641	599	556	567
Municipal duty on buildings (business)	25	366	1 165	1 560	2 244	3 269	2 789	2 416	2 245	2 242
4110 Households	..	..	..	..	..	..	..	..	..	..

	1965	1980	1990	2000	2007	2010	2013	2015	2019	2020
4120 Others	..	..	..	..	..	..	..	..	..	..
4200 Recurrent taxes on net wealth	306	963	934	0	0	0	0	0	0	0
4210 Individual	306	963	934	..	..	..	..	..	..	..
4220 Corporate	0	0	0	..	..	..	..	..	..	..
4300 Estate, inheritance and gift taxes	137	738	2 197	2 863	3 896	3 646	3 940	5 177	8 571	6 676
4310 Estate and inheritance taxes	..	..	..	..	..	..	..	..	..	..
4320 Gift taxes	..	..	..	..	..	..	..	..	..	..
4400 Taxes on financial and capital transactions	219	2 313	4 166	4 171	8 659	5 726	4 685	5 907	7 214	7 372
Stamp duties	214	2 243	2 829	4 125	8 574	5 695	4 664	5 879	7 165	7 313
Duty on share capital creation	0	32	500	0	0	0	0	0	0	0
Duty to land registry office	5	38	28	46	85	30	21	28	49	59
Duty on transfers of shares	0	0	809	0	0	0	0	0	0	0
4500 Non-recurrent taxes	0	116	81	140	6	0	0	0	0	0
4510 On net wealth	..	0	0	0	0	0	..	..	..	..
4520 Other non-recurrent taxes	..	116	81	140	6	0	..	..	..	..
4600 Other recurrent taxes on property	0	0	0	0	0	0	0	0	0	0
5000 Taxes on goods and services	**8 727**	**63 437**	**129 630**	**208 826**	**286 136**	**273 982**	**293 170**	**304 823**	**333 822**	**339 547**
5100 Taxes on production, sale, transfer, etc.	8 239	60 545	123 645	197 991	267 325	254 303	270 493	281 109	308 401	314 865
5110 General taxes	2 139	37 727	80 650	121 955	174 639	171 583	181 378	191 479	223 180	231 628
5111 Value added taxes	2 139	37 727	72 120	121 955	174 639	171 583	181 378	191 479	223 180	231 628
5112 Sales tax	0	0	0	0	0	0	0	0	0	0
5113 Other	0	0	8 530	0	0	0	0	0	0	0
Labour market contrib. concerning imports	..	..	4 903	..	..	..	..	..	..	..
Labour market contrib. concerning value added	..	..	3 627	..	..	..	..	..	..	..
5120 Taxes on specific goods and services	6 100	22 817	42 995	76 036	92 686	82 720	89 116	89 630	85 221	83 237
5121 Excise duties	5 466	20 473	38 339	68 977	82 861	74 032	81 894	81 893	76 758	75 482
Duty on petrol	1 016	3 713	5 637	10 005	9 154	8 029	7 286	7 348	7 658	7 055
Motor vehicle registration duty	818	2 989	7 917	13 858	24 289	13 586	15 218	17 988	20 307	18 683
Cigarettes and tobacco duties	1 469	4 472	6 516	7 489	7 201	8 283	8 417	7 658	7 830	8 809
Duties on cigars, cheroots and cigarillos	234	220	128	80	40	32	47	113	46	51
Sale of revenue labels	0	3	10	13	13	5	4	4	0	0
Sales duties on chocolate and sugar	254	331	801	1 205	1 289	1 470	2 020	2 156	2 191	2 285
Raw material duty on chocolate and sugar	11	14	54	60	93	144	180	187	94	0
Special tax on chocolate and sugar	0	2	13	76	46	51	68	103	93	121
Duty on ice-cream	33	58	135	168	180	201	297	297	356	408
Duty on coffee	5	249	224	266	250	243	271	280	277	274
Duty on mineral water	68	195	466	505	418	383	374	0	0	0
Duty on beer	622	1 983	3 100	1 510	1 080	895	977	916	810	781
Duty on wine	122	611	1 448	1 166	1 032	1 071	1 674	1 764	1 664	1 803
Duty on spirits	412	1 432	1 982	1 756	1 213	1 028	1 127	1 201	1 205	1 179
Duty on restaurant sales of alcoholic bev.	150	0	0	0	0	0	0	0	0	0
Duty on wireless sets	55	67	0	0	0	0	0	0	0	0
Duty on television sets	0	93	-18	0	0	0	0	0	0	0
Duty on video recorders	0	17	-15	0	0	0	0	0	0	0
Duty on major household appliances	0	199	-10	0	0	0	0	0	0	0
Duty on grammophone records	10	46	84	0	0	0	0	0	0	0
Duty on playing cards	1	2	0	0	0	0	0	0	0	0
Duty on matches	5	3	-1	0	0	0	0	0	0	0
Duty on lighters	1	8	-4	0	0	0	0	0	0	0
Duty on electric bulbs	36	67	152	176	211	117	95	86	42	38
Duty on perfumery and toilet articles	91	214	506	0	0	0	0	0	0	0
Duty on almanacs	3	0	0	0	0	0	0	0	0	0
Duty on salmon	0	1	0	0	0	0	0	0	0	0
Duty on paper and cardboard	45	0	0	0	0	0	0	0	0	0
Duty on sugar	0	174	-8	0	0	0	0	0	0	0
Duty on tea	0	12	10	8	8	8	8	8	0	0
Duty on electricity	0	1 222	4 317	7 430	8 665	10 195	10 013	11 501	11 178	11 203
Duty on certain oil products	0	1 719	2 938	6 757	8 549	8 623	9 306	9 347	9 971	9 467
Duty on certain retail containers	0	100	397	594	727	706	715	316	244	132
Duty on gas	0	56	47	0	0	0	0	0	0	0
Duty on extraction and import of raw materials	0	16	129	172	220	119	132	148	163	183
Duty on disposable tableware	0	0	72	65	126	120	121	138	140	267
Duty on insecticides, herbicides, etc.	0	0	13	366	449	466	656	598	590	563
Duty on videotapes	0	0	0	0	0	0	0	0	0	0
Duty on coal, etc.	0	0	849	1 217	1 450	2 587	2 991	2 255	1 766	1 600
Other duties on goods and services	5	186	20	53	147	189	-13	186	178	136
Duty on waste	0	0	404	1 025	1 225	51	167	130	120	158
Duty on CFC	0	0	27	0	53	56	82	65	45	41
Duty on CO2	0	0	0	4 883	5 108	5 822	5 762	3 652	3 565	3 306
Duty on cigarette paper	0	0	0	68	32	28	36	38	32	30
Duty on rechargeable Ni-Cd batteries	0	0	0	21	17	4	3	2	1	1
Duty on piped water	0	0	0	1 357	1 371	1 334	1 584	1 688	1 673	1 687

	1965	1980	1990	2000	2007	2010	2013	2015	2019	2020
Duty on carrier bags made of paper, plastic, etc.	0	0	0	178	210	201	186	208	166	324
Duty on tires	0	0	0	29	45	62	50	57	47	56
Duty on sulphur	0	0	0	165	108	48	51	42	33	35
Duty on chlorinated solvents	0	0	0	2	0	0	0	0	0	0
Duty on natural gas	0	0	0	2 532	3 375	4 524	5 255	3 160	2 781	2 784
Duty on nitrogen	0	0	0	30	27	26	21	17	14	15
Duty on specific growth stimulants	0	0	0	0	0	0	0	0	0	0
Duty on PVC-film	0	0	0	7	12	11	10	11	0	0
Duty on PVC and phathalates	0	0	0	31	42	23	18	19	0	0
Duty on lead accumulators	0	0	0	14	0	0	0	0	0	0
Duty on mineral phosphorus	0	0	0	0	51	51	49	52	25	0
Surcharge on alcoholic soft drinks	0	0	0	0	17	26	33	33	0	0
Duty on nitrogen oxides	0	0	0	0	0	212	870	820	152	155
Duty on saturated fat	0	0	0	0	0	0	0	0	0	0
Duty on PSO (Public Service Obligations)	0	0	0	3 641	4 319	3 004	5 734	7 302	1 301	1 853
5122 Profits of fiscal monopolies	16	183	404	1 402	1 648	1 481	1 339	1 230	1 989	1 574
5123 Customs and import duties	556	1 113	1 849	2 325	3 282	3 242	2 824	3 285	3 129	3 089
Customs duties	0	1 032	1 779	2 325	3 282	3 242	2 824	3 285	3 129	3 089
Temporary import surcharge	556	0	0	0	0	0	0	0	0	0
Import duties on agricultural produce	0	81	70	0	0	0	0	0	0	0
5124 Taxes on exports	0	0	0	0	0	0	0	0	0	0
5125 Taxes on investment goods	0	0	0	0	0	0	0	0	0	0
5126 Taxes on specific services	62	771	1 567	3 019	4 525	3 932	3 008	3 189	3 346	3 092
Sales tax on gambling stakes races	17	28	20	12	18	16	15	14	0	0
Tax on football pools	31	152	284	942	1 143	1 071	0	0	0	0
Tax on cinema tickets	14	0	0	0	0	0	0	0	0	0
Duty on motor vehicle compl. insurance	0	470	923	1 327	2 104	1 854	1 598	1 529	1 478	1 444
Duty on insurance on pleasure boats	0	13	57	66	100	122	127	126	93	104
Duty on charter flight	0	109	283	0	0	0	0	0	0	0
Turnover tax on 6-win horse race betting	0	0	0	0	0	0	0	0	0	0
Duty on casinos	0	0	0	180	261	173	192	200	198	132
Passenger duty	0	0	0	477	6	0	0	0	0	0
Duty on the Danish State Lottery	0	0	0	16	35	41	42	44	44	45
Duty on slot machines	0	0	0	0	858	656	545	618	569	414
Duty on gambling	0	0	0	0	0	0	288	397	490	459
Duty on online casinos	0	0	0	0	0	0	202	261	475	495
5127 Other taxes on internat. trade and transactions	0	0	0	0	0	0	0	0	0	0
5128 Other taxes	0	277	837	312	370	33	51	33	0	0
Duty paid to ECSC	..	4	5	0	0	0	0	0	..	..
Sugar storing duty	..	83	113	62	0	0	0	0	..	..
Duty on the production of sugar	..	81	145	249	-26	33	51	33	..	..
Duty on milk co-reponsibility levy	..	109	255	0	0	0	0	0	..	..
Grain co-reponsibility levy	..	0	319	0	0	0	0	0	..	..
Restructuring scheme for EU sugar system	..	0	0	0	397	0	0	0	..	..
5130 Unallocable between 5110 and 5120	0	0	0	0	0	0	0	0	0	0
5200 Taxes on use of goods and perform activities	488	2 893	4 410	7 468	14 088	14 731	16 180	16 537	16 099	15 076
5210 Recurrent taxes	488	2 893	4 410	7 468	14 088	14 731	15 966	16 171	14 859	13 836
5211 Paid by households: motor vehicles	199	1 874	2 922	5 485	7 105	7 614	8 094	8 136	7 298	7 177
Weight duty automobiles	199	1 874	2 922	5 318	6 954	7 467	7 936	7 859	7 048	6 917
Recycling fee on cars	0	0	0	167	151	147	158	277	251	259
5212 Paid by others: motor vehicles	287	1 014	1 441	1 919	3 125	2 980	3 336	3 483	3 935	3 908
Weight duty automobiles	287	1 014	1 441	1 612	2 652	2 611	2 952	3 088	3 416	3 352
Road charges	0	0	0	307	473	370	383	395	519	555
5213 Paid in respect of other goods	2	5	47	64	3 858	4 137	4 537	4 552	3 626	2 752
5220 Non-recurrent taxes	0	0	0	0	0	0	214	365	1 240	1 240
5300 Unallocable between 5100 and 5200	0	0	1 575	3 368	4 724	4 948	6 497	7 177	9 322	9 606
6000 Other taxes	**0**	**0**	**0**	**391**	**190**	**206**	**152**	**320**	**289**	**258**
6100 Paid solely by business	..	..	..	391	190	206	152	320	289	258
6200 Other	..	..	..	0	0	0	0	0	0	0
Memorandum item										
Customs duties collected on behalf of the EU	..	..	1 779	2 325	3 282	3 242	2 824	3 285	3 129	3 089
Non-wastable tax credits										
Non-wastable tax credits against 1110	..	..	..	..	..	4 960	5 515	4 228	3 099	3 028
Tax expenditure component	..	..	..	..	..	4 712	5 240	4 016	2 944	2 876
Transfer component	..	..	..	..	..	248	276	211	155	151
Non-wastable tax credits against 1210	..	..	..	..	..	0	0	0	0	0
Tax expenditure component	..	..	..	..	..	..	..	..	..	..
Transfer component	..	..	..	..	..	..	..	..	..	..
Total tax revenue on cash basis	**..**	**..**	**..**	**..**	**..**	**..**	**..**	**..**	**..**	**..**
Total tax revenue on accrual basis	**20 821**	**166 358**	**382 232**	**623 911**	**809 988**	**813 972**	**901 001**	**957 281**	**1 094 118**	**1 105 573**

	1965	1980	1990	2000	2007	2010	2013	2015	2019	2020
Conciliation with National Accounts										
Additional taxes included in National Accounts	0	0	..	..	..	..	..	..	..	..
Taxes excluded from National Accounts	0	0	..	..	..	..	..	..	..	..
Difference in treatment of tax credits	0	0	0	0	0	4 712	5 240	4 016	2 944	2 876
Capital transfer for uncollected revenue	0	-1 374	-2 387	-1 917	-2 726	-3 475	-15 512	-19 396	-10 370	-10 754
Voluntary social security contributions	0	1 673	8 087	16 633	17 061	17 192	14 655	14 721	14 792	14 873
Miscellaneous differences	0	0	..	..	..	..	..	..	..	..
National Accounts: Taxes and actual social contributions	20 821	166 657	387 932	638 626	824 323	832 401	905 384	956 623	1 101 485	1 112 568
Imputed social contributions	0	5 958	4 592	6 223	5 693	5 356	4 520	4 067	3 227	3 094
National Accounts: Taxes and all social contributions	20 821	172 615	392 525	644 849	830 017	837 758	909 904	960 690	1 104 712	1 115 662

.. Not available
Note: Year ending 31st December.
The figures are on an accrual basis.
Heading 2300 includes a small amount of voluntary contributions which cannot be isolated.
Source: Statistics Denmark.

StatLink https://stat.link/uczatn

Table 5.10. Estonia: Details of tax revenue, 1965-2020

Million EUR

	1965	1980	1990	2000	2007	2010	2013	2015	2019	2020
Total tax revenue	..	..	..	**1 919**	**5 082**	**4 894**	**5 988**	**6 874**	**9 298**	**9 134**
Total tax revenue exclusive of taxes collected for the EU	..	..	..	**1 919**	**5 047**	**4 870**	**5 960**	**6 840**	**9 239**	**9 084**
1000 Taxes on income, profits and capital gains	..	..	..	**476**	**1 197**	**970**	**1 357**	**1 607**	**2 041**	**2 102**
1100 Of individuals	..	..	..	421	936	776	1 031	1 182	1 532	1 652
1110 On income and profits	..	..	..	421	936	776	1 031	1 182	1 532	1 652
1120 On capital gains	..	..	..	0	0	0	0	0	0	0
1200 Corporate	..	..	..	55	261	194	327	424	509	450
1210 On profits	..	..	..	55	65	35	62	38	94	82
1220 On capital gains	..	..	..	0	196	159	265	386	416	368
1300 Unallocable between 1100 and 1200	..	..	..	0	0	0	0	0	0	0
2000 Social security contributions	..	..	..	**674**	**1 683**	**1 879**	**2 077**	**2 300**	**3 256**	**3 331**
2100 Employees	..	..	..	0	28	116	109	99	136	139
2110 On a payroll basis	..	..	..	..	28	116	109	99	136	139
2120 On an income tax basis	..	..	..	..	0	0	0	0	0	0
2200 Employers	..	..	..	662	1 635	1 742	1 949	2 181	3 101	2 974
2210 On a payroll basis	..	..	..	662	1 635	1 742	1 949	2 181	3 101	2 974
2220 On an income tax basis	..	..	..	0	0	0	0	0	0	0
2300 Self-employed or non-employed	..	..	..	12	21	21	19	20	20	217
2310 On a payroll basis	..	..	..	12	21	21	19	20	20	217
2320 On an income tax basis	..	..	..	0	0	0	0	0	0	0
2400 Unallocable between 2100, 2200 and 2300	..	..	..	0	0	0	0	0	0	0
2410 On a payroll basis	..	..	..	..	..	..	..	..	..	..
2420 On an income tax basis	..	..	..	..	..	..	..	..	..	..
3000 Taxes on payroll and workforce	..	..	..	**0**	**0**	**0**	**0**	**0**	**0**	**0**
4000 Taxes on property	..	..	..	**24**	**35**	**51**	**57**	**58**	**58**	**58**
4100 Recurrent taxes on immovable property	..	..	..	24	35	51	57	58	58	58
Land tax	..	..	..	24	35	51	57	58	58	58
4110 Households	..	..	..	..	..	..	..	..	..	..
4120 Others	..	..	..	..	..	..	..	..	..	..
4200 Recurrent taxes on net wealth	..	..	..	0	0	0	0	0	0	0
4210 Individual	..	..	..	..	..	..	..	..	..	..
4220 Corporate	..	..	..	..	..	..	..	..	..	..
4300 Estate, inheritance and gift taxes	..	..	..	0	0	0	0	0	0	0
4310 Estate and inheritance taxes	..	..	..	..	..	..	..	..	..	..
4320 Gift taxes	..	..	..	..	..	..	..	..	..	..
4400 Taxes on financial and capital transactions	..	..	..	0	0	0	0	0	0	0
4500 Non-recurrent taxes	..	..	..	0	0	0	0	0	0	0
4510 On net wealth	..	..	..	..	..	..	..	..	..	..
4520 Other non-recurrent taxes	..	..	..	..	..	..	..	..	..	..
4600 Other recurrent taxes on property	..	..	..	0	0	0	0	0	0	0
5000 Taxes on goods and services	..	..	..	**745**	**2 166**	**1 993**	**2 496**	**2 909**	**3 943**	**3 643**
5100 Taxes on production, sale, transfer, etc.	..	..	..	723	2 099	1 938	2 431	2 829	3 725	3 438
5110 General taxes	..	..	..	521	1 423	1 263	1 558	1 873	2 483	2 439
5111 Value added taxes	..	..	..	520	1 423	1 257	1 558	1 873	2 483	2 439
5112 Sales tax	..	..	..	0	0	6	0	0	0	0
5113 Other	..	..	..	0	0	0	0	0	0	0
5120 Taxes on specific goods and services	..	..	..	202	675	675	873	956	1 243	999
5121 Excise duties	..	..	..	183	577	619	796	869	1 128	897
Alcohol	..	..	..	62	153	154	212	207	225	211
Tobacco	..	..	..	36	134	91	169	183	231	231
Fuel	..	..	..	76	290	343	383	444	638	437
Motor vehicle	..	..	..	9	0	0	0	0	0	0
Package	..	..	..	0	0	0	0	1	0	0
Fur	..	..	..	0	0	0	0	0	0	0
Electricity	..	..	..	0	0	31	33	34	34	18
5122 Profits of fiscal monopolies	..	..	..	0	0	0	0	0	0	0
5123 Customs and import duties	..	..	..	2	35	24	29	34	52	42
5124 Taxes on exports	..	..	..	0	0	0	0	0	0	0
5125 Taxes on investment goods	..	..	..	0	0	0	0	0	0	0
5126 Taxes on specific services	..	..	..	17	64	33	48	53	62	60
Gambling tax	..	..	..	7	30	21	22	23	30	28
Advertising tax	..	..	..	1	3	2	4	4	6	0
Postal service payment	..	..	..	0	0	0	0	0	0	5
Liquid fuel stockpiling fee	..	..	..	0	2	5	6	5	5	4
Contributions to the Guarantee Fund	..	..	..	9	29	5	17	20	21	23
5127 Other taxes on internat. trade and transactions	..	..	..	0	0	0	0	0	0	0
5128 Other taxes	..	..	..	0	0	0	0	0	0	0
5130 Unallocable between 5110 and 5120	..	..	..	0	0	0	0	0	0	0

	1965	1980	1990	2000	2007	2010	2013	2015	2019	2020
5200 Taxes on use of goods and perform activities	..	..	..	22	68	55	65	80	217	204
5210 Recurrent taxes	..	..	..	22	68	55	65	73	77	61
Car registration fee	..	..	..	2	5	4	7	7	8	6
Heavy vehicle tax	..	..	..	0	4	4	4	5	5	5
5211 Paid by households: motor vehicles	..	..	..	..	..	..	..	..	..	..
5212 Paid by others: motor vehicles	..	..	..	..	..	..	..	..	..	..
5213 Paid in respect of other goods	..	..	..	20	58	47	55	61	64	50
Business and professional licenses	..	..	..	3	2	1	1	1	4	4
Pollution fee	..	..	..	10	44	31	37	44	44	29
Specific use of water	..	..	..	4	9	13	14	13	13	14
Fees for closure of roads, streets and squares	..	..	..	0	1	1	1	2	2	2
Fishing fees	..	..	..	1	1	1	2	2	2	2
Tax on motor vehicle	..	..	..	2	0	0	0	0	0	0
Boat tax	..	..	..	0	0	0	0	0	0	0
Animal tax	..	..	..	0	0	0	0	0	0	0
5220 Non-recurrent taxes	..	..	..	0	0	0	0	7	140	143
Revenue from the sale of emission permits	..	..	..	..	..	..	..	7	140	143
5300 Unallocable between 5100 and 5200	..	..	..	0	0	0	0	0	0	0
6000 Other taxes	**..**	**..**	**..**	**0**	**0**	**0**	**0**	**0**	**0**	**0**
6100 Paid solely by business	..	..	..	..	..	..	..	..	..	..
6200 Other	..	..	..	..	..	..	..	..	..	..
Other taxes	..	..	..	..	..	..	..	..	..	..
Memorandum item										
Customs duties collected on behalf of the EU	..	..	..	..	35	24	29	34	52	42
SRF contributions collected on behalf of the EU	..	..	..	..	..	..	..	..	7	8
Total tax revenue on cash basis	**..**	**..**	**..**	**1 907**	**5 003**	**4 921**	**5 964**	**6 848**	**9 195**	**9 204**
Total tax revenue on accrual basis	**..**	**..**	**..**	**1 919**	**5 082**	**4 894**	**5 988**	**6 874**	**9 298**	**9 134**
Conciliation with National Accounts										
Additional taxes included in National Accounts	..	..	..	0	0	0	0	0	0	0
Taxes excluded from National Accounts	..	..	..	0	0	0	0	0	0	0
Difference in treatment of tax credits	..	..	..	0	0	0	0	0	0	0
Capital transfer for uncollected revenue	..	..	..	0	0	0	0	0	0	0
Voluntary social security contributions	..	..	..	0	0	0	0	0	0	0
Miscellaneous differences	..	..	..	0	0	0	0	0	0	0
National Accounts: Taxes and actual social contributions	..	..	..	1 919	5 082	4 894	5 988	6 874	9 298	9 134
Imputed social contributions	..	..	..	4	20	30	38	49	73	86
National Accounts: Taxes and all social contributions	..	..	..	1 922	5 102	4 924	6 026	6 923	9 371	9 220

.. Not available
Note: Year ending 31st December.
Data on an accrual basis.
Source: Statistics Estonia.

StatLink https://stat.link/fx2sq7

Table 5.11. Finland: Details of tax revenue, 1965-2020

Million EUR

	1965	1980	1990	2000	2007	2010	2013	2015	2019	2020
Total tax revenue	**1 362**	**11 895**	**39 052**	**62 435**	**77 447**	**76 315**	**88 688**	**92 003**	**101 439**	**99 610**
Total tax revenue exclusive of taxes collected for the EU	..	..	**39 052**	**62 296**	**77 247**	**76 163**	**88 521**	**91 760**	**101 036**	**99 201**
1000 Taxes on income, profits and capital gains	**564**	**4 654**	**15 323**	**26 910**	**30 358**	**27 104**	**30 797**	**32 371**	**35 470**	**34 962**
1100 Of individuals	453	4 248	13 562	19 118	23 396	22 545	25 998	27 824	29 401	29 873
1110 On income and profits	453	4 234	13 520	19 118	23 396	22 545	25 998	27 824	29 401	29 873
Tax on income	125	1 827	5 917	9 036	9 086	6 465	7 903	9 138	9 986	9 360
The final withdrawal tax on interest income	0	0	0	92	254	205	207	110	39	36
Communal tax	279	2 376	7 603	9 990	14 056	15 875	17 888	18 576	19 376	20 477
Seaman's tax	3	31	0	0	0	0	0	0	0	0
National pension contributions	32	0	0	0	0	0	0	0	0	0
National health insurance contributions	15	0	0	0	0	0	0	0	0	0
1120 On capital gains	0	14	42	0	0	0	0	0	0	0
Tax on lottery prizes	..	14	42	..	..	..	..	..	..	..
1200 Corporate	111	405	1 761	7 792	6 962	4 559	4 799	4 547	6 069	5 089
1210 On profits	111	405	1 761	7 792	6 962	4 559	4 799	4 547	6 069	5 089
Tax on income	72	202	1 001	4 758	5 298	2 972	3 227	2 761	4 151	2 933
Communal tax	36	187	699	2 900	1 541	1 471	1 456	1 668	1 918	2 156
Church tax	3	16	61	134	123	116	116	118	0	0
1220 On capital gains	0	0	0	0	0	0	0	0	0	0
1300 Unallocable between 1100 and 1200	0	0	0	0	0	0	0	0	0	0
2000 Social security contributions	**93**	**2 776**	**10 012**	**15 756**	**21 384**	**22 648**	**25 632**	**26 639**	**28 295**	**27 326**
2100 Employees	1	394	1 152	2 926	4 050	4 710	5 811	6 364	8 546	8 553
For employment pension schemes	1	10	23	2 120	2 950	3 386	4 235	4 714	6 078	6 239
For unemployment schemes	0	0	0	435	369	267	457	489	1 379	1 072
2110 On a payroll basis	..	10	23	2 565	3 319	3 653	4 692	5 203	7 457	7 311
2120 On an income tax basis	..	384	1 129	361	731	1 057	1 119	1 161	1 089	1 242
National pension contributions	..	251	502	2	0	0	0	0	0	0
National health insurance contributions	..	133	627	359	731	1 057	1 119	1 161	1 089	1 242
2200 Employers	93	2 230	8 127	11 571	15 715	16 041	17 888	18 232	17 778	16 704
For national pension schemes	29	685	1 502	1 566	1 331	0	0	0	0	0
For national health insurance	10	244	792	839	1 142	1 590	1 612	1 662	694	1 197
For unemployment schemes	3	106	206	1 143	1 346	1 377	1 775	1 676	1 260	1 006
For employment pension schemes	50	1 195	5 627	8 023	11 896	13 074	14 501	14 894	15 824	14 501
For accident and group life insurance premiums	0	0	0	0	0	0	0	0	0	0
2210 On a payroll basis	..	2 230	8 127	11 571	15 715	16 041	17 888	18 232	17 778	16 704
2220 On an income tax basis	..	0	0	0	0	0	0	0	0	0
2300 Self-employed or non-employed	0	152	733	1 259	1 619	1 897	1 933	2 043	1 971	2 069
For employment pension schemes	..	84	394	576	817	932	1 187	1 269	1 245	1 241
2310 On a payroll basis	..	84	394	576	817	932	1 187	1 269	1 245	1 241
2320 On an income tax basis	..	68	339	683	802	965	746	774	726	828
National pension contributions	..	43	151	5	0	0	0	0	0	0
National health insurance contributions	..	25	188	678	802	965	746	774	726	828
2400 Unallocable between 2100, 2200 and 2300	0	0	0	0	0	0	0	0	0	0
2410 On a payroll basis	..	..	..	..	..	..	..	..	..	..
2420 On an income tax basis	..	..	..	..	..	..	..	..	..	..
3000 Taxes on payroll and workforce	**70**	**22**	**0**	**0**	**0**	**0**	**0**	**0**	**0**	**0**
Soc. Sec. contr. for children allowance	70	22	..	..	..	..	..	..	..	..
4000 Taxes on property	**54**	**221**	**956**	**1 518**	**2 012**	**2 087**	**2 599**	**3 017**	**3 477**	**3 569**
4100 Recurrent taxes on immovable property	0	0	76	570	855	1 169	1 363	1 603	1 871	1 950
4110 Households	..	..	46	273	405	576	623	733	860	899
4120 Others	..	..	30	297	450	593	740	870	1 011	1 051
4200 Recurrent taxes on net wealth	24	24	27	179	0	0	0	0	0	0
4210 Individual	11	23	25	175	..	..	..	..	..	..
4220 Corporate	13	2	2	4	..	..	..	..	..	..
4300 Estate, inheritance and gift taxes	3	26	146	368	459	387	646	631	749	797
4310 Estate and inheritance taxes	3	21	121	307	384	324	541	528	612	650
4320 Gift taxes	1	5	25	61	75	63	105	103	137	147
4400 Taxes on financial and capital transactions	27	170	707	401	698	531	590	783	857	822
Stamp duty excluded entertainment	27	170	688	-20	0	0	0	0	0	0
Credit tax	0	0	19	0	0	0	0	0	0	0
Transfer tax	0	0	0	421	698	531	590	783	857	822
4500 Non-recurrent taxes	0	0	0	0	0	0	0	0	0	0
4510 On net wealth	..	..	..	..	..	..	..	..	..	..
4520 Other non-recurrent taxes	..	..	..	..	..	..	..	..	..	..
4600 Other recurrent taxes on property	0	0	0	0	0	0	0	0	0	0
5000 Taxes on goods and services	**578**	**4 202**	**12 711**	**18 221**	**23 624**	**24 407**	**29 596**	**29 895**	**34 146**	**33 680**
5100 Taxes on production, sale, transfer, etc.	570	4 158	12 555	17 781	22 953	23 642	28 662	28 836	32 667	32 224
5110 General taxes	251	2 062	7 519	10 869	15 207	15 533	18 888	18 974	21 974	22 005

	1965	1980	1990	2000	2007	2010	2013	2015	2019	2020
5111 Value added taxes	251	2 062	7 519	10 869	15 207	15 533	18 888	18 974	21 974	22 005
Value added taxes	251	2 062	7 519	9 616	13 657	13 691	16 561	16 680	18 929	18 802
VAT repayments of local government	0	0	0	849	1 550	1 842	2 327	2 294	3 045	3 203
Social Insur. Institutions' part of VAT revenue	0	0	0	404	0	0	0	0	0	0
5112 Sales tax	0	0	0	0	0	0	0	0	0	0
5113 Other	0	0	0	0	0	0	0	0	0	0
Suppl. sales tax on consumer durables	..	..	..	..	..	..	..	..	..	..
5120 Taxes on specific goods and services	319	2 096	5 036	6 912	7 746	8 109	9 774	9 862	10 693	10 219
5121 Excise duties	183	1 615	3 813	5 613	6 013	6 286	7 511	7 678	8 118	8 006
Excise on tobacco products	52	206	473	561	622	655	852	885	1 019	1 054
Excise on sweetments	6	23	26	0	0	0	0	0	0	0
Excise on medium, strong beer	3	109	419	0	0	0	0	0	0	0
Excise on non-alcoholic beverages	2	17	22	32	35	37	204	250	180	209
Excise on certain foodstuffs	3	218	36	0	0	0	0	0	0	0
Excise on liquid fuels	58	504	986	2 583	2 907	3 167	3 925	4 054	4 294	4 253
Excise on motor cars	28	238	697	1 059	1 217	941	931	882	886	713
Tax on alcoholic beverages	29	353	813	1 239	1 016	1 279	1 355	1 356	1 483	1 521
Levies on pharmacy	2	16	46	85	113	122	153	165	188	198
Levies for price reduction on butter	0	3	0	0	0	0	0	0	0	0
Levies for marketing of milk	0	12	58	0	0	0	0	0	0	0
Excise on margarines	0	18	55	0	0	0	0	0	0	0
Stock-building levies on liquid fuels	0	15	44	46	50	48	45	43	43	40
Excise on sugar products	0	18	34	0	0	0	0	0	0	0
Excise on feeding stuffs	0	0	0	0	0	0	0	0	0	0
Excise on fertilizers	0	21	21	0	0	0	0	0	0	0
Excise on oil-based concentrated feed	0	1	0	0	0	0	0	0	0	0
Excise on protein feed	0	0	0	0	0	0	0	0	0	0
Equalization fee agricultural products	0	8	29	0	0	0	0	0	0	0
Excise on albumen	0	0	30	0	0	0	0	0	0	0
Tax on electricity	0	65	0	0	0	0	0	0	0	0
Oil damage levy	0	0	7	5	8	20	27	24	7	2
Oil waste levy	0	0	4	3	4	4	4	4	4	0
Price difference compensations	0	-231	0	0	0	0	0	0	0	0
The milk quota charge	0	0	6	0	0	0	0	0	0	0
Levies for marketing of special agric. prod.	0	0	0	0	0	0	0	0	0	0
Excise on phosphorous fertilizers	0	0	7	0	0	0	0	0	0	0
Excise on certain beverage packages	0	0	0	0	41	13	15	15	14	16
5122 Profits of fiscal monopolies	38	86	202	0	0	0	0	0	0	0
Excess profits on alcohol	38	86	202	..	..	..	..	..	..	..
5123 Customs and import duties	88	235	423	130	199	151	166	166	187	174
Import duties	62	126	232	0	0	0	0	0	0	0
Import levies on agricultural products	26	6	12	0	0	0	0	0	0	0
Local import duties (Town dues)	1	0	0	0	0	0	0	0	0	0
Import levies price stabilisation fund	0	3	0	0	0	0	0	0	0	0
Agricultural levies	0	0	0	0	0	0	0	0	0	0
Equalization tax	0	100	179	0	0	0	0	0	0	0
Custom duties	..	..	0	130	199	151	166	166	187	174
5124 Taxes on exports	0	0	0	0	0	0	0	0	0	0
Export duties	..	..	..	..	..	..	..	..	..	..
Levies on export	..	..	..	..	..	..	..	..	..	..
Counter-cyclical tax exports	..	..	..	..	..	..	..	..	..	..
5125 Taxes on investment goods	0	0	0	0	0	0	0	0	0	0
Investment tax on buildings	..	..	..	..	..	..	..	..	..	..
5126 Taxes on specific services	9	161	598	1 160	1 533	1 671	2 096	2 017	2 388	2 039
Net revenue of betting	8	94	328	704	807	874	948	967	1 099	746
Tax on motion pictures	0	0	0	0	0	0	0	0	0	0
Stamp duties on entertainment	2	5	0	0	0	0	0	0	0	0
Fire protection levy	0	3	7	6	8	9	10	11	11	11
Tax on waste	0	0	0	33	56	42	56	32	3	7
Rail tax	0	0	0	0	18	18	19	6	0	0
Tax on insurance premiums	0	58	263	337	509	584	712	777	789	820
Tax on lottery prizes	0	0	0	80	135	144	217	222	217	163
Tax on telecommunications	0	0	0	0	0	0	0	0	0	0
Bank tax	0	0	0	0	0	0	134	-74	-3	-2
Contributions to the Resolution Fund	..	..	0	0	0	0	0	76	216	235
Contributions to the Deposit Guarantee Fund	..	..	0	0	0	0	0	0	56	59
5127 Other taxes on internat. trade and transactions	0	0	0	0	0	0	0	0	0	0
Tax on charter flights	..	..	..	..	..	..	..	..	..	..
5128 Other taxes	0	0	0	9	1	1	1	1	0	0
Sugar levy	..	..	..	9	1	1	1	1	..	..
Steel and coal levy	..	..	..	0	0	0	0	0	..	..
5130 Unallocable between 5110 and 5120	0	0	0	0	0	0	0	0	0	0

	1965	1980	1990	2000	2007	2010	2013	2015	2019	2020
5200 Taxes on use of goods and perform activities	8	44	156	440	671	765	934	1 059	1 479	1 456
5210 Recurrent taxes	8	44	156	423	637	725	897	960	1 189	1 208
5211 Paid by households: motor vehicles	0	2	5	165	486	541	696	748	949	965
5212 Paid by others: motor vehicles	7	32	135	235	126	150	170	182	201	203
5213 Paid in respect of other goods	1	10	16	23	25	34	31	30	39	40
Dog licenses	1	2	4	5	3	2	2	1	0	0
Hunting and fishing licenses	1	7	12	17	17	24	23	22	27	28
Seamens welfare and rescue levy	0	0	0	1	1	1	1	0	0	0
Nuclear energy research levy	0	0	0	0	4	7	5	7	12	12
5220 Non-recurrent taxes	0	0	0	17	34	40	37	99	290	248
Vehicle registration tax	..	..	..	17	34	40	37	36	27	27
Income from auction of emission allowances	..	..	..	0	0	0	0	63	263	221
5300 Unallocable between 5100 and 5200	0	0	0	0	0	0	0	0	0	0
6000 Other taxes	**2**	**21**	**50**	**30**	**69**	**69**	**64**	**81**	**51**	**73**
6100 Paid solely by business	0	0	0	0	0	0	0	0	0	0
6200 Other	2	21	50	30	69	69	64	81	51	73
Memorandum items										
Customs duties collected on behalf of the EU	..	..	..	130	199	151	166	166	187	174
SRF contributions collected on behalf of the EU	..	..	..	..	..	..	..	76	216	235
Total tax revenue on cash basis	**1 362**	**11 895**	**39 396**	**61 638**	**77 110**	**76 176**	**88 425**	**91 846**	**101 219**	**98 048**
Total tax revenue on accrual basis	**..**	**..**	**39 052**	**62 435**	**77 447**	**76 315**	**88 688**	**92 003**	**101 439**	**99 610**
Conciliation with National Accounts										
Additional taxes included in National Accounts	..	0	0	0	0	0	0	0	0	0
Taxes excluded from National Accounts	..	0	0	0	0	0	0	0	0	0
Difference in treatment of tax credits	..	0	0	0	0	0	0	0	0	0
Capital transfer for uncollected revenue	..	0	0	0	0	0	0	0	0	0
Voluntary social security contributions	..	262	632	236	228	254	270	303	246	235
Miscellaneous differences	..	0	0	0	0	0	0	0	0	0
National Accounts: Taxes and actual social contributions	..	12 157	39 684	62 671	77 675	76 569	88 958	92 306	101 685	99 845
Imputed social contributions	..	513	688	30	0	0	0	0	..	..
National Accounts: Taxes and all social contributions	..	12 670	40 372	62 701	77 675	76 569	88 958	92 306	101 685	99 845

.. Not available
Note: Year ending 31st December.
From 1988 data are on accrual basis.
The comparability of the time series to earlier years is slightly lower.
Headings 2120 and 2320: The breakdown of contributions paid by employees and self-employed or non-employed is estimated, except for the healthcare fee of students in higher education included also into 2320 (in effect from 2021).
Headings 4110 and 4120: The breakdown of contributions paid by households and others is estimated.
Heading 4400: Negative values in Stamp duties are due to repayments during transition time from Stamp duties to Transfer tax.
Heading 5121: Negative items in Price difference compensations were due to subsidies under the price compensation scheme, which could be offset against any positive tax liability.
Heading 5126: Negative values are due to repayments temporary bank tax.
Heading 5212: Prior to 1990, a part of the tax was paid by households.
Source: Statistics Finland, basing on data from State Treasury, Tax Administration, Finnish Customs, Finnish Transport and Communication Agency, Financial Stability Authority and Financial Supervisory Authority. Supplementary information from unpublished sources.

StatLink https://stat.link/v5ytwn

Table 5.12. France: Details of tax revenue, 1965-2020

Million EUR

	1965	1980	1990	2000	2007	2010	2013	2015	2019	2020
Total tax revenue	**25 776**	**178 576**	**433 771**	**645 528**	**831 226**	**846 318**	**966 817**	**1 002 131**	**1 098 902**	**1 058 387**
Total tax revenue exclusive of taxes collected for the EU	..	..	..	**643 655**	**829 411**	**844 346**	**964 743**	**999 064**	**1 094 291**	**1 053 334**
1000 Taxes on income, profits and capital gains	**4 095**	**30 019**	**69 649**	**160 363**	**197 939**	**191 085**	**235 964**	**234 532**	**282 086**	**276 718**
1100 Of individuals	2 736	20 734	46 272	115 885	141 405	144 165	179 715	188 357	227 806	222 907
1110 On income and profits	2 723	20 674	46 252	115 884	141 405	144 165	179 715	188 357	227 806	222 907
Tax on individual income	..	18 207	39 237	49 548	48 597	49 575	70 098	72 750	77 681	75 556
Tax on non business profits	..	51	189	293	559	446	598	927	979	694
Tax on financial assets	..	2 333	3 971	0	0	0	0	0	0	0
CSG, CRDS, social security contributions for the benefit of the FSV, FNAL and / or the FS	..	0	0	65 953	92 204	93 972	108 247	113 065	135 098	131 852
Flat-rate tax on precious metals	..	70	58	47	37	52	69	71	104	79
Tax on multiple wages	..	7	20	38	0	0	0	0	0	0
Solidarity levy	..	0	2 207	5	0	82	381	0	10 537	10 292
Others	..	6	571	0	8	38	322	1 544	3 407	4 434
1120 On capital gains	14	59	20	1	0	0	0	0	0	0
On capital gains	..	0	0	0	..	..	..	..	..	..
Levies on construction profits	..	59	20	1	..	..	..	..	..	..
1200 Corporate	1 358	9 158	23 117	44 478	56 534	46 920	56 249	46 175	54 280	53 811
1210 On profits	1 358	9 158	23 117	44 478	56 534	46 920	56 249	46 175	54 280	53 811
Corporations' tax (excluding tax credits to reduce or remove the taxation)	..	8 524	20 804	39 755	51 063	39 095	46 474	39 579	48 670	49 942
3% tax on dividends	..	0	0	0	0	0	1 943	2 165	0	0
Tax on financial assets	..	487	1 333	1 460	3 492	5 952	5 894	3 325	4 339	1 575
Precount on distributed profits (exceptional levy of 25% since 2005)	..	36	247	1 135	88	28	-6	4	-131	0
Exceptional levies on temporary work corporations	..	0	0	0	0	0	0	0	0	0
Social contribution on corporation profits	..	0	0	589	158	842	1 160	971	1 240	1 171
Annual flat-rate tax	..	111	658	1 484	1 656	599	680	4	1	1
Exceptionnal levies on insurances	..	0	61	55	64	94	104	127	161	1 122
Other	..	0	14	0	13	310	0	0	0	0
1220 On capital gains	0	0	0	0	0	0	0	0	0	0
1300 Unallocable between 1100 and 1200	0	127	260	0	0	0	0	0	0	0
2000 Social security contributions	**8 804**	**76 235**	**191 141**	**231 875**	**307 663**	**323 816**	**356 934**	**370 375**	**363 817**	**348 335**
2100 Employees	1 701	19 851	57 347	57 686	76 815	78 268	88 097	93 767	87 940	84 244
Actual cotisations	0	19 851	57 347	57 686	76 815	78 268	88 097	93 767	87 940	84 244
2110 On a payroll basis	0	0	0	57 686	76 815	78 268	88 097	93 767	87 940	84 244
2120 On an income tax basis	0	0	0	0	0	0	0	0	0	0
2200 Employers	6 525	50 742	118 079	159 476	208 688	219 687	240 672	248 173	247 437	236 893
Actual cotisations	0	50 742	118 079	159 476	208 688	219 687	240 672	248 173	247 437	236 893
2210 On a payroll basis	0	0	0	159 476	208 688	219 687	240 672	248 173	247 437	236 893
2220 On an income tax basis	0	0	0	0	0	0	0	0	0	0
2300 Self-employed or non-employed	578	5 642	15 714	14 713	22 160	25 861	28 165	28 435	28 440	27 198
Actual cotisations	..	5 642	15 714	14 713	22 160	25 861	28 165	28 435	28 440	27 198
2310 On a payroll basis	0	0	0	14 713	22 160	25 861	28 165	28 435	28 440	27 198
2320 On an income tax basis	0	0	0	0	0	0	0	0	0	0
2400 Unallocable between 2100, 2200 and 2300	0	0	0	0	0	0	0	0	0	0
2410 On a payroll basis	0	0	0	..	..	..	..	..	..	..
2420 On an income tax basis	0	0	0	..	..	..	..	..	..	..
3000 Taxes on payroll and workforce	**1 189**	**3 935**	**8 254**	**14 916**	**22 874**	**26 926**	**33 595**	**34 574**	**43 522**	**43 656**
Tax on wages	0	2 413	5 208	7 583	10 272	11 440	13 127	13 165	13 533	14 537
Corporate social contributions	0	0	0	0	0	657	4 654	5 019	5 251	5 428
Apprenticeship tax	0	172	101	102	964	1 130	1 317	1 436	3 758	0
Tax benefitting the wage garantee scheme (AGS): royalties for concessions, patents, licenses, trademarks, processes, rights and similar values	0	263	379	551	736	1 759	1 435	1 479	841	798
Tax on vocational training	0	236	30	97	19	13	17	17	5 447	8 442
Tax benefitting the FNAL: ACOSS (employer contributions)	0	120	754	1 506	2 412	2 465	3 123	2 929	2 855	2 978
Tax benefitting the transports union	0	731	1 600	3 786	5 738	6 344	7 326	7 842	9 402	9 185
Payment benefitting the UNEDIC	0	0	23	24	0	0	0	0	0	0
Tax on re-employed pensioners income	0	0	0	0	0	0	0	0	0	0
Providence contribution	0	0	0	415	773	1 120	496	415	331	283
Others	0	0	159	851	100	81	49	27	26	11
Taxes benefitting the national solidarity fund for autonomy (CNSA)	0	0	0	0	1 860	1 917	2 051	1 891	2 049	1 993
Employers' contribution to the early retirement of asbestos workers regime (FCAATA)	0	0	0	0	0	0	0	0	0	0
Exceptional levy on high wages	0	0	0	0	0	0	0	354	29	1
4000 Taxes on property	**1 105**	**8 591**	**27 434**	**44 070**	**65 318**	**70 613**	**81 343**	**89 311**	**94 802**	**91 679**
4100 Recurrent taxes on immovable property	506	5 358	14 808	27 340	39 875	47 589	54 545	57 431	57 572	54 847

	1965	1980	1990	2000	2007	2010	2013	2015	2019	2020
4110 Households	198	4 454	11 493	20 186	30 584	36 480	41 818	43 861	42 235	39 231
Council tax	0	2 306	5 100	8 366	12 433	15 254	17 470	18 424	13 928	10 456
Tax on real-estate properties	0	1 034	4 040	8 460	11 983	14 403	16 539	17 557	19 936	20 309
Waste collection tax	0	534	1 219	3 103	5 117	5 699	6 552	6 567	7 027	7 155
Tax on non-developped land	0	506	979	172	851	919	955	980	998	1 001
Chamber of Agriculture tax	0	0	0	53	59	61	62	61	56	55
Street-cleaning tax	0	0	0	68	74	75	109	109	112	111
Other taxes	0	74	156	-36	67	69	131	163	178	144
4120 Others	308	904	3 315	7 154	9 291	11 109	12 727	13 570	15 337	15 616
Tax on real-estate properties	0	759	3 032	6 256	9 054	10 865	12 477	13 246	15 039	15 321
Tax on non-developped land	0	127	245	688	0	0	0	0	0	0
Chamber of Agriculture tax	0	18	39	210	237	244	250	242	222	219
Other taxes	0	0	0	0	0	0	0	82	76	76
4200 Recurrent taxes on net wealth	0	0	2 615	2 440	4 390	4 461	4 372	5 224	2 054	1 999
4210 Individual	..	..	938	2 440	4 390	4 461	4 372	5 224	2 054	1 999
4220 Corporate	..	..	1 677	0	0	0	0	0	0	0
4300 Estate, inheritance and gift taxes	145	1 010	4 124	6 907	8 910	7 738	10 456	12 317	15 252	15 039
4310 Estate and inheritance taxes	140	875	3 490	5 508	7 853	6 862	9 368	10 690	12 311	12 578
Inheritance taxes	0	861	3 453	5 428	7 794	6 806	8 433	10 540	12 208	12 527
Various receipts and tax fines	0	14	37	80	59	56	935	150	103	51
4320 Gift taxes	5	135	634	1 399	1 057	876	1 088	1 627	2 941	2 461
Donations	0	113	568	1 399	1 057	876	1 088	1 627	2 941	2 461
Various receipts and tax fines	0	0	0	0	0	0	0	0	0	0
Other taxes	0	22	66	0	0	0	0	0	0	0
4400 Taxes on financial and capital transactions	447	2 224	5 886	7 383	12 143	10 825	11 970	14 339	19 924	19 794
Debts, annuities, officies	0	30	209	279	443	279	359	335	428	322
Business assets	0	253	518	199	268	154	135	132	159	159
Tangible movable assets	0	14	18	0	0	1	0	1	0	0
Properties and real property rights	0	63	4	2	2	3	1	1	0	0
Agreements and civil acts between companies	0	95	218	4	5	8	6	7	0	0
Various receipts and tax fines	0	35	60	367	179	253	4	6	15	3
Judicial and extra-judicial documents	0	6	10	0	0	0	0	0	0	0
Land registration tax	0	781	38	68	130	140	703	770	1 034	991
Various stamps and fees	0	94	242	0	0	0	0	0	0	0
Taxes on stock exchange transactions	0	168	525	407	271	0	0	0	0	0
Tax on financial transactions	0	0	0	0	0	0	697	917	906	1 290
Additional registration taxes	0	679	4 002	5 339	10 396	9 567	9 538	11 618	16 844	16 549
Other taxes and receipts	0	5	44	718	449	420	527	552	538	480
4500 Non-recurrent taxes	8	0	0	0	0	0	0	0	0	0
4510 On net wealth	8	..	..	..	..	..	..	..	..	..
4520 Other non-recurrent taxes	0	..	..	..	..	..	..	..	..	..
4600 Other recurrent taxes on property	0	0	0	0	0	0	0	0	0	0
5000 Taxes on goods and services	**9 902**	**54 317**	**123 235**	**170 220**	**210 205**	**224 637**	**248 337**	**261 968**	**302 425**	**285 486**
5100 Taxes on production, sale, transfer, etc.	9 676	52 719	119 201	163 520	202 109	215 844	238 774	251 793	290 464	274 374
5110 General taxes	5 994	37 760	81 341	110 296	142 033	151 565	163 103	169 913	194 261	182 045
5111 Value added taxes	5 173	37 282	79 972	107 511	137 137	136 129	145 264	152 550	174 894	162 577
VAT (general budget)	0	36 895	78 902	103 054	136 927	135 578	144 490	151 680	173 953	161 537
VAT (BAPSA)	0	62	101	4 111	0	0	0	0	0	0
Other VAT	0	325	969	0	0	0	0	0	0	0
Sub-compensations of agricultural VAT	0	0	0	346	138	330	462	381	406	407
Value added taxes on subsidies	0	0	0	0	72	221	312	489	535	633
5112 Sales tax	822	0	0	0	0	0	0	0	0	0
5113 Other	0	477	1 369	2 784	4 896	15 436	17 839	17 363	19 367	19 468
Social solidarity contribution	..	477	1 369	2 784	4 896	5 090	5 671	4 390	3 899	4 107
Contributions on the value added of the corporations	..	..	..	0	0	10 346	12 168	12 973	15 191	14 986
Tax on digital services	..	..	..	0	0	0	0	0	277	375
5120 Taxes on specific goods and services	3 682	14 960	37 860	53 225	60 076	64 279	75 671	81 880	96 203	92 329

	1965	1980	1990	2000	2007	2010	2013	2015	2019	2020
5121 Excise duties	2 775	11 013	26 834	39 850	44 013	45 770	52 343	56 660	64 796	61 310
Excise tax on energy products	0	7 136	17 476	23 493	24 318	23 577	23 693	26 238	31 438	27 018
Exceptional levies on oil product corporations	0	0	0	0	0	0	0	0	0	0
Taxes on wines, ciders and meads	0	97	174	0	121	121	486	501	572	533
Taxes on alcohol	0	1 238	1 593	3 025	484	2 482	2 950	2 956	2 900	2 909
Taxes on beer and mineral water	0	58	91	20	409	538	803	931	1 114	1 048
Other taxes and receipts	0	136	38	19	2 169	100	90	110	76	61
Taxes on tobaccos and matches	0	1 188	2 989	7 965	9 659	11 083	12 227	12 318	13 682	15 416
Fines and confiscations	0	2	1	0	0	0	0	0	0	0
Gold and silver warranty	0	6	19	29	2	0	0	0	0	0
ANDA taxes	0	84	147	89	0	0	0	0	0	0
Tax on health protection and the organisation of meat markets	0	0	0	48	46	43	41	43	41	41
Tax on cereals	0	147	275	19	19	24	18	14	4	4
Fees on tobacco stores	0	0	0	0	0	0	0	0	0	0
Fees on potash salt	0	0	0	0	0	0	0	0	0	0
Tax on flour	0	0	0	38	0	0	0	0	0	0
Fees included in fuel price	0	36	32	453	485	495	499	493	558	499
National Book Fund tax	0	7	17	0	0	0	0	0	0	0
Tax on logging products	0	11	0	0	0	0	0	0	0	0
Mining fees	0	16	59	43	23	25	22	16	19	18
Tax on electricity and heating	0	426	1 340	1 061	2 990	3 717	7 253	8 703	9 955	9 434
Surtax on appetizers	0	12	17	0	0	0	0	0	0	0
Pharmaceutical taxes	0	4	559	0	0	0	0	0	0	0
Tax on beet, sugar and alcohol	0	22	400	0	0	0	0	0	0	0
Solidarity tax on oil seeds	0	8	41	0	0	0	0	0	0	0
Tax on food fats	0	32	89	99	0	0	0	0	0	0
National Literature Fund tax	0	23	0	0	0	0	0	0	0	0
Tax on water consumption	0	34	51	74	5	11	1	2	0	0
Tax on meat	0	25	36	0	19	1	1	0	0	0
Tax on pollution, distribution, collection and extraction of water	0	217	609	1 624	1 821	1 763	2 175	2 268	2 237	2 175
Sugar market fund tax	0	0	0	0	0	0	0	0	0	0
Exceptional contribution on pharmacies and laboratories	0	16	0	522	0	0	0	0	0	0
Local tax	0	5	8	241	247	325	127	126	64	95
Contribution of low voltage electric energy suppliers	0	0	0	183	322	324	374	375	378	376
ADEME tax	0	0	0	80	212	489	499	449	0	0
Dock dues	0	0	0	449	544	581	386	422	466	467
General tax on polluting activities	0	0	0	6	16	16	205	117	331	268
Tax on oil products	0	0	0	0	0	0	367	379	401	384
Other taxes	0	30	772	78	102	55	126	199	560	564
Tax benefitting the French petrol institute (IFP)	0	0	0	193	0	0	0	0	0	0
5122 Profits of fiscal monopolies	0	0	0	0	0	0	0	0	0	0
5123 Customs and import duties	471	966	1 669	1 810	2 043	2 180	2 605	2 665	2 848	2 873
Import duties (State)	0	0	0	0	0	0	0	0	0	0
Import duties (UE)	0	873	1 623	0	0	0	0	0	0	0
Dock dues	0	0	0	267	327	361	627	678	765	768
Other taxes	0	94	46	30	59	67	136	55	56	40
5124 Taxes on exports	0	75	15	0	0	0	0	0	0	0
Agricultural levies (State part)	..	0	0	..	..	..	..	..	..	..
Agricultural levies (EU part)	..	75	15	..	..	..	..	..	..	..
5125 Taxes on investment goods	0	0	0	0	0	0	0	0	0	0

	1965	1980	1990	2000	2007	2010	2013	2015	2019	2020
5126 Taxes on specific services	431	2 690	8 373	11 204	14 007	16 274	20 656	22 501	28 559	28 146
Levies on horse-race bets	0	446	545	502	719	626	434	446	421	362
Levies on gambling casinos	0	0	0	727	1 022	748	708	691	803	476
Levies on the French national lottery	0	200	702	1 305	1 982	1 800	1 941	2 118	2 593	2 107
Exceptionnal levies on banks and lending institutions	0	0	0	0	0	0	0	0	0	0
Tax on insurance policies	0	1 292	4 782	5 097	6 571	7 099	9 973	10 386	11 407	12 205
Tax on leases	0	264	633	573	29	-5	-1	0	0	0
Taxes on funerals	0	11	32	14	11	12	12	12	13	15
Stamp taxes for transportation contracts	0	9	77	10	0	0	0	0	0	0
Tax on expertise and technical checks	0	0	0	0	0	0	0	0	0	0
ANAEM tax	0	0	0	33	58	129	145	146	115	115
Tax on the use of inland waterways	0	0	0	104	157	169	192	183	176	167
Other various taxes	0	98	272	273	449	1 007	547	798	2 686	2 735
Taxes on entertainment	0	75	195	274	372	425	799	785	1 238	1 053
Insurances contributions to the guarantee funds	0	32	135	223	274	323	387	450	766	783
Tax on automobile insurance	0	0	0	55	0	0	0	0	0	0
Additional contribution on insurance contracts to the FNGCA	0	0	0	261	96	101	120	125	60	60
National fund for housing improvement, 5% levy	0	114	258	678	604	604	726	932	992	1 000
Movie-making corporations contributions to the CNC	0	52	207	397	144	766	735	695	741	616
Agricultural insurances fund tax on food	0	0	0	0	0	0	0	0	0	0
National Sports Fund tax	0	3	0	0	0	0	0	0	0	0
Annuities and pensions upgrading fund tax	0	15	0	0	0	0	0	0	0	0
Annual tax on outstanding loans	0	0	0	0	0	0	0	0	0	0
Tax on advertisement	0	0	26	52	38	156	219	232	247	173
Levies on mortgage recording officers wages	0	67	188	0	0	0	0	0	0	0
Tax on safety and security	0	0	0	220	353	459	521	574	773	261
Tax on systemic risk	0	0	0	0	0	0	899	591	29	28
CMU tax on mutual insurances	0	0	0	247	560	1 637	1 851	1 909	2 430	2 531
Major natural disasters prevention fund (FPRNM) tax	0	0	0	0	0	0	197	205	137	137
SRF Contributions collected for the EU	..	..	..	..	..	..	..	916	2 419	2 988
Other taxes	0	10	320	159	568	218	251	307	513	334
5127 Other taxes on internat. trade and transactions	0	0	0	0	0	0	0	0	0	0
5128 Other taxes	5	215	970	360	13	55	67	54	0	0
Co-responsibility tax on milk	0	48	119	0	0	0	0	0	..	..
Co-responsibility tax on cereals	0	0	520	0	0	0	0	0	..	..
European Coal and Steel Community levy	0	14	0	0	0	0	0	0	..	..
Collector of customs	0	9	24	0	0	0	0	0	..	..
Various taxes (local government)	0	0	0	0	0	0	0	0	..	..
Contributions on sugar	0	68	185	270	0	42	54	41	..	..
Sugar market fund tax	0	76	120	76	0	0	0	0	..	..
Other taxes	0	0	2	14	13	13	13	13	..	..
5130 Unallocable between 5110 and 5120	0	0	0	0	0	0	0	0	0	0
5200 Taxes on use of goods and perform activities	226	1 598	4 034	6 700	8 096	8 793	9 563	10 175	11 961	11 112
5210 Recurrent taxes	178	1 226	3 024	4 909	5 264	5 338	5 715	5 681	6 177	5 677
5211 Paid by households: motor vehicles	27	545	1 236	126	0	0	0	0	0	0
Tax differential (central and local government)	0	545	1 236	126	..	..	..	..	..	..
5212 Paid by others: motor vehicles	79	545	1 086	1 280	1 559	1 269	1 181	1 028	917	927
Tax on corporation vehicles	0	197	345	644	891	992	876	753	767	801
Tax on vehicles (central and local government)	0	348	741	636	668	277	305	275	150	126
5213 Paid in respect of other goods	72	136	702	3 503	3 705	4 069	4 534	4 653	5 260	4 750
Special tax on use of roads	0	0	0	420	526	539	573	574	640	530
Weighing tax	0	17	14	0	0	0	0	0	0	0
Various taxes (local government)	0	7	33	0	0	0	0	0	0	0
Tax on video recorders	0	0	0	0	0	0	0	0	0	0
Fee on nuclear power plants monitoring	0	8	41	0	0	0	0	0	0	0
Tax on use of slaughterhouses	0	19	13	0	0	0	0	0	0	0
Corporation contributions on medicines preparation	0	0	20	238	0	379	213	255	252	269
Tax on electric pylons	0	1	66	128	183	213	244	231	272	283
Beverage licences	0	8	22	23	0	0	0	0	0	0
Gallicisation and navigation annual right (DAFN)	0	0	0	0	0	39	37	37	38	38
Fees on radio frequencies use	0	0	0	191	280	275	262	187	270	240
Contribution to public broadcasting	..	..	..	2 099	2 255	2 472	2 866	3 012	3 147	3 048
Other taxes	0	75	493	404	461	152	339	357	641	342

	1965	1980	1990	2000	2007	2010	2013	2015	2019	2020
5220 Non-recurrent taxes	47	372	1 010	1 791	2 832	3 455	3 848	4 494	5 784	5 435
Entry into service receipt	0	75	0	0	0	0	0	0	0	0
Carbon emission allowances	..	..	..	0	0	0	48	215	828	727
Beverage taxes and licences	0	0	0	3	0	0	0	0	0	0
Fee for the right to build	0	79	53	72	0	18	18	0	0	0
Building permit tax	0	146	263	305	848	1 252	1 381	1 839	2 164	2 048
Car registration tax	0	0	0	1 373	1 939	1 917	2 042	2 086	2 299	2 091
Tax on exceeding the density legal ceiling	0	38	270	38	45	82	82	52	0	0
Additional tax on car registration	0	0	0	0	0	186	277	302	493	569
Other taxes	0	35	423	0	0	0	0	0	0	0
5300 Unallocable between 5100 and 5200	0	0	0	0	0	0	0	0	0	0
6000 Other taxes	**681**	**5 480**	**14 060**	**24 084**	**27 227**	**9 241**	**10 644**	**11 371**	**12 250**	**12 513**
6100 Paid solely by business	678	5 480	14 060	22 398	27 219	9 235	10 638	11 365	12 227	12 491
National Institute of intellectual property (INPI) tax on services	0	43	67	115	156	165	180	193	231	234
Tax on general charges	0	0	0	0	0	0	0	0	0	0
Tax on the use of fixed assets	0	5 152	13 381	19 641	22 035	0	0	0	0	0
Tax on union benefits (local government)	0	36	197	293	0	0	0	0	0	0
Various taxes (central government)	0	0	0	61	236	255	478	649	813	848
Annual tax on outstanding loans	0	110	0	0	0	0	0	0	0	0
Exceptionnal levies on insurance corporations	0	0	0	0	0	0	0	0	0	0
Fees of the chambers of commerce and industry	0	36	125	155	203	275	233	253	200	201
Payments of industrial enterprises to the benefit of the FNE	0	4	240	204	33	10	3	0	0	0
Other taxes	0	98	50	1 127	3 721	1 078	727	1 269	1 046	999
(ANDA) and (ADAR) tax	0	0	0	32	0	0	0	0	0	0
Property contributions of the corporations	..	..	..	0	0	10 346	12 168	12 973	15 191	14 986
Flat-rate tax on network corporations	0	0	0	0	0	1 223	1 206	1 297	1 408	1 444
Exit tax on insurance	0	0	0	0	0	0	0	0	0	0
Fees of the chambers of commerce and industry	0	0	0	770	835	1 103	1 323	458	655	642
Employers' contribution on stock options	0	0	0	0	0	185	380	490	567	755
Tax on railway companies profit	0	0	0	0	0	0	200	400	226	226
6200 Other	3	0	0	1 686	8	6	6	6	23	22
Other taxes	0	..	..	1 686	8	6	6	6	23	22
Sectors accounts differential	0	..	..	0	0	0	0	0	0	0
Memorandum items										
Customs duties collected on behalf of the EU	..	..	..	1 513	1 657	1 752	1 842	1 932	2 027	2 065
SRF contributions collected on behalf of the EU	..	..	..	..	..	..	..	916	2 419	2 988
Non-wastable tax credits										
Non-wastable tax credits against 1110	..	..	..	0	7 663	10 761	8 214	8 041	8 473	7 848
Tax component	..	..	..	..	..	8 234	6 755	5 669	6 245	6 365
Transfer component	..	..	..	..	..	2 527	1 459	2 372	2 228	1 483
Non-wastable tax credits against 1210	..	..	..	457	1 860	6 655	5 466	18 618	26 885	18 209
Tax component	..	..	..	..	..	1 277	3 572	10 560	10 661	5 349
Transfer component	..	..	..	..	..	5 378	1 894	8 058	16 224	12 860
Non-wastable tax credits against 3000	..	..	..	0	0	0	0	0	578	0
Tax expenditure component	..	..	..	..	..	..	..	..	578	..
Transfer component	..	..	..	..	..	..	..	..	0	..
Total tax revenue on cash basis	**25 776**	**178 576**	**433 771**	**642 156**	**825 954**	**840 905**	**960 513**	**995 462**	**1 100 141**	**1 047 573**
Total tax revenue on accrual basis	**..**	**..**	**..**	**645 528**	**831 226**	**846 318**	**966 817**	**1 002 131**	**1 098 902**	**1 058 387**
Conciliation with National Accounts										
Additional taxes included in National Accounts	..	..	..	0	0	0	0	0	0	0
Tax excluded from national accounts	..	..	..	-3 171	-5 191	-5 774	-6 661	-6 676	-7 139	-7 266
Waste collection tax	..	..	..	-3 103	-5 117	-5 699	-6 552	-6 567	-7 027	-7 155
Tax on electric pylons	..	..	..	0	0	0	0	0	0	0
Street-cleaning tax	..	..	..	-68	-74	-75	-109	-109	-112	-111
Difference in treatment of tax credits	..	..	..	0	0	9 511	10 327	16 229	17 484	11 714
Capital transfer for uncollected revenue	..	..	..	-3 372	-5 272	-5 413	-6 304	-6 669	-4 761	-10 814
Voluntary social security contributions	..	..	..	0	0	0	0	0	0	0
Miscellaneous differences	..	..	..	0	0	0	0	0	0	0
National Accounts: taxes and actual social contributions	..	..	..	638 985	820 763	844 642	964 179	1 005 015	1 104 486	1 052 021
Imputed social contributions	..	..	..	25 875	33 510	38 028	41 947	42 655	43 965	44 458
National Accounts: taxes and all social contributions	..	..	..	664 860	854 273	882 670	1 006 126	1 047 670	1 148 451	1 096 479

.. Not available

Note: Calendar year ending on December 31st.

From 1992, the data are on an accrual basis.

From 1970, figures were calculated according to the new System of National Accounts and are not, therefore, comparable to those of the previous years.

The section 2000 includes certain voluntary contributions.

Source: National accounts for France, Insee.

StatLink https://stat.link/ud1ein

Table 5.13. Germany: Details of tax revenue, 1965-2020

Million EUR

	1965	1980	1990	2000	2007	2010	2013	2015	2019	2020
Total tax revenue	**74 359**	**287 373**	**454 764**	**767 045**	**884 216**	**911 161**	**1 038 904**	**1 128 773**	**1 341 320**	**1 291 049**
Total tax revenue exclusive of taxes collected for the EU	..	..	**450 620**	**763 300**	**880 273**	**906 897**	**1 034 589**	**1 121 962**	**1 334 206**	**1 284 104**
1000 Taxes on income, profits and capital gains	**25 059**	**100 821**	**147 257**	**231 249**	**273 596**	**257 817**	**319 926**	**351 386**	**436 763**	**404 583**
1100 Of individuals	19 254	85 134	125 296	194 173	218 848	219 387	270 179	299 362	367 218	348 944
1110 On income and profits	19 254	85 134	125 296	194 173	218 848	219 387	270 179	299 362	367 218	348 944
Taxes on wages and salaries	8 558	57 039	90 801	135 733	146 365	145 202	174 512	194 116	236 355	228 377
Assessed income tax	7 567	18 813	18 672	12 225	25 341	31 346	42 586	48 902	63 781	59 447
Withholding tax on dividends	691	2 135	5 538	13 515	13 572	12 982	17 258	17 944	23 486	21 498
Supplementary tax	0	0	0	10 347	10 907	10 706	13 085	14 555	17 829	17 105
Enterprise tax	2 438	7 147	10 285	16 486	14 630	13 709	17 305	18 553	22 193	18 112
Stabilisation tax	0	0	0	0	0	0	0	0	0	0
Withholding tax on interest	0	0	0	5 867	8 033	5 442	5 433	5 292	3 574	4 405
1120 On capital gains	0	0	0	0	0	0	0	0	0	0
1200 Corporate	5 806	15 686	21 961	37 076	54 748	38 430	49 747	52 024	69 545	55 639
1210 On profits	5 806	15 686	21 961	37 076	54 748	38 430	49 747	52 024	69 545	55 639
Corporation tax	4 177	10 902	15 385	23 575	23 386	12 516	19 762	20 178	32 284	24 514
Supplementary tax	0	20	1	1 494	1 550	982	1 337	1 409	1 896	1 460
Sacrifice for Berlin	3	0	0	0	0	0	0	0	0	0
Enterprise tax	1 625	4 765	6 576	10 540	25 486	22 002	25 722	27 589	33 441	27 293
Stabilisation tax	0	0	0	0	0	0	0	0	0	0
Withholding tax on interest	0	0	0	1 467	4 326	2 930	2 926	2 848	1 924	2 372
1220 On capital gains	0	0	0	0	0	0	0	0	0	0
1300 Unallocable between 1100 and 1200	0	0	0	0	0	0	0	0	0	0
2000 Social security contributions	**19 876**	**98 659**	**170 449**	**299 440**	**320 750**	**354 320**	**392 378**	**424 841**	**508 124**	**512 122**
2100 Employees	8 723	43 833	73 580	131 610	139 927	152 843	171 657	186 305	220 204	217 235
Payments by employees total	8 723	43 833	73 580	131 610	139 927	152 843	171 657	186 305	220 204	217 235
2110 On a payroll basis	..	..	..	131 610	139 927	152 843	171 657	186 305	220 204	217 235
2120 On an income tax basis	..	..	..	0	0	0	0	0	0	0
2200 Employers	10 693	52 985	86 659	147 410	151 094	165 476	181 782	196 679	238 358	244 692
Payments by employers total	10 693	52 985	86 659	147 410	151 094	165 476	181 782	196 679	238 358	244 692
2210 On a payroll basis	..	..	..	147 410	151 094	165 476	181 782	196 679	238 358	244 692
2220 On an income tax basis	..	..	..	0	0	0	0	0	0	0
2300 Self-employed or non-employed	460	1 841	10 210	20 420	29 729	36 001	38 939	41 857	49 562	50 195
Payments total	460	1 841	10 210	20 420	29 729	36 001	38 939	41 857	49 562	50 195
2310 On a payroll basis	..	..	..	20 420	29 729	36 001	38 939	41 857	49 562	50 195
2320 On an income tax basis	..	..	..	0	0	0	0	0	0	0
2400 Unallocable between 2100, 2200 and 2300	0	0	0	0	0	0	0	0	0	0
2410 On a payroll basis	..	..	..	..	..	..	..	..	..	..
2420 On an income tax basis	..	..	..	..	..	..	..	..	..	..
3000 Taxes on payroll and workforce	**477**	**445**	**0**	**0**	**0**	**0**	**0**	**0**	**0**	**0**
Payroll tax	477	445	..	..	..	..	..	..	..	..
4000 Taxes on property	**4 313**	**9 414**	**15 321**	**17 505**	**21 873**	**21 012**	**26 104**	**32 440**	**38 680**	**42 427**
4100 Recurrent taxes on immovable property	1 079	2 968	4 461	8 849	10 713	11 315	12 377	13 215	14 439	14 675
4110 Households	644	1 187	1 784	3 540	4 285	4 526	4 951	5 286	5 776	5 870
4120 Others	435	1 780	2 676	5 309	6 428	6 789	7 426	7 929	8 663	8 805
4200 Recurrent taxes on net wealth	2 530	4 362	6 213	433	5	2	700	1 686	1 466	1 517
4210 Individual	973	977	1 425	191	2	1	0	-1	0	0
General wealth tax	471	954	1 425	191	2	1	..	-1	..	..
Equalization of war burden	502	23	0	0	0	0	..	0	..	..
4220 Corporate	1 557	3 385	4 788	242	3	1	700	1 687	1 466	1 517
General wealth tax	490	1 431	1 813	242	3	1	0	-1	0	0
Equalization of war burden	350	15	0	0	0	0	0	0	0	0
Enterprise tax	717	1 939	2 975	0	0	0	0	0	0	0
Bank levy	0	0	0	0	0	0	520	0	14	21
Contribution to Deposit Protection Fund	0	0	0	0	0	0	180	1 688	1 452	1 496
4300 Estate, inheritance and gift taxes	162	520	1 545	2 982	4 203	4 405	4 633	6 290	6 986	8 657
4310 Estate and inheritance taxes	134	416	1 359	2 624	3 699	3 876	4 077	5 535	6 148	7 618
4320 Gift taxes	28	104	186	358	504	529	556	755	838	1 039
4400 Taxes on financial and capital transactions	542	1 564	3 103	5 241	6 952	5 290	8 394	11 249	15 789	17 578
Real property transfer tax	150	521	1 999	5 081	6 952	5 290	8 394	11 249	15 789	17 578
Additional real property transfer	198	680	148	160	0	0	0	0	0	0
Capital transfer tax	111	200	807	0	0	0	0	0	0	0
Bill of exchange tax	83	163	149	0	0	0	0	0	0	0
4500 Non-recurrent taxes	0	0	0	0	0	0	0	0	0	0
4510 On net wealth	..	..	..	..	..	..	..	..	..	..
4520 Other non-recurrent taxes	..	..	..	..	..	..	..	..	..	..
4600 Other recurrent taxes on property	0	0	0	0	0	0	0	0	0	0
5000 Taxes on goods and services	**24 462**	**77 863**	**121 577**	**218 686**	**267 901**	**277 912**	**300 368**	**319 890**	**357 434**	**331 709**

	1965	1980	1990	2000	2007	2010	2013	2015	2019	2020
5100 Taxes on production, sale, transfer, etc.	23 079	74 406	117 209	211 444	251 558	261 160	281 997	301 101	337 086	310 695
5110 General taxes	12 235	47 779	75 459	140 871	170 387	180 533	197 326	211 936	244 433	221 882
5111 Value added taxes	0	47 779	75 459	140 871	170 387	180 533	197 326	211 936	244 433	221 882
5112 Sales tax	0	0	0	0	0	0	0	0	0	0
5113 Other	12 235	0	0	0	0	0	0	0	0	0
Turnover tax old	11 028	..	..	..	..	..	..	..	..	..
Old turnover tax on import	1 208	..	..	..	..	..	..	..	..	..
5120 Taxes on specific goods and services	10 844	26 627	41 750	70 573	80 819	80 287	84 383	88 873	92 365	88 525
5121 Excise duties	8 213	20 566	31 158	57 224	63 780	63 438	64 623	65 332	66 187	63 192
Duty on mineral oils	3 798	10 917	17 701	37 826	38 877	39 601	39 260	39 605	40 837	37 703
Duty on power	0	0	0	3 356	6 439	6 167	6 987	6 560	6 696	6 569
Duty on tobacco	2 402	5 771	8 898	11 443	14 108	13 453	14 131	14 963	14 469	14 789
Duty on alcohol	771	1 986	2 162	2 151	2 169	2 049	2 100	2 075	2 116	2 098
Duty on beer	501	645	693	843	750	708	675	679	604	572
Duty on coffee	488	756	986	1 087	985	998	1 030	1 034	1 069	1 070
Duty on sugar	59	72	79	0	0	0	0	0	0	0
Duty on tea	16	32	31	0	0	0	0	0	0	0
Duty on salt	20	20	23	0	0	0	0	0	0	0
Duty on electric lamps	34	63	83	0	0	0	0	0	0	0
Duty on playing cards	2	4	0	0	0	0	0	0	0	0
Duty on beverages	46	22	8	6	1	0	0	0	0	0
Duty on acetic acid	3	2	0	0	0	0	0	0	0	0
Duty on champagne	69	274	494	512	451	462	440	416	396	391
Duty on matches	5	2	0	0	0	0	0	0	0	0
Duty on ice cream	1	0	0	0	0	0	0	0	0	0
5122 Profits of fiscal monopolies	8	2	0	0	0	0	0	0	0	0
5123 Customs and import duties	1 658	3 125	3 847	3 394	3 972	4 234	4 251	5 195	5 117	4 715
Monetary compensation accounts	0	368	1	0	0	0	0	0	0	0
Customs (mainly EU)	1 294	2 353	3 662	3 394	3 972	4 234	4 251	5 195	5 117	4 715
Agricultural levies EU	364	404	184	0	0	0	0	0	0	0
5124 Taxes on exports	0	0	0	0	0	0	0	0	0	0
5125 Taxes on investment goods	0	0	0	0	0	0	0	0	0	0
5126 Taxes on specific services	942	2 689	6 443	9 599	13 095	12 583	15 443	18 306	21 059	20 617
Duty transport goods on residents	0	0	0	0	0	0	0	0	0	0
Transport tax	452	0	0	0	0	0	0	0	0	0
Insurance tax	198	910	2 266	7 243	10 410	10 261	11 588	12 445	14 179	14 551
Fire insurance tax	33	124	200	288	319	326	392	413	482	510
Entertainment tax	55	44	140	267	210	376	708	881	997	746
Taxes on betting and gambling	204	655	1 046	1 801	1 702	1 412	1 635	1 711	1 974	2 043
Tax on electricity bills	0	956	2 792	0	0	0	0	0	0	0
Aviation tax	0	0	0	0	0	0	955	1 027	1 168	349
Gaming casinos levy	0	0	0	0	454	208	165	251	262	188
SRF Contributions	..	..	..	..	..	..	..	1 578	1 997	2 230
5127 Other taxes on internat. trade and transactions	0	0	4	5	1	2	2	2	2	1
5128 Other taxes	24	244	298	351	-29	30	64	38	0	0
Levies CECA	24	56	36	0	0	0	0	0	..	..
Cotisation sugar EU	0	112	224	351	-29	30	64	38	..	..
Levy on milk	0	75	38	0	0	0	0	0	..	..
5130 Unallocable between 5110 and 5120	0	0	0	0	352	340	288	292	288	288
Contributions to the German National Petroleum Stockpiling Agency	..	..	..	..	352	340	288	292	288	288
5200 Taxes on use of goods and perform activities	1 383	3 457	4 368	7 242	16 343	16 752	18 371	18 789	20 348	21 014
5210 Recurrent taxes	1 369	3 454	4 368	7 239	16 343	16 189	17 699	18 034	17 597	17 931
5211 Paid by households: motor vehicles	614	1 892	2 950	5 177	6 823	6 447	6 393	6 992	7 338	7 439
5212 Paid by others: motor vehicles	728	1 475	1 300	1 838	2 075	2 041	2 097	1 812	2 034	2 089
5213 Paid in respect of other goods	27	87	118	224	7 445	7 701	9 209	9 230	8 225	8 403
Dog taxes	24	75	101	198	240	258	299	322	370	380
Hunting and fishing taxes	4	13	17	26	23	19	10	10	8	8
Nuclear fuel tax	0	0	0	0	0	0	1 285	1 018	0	0
Licence fee (private households)	0	0	0	0	6 464	6 681	6 914	7 155	7 125	7 278
Licence fee (companies)	0	0	0	0	718	743	701	725	722	737
5220 Non-recurrent taxes	14	3	1	3	0	563	672	755	2 751	3 083
Non-recurrent taxes	..	..	0	0	..	0	0	0	0	0
CO2 emission certificates	..	..	0	0	..	563	672	755	2 751	3 083
5300 Unallocable between 5100 and 5200	0	0	0	0	0	0	0	0	0	0
6000 Other taxes	**172**	**172**	**160**	**165**	**96**	**100**	**128**	**216**	**319**	**208**
6100 Paid solely by business	0	0	0	0	0	0	0	0	0	0
6200 Other	172	172	160	165	96	100	128	216	319	208

	1965	1980	1990	2000	2007	2010	2013	2015	2019	2020
Memorandum items										
Customs duties collected on behalf of the EU	..	..	3 662	3 394	3 972	4 234	4 251	5 195	5 117	4 715
SRF contributions collected on behalf of the EU	..	..	..	..	..	..	..	1 578	1 997	2 230
Taxes and compulsory social security contributions paid by EU civil servants	..	..	..	..	..	..	39	43	53	56
Taxes paid by EU civil servants: income taxes	..	..	..	..	..	..	20	22	27	29
Taxes paid by EU civil servants: compulsory social security contributions	..	..	..	..	..	..	19	21	26	27
Non-wastable tax credits										
Non-wastable tax credits against 1110	..	..	..	38 356	43 602	45 475	41 890	41 951	45 153	51 861
Tax expenditure component	..	..	..	..	29 499	28 268	26 275	26 817	29 273	31 527
Transfer component	..	..	..	..	14 104	17 207	15 616	15 134	15 880	20 334
Non-wastable tax credits against 1210	..	..	..	962	804	802	426	200	44	-2
Tax expenditure component	..	..	..	..	348	326	172	120	40	0
Transfer component	..	..	..	..	456	474	254	80	6	-2
Total tax revenue on cash basis	**74 359**	**287 373**	**454 764**	**767 045**	**881 517**	**911 154**	**1 037 607**	**1 126 986**	**1 338 427**	**1 289 798**
Total tax revenue on accrual basis	**..**	**..**	**..**	**..**	**884 216**	**911 161**	**1 038 904**	**1 128 773**	**1 341 320**	**1 291 049**
Conciliation with National Accounts										
Additional taxes included in National Accounts	..	..	..	..	2 406	2 067	2 411	2 856	2 450	2 419
Several duties, administrative fees and other revenues	..	..	..	..	2 406	2 067	2 411	2 856	2 450	2 419
Taxes excluded from National Accounts	..	..	..	..	0	0	0	0	..	..
Difference in treatment of tax credits	..	..	..	..	12 623	9 230	6 358	5 619	5 720	7 311
Capital transfer for uncollected revenue	..	..	..	..	0	0	0	0	..	..
Voluntary social security contributions	..	..	..	..	21 409	5 102	5 352	6 068	7 262	7 378
Miscellaneous differences	..	..	..	..	33 134	34 234	34 081	35 455	42 922	47 419
National Accounts: Taxes and actual social contributions	..	..	..	..	953 788	961 794	1 087 106	1 178 771	1 399 674	1 355 576
Imputed social contributions	..	..	..	..	29 509	32 687	33 506	34 542	40 053	41 414
National Accounts: Taxes and all social contributions	..	..	..	..	983 297	994 481	1 120 612	1 213 313	1 439 727	1 396 990

.. Not available
Note: Year ending 31st December.
From 2002 data are on accrual basis.
The tax revenues for Germany refer to the old Länder until 1990 and to all Germany beginning in 1991.
Heading 1000: In the years up to 2000, the revenues shown take into account the whole amount of non-wastable tax credits including that part paid out by the tax authorities which should, under the OECD criteria, be treated as expenditure. From 2001, the data necessary to make the adjustment have become available and the revenue figures comply with the OECD criteria from that year.
Heading for non-wastable tax credits against 1110 comprise child tax credits (paid out of wage tax revenue), tax credits for owner occupied housing (paid out of assessed income tax revenue), retirement allowance ("Riester allowance", paid out of wage tax revenue), investment tax credits for unincorporated businesses (for investment in former East Germany; paid out of assessed income tax revenue), research allowance for unincorporated businesses (paid out of assessed income tax revenue) and employee savings allowance.
Heading for non-wastable tax credits against 1210 are investment tax credits for incorporated businesses (for investment in former East Germany; paid out of corporate income tax revenue) and research allowance for incorporated businesses (paid out of corporate income tax revenue).
Source: *Finanzbericht*, Bonn; Tax Statistics. Unpublished estimates by the Ministry of Finance.

StatLink https://stat.link/3swnhb

Table 5.14. Greece: Details of tax revenue, 1965-2020

Million EUR

	1965	1980	1990	2000	2007	2010	2013	2015	2019	2020
Total tax revenue	**116**	**1 475**	**11 472**	**47 211**	**73 990**	**72 414**	**64 560**	**64 510**	**72 387**	**64 248**
Total tax revenue exclusive of taxes collected for the EU	**..**	**..**	**11 361**	**46 990**	**73 683**	**72 134**	**64 410**	**64 235**	**72 004**	**63 906**
1000 Taxes on income, profits and capital gains	**11**	**286**	**2 283**	**12 662**	**17 176**	**15 953**	**14 015**	**14 586**	**15 642**	**13 111**
1100 Of individuals	8	220	1 619	6 127	10 554	9 015	10 780	10 155	11 001	10 447
1110 On income and profits	8	220	1 619	6 102	10 500	8 948	10 698	10 047	10 855	10 359
Personal income tax	..	..	1 414	..	..	..	..	..	..	..
Receipts from previous years	..	..	62	..	..	..	..	..	..	..
Agricultural social security fund	..	..	143	..	..	..	..	..	..	..
1120 On capital gains	0	0	0	25	54	67	82	108	146	88
1200 Corporate	2	56	631	5 625	5 304	5 717	2 071	3 800	4 071	1 999
1210 On profits	2	56	631	5 625	5 304	5 717	2 071	3 800	4 071	1 999
Corporation income tax	2	39	553	..	..	..	..	..	..	..
Receipts from previous years	0	8	33	..	..	..	..	..	..	..
Agricultural social security fund	0	9	46	..	..	..	..	..	..	..
1220 On capital gains	0	0	0	0	0	0	0	0	0	0
1300 Unallocable between 1100 and 1200	1	10	32	910	1 318	1 221	1 164	631	570	665
Extraordinary taxes	0	10	32	..	..	..	..	..	..	..
Other taxes on income and profits	1	0	0	..	..	..	..	..	..	..
2000 Social security contributions	**37**	**485**	**3 466**	**14 284**	**24 940**	**24 748**	**19 354**	**18 807**	**22 260**	**21 352**
2100 Employees	15	214	1 735	7 629	13 417	13 292	10 881	11 095	12 063	11 622
2110 On a payroll basis	..	..	..	..	..	..	..	..	..	..
2120 On an income tax basis	..	..	..	..	..	..	..	..	..	..
2200 Employers	14	213	1 728	6 655	11 523	11 456	8 473	7 712	10 197	9 730
2210 On a payroll basis	..	..	..	..	..	..	..	..	..	..
2220 On an income tax basis	..	..	..	..	..	..	..	..	..	..
2300 Self-employed or non-employed	0	0	3	0	0	0	0	0	0	0
2310 On a payroll basis	..	..	..	..	..	..	..	..	..	..
2320 On an income tax basis	..	..	..	..	..	..	..	..	..	..
2400 Unallocable between 2100, 2200 and 2300	7	58	0	0	0	0	0	0	0	0
2410 On a payroll basis	..	..	..	..	..	..	..	..	..	..
2420 On an income tax basis	..	..	..	..	..	..	..	..	..	..
3000 Taxes on payroll and workforce	**1**	**27**	**79**	**0**	**0**	**0**	**0**	**0**	**0**	**0**
4000 Taxes on property	**11**	**68**	**532**	**3 631**	**4 908**	**3 741**	**5 698**	**5 418**	**5 602**	**5 038**
4100 Recurrent taxes on immovable property	0	4	22	372	709	553	2 619	3 592	3 268	3 064
4110 Households	0	3	22	..	..	..	..	..	..	..
4120 Others	0	1	0	..	..	..	..	..	..	..
Taxes on immovable property	0	0	..	..	..	..	..	..	..	..
4200 Recurrent taxes on net wealth	0	0	0	714	1 208	1 272	1 084	1 083	1 193	1 161
4210 Individual	..	..	..	..	..	..	..	..	..	..
4220 Corporate	..	..	..	..	..	..	..	..	..	..
4300 Estate, inheritance and gift taxes	1	18	141	372	208	165	99	134	244	169
4310 Estate and inheritance taxes	1	13	85	..	..	..	..	..	..	..
4320 Gift taxes	0	4	55	..	..	..	..	..	..	..
4400 Taxes on financial and capital transactions	10	44	368	2 035	2 556	1 146	615	547	869	630
Stamp and transaction taxes	10	41	368	2 035	2 556	1 146	615	547	869	630
Receipts from previous years	0	3	0	0	0	0	0	0	0	0
4500 Non-recurrent taxes	0	2	1	27	0	1	0	0	0	0
4510 On net wealth	0	0	0	..	..	..	..	..	..	..
4520 Other non-recurrent taxes	0	2	1	..	..	..	..	..	..	..
4600 Other recurrent taxes on property	0	0	0	111	227	604	1 281	62	28	14
5000 Taxes on goods and services	**57**	**608**	**5 109**	**16 634**	**26 966**	**27 972**	**25 493**	**25 699**	**28 883**	**24 747**
5100 Taxes on production, sale, transfer, etc.	51	564	4 881	14 797	24 541	25 505	21 536	21 480	24 892	21 139
5110 General taxes	12	194	3 040	9 234	17 020	16 504	13 100	13 077	15 474	13 007
5111 Value added taxes	0	0	2 821	8 927	16 511	15 958	12 593	12 885	15 390	12 925
5112 Sales tax	9	185	123	0	0	0	0	0	0	0
5113 Other	2	9	96	307	509	546	507	192	84	82
Other taxes on goods and services	1	9	34	307	509	546	507	192	84	82
Receipts from previous years	1	0	62	0	0	0	0	0	0	0
5120 Taxes on specific goods and services	39	370	1 789	5 526	7 407	8 922	8 327	8 302	9 373	8 097
5121 Excise duties	20	165	1 372	4 069	5 876	7 567	6 997	6 929	7 215	6 349
Duty on tobacco products	8	45	357	1 769	2 657	2 712	2 506	2 365	2 207	2 081
Duty on alcohol and spirits	1	7	50	262	334	501	417	393	504	375
Duty on mineral oil	7	75	637	2 016	2 878	4 242	3 894	3 971	4 182	3 607
Duty on sugar	3	6	0	0	0	0	0	0	0	0
Duty on coton and other products	0	30	328	22	7	112	180	200	322	286
5122 Profits of fiscal monopolies	2	6	0	0	0	0	0	0	0	0

	1965	1980	1990	2000	2007	2010	2013	2015	2019	2020
5123 Customs and import duties	12	94	112	220	314	279	153	181	299	255
Import duties	11	90	111	220	314	279	153	181	299	255
Agricultural social security fund	1	5	1	0	0	0	0	0	0	0
5124 Taxes on exports	0	1	1	0	0	0	0	0	0	0
5125 Taxes on investment goods	0	0	0	0	0	0	0	0	0	0
5126 Taxes on specific services	2	47	293	1 237	1 217	1 076	1 177	1 192	1 859	1 493
5127 Other taxes on internat. trade and transactions	0	0	0	0	0	0	0	0	0	0
5128 Other taxes	4	58	10	0	0	0	0	0	0	0
Agricultural social security fund	2	..	0	..	..	..	..	..	..	..
Other taxes	2	..	0	..	..	..	..	..	..	..
5130 Unallocable between 5110 and 5120	0	0	52	37	114	79	109	101	45	35
5200 Taxes on use of goods and perform activities	6	44	228	1 320	2 169	1 682	2 954	3 217	3 258	2 945
5210 Recurrent taxes	5	24	219	1 320	2 169	1 682	2 954	3 217	3 258	2 945
Motor vehicle tax	5	0	0	0	0	0	0	0	0	0
5211 Paid by households: motor vehicles	..	23	210	281	598	825	781	780	819	789
5212 Paid by others: motor vehicles	..	0	8	735	1 182	272	120	207	301	240
5213 Paid in respect of other goods	0	1	1	304	389	585	2 053	2 230	2 138	1 916
Taxes on boats/ships	0	0	1	..	..	..	..	..	..	..
5220 Non-recurrent taxes	1	20	9	0	0	0	0	0	0	0
Exceptional tax on construction of buildings	0	..	9	..	..	..	..	..	..	..
Building permits	0	..	0	..	..	..	..	..	..	..
5300 Unallocable between 5100 and 5200	0	0	0	517	256	785	1 003	1 002	733	663
6000 Other taxes	**0**	**1**	**3**	**0**	**0**	**0**	**0**	**0**	**0**	**0**
6100 Paid solely by business	..	0	0	..	..	..	..	..	..	..
6200 Other	..	1	3	..	..	..	..	..	..	..
Memorandum items										
Customs duties collected on behalf of the EU	..	..	100	210	307	278	148	181	299	255
SRF contributions collected on behalf of the EU	..	..	..	..	..	..	..	92	84	87
Total tax revenue on cash basis	**116**	**1 475**	**11 472**	**45 979**	**72 429**	**73 083**	**62 632**	**63 210**	**71 533**	**62 166**
Total tax revenue on accrual basis	**..**	**..**	**..**	**47 211**	**73 990**	**72 414**	**64 560**	**64 510**	**72 387**	**64 248**
Conciliation with National Accounts										
Additional taxes included in National Accounts	..	..	..	0	0	0	0	0	0	0
Taxes excluded from National Accounts	..	..	..	0	0	0	0	0	0	0
Difference in treatment of tax credits	..	..	..	0	0	0	0	0	0	0
Capital transfer for uncollected revenue	..	..	..	0	0	0	0	0	0	0
Tax (Employer's actual social contributions)	..	..	..	..	..	..	..	..	..	..
Tax (Employee's actual social contributions)	..	..	..	..	..	..	..	..	..	..
Voluntary social security contributions	..	..	..	0	0	0	0	0	0	0
Miscellaneous differences	..	..	..	0	0	0	0	0	0	0
National Accounts: Taxes and actual social contributions	..	..	..	47 211	73 990	72 414	64 560	64 510	72 387	64 248
Imputed social contributions	..	..	..	2 055	3 952	4 952	5 101	5 615	4 394	4 086
National Accounts: Taxes and all social contributions	..	..	..	49 266	77 942	77 366	69 661	70 125	76 781	68 334

.. Not available

Note: Year ending 31st December.

From 1998 data are on accrual basis.

Source: Ministry of Finance, General accounting Office, Directorate of General Government Budget in collaboration with the National Statistical Authority (ELSTAT).

StatLink https://stat.link/vbogr0

Table 5.15. Hungary: Details of tax revenue, 1965-2020

Million HUF

	1965	1980	1990	2000	2007	2010	2013	2015	2019	2020
Total tax revenue	..	..	..	**5 132 570**	**10 098 955**	**10 121 687**	**11 668 441**	**13 519 622**	**17 308 702**	**17 425 586**
Total tax revenue exclusive of taxes collected for the EU	..	..	..	**5 132 570**	**10 055 315**	**10 096 033**	**11 641 223**	**13 479 897**	**17 244 422**	**17 362 091**
1000 Taxes on income, profits and capital gains	..	..	..	**1 247 420**	**2 539 389**	**2 093 830**	**2 009 010**	**2 425 958**	**3 045 893**	**3 165 880**
1100 Of individuals	..	..	..	954 698	1 838 563	1 764 082	1 604 686	1 824 671	2 457 567	2 543 593
1110 On income and profits	..	..	..	954 698	1 838 563	1 764 082	1 604 686	1 824 671	2 457 567	2 543 593
1120 On capital gains	..	..	..	0	0	0	0	0	0	0
1200 Corporate	..	..	..	292 722	700 826	329 748	404 324	601 287	588 326	622 287
Corporate income tax	..	..	..	292 722	510 781	323 370	322 467	539 777	534 518	549 822
Research and development fund levy	..	..	..	0	0	0	0	0	0	0
Financial institutions' special tax	..	..	..	0	10 890	21 618	27 686	19 902	8 253	8 842
Separate tax for companies	..	..	..	0	178 598	-32 390	0	0	0	0
Medicine tax	..	..	..	0	558	163	111	0	0	0
Energy corporations' special tax	..	..	..	0	0	16 987	54 060	41 608	45 555	63 623
1210 On profits	..	..	..	..	..	..	..	..	..	..
1220 On capital gains	..	..	..	..	..	..	..	..	..	..
1300 Unallocable between 1100 and 1200	..	..	..	0	0	0	0	0	0	0
Interest withholding	..	..	..	..	..	..	..	..	..	..
2000 Social security contributions	..	..	..	**1 506 755**	**3 402 194**	**3 179 509**	**3 899 154**	**4 433 464**	**5 545 481**	**5 364 764**
2100 Employees	..	..	..	275 323	941 682	1 112 583	1 592 995	1 770 923	2 771 550	2 813 766
Pensions	..	..	..	150 585	336 855	537 556	875 371	969 908	1 481 874	1 539 523
Health	..	..	..	81 874	513 633	467 208	591 224	656 147	1 003 683	1 046 999
Unemployment	..	..	..	42 864	91 194	107 819	126 400	144 868	285 993	227 244
2110 On a payroll basis	..	..	..	..	..	..	..	..	..	..
2120 On an income tax basis	..	..	..	..	..	..	..	..	..	..
2200 Employers	..	..	..	1 213 190	2 402 941	2 043 771	2 280 505	2 637 330	2 745 966	2 521 692
Pensions	..	..	..	734 456	1 508 490	1 800 864	2 254 959	2 235 536	1 961 423	1 781 794
Health	..	..	..	385 019	693 705	169 202	25 546	398 618	783 108	738 506
Unemployment	..	..	..	93 715	200 746	73 705	0	3 176	1 435	1 392
2210 On a payroll basis	..	..	..	..	..	..	..	..	..	..
2220 On an income tax basis	..	..	..	..	..	..	..	..	..	..
2300 Self-employed or non-employed	..	..	..	873	2 534	0	0	0	0	0
Pensions: of which	..	..	..	0	0	..	..	..	..	..
Self-employed	..	..	..	0	0	..	..	..	..	..
Unemployed	..	..	..	0	0	..	..	..	..	..
Retired	..	..	..	0	0	..	..	..	..	..
Other	..	..	..	0	0	..	..	..	..	..
Health: of which	..	..	..	873	2 534	..	..	..	..	..
Self-employed	..	..	..	873	2 534	..	..	..	..	..
Unemployed	..	..	..	0	0	..	..	..	..	..
Retired	..	..	..	0	0	..	..	..	..	..
Other	..	..	..	0	0	..	..	..	..	..
2310 On a payroll basis	..	..	..	..	..	..	..	..	..	..
2320 On an income tax basis	..	..	..	..	..	..	..	..	..	..
2400 Unallocable between 2100, 2200 and 2300	..	..	..	17 368	55 037	23 155	25 654	25 211	27 965	29 306
2410 On a payroll basis	..	..	..	..	..	..	..	..	..	..
2420 On an income tax basis	..	..	..	..	..	..	..	..	..	..
3000 Taxes on payroll and workforce	..	..	..	**183 430**	**82 068**	**113 689**	**206 426**	**241 750**	**494 906**	**501 324**
Rehabilitation contribution	..	..	..	2 184	13 559	56 004	64 400	67 460	102 990	107 943
Training levy	..	..	..	13 186	36 612	47 083	89 348	96 427	145 280	140 513
Wage guarantee contribution	..	..	..	0	0	0	0	0	0	0
Communal tax on enterprises	..	..	..	1 192	1 261	1 170	2	0	0	0
Health contribution	..	..	..	166 869	20 427	0	0	0	0	0
Medicine tax	..	..	..	0	10 209	9 431	9 547	10 283	10 179	9 543
Tax on home-workers	..	..	..	0	0	1	23	29	24	20
Lump sum tax for small taxpayers	..	..	..	0	0	0	31 241	55 409	161 207	158 736
Small business tax	..	..	..	0	0	0	11 865	12 142	75 226	84 569
4000 Taxes on property	..	..	..	**89 024**	**202 711**	**312 059**	**388 824**	**437 329**	**446 471**	**507 379**
4100 Recurrent taxes on immovable property	..	..	..	30 810	72 071	92 525	190 249	200 906	221 441	224 590
Land tax	..	..	..	0	0	0	0	0	0	0
Building tax	..	..	..	22 262	54 556	71 025	102 719	111 963	127 594	130 529
Development land tax	..	..	..	3 099	6 900	9 861	19 395	19 102	24 095	26 168
Communal tax on recreational howes	..	..	..	893	1 412	1 515	21	26	0	0
Communal tax on households	..	..	..	4 557	9 069	10 124	13 175	13 451	14 566	14 770
Luxury tax	..	..	..	0	134	0	0	0	0	0
Public utility tax	..	..	..	0	0	0	54 939	55 906	54 509	52 502
Community tax	..	..	..	0	0	0	0	458	677	621
4110 Households	..	..	..	..	..	..	..	..	..	..
4120 Others	..	..	..	..	..	..	..	..	..	..

	1965	1980	1990	2000	2007	2010	2013	2015	2019	2020
4200 Recurrent taxes on net wealth	..	..	..	0	0	135 652	128 560	135 661	44 894	108 104
Surtax payable by financial institutions	..	..	..	..	..	135 652	128 560	135 661	44 894	108 104
4210 Individual	..	..	..	..	..	..	..	..	..	..
4220 Corporate	..	..	..	..	..	..	..	..	..	..
4300 Estate, inheritance and gift taxes	..	..	..	5 460	13 175	6 264	5 307	7 373	11 428	9 493
4310 Estate and inheritance taxes	..	..	..	4 020	10 775	4 243	4 097	6 230	9 758	8 026
Inheritance tax-local	..	..	..	2 010	4 658	1 858	0	0	0	0
Inheritance tax-central	..	..	..	2 010	6 117	2 385	4 097	6 230	9 758	8 026
4320 Gift taxes	..	..	..	1 440	2 400	2 021	1 210	1 143	1 670	1 467
Gift tax-local	..	..	..	720	1 038	885	0	0	0	0
Gift tax-central	..	..	..	720	1 363	1 136	1 210	1 143	1 670	1 467
4400 Taxes on financial and capital transactions	..	..	..	52 754	117 465	77 618	64 708	93 389	168 708	165 192
Property transfer tax-local	..	..	..	26 349	50 783	33 990	0	0	0	0
Property transfer tax-central	..	..	..	26 405	66 682	43 628	64 708	93 389	168 708	165 192
4500 Non-recurrent taxes	..	..	..	0	0	0	0	0	0	0
4510 On net wealth	..	..	..	..	..	..	..	..	..	..
4520 Other non-recurrent taxes	..	..	..	..	..	..	..	..	..	..
4600 Other recurrent taxes on property	..	..	..	0	0	0	0	0	0	0
5000 Taxes on goods and services	**..**	**..**	**..**	**2 081 439**	**3 832 361**	**4 383 865**	**5 127 520**	**5 936 435**	**7 742 057**	**7 863 946**
5100 Taxes on production, sale, transfer, etc.	..	..	..	2 052 712	3 751 218	4 272 312	5 002 824	5 798 298	7 524 731	7 645 017
5110 General taxes	..	..	..	1 340 572	2 622 027	3 010 781	3 414 342	4 099 741	5 527 475	5 632 941
5111 Value added taxes	..	..	..	1 153 750	2 013 271	2 325 608	2 693 555	3 309 540	4 526 757	4 717 048
5112 Sales tax	..	..	..	0	0	37 795	47 927	50 635	90 743	96 406
Public health product tax	..	..	..	..	..	0	19 090	29 882	54 912	57 685
Hydrocarbons stockholding fee	..	..	..	..	..	37 795	28 837	20 753	35 831	38 721
5113 Other	..	..	..	186 823	608 756	647 378	672 860	739 566	909 975	819 487
Local tax on company sales	..	..	..	186 823	427 134	443 093	500 868	584 380	788 308	729 000
Simplified business tax	..	..	..	0	152 812	181 880	110 021	89 406	43 364	1 690
Research and development contribution	..	..	..	0	28 810	22 405	61 971	65 780	78 303	88 797
5120 Taxes on specific goods and services	..	..	..	712 140	1 129 192	1 261 531	1 588 482	1 698 557	1 997 256	2 012 076
5121 Excise duties	..	..	..	533 502	969 730	929 881	992 269	1 119 189	1 303 858	1 318 427
Road fund petrol tax	..	..	..	0	0	0	0	0	0	0
Alcohol production duty	..	..	..	3 848	5 621	3 021	196	8 007	7 640	6 535
Water fund tax	..	..	..	6 017	13 171	14 444	13 164	12 305	12 513	12 632
Forestry fund tax	..	..	..	2 858	3 353	284	0	0	0	0
Environment petrol tax	..	..	..	14 837	19 447	17 274	46 711	65 534	80 511	74 825
Budget excises (central budget)	..	..	..	505 942	916 869	877 778	915 546	1 015 555	1 184 136	1 207 253
Coffee	..	..	..	3 200	0	0	0	0	0	0
Alcohol	..	..	..	53 500	88 600	83 078	85 487	87 369	90 126	90 640
Tobacco	..	..	..	107 000	252 400	251 778	312 509	321 922	369 155	409 123
Petrol	..	..	..	156 000	218 200	216 728	189 755	206 220	238 390	227 025
Diesel	..	..	..	157 000	256 600	293 588	308 736	375 026	459 013	459 231
Other oil	..	..	..	6 000	2 200	2 567	3 451	3 608	2 364	1 711
Other budget excises	..	..	..	30 343	93 442	30 039	15 608	21 410	25 088	19 523
Energy tax	..	..	..	0	11 269	17 080	16 652	17 788	19 058	17 182
5122 Profits of fiscal monopolies	..	..	..	0	0	0	0	0	0	0
5123 Customs and import duties	..	..	..	137 730	37 174	33 446	35 307	52 395	80 315	79 357
Customs duties	..	..	..	137 730	37 174	33 446	35 307	52 395	80 315	79 357
5124 Taxes on exports	..	..	..	0	0	0	0	0	0	0
5125 Taxes on investment goods	..	..	..	0	0	0	0	0	0	0

	1965	1980	1990	2000	2007	2010	2013	2015	2019	2020
5126 Taxes on specific services	..	..	..	40 908	106 629	297 554	507 201	465 479	587 967	590 136
Gambling tax	..	..	..	27 935	71 804	62 718	41 316	44 972	39 656	48 956
Tourism tax	..	..	..	4 379	0	0	0	0	0	0
Communal tourism tax	..	..	..	2 943	4 935	5 798	8 411	10 475	16 249	3 953
Cultural contribution	..	..	..	4 387	8 432	1 096	105	127	0	0
Pork slaughterhouse tax	..	..	..	32	0	0	0	0	0	0
Breeding contribution	..	..	..	899	919	0	0	0	0	0
Medicine tax	..	..	..	0	19 789	28 104	40 496	45 529	51 318	53 064
Surtax payable by financial institutions	..	..	..	0	0	39 611	1 217	4 155	3 428	3 513
Specific sectors' surtax	..	..	..	0	0	151 693	9 815	285	94	0
Telecommunication services tax	..	..	..	0	0	0	50 176	54 516	53 412	58 709
Accident tax	..	..	..	0	0	0	23 313	27 694	5 125	-10
Insurance tax	..	..	..	0	0	4 018	28 088	30 108	87 784	97 220
Financial transaction levy	..	..	..	0	0	0	289 321	205 616	245 548	213 979
Waste dumping contribution	..	..	..	0	0	0	6 639	11 123	16 177	15 473
Advertising tax	..	..	..	0	0	0	0	5 675	6 451	0
Protection Fund levies (BEVA)	..	..	..	0	0	1 036	1 000	2 600	7 328	7 624
Protection Fund levies (OBA)	..	..	..	0	0	2 435	7 299	14 391	10 041	10 027
Protection Fund levies (Resolution Fund)	..	..	..	0	0	0	0	7 290	12 114	16 576
Protection Fund levies (SZHTKA)	..	..	..	0	0	0	5	923	1 166	1 226
Protection Fund levies (KA)	..	..	..	0	0	0	0	0	4 765	4 744
Tourism development contribution	..	..	..	0	0	0	0	0	27 311	7 445
Protection Fund Levies (PGA)	..	..	..	332	750	1 045	0	0	0	0
Retail tax	..	..	..	0	0	0	0	0	0	47 637
5127 Other taxes on internat. trade and transactions	..	..	..	0	0	0	0	0	0	0
Previous differential producer's turnover tax	..	..	..	..	..	..	..	..	..	..
5128 Other taxes	..	..	..	0	15 659	650	53 705	61 494	25 116	24 156
Sugar duty	..	..	..	..	15 659	650	881	765	0	0
Payments by companies in the energy sector (MAVIR)	..	..	..	..	0	0	52 824	60 729	25 116	24 156
5130 Unallocable between 5110 and 5120	..	..	..	0	0	0	0	0	0	0
5200 Taxes on use of goods and perform activities	..	..	..	28 727	81 143	111 553	124 696	138 137	217 326	218 929
5210 Recurrent taxes	..	..	..	25 454	74 268	106 903	121 126	130 238	201 235	206 069
Tax on domestically registered vehicles-local	..	..	..	12 622	62 432	71 112	69 248	73 248	84 095	85 563
Tax on domestically registered vehicles-extra budget	..	..	..	0	0	0	0	0	0	0
Tax on domestically registered vehicles-central	..	..	..	8 250	0	79	0	0	0	0
Tax on foreign registered vehicles extra budget fund	..	..	..	0	0	0	0	0	0	0
Tax on foreign registered vehicles-central	..	..	..	3 078	1 655	1 397	0	0	0	0
Company car tax	..	..	..	0	0	25 867	32 935	31 570	36 928	37 511
5211 Paid by households: motor vehicles	..	..	..	0	0	0	0	0	0	0
5212 Paid by others: motor vehicles	..	..	..	0	0	0	0	0	0	0
5213 Paid in respect of other goods	..	..	..	1 504	10 181	8 448	18 943	25 420	80 212	82 995
Environmental protection charge	..	..	..	5	13	27	0	0	0	0
Fishing development contribution	..	..	..	40	104	0	0	0	0	0
Environmental pollution charge	..	..	..	0	8 785	7 653	7 861	6 680	6 413	6 357
Air pollution levy	..	..	..	751	610	53	0	0	0	0
Water pollution levy	..	..	..	225	186	0	0	0	0	0
Toxic waste levy	..	..	..	65	42	130	0	0	0	0
Noise abatement levy	..	..	..	13	8	19	0	0	0	0
Unidentified environmental protection levies paid to local governments	..	..	..	404	433	566	521	265	144	155
Sale of emission allowances	..	..	..	0	0	0	10 561	17 479	72 223	74 177
Concession fees (tobacco shops)	..	..	..	0	0	0	0	996	1 432	2 306
5220 Non-recurrent taxes	..	..	..	3 273	6 875	4 650	3 570	7 899	16 091	12 860
Land protection levy	..	..	..	1 640	3 777	2 488	1 881	3 610	8 331	5 776
Vehicle weight fee	..	..	..	805	1 288	820	624	0	2 948	2 059
Game protection contribution	..	..	..	178	176	1	0	0	0	0
Casino license fee	..	..	..	650	1 635	1 341	1 065	4 289	4 812	5 025
5300 Unallocable between 5100 and 5200	..	..	..	0	0	0	0	0	0	0
6000 Other taxes	**..**	**..**	**..**	**24 503**	**40 232**	**38 735**	**37 507**	**44 686**	**33 894**	**22 293**
Unallocable tax penalties	..	..	..	23 546	33 321	36 250	37 507	35 530	25 751	22 293
6100 Paid solely by business	..	..	..	957	6 911	2 485	0	9 156	8 143	0
Nuclear contribution	..	..	..	957	6 711	2 485	..	9 156	8 143	..
Medicine tax	..	..	..	0	200	0	..	0	0	..
6200 Other	..	..	..	0	0	0	0	0	0	0
Memorandum item										
Customs duties collected on behalf of the EU	..	..	..	..	27 981	25 004	26 337	38 960	64 280	63 495
Total tax revenue on cash basis	**..**	**..**	**..**	**5 132 570**	**10 020 734**	**10 137 257**	**11 480 296**	**13 218 609**	**16 799 260**	**16 994 769**
Total tax revenue on accrual basis	**..**	**..**	**..**	**..**	**10 098 955**	**10 121 687**	**11 668 441**	**13 519 622**	**17 308 702**	**17 425 586**

	1965	1980	1990	2000	2007	2010	2013	2015	2019	2020
Conciliation with National Accounts										
Additional taxes included in National Accounts	..	..	..	..	45 120	49 057	73 565	76 364	38 847	32 597
Social security contributions	..	..	..	..	0	11 675	36 063	40 688	3 386	84
Duty for state procedures	..	..	..	..	45 084	37 331	37 417	35 653	35 443	32 498
Other taxes	..	..	..	..	36	51	85	23	18	15
Taxes excluded from National Accounts	..	..	..	..	-49 439	-53 707	-51 838	-48 414	-38 432	-35 100
Water fund tax	..	..	..	..	-13 171	-14 444	-13 164	-12 305	-12 513	-12 632
Tax on foreign registered vehicles	..	..	..	..	-1 655	-1 397	0	0	0	0
Environmental protection fee	..	..	..	..	-446	-593	-520	-265	-144	-155
Air pollution levy	..	..	..	..	-610	-53	0	0	0	0
Water pollution levy	..	..	..	..	-186	0	0	0	0	0
Toxic waste levy	..	..	..	..	-42	-130	0	0	0	0
Noise abatement levy	..	..	..	..	-8	-19	0	0	0	0
Vehicle weight fee	..	..	..	..	0	-820	-624	0	0	0
Unallocable tax penalties	..	..	..	..	-33 320	-36 250	-37 507	-35 530	-25 751	-22 293
Tax on home-workers	..	..	..	..	0	-1	-23	-29	-24	-20
Specific sectors' surtax correction	..	..	..	..	0	0	0	-285	0	0
Difference in treatment of tax credits	..	..	..	..	0	0	0	0	0	0
Capital transfer for uncollected revenue	..	..	..	..	0	0	0	0	0	0
Voluntary social security contributions	..	..	..	..	1 762	1 693	1 523	1 229	983	953
Miscellaneous differences	..	..	..	..	-2 687	-28	2	-43	190	1 433
Inheritance tax	..	..	..	..	0	0	0	0	0	0
Gift tax	..	..	..	..	0	0	0	0	0	0
Property transfer tax	..	..	..	..	0	0	0	0	0	0
Rounding	..	..	..	..	4	-2	2	0	-1	-1
Taxes on income and profits	..	..	..	..	-2 087	0	0	0	0	0
Corporate income tax	..	..	..	..	0	0	0	0	0	0
Customs duties	..	..	..	..	-603	-26	0	-43	191	1 434
Vehicle weight fee	..	..	..	..	0	0	0	0	0	0
Environment petrol tax	..	..	..	..	0	0	0	0	0	0
Social security contributions	..	..	..	..	0	0	0	0	0	0
Credit institutions' special tax	..	..	..	..	0	0	0	0	0	0
National Accounts: Taxes and actual social contributions	..	..	..	..	10 093 712	10 118 702	11 691 693	13 548 758	17 310 290	17 425 469
Imputed social contributions	..	..	..	..	21 113	24 841	21 669	28 783	21 940	28 280
National Accounts: Taxes and all social contributions	..	..	..	..	10 114 825	10 143 543	11 713 362	13 577 541	17 332 230	17 453 749

.. Not available
Note: Year ending 31st December.
From 2002 onwards, data are on accrual basis, except for the preliminary year, which is on a cash basis.
Heading 5121: the aggregate figure for excise tax revenues is on a cash basis. Revenue from specific excises is in several cases reported on an accrual basis.
Tax base for "Environment petrol tax" is broader than petrol only.
Source: Ministry of Finance, Economic Department.

StatLink https://stat.link/j8es0y

Table 5.16. Iceland: Details of tax revenue, 1965-2020

Million ISK

	1965	1980	1990	2000	2007	2010	2013	2015	2019	2020
Total tax revenue	**60**	**4 731**	**114 932**	**254 571**	**532 769**	**541 578**	**676 142**	**812 002**	**1 061 978**	**1 061 089**
1000 Taxes on income, profits and capital gains	**13**	**1 211**	**34 106**	**101 488**	**241 378**	**239 664**	**315 577**	**380 979**	**530 192**	**542 035**
1100 Of individuals	12	1 092	30 908	88 492	180 070	197 318	258 623	297 979	435 351	457 255
1110 On income and profits	..	..	30 908	88 492	180 070	197 318	258 623	297 979	435 351	457 255
1120 On capital gains	..	..	..	0	0	0	0	0	0	0
1200 Corporate	1	119	3 198	8 371	32 555	14 609	40 479	52 544	62 972	64 447
1210 On profits	..	..	3 198	8 371	32 555	14 609	40 479	52 544	62 972	64 447
1220 On capital gains	..	..	..	0	0	0	0	0	0	0
1300 Unallocable between 1100 and 1200	0	0	0	4 625	28 754	27 737	16 475	30 457	31 868	20 333
2000 Social security contributions	**5**	**102**	**3 607**	**19 680**	**39 594**	**63 599**	**69 899**	**79 707**	**97 423**	**88 364**
2100 Employees	0	0	315	..	..	..	..	..	..	..
2110 On a payroll basis	..	..	..	..	..	..	..	..	..	..
2120 On an income tax basis	..	..	..	..	..	..	..	..	..	..
2200 Employers	5	102	3 292	..	..	..	..	..	..	..
2210 On a payroll basis	..	..	..	..	..	..	..	..	..	..
2220 On an income tax basis	..	..	..	..	..	..	..	..	..	..
2300 Self-employed or non-employed	0	0	0	..	..	..	..	..	..	..
2310 On a payroll basis	..	..	..	..	..	..	..	..	..	..
2320 On an income tax basis	..	..	..	..	..	..	..	..	..	..
2400 Unallocable between 2100, 2200 and 2300	0	0	0	19 680	39 594	63 599	69 899	79 707	97 423	88 364
2410 On a payroll basis	..	..	..	19 680	39 594	63 599	69 899	79 707	97 423	88 364
2420 On an income tax basis	..	..	..	0	0	0	0	0	0	0
3000 Taxes on payroll and workforce	**1**	**180**	**4 071**	**184**	**1 519**	**2 827**	**6 534**	**6 638**	**9 124**	**9 233**
4000 Taxes on property	**2**	**297**	**9 689**	**16 839**	**23 039**	**35 412**	**42 520**	**39 160**	**58 366**	**66 312**
4100 Recurrent taxes on immovable property	1	138	4 131	10 107	20 567	28 542	30 664	34 879	52 522	56 040
4110 Households	0	50	1 862	..	..	..	..	..	..	..
4120 Others	1	88	2 269	..	..	..	..	..	..	..
4200 Recurrent taxes on net wealth	0	69	2 402	5 173	-8	3 849	8 886	657	10	34
4210 Individual	..	29	1 476	..	..	..	..	..	..	..
4220 Corporate	..	40	926	..	..	..	..	..	..	..
4300 Estate, inheritance and gift taxes	0	6	235	765	1 663	2 613	2 437	2 919	4 668	9 059
4310 Estate and inheritance taxes	0	6	235	765	1 663	2 613	2 437	2 919	4 668	9 059
4320 Gift taxes	0	0	0	0	0	0	0	0	0	0
4400 Taxes on financial and capital transactions	1	84	2 921	0	0	0	0	0	0	0
4500 Non-recurrent taxes	0	0	0	113	460	146	233	362	623	612
4510 On net wealth	..	..	..	0	0	0	0	0	0	0
4520 Other non-recurrent taxes	..	..	..	113	460	146	233	362	623	612
4600 Other recurrent taxes on property	0	0	0	681	356	263	299	343	542	567
5000 Taxes on goods and services	**37**	**2 834**	**58 943**	**115 389**	**225 480**	**194 088**	**230 592**	**267 155**	**348 278**	**335 971**
5100 Taxes on production, sale, transfer, etc.	37	2 778	56 564	103 813	202 449	182 953	219 244	254 422	325 802	312 821
5110 General taxes	10	1 368	37 084	75 811	148 085	126 351	153 800	188 001	248 554	239 773
5111 Value added taxes	0	0	32 698	72 668	138 601	123 695	149 828	183 674	243 285	233 732
5112 Sales tax	10	1 368	4 386	0	0	0	0	0	0	0
5113 Other	0	0	0	3 143	9 484	2 656	3 973	4 327	5 269	6 040
5120 Taxes on specific goods and services	27	1 410	19 480	28 002	54 364	56 603	65 444	66 421	77 248	73 049
5121 Excise duties	1	311	2 346	23 585	45 891	46 711	55 171	56 909	66 833	64 251
5122 Profits of fiscal monopolies	5	263	5 986	0	0	0	0	0	0	0
5123 Customs and import duties	20	715	9 181	2 702	5 446	5 952	5 815	4 989	3 430	2 575
5124 Taxes on exports	1	2	0	0	0	0	0	0	0	0
5125 Taxes on investment goods	0	0	0	0	0	0	0	0	0	0
5126 Taxes on specific services	1	69	1 404	1 715	3 026	3 940	4 457	4 523	6 986	6 223
5127 Other taxes on internat. trade and transactions	0	50	563	0	0	0	0	0	0	0
5128 Other taxes	0	0	0	0	0	0	0	0	0	0
5130 Unallocable between 5110 and 5120	0	0	0	0	0	0	0	0	0	0
5200 Taxes on use of goods and perform activities	1	56	2 379	11 576	23 032	11 135	11 347	12 733	22 476	23 150
5210 Recurrent taxes	1	56	2 379	..	..	..	..	..	..	..
5211 Paid by households: motor vehicles	0	10	970	..	..	..	..	..	..	..
5212 Paid by others: motor vehicles	0	41	1 331	..	..	..	..	..	..	..
5213 Paid in respect of other goods	0	5	78	..	..	..	..	..	..	..
5220 Non-recurrent taxes	0	0	0	..	..	..	..	..	..	..
5300 Unallocable between 5100 and 5200	0	0	0	0	0	0	0	0	0	0
6000 Other taxes	**2**	**107**	**4 516**	**991**	**1 758**	**5 988**	**11 020**	**38 364**	**18 594**	**19 174**
6100 Paid solely by business	2	107	4 145	418	628	763	5 255	32 477	11 629	12 046
6200 Other	0	0	371	573	1 130	5 225	5 766	5 887	6 966	7 127

	1965	1980	1990	2000	2007	2010	2013	2015	2019	2020
Non-wastable tax credits										
Non-wastable tax credits against 1110	..	..	..	..	..	..	0	0	0	0
Tax expenditure component	..	..	..	..	..	..	..	..	..	..
Transfer component	..	..	..	..	..	..	..	..	..	..
Non-wastable tax credits against 1210	..	..	..	..	..	..	1 025	1 190	3 577	4 361
Tax expenditure component	..	..	..	..	..	..	127	173	608	824
Transfer component	..	..	..	..	..	..	898	1 017	2 969	4 362
Total tax revenue on cash basis	**60**	**4 731**	**114 932**	**..**	**..**	**..**	**..**	**..**	**..**	**..**
Total tax revenue on accrual basis	**..**	**..**	**..**	**254 571**	**532 769**	**541 578**	**676 142**	**812 002**	**1 061 978**	**1 061 089**
Conciliation with National Accounts										
Additional taxes included in National Accounts	..	..	..	0	0	0	0	0	0	0
Taxes excluded from National Accounts	..	..	..	-765	-1 663	-2 613	-2 437	-2 919	-4 668	-9 059
Estate and inheritance taxes (4310)	..	..	..	-765	-1 663	-2 613	-2 437	-2 919	-4 668	-9 059
Difference in treatment of tax credits	..	..	..	0	0	0	0	0	0	0
Capital transfer for uncollected revenue	..	..	..	0	0	0	0	0	0	0
Voluntary social security contributions	..	..	..	0	0	0	0	0	0	0
Miscellaneous differences	..	..	..	0	0	0	0	0	0	0
National Accounts: Taxes and actual social contributions	..	..	..	253 806	531 105	538 964	673 704	809 084	1 057 310	1 052 029
Imputed social contributions	..	..	..	0	0	0	0	0	0	0
National Accounts: Taxes and all social contributions	..	..	..	253 806	531 105	538 964	673 704	809 084	1 057 310	1 052 029

.. Not available

Note: Year ending 31st December.

From 1998 data are on accrual basis.

Source: Statistics Iceland.

StatLink https://stat.link/ci0gwu

Table 5.17. Ireland: Details of tax revenue, 1965-2020

Million EUR

	1965	1980	1990	2000	2007	2010	2013	2015	2019	2020
Total tax revenue	**317**	**4 046**	**12 260**	**33 363**	**60 790**	**46 399**	**51 459**	**60 898**	**77 962**	**74 034**
Total tax revenue exclusive of taxes collected for the EU	..	..	**12 075**	**33 155**	**60 517**	**46 170**	**51 212**	**60 572**	**77 505**	**73 624**
1000 Taxes on income, profits and capital gains	**82**	**1 478**	**4 662**	**14 551**	**25 364**	**18 617**	**21 298**	**26 599**	**35 560**	**36 333**
1100 Of individuals	53	1 294	4 059	10 650	18 970	14 665	17 020	19 722	24 671	24 380
1110 On income and profits	53	1 286	4 023	9 876	15 872	14 320	16 652	19 053	23 599	23 428
Income tax	66	1 286	4 023	9 876	15 872	14 320	16 652	19 053	23 599	23 428
Surtax	3	0	0	0	0	0	0	0	0	0
Income tax paid by corporations	-17	0	0	0	0	0	0	0	0	0
1120 On capital gains	0	8	36	774	3 097	345	369	669	1 072	952
1200 Corporate	29	184	603	3 900	6 395	3 945	4 273	6 873	10 888	11 954
1210 On profits	29	184	603	3 900	6 395	3 945	4 273	6 873	10 888	11 954
Corporation profits tax	12	2	0	0	0	0	0	0	0	0
Corporation tax	0	176	603	3 885	6 393	3 944	4 272	6 872	10 887	11 953
Income tax paid by corporation	17	0	0	0	0	0	0	0	0	0
Agricultural produce duty	0	6	0	14	1	1	1	1	1	1
1220 On capital gains	0	0	0	0	0	0	0	0	0	0
1300 Unallocable between 1100 and 1200	0	0	0	2	0	7	4	4	0	0
2000 Social security contributions	**21**	**578**	**1 729**	**3 966**	**8 143**	**8 458**	**8 871**	**9 999**	**13 110**	**12 285**
2100 Employees	10	190	570	962	1 926	3 195	3 141	3 327	3 977	3 785
2110 On a payroll basis	..	..	570	962	1 926	3 195	3 141	3 327	3 977	3 785
2120 On an income tax basis	..	..	0	0	0	0	0	0	0	0
2200 Employers	10	380	1 092	2 814	5 796	4 932	5 326	6 211	8 501	7 868
2210 On a payroll basis	..	..	1 092	2 814	5 796	4 932	5 326	6 211	8 501	7 868
2220 On an income tax basis	..	..	0	0	0	0	0	0	0	0
2300 Self-employed or non-employed	0	8	67	190	421	331	403	460	632	632
2310 On a payroll basis	..	..	67	190	421	331	403	460	632	632
2320 On an income tax basis	..	..	0	0	0	0	0	0	0	0
2400 Unallocable between 2100, 2200 and 2300	0	0	0	0	0	0	0	0	0	0
2410 On a payroll basis	..	..	..	..	..	..	..	..	..	..
2420 On an income tax basis	..	..	..	..	..	..	..	..	..	..
3000 Taxes on payroll and workforce	**0**	**9**	**159**	**15**	**411**	**310**	**314**	**357**	**774**	**717**
4000 Taxes on property	**48**	**213**	**569**	**1 902**	**4 789**	**2 389**	**3 632**	**3 918**	**4 435**	**3 687**
4100 Recurrent taxes on immovable property	39	139	312	587	1 233	1 322	1 724	1 864	1 933	1 215
4110 Households	..	..	..	..	..	..	..	..	..	..
4120 Others	..	..	..	..	..	..	..	..	..	..
4200 Recurrent taxes on net wealth	0	1	0	0	0	0	536	169	0	0
4210 Individual	..	..	..	..	..	..	0	0	0	0
4220 Corporate	..	..	..	..	..	..	536	169	0	0
4300 Estate, inheritance and gift taxes	6	14	48	225	405	235	278	401	531	505
4310 Estate and inheritance taxes	6	14	45	210	337	192	259	365	467	499
Estate duty	5	..	0	0	0	0	0	0	0	0
Legacy duty	1	..	0	0	0	0	0	0	0	0
Succession duty	0	..	0	0	0	0	0	0	0	0
4320 Gift taxes	0	0	3	15	68	43	20	36	64	6
4400 Taxes on financial and capital transactions	3	59	209	1 090	3 151	832	1 093	1 484	1 971	1 968
Stamp duty	3	59	209	1 090	3 151	832	1 093	1 484	1 971	1 968
4500 Non-recurrent taxes	0	0	0	0	0	0	0	0	0	0
4510 On net wealth	..	..	..	..	..	..	..	..	..	..
4520 Other non-recurrent taxes	..	..	..	..	..	..	..	..	..	..
4600 Other recurrent taxes on property	0	0	0	0	0	0	0	0	0	0
5000 Taxes on goods and services	**167**	**1 769**	**5 140**	**12 929**	**22 082**	**16 619**	**17 321**	**20 013**	**24 078**	**21 002**
5100 Taxes on production, sale, transfer, etc.	155	1 741	4 939	12 374	20 982	15 319	15 789	18 036	22 263	19 183
5110 General taxes	18	597	2 500	7 643	14 355	10 067	10 372	11 831	15 271	12 753
5111 Value added taxes	0	597	2 500	7 643	14 355	10 067	10 372	11 831	15 271	12 753
Value added tax	..	597	2 500	7 643	14 355	10 067	10 372	11 831	15 271	12 753
5112 Sales tax	18	0	0	0	0	0	0	0	0	0
Turnover tax	18	..	..	..	..	..	..	..	..	..
Wholesale tax	0	..	..	..	..	..	..	..	..	..
5113 Other	0	0	0	0	0	0	0	0	0	0
5120 Taxes on specific goods and services	137	1 143	2 439	4 731	6 627	5 252	5 417	6 205	6 992	6 430

	1965	1980	1990	2000	2007	2010	2013	2015	2019	2020
5121 Excise duties	124	1 045	2 084	4 402	6 125	4 859	5 013	5 474	5 974	5 470
Beer	19	192	356	475	459	316	363	418	421	348
Oils	31	330	745	1 491	2 204	2 099	2 035	2 120	2 165	1 805
Spirits	16	148	153	241	363	244	282	313	375	379
Table waters	0	11	23	0	0	0	0	0	0	0
Tobacco	50	187	419	1 035	1 192	1 160	1 064	1 055	1 137	1 202
Wine, cider, perry	1	18	46	154	297	266	354	414	433	478
Motor vehicle (incl. tyres)	7	148	331	985	1 554	395	459	702	950	717
Others	1	11	11	20	57	379	457	451	493	541
5122 Profits of fiscal monopolies	0	0	0	0	0	0	0	0	0	0
5123 Customs and import duties	10	62	147	208	273	229	247	327	342	272
5124 Taxes on exports	0	0	0	0	0	0	0	0	0	0
UE agriculture levies	..	..	0	..	..	..	..	..	..	..
5125 Taxes on investment goods	0	0	0	0	0	0	0	0	0	0
5126 Taxes on specific services	3	21	171	122	229	164	157	404	676	688
Duty on betting	2	19	37	59	36	30	26	37	110	83
Sweepstakes duty	1	1	0	0	0	0	0	0	0	0
Bank levy	0	0	46	61	66	-70	-23	190	398	427
Other	0	1	88	2	127	204	154	178	168	178
5127 Other taxes on internat. trade and transactions	0	0	0	0	0	0	0	0	0	0
5128 Other taxes	0	14	37	0	0	0	0	0	0	0
5130 Unallocable between 5110 and 5120	0	0	0	0	0	0	0	0	0	0
5200 Taxes on use of goods and perform activities	11	28	201	555	1 100	1 300	1 532	1 977	1 815	1 819
5210 Recurrent taxes	11	28	201	555	1 100	1 300	1 532	1 977	1 815	1 819
5211 Paid by households: motor vehicles	6	14	100	373	723	768	888	904	795	756
5212 Paid by others: motor vehicles	5	11	82	124	239	256	284	281	241	235
5213 Paid in respect of other goods	0	3	20	58	138	276	360	792	779	828
5220 Non-recurrent taxes	0	0	0	0	0	0	0	0	0	0
5300 Unallocable between 5100 and 5200	0	0	0	0	0	0	0	0	0	0
6000 Other taxes	**0**	**0**	**0**	**0**	**0**	**6**	**23**	**12**	**5**	**9**
6100 Paid solely by business	..	..	..	..	..	0	0	0	0	0
6200 Other	..	..	..	..	..	6	23	12	5	9
Memorandum items										
Customs duties collected on behalf of the EU	..	..	148	208	273	229	247	327	342	272
SRF contributions collected on behalf of the EU	..	..	..	..	..	..	..	..	114	138
Non-wastable tax credits										
Non-wastable tax credits against 1110	..	..	..	..	843	1 073	816	555	413	400
Tax expenditure component	..	..	..	..	843	1 073	816	555	413	400
Transfer component	..	..	..	..	0	0	0	0	0	0
Total tax revenue on cash basis	**317**	**4 046**	**12 260**	**32 997**	**60 836**	**46 609**	**51 491**	**60 867**	**77 815**	**73 733**
Total tax revenue on accrual basis	**..**	**..**	**..**	**33 363**	**60 790**	**46 399**	**51 459**	**60 898**	**77 962**	**74 034**
Conciliation with National Accounts										
Additional taxes included in National Accounts	..	..	..	0	0	178	178	177	185	185
Taxes excluded from National Accounts	..	..	..	0	0	0	0	0	0	0
Difference in treatment of tax credits	..	..	..	0	0	0	0	0	0	0
Capital transfer for uncollected revenue	..	..	..	0	0	0	0	0	0	0
Voluntary social security contributions	..	..	..	0	0	0	0	0	0	0
Miscellaneous differences	..	..	..	0	0	0	0	0	0	0
National Accounts: Taxes and actual social contributions	..	..	..	33 363	60 790	46 577	51 637	61 075	78 147	74 219
Imputed social contributions	..	..	..	1 366	2 579	1 053	2 064	2 223	2 917	3 144
National Accounts: Taxes and all social contributions	..	..	..	34 729	63 369	47 630	53 700	63 298	81 064	77 362

.. Not available

Note: The personal income tax data shown for the country table for Ireland is different to the ESA2010 presentation as the expenditure component of the payable tax credits are excluded in accordance with the OECD Interpretative Guide.

The data for years 1965 to 1973 are on fiscal year basis (commencing on 1st April) and are therefore not strictly comparable with the data for later years, which are on a calendar year basis.

From 1998, data are on accrual basis.

Heading 1200: Capital gains taxes paid by corporations are included in heading 1210.

Heading 2100: Includes contributions by self-employed and certain voluntary contributions.

Heading 2200: Since 1976 income tax paid by corporations and corporation profits tax have been replaced by corporation tax.

Heading 5111: Includes arrears of the wholesale and turnover taxes.

Tax receipts in 1988 were inflated by the success of the new arrangements for assessment and collection of tax.These arrangements included an amnesty for tax arrears paid by 30th September. This amnesty waived penalities and interest charge tax. It resulted in payments of 631 millons of euros spread across the main tax headings.

Source: Annual Report of he Revenue Commissioners, Financial Accounts and National Income and Expenditure Accounts.

StatLink https://stat.link/kw72fx

Table 5.18. Israel: Details of tax revenue, 1965-2020

Million ILS

	1965	1980	1990	2000	2007	2010	2013	2015	2019	2020
Total tax revenue	..	..	..	**189 300**	**252 028**	**269 672**	**326 855**	**366 044**	**430 461**	**420 585**
1000 Taxes on income, profits and capital gains	..	..	..	**74 551**	**91 530**	**78 265**	**101 481**	**113 966**	**140 453**	**139 321**
1100 Of individuals	..	..	..	54 753	56 434	48 214	57 311	70 885	89 493	91 900
1110 On income and profits	..	..	..	53 698	55 213	47 550	55 831	68 455	86 593	88 630
On wages – deduction at source	..	..	..	45 278	45 515	40 159	46 458	54 087	68 041	70 414
On self employement income – deduction at source	..	..	..	688	0	853	1 051	0	83	96
On self employement income – other	..	..	..	7 731	9 698	6 538	8 322	14 368	18 469	18 120
1120 On capital gains	..	..	..	1 055	1 221	664	1 480	2 430	2 900	3 270
1200 Corporate	..	..	..	18 001	30 210	23 113	36 639	34 676	43 291	38 831
1210 On profits	..	..	..	16 109	27 582	22 291	33 959	33 446	41 731	37 071
Deduction at source	..	..	..	361	0	520	751	0	41	49
In lieu of VAT on the profits of Financial Institutions	..	..	..	1 290	2 200	1 920	2 560	1 890	2 500	2 700
Other	..	..	..	14 458	25 382	19 850	30 648	31 556	39 190	34 322
1220 On capital gains	..	..	..	1 892	2 628	822	2 680	1 230	1 560	1 760
1300 Unallocable between 1100 and 1200	..	..	..	1 797	4 886	6 938	7 531	8 405	7 669	8 590
Tax deducted at the source on the capital market	..	..	..	1 797	4 886	6 938	7 531	8 405	7 669	8 590
2000 Social security contributions	..	..	..	**27 565**	**37 909**	**45 343**	**53 364**	**59 561**	**74 420**	**73 031**
2100 Employees	..	..	..	15 771	23 093	27 788	31 537	34 692	41 852	40 797
2110 On a payroll basis	..	..	..	15 771	23 093	27 788	31 537	34 692	41 852	40 797
2120 On an income tax basis	..	..	..	0	0	0	0	0	0	0
2200 Employers	..	..	..	8 182	9 960	11 427	15 026	17 247	23 105	22 564
2210 On a payroll basis	..	..	..	8 182	9 960	11 427	15 026	17 247	23 105	22 564
2220 On an income tax basis	..	..	..	0	0	0	0	0	0	0
2300 Self-employed or non-employed	..	..	..	3 612	4 856	6 128	6 802	7 622	9 464	9 670
2310 On a payroll basis	..	..	..	3 612	4 856	6 128	6 802	7 622	9 464	9 670
2320 On an income tax basis	..	..	..	0	0	0	0	0	0	0
2400 Unallocable between 2100, 2200 and 2300	..	..	..	0	0	0	0	0	0	0
2410 On a payroll basis	..	..	..	..	..	..	..	..	..	..
2420 On an income tax basis	..	..	..	..	..	..	..	..	..	..
3000 Taxes on payroll and workforce	..	..	..	**6 850**	**9 920**	**10 280**	**12 780**	**13 770**	**16 168**	**16 191**
Employers tax on the the non-profit sector other than govt	..	..	..	1 250	1 500	320	390	410	555	472
In lieu of VAT on the wage-bill in the non-profit sector	..	..	..	4 260	6 580	7 650	9 540	10 320	12 521	12 716
In lieu VAT on the wage-bill in Financial Institutions	..	..	..	1 340	1 840	2 310	2 850	3 040	3 092	3 003
4000 Taxes on property	..	..	..	**17 987**	**25 049**	**30 029**	**34 144**	**40 609**	**45 794**	**43 409**
4100 Recurrent taxes on immovable property	..	..	..	11 311	16 156	18 768	21 499	23 702	27 105	25 031
Land tax	..	..	..	442	52	48	59	44	25	10
4110 Households	..	..	..	0	0	0	0	0	0	0
4120 Others	..	..	..	10 869	16 104	18 720	21 440	23 658	27 080	25 022
4200 Recurrent taxes on net wealth	..	..	..	0	0	0	0	0	0	0
4210 Individual	..	..	..	..	..	..	..	..	..	..
4220 Corporate	..	..	..	..	..	..	..	..	..	..
4300 Estate, inheritance and gift taxes	..	..	..	0	0	0	0	0	0	0
4310 Estate and inheritance taxes	..	..	..	..	..	..	..	..	..	..
4320 Gift taxes	..	..	..	..	..	..	..	..	..	..
4400 Taxes on financial and capital transactions	..	..	..	3 181	3 555	4 071	4 532	6 732	6 923	6 864
Transaction tax on the buyer of real estate	..	..	..	1 972	3 084	4 024	4 513	6 731	6 917	6 864
Transaction tax on the seller of real estate	..	..	..	206	404	27	19	1	6	0
Stamp tax	..	..	..	1 003	67	20	0	0	0	0
4500 Non-recurrent taxes	..	..	..	3 495	5 338	7 190	8 114	10 175	11 766	11 514
4510 On net wealth	..	..	..	0	0	0	0	0	0	0
4520 Other non-recurrent taxes	..	..	..	3 495	5 338	7 190	8 114	10 175	11 766	11 514
Capital gains tax on real estate	..	..	..	3 495	5 338	7 190	8 114	10 175	11 766	11 514
4600 Other recurrent taxes on property	..	..	..	0	0	0	0	0	0	0
5000 Taxes on goods and services	..	..	..	**62 347**	**87 621**	**105 756**	**125 086**	**138 138**	**153 626**	**148 633**
5100 Taxes on production, sale, transfer, etc.	..	..	..	57 887	81 108	98 094	116 334	128 277	143 066	138 750
5110 General taxes	..	..	..	49 876	67 570	79 947	97 356	107 765	120 541	118 854
5111 Value added taxes	..	..	..	39 805	53 983	65 510	81 523	90 824	102 463	100 373
5112 Sales tax	..	..	..	10 071	13 587	14 437	15 833	16 941	18 078	18 481
On domestic production	..	..	..	662	287	291	457	450	287	303
On imports	..	..	..	9 409	13 300	14 146	15 376	16 491	17 791	18 178
5113 Other	..	..	..	0	0	0	0	0	0	0
5120 Taxes on specific goods and services	..	..	..	8 012	13 538	18 147	18 978	20 512	22 525	19 896
5121 Excise duties	..	..	..	6 595	11 323	15 458	16 680	17 642	19 509	17 021
On domestically refined fuel	..	..	..	5 666	10 590	14 637	15 876	17 008	18 966	16 526
On domestically processed tobacco products	..	..	..	929	733	821	804	634	543	495
5122 Profits of fiscal monopolies	..	..	..	0	0	0	0	0	0	0
5123 Customs and import duties	..	..	..	1 417	2 215	2 689	2 298	2 870	3 016	2 875
5124 Taxes on exports	..	..	..	0	0	0	0	0	0	0

	1965	1980	1990	2000	2007	2010	2013	2015	2019	2020
5125 Taxes on investment goods	..	..	..	0	0	0	0	0	0	0
5126 Taxes on specific services	..	..	..	0	0	0	0	0	0	0
5127 Other taxes on internat. trade and transactions	..	..	..	0	0	0	0	0	0	0
5128 Other taxes	..	..	..	0	0	0	0	0	0	0
5130 Unallocable between 5110 and 5120	..	..	..	0	0	0	0	0	0	0
5200 Taxes on use of goods and perform activities	..	..	..	4 460	6 512	7 663	8 752	9 861	10 560	9 884
5210 Recurrent taxes	..	..	..	4 460	6 512	7 663	8 752	9 861	10 560	9 884
5211 Paid by households: motor vehicles	..	..	..	1 436	1 895	2 274	2 249	2 515	2 966	2 868
5212 Paid by others: motor vehicles	..	..	..	479	632	758	1 580	1 723	1 927	1 864
5213 Paid in respect of other goods	..	..	..	2 546	3 986	4 630	4 923	5 623	5 668	5 152
Licences collected by the Ministry of Transportation	..	..	..	257	535	350	132	196	165	64
Licences collected by the Ministry of Communication	..	..	..	151	0	274	299	338	371	356
Licences collected by other ministries	..	..	..	1 587	2 597	2 989	3 245	3 781	3 624	3 331
Business and professional licences paid locally	..	..	..	500	769	917	1 122	1 181	1 353	1 250
Other local authority fees	..	..	..	51	86	101	125	128	155	150
5220 Non-recurrent taxes	..	..	..	0	0	0	0	0	0	0
5300 Unallocable between 5100 and 5200	..	..	..	0	0	0	0	0	0	0
6000 Other taxes	**..**	**..**	**..**	**0**	**0**	**0**	**0**	**0**	**0**	**0**
6100 Paid solely by business	..	..	..	..	..	..	..	..	..	..
6200 Other	..	..	..	..	..	..	..	..	..	..
Non-wastable tax credits										
Non-wastable tax credits against 1110	..	..	..	..	..	87	911	1 415	1 327	1 283
Tax expenditure component	..	..	..	..	..	84	879	1 348	1 327	1 283
Transfer component	..	..	..	..	..	3	32	67	0	0
Non-wastable tax credits against 1210	..	..	..	..	..	0	0	0	0	0
Tax expenditure component	..	..	..	..	..	..	..	..	..	..
Transfer component	..	..	..	..	..	..	..	..	..	..
Total tax revenue on cash basis	**..**	**..**	**..**	**189 300**	**252 028**	**269 672**	**326 855**	**366 044**	**430 461**	**420 585**
Total tax revenue on accrual basis	**..**	**..**	**..**	**..**	**..**	**..**	**..**	**..**	**..**	**..**
Conciliation with National Accounts										
Additional taxes included in National Accounts	..	..	..	0	0	0	0	0	0	0
Taxes excluded from National Accounts	..	..	..	..	..	..	..	..	..	..
Difference in treatment of tax credits	..	..	..	..	..	..	..	..	..	..
Capital transfer for uncollected revenue	..	..	..	..	..	..	..	..	..	..
Voluntary social security contributions	..	..	..	..	..	..	..	..	..	..
Miscellaneous differences	..	..	..	..	..	..	..	..	..	..
National Accounts: Taxes and actual social contributions	..	..	..	189 300	252 028	269 672	326 855	366 044	430 461	420 585
Imputed social contributions	..	..	..	6 172	7 131	8 203	9 084	9 186	9 072	8 826
National Accounts: Taxes and all social contributions	..	..	..	195 472	259 159	277 875	335 940	375 230	439 533	429 411

.. Not available

Note: Year ending 31st December.

Data are on a cash basis.

Source: Israel Central Bureau of Statistics and Israel Ministry of Finance.

StatLink https://stat.link/je3bw6

Table 5.19. Italy: Details of tax revenue, 1965-2020

Million EUR

	1965	1980	1990	2000	2007	2010	2013	2015	2019	2020
Total tax revenue	**5 505**	**60 422**	**265 116**	**503 096**	**671 189**	**671 912**	**706 829**	**711 114**	**759 445**	**706 743**
Total tax revenue exclusive of taxes collected for the EU	**..**	**..**	**263 829**	**501 560**	**668 928**	**669 687**	**704 939**	**706 522**	**756 285**	**703 791**
1000 Taxes on income, profits and capital gains	**982**	**18 821**	**96 707**	**166 912**	**226 498**	**219 547**	**233 294**	**225 934**	**239 859**	**231 868**
1100 Of individuals	603	13 940	69 654	124 918	172 136	180 512	185 996	184 622	196 283	189 206
1110 On income and profits	603	13 796	68 786	124 233	172 122	180 505	185 991	184 619	196 283	189 206
Personal income tax	0	11 538	57 318	121 211	162 644	173 991	175 921	173 007	185 726	178 938
Local income tax paid by households	0	829	4 492	67	0	0	0	0	0	0
Tax on income from investments (60%)	319	55	15	0	0	0	11	80	47	53
10% Surcharge on income	94	37	5	0	0	0	0	0	0	0
10% proportional surcharge	1	0	0	0	0	0	0	0	0	0
Withholding tax on company dividends paid by households	23	51	496	110	542	393	564	875	1 751	1 742
Law 1177 proportional surcharge (60%)	39	0	1	0	0	0	0	0	0	0
Direct taxes 5% proportional surcharge (60%)	0	8	72	0	0	0	0	0	0	0
Additional Treasury increase (60%)	23	6	1	0	0	0	0	0	0	0
Decree 1132 revenues (60%)	0	0	0	0	0	0	0	0	0	0
Tax on households	65	7	0	0	0	0	0	0	0	0
Rental value tax	2	0	0	0	0	0	0	0	0	0
Driving licence tax	1	0	0	0	0	0	0	0	0	0
Municipal surcharge on buildings (40%)	37	5	0	22	0	0	0	0	0	0
Withholding tax on income from deposits paid by households	0	1 206	6 223	2 823	8 402	5 440	8 994	10 076	7 798	7 583
Direct taxes refund (60%)	0	0	41	0	0	0	0	0	0	0
Other	0	53	123	0	534	681	501	581	962	890
1120 On capital gains	0	144	867	685	14	7	5	3	0	0
Tax on capital gains on land	..	0	0	0	0	0	0	0	..	..
Municipal capital gains tax on buildings paid by households (60%)	..	144	867	685	14	7	5	3	..	..
1200 Corporate	379	4 710	26 605	34 699	50 529	36 740	41 194	33 530	35 176	34 162
1210 On profits	379	4 494	26 027	34 242	50 520	36 736	41 190	33 528	35 172	34 160
Corporation tax	0	1 245	9 042	28 877	47 192	34 841	39 160	31 927	32 781	31 936
Municipal surcharge on buildings (60%)	37	8	0	32	0	0	0	0	0	0
Tax on income from investments (40%)	213	37	10	0	0	0	8	54	31	36
Company franchise and liabilities tax	88	12	2	0	0	0	0	0	0	0
Law 1177 proportional surcharge (40%)	26	0	0	0	0	0	0	0	0	0
Direct taxes 5% proportional surcharge (40%)	0	20	48	0	0	0	0	0	0	0
Decree 1132 revenues (40%)	0	0	0	0	0	0	0	0	0	0
Additional Treasury increase (40%)	15	4	0	0	0	0	0	0	0	0
Withholding tax on company dividends paid by firms	0	77	745	166	0	0	0	0	0	0
Withholding tax on income from deposits paid by firms	0	1 810	9 334	4 235	2 370	605	1 464	759	472	592
Local income tax paid by firms	0	1 245	6 738	100	15	13	12	12	6	4
Direct taxes refund (40%)	0	0	27	0	0	0	0	0	0	0
Other	0	36	82	832	943	1 277	546	776	1 882	1 592
1220 On capital gains	0	216	578	457	9	4	4	2	4	2
Municipal capital gains tax on buildings paid by firms (40%)	..	216	578	457	9	4	4	2	4	2
1300 Unallocable between 1100 and 1200	0	171	448	7 295	3 833	2 295	6 104	7 782	8 399	8 500
Refunds tax on income	..	-240	-1 768	-5 175	0	0	0	0	0	0
Other	..	412	2 216	12 470	3 833	2 295	6 104	7 782	8 399	8 500
2000 Social security contributions	**1 881**	**22 976**	**87 256**	**143 629**	**200 772**	**209 122**	**210 462**	**214 376**	**237 290**	**224 781**
2100 Employees	..	4 171	16 753	27 333	35 715	37 598	39 284	39 805	44 486	41 351
2110 On a payroll basis	..	..	..	27 333	35 715	37 598	39 284	39 805	44 486	41 351
2120 On an income tax basis	..	..	..	0	0	0	0	0	0	0
2200 Employers	..	17 152	62 540	99 904	137 924	144 281	141 629	143 273	158 616	149 824
2210 On a payroll basis	..	..	..	99 904	137 924	144 281	141 629	143 273	158 616	149 824
2220 On an income tax basis	..	..	..	0	0	0	0	0	0	0
2300 Self-employed or non-employed	..	1 654	7 962	16 392	27 133	27 243	29 549	31 298	34 188	33 606
2310 On a payroll basis	..	..	..	16 392	27 133	27 243	29 549	31 298	34 188	33 606
2320 On an income tax basis	..	..	..	0	0	0	0	0	0	0
2400 Unallocable between 2100, 2200 and 2300	1 881	0	0	0	0	0	0	0	0	0
2410 On a payroll basis	..	..	..	..	..	..	..	..	..	..
2420 On an income tax basis	..	..	..	..	..	..	..	..	..	..
3000 Taxes on payroll and workforce	**0**	**387**	**890**	**0**	**0**	**0**	**0**	**0**	**0**	**0**
Contributions to GESCAL	..	387	890	..	..	..	..	..	..	..
4000 Taxes on property	**397**	**2 248**	**5 983**	**23 360**	**32 646**	**32 441**	**43 883**	**46 259**	**43 243**	**40 443**

	1965	1980	1990	2000	2007	2010	2013	2015	2019	2020
4100 Recurrent taxes on immovable property	96	7	1	9 354	12 778	9 663	20 748	25 558	22 002	21 270
Income tax on landowners	2	0	0	0	0	0	0	0	0	0
Income tax on buildings	12	2	1	0	0	0	0	0	0	0
Income tax on luxury buildings	1	0	0	0	0	0	0	0	0	0
Surcharge on land (provincial)	16	0	0	0	0	0	0	0	0	0
Surcharge on land (municipal)	18	0	0	0	0	0	0	0	0	0
Surcharge on buildings (provincial)	26	2	0	0	0	0	0	0	0	0
Surcharge on buildings (municipal)	21	3	0	0	0	0	0	0	0	0
Municipal real estate tax	0	0	0	9 354	12 778	9 663	20 748	20 798	20 824	21 137
Tax on indivisible services (TASI)	0	0	0	0	0	0	0	4 760	1 178	133
4110 Households	..	..	..	..	..	..	..	..	..	..
4120 Others	..	..	..	..	..	..	..	..	..	..
4200 Recurrent taxes on net wealth	0	0	0	14	1	2 118	2 547	231	226	427
4210 Individual	..	..	..	5	0	0	0	0	0	0
4220 Corporate	..	..	..	9	1	2 118	2 547	231	226	427
4300 Estate, inheritance and gift taxes	47	128	376	1 005	149	483	622	674	798	396
Inheritance and gift duty	33	119	376	1 005	149	483	622	674	798	396
Estate duty	11	9	0	0	0	0	0	0	0	0
Proportional surcharge and premium	3	0	0	0	0	0	0	0	0	0
4310 Estate and inheritance taxes	..	..	..	..	..	..	..	..	..	..
4320 Gift taxes	..	..	..	..	..	..	..	..	..	..
4400 Taxes on financial and capital transactions	255	2 113	5 606	12 320	18 256	17 365	17 092	17 245	18 800	17 252
Registration tax	120	1 048	2 421	6 794	9 410	9 019	7 353	7 625	9 587	8 118
Mortgage taxes and land registry duties	22	190	469	1 067	2 525	2 071	1 841	1 529	1 625	1 464
5% proportional surcharge	6	0	0	0	0	0	0	0	0	0
Additional surcharge	4	0	0	0	0	0	0	0	0	0
Stamp duties and surcharges accruing on cadastral acts	104	751	2 185	4 459	6 321	6 275	7 898	7 600	7 190	7 261
Other	0	123	530	0	0	0	0	491	398	409
4500 Non-recurrent taxes	0	0	0	98	151	916	985	309	228	121
4510 On net wealth	..	..	..	0	0	0	0	0	0	0
4520 Other non-recurrent taxes	..	..	..	98	151	916	985	309	228	121
4600 Other recurrent taxes on property	0	0	0	569	1 311	1 896	1 889	2 242	1 189	977
5000 Taxes on goods and services	**2 173**	**15 990**	**74 280**	**141 852**	**171 869**	**178 863**	**187 210**	**196 473**	**214 775**	**190 248**
5100 Taxes on production, sale, transfer, etc.	2 037	15 251	67 083	127 281	155 191	160 775	164 597	174 443	187 651	164 766
Direct taxes refund	0	-73	-86	0	0	0	0	0	0	0
5110 General taxes	710	9 438	38 940	77 473	95 623	97 586	93 921	100 692	111 464	99 902
5111 Value added taxes	0	9 438	38 940	77 473	95 623	97 586	93 921	100 692	111 464	99 669
VAT	..	9 438	38 940	77 473	95 623	97 586	93 921	100 692	111 464	99 669
5112 Sales tax	0	0	0	0	0	0	0	0	0	0
5113 Other	710	0	0	0	0	0	0	0	0	233
General tax on receipts	662	..	..	..	..	..	..	..	..	0
Compensation tax on imported products	48	..	..	..	..	..	..	..	..	0
Digital Services Tax	..	..	..	..	..	..	..	..	..	233
5120 Taxes on specific goods and services	1 327	5 886	28 048	49 808	59 568	63 189	70 676	73 751	76 187	64 864
5121 Excise duties	816	4 088	20 304	31 479	32 904	36 414	45 720	46 238	47 108	40 119
Duty on mineral oils	465	3 462	15 928	22 172	23 252	22 884	26 332	25 759	25 907	21 454
Duty on spirits	27	87	206	486	595	570	571	600	652	593
Duty on beer	12	54	172	242	489	476	532	633	709	624
Duty on sugars	22	25	68	120	0	5	10	5	0	0
Duty on electricity	20	51	2 018	3 079	3 034	7 152	13 542	15 246	15 150	13 507
Duty on bananas	9	53	97	0	0	0	0	0	0	0
Duty on coffee	31	60	74	0	0	0	0	0	0	0
Duty on cocoa	3	4	7	0	0	0	0	0	0	0
Duty on olive oil	0	0	0	0	0	0	0	0	0	0
Other duty	44	190	1 037	5 201	5 385	5 268	4 659	3 898	4 666	3 922
Alcohol, spirits, liquor	5	0	0	0	0	0	0	0	0	0
On matches and flints	13	22	47	0	0	0	0	0	0	0
Meat	26	0	0	0	0	0	0	0	0	0
In-bond surcharge	0	81	650	174	143	54	67	90	17	12
Combustible materials	39	0	0	0	0	0	0	0	0	0
Construction materials	30	0	0	0	0	0	0	0	0	0
Excise duty on sound and video	3	0	0	0	0	0	0	0	0	0
Tax on phonograph records	1	0	0	0	0	0	0	0	0	0
Stamp duty on playing cards	1	0	0	0	0	0	0	0	0	0
Other	66	0	0	5	6	5	7	7	7	7
5122 Profits of fiscal monopolies	303	1 033	3 248	7 718	10 440	10 983	10 683	10 711	10 653	10 539
Duty on tobacco	292	1 033	3 248	7 712	10 436	10 978	10 679	10 710	10 652	10 538
On salt	10	0	0	0	0	0	0	0	0	0
Duty on products of Monopoli di Stato	1	0	0	6	4	5	4	1	1	1

	1965	1980	1990	2000	2007	2010	2013	2015	2019	2020
5123 Customs and import duties	142	261	1 164	1 536	2 261	2 225	1 890	2 246	2 314	1 971
Common Customs tariff (CEE)	0	0	836	1 536	2 261	2 225	1 890	2 246	2 314	1 971
Customs and shipping duties	115	14	0	0	0	0	0	0	0	0
Administrative services duties	11	0	0	0	0	0	0	0	0	0
Tax on agriculture	15	228	207	0	0	0	0	0	0	0
Other duties	0	9	68	0	0	0	0	0	0	0
Compensatory amounts	0	9	53	0	0	0	0	0	0	0
5124 Taxes on exports	0	0	0	0	0	0	0	0	0	0
5125 Taxes on investment goods	0	0	0	0	0	0	0	0	0	0
5126 Taxes on specific services	67	483	3 141	9 029	13 932	13 567	12 383	14 556	16 112	12 235
Entertainment tax	20	59	167	118	68	58	42	40	32	15
Stamp duty	6	0	0	0	0	0	0	0	0	0
Tax on advertisements	6	56	168	389	392	384	424	405	455	374
Tax on lotto, lotteries, betting and Totocalcio game	3	123	617	4 164	7 144	7 983	7 088	7 488	10 514	6 930
Casino takings, special duties, etc.	0	0	0	158	152	192	130	112	106	45
Single tax on games of skill and betting-levied indirectly	9	74	476	487	405	242	85	116	181	214
Aerotaxi passengers tax	0	0	0	0	0	0	7	8	9	5
Local tax (including insurance)	23	171	1 714	3 713	5 771	4 708	4 607	3 835	3 969	3 671
Bank levy for the National Resolution Fund	..	..	0	0	0	0	0	2 552	846	981
5127 Other taxes on internat. trade and transactions	0	0	0	0	0	0	0	0	0	0
Special Duty on foreign payments and currency selling	..	..	..	..	..	..	..	..	..	..
5128 Other taxes	0	21	192	46	31	0	0	0	0	0
ECSC taxes and contributions on sugar and other levies	..	21	121	0	0	..	..	..	..	..
Other	..	0	70	46	31	..	..	..	..	..
Bank cont. to the unique European Resolution Fund	..	0	0	0	0	..	..	..	..	..
5130 Unallocable between 5110 and 5120	0	0	180	0	0	0	0	0	0	0
5200 Taxes on use of goods and perform activities	136	456	4 474	8 479	10 550	10 531	11 352	11 130	14 021	12 800
5210 Recurrent taxes	136	456	4 474	8 479	10 550	1 155	1 359	1 653	1 904	1 571
Public motor vehicle register tax	64	152	967	1 034	1 326	1 155	1 359	1 653	1 904	1 571
Tax on vehicles 5% proportional surcharge	3	13	450	0	0	0	0	0	0	0
Surcharge on diesel cars	0	66	683	0	0	0	0	0	0	0
Surcharge on gas cars	0	0	171	0	0	0	0	0	0	0
5211 Paid by households: motor vehicles	..	..	..	3 433	4 652	4 628	4 487	4 710	5 323	4 713
5212 Paid by others: motor vehicles	..	..	..	1 006	1 332	1 300	1 395	1 446	1 394	1 235
Motor vehicle duty paid by firms	..	..	..	1 006	1 332	1 300	1 395	1 446	1 394	1 235
5213 Paid in respect of other goods	67	225	2 203	3 006	3 240	3 448	4 111	3 321	5 400	5 281
Law 1177 proportional surcharge	22	0	0	0	0	0	0	0	0	0
Taxes on signs	2	4	0	0	0	0	0	0	0	0
Tax on dog tags	0	7	12	0	0	0	0	0	0	0
Tax on hunting and fishing	0	0	0	0	0	0	0	0	0	0
Duty on official franchises	43	215	2 191	3 006	3 240	3 448	4 111	3 321	3 482	3 381
Television tax (households)	0	0	0	0	0	0	0	0	1 918	1 900
5220 Non-recurrent taxes	0	0	0	0	0	0	0	0	0	0
Motor vehicles, airplanes	..	..	..	..	..	..	..	..	..	..
Pro-Friuli tax on vehicles	..	..	..	..	..	..	..	..	..	..
5300 Unallocable between 5100 and 5200	0	283	2 724	6 092	6 128	7 557	11 261	10 900	13 103	12 682
Indirect taxes refund	..	0	160	288	616	693	477	715	788	524
Other	..	283	2 564	5 804	5 512	6 864	10 784	10 185	12 315	12 158
6000 Other taxes	**72**	**0**	**0**	**27 343**	**39 404**	**31 939**	**31 980**	**28 072**	**24 278**	**19 403**
6100 Paid solely by business	0	..	..	27 343	39 404	31 939	31 980	28 072	24 278	19 403
6200 Other	72	..	..	0	0	0	0	0	0	0
Capital levies	2	..	..	..	..	..	..	..	..	..
Other taxes	71	..	..	..	..	..	..	..	..	..
Memorandum items										
Customs duties collected on behalf of the EU	..	..	836	1 536	2 261	2 225	1 890	2 246	2 314	1 971
SRF contributions collected on behalf of the EU	..	..	..	..	..	..	..	2 346	846	981
Taxes and compulsory social security contributions paid by EU civil servants	..	..	..	..	..	..	55	61	72	77
Taxes paid by EU civil servants: income taxes	..	..	..	..	..	..	28	31	37	39
Taxes paid by EU civil servants: compulsory social security contributions	..	..	..	..	..	..	27	30	35	38
Non-wastable tax credits										
Non-wastable tax credits against 1110	..	..	..	..	0	0	357	9 793	10 085	11 667
Tax expenditure component	..	..	..	..	..	-109	206	8 615	8 917	10 362
Transfer component	..	..	..	..	..	109	151	1 178	1 167	1 305
Non-wastable tax credits against 1210	..	..	..	..	0	0	2 401	4 866	308	469
Tax expenditure component	..	..	..	..	..	..	0	0	0	0
Transfer component	..	..	..	..	..	..	2 401	4 866	308	469
Total tax revenue on cash basis	**5 505**	**60 422**	**265 116**	**488 738**	**653 836**	**659 704**	**689 299**	**711 837**	**754 038**	**715 825**
Total tax revenue on accrual basis	**..**	**..**	**..**	**503 096**	**671 189**	**671 912**	**706 829**	**711 114**	**759 445**	**706 743**

	1965	1980	1990	2000	2007	2010	2013	2015	2019	2020
Conciliation with National Accounts										
Additional taxes included in National Accounts	..	..	..	0	0	0	0	0	0	0
Taxes excluded from National Accounts	..	..	..	-5 416	-5 470	-6 538	-9 786	-9 801	-10 949	-10 622
The tax for the urban solid waste disposal (TARSU)	..	..	..	-4 387	-4 443	-5 519	-8 363	-8 519	-9 459	-9 381
Other	..	..	..	-1 029	-1 027	-1 019	-1 423	-1 282	-1 490	-1 241
Difference in treatment of tax credits	..	..	..	0	0	-109	206	8 615	8 917	10 362
Capital transfer for uncollected revenue	..	..	..	0	0	0	0	0	0	0
Voluntary social security contributions	..	..	..	464	567	561	738	750	764	724
Miscellaneous differences	..	..	..	0	0	0	0	0	0	0
National Accounts: Taxes and actual social contributions	..	..	..	498 144	666 286	665 826	697 987	710 678	758 177	707 207
Imputed social contributions	..	..	..	3 884	3 980	3 984	4 093	3 938	4 151	4 190
National Accounts: Taxes and all social contributions	..	..	..	502 028	670 266	669 810	702 080	714 616	762 328	711 397

.. Not available

Note: The tax year ends in December 31th.

As from 2000, revenues data are computed on accrual basis.

As from 1997, revenues data are based on data provided to the European Union as for the Treaty of Maastricht excessive deficit procedure.

Section 6000: Regional Tax on Productive Activities (IRAP); it is a tax on the value of production therefore its taxable base is different from other groups tax bases.

Regarding the section "Taxes excluded National Accounts" the item "Others" includes: tax on the public areas utilization and tax on the collection and disposal of waste water.

Source: *Ministero dell'economia e delle finanze; Istituto nazionale di statistica*.

StatLink https://stat.link/nq5c0j

Table 5.20. Japan: Details of tax revenue, 1965-2020

Billion JPY

	1965	1980	1990	2000	2007	2010	2013	2015	2019	2020
Total tax revenue	**6 172**	**62 443**	**130 843**	**136 236**	**146 248**	**132 484**	**146 405**	**163 533**	**175 380**	**177 308**
1000 Taxes on income, profits and capital gains	**2 708**	**28 800**	**65 682**	**47 398**	**53 174**	**40 034**	**47 534**	**50 969**	**53 994**	**53 934**
1100 Of individuals	1 338	15 180	36 394	28 677	28 600	24 663	28 150	30 847	32 947	33 189
1110 On income and profits	1 338	15 180	36 394	28 677	28 600	24 663	28 150	30 847	32 947	33 189
Income tax	970	10 800	25 996	18 789	16 080	12 984	15 865	18 178	19 571	19 591
Prefectural inhabitants tax	123	1 415	3 675	3 621	5 008	4 699	5 090	5 252	4 840	4 955
Municipal inhabitants tax	220	2 890	6 475	6 044	7 294	6 795	7 015	7 224	8 325	8 427
Enterprise tax	25	75	249	223	218	184	181	194	211	216
1120 On capital gains	0	0	0	0	0	0	0	0	0	0
1200 Corporate	1 370	13 620	29 288	18 721	24 573	15 372	19 384	20 122	21 046	20 745
1210 On profits	1 370	13 620	29 288	18 721	24 573	15 372	19 384	20 122	21 046	20 745
Corporation tax	927	8 923	18 384	11 747	14 744	8 968	11 698	10 832	10 797	11 235
Prefectural inhabitants tax	53	557	1 414	879	1 206	777	854	859	821	548
Municipal inhabitants tax	85	1 297	3 198	2 176	3 015	1 954	2 157	2 324	2 395	1 813
Enterprise tax	305	2 843	6 293	3 918	5 608	2 253	2 674	3 510	4 385	4 082
Local special corporate tax	0	0	0	0	0	1 420	2 001	2 081	2 044	978
Local corporate tax	0	0	0	0	0	0	0	516	604	1 418
Special corporate enterprise tax	..	..	0	0	0	0	0	0	0	672
1220 On capital gains	0	0	0	0	0	0	0	0	0	0
1300 Unallocable between 1100 and 1200	0	0	0	0	0	0	0	0	0	0
2000 Social security contributions	**1 344**	**18 178**	**34 613**	**47 968**	**53 325**	**54 461**	**59 803**	**64 465**	**71 993**	**71 550**
2100 Employees	446	6 393	13 895	19 830	21 975	23 593	25 984	28 224	31 954	31 839
2110 On a payroll basis	..	..	13 895	19 830	21 975	23 593	25 984	28 224	31 954	31 839
2120 On an income tax basis	..	..	0	0	0	0	0	0	0	0
2200 Employers	588	9 267	16 649	22 456	24 243	24 674	27 143	29 479	33 488	33 245
2210 On a payroll basis	..	..	16 649	22 456	24 243	24 674	27 143	29 479	33 488	33 245
2220 On an income tax basis	..	..	0	0	0	0	0	0	0	0
2300 Self-employed or non-employed	107	2 518	4 069	5 683	7 108	6 194	6 676	6 763	6 552	6 465
2310 On a payroll basis	..	..	4 069	5 683	7 108	6 194	6 676	6 763	6 552	6 465
2320 On an income tax basis	..	..	0	0	0	0	0	0	0	0
2400 Unallocable between 2100, 2200 and 2300	203	0	0	0	0	0	0	0	0	0
2410 On a payroll basis	..	..	..	..	..	..	..	..	..	..
2420 On an income tax basis	..	..	..	..	..	..	..	..	..	..
3000 Taxes on payroll and workforce	**0**	**0**	**0**	**0**	**0**	**0**	**0**	**0**	**0**	**0**
4000 Taxes on property	**498**	**5 114**	**12 296**	**14 294**	**13 138**	**12 878**	**12 940**	**13 400**	**14 340**	**14 328**
4100 Recurrent taxes on immovable property	319	3 326	7 099	10 414	9 949	10 225	9 882	10 005	10 612	10 719
Prefectural property tax	4	8	15	11	14	5	2	2	8	9
Municipal property tax	296	2 784	6 023	9 041	8 729	8 961	8 653	8 755	9 286	9 380
City planning tax	19	469	942	1 318	1 202	1 256	1 227	1 244	1 318	1 330
Special landholding tax	0	65	118	43	4	3	1	3	0	0
Water and land utilization tax	0	0	0	0	0	0	0	0	0	0
Land value tax	0	0	0	1	0	0	0	0	0	0
4110 Households	..	..	..	..	..	..	..	..	..	..
4120 Others	..	..	..	..	..	..	..	..	..	..
4200 Recurrent taxes on net wealth	0	0	0	0	0	0	0	0	0	0
4210 Individual	..	..	..	..	..	..	..	..	..	..
4220 Corporate	..	..	..	..	..	..	..	..	..	..
4300 Estate, inheritance and gift taxes	44	441	1 918	1 782	1 503	1 250	1 574	1 968	2 301	2 315
4310 Estate and inheritance taxes	34	375	..	..	..	..	..	..	..	..
Inheritance tax	34	375	..	..	..	..	..	..	..	..
4320 Gift taxes	10	65	..	..	..	..	..	..	..	..
Tax on gifts	10	65	..	..	..	..	..	..	..	..
4400 Taxes on financial and capital transactions	135	1 347	3 280	2 099	1 686	1 403	1 483	1 426	1 427	1 294
Bourse tax	3	15	41	0	0	0	0	0	0	0
Securities transaction	8	209	748	0	0	0	0	0	0	0
Bank of Japan note issue tax	0	0	0	0	0	0	0	0	0	0
Stamp revenues	83	841	1 894	1 532	1 202	1 024	1 126	1 050	1 023	920
Real property acquisition tax	41	282	596	567	485	379	357	377	404	374
4500 Non-recurrent taxes	0	0	0	0	0	0	0	0	0	0
4510 On net wealth	..	..	..	..	..	..	..	..	..	..
4520 Other non-recurrent taxes	..	..	..	..	..	..	..	..	..	..
4600 Other recurrent taxes on property	0	0	0	0	0	0	0	0	0	0
5000 Taxes on goods and services	**1 620**	**10 200**	**17 917**	**26 227**	**26 256**	**24 730**	**25 744**	**34 286**	**34 599**	**37 053**
5100 Taxes on production, sale, transfer, etc.	1 544	8 822	15 647	23 180	23 241	22 160	23 313	31 871	32 046	34 433
5110 General taxes	0	0	5 778	12 350	12 841	12 675	13 479	22 400	23 148	26 395
5111 Value added taxes	..	..	5 778	12 350	12 841	12 675	13 479	22 400	23 148	26 395
5112 Sales tax	..	..	0	0	0	0	0	0	0	0
5113 Other	..	..	0	0	0	0	0	0	0	0
5120 Taxes on specific goods and services	1 544	8 822	9 868	10 830	10 400	9 485	9 834	9 470	8 898	8 038

	1965	1980	1990	2000	2007	2010	2013	2015	2019	2020
5121 Excise duties	1 062	6 674	8 637	9 837	9 374	8 622	8 728	8 351	7 891	7 167
Liquor tax	353	1 424	1 935	1 816	1 524	1 389	1 371	1 338	1 247	1 134
Sugar excises	29	43	0	0	0	0	0	0	0	0
Local gasoline tax	46	278	361	296	302	294	275	264	244	220
Gasoline tax	254	1 547	2 007	2 769	2 820	2 750	2 574	2 465	2 281	2 058
Liquefied petroleum gas tax	0	30	31	28	27	24	21	18	14	9
Aviation fuel tax	0	58	76	104	104	89	67	66	65	11
Commodity tax	138	1 038	5	0	0	0	0	0	0	0
Playing-card tax	1	1	0	0	0	0	0	0	0	0
Prefectural tobacco tax	44	229	361	282	278	256	173	153	140	134
Municipal tobacco tax	73	402	636	865	853	788	983	936	854	817
Timber delivery tax	3	3	0	0	0	0	0	0	0	0
Mineral product tax	2	5	3	2	2	2	2	2	2	2
Electricity and gas tax	54	386	0	0	0	0	0	0	0	0
Diesel oil tax	65	447	834	1 208	1 034	918	943	925	945	910
Vehicle acquisition tax	0	270	613	464	425	192	193	137	104	0
Promotion of power resources development tax	0	109	295	375	352	349	328	316	316	311
Petroleum and coal tax	0	404	487	489	513	502	600	630	638	608
Tobacco tax	0	0	996	876	925	908	1 038	954	874	840
Special tobacco tax	0	0	0	264	214	163	161	148	124	112
International tourist tax	..	..	0	0	0	0	0	0	44	1
5122 Profits of fiscal monopolies	179	808	0	0	0	0	0	0	0	0
Monopoly profits	179	808	..	..	..	..	..	..	..	..
5123 Customs and import duties	222	786	928	877	941	786	1 034	1 049	941	820
Customs duty	222	786	928	877	941	786	1 034	1 049	941	820
5124 Taxes on exports	0	0	0	0	0	0	0	0	0	0
5125 Taxes on investment goods	0	0	0	0	0	0	0	0	0	0
5126 Taxes on specific services	81	554	303	116	85	77	71	70	66	52
Travel tax	4	64	0	0	0	0	0	0	0	0
Admission tax	10	5	0	0	0	0	0	0	0	0
Local entertainment tax	10	74	0	0	0	0	0	0	0	0
Golf course utilization tax	0	0	90	81	60	55	49	48	43	39
Meal and lodging tax	56	398	0	0	0	0	0	0	0	0
Special local consumption tax	0	0	195	12	0	0	0	0	0	0
Bathing tax	1	13	18	23	25	22	22	23	23	12
5127 Other taxes on internat. trade and transactions	0	0	0	0	0	0	0	0	0	0
5128 Other taxes	0	0	0	0	0	0	0	0	0	0
5130 Unallocable between 5110 and 5120	0	0	0	0	0	0	0	0	0	0
5200 Taxes on use of goods and perform activities	76	1 378	2 270	3 047	3 015	2 570	2 431	2 416	2 553	2 620
5210 Recurrent taxes	69	1 358	2 250	3 027	2 993	2 548	2 409	2 393	2 530	2 599
Automobile tax	55	781	1 276	1 765	1 717	1 616	1 574	1 543	1 588	1 623
Light vehicle tax	13	43	88	125	164	178	189	200	269	285
Motor vehicle tonnage tax	0	527	881	1 134	1 110	753	643	649	671	690
Hunter licence tax	0	3	2	2	0	0	0	0	0	0
Hunting tax	0	3	2	1	2	2	2	1	1	1
Mine lot tax	1	1	1	1	0	0	0	0	0	0
5211 Paid by households: motor vehicles	..	..	..	..	..	..	..	..	..	..
5212 Paid by others: motor vehicles	..	..	..	..	..	..	..	..	..	..
5213 Paid in respect of other goods	..	..	..	..	..	..	..	..	..	..
5220 Non-recurrent taxes	7	20	20	20	22	21	22	22	23	21
5300 Unallocable between 5100 and 5200	0	0	0	0	0	0	0	0	0	0
6000 Other taxes	**2**	**151**	**335**	**348**	**356**	**381**	**384**	**413**	**454**	**444**
6100 Paid solely by business	0	139	288	324	313	330	348	361	387	385
Business office tax	..	139	288	324	313	330	348	361	387	385
6200 Other	2	12	47	24	43	52	36	52	68	60
Taxes not in local tax law	2	12	47	24	43	52	36	52	67	60
Other	0	0	0	0	0	0	0	0	1	0
Total tax revenue on cash basis	**6 172**	**62 443**	**..**	**..**	**..**	**..**	**..**	**..**	**..**	**..**
Total tax revenue on accrual basis	**..**	**..**	**130 843**	**136 236**	**146 248**	**132 484**	**146 405**	**163 533**	**175 380**	**177 308**
Conciliation with National Accounts										
Additional taxes included in National Accounts	..	..	..	..	..	..	..	..	..	..
Taxes excluded from National Accounts	..	..	..	..	..	..	..	..	..	..
Difference in treatment of tax credits	..	..	..	..	..	..	..	..	..	..
Capital transfer for uncollected revenue	..	..	..	..	..	..	..	..	..	..
Voluntary social security contributions	..	..	..	..	..	..	..	..	..	..
Miscellaneous differences	..	..	..	..	..	..	..	..	..	..
National Accounts: Taxes and actual social contributions	..	..	..	..	..	..	..	..	..	..
Imputed social contributions	..	..	..	..	..	..	..	..	..	..
National Accounts: Taxes and all social contributions	..	..	..	..	..	..	..	..	..	..

.. Not available

Note: Data are on a fiscal year basis beginning 1st April.
From 1990, data are on accrual basis.
The figures for different groups of taxes are reported on different reporting bases, namely: Social security contributions (heading 2000) : in principle accrual basis, Central government taxes : accrual basis (revenues accrued during the fiscal year plus cash receipts collected before the end of May (the end of April until 1977), Local government taxes : accrual basis (due to be paid during the fiscal year and cash receipts collected before the end of May).
Heading 2000 includes some unidentifiable voluntary contributions.
Heading 2300: Includes contributions to the National pension, National Health Insurance and the Farmer's pension fund.
Heading 4100: Municipal property tax, includes Prefectural property tax from 1990 to 1994 because data is not available to provide a breakdown.
Heading 5121: Municipal tobacco tax, includes Prefectural tobacco tax from 1990 to 1994 because data is not available to provide a breakdown.
Heading 5121: In sub-item Petroleum and coal tax, the data before 2003 refer to petroleum tax.
Source: Tax Bureau, Ministry of Finance.

StatLink https://stat.link/td4xr3

Table 5.21. Korea: Details of tax revenue, 1965-2020

Billion KRW

	1965	1980	1990	2000	2007	2010	2013	2015	2019	2020
Total tax revenue	..	**6 687**	**37 262**	**136 295**	**258 571**	**295 968**	**347 332**	**393 559**	**523 985**	**538 450**
1000 Taxes on income, profits and capital gains	..	**1 704**	**12 203**	**39 254**	**82 239**	**82 905**	**101 792**	**119 151**	**174 040**	**166 564**
1100 Of individuals	..	766	7 440	19 950	43 276	42 098	53 311	67 600	91 714	101 286
1110 On income and profits	..	766	6 327	18 569	31 984	33 935	46 654	55 744	75 613	77 630
Income tax	..	0	0	0	0	0	0	0	0	0
Dividends and interest income tax	..	0	0	0	4 682	4 425	4 889	4 561	5 577	5 830
Wages and salaries income tax	..	0	0	0	14 124	15 517	21 931	27 055	38 466	40 905
Other income tax	..	0	0	0	2 607	2 986	3 432	4 467	6 640	6 645
Global income tax	..	661	4 723	16 128	6 151	6 369	10 901	12 784	16 778	16 073
Defence tax on income tax	..	105	938	0	0	0	0	0	0	0
Education tax on income tax	..	0	325	0	0	0	0	0	0	0
Rural dev. tax on interest, bus. Inc. & cap. gains relief	..	0	0	156	160	179	124	105	139	225
Inhabitant tax on income tax (local)	..	0	341	2 285	4 260	4 459	5 377	6 772	8 013	7 952
1120 On capital gains	..	0	1 113	1 381	11 292	8 163	6 657	11 856	16 101	23 656
Capital gains tax	..	..	1 113	1 381	11 292	8 163	6 657	11 856	16 101	23 656
1200 Corporate	..	738	4 757	19 271	38 963	40 807	48 481	51 551	82 326	65 278
1210 On profits	..	738	4 757	19 271	38 963	40 807	48 481	51 551	82 326	65 278
Corporation tax - withholding	..	..	677	8 577	8 360	9 095	12 176	12 317	14 168	13 179
Corporation tax - final returns	..	..	2 549	9 302	27 057	28 173	31 679	32 713	58 006	42 335
Defence tax on corporation tax	..	..	1 323	0	0	0	0	0	0	0
Inhabitant tax on corporation tax (local)	..	..	207	1 142	3 152	3 094	4 118	6 217	9 729	9 293
Rural development tax corporate income	..	..	0	251	394	445	508	304	423	471
Excess profit tax	..	0	0	0	0	0	0	0	0	0
1220 On capital gains	..	0	0	0	0	0	0	0	0	0
Capital gains tax	..	..	..	..	..	..	..	..	..	..
1300 Unallocable between 1100 and 1200	..	199	6	33	0	0	0	0	0	0
Business income tax	..	0	0	0	..	..	..	..	..	..
Real estate income tax	..	0	0	0	..	..	..	..	..	..
Defence tax on real estate & business income	..	0	0	0	..	..	..	..	..	..
Rural dev. tax on bus. inc. & cap. gains relief	..	0	0	30	..	..	..	..	..	..
Inhabitant tax before 1990 (local)	..	117	0	0	..	..	..	..	..	..
Farm land tax (local)	..	83	6	3	..	..	..	..	..	..
Inhabitant tax on farm land tax (local)	..	0	0	0	..	..	..	..	..	..
2000 Social security contributions	..	**73**	**3 760**	**22 759**	**53 588**	**69 090**	**91 596**	**104 693**	**140 071**	**150 854**
2100 Employees	..	0	1 464	8 578	21 773	28 213	38 396	44 281	60 682	65 384
Veterans' relief fund	..	0	0	0	0	0	0	0	0	0
Soldiers' annuity fund	..	0	0	0	0	0	0	0	0	0
Unemployment assurance	..	0	0	598	1 164	1 358	2 418	3 076	4 027	4 895
National welfare pension fund	..	0	429	4 325	9 338	11 004	13 890	15 821	20 630	21 722
Social benefit fund	..	0	0	0	0	0	0	0	0	0
Health Insurance	..	0	483	2 066	8 180	11 783	17 128	19 868	27 911	30 184
Teachers' pensions	..	0	86	279	581	868	1 077	1 125	1 678	1 780
Government employees pensions	..	0	406	1 144	2 202	2 878	3 435	3 876	5 796	6 134
Military personal pensions	..	0	60	166	308	322	448	515	640	669
2110 On a payroll basis	..	..	..	8 578	21 773	28 213	38 396	44 281	60 682	65 384
2120 On an income tax basis	..	..	..	0	0	0	0	0	0	0
2200 Employers	..	73	1 694	9 409	23 557	30 856	41 518	47 846	63 780	67 676
Ind. works' insurance fund	..	73	550	1 876	4 431	4 632	5 436	6 062	7 539	7 088
Soldiers' annuity fund	..	0	0	0	0	0	0	0	0	0
Pneumoconiosis fund	..	0	0	0	0	0	0	0	0	0
Unemployment insurance	..	0	0	1 449	2 474	2 860	4 545	5 499	7 063	8 024
Veterans' relief fund	..	0	0	0	0	0	0	0	0	0
National welfare pension fund	..	0	430	4 340	9 383	11 052	13 958	15 895	20 631	21 722
Social benefit fund	..	0	0	0	0	0	0	0	0	0
Health Insurance	..	0	658	1 547	6 844	11 718	16 826	19 493	27 110	29 288
Teachers' pensions	..	0	56	197	425	594	753	897	1 437	1 554
Government employees pensions	..	0	0	0	0	0	0	0	0	0
2210 On a payroll basis	..	..	..	9 409	23 557	30 856	41 518	47 846	63 780	67 676
2220 On an income tax basis	..	..	..	0	0	0	0	0	0	0
2300 Self-employed or non-employed	..	0	602	4 772	8 258	10 021	11 682	12 566	15 609	17 794
2310 On a payroll basis	..	..	0	0	0	0	0	0	0	0
2320 On an income tax basis	..	..	602	4 772	8 258	10 021	11 682	12 566	15 609	17 794
2400 Unallocable between 2100, 2200 and 2300	..	0	0	0	0	0	0	0	0	0
2410 On a payroll basis	..	..	..	..	..	..	..	..	..	..
2420 On an income tax basis	..	..	..	..	..	..	..	..	..	..
3000 Taxes on payroll and workforce	..	**34**	**153**	**258**	**619**	**714**	**981**	**1 122**	**1 597**	**1 607**
Workshop tax on workforce (local)	..	31	124	258	619	714	981	1 122	1 597	1 607
Vocational training promotion fund	..	3	29	0	0	0	0	0	0	0
4000 Taxes on property	..	**537**	**4 389**	**16 846**	**33 109**	**33 516**	**35 847**	**48 625**	**59 732**	**76 512**

	1965	1980	1990	2000	2007	2010	2013	2015	2019	2020
4100 Recurrent taxes on immovable property	..	183	980	3 385	9 196	9 270	10 809	12 486	17 750	20 044
Property tax (local)	..	119	227	728	3 755	4 817	8 267	9 294	12 677	13 773
City planning tax on urban real estate (local)	..	51	244	815	1 883	2 465	0	0	0	0
Community facilities tax (local)	..	13	86	341	543	650	912	1 351	1 681	1 777
Tax on excessive land holdings (local)	..	0	1	0	0	0	0	0	0	0
Tax on aggregate land holdings (local)	..	0	400	1 282	5	0	0	0	0	0
Rural dev. tax on local agg. land holdings tax	..	0	0	81	1	0	0	0	0	0
Tax on excessively increased land value	..	0	0	0	0	0	0	0	0	0
Comprehensive real estate tax	..	0	0	0	2 414	1 029	1 224	1 399	2 671	3 601
Rural dev. tax on comprehensive real estate tax	..	0	0	0	483	208	250	267	505	680
4110 Households	..	..	0	0	0	0	0	0	0	0
4120 Others	..	..	22	138	112	101	156	175	216	213
Workshop tax on property (local)	..	..	22	138	112	101	156	175	216	213
4200 Recurrent taxes on net wealth	..	0	0	0	0	0	0	0	0	0
4210 Individual	..	..	..	..	..	..	..	..	..	..
4220 Corporate	..	..	..	..	..	..	..	..	..	..
4300 Estate, inheritance and gift taxes	..	12	354	989	2 842	3 076	4 290	5 044	8 329	10 375
4310 Estate and inheritance taxes	..	5	85	449	1 059	1 203	1 587	1 944	3 154	3 904
Inheritance tax	..	3	71	449	1 059	1 203	1 587	1 944	3 154	3 904
Defence tax on inheritance tax	..	2	14	0	0	0	0	0	0	0
4320 Gift taxes	..	7	269	540	1 783	1 873	2 703	3 100	5 175	6 471
Gift tax	..	7	225	540	1 783	1 873	2 703	3 100	5 175	6 471
Defence tax on gift tax	..	0	44	0	0	0	0	0	0	0
4400 Taxes on financial and capital transactions	..	319	2 960	11 935	21 071	21 170	20 748	31 095	33 653	46 093
Registration tax (local)	..	122	1 378	4 528	7 254	7 370	1 312	1 831	1 837	2 053
Registration tax	..	0	0	0	0	0	0	0	0	0
Defence tax on registration tax	..	0	0	0	0	0	0	0	0	0
Rural dev. tax on local acquisition tax	..	0	0	246	627	632	874	969	947	1 164
Rural dev. tax on local registration tax	..	0	0	66	143	144	1	1	0	0
Securities transactions tax	..	0	224	2 736	3 469	3 667	3 077	4 670	4 473	8 759
Rural dev. tax on securities transaction tax	..	0	0	823	1 729	2 010	1 529	1 861	1 635	3 616
Acquisition tax (local)	..	163	1 165	3 148	7 261	6 825	13 318	20 810	23 915	29 536
Stamp tax	..	34	193	388	588	522	637	953	846	965
4500 Non-recurrent taxes	..	22	95	537	0	0	0	0	0	0
Asset revaluation tax	..	22	95	537	..	..	..	..	..	..
4510 On net wealth	..	..	0	0	..	..	..	..	..	..
4520 Other non-recurrent taxes	..	..	0	0	..	..	..	..	..	..
4600 Other recurrent taxes on property	..	0	0	0	0	0	0	0	0	0
5000 Taxes on goods and services	**..**	**4 190**	**16 497**	**52 271**	**80 861**	**99 769**	**106 717**	**110 326**	**135 276**	**131 353**
5100 Taxes on production, sale, transfer, etc.	..	4 114	16 024	50 023	78 414	96 573	99 970	103 254	127 551	123 219
5110 General taxes	..	1 471	6 964	23 212	40 942	51 800	59 105	60 162	82 174	81 452
5111 Value added taxes	..	1 471	6 964	23 212	40 942	51 800	59 105	60 162	82 174	81 452
Value added tax	..	1 471	6 964	23 212	40 942	51 800	59 105	60 162	82 174	81 452
5112 Sales tax	..	0	0	0	0	0	0	0	0	0
Business tax	..	..	..	..	..	..	..	..	..	..
5113 Other	..	0	0	0	0	0	0	0	0	0
5120 Taxes on specific goods and services	..	2 643	9 059	26 811	37 472	44 773	40 865	43 092	45 377	41 767
5121 Excise duties	..	1 029	4 924	18 155	27 880	31 340	27 661	31 857	34 691	33 013
Commodity tax	..	0	0	0	0	0	0	0	0	0
Defence tax on commodity tax	..	0	0	0	0	0	0	0	0	0
Liquor tax	..	298	1 022	1 963	2 268	2 878	2 947	3 228	3 504	3 008
Defence tax on liquor tax	..	78	0	0	0	0	0	0	0	0
Education tax on liquor tax	..	0	81	516	580	724	764	808	844	733
Textile tax	..	0	0	0	0	0	0	0	0	0
Petroleum tax	..	0	0	0	0	0	0	0	0	0
Transport tax on petrol products	..	0	0	8 404	11 464	13 970	13 248	14 055	14 563	13 938
Education tax on transport tax	..	0	0	1 247	1 715	2 133	1 895	2 154	2 190	2 041
Electricity and gas tax	..	0	0	0	0	0	0	0	0	0
Special excise tax	..	583	1 912	2 985	5 161	5 066	5 484	8 001	9 719	9 218
Defence tax on special excise tax	..	70	337	0	0	0	0	0	0	0
Education tax on special excise tax	..	0	0	498	607	501	485	515	455	440
Rural development on special excise tax	..	0	0	37	54	24	56	61	58	57
Tobacco sales tax (local)	..	0	0	0	0	0	0	0	0	0
Tobacco consumption tax (local)	..	0	1 572	2 251	2 761	2 875	2 782	3 035	3 358	3 578
Motor fuel tax (local)	..	0	0	254	3 270	3 169	0	0	0	0
5122 Profits of fiscal monopolies	..	510	0	0	0	0	0	0	0	0
Monopoly profit	..	510	..	..	..	..	..	..	..	..

	1965	1980	1990	2000	2007	2010	2013	2015	2019	2020
5123 Customs and import duties	..	1 014	3 692	5 936	7 690	11 046	11 012	8 907	8 250	7 413
Customs duties	..	762	2 765	5 800	7 411	10 666	10 562	8 495	7 882	7 059
Defence tax on customs duties	..	248	919	0	0	0	0	0	0	0
Special customs duties	..	0	0	0	0	0	0	0	0	0
Tonnage tax	..	0	0	0	0	0	0	0	0	0
Education tax on imports	..	0	7	99	234	336	429	390	345	341
Rural dev. tax on customs exemptions	..	0	0	37	45	44	21	22	23	13
Previous year receipts	..	4	0	0	0	0	0	0	0	0
5124 Taxes on exports	..	0	0	0	0	0	0	0	0	0
5125 Taxes on investment goods	..	0	0	0	0	0	0	0	0	0
5126 Taxes on specific services	..	90	444	2 720	1 902	2 387	2 192	2 328	2 436	1 341
Telephone tax	..	50	262	1 457	0	0	0	0	0	0
Defence tax on telephone tax	..	33	0	0	0	0	0	0	0	0
Entertainment tax	..	0	0	0	0	0	0	0	0	0
Defence tax on entertainment tax	..	0	0	0	0	0	0	0	0	0
Entertainment tax (local)	..	0	0	0	0	0	0	0	0	0
Travel tax	..	0	0	0	0	0	0	0	0	0
Admission tax	..	0	0	0	0	0	0	0	0	0
Defence tax on admission tax	..	0	0	0	0	0	0	0	0	0
Education tax on banking & insurance	..	0	108	473	721	951	938	1 004	1 277	1 138
Horse race tax (local)	..	3	56	566	864	1 068	1 042	1 089	970	169
Rural dev. tax on horse race tax	..	0	0	84	165	215	212	235	189	34
Butchery tax (local)	..	5	18	51	52	58	0	0	0	0
Regional development tax (local)	..	0	0	89	100	95	0	0	0	0
5127 Other taxes on internat. trade and transactions	..	0	0	0	0	0	0	0	0	0
5128 Other taxes	..	0	0	0	0	0	0	0	0	0
5130 Unallocable between 5110 and 5120	..	0	0	0	0	0	0	0	0	0
5200 Taxes on use of goods and perform activities	..	75	474	2 248	2 447	3 196	6 747	7 072	7 725	8 134
5210 Recurrent taxes	..	75	474	2 248	2 447	3 196	6 747	7 072	7 725	8 134
License tax (local)	..	18	48	241	77	76	0	0	0	0
Automobile tax (local)	..	57	426	2 007	2 370	3 120	6 747	7 072	7 725	8 134
5211 Paid by households: motor vehicles	..	..	..	..	..	..	..	..	..	..
5212 Paid by others: motor vehicles	..	..	..	..	..	..	..	..	..	..
5213 Paid in respect of other goods	..	..	..	..	..	..	..	..	..	..
5220 Non-recurrent taxes	..	0	0	0	0	0	0	0	0	0
5300 Unallocable between 5100 and 5200	..	0	0	0	0	0	0	0	0	0
6000 Other taxes	**..**	**150**	**259**	**4 907**	**8 155**	**9 974**	**10 399**	**9 642**	**13 269**	**11 560**
6100 Paid solely by business	..	0	0	0	0	0	0	0	0	0
6200 Other	..	150	259	4 907	8 155	9 974	10 399	9 642	13 269	11 560
Unallocable tax revenue	..	143	0	0	0	0	0	0	0	0
Previous year tax	..	0	213	1 474	2 965	4 449	4 774	3 435	5 873	4 165
Previous year tax (local)	..	6	47	474	672	654	601	392	719	259
Unallocable defence tax	..	0	0	-3	0	0	0	0	0	0
Education tax on local taxes	..	0	0	2 962	4 518	4 871	5 024	5 815	6 677	7 136
Total tax revenue on cash basis	**..**	**6 687**	**37 262**	**136 295**	**258 571**	**295 968**	**347 332**	**393 559**	**523 985**	**538 450**
Total tax revenue on accrual basis	**..**	**..**	**..**	**..**	**..**	**..**	**..**	**..**	**..**	**..**
Conciliation with National Accounts										
Additional taxes included in National Accounts	..	..	..	..	..	..	..	..	..	..
Taxes excluded from National Accounts	..	..	..	..	..	..	..	..	..	..
Difference in treatment of tax credits	..	..	..	..	..	..	..	..	..	..
Capital transfer for uncollected revenue	..	..	..	..	..	..	..	..	..	..
Voluntary social security contributions	..	..	..	..	..	..	..	..	..	..
Miscellaneous differences	..	..	..	..	..	..	..	..	..	..
National Accounts: Taxes and actual social contributions	..	..	..	..	..	..	..	..	..	..
Imputed social contributions	..	..	..	..	..	..	..	..	..	..
National Accounts: Taxes and all social contributions	..	..	..	..	..	..	..	..	..	..

.. Not available

Note: Year ending 31st December.

Data are on cash basis.

Heading 2000: From 1997 the contributions to the three funds (civil servant pension fund, private school teachers pension fund and medical insurance fund) are classified as security social contributions. The reasons for the change are that the contributions either became mandatory or the fund started to be managed by public authorities in that year, thereby meeting the OECD definition of social security contributions.

Heading 2200: From 2007, this includes long-term care insurance.

Source: Ministry of Finance and Economy, Ministry of Home Affairs.

StatLink https://stat.link/90pci1

Table 5.22. Latvia: Details of tax revenue, 1965-2020

Million EUR

	1965	1980	1990	2000	2007	2010	2013	2015	2019	2020
Total tax revenue	..	..	..	**1 995**	**6 401**	**5 162**	**6 695**	**7 320**	**9 482**	**9 357**
Total tax revenue exclusive of taxes collected for the EU	..	..	..	**1 995**	**6 362**	**5 137**	**6 667**	**7 272**	**9 426**	**9 304**
1000 Taxes on income, profits and capital gains	..	..	..	**480**	**1 857**	**1 292**	**1 690**	**1 833**	**2 026**	**2 021**
1100 Of individuals	..	..	..	376	1 287	1 116	1 320	1 445	1 978	1 808
1110 On income and profits	..	..	..	376	1 287	1 116	1 320	1 445	1 978	1 808
Personal income tax	..	..	..	376	1 287	1 116	1 320	1 445	1 978	1 808
Solidarity tax	..	..	..	0	0	0	0	0	1	0
1120 On capital gains	..	..	..	0	0	0	0	0	0	0
1200 Corporate	..	..	..	105	570	175	370	389	48	213
1210 On profits	..	..	..	105	570	175	370	389	48	213
1220 On capital gains	..	..	..	0	0	0	0	0	0	0
1300 Unallocable between 1100 and 1200	..	..	..	0	0	0	0	0	0	0
2000 Social security contributions	..	..	..	**669**	**1 774**	**1 554**	**1 933**	**2 030**	**2 911**	**2 937**
2100 Employees	..	..	..	167	479	389	531	585	847	841
2110 On a payroll basis	..	..	..	167	479	389	531	585	847	841
2120 On an income tax basis	..	..	..	0	0	0	0	0	0	0
2200 Employers	..	..	..	501	1 283	1 155	1 391	1 432	2 037	2 068
2210 On a payroll basis	..	..	..	501	1 283	1 155	1 391	1 432	2 037	2 068
2220 On an income tax basis	..	..	..	0	0	0	0	0	0	0
2300 Self-employed or non-employed	..	..	..	1	12	9	11	12	27	29
2310 On a payroll basis	..	..	..	1	12	9	11	12	27	29
2320 On an income tax basis	..	..	..	0	0	0	0	0	0	0
2400 Unallocable between 2100, 2200 and 2300	..	..	..	0	0	0	0	0	0	0
2410 On a payroll basis	..	..	..	..	..	..	..	..	..	..
2420 On an income tax basis	..	..	..	..	..	..	..	..	..	..
3000 Taxes on payroll and workforce	..	..	..	**0**	**4**	**3**	**3**	**3**	**3**	**3**
Risk duty of business	..	..	..	..	4	3	3	3	3	3
4000 Taxes on property	..	..	..	**76**	**195**	**157**	**221**	**249**	**287**	**281**
4100 Recurrent taxes on immovable property	..	..	..	63	106	128	173	197	226	222
4110 Households	..	..	..	0	0	0	22	24	40	39
4120 Others	..	..	..	63	106	128	151	173	187	183
Tax on property	..	..	..	63	106	128	151	173	187	183
Tax on land	..	..	..	0	0	0	0	0	0	0
4200 Recurrent taxes on net wealth	..	..	..	0	0	0	0	0	0	0
4210 Individual	..	..	..	..	..	..	..	..	..	..
4220 Corporate	..	..	..	..	..	..	..	..	..	..
4300 Estate, inheritance and gift taxes	..	..	..	0	3	3	5	7	11	12
4310 Estate and inheritance taxes	..	..	..	..	3	3	5	7	11	12
Duty for legacies and donations	..	..	..	..	0	2	3	4	9	9
Stamp duty for transactions made in Land Register in relation to legacies and donations	..	..	..	..	1	0	0	1	1	1
Duty for consolidation of ownership and legal clients in Land Register anent legacies and donations	..	..	..	..	2	2	2	2	2	2
4320 Gift taxes	..	..	..	..	0	0	0	0	0	0
4400 Taxes on financial and capital transactions	..	..	..	13	86	26	43	42	45	44
Duties on transactions with privatization vouchers	..	..	..	0	0	0	0	0	0	0
Stamp duty for transactions made in Land Register, which have been collected from juridical persons, except legacies and donations	..	..	..	0	1	1	1	1	1	1
Duty for consolidation of ownership and legal liens in Land Register, which have been collected from juridical persons, except legacies and donations	..	..	..	4	27	13	17	18	19	18
Stamp duty for transactions made in Land Register, which have been collected from physical persons, except legacies and donations	..	..	..	1	8	1	2	2	2	2
Duty for consolidation of ownership and legal liens in Land Register, which have been collected from physical persons, except legacies and donations	..	..	..	7	51	11	23	20	23	23
4500 Non-recurrent taxes	..	..	..	0	0	0	0	3	4	3
4510 On net wealth	..	..	..	..	..	..	..	0	0	0
4520 Other non-recurrent taxes	..	..	..	..	..	..	..	3	4	3
The payment made by a foreigner before receiving temporary residence permit	..	..	..	..	..	..	..	3	4	3
4600 Other recurrent taxes on property	..	..	..	0	0	0	0	0	0	0
5000 Taxes on goods and services	..	..	..	**770**	**2 572**	**2 157**	**2 849**	**3 205**	**4 254**	**4 114**
5100 Taxes on production, sale, transfer, etc.	..	..	..	739	2 515	2 031	2 695	3 052	3 977	3 896
5110 General taxes	..	..	..	476	1 753	1 301	1 855	2 130	2 783	2 720
5111 Value added taxes	..	..	..	476	1 727	1 202	1 690	1 876	2 632	2 571
5112 Sales tax	..	..	..	0	0	0	0	31	0	0
Subsidised electricity tax	..	..	..	..	..	..	..	31	..	..

	1965	1980	1990	2000	2007	2010	2013	2015	2019	2020
5113 Other	..	..	..	0	27	99	165	223	150	149
Mandatory procurement public service obligation fee	..	..	..	..	27	99	165	223	150	149
5120 Taxes on specific goods and services	..	..	..	262	761	730	840	922	1 194	1 176
5121 Excise duties	..	..	..	232	626	645	742	807	1 068	1 065
Excise duty on alcoholic beverages	..	..	..	63	127	111	124	128	200	189
Excise duty on beer	..	..	..	4	15	25	24	27	54	52
Excise duty on oil products	..	..	..	124	359	360	388	428	542	560
Excise duty on tobacco	..	..	..	27	92	130	160	178	228	223
Excise duty on other products	..	..	..	14	32	18	24	25	17	18
Excise duty on coffee and non alcoholic beverages	..	..	..	6	8	13	14	14	17	18
Excise duty / Tax on cars and motorcycles	..	..	..	8	24	5	10	11	0	0
Excise duty on natural gas	..	..	..	0	0	1	22	20	22	17
Tax on electricity	..	..	..	0	1	1	1	2	5	5
5122 Profits of fiscal monopolies	..	..	..	0	0	0	0	0	0	0
5123 Customs and import duties	..	..	..	21	70	38	29	43	52	48
Customs duties	..	..	..	21	40	25	28	40	50	48
Levies on imported agricultural products	..	..	..	0	2	0	0	0	0	0
Excise duty of imported goods for omission for free turnover	..	..	..	0	28	14	2	3	2	0
5124 Taxes on exports	..	..	..	0	0	0	0	0	0	0
5125 Taxes on investment goods	..	..	..	0	0	0	0	0	0	0
5126 Taxes on specific services	..	..	..	10	66	47	68	72	74	63
Taxes on lotteries and gambling	..	..	..	7	42	22	29	32	47	34
Financial stability fee	..	..	..	0	0	0	5	4	7	6
Passenger departure duty	..	..	..	3	0	0	0	0	0	0
Contributions to the EU Single Resolution Fund	..	..	..	0	0	0	0	8	6	4
Contributions to the fund for the protection of the insured	..	..	..	0	1	1	1	1	0	0
Contributions to the deposit guarantee fund	..	..	..	0	22	24	32	28	14	18
Other special target State duties	..	..	..	0	0	0	0	0	0	1
5127 Other taxes on internat. trade and transactions	..	..	..	0	0	0	0	0	0	0
5128 Other taxes	..	..	..	0	0	0	0	0	0	0
5130 Unallocable between 5110 and 5120	..	..	..	0	0	0	0	0	0	0
5200 Taxes on use of goods and perform activities	..	..	..	32	57	126	154	153	277	219
5210 Recurrent taxes	..	..	..	32	57	73	140	142	171	177
5211 Paid by households: motor vehicles	..	..	..	12	16	34	48	54	64	66
Vehicle tax for vehicles which have been registered on physical persons	..	..	..	0	0	0	48	54	64	66
Annual vehicle duty for vehicles which have been registered on physical persons	..	..	..	12	16	34	0	0	0	0
5212 Paid by others: motor vehicles	..	..	..	0	20	22	45	46	52	53
Tax on cars belonging to enterprises	..	..	..	..	0	0	21	20	21	22
Vehicle tax for vehicles which have been registered on judical persons	..	..	..	..	0	0	24	26	31	31
Annual vehicle duty for vehicles which have been registered on judical persons	..	..	..	..	20	22	0	0	0	0
5213 Paid in respect of other goods	..	..	..	20	21	17	47	42	55	58
Duty for keeping animals	..	..	..	0	0	0	0	0	0	0
Income from lease of reservoirs and fishing rights and non-production use of fishing rights (fishing cards)	..	..	..	0	0	0	1	1	1	1
Business and professional licences	..	..	..	5	6	4	27	20	23	23
State duties and payments for issue of special permits (licences) and registration of documents that commensurate correspondence of professional qualification	..	..	..	1	0	0	0	0	0	0
Lottery and gambling state duty	..	..	..	1	4	2	2	2	4	4
Gambling equipment marking duty	..	..	..	0	1	1	0	0	0	0
Payment for rental of commercial fishing rights	..	..	..	0	0	0	0	1	1	0
Lottery of goods and services organization duty	..	..	..	2	0	0	0	0	0	0
State duty for using numerative rights	..	..	..	0	0	0	0	0	0	0
State duty for keeping oil products` security reserves	..	..	..	0	0	0	24	16	19	18
Tax on natural resources	..	..	..	15	15	12	19	22	30	34
State fee from weapon	..	..	..	0	0	0	0	0	0	0
5220 Non-recurrent taxes	..	..	..	0	0	53	14	11	105	42
Revenue from state-owned greenhouse gas emission unit trade	..	..	..	..	..	53	14	0	0	0
Payment for emission quota trading	..	..	..	..	..	0	0	11	105	42
The fee for the appeal of procurement	..	..	..	..	..	0	0	0	0	0
5300 Unallocable between 5100 and 5200	..	..	..	0	0	0	0	0	0	0
6000 Other taxes	**..**	**..**	**..**	**0**	**0**	**0**	**0**	**0**	**0**	**0**
6100 Paid solely by business	..	..	..	..	..	..	..	..	..	..
6200 Other	..	..	..	..	..	..	..	..	..	..

	1965	1980	1990	2000	2007	2010	2013	2015	2019	2020
Memorandum items										
Customs duties collected on behalf of the EU	..	..	..	..	37	25	28	40	50	48
SRF contributions collected on behalf of the EU	..	..	..	..	..	..	..	8	6	4
Total tax revenue on cash basis	**..**	**..**	**..**	**..**	**..**	**..**	**..**	**..**	**..**	**..**
Total tax revenue on accrual basis	**..**	**..**	**..**	**1 995**	**6 401**	**5 162**	**6 695**	**7 320**	**9 482**	**9 357**
Conciliation with National Accounts										
Additional taxes included in National Accounts	..	..	..	14	1	1	0	0	0	0
Taxes excluded from National Accounts	..	..	..	0	0	0	0	0	0	0
Difference in treatment of tax credits	..	..	..	0	0	0	0	0	0	0
Capital transfer for uncollected revenue	..	..	..	0	0	0	0	0	0	0
Voluntary social security contributions	..	..	..	0	0	0	0	0	0	0
Miscellaneous differences	..	..	..	0	0	0	0	0	0	0
National Accounts: Taxes and actual social contributions	..	..	..	2 009	6 402	5 163	6 695	7 320	9 482	9 357
Imputed social contributions	..	..	..	12	51	36	59	80	149	128
National Accounts: Taxes and all social contributions	..	..	..	2 022	6 453	5 199	6 754	7 401	9 630	9 484

.. Not available
Note: Year ending 31st December.
Data on accrual basis.
Source: Ministry of Finance.

StatLink https://stat.link/pw92xm

Table 5.23. Lithuania: Details of tax revenue, 1965-2020

Million EUR

	1965	1980	1990	2000	2007	2010	2013	2015	2019	2020
Total tax revenue	..	..	..	**4 154**	**8 730**	**7 961**	**9 445**	**10 826**	**14 817**	**15 327**
Total tax revenue exclusive of taxes collected for the EU	..	..	..	**4 154**	**8 656**	**7 908**	**9 370**	**10 716**	**14 687**	**15 193**
1000 Taxes on income, profits and capital gains	..	..	..	**1 111**	**2 625**	**1 281**	**1 726**	**2 013**	**4 288**	**4 296**
1100 Of individuals	..	..	..	1 020	1 891	1 005	1 250	1 440	3 529	3 517
1110 On income and profits	..	..	..	1 020	1 810	972	1 226	1 390	3 529	3 517
Tax on payroll and workforce	..	..	..	950	1 628	793	1 008	1 148	2 990	3 517
Tax on income from individual activities	..	..	..	40	81	36	48	55	110	0
Tax on capital income	..	..	..	31	102	143	170	187	429	0
1120 On capital gains	..	..	..	0	81	33	24	50	0	0
1200 Corporate	..	..	..	90	734	276	477	574	759	780
1210 On profits	..	..	..	90	734	276	477	574	759	780
1220 On capital gains	..	..	..	0	0	0	0	0	0	0
1300 Unallocable between 1100 and 1200	..	..	..	0	0	0	0	0	0	0
2000 Social security contributions	..	..	..	**1 362**	**2 643**	**3 293**	**3 791**	**4 338**	**4 743**	**5 127**
2100 Employees	..	..	..	107	233	641	763	873	3 605	3 872
2110 On a payroll basis	..	..	..	107	233	641	763	873	3 605	3 872
2120 On an income tax basis	..	..	..	0	0	0	0	0	0	0
2200 Employers	..	..	..	1 119	2 180	2 109	2 526	2 916	359	378
2210 On a payroll basis	..	..	..	1 119	2 180	2 109	2 526	2 916	359	378
2220 On an income tax basis	..	..	..	0	0	0	0	0	0	0
2300 Self-employed or non-employed	..	..	..	135	230	544	502	549	779	877
2310 On a payroll basis	..	..	..	135	230	544	502	549	779	877
2320 On an income tax basis	..	..	..	0	0	0	0	0	0	0
2400 Unallocable between 2100, 2200 and 2300	..	..	..	0	0	0	0	0	0	0
2410 On a payroll basis	..	..	..	..	..	..	..	..	..	..
2420 On an income tax basis	..	..	..	..	..	..	..	..	..	..
3000 Taxes on payroll and workforce	..	..	..	**0**	**0**	**0**	**0**	**0**	**0**	**0**
4000 Taxes on property	..	..	..	**62**	**83**	**103**	**97**	**126**	**145**	**147**
4100 Recurrent taxes on immovable property	..	..	..	61	82	102	96	125	143	145
4110 Households	..	..	..	3	6	7	8	17	39	40
4120 Others	..	..	..	58	76	95	88	108	105	105
Tax on land from corporations	..	..	..	3	8	9	10	10	6	6
Tax on immovable property	..	..	..	55	69	86	77	98	99	99
4200 Recurrent taxes on net wealth	..	..	..	0	0	0	0	0	0	0
4210 Individual	..	..	..	..	..	..	..	..	..	..
4220 Corporate	..	..	..	..	..	..	..	..	..	..
4300 Estate, inheritance and gift taxes	..	..	..	1	2	1	1	1	2	2
4310 Estate and inheritance taxes	..	..	..	1	2	1	1	1	2	2
4320 Gift taxes	..	..	..	0	0	0	0	0	0	0
4400 Taxes on financial and capital transactions	..	..	..	0	0	0	0	0	0	0
4500 Non-recurrent taxes	..	..	..	0	0	0	0	0	0	0
4510 On net wealth	..	..	..	..	..	..	..	..	..	..
4520 Other non-recurrent taxes	..	..	..	..	..	..	..	..	..	..
4600 Other recurrent taxes on property	..	..	..	0	0	0	0	0	0	0
5000 Taxes on goods and services	..	..	..	**1 619**	**3 378**	**3 284**	**3 830**	**4 348**	**5 640**	**5 756**
5100 Taxes on production, sale, transfer, etc.	..	..	..	1 556	3 298	3 202	3 753	4 275	5 541	5 642
5110 General taxes	..	..	..	1 086	2 339	2 183	2 611	2 913	3 876	3 931
5111 Value added taxes	..	..	..	1 005	2 330	2 180	2 611	2 889	3 850	3 907
5112 Sales tax	..	..	..	0	0	0	0	0	0	0
5113 Other	..	..	..	81	8	3	0	24	26	24
Deductions from revenue according to the RoL on the financing of road maintence and development	..	..	..	81	0	0	..	0	0	0
Deductions from revenue according to the RoL Forestry Law	..	..	..	0	0	0	..	24	26	24
Turnover tax on goods	..	..	..	0	0	0	..	0	0	0
Deductions from Ignalina nuclear power plant income generated by sales of electricity	..	..	..	0	8	3	..	0	0	0
Turnover tax on publications of erotic and violent nature	..	..	..	0	0	0	..	0	0	0
Turnover tax on motor cars	..	..	..	0	0	0	..	0	0	0
Turnover tax on goods containing ethyl	..	..	..	0	0	0	..	0	0	0
5120 Taxes on specific goods and services	..	..	..	470	960	1 019	1 141	1 362	1 665	1 711

	1965	1980	1990	2000	2007	2010	2013	2015	2019	2020
5121 Excise duties	..	..	..	428	835	903	996	1 165	1 503	1 546
Alcoholic beverages	..	..	..	10	2	10	12	6	20	17
Manufactured tabacco	..	..	..	41	121	170	209	270	300	306
Oil and other oil products	..	..	..	230	451	487	534	619	835	858
Electricity	..	..	..	2	0	3	3	4	2	2
Luxury cars	..	..	..	1	0	0	0	0	0	0
Sugar	..	..	..	25	13	1	7	1	0	0
Other former minor excises	..	..	..	5	0	0	0	0	0	0
Wine and sparkling wine	..	..	..	6	23	30	31	36	48	49
Beer	..	..	..	24	38	44	38	50	84	84
Other alcoholic beverages	..	..	..	84	186	158	162	179	213	231
5122 Profits of fiscal monopolies	..	..	..	0	0	0	0	0	0	0
5123 Customs and import duties	..	..	..	41	61	53	68	99	122	128
Taxes on international trades and transactions	..	..	..	41	0	0	0	0	0	0
Imported sugar tax	..	..	..	0	0	0	0	0	0	0
Custom duties collected for the EU	..	..	..	0	61	53	68	99	122	128
5124 Taxes on exports	..	..	..	0	0	0	0	0	0	0
5125 Taxes on investment goods	..	..	..	0	0	0	0	0	0	0
5126 Taxes on specific services	..	..	..	0	64	63	77	98	39	37
Tax on lotteries and gambling	..	..	..	..	9	8	12	15	19	17
Contributions to the Guarantee Fund	..	..	..	..	11	5	12	16	0	0
Deposit and investment insurance tax	..	..	..	..	43	48	52	56	11	13
Resolution Fund	..	..	..	..	0	0	0	10	8	6
Other taxes on specific services	..	..	..	..	0	1	2	1	2	2
5127 Other taxes on internat. trade and transactions	..	..	..	0	0	0	0	0	0	0
5128 Other taxes	..	..	..	0	0	0	0	0	0	0
5130 Unallocable between 5110 and 5120	..	..	..	0	0	0	0	0	0	0
5200 Taxes on use of goods and perform activities	..	..	..	64	80	83	78	74	99	114
5210 Recurrent taxes	..	..	..	64	80	83	78	74	99	114
5211 Paid by households: motor vehicles	..	..	..	0	0	0	0	0	0	0
5212 Paid by others: motor vehicles	..	..	..	7	30	13	31	32	38	51
Car registration taxes	..	..	..	0	0	0	15	15	18	30
Conveyance taxes	..	..	..	7	30	13	16	17	20	21
5213 Paid in respect of other goods	..	..	..	57	50	70	47	42	61	64
Pollution taxes	..	..	..	6	18	7	19	13	20	20
Payments by households for licences (not for business purposes)	..	..	..	5	3	6	2	2	2	2
Tax on market place	..	..	..	2	0	0	0	0	0	0
State-imposed fees and charges	..	..	..	34	22	44	6	5	6	6
Other taxes on production	..	..	..	10	6	13	21	22	33	36
5220 Non-recurrent taxes	..	..	..	0	0	0	0	0	0	0
5300 Unallocable between 5100 and 5200	..	..	..	0	0	0	0	0	0	0
6000 Other taxes	**..**	**..**	**..**	**0**	**0**	**0**	**0**	**0**	**0**	**0**
6100 Paid solely by business	..	..	..	..	..	..	..	..	..	..
6200 Other	..	..	..	..	..	..	..	..	..	..
Memorandum items										
Customs duties collected on behalf of the EU	..	..	..	..	61	53	68	99	122	128
SRF contributions collected on behalf of the EU	..	..	..	..	..	..	..	10	8	6
Total tax revenue on cash basis	**..**	**..**	**..**	**..**	**..**	**..**	**..**	**..**	**..**	**..**
Total tax revenue on accrual basis	**..**	**..**	**..**	**4 154**	**8 730**	**7 961**	**9 445**	**10 826**	**14 817**	**15 327**
Conciliation with National Accounts										
Additional taxes included in National Accounts	..	..	..	0	0	0	0	0	0	0
Taxes excluded from National Accounts	..	..	..	0	0	0	0	0	0	0
Difference in treatment of tax credits	..	..	..	0	0	0	0	0	0	0
Capital transfer for uncollected revenue	..	..	..	-39	-9	-32	-17	-18	-25	-69
Voluntary social security contributions	..	..	..	0	2	2	3	2	2	0
Miscellaneous differences	..	..	..	0	0	0	0	0	0	0
National Accounts: Taxes and actual social contributions	..	..	..	4 115	8 723	7 932	9 430	10 811	14 794	15 258
Imputed social contributions	..	..	..	3	91	103	99	116	160	171
National Accounts: Taxes and all social contributions	..	..	..	4 118	8 814	8 035	9 529	10 927	14 954	15 429

.. Not available

Note: Year ending 31st December.

Data on an accrual basis.

Source: Ministry of Finance.

StatLink https://stat.link/53ap82

Table 5.24. Luxembourg: Details of tax revenue, 1965-2020

Million EUR

	1965	1980	1990	2000	2007	2010	2013	2015	2019	2020
Total tax revenue	**266**	**1 543**	**3 671**	**8 510**	**13 456**	**15 117**	**17 777**	**18 830**	**24 696**	**24 697**
Total tax revenue exclusive of taxes collected for the EU	..	..	**3 654**	**8 482**	**13 432**	**15 099**	**17 761**	**18 777**	**24 530**	**24 488**
1000 Taxes on income, profits and capital gains	**95**	**667**	**1 476**	**3 106**	**4 654**	**5 467**	**6 274**	**7 011**	**9 678**	**9 370**
1100 Of individuals	66	417	884	1 573	2 677	3 156	4 061	4 716	5 917	6 290
1110 On income and profits	66	417	884	1 573	2 677	3 156	4 061	4 716	5 917	6 290
Personal income tax - fixed by assessment	27	106	184	258	389	540	666	721	782	874
Supplementary solidarity income tax	0	10	41	37	59	74	268	305	381	410
Tax on wages and salaries	36	287	601	1 177	1 909	2 136	2 797	3 227	4 146	4 468
Withholding tax on income from capital	2	11	52	88	188	315	223	313	516	456
Special tax on company directors fees	1	2	5	11	20	26	38	44	57	53
Tax on certain income of non-residents	0	1	1	2	1	1	1	1	2	1
Tax withheld on savings income (non-residents)	0	0	0	0	51	33	40	0	0	0
Withholding tax on interest	0	0	0	0	60	31	28	20	30	21
Crisis tax	0	0	0	0	0	0	0	0	0	0
Temporary budgetary balance tax	0	0	0	0	0	0	0	85	2	1
Tax withheld on contributions to a registered supplementary pension plan for self-employed persons	..	..	0	0	0	0	0	0	1	6
1120 On capital gains	0	0	0	0	0	0	0	0	0	0
Tax on betting gains	..	..	..	..	..	..	..	..	..	..
1200 Corporate	29	250	592	1 533	1 977	2 311	2 213	2 295	3 761	3 080
1210 On profits	29	250	592	1 533	1 977	2 311	2 213	2 295	3 761	3 080
Corporation tax	18	168	376	1 031	1 381	1 646	1 530	1 569	2 460	1 965
Supplementary solidarity corporation tax	0	2	8	43	58	61	113	120	192	146
Trade tax	0	80	209	460	538	603	569	606	1 110	969
1220 On capital gains	0	0	0	0	0	0	0	0	0	0
1300 Unallocable between 1100 and 1200	0	0	0	0	0	0	0	0	0	0
2000 Social security contributions	**86**	**443**	**1 011**	**2 224**	**3 710**	**4 387**	**5 132**	**5 548**	**6 862**	**7 216**
2100 Employees	32	175	388	993	1 691	2 017	2 308	2 498	3 164	3 345
2110 On a payroll basis	..	175	388	993	1 691	2 017	2 308	2 498	3 164	3 345
2120 On an income tax basis	..	0	0	0	0	0	0	0	0	0
2200 Employers	49	243	494	964	1 580	1 888	2 157	2 335	2 847	2 959
2210 On a payroll basis	..	243	494	964	1 580	1 888	2 157	2 335	2 847	2 959
2220 On an income tax basis	..	0	0	0	0	0	0	0	0	0
2300 Self-employed or non-employed	5	25	129	266	438	482	667	715	851	911
2310 On a payroll basis	..	25	129	266	438	482	667	715	851	911
2320 On an income tax basis	..	0	0	0	0	0	0	0	0	0
2400 Unallocable between 2100, 2200 and 2300	0	0	0	0	0	0	0	0	0	0
2410 On a payroll basis	..	..	..	..	..	..	..	..	..	..
2420 On an income tax basis	..	..	..	..	..	..	..	..	..	..
3000 Taxes on payroll and workforce	**2**	**10**	**0**	**0**	**0**	**0**	**0**	**0**	**0**	**0**
Payroll tax	2	10	..	..	..	..	..	..	..	..
4000 Taxes on property	**16**	**87**	**309**	**910**	**1 294**	**1 062**	**1 296**	**1 715**	**2 416**	**2 463**
4100 Recurrent taxes on immovable property	4	9	14	21	27	29	33	36	38	39
Taxes on ownership of lands and buildings	4	9	14	21	27	29	33	36	38	39
4110 Households	..	..	..	..	..	..	..	..	..	..
4120 Others	..	..	..	..	..	..	..	..	..	..
4200 Recurrent taxes on net wealth	7	44	172	633	878	831	980	1 318	1 844	1 852
4210 Individual	0	0	0	0	0	0	0	0	0	0
Wealth tax	..	..	..	..	..	..	..	..	..	..
4220 Corporate	7	44	172	633	878	831	980	1 318	1 844	1 852
Wealth tax	2	15	58	152	172	208	269	385	771	780
Holding tax	3	29	114	481	706	622	710	933	1 073	1 072
4300 Estate, inheritance and gift taxes	1	5	11	23	47	50	72	74	114	84
4310 Estate and inheritance taxes	1	5	11	23	47	50	72	74	114	84
4320 Gift taxes	0	0	0	0	0	0	0	0	0	0
4400 Taxes on financial and capital transactions	4	30	112	232	343	152	212	287	420	487
Registration taxes	4	26	94	208	288	116	164	221	319	381
Mortgage taxes	1	3	9	12	29	21	28	39	64	72
Stamp duties	0	2	2	5	7	5	7	8	9	9
Tax on contruction in dense sectors	0	0	0	0	1	1	1	2	3	3
Tax on sale of real estate	0	0	6	7	17	8	10	16	23	22
Mortgage tax on salaries	0	0	1	1	1	1	1	1	1	1
Building permits	0	0	0	0	0	0	0	0	0	0
Infrastructure tax	0	0	0	0	0	0	0	0	0	0
Authorisation taxes on oil tanks	0	0	0	0	0	0	0	0	0	0
Tax on secondary residence	0	0	0	0	0	1	0	0	0	0
4500 Non-recurrent taxes	0	0	0	0	0	0	0	0	0	0
4510 On net wealth	..	..	..	..	..	..	..	..	..	..

	1965	1980	1990	2000	2007	2010	2013	2015	2019	2020
4520 Other non-recurrent taxes	..	..	..	..	..	..	..	..	..	..
4600 Other recurrent taxes on property	0	0	0	0	0	0	0	0	0	0
5000 Taxes on goods and services	**66**	**336**	**868**	**2 260**	**3 784**	**4 180**	**5 052**	**4 528**	**5 711**	**5 626**
5100 Taxes on production, sale, transfer, etc.	62	327	848	2 229	3 709	4 105	4 969	4 442	5 614	5 530
5110 General taxes	33	179	443	1 127	2 231	2 616	3 399	2 946	3 637	3 674
5111 Value added taxes	0	179	443	1 127	2 231	2 616	3 399	2 946	3 637	3 674
VAT own resources	..	18	75	92	50	41	49	45	64	56
5112 Sales tax	0	0	0	0	0	0	0	0	0	0
5113 Other	33	0	0	0	0	0	0	0	0	0
Turnover tax	33	..	..	..	..	..	..	..	..	..
5120 Taxes on specific goods and services	30	148	404	1 103	1 478	1 489	1 570	1 496	1 977	1 855
5121 Excise duties	26	134	365	1 036	1 394	1 401	1 484	1 374	1 674	1 516
Excise duties on mineral oils	1	1	10	100	135	145	197	184	221	180
Excise duties on tobacco (part on national production)	..	0	8	24	66	70	85	81	159	176
Autonomous excise duties on mineral oils	..	76	173	414	559	536	530	495	551	436
Tax on the consumption of national alcoholic beverages and spirits	1	5	19	20	21	20	25	28	46	47
Excise duties on tobacco	..	40	141	407	418	422	445	394	462	481
Supplementary tax on fuel	..	0	0	59	145	132	126	117	135	106
Tax on control of domestic fuel	..	0	0	2	3	3	2	2	2	2
Excise duty on liquefied petroleum	..	0	0	0	0	0	0	0	0	0
Excise duty on benzol	..	0	0	1	1	1	1	1	1	1
Excise duties on imported alcoholic beverages	..	3	5	5	6	5	7	8	13	13
Excise duties on beers (national production)	..	4	2	3	4	4	4	5	4	3
Excise duty on fermented fruit beverages	..	2	3	0	0	0	0	0	0	0
Excise duties on fermented sparkling beverages	..	0	1	0	0	0	0	0	0	0
Excise duty on sugar	..	0	1	0	0	0	0	0	0	0
Excise UEBL	..	0	0	0	0	0	0	0	0	0
Excise duties on nationally produced alcoholic beverages	..	1	1	0	0	0	0	0	0	0
Excise duty on Kyoto	..	0	0	0	37	62	62	58	80	70
Excise duty on alcopops	..	0	0	0	0	0	0	0	0	0
CO2 tax	..	0	0	0	0	0	0	0	0	0
5122 Profits of fiscal monopolies	0	0	0	0	0	0	0	0	0	0
5123 Customs and import duties	1	5	11	27	24	18	16	23	26	24
Levies on imported agricultural products	1	0	0	0	1	0	0	0	0	0
Customs duty	0	0	0	0	0	0	0	0	0	0
Customs duty + mobiles + C.E.C.A. + anti-dumping	0	4	11	27	23	18	15	23	26	24
Agricultural compensatory amounts	0	0	0	0	0	0	0	0	0	0
5124 Taxes on exports	0	0	0	0	0	0	0	0	0	0
5125 Taxes on investment goods	0	0	0	0	0	0	0	0	0	0
5126 Taxes on specific services	2	6	22	39	60	69	70	98	277	316
Tax on betting stakes	0	0	0	0	0	0	0	0	0	0
Tax on insurance	1	5	15	23	32	40	45	46	59	61
Tax on transport	1	0	0	0	0	0	0	0	0	0
Tourist tax	0	0	1	1	2	2	2	3	3	1
Tax on national lottery	0	0	3	4	3	3	0	0	0	0
Tax on casino gambling	0	0	3	9	21	23	21	19	22	12
Tax on bank notes	0	0	0	0	0	0	0	0	0	0
Entertainment tax	0	1	1	2	2	1	2	2	1	0
Contributions to FGDL	0	0	0	0	0	0	0	0	45	50
Contributions to FRL	..	..	0	0	0	0	0	29	139	185
Special tax for insurers in the interest of the rescue service	0	0	0	0	0	0	0	0	6	6
5127 Other taxes on internat. trade and transactions	0	0	0	0	0	0	0	0	0	0
5128 Other taxes	0	4	6	1	0	1	1	1	0	0
C.E.C.A.	..	3	4	0	0	0	0	0	..	..
Co-responsibility tax on milk	..	1	2	1	0	1	1	1	..	..
Co-responsibility tax on cereals	..	0	0	0	0	0	0	0	..	..
5130 Unallocable between 5110 and 5120	0	0	0	0	0	0	0	0	0	0
5200 Taxes on use of goods and perform activities	3	9	20	30	75	75	83	86	97	97
5210 Recurrent taxes	3	8	18	28	68	68	72	71	70	71
5211 Paid by households: motor vehicles	2	4	9	16	39	39	40	41	40	41
5212 Paid by others: motor vehicles	1	4	7	11	26	26	27	28	27	28
5213 Paid in respect of other goods	0	0	1	2	2	3	4	3	3	3
Tax on licenced premises	0	0	0	0	1	1	1	1	1	0
Ship registration tax	0	0	0	1	1	1	2	1	1	1
Dog tax	0	0	1	1	1	1	1	1	1	1
Tax on peddling	0	0	0	0	0	0	0	0	0	0
Tax on ships	0	0	0	0	0	0	0	0	0	0

	1965	1980	1990	2000	2007	2010	2013	2015	2019	2020
5220 Non-recurrent taxes	0	0	2	2	7	7	11	15	27	26
Emission permits	..	..	0	0	0	0	5	7	17	17
Car registration taxes	..	..	2	2	7	7	6	8	10	9
5300 Unallocable between 5100 and 5200	0	0	0	0	0	0	0	0	0	0
6000 Other taxes	**0**	**0**	**7**	**11**	**14**	**22**	**23**	**28**	**29**	**23**
6100 Paid solely by business	..	0	6	11	13	16	15	28	29	23
Supplementary tax on electricity	..	0	0	2	2	2	2	2	2	2
Tax on distribution of electricity	..	0	3	4	1	1	1	1	1	1
Tax on production of electricity	..	0	2	2	1	1	1	0	2	0
Tax on natural gas consumption	..	0	0	0	3	4	5	4	5	4
Tax on enterprise register	..	0	1	1	0	0	0	0	0	0
Tax concerning foreign affairs departments	..	0	0	0	2	5	5	4	5	6
Chancellery stamps	..	0	1	2	4	3	2	1	2	1
VAT reclassified as tax on production	..	0	0	1	1	1	1	1	1	2
Under-compensation of VAT (flat rate system)	..	0	2	0	0	0	0	0	0	0
Tax on water	..	0	2	0	0	0	0	0	0	0
6200 Other	..	0	0	0	0	0	0	0	0	0
Memorandum items										
Customs duties collected on behalf of the EU	..	..	11	27	23	18	15	23	26	24
SRF contributions collected on behalf of the EU	..	..	..	..	..	..	..	29	139	185
Taxes and compulsory social security contributions paid by EU civil servants	..	..	140	133	339	420	401	450	587	608
Taxes paid by EU civil servants: income taxes	..	..	37	55	103	112	112	125	165	171
Taxes paid by EU civil servants: compulsory social security contributions	..	..	103	77	236	308	289	325	422	437
Non-wastable tax credits										
Non-wastable tax credits against 1110	..	..	..	..	..	..	..	198	191	189
Tax expenditure component	..	..	..	..	..	..	..	..	..	..
Transfer component	..	..	..	..	..	..	..	..	..	..
Total tax revenue on cash basis	**266**	**1 543**	**3 722**	**8 612**	**13 385**	**14 746**	**17 800**	**19 087**	**25 178**	**24 715**
Total tax revenue on accrual basis	**..**	**..**	**3 671**	**8 510**	**13 456**	**15 117**	**17 777**	**18 830**	**24 696**	**24 697**
Conciliation with National Accounts										
Additional taxes included in National Accounts	..	..	0	0	0	0	0	0	0	0
Tax excluded from national accounts	..	..	0	0	0	0	0	0	0	0
Difference in treatment of tax credits	..	..	0	0	0	0	0	0	0	0
Capital transfer for uncollected revenue	..	..	0	0	0	0	-13	-1	-10	-17
Voluntary social security contributions	..	..	4	18	18	28	33	38	48	52
Miscellaneous differences	..	..	0	0	0	0	0	0	0	0
National Accounts: taxes and actual social contributions	..	..	3 675	8 528	13 474	15 146	17 797	18 867	24 733	24 732
Imputed social contributions	..	..	267	288	429	505	605	669	814	855
National Accounts: taxes and all social contributions	..	..	3 941	8 816	13 903	15 651	18 402	19 536	25 547	25 587

.. Not available

Note: The civil year ends December 31st.

Data are on an accrual basis.

Under the heading 2000, the difference between the total social security contributions and those collected by the social security parastatals corresponds to the levy for realignment of pensions operated on the remuneration and pensions of employees and former agents of P&T and BCEE; one of these establishments belonging to the "non-corporate and quasi-corporate sector" and the other to the "credit institutions sector".

Compulsory social security contributions paid by EU civil servants include imputed social security contributions.

Source: General account of the State.

StatLink https://stat.link/bxl9au

Table 5.25. Mexico: Details of tax revenue, 1965-2020

Million MXN

	1965	1980	1990	2000	2007	2010	2013	2015	2019	2020
Total tax revenue	..	**771**	**102 005**	**767 216**	**1 382 103**	**1 716 243**	**2 165 501**	**2 953 480**	**3 995 654**	**4 148 699**
1000 Taxes on income, profits and capital gains	..	**230**	**34 673**	**276 548**	**554 099**	**683 604**	**957 213**	**1 230 555**	**1 694 143**	**1 768 161**
1100 Of individuals	..	..	..	..	238 938	313 473	425 621	609 384	829 501	872 598
Tax on income of individuals	..	..	..	..	238 938	313 473	425 621	609 384	829 501	872 598
1110 On income and profits	..	..	..	..	..	..	..	..	..	..
1120 On capital gains	..	..	..	..	..	..	..	..	..	..
1200 Corporate	..	..	..	..	217 790	246 745	392 199	592 443	803 643	832 120
Tax on income of corporations	..	..	..	..	217 790	246 745	392 199	592 443	803 643	832 120
1210 On profits	..	..	..	..	..	..	..	..	..	..
1220 On capital gains	..	..	..	..	..	..	..	..	..	..
1300 Unallocable between 1100 and 1200	..	230	34 673	276 548	97 370	123 386	139 393	28 728	60 999	63 443
Tax on income	..	..	..	244 841	54 785	66 937	89 028	36 268	54 686	58 196
Tax on asset	..	..	..	13 913	15 670	-624	-1 325	-502	-585	-1 245
Credit on salary	..	..	..	17 794	23 177	9 708	1 274	993	1 290	479
Oil yields tax	..	..	..	0	3 738	2 296	3 210	0	0	0
IETU	..	..	..	0	0	45 069	47 205	-11 777	-195	-888
Imposed by activity exploration and extraction of hydrocarbon	..	..	..	0	0	0	0	3 746	5 803	6 902
2000 Social security contributions	..	**109**	**17 165**	**138 223**	**236 727**	**277 459**	**351 993**	**409 249**	**552 058**	**576 019**
2100 Employees	..	..	..	..	..	..	..	..	..	..
2110 On a payroll basis	..	..	..	..	..	..	..	..	..	..
2120 On an income tax basis	..	..	..	..	..	..	..	..	..	..
2200 Employers	..	..	..	..	..	..	..	..	..	..
2210 On a payroll basis	..	..	..	..	..	..	..	..	..	..
2220 On an income tax basis	..	..	..	..	..	..	..	..	..	..
2300 Self-employed or non-employed	..	..	..	..	..	..	..	..	..	..
2310 On a payroll basis	..	..	..	..	..	..	..	..	..	..
2320 On an income tax basis	..	..	..	..	..	..	..	..	..	..
2400 Unallocable between 2100, 2200 and 2300	..	109	17 165	138 223	236 727	277 459	351 993	409 249	552 058	576 019
2410 On a payroll basis	..	..	..	138 223	236 727	277 459	351 993	409 249	552 058	576 019
2420 On an income tax basis	..	..	..	0	0	0	0	0	0	0
3000 Taxes on payroll and workforce	..	**8**	**1 797**	**11 217**	**28 071**	**36 911**	**53 042**	**70 221**	**101 284**	**105 456**
Substitute tax on salary	..	..	..	0	0	0	0	0	0	0
Payroll tax	..	..	..	11 101	20 277	27 813	41 184	69 866	100 798	104 825
Tax on remuneration to the personal work	..	..	..	65	7 578	8 841	11 645	152	298	407
Tax on professions and fees	..	..	..	36	68	71	50	106	121	177
Tax on operations by contract	..	..	..	15	148	186	163	96	67	47
4000 Taxes on property	..	**15**	**1 914**	**13 964**	**33 161**	**38 955**	**46 238**	**57 673**	**79 262**	**79 237**
4100 Recurrent taxes on immovable property	..	10	1 036	9 948	19 425	25 724	31 338	37 961	50 540	52 728
4110 Households	..	0	0	0	0	0	0	0	0	0
4120 Others	..	10	1 036	9 948	19 425	25 724	31 338	37 961	50 540	52 728
Property tax	..	..	..	9 948	19 425	25 724	31 338	37 961	50 540	52 728
4200 Recurrent taxes on net wealth	..	0	0	0	0	0	0	0	0	0
4210 Individual	..	..	..	..	..	..	..	..	..	..
4220 Corporate	..	..	..	..	..	..	..	..	..	..
4300 Estate, inheritance and gift taxes	..	0	8	0	0	0	0	0	0	0
4310 Estate and inheritance taxes	..	..	8	..	..	..	..	..	..	..
4320 Gift taxes	..	..	0	..	..	..	..	..	..	..
4400 Taxes on financial and capital transactions	..	5	870	4 017	13 736	13 231	14 900	19 712	28 722	26 509
Alienation of immovable property	..	..	..	1 763	1 076	1 122	1 271	1 595	1 939	1 982
Transfer of ownership of real estate	..	..	..	2 236	8 147	5 027	4 518	6 671	8 385	12 072
Purchasing property	..	..	..	18	4 513	7 082	9 110	11 447	18 397	12 456
4500 Non-recurrent taxes	..	0	0	0	0	0	0	0	0	0
4510 On net wealth	..	..	..	..	..	..	..	..	..	..
4520 Other non-recurrent taxes	..	..	..	..	..	..	..	..	..	..
4600 Other recurrent taxes on property	..	0	0	0	0	0	0	0	0	0
5000 Taxes on goods and services	..	**395**	**44 837**	**319 612**	**513 140**	**651 915**	**715 811**	**1 141 170**	**1 504 252**	**1 544 156**
5100 Taxes on production, sale, transfer, etc.	..	388	44 171	310 325	491 928	630 123	696 150	1 120 610	1 486 758	1 527 674
5110 General taxes	..	121	26 635	189 606	409 013	504 509	556 794	707 213	933 327	987 525
5111 Value added taxes	..	120	26 635	189 606	409 013	504 509	556 794	707 213	933 327	987 525
5112 Sales tax	..	0	0	0	0	0	0	0	0	0
5113 Other	..	1	0	0	0	0	0	0	0	0
5120 Taxes on specific goods and services	..	265	17 519	120 720	82 915	125 614	139 356	413 397	553 432	540 149
5121 Excise duties	..	45	10 072	86 163	47 008	86 098	104 111	361 538	470 993	469 040
Special tax on production and services	..	..	..	81 544	41 532	81 427	97 860	354 294	460 496	460 674
Tax on new automobiles	..	..	..	4 619	5 476	4 671	6 252	7 244	10 497	8 366
Tax on luxury goods and services	..	..	..	0	0	0	0	0	0	0
5122 Profits of fiscal monopolies	..	0	0	0	0	0	0	0	0	0

	1965	1980	1990	2000	2007	2010	2013	2015	2019	2020
5123 Customs and import duties	..	45	6 998	33 285	33 344	26 602	32 324	45 366	66 295	59 247
Step customs officer	..	..	..	423	1 156	2 071	3 065	1 270	1 554	1 309
Import taxes	..	..	..	32 861	32 188	24 531	29 260	44 096	64 741	57 938
5124 Taxes on exports	..	2	75	4	3	0	1	1	0	0
Tax on exports	..	..	..	4	3	0	1	1	0	0
5125 Taxes on investment goods	..	0	0	0	0	0	0	0	0	0
5126 Taxes on specific services	..	8	132	1 042	2 146	10 958	-967	1 763	9 196	5 625
IDE	..	8	..	0	0	8 022	-5 988	-3 323	-405	-252
Tax on lodging	..	0	..	504	1 059	1 384	1 890	2 561	4 254	2 500
Public entertainment tax	..	0	..	240	365	462	566	689	924	467
Tax on lotteries, raffles and gambling	..	0	..	267	705	923	1 213	1 416	3 403	2 114
Tax on commercials	..	0	..	4	17	166	203	210	376	0
Various indirect taxes	..	0	..	28	0	1	1 149	209	644	795
5127 Other taxes on internat. trade and transactions	..	0	0	0	0	0	0	0	0	0
5128 Other taxes	..	165	242	226	414	1 956	3 886	4 730	6 947	6 238
Mining fees	..	..	..	226	414	1 956	3 886	4 730	6 947	6 238
5130 Unallocable between 5110 and 5120	..	2	17	0	0	0	0	0	0	0
5200 Taxes on use of goods and perform activities	..	7	666	9 287	21 212	21 793	19 661	20 560	17 494	16 482
5210 Recurrent taxes	..	7	666	9 287	21 212	21 793	19 661	20 560	17 494	16 482
5211 Paid by households: motor vehicles	..	3	567	8 878	20 692	21 319	19 174	19 880	16 624	15 699
Tax on motor vehicules	..	..	..	8 878	20 692	21 319	19 174	19 880	16 624	15 699
5212 Paid by others: motor vehicles	..	0	0	301	275	281	357	439	645	437
Tax on federal auto transport	..	..	..	301	275	281	357	439	645	437
5213 Paid in respect of other goods	..	4	99	108	246	193	130	240	225	347
Sport fishing	..	..	..	40	98	59	50	62	73	55
Sport hunting	..	..	..	3	0	0	0	0	0	0
Tax on commercial activities	..	..	..	63	147	50	26	64	41	159
Trade in books and magazines	..	..	..	0	0	0	3	1	0	0
Tax on industrial activities	..	..	..	2	0	82	49	93	92	113
Mining	..	..	..	0	0	1	1	21	17	19
5220 Non-recurrent taxes	..	0	0	0	0	0	0	0	0	0
5300 Unallocable between 5100 and 5200	..	0	0	0	0	0	0	0	0	0
6000 Other taxes	**..**	**14**	**1 619**	**7 651**	**16 905**	**27 398**	**41 204**	**44 612**	**64 654**	**75 671**
6100 Paid solely by business	..	0	0	0	0	0	0	0	0	0
6200 Other	..	14	1 619	7 651	16 905	27 398	41 204	44 612	64 654	75 671
Accessories	..	..	..	5 504	12 403	22 206	25 301	23 211	41 063	56 793
Unallocable between 1000 and 5000 caused in exercices fiscal previous liquidation slopes or of payment	..	..	..	374	222	30	1 618	4 168	79	218
Additional state and local taxes	..	..	..	1 773	4 280	5 162	14 285	17 232	23 512	18 660
Non-wastable tax credits										
Non-wastable tax credits against 1000	..	..	..	..	59 065	40 344	41 800	43 806	50 649	50 476
Tax expenditure component	..	..	..	..	35 888	30 635	40 526	42 813	49 359	49 997
Transfer component	..	..	..	..	23 177	9 708	1 274	993	1 290	479
Total tax revenue on cash basis	**..**	**771**	**102 005**	**767 216**	**1 382 103**	**1 716 243**	**2 165 501**	**2 953 480**	**3 995 654**	**4 148 699**
Total tax revenue on accrual basis	**..**	**..**	**..**	**..**	**..**	**..**	**..**	**..**	**..**	**..**
Conciliation with National Accounts										
Additional taxes included in National Accounts	..	..	..	..	..	..	..	..	..	..
Taxes excluded from National Accounts	..	..	..	..	..	..	..	..	..	..
Difference in treatment of tax credits	..	..	..	..	..	..	..	..	..	..
Capital transfer for uncollected revenue	..	..	..	..	..	..	..	..	..	..
Voluntary social security contributions	..	..	..	..	..	..	..	..	..	..
Miscellaneous differences	..	..	..	..	..	..	..	..	..	..
National Accounts: Taxes and actual social contributions	..	..	..	..	..	..	..	..	..	..
Imputed social contributions	..	..	..	..	..	..	..	..	..	..
National Accounts: Taxes and all social contributions	..	..	..	..	..	..	..	..	..	..

.. Not available

Note: Year ending 31st December.

Data are on cash basis.

Source: Ministry of Finance, Economic Department.

StatLink https://stat.link/ula0fe

Table 5.26. Netherlands: Details of tax revenue, 1965-2020

Million EUR

	1965	1980	1990	2000	2007	2010	2013	2015	2019	2020
Total tax revenue	**10 860**	**69 982**	**104 419**	**166 824**	**220 950**	**227 911**	**238 488**	**255 348**	**319 236**	**318 601**
Total tax revenue exclusive of taxes collected for the EU	..	..	**102 926**	**165 227**	**218 926**	**225 943**	**236 479**	**252 272**	**315 652**	**315 077**
1000 Taxes on income, profits and capital gains	**3 884**	**22 998**	**33 689**	**43 256**	**62 463**	**63 581**	**59 085**	**70 849**	**99 003**	**97 810**
1100 Of individuals	3 008	18 383	25 806	25 116	41 414	48 992	44 830	52 405	68 968	73 116
1110 On income and profits	3 007	18 364	25 757	25 057	41 276	48 771	44 592	52 167	68 811	72 937
Income tax	1 359	2 895	2 455	-880	2 294	2 076	-1 337	-2 566	4 858	8 109
Wage tax	1 466	14 984	22 258	24 433	37 729	46 102	45 546	53 953	61 757	62 077
Dividend tax	123	486	1 044	1 504	1 253	593	383	780	2 196	2 751
Directors tax	14	0	0	0	0	0	0	0	0	0
Inhabited house tax	45	0	0	0	0	0	0	0	0	0
1120 On capital gains	1	18	50	59	138	221	238	238	157	179
Tax on games of chance	1	18	50	59	138	221	238	238	157	179
1200 Corporate	876	4 615	7 882	18 140	21 049	14 589	14 255	18 444	30 035	24 694
1210 On profits	876	4 615	7 882	18 140	21 049	14 589	14 255	18 444	30 035	24 694
Corporate income and dividend taxes	876	4 615	7 882	18 140	21 049	14 589	14 255	18 444	30 035	24 694
1220 On capital gains	0	0	0	0	0	0	0	0	0	0
1300 Unallocable between 1100 and 1200	0	0	0	0	0	0	0	0	0	0
2000 Social security contributions	**3 342**	**26 641**	**39 075**	**64 522**	**77 072**	**82 732**	**97 372**	**96 426**	**109 298**	**108 685**
2100 Employees	1 659	11 018	24 109	35 305	40 918	41 637	49 327	48 213	40 695	40 295
2110 On a payroll basis	..	..	..	35 305	40 918	41 637	49 327	48 213	40 695	40 295
2120 On an income tax basis	..	..	..	0	0	0	0	0	0	0
2200 Employers	1 371	12 465	7 837	18 671	25 925	29 351	31 603	34 614	43 693	44 135
2210 On a payroll basis	..	..	..	18 671	25 925	29 351	31 603	34 614	43 693	44 135
2220 On an income tax basis	..	..	..	0	0	0	0	0	0	0
2300 Self-employed or non-employed	311	3 158	7 129	10 546	10 229	11 744	16 442	13 599	24 910	24 255
2310 On a payroll basis	..	..	..	0	0	0	0	0	0	0
2320 On an income tax basis	..	..	..	10 546	10 229	11 744	16 442	13 599	24 910	24 255
2400 Unallocable between 2100, 2200 and 2300	0	0	0	0	0	0	0	0	0	0
2410 On a payroll basis	..	..	..	..	..	..	..	..	..	..
2420 On an income tax basis	..	..	..	..	..	..	..	..	..	..
3000 Taxes on payroll and workforce	**0**	**0**	**0**	**0**	**0**	**0**	**0**	**0**	**0**	**0**
4000 Taxes on property	**476**	**2 509**	**3 816**	**8 797**	**10 363**	**8 770**	**8 084**	**9 768**	**12 179**	**13 544**
4100 Recurrent taxes on immovable property	111	1 021	1 711	3 094	3 488	4 241	5 249	6 382	7 385	7 910
Municipal immovable property tax	-59	821	1 398	..	..	..	..	..	..	..
Other municipal taxes	66	5	18	..	..	..	..	..	..	..
Contributions polder boards	44	195	295	..	..	..	..	..	..	..
Tax on land	59	0	0	..	..	..	..	..	..	..
4110 Households	..	..	..	1 806	1 642	2 058	2 802	3 741	4 417	4 769
Municipal immovable property tax	..	..	..	1 651	1 368	1 553	1 754	1 882	2 125	2 243
Contributions polder boards	..	..	..	155	274	429	492	514	606	638
Levies on social housing corporations	..	..	..	0	0	76	556	1 345	1 686	1 888
4120 Others	..	..	..	1 288	1 846	2 183	2 447	2 641	2 968	3 141
Municipal immovable property tax	..	..	..	893	1 319	1 488	1 686	1 809	2 041	2 156
Contributions polder boards	..	..	..	395	527	695	761	832	927	985
4200 Recurrent taxes on net wealth	86	517	554	824	30	23	1	0	0	0
4210 Individual	86	517	554	824	30	23	1	..	..	..
Property tax of individuals	86	517	554	824	30	23	1	..	..	..
4220 Corporate	0	0	0	0	0	0	0	..	..	..
4300 Estate, inheritance and gift taxes	117	336	522	1 483	1 877	1 721	1 730	1 614	1 777	2 081
4310 Estate and inheritance taxes	..	304	472	1 303	1 877	1 721	1 730	1 614	1 777	2 081
Estate tax	..	0	0	0	0	0	0	0	0	0
Inheritance tax	..	304	472	1 303	1 877	1 721	1 730	1 614	1 777	2 081
4320 Gift taxes	..	32	50	180	0	0	0	0	0	0
4400 Taxes on financial and capital transactions	162	635	1 030	3 396	4 968	2 785	1 104	1 772	3 017	3 553
Stamp duties	44	0	0	0	0	0	0	0	0	0
Registration duties	118	0	0	0	0	0	0	0	0	0
Tax on legal transactions	0	635	1 030	0	0	0	0	0	0	0
Real estate transfer tax	0	0	0	2 804	4 925	2 785	1 104	1 772	3 017	3 553
Tax on capital formation	0	0	0	592	43	0	0	0	0	0
4500 Non-recurrent taxes	0	0	0	0	0	0	0	0	0	0
4510 On net wealth	..	..	..	..	..	..	..	..	..	..
4520 Other non-recurrent taxes	..	..	..	..	..	..	..	..	..	..
4600 Other recurrent taxes on property	0	0	0	0	0	0	0	0	0	0
5000 Taxes on goods and services	**3 110**	**17 675**	**27 585**	**49 472**	**70 084**	**71 866**	**72 824**	**77 889**	**97 978**	**97 033**
5100 Taxes on production, sale, transfer, etc.	2 943	16 204	25 067	44 871	63 673	64 247	65 030	69 315	88 461	87 507
5110 General taxes	1 344	11 081	17 216	28 857	42 884	42 674	42 459	44 922	58 186	59 038
5111 Value added taxes	0	11 081	17 216	28 849	42 873	42 654	42 424	44 879	58 115	58 971
5112 Sales tax	0	0	0	0	0	0	0	0	0	0

	1965	1980	1990	2000	2007	2010	2013	2015	2019	2020
5113 Other	1 344	0	0	8	11	20	35	43	71	67
Turnover tax	1 344	..	..	..	..	..	..	..	..	..
5120 Taxes on specific goods and services	1 600	5 123	7 850	16 014	20 789	21 573	22 571	24 393	30 275	28 469
5121 Excise duties	880	3 789	5 985	13 755	17 724	18 392	17 309	18 020	22 039	20 410
Excise on spirits	129	463	422	397	335	331	306	314	331	321
Excise on beer	34	123	259	263	310	389	413	451	422	384
Excise on sugar	45	9	27	0	0	0	0	0	0	0
Excise on tobacco	307	839	948	1 590	2 136	2 437	2 228	2 222	2 547	3 178
Excise on wine	14	82	91	173	257	304	348	354	330	329
Registration tax on motor vehicles	0	613	1 189	2 875	3 647	2 096	1 159	1 462	2 347	1 501
Excise on soft drinks	0	59	186	216	155	156	154	207	269	269
Levies for nuclear reactor	0	0	0	0	0	0	0	0	0	0
Excise on petrol	310	1 280	1 684	3 151	4 010	4 086	3 960	4 109	4 574	3 888
Excise on other mineral oils	41	295	808	2 139	2 965	3 573	3 630	3 757	3 887	3 483
Levies on air pollution	0	27	304	0	0	0	0	0	0	0
Taxes on pollution/resources	0	0	68	462	456	655	144	345	502	532
Levies on energy	0	0	0	2 387	3 333	4 250	4 856	4 679	6 698	6 409
Other excise duties and consumption taxes	0	0	0	0	0	0	0	0	0	0
Other environmental taxes	0	0	0	34	35	15	10	14	22	21
Strategic stockpile tax on mineral oils	0	0	0	68	85	100	101	106	110	95
5122 Profits of fiscal monopolies	0	0	0	0	0	0	0	0	0	0
5123 Customs and import duties	702	971	1 375	1 310	1 679	1 732	1 756	2 266	2 709	2 533
EU levies on food products	338	295	168	0	0	0	0	0	0	0
MCA levy	0	9	0	0	0	0	0	0	0	0
Remaining import duties	364	667	1 207	0	0	0	0	0	0	0
Custom duties collected for the EU	..	..	0	1 310	1 679	1 732	1 756	2 266	2 709	2 533
5124 Taxes on exports	0	0	0	0	0	0	0	0	0	0
5125 Taxes on investment goods	0	77	0	0	0	0	0	0	0	0
Selective investment regulation levy	..	77	..	..	..	..	..	..	..	..
5126 Taxes on specific services	16	222	372	662	1 041	1 213	3 253	3 751	5 284	5 283
Tax on fire insurance	2	0	0	0	0	0	0	0	0	0
Entertainment tax	14	0	0	0	0	0	0	0	0	0
Tax on insurances	0	209	340	512	807	861	2 343	2 375	2 880	3 048
Tourist tax	0	14	32	83	125	131	164	206	342	211
Tax on games of chance	0	0	0	67	109	221	239	238	415	181
Flight tax	0	0	0	0	0	0	0	0	0	0
Bank levies	0	0	0	0	0	0	507	478	1 015	1 095
Contribution to EU Single Resolution Fund	..	..	0	0	0	0	0	454	632	748
5127 Other taxes on internat. trade and transactions	0	0	0	0	0	0	0	0	0	0
5128 Other taxes	1	64	118	287	345	236	253	356	243	243
ESCC levy	1	5	0	0	0	0	0	0	0	0
Sugar contribution	0	23	36	0	0	0	0	0	0	0
Milk levy	0	36	82	0	0	0	0	0	0	0
EU levies on food products	0	0	0	273	345	236	253	356	243	243
Sugar storage duty	0	0	0	14	0	0	0	0	0	0
5130 Unallocable between 5110 and 5120	0	0	0	0	0	0	0	0	0	0
5200 Taxes on use of goods and perform activities	167	1 470	2 518	4 601	6 411	7 619	7 794	8 574	9 517	9 526
5210 Recurrent taxes	165	1 470	2 518	4 601	6 411	7 619	7 751	8 410	8 993	9 083
5211 Paid by households: motor vehicles	27	463	799	2 288	3 211	4 084	4 008	4 470	4 752	4 784
Motor vehicle tax	27	427	744	2 288	3 211	4 084	4 008	4 470	4 752	4 784
Motor vehicle licence	0	36	54	0	0	0	0	0	0	0
5212 Paid by others: motor vehicles	132	604	1 044	554	760	976	959	1 069	1 137	1 144
Motor vehicle tax	132	590	1 026	554	760	976	959	1 069	1 137	1 144
Motor vehicle licence	0	14	18	0	0	0	0	0	0	0
Heavy motor vehicle tax	0	0	0	0	0	0	0	0	0	0
5213 Paid in respect of other goods	6	404	676	1 759	2 440	2 559	2 784	2 871	3 104	3 155
Dog licences	3	23	27	40	54	59	67	65	52	50
Commuter tax	0	5	5	12	21	25	29	29	35	39
Levies on water pollution	1	372	644	1 003	1 220	1 127	1 182	1 212	1 339	1 351
Permission to sell spirits	2	5	0	0	0	0	0	0	0	0
Sewerage charges	0	0	0	650	1 094	1 304	1 463	1 531	1 669	1 702
Levies on manure surplus	0	0	0	18	-4	2	4	3	7	12
Noise nuisance tax civil aviation	0	0	0	36	55	42	39	31	2	1
5220 Non-recurrent taxes	2	0	0	0	0	0	43	164	524	443
Emission permits	..	..	..	..	..	..	43	164	524	443
5300 Unallocable between 5100 and 5200	0	0	0	0	0	0	0	0	0	0
6000 Other taxes	**48**	**159**	**254**	**777**	**968**	**962**	**1 123**	**416**	**778**	**1 529**
6100 Paid solely by business	48	159	254	410	322	326	139	0	0	0
Administrative levies	48	159	254	410	322	326	139	..	..	..

	1965	1980	1990	2000	2007	2010	2013	2015	2019	2020
6200 Other	0	0	0	367	646	636	984	416	778	1 529
Employers tax	..	..	..	331	497	609	804	208	496	1 226
Tax revenue from Caribbean Netherlands	..	..	..	0	0	13	100	128	161	148
Other taxes on wealth	..	..	..	36	149	14	80	80	121	155
Memorandum items										
Customs duties collected on behalf of the EU	..	..	..	1 310	1 679	1 732	1 756	2 266	2 709	2 533
SRF contributions collected on behalf of the EU	..	..	..	..	..	..	..	454	632	748
Total tax revenue on cash basis	**10 860**	**69 982**	**104 419**	**165 503**	**..**	**..**	**..**	**..**	**..**	**..**
Total tax revenue on accrual basis	**..**	**..**	**..**	**166 824**	**220 950**	**227 911**	**238 488**	**255 348**	**319 236**	**318 601**
Conciliation with National Accounts										
Additional taxes included in National Accounts	..	..	..	1 400	0	0	0	0	0	0
Wage Tax reductions	..	..	..	1 400	..	..	..	..	..	..
Taxes excluded from National Accounts	..	..	..	0	0	0	0	0	0	0
Difference in treatment of tax credits	..	..	..	0	0	0	0	0	0	0
Capital transfer for uncollected revenue	..	..	..	0	0	0	0	0	0	0
Voluntary social security contributions	..	..	..	0	0	0	0	0	0	0
Miscellaneous differences	..	..	..	-70	0	0	0	0	0	0
National Accounts: Taxes and actual social contributions	..	..	..	168 154	220 950	227 911	238 488	255 348	319 236	318 601
Imputed social contributions	..	..	..	3 808	3 509	3 545	3 414	3 160	3 852	3 801
National Accounts: Taxes and all social contributions	..	..	..	171 962	224 459	231 456	241 902	258 508	323 088	322 402

.. Not available

Note: Year ending 31st December.

From 1999 data are on accrual basis.

Heading 2000: From 1998 the figures include some violuntary contributions and the breakdown between premiums paid by employees (2100) and by self-employed / non-employed has been estimated. This is also the case for the breakdown between premiums paid on a payroll or on an income tax basis for those years where both apply.

Heading 4100: From 1992, there was a structural break in the data for the 'municipal immovable property tax'. The tax ceased to be collected by the central government at that time and the figures are presented on a different type of statistical registration (no longer cash basis).

Heading 5110: Includes 358 millions of euros (1969) and 186 millions of euros (1970) in respect of deduction of turnover tax on stocks existing at 1st January 1969.

Heading 5213: Small amounts (less than 2.3 million euros) of hunting and fishing licence receipts which should be classified here have been omitted.

Source: Social security contributions and local taxes: Central Bureau of Statistics.

Other taxes: Ministry of Finance.

StatLink https://stat.link/7zrpy6

Table 5.27. New Zealand: Details of tax revenue, 1965-2020

Million NZD

	1965	1980	1990	2000	2007	2010	2013	2015	2019	2020
Total tax revenue	**1 001**	**7 594**	**27 471**	**39 765**	**64 046**	**62 310**	**72 187**	**81 499**	**99 620**	**115 600**
1000 Taxes on income, profits and capital gains	**606**	**5 299**	**16 370**	**23 861**	**40 308**	**33 494**	**39 415**	**44 723**	**54 913**	**65 298**
1100 Of individuals	394	4 679	13 177	17 126	26 965	23 519	26 555	30 297	39 574	44 494
1110 On income and profits	394	4 679	13 177	17 126	26 965	23 519	26 555	30 297	39 574	44 494
1120 On capital gains	0	0	0	0	0	0	0	0	0	0
1200 Corporate	207	589	1 780	4 914	9 069	7 609	10 344	11 407	12 415	17 819
1210 On profits	207	589	1 780	4 914	9 069	7 609	10 344	11 407	12 415	17 819
1220 On capital gains	0	0	0	0	0	0	0	0	0	0
1300 Unallocable between 1100 and 1200	5	31	1 413	1 821	4 274	2 366	2 516	3 019	2 924	2 985
NRWT	5	24	277	760	1 506	467	427	733	570	470
Property speculation	0	0	0	0	0	0	0	0	0	0
Absentee income tax	0	7	0	0	0	0	0	0	0	0
Interest	0	0	1 028	990	2 699	1 704	1 643	1 660	1 528	999
Dividends	0	0	83	71	69	195	446	626	826	1 516
Other	0	0	25	0	0	0	0	0	0	0
2000 Social security contributions	**0**	**0**	**0**	**0**	**0**	**0**	**0**	**0**	**0**	**0**
2100 Employees	0	0	0	0	0	0	0	0	0	0
2110 On a payroll basis	..	..	..	..	..	..	..	..	..	..
2120 On an income tax basis	..	..	..	..	..	..	..	..	..	..
2200 Employers	0	0	0	0	0	0	0	0	0	0
2210 On a payroll basis	..	..	..	..	..	..	..	..	..	..
2220 On an income tax basis	..	..	..	..	..	..	..	..	..	..
2300 Self-employed or non-employed	0	0	0	0	0	0	0	0	0	0
2310 On a payroll basis	..	..	..	..	..	..	..	..	..	..
2320 On an income tax basis	..	..	..	..	..	..	..	..	..	..
2400 Unallocable between 2100, 2200 and 2300	0	0	0	0	0	0	0	0	0	0
2410 On a payroll basis	..	..	..	..	..	..	..	..	..	..
2420 On an income tax basis	..	..	..	..	..	..	..	..	..	..
3000 Taxes on payroll and workforce	**0**	**0**	**0**	**0**	**0**	**0**	**0**	**0**	**0**	**0**
4000 Taxes on property	**116**	**602**	**1 880**	**2 112**	**3 417**	**4 119**	**4 585**	**5 046**	**6 138**	**6 361**
4100 Recurrent taxes on immovable property	84	515	1 722	2 049	3 322	4 031	4 492	4 962	6 037	6 273
Local govt rates and services	81	503	1 550	2 049	3 322	4 031	4 492	4 962	6 037	6 273
Land tax	3	12	172	0	0	0	0	0	0	0
4110 Households	..	..	0	..	..	..	..	..	..	..
4120 Others	..	..	172	..	..	..	..	..	..	..
4200 Recurrent taxes on net wealth	0	0	0	0	0	0	0	0	0	0
4210 Individual	..	..	..	..	..	..	..	..	..	..
4220 Corporate	..	..	..	..	..	..	..	..	..	..
4300 Estate, inheritance and gift taxes	23	39	80	2	3	2	0	0	0	0
4310 Estate and inheritance taxes	21	37	74	0	0	0	..	..	..	..
4320 Gift taxes	2	2	6	2	3	2	..	..	..	..
4400 Taxes on financial and capital transactions	9	48	78	61	92	86	93	84	101	88
Instrument duty	7	40	62	51	85	82	91	84	101	88
Cheque duty	2	8	16	10	7	4	2	0	0	0
4500 Non-recurrent taxes	0	0	0	0	0	0	0	0	0	0
4510 On net wealth	..	..	..	..	..	..	..	..	..	..
4520 Other non-recurrent taxes	..	..	..	..	..	..	..	..	..	..
4600 Other recurrent taxes on property	0	0	0	0	0	0	0	0	0	0
5000 Taxes on goods and services	**280**	**1 693**	**9 220**	**13 792**	**20 290**	**24 692**	**28 184**	**31 728**	**38 567**	**43 940**
5100 Taxes on production, sale, transfer, etc.	262	1 624	8 680	12 887	18 832	23 107	26 344	29 584	35 996	41 122
5110 General taxes	77	776	6 163	9 885	15 046	19 143	22 063	24 587	30 259	35 397
5111 Value added taxes	0	0	6 163	9 885	15 046	19 143	22 063	24 587	30 259	35 397
5112 Sales tax	77	776	0	0	0	0	0	0	0	0
Motor vehicles	..	231	..	..	..	..	..	..	..	..
Other sales tax	..	544	..	..	..	..	..	..	..	..
5113 Other	0	0	0	0	0	0	0	0	0	0
5120 Taxes on specific goods and services	186	849	2 517	3 002	3 786	3 964	4 281	4 997	5 737	5 725

	1965	1980	1990	2000	2007	2010	2013	2015	2019	2020
5121 Excise duties	124	548	1 929	2 148	1 627	1 782	1 854	2 280	2 460	2 111
On alcoholic beverages	37	84	411	436	573	622	650	672	710	780
Beer	33	64	0	201	290	207	250	262	268	308
Wine	0	0	0	100	163	181	204	216	221	229
Spirits	4	20	0	135	120	234	196	194	221	243
Tobacco	33	99	568	764	159	220	273	362	485	45
Motor vehicles	0	0	7	0	0	0	0	0	0	0
Refined sugar	2	0	0	0	0	0	0	0	0	0
CA petroleum fuels	0	140	835	810	819	872	865	1 185	1 075	1 084
NRF fuel excise	49	121	0	0	0	0	0	0	0	0
Local petroleum fuels	0	18	21	27	30	32	31	33	167	179
CA mileage tax	0	0	0	0	0	0	0	0	0	0
NRF mileage tax	3	0	0	0	0	0	0	0	0	0
Road user charges	0	68	0	0	0	0	0	0	0	0
Energy resources levy	0	20	87	111	46	36	35	28	23	23
5122 Profits of fiscal monopolies	0	0	0	0	0	0	0	0	0	0
5123 Customs and import duties	49	231	505	648	1 857	1 916	2 160	2 442	3 001	3 292
5124 Taxes on exports	0	0	0	0	0	0	0	0	0	0
5125 Taxes on investment goods	0	0	0	0	0	0	0	0	0	0
5126 Taxes on specific services	13	57	83	206	302	266	267	275	276	322
Lottery (national)	1	6	26	167	290	253	254	260	266	314
Lottery (overseas)	0	0	0	0	0	0	0	0	0	0
Racing	12	46	57	39	12	13	13	15	10	8
Film hire tax	0	1	0	0	0	0	0	0	0	0
Domestic air travel tax	0	3	0	0	0	0	0	0	0	0
5127 Other taxes on internat. trade and transactions	0	12	0	0	0	0	0	0	0	0
Foreign fishing vessels tax	..	0	..	..	..	..	..	..	..	..
Foreign travel tax	..	0	..	..	..	..	..	..	..	..
International departure tax	..	12	..	..	..	..	..	..	..	..
5128 Other taxes	0	0	0	0	0	0	0	0	0	0
5130 Unallocable between 5110 and 5120	0	0	0	0	0	0	0	0	0	0
5200 Taxes on use of goods and perform activities	18	69	539	905	1 458	1 585	1 840	2 144	2 571	2 818
5210 Recurrent taxes	18	69	539	905	1 458	1 585	1 840	2 144	2 571	2 818
Motor vehicle registration	7	47	154	181	226	172	187	214	226	231
Heavy traffic fees	8	0	285	532	851	1 016	1 205	1 381	1 716	1 930
Accident compensation levies	0	0	0	0	0	0	0	0	0	0
5211 Paid by households: motor vehicles	0	0	0	0	0	0	0	0	0	0
5212 Paid by others: motor vehicles	0	0	0	0	0	0	0	0	0	0
5213 Paid in respect of other goods	3	23	100	192	381	397	448	549	629	657
Local authority fees and charges	3	23	100	192	381	397	448	549	629	657
5220 Non-recurrent taxes	0	0	0	0	0	0	0	0	0	0
5300 Unallocable between 5100 and 5200	0	0	0	0	0	0	0	0	0	0
6000 Other taxes	**0**	**0**	**1**	**0**	**31**	**5**	**3**	**2**	**2**	**1**
6100 Paid solely by business	..	..	0	..	0	0	0	0	0	0
6200 Other	..	..	1	..	31	5	3	2	2	1
Non-wastable tax credits										
Non-wastable tax credits against 1110	..	..	..	1 057	2 568	2 794	2 582	2 352	3 016	2 958
Tax expenditure component	..	..	..	311	873	950	1 349	1 254	1 532	1 520
Transfer component	..	..	..	746	1 695	1 844	1 233	1 098	1 484	1 438
Non-wastable tax credits against 1210	..	..	..	0	0	0	0	0	0	0
Tax expenditure component	..	..	..	..	..	..	..	..	..	..
Transfer component	..	..	..	..	..	..	..	..	..	..
Total tax revenue on cash basis	**1 001**	**7 594**	**27 471**	**39 276**	**64 273**	**62 053**	**73 172**	**82 481**	**100 104**	**114 309**
Total tax revenue on accrual basis	**..**	**..**	**..**	**39 765**	**64 046**	**62 310**	**72 187**	**81 499**	**99 620**	**115 600**
Conciliation with National Accounts										
Additional taxes included in National Accounts	..	..	..	..	0	0	2 397	3 858	4 673	4 248
Taxes excluded from National Accounts	..	..	..	..	0	0	-4 955	-6 903	-8 497	-9 821
Difference in treatment of tax credits	..	..	..	..	873	950	1 349	1 254	1 532	1 520
Capital transfer for uncollected revenue	..	..	..	..	0	0	0	0	0	0
Voluntary social security contributions	..	..	..	..	0	0	0	0	0	0
Miscellaneous differences	..	..	..	..	0	0	461	-1 602	6 760	-8 389
National Accounts: Taxes and actual social contributions	..	..	..	..	64 919	63 260	71 439	78 106	104 088	103 158
Imputed social contributions	..	..	..	..	0	0	2 617	2 063	2 199	2 221
National Accounts: Taxes and all social contributions	..	..	..	..	64 919	63 260	74 056	80 169	106 287	105 379

.. Not available

Note: For the years before 1989 data are on a fiscal year basis ending 31st March. The figures provided for 1989 and onwards relate to the financial year ending 30th June of the following year.
From 1993, data are on accrual basis.
Heading 1000: Tax credits to exporters under the export incentives schemes are non-wastable, but that part of the excess of taxliability paid out to taxpayers is not identifiable.
Heading 1100: The figures up to 1969 include revenues collected by a social security income tax. The base of this tax was the same as the ordinary income tax base and the two have now been incorporated into a single income tax.
Heading 5121: From October 1986 incorporates that portion of the selective impost on wine, spirits, tobacco and motor vehicles which was formerly collected and reported as sales tax. The revenue collected on those imported goods which are subject to the equivalent of the domestic excise has been classified as excise duty. In this respect, there is a discontinuity between the excises recorded before and after October 1986.
Heading 5210: The other local authority licence fees include some small items which could be regarded as non-tax revenues.
Heading for non-wastable tax credits 1110 comprises four Family assistance tax credits. The total in item 1100 is net of the tax expenditure component but not net of the transfer component.
Source: Statistics New Zealand.

StatLink https://stat.link/debat5

Table 5.28. Norway: Details of tax revenue, 1965-2020

Million NOK

	1965	1980	1990	2000	2007	2010	2013	2015	2019	2020
Total tax revenue	**16 842**	**133 499**	**301 812**	**627 989**	**987 278**	**1 083 337**	**1 222 890**	**1 195 354**	**1 427 835**	**1 323 112**
1000 Taxes on income, profits and capital gains	**7 316**	**55 837**	**106 290**	**284 189**	**474 460**	**512 244**	**558 171**	**475 374**	**583 628**	**470 512**
1100 Of individuals	6 671	38 018	79 068	152 013	219 726	256 544	304 409	335 199	369 790	389 129
1110 On income and profits	6 671	38 018	79 068	152 013	219 726	256 544	304 409	335 199	369 790	389 129
Employee social security contributions	1 305	0	0	0	0	0	0	0	0	0
Income taxes	5 366	38 018	79 068	152 013	219 726	256 544	304 409	335 199	369 790	389 129
1120 On capital gains	0	0	0	0	0	0	0	0	0	0
1200 Corporate	645	17 819	27 222	132 176	254 734	255 700	253 762	140 175	213 838	81 383
1210 On profits	..	..	..	132 176	254 734	255 700	253 762	140 175	213 838	81 383
1220 On capital gains	..	..	..	0	0	0	0	0	0	0
1300 Unallocable between 1100 and 1200	0	0	0	0	0	0	0	0	0	0
2000 Social security contributions	**2 009**	**28 205**	**79 362**	**132 170**	**204 473**	**243 002**	**292 461**	**325 130**	**377 057**	**381 838**
2100 Employees	0	6 639	25 345	45 162	68 518	81 032	98 124	112 662	130 878	134 450
2110 On a payroll basis	..	..	..	45 162	68 518	81 032	98 124	112 662	130 878	134 450
2120 On an income tax basis	..	..	..	0	0	0	0	0	0	0
2200 Employers	1 716	20 454	50 116	79 242	124 178	148 047	177 458	190 923	220 966	222 175
2210 On a payroll basis	..	..	..	79 242	124 178	148 047	177 458	190 923	220 966	222 175
2220 On an income tax basis	..	..	..	0	0	0	0	0	0	0
2300 Self-employed or non-employed	293	1 112	3 901	7 766	11 777	13 923	16 879	21 545	25 213	25 213
2310 On a payroll basis	..	..	..	7 766	11 777	13 923	16 879	21 545	25 213	25 213
2320 On an income tax basis	..	..	..	0	0	0	0	0	0	0
2400 Unallocable between 2100, 2200 and 2300	0	0	0	0	0	0	0	0	0	0
2410 On a payroll basis	..	..	..	..	..	..	..	..	..	..
2420 On an income tax basis	..	..	..	..	..	..	..	..	..	..
3000 Taxes on payroll and workforce	**0**	**0**	**0**	**0**	**0**	**0**	**0**	**0**	**2 011**	**2 065**
4000 Taxes on property	**523**	**2 295**	**8 887**	**14 422**	**26 601**	**28 547**	**34 810**	**34 021**	**46 334**	**44 693**
4100 Recurrent taxes on immovable property	100	431	2 216	2 724	5 571	7 109	8 879	11 177	14 748	14 818
4110 Households	..	431	2 216	2 724	2 149	3 024	3 693	5 437	7 680	7 224
4120 Others	..	0	0	0	3 422	4 085	5 186	5 740	7 068	7 594
4200 Recurrent taxes on net wealth	341	1 450	5 118	7 703	12 900	13 193	16 376	14 123	21 232	18 459
4210 Individual	235	907	3 692	6 869	10 746	12 169	14 039	12 902	16 599	16 200
4220 Corporate	106	543	1 426	834	2 154	1 024	2 337	1 221	4 633	2 259
4300 Estate, inheritance and gift taxes	45	122	446	1 273	2 576	2 377	2 246	295	44	64
4310 Estate and inheritance taxes	..	122	446	1 273	2 576	2 377	2 246	295	44	64
4320 Gift taxes	..	0	0	0	0	0	0	0	0	0
4400 Taxes on financial and capital transactions	37	292	1 107	2 722	5 554	5 868	7 309	8 426	10 310	11 352
4500 Non-recurrent taxes	0	0	0	0	0	0	0	0	0	0
4510 On net wealth	..	..	..	..	..	..	..	..	..	..
4520 Other non-recurrent taxes	..	..	..	..	..	..	..	..	..	..
4600 Other recurrent taxes on property	0	0	0	0	0	0	0	0	0	0
5000 Taxes on goods and services	**6 928**	**47 154**	**107 262**	**197 208**	**281 744**	**299 544**	**337 448**	**360 829**	**418 805**	**424 004**
5100 Taxes on production, sale, transfer, etc.	6 720	45 882	102 901	185 921	266 456	284 646	321 557	342 410	398 944	403 893
5110 General taxes	3 622	24 350	56 656	124 985	189 424	201 802	235 771	256 029	308 280	312 936
5111 Value added taxes	0	24 350	56 656	124 166	188 705	201 184	234 941	255 182	307 000	311 600
Value added tax	..	24 350	56 656	124 166	188 705	201 184	234 941	255 182	307 000	311 600
5112 Sales tax	0	0	0	0	719	618	0	0	1 280	1 336
5113 Other	3 622	0	0	819	0	0	830	847	0	0
5120 Taxes on specific goods and services	3 098	21 532	46 245	60 936	77 032	82 844	85 786	86 381	90 664	90 957
5121 Excise duties	2 338	14 914	37 453	54 871	71 047	76 328	78 515	78 845	79 654	81 662
Stamp duty on tobacco	392	1 076	3 750	6 806	6 815	7 768	6 375	7 219	6 313	9 127
Taxes on spirits and wines	449	2 013	3 454	5 217	0	0	0	0	0	0
Excise on beer	162	605	2 195	3 650	0	0	0	0	0	0
Excise on petrol	480	2 310	7 057	9 756	8 132	7 373	6 417	5 711	5 239	4 409
Vehicles transfer tax	395	2 761	4 554	10 956	22 898	21 835	22 229	19 355	14 418	10 793
Chocolate and sweets	123	247	551	789	1 078	1 173	1 261	1 324	1 458	1 516
Sugar	0	0	217	230	192	196	201	206	191	205
Non-alcoholic beverages	38	120	487	1 113	1 024	1 739	1 803	1 972	3 071	3 057
Electric energy	89	1 515	3 414	5 091	7 079	8 110	8 656	9 233	11 393	11 322
Oil and gas products	0	3 703	8 729	88	92	98	108	103	112	111
Sales of radio and tv sets	0	163	220	920	0	0	0	0	0	0
Mineral oil	0	113	1 098	490	685	1 419	1 383	1 986	1 912	1 770
Cosmetics	0	0	0	159	0	0	0	0	0	0
Recording equipment	0	0	92	35	0	0	0	0	0	0
Others	210	288	1 635	1 249	1 821	1 965	2 060	2 535	2 915	3 346
Taxes on alcoholic beverages	0	0	0	0	10 338	11 317	12 602	12 969	14 518	17 976
Excise on diesel	0	0	0	4 802	6 424	8 653	10 507	10 267	10 040	9 588
Tax on Co2 emissions, petroleum sector excepted	0	0	0	3 520	4 469	4 682	4 913	5 965	8 074	8 442

	1965	1980	1990	2000	2007	2010	2013	2015	2019	2020
5122 Profits of fiscal monopolies	31	395	751	2 534	2 902	3 433	3 751	3 869	5 168	5 311
Profits state wine monopoly	31	30	67	41	32	44	36	0	0	0
Norsk tipping	0	365	684	2 493	2 870	3 389	3 715	3 869	5 168	5 311
5123 Customs and import duties	634	697	1 360	1 944	2 132	2 505	3 111	3 305	3 403	3 588
Customs revenue	615	689	1 305	1 944	2 132	2 505	3 111	3 305	3 403	3 588
Loading and lighthouse dues	11	0	0	0	0	0	0	0	0	0
Other import duties	8	8	55	0	0	0	0	0	0	0
5124 Taxes on exports	7	105	227	0	112	151	177	178	322	316
5125 Taxes on investment goods	0	4 274	4 454	0	0	0	0	0	0	0
5126 Taxes on specific services	88	195	1 233	1 386	131	114	140	138	2 058	21
Excise on race tracks	9	25	15	88	119	114	140	138	127	21
Taxes on specific services	34	49	150	1 298	0	0	0	0	1 931	0
Pengelotteriet (national lotteries)	45	121	462	0	0	0	0	0	0	0
Excise on lotto games	0	0	606	0	12	0	0	0	0	0
5127 Other taxes on internat. trade and transactions	0	0	0	0	0	0	0	0	0	0
5128 Other taxes	0	952	767	201	708	313	92	46	59	59
5130 Unallocable between 5110 and 5120	0	0	0	0	0	0	0	0	0	0
5200 Taxes on use of goods and perform activities	208	1 272	4 361	11 287	15 288	14 898	15 891	18 419	19 861	20 111
5210 Recurrent taxes	208	1 272	4 361	11 287	15 288	13 423	15 603	17 635	17 521	17 735
5211 Paid by households: motor vehicles	88	458	1 789	4 435	6 699	7 157	8 007	8 400	7 613	7 640
5212 Paid by others: motor vehicles	108	696	2 072	1 346	712	539	494	352	335	330
5213 Paid in respect of other goods	12	118	500	5 506	7 877	5 727	7 102	8 883	9 573	9 765
CO2 tax	0	0	0	3 047	3 385	2 166	3 293	4 906	5 478	5 713
Excise on pharmacies	6	32	59	105	153	80	78	99	74	64
Others	6	86	441	2 354	3 132	3 394	3 666	3 809	3 956	3 933
Tax on emissions of NOX	0	0	0	0	1 207	87	65	69	65	55
5220 Non-recurrent taxes	0	0	0	0	0	1 475	288	784	2 340	2 376
5300 Unallocable between 5100 and 5200	0	0	0	0	0	0	0	0	0	0
6000 Other taxes	**66**	**8**	**11**	**0**	**0**	**0**	**0**	**0**	**0**	**0**
6100 Paid solely by business	0	3	2	..	..	..	..	..	..	..
6200 Other	66	5	9	..	..	..	..	..	..	..
Non-wastable tax credits										
Non-wastable tax credits against 1210	..	..	..	..	994	1 229	1 576	2 959	4 183	4 003
Tax expenditure component	..	..	..	..	350	75	307	484	830	830
Transfer component	..	..	..	..	644	1 154	1 269	2 475	3 353	3 173
Total tax revenue on cash basis	**16 842**	**133 499**	**301 812**	**575 989**	**0**	**0**	**0**	**0**	**1 434 405**	**1 361 127**
Total tax revenue on accrual basis	**..**	**..**	**..**	**627 989**	**987 278**	**1 083 337**	**1 222 890**	**1 195 354**	**1 427 835**	**1 323 112**
Conciliation with National Accounts										
Additional taxes included in National Accounts	..	..	1 485	2 773	3 288	4 022	4 560	4 674	4 904	0
Taxes excluded from National Accounts	..	..	..	0	0	0	0	0	0	0
Difference in treatment of tax credits	..	..	..	0	350	75	307	484	830	830
Capital transfer for uncollected revenue	..	..	..	0	0	0	0	0	0	0
Voluntary social security contributions	..	..	..	0	0	0	0	0	0	0
Miscellaneous differences	..	..	..	0	0	0	0	0	0	0
National Accounts: Taxes and actual social contributions	..	..	..	630 762	990 916	1 087 434	1 227 757	1 200 512	1 433 569	1 323 942
Imputed social contributions	..	..	..	2 076	2 931	3 164	3 628	3 870	5 803	5 932
National Accounts: Taxes and all social contributions	..	..	..	632 838	993 847	1 090 598	1 231 385	1 204 382	1 439 372	1 329 874

.. Not available

Note: Year ending 31st December.

From 2000, data are on accrual basis.

Heading 5211: Up to 1971 this item contains motor vehicle licences paid by both households and enterprises.

Heading 5121: From 2005, taxes on alcoholic beverages include both 'taxes on spirits and wines' and 'excise on beer'.

Heading 5125: From 1998, revenue from taxes on investments goods is included in item 5121 "Others".

Source: Statistics Norway; National Accounts.

StatLink https://stat.link/idah9y

Table 5.29. Poland: Details of tax revenue, 1965-2020

Million PLN

	1965	1980	1990	2000	2007	2010	2013	2015	2019	2020
Total tax revenue	..	..	..	**247 064**	**412 656**	**454 660**	**530 086**	**586 263**	**808 079**	**834 476**
Total tax revenue exclusive of taxes collected for the EU	..	..	..	**247 064**	**410 945**	**452 961**	**527 935**	**583 369**	**803 616**	**830 082**
1000 Taxes on income, profits and capital gains	..	..	..	**50 268**	**93 795**	**91 026**	**103 567**	**117 078**	**172 539**	**175 845**
1100 Of individuals	..	..	..	32 415	61 471	62 901	74 216	83 974	121 932	122 973
Individual income tax	..	..	..	32 415	61 403	62 818	74 124	83 861	121 755	122 817
Tax on winnings from lottery or gambling	..	..	..	0	68	83	92	113	177	156
1110 On income and profits	..	..	..	..	..	..	..	..	..	..
1120 On capital gains	..	..	..	..	..	..	..	..	..	..
1200 Corporate	..	..	..	17 853	32 324	28 125	29 351	33 104	50 607	52 872
1210 On profits	..	..	..	..	..	..	..	..	..	..
1220 On capital gains	..	..	..	..	..	..	..	..	..	..
1300 Unallocable between 1100 and 1200	..	..	..	0	0	0	0	0	0	0
2000 Social security contributions	..	..	..	**97 411**	**141 457**	**157 432**	**204 600**	**225 711**	**305 353**	**318 637**
2100 Employees	..	..	..	42 606	51 745	60 278	83 429	92 052	128 664	132 901
2110 On a payroll basis	..	..	..	..	..	..	..	..	..	..
2120 On an income tax basis	..	..	..	..	..	..	..	..	..	..
2200 Employers	..	..	..	41 834	56 016	66 712	81 114	89 570	116 901	121 101
2210 On a payroll basis	..	..	..	..	..	..	..	..	..	..
2220 On an income tax basis	..	..	..	..	..	..	..	..	..	..
2300 Self-employed or non-employed	..	..	..	12 971	33 696	30 442	40 057	44 089	59 788	64 635
2310 On a payroll basis	..	..	..	..	..	..	..	..	..	..
2320 On an income tax basis	..	..	..	..	..	..	..	..	..	..
2400 Unallocable between 2100, 2200 and 2300	..	..	..	0	0	0	0	0	0	0
2410 On a payroll basis	..	..	..	..	..	..	..	..	..	..
2420 On an income tax basis	..	..	..	..	..	..	..	..	..	..
3000 Taxes on payroll and workforce	..	..	..	**1 628**	**3 081**	**3 720**	**3 998**	**4 028**	**5 928**	**7 683**
Rehabilitation fund contribution	..	..	..	1 508	2 860	3 370	3 633	3 621	4 737	4 937
Wage guarantee fund contribution	..	..	..	120	221	350	365	407	424	416
Receipts from employers' obligatory payments to the Fundusz Solidarnościowy	..	..	..	0	0	0	0	0	767	2 330
4000 Taxes on property	..	..	..	**10 584**	**17 116**	**19 068**	**23 120**	**24 637**	**28 993**	**30 293**
4100 Recurrent taxes on immovable property	..	..	..	8 404	13 515	16 399	20 747	22 206	25 201	26 454
Agricultural tax-local	..	..	..	720	906	969	1 666	1 579	1 527	1 628
Forest tax-local	..	..	..	96	157	165	228	230	298	301
Real estate tax-local	..	..	..	7 588	12 452	15 265	18 853	20 397	23 376	24 525
4110 Households	..	..	..	2 348	3 613	4 555	6 289	6 549	7 436	7 796
4120 Others	..	..	..	6 056	9 902	11 844	14 458	15 657	17 765	18 658
4200 Recurrent taxes on net wealth	..	..	..	0	0	0	0	0	0	0
4210 Individual	..	..	..	..	..	..	..	..	..	..
4220 Corporate	..	..	..	..	..	..	..	..	..	..
4300 Estate, inheritance and gift taxes	..	..	..	172	328	290	252	246	325	313
Inheritance and gift tax-local	..	..	..	172	328	290	252	246	325	313
4310 Estate and inheritance taxes	..	..	..	..	..	..	..	..	..	..
4320 Gift taxes	..	..	..	..	..	..	..	..	..	..
4400 Taxes on financial and capital transactions	..	..	..	2 008	3 273	2 379	2 121	2 185	3 467	3 526
Tax on civil law transactions and stamp tax	..	..	..	2 008	3 273	2 379	2 121	2 185	3 467	3 526
4500 Non-recurrent taxes	..	..	..	0	0	0	0	0	0	0
4510 On net wealth	..	..	..	..	..	..	..	..	..	..
4520 Other non-recurrent taxes	..	..	..	..	..	..	..	..	..	..
4600 Other recurrent taxes on property	..	..	..	0	0	0	0	0	0	0
5000 Taxes on goods and services	..	..	..	**86 880**	**156 683**	**182 820**	**193 776**	**214 162**	**294 143**	**301 032**
5100 Taxes on production, sale, transfer, etc.	..	..	..	84 885	151 804	176 044	188 331	206 197	281 787	283 819
5110 General taxes	..	..	..	51 615	97 848	109 717	116 607	125 895	182 147	185 964
5111 Value added taxes	..	..	..	51 615	97 848	109 717	116 607	125 895	182 147	185 964
5112 Sales tax	..	..	..	0	0	0	0	0	0	0
5113 Other	..	..	..	0	0	0	0	0	0	0
Turnover tax, of which:	..	..	..	..	..	..	..	..	..	..
On spirits	..	..	..	..	..	..	..	..	..	..
On fuels	..	..	..	..	..	..	..	..	..	..
On tobacco	..	..	..	..	..	..	..	..	..	..
5120 Taxes on specific goods and services	..	..	..	33 270	53 956	66 327	71 724	80 302	99 640	97 855

	1965	1980	1990	2000	2007	2010	2013	2015	2019	2020
5121 Excise duties	..	..	..	27 170	49 376	62 016	66 310	70 632	83 854	81 756
On domestic excise products, of which:	..	..	..	24 213	45 752	58 935	60 774	62 442	79 127	77 649
On spirits	..	..	..	4 309	5 000	6 154	7 393	6 655	8 202	8 202
On fuels	..	..	..	11 056	22 128	26 545	28 184	29 874	43 078	43 078
On tobacco	..	..	..	6 143	11 973	17 348	18 126	17 788	20 752	20 752
On beer	..	..	..	1 758	2 975	3 303	3 473	3 547	3 328	3 328
On wine	..	..	..	459	378	315	219	246	218	218
On other products	..	..	..	488	3 298	5 270	3 379	4 332	3 549	2 071
On imported excise products, of which:	..	..	..	2 957	3 624	3 081	5 536	8 190	4 727	4 107
On spirits	..	..	..	90	253	311	279	267	400	400
On fuels	..	..	..	2 031	2 045	1 051	3 481	5 650	966	966
On tobacco	..	..	..	18	214	114	62	86	45	45
On beer	..	..	..	26	12	14	43	53	64	64
On wine	..	..	..	71	106	133	149	139	181	181
On other products	..	..	..	721	994	1 458	1 522	1 995	3 071	2 451
5122 Profits of fiscal monopolies	..	..	..	0	0	0	0	0	0	0
5123 Customs and import duties	..	..	..	5 038	1 711	1 627	1 977	2 823	4 463	4 394
5124 Taxes on exports	..	..	..	0	0	0	0	0	0	0
5125 Taxes on investment goods	..	..	..	0	0	0	0	0	0	0
5126 Taxes on specific services	..	..	..	1 062	1 297	1 974	2 534	5 795	10 211	10 582
Taxes and payments of financial institutions	..	..	..	443	189	375	1 077	4 472	3 076	3 485
Gambling tax	..	..	..	619	1 108	1 599	1 457	1 323	2 319	2 366
Tax from some financial institutions	..	..	..	0	0	0	0	0	4 816	4 731
5127 Other taxes on internat. trade and transactions	..	..	..	0	0	0	0	0	0	0
5128 Other taxes	..	..	..	0	1 572	710	903	1 052	1 112	1 123
5130 Unallocable between 5110 and 5120	..	..	..	0	0	0	0	0	0	0
5200 Taxes on use of goods and perform activities	..	..	..	1 995	4 879	6 776	5 445	7 965	12 356	17 213
5210 Recurrent taxes	..	..	..	433	2 383	3 667	3 432	4 317	4 377	3 596
5211 Paid by households: motor vehicles	..	..	..	0	0	0	0	0	0	0
5212 Paid by others: motor vehicles	..	..	..	0	0	0	0	0	0	0
5213 Paid in respect of other goods	..	..	..	433	2 383	3 667	3 432	4 317	4 377	3 596
5220 Non-recurrent taxes	..	..	..	1 562	2 496	3 109	2 013	3 648	7 979	13 617
5300 Unallocable between 5100 and 5200	..	..	..	0	0	0	0	0	0	0
6000 Other taxes	**..**	**..**	**..**	**293**	**524**	**594**	**1 025**	**647**	**1 123**	**986**
Abolished taxes	..	..	..	0	0	0	0	0	0	0
6100 Paid solely by business	..	..	..	0	0	0	0	0	0	0
6200 Other	..	..	..	293	524	594	1 025	647	1 123	986
Memorandum item										
Customs duties collected on behalf of the EU	..	..	..	..	1 711	1 627	1 977	2 823	4 463	4 394
Total tax revenue on cash basis	**..**	**..**	**..**	**..**	**..**	**..**	**..**	**..**	**..**	**..**
Total tax revenue on accrual basis	**..**	**..**	**..**	**247 064**	**412 656**	**454 660**	**530 086**	**586 263**	**808 079**	**834 476**
Conciliation with National Accounts										
Additional taxes included in National Accounts	..	..	..	..	..	..	..	..	..	..
Taxes excluded from National Accounts	..	..	..	..	..	..	..	..	..	..
Difference in treatment of tax credits	..	..	..	..	..	..	..	..	..	..
Capital transfer for uncollected revenue	..	..	..	1 025	1 371	1 406	2 005	2 229	3 035	3 201
Voluntary social security contributions	..	..	..	..	..	..	34	49	46	48
Miscellaneous differences	..	..	..	..	..	..	..	..	..	..
National Accounts: Taxes and actual social contributions	..	..	..	246 039	411 285	453 254	528 115	584 083	805 090	831 323
Imputed social contributions	..	..	..	777	10 848	13 841	16 603	17 423	19 465	20 464
National Accounts: Taxes and all social contributions	..	..	..	252 943	422 133	467 095	544 718	601 506	824 555	851 787

.. Not available

Note: Year ending 31st December.

From 2002, data are on accrual basis.

Source: Ministry of Finance, Economic Department.

StatLink https://stat.link/l9oauh

Table 5.30. Portugal: Details of tax revenue, 1965-2020

Million EUR

	1965	1980	1990	2000	2007	2010	2013	2015	2019	2020
Total tax revenue	**99**	**1 798**	**14 825**	**39 705**	**55 885**	**54 541**	**57 913**	**61 788**	**73 955**	**70 541**
Total tax revenue exclusive of taxes collected for the EU	**..**	**..**	**14 675**	**39 501**	**55 695**	**54 363**	**57 769**	**61 630**	**73 602**	**70 209**
1000 Taxes on income, profits and capital gains	**24**	**355**	**3 805**	**11 691**	**15 546**	**14 585**	**18 664**	**18 762**	**20 262**	**19 549**
1100 Of individuals	..	..	2 350	6 768	9 328	9 637	13 119	13 149	13 580	14 009
Individual income tax	..	..	2 350	6 768	9 328	9 637	13 119	13 149	13 580	14 009
1110 On income and profits	..	..	..	..	..	..	..	..	..	..
1120 On capital gains	..	..	..	..	..	..	..	..	..	..
1200 Corporate	..	..	1 182	4 744	6 128	4 936	5 545	5 614	6 682	5 540
Corporate income tax	..	..	1 088	4 457	5 815	4 670	5 327	5 405	6 308	5 193
Local corporate income tax ("Derrama")	..	..	84	287	313	266	217	208	374	347
Other	..	..	11	0	0	0	0	0	0	0
1210 On profits	..	..	..	..	..	..	..	..	..	..
1220 On capital gains	..	..	..	..	..	..	..	..	..	..
1300 Unallocable between 1100 and 1200	24	355	273	178	90	12	0	0	0	0
Tax on wages and professional income	2	93	9	0	0	0	0	0	..	..
Industrial tax	7	108	129	0	0	0	0	0	..	..
Tax on income from movable capital	2	71	1	0	0	0	0	0	..	..
Property income tax	3	23	17	0	0	0	0	0	..	..
Agricultural income tax	0	0	1	0	0	0	0	0	..	..
Complementary income ax	4	43	58	0	0	0	0	0	..	..
Tax on capital gains	0	3	1	0	0	0	0	0	..	..
Taxes abolished by DL 442-A/88 and DL 442-B/88	0	0	0	0	0	0	0	0	..	..
Other	6	15	58	178	90	12	0	0	..	..
2000 Social security contributions	**22**	**531**	**4 026**	**10 168**	**14 305**	**15 462**	**15 139**	**16 182**	**20 602**	**20 914**
2100 Employees	8	203	1 470	4 286	6 344	6 670	6 403	6 992	8 170	8 294
2110 On a payroll basis	8	203	1 470	4 286	6 344	6 670	6 403	6 992	8 170	8 294
Compulsory employee's social contributions	8	203	1 470	4 286	6 344	6 670	6 403	6 992	8 170	8 294
2120 On an income tax basis	0	0	0	0	0	0	0	0	0	0
2200 Employers	13	318	2 413	5 882	7 961	8 792	8 736	9 191	12 432	12 620
2210 On a payroll basis	13	318	2 413	5 882	7 961	8 792	8 736	9 191	12 432	12 620
Employers' social contributions	13	318	2 413	5 882	7 961	8 792	8 736	9 191	12 432	12 620
2220 On an income tax basis	0	0	0	0	0	0	0	0	0	0
2300 Self-employed or non-employed	0	10	143	0	0	0	0	0	0	0
Compulsory social contributions by self-employed	0	10	143	..	..	..	..	..	..	..
2310 On a payroll basis	..	..	0	..	..	..	..	..	..	..
2320 On an income tax basis	..	..	0	..	..	..	..	..	..	..
2400 Unallocable between 2100, 2200 and 2300	0	0	0	0	0	0	0	0	0	0
2410 On a payroll basis	..	..	..	..	..	..	..	..	..	..
2420 On an income tax basis	..	..	..	..	..	..	..	..	..	..
3000 Taxes on payroll and workforce	**1**	**47**	**0**	**0**	**0**	**0**	**0**	**0**	**0**	**0**
Contributions for Unemployment Fund	1	47	..	..	..	..	..	..	..	..
Stamp duty on wages and salaries	0	0	..	..	..	..	..	..	..	..
4000 Taxes on property	**5**	**26**	**402**	**1 468**	**2 330**	**2 028**	**1 915**	**2 307**	**3 078**	**2 928**
4100 Recurrent taxes on immovable property	0	0	133	508	1 008	1 112	1 339	1 535	1 699	1 635
Real estate tax	..	..	133	508	1 008	1 112	1 339	1 535	1 699	1 635
4110 Households	..	..	..	..	..	..	..	..	..	..
4120 Others	..	..	..	..	..	..	..	..	..	..
4200 Recurrent taxes on net wealth	0	0	0	0	0	0	0	0	0	0
4210 Individual	..	..	..	..	..	..	..	..	..	..
4220 Corporate	..	..	..	..	..	..	..	..	..	..
4300 Estate, inheritance and gift taxes	2	4	74	103	10	85	2	0	0	0
Inheritance and gift taxes	2	4	74	103	10	85	2	..	..	0
4310 Estate and inheritance taxes	..	..	0	103	10	85	2	..	..	0
4320 Gift taxes	..	..	0	0	0	0	0	..	..	0
4400 Taxes on financial and capital transactions	2	21	195	857	1 312	831	575	772	1 379	1 293
Real estate transfer tax	2	21	195	674	973	595	356	569	1 020	949
Stamp duty on registrations and mortgages	0	0	0	34	45	35	28	49	20	19
Stamp duty on the raising of capital	0	0	0	0	9	1	0	0	0	0
Stamp duty on real estate transactions	0	0	0	150	285	201	191	154	339	325
4500 Non-recurrent taxes	0	0	0	0	0	0	0	0	0	0
4510 On net wealth	..	..	..	..	..	..	..	..	..	..
4520 Other non-recurrent taxes	..	..	..	..	..	..	..	..	..	..
4600 Other recurrent taxes on property	0	0	0	0	0	0	0	0	0	0
5000 Taxes on goods and services	**47**	**837**	**6 555**	**16 155**	**23 166**	**22 023**	**21 554**	**23 957**	**29 438**	**26 458**
5100 Taxes on production, sale, transfer, etc.	44	810	6 440	15 847	22 708	21 433	20 727	23 094	28 086	25 176
5110 General taxes	0	290	2 906	9 733	14 333	13 527	13 710	15 368	18 786	16 803
5111 Value added taxes	0	0	2 899	9 733	14 333	13 527	13 710	15 368	18 786	16 803
VAT	..	..	2 899	9 733	14 333	13 527	13 710	15 368	18 786	16 803

	1965	1980	1990	2000	2007	2010	2013	2015	2019	2020
5112 Sales tax	0	290	7	0	0	0	0	0	0	0
General sales tax	..	290	7	..	..	..	..	..	..	..
5113 Other	0	0	0	0	0	0	0	0	0	0
5120 Taxes on specific goods and services	44	519	3 534	6 113	8 374	7 906	7 017	7 726	9 300	8 373
5121 Excise duties	15	295	2 052	4 496	5 937	5 653	4 677	5 211	6 198	5 490
Excise duties on tobacco	3	62	362	1 077	1 165	1 496	1 387	1 357	1 484	1 474
Excise duties on beer	1	0	55	87	97	80	75	75	93	73
Tax on motor vehicle sales	1	59	304	1 239	1 221	832	360	585	743	447
Tax on oil products	6	166	1 251	1 969	3 320	3 126	2 740	3 069	3 642	3 298
Excise duties on alcoholic beverages	0	0	23	123	126	112	108	115	143	113
Excise duties on alcohol	0	0	0	1	1	1	1	0	1	1
Tax on sugary soft drinks	0	0	0	0	0	0	0	0	64	53
Other	4	7	59	0	6	6	4	11	28	30
5122 Profits of fiscal monopolies	0	0	0	261	521	425	538	582	779	629
5123 Customs and import duties	21	96	511	204	190	177	144	158	229	203
Import levies	14	36	392	0	0	0	0	0	0	0
Import surtax	0	26	1	0	0	0	0	0	0	0
Agricultural Levies	..	..	0	30	29	20	25	0	0	0
Levy on sugar and isoglucse	..	..	0	4	5	0	0	0	0	0
Other	6	34	119	0	0	0	0	0	0	0
Custom duties collected for the EU	..	..	0	170	156	157	119	158	229	203
5124 Taxes on exports	0	0	0	0	0	0	0	0	0	0
Taxes on Oporto wine exports	0	0	..	..	..	..	..	..	..	..
Other	0	0	..	..	..	..	..	..	..	..
5125 Taxes on investment goods	0	0	0	0	0	0	0	0	0	0
5126 Taxes on specific services	1	38	547	1 116	1 679	1 539	1 493	1 523	1 879	1 845
Tax on insurance premiums	0	6	47	131	170	215	200	218	277	286
Stamp duty on bank transactions	1	24	405	330	694	619	508	464	608	583
Stamp duty on debt related operations, interest and leasing of buildings	0	0	22	258	386	293	212	144	145	139
Stamp duty on insurance premiums	0	0	0	248	335	325	308	313	401	385
Bank levies	0	0	0	100	48	46	238	353	378	412
Other	2	8	73	47	46	40	29	30	70	40
5127 Other taxes on internat. trade and transactions	0	0	0	0	0	0	0	0	0	0
5128 Other taxes	6	91	424	36	48	111	166	251	215	206
Stamp taxes (miscellaneous)	6	91	424	36	48	111	166	251	215	206
Other	0	0	0	0	0	0	0	0	0	0
5130 Unallocable between 5110 and 5120	0	0	0	0	0	0	0	0	0	0
5200 Taxes on use of goods and perform activities	4	27	115	267	427	573	802	850	1 339	1 274
5210 Recurrent taxes	4	27	115	267	427	573	768	770	1 099	1 016
5211 Paid by households: motor vehicles	0	4	15	55	94	139	225	209	252	230
Local tax on vehicles	..	4	15	55	94	139	225	209	252	230
5212 Paid by others: motor vehicles	2	10	20	67	132	180	303	330	463	453
Local tax on vehicles	0	2	6	0	0	0	0	0	0	0
Road taxes	2	8	14	67	132	180	303	330	463	453
5213 Paid in respect of other goods	2	13	80	145	202	255	240	232	383	333
Gambling tax	0	3	72	110	140	143	107	108	222	219
Tax on the use, carrying and possession of weapons	0	0	1	3	6	4	7	5	8	4
Tax on motor vehicles - compensation	2	8	0	0	0	0	0	0	0	0
Hunting and fishery licenses	0	1	4	1	7	12	12	13	14	11
Fee for the use of water resources	0	0	0	0	2	19	23	19	22	21
Other	0	1	2	31	47	76	92	88	118	78
5220 Non-recurrent taxes	0	0	0	0	0	0	34	80	240	258
Special tax on motor vehicles	..	..	0	..	..	..	0	0	0	0
Emissions Permits	..	..	0	..	..	..	34	80	240	258
5300 Unallocable between 5100 and 5200	0	0	0	41	31	17	25	13	13	7
Miscellaneous taxes on production	..	..	..	41	31	17	25	13	13	7
6000 Other taxes	**0**	**3**	**37**	**224**	**539**	**442**	**641**	**580**	**576**	**692**
6100 Paid solely by business	0	2	17	90	200	210	214	341	317	442
General services and licenses granted to corporations	0	2	17	90	200	210	214	341	317	442
6200 Other	0	0	20	134	339	231	427	239	259	250
Fees collected by courts of justice	0	0	0	128	328	215	401	237	256	248
Miscellaneous taxes	0	0	20	5	11	17	25	1	2	2
Memorandum items										
Customs duties collected on behalf of the EU	..	..	..	170	156	157	119	158	229	203
SRF contributions collected on behalf of the EU	..	..	..	..	..	..	..	..	124	128
Total tax revenue on cash basis	**99**	**1 798**	**14 825**	**..**	**..**	**..**	**..**	**..**	**..**	**..**
Total tax revenue on accrual basis	**..**	**..**	**..**	**39 705**	**55 885**	**54 541**	**57 913**	**61 788**	**73 955**	**70 541**

	1965	1980	1990	2000	2007	2010	2013	2015	2019	2020
Conciliation with National Accounts										
Additional taxes included in National Accounts	..	..	..	5	7	14	14	18	20	21
Taxes excluded from National Accounts	..	..	0	0	0	0	0	0	0	0
Difference in treatment of tax credits	..	..	0	0	0	0	0	0	0	0
Capital transfer for uncollected revenue	..	..	0	0	0	0	0	0	0	0
Voluntary social security contributions	..	..	0	0	0	0	0	0	0	0
Miscellaneous differences	..	..	0	0	0	0	0	0	0	0
National Accounts: Taxes and actual social contributions	..	..	..	39 710	55 892	54 555	57 927	61 806	73 975	70 562
Imputed social contributions	..	..	..	3 292	5 592	5 906	5 311	4 602	4 758	4 691
National Accounts: Taxes and all social contributions	..	..	..	43 002	61 484	60 461	63 238	66 408	78 733	75 253

.. Not available
Note: Fiscal year ending 31 December.
From 1995, data are on accrual basis.
Source: Instituto Nacional de Estatística.

StatLink https://stat.link/q30lhm

Table 5.31. Slovak Republic: Details of tax revenue, 1965-2020

Million EUR

	1965	1980	1990	2000	2007	2010	2013	2015	2019	2020
Total tax revenue	..	..	..	**10 648**	**18 456**	**19 159**	**23 082**	**26 049**	**32 494**	**32 401**
Total tax revenue exclusive of taxes collected for the EU	..	..	..	**10 648**	**18 321**	**19 016**	**22 967**	**25 930**	**32 348**	**32 263**
1000 Taxes on income, profits and capital gains	..	..	..	**2 181**	**3 844**	**3 601**	**4 471**	**5 542**	**6 658**	**6 535**
1100 Of individuals	..	..	..	1 055	1 820	1 790	2 175	2 464	3 534	3 500
1110 On income and profits	..	..	..	1 055	1 820	1 790	2 175	2 464	3 534	3 500
Wages and salaries withholding	..	..	..	0	0	0	0	0	0	0
Of unicorporated individuals	..	..	..	0	0	0	0	0	0	0
1120 On capital gains	..	..	..	0	0	0	0	0	0	0
1200 Corporate	..	..	..	813	1 835	1 659	2 118	2 917	2 878	2 800
1210 On profits	..	..	..	0	0	0	0	0	0	0
1220 On capital gains	..	..	..	0	0	0	0	0	0	0
1300 Unallocable between 1100 and 1200	..	..	..	314	189	152	178	162	246	235
2000 Social security contributions	..	..	..	**4 409**	**7 244**	**8 154**	**9 847**	**10 897**	**14 085**	**14 233**
2100 Employees	..	..	..	901	1 700	2 077	2 238	2 410	3 435	3 477
Retirement	..	..	..	0	0	0	0	0	0	0
State employment policy	..	..	..	0	0	0	0	0	0	0
Health insurance	..	..	..	0	0	0	0	0	0	0
Sick leave	..	..	..	0	0	0	0	0	0	0
2110 On a payroll basis	..	..	..	901	1 700	2 077	2 238	2 410	3 435	3 477
2120 On an income tax basis	..	..	..	0	0	0	0	0	0	0
2200 Employers	..	..	..	2 850	3 914	4 579	5 556	6 319	8 539	8 654
Retirement	..	..	..	0	0	0	0	0	0	0
State employment policy	..	..	..	0	0	0	0	0	0	0
Health insurance	..	..	..	0	0	0	0	0	0	0
Sick leave	..	..	..	0	0	0	0	0	0	0
2210 On a payroll basis	..	..	..	2 850	3 914	4 579	5 556	6 319	8 539	8 654
2220 On an income tax basis	..	..	..	0	0	0	0	0	0	0
2300 Self-employed or non-employed	..	..	..	658	1 631	1 498	2 054	2 168	2 111	2 103
Retirement	..	..	..	0	0	0	0	0	0	0
State employment policy	..	..	..	0	0	0	0	0	0	0
Health insurance	..	..	..	0	0	0	0	0	0	0
Sick leave	..	..	..	0	0	0	0	0	0	0
2310 On a payroll basis	..	..	..	658	1 631	1 498	2 054	2 168	2 111	2 103
2320 On an income tax basis	..	..	..	0	0	0	0	0	0	0
2400 Unallocable between 2100, 2200 and 2300	..	..	..	0	0	0	0	0	0	0
2410 On a payroll basis	..	..	..	..	..	..	..	..	..	..
2420 On an income tax basis	..	..	..	..	..	..	..	..	..	..
3000 Taxes on payroll and workforce	..	..	..	**0**	**0**	**0**	**0**	**0**	**0**	**0**
4000 Taxes on property	..	..	..	**194**	**245**	**277**	**327**	**335**	**378**	**438**
4100 Recurrent taxes on immovable property	..	..	..	143	243	277	327	335	378	438
4110 Households	..	..	..	28	22	25	28	29	35	36
4120 Others	..	..	..	114	222	252	299	306	343	402
4200 Recurrent taxes on net wealth	..	..	..	0	0	0	0	0	0	0
4210 Individual	..	..	..	..	..	..	..	..	..	..
4220 Corporate	..	..	..	..	..	..	..	..	..	..
4300 Estate, inheritance and gift taxes	..	..	..	8	0	0	0	0	0	0
4310 Estate and inheritance taxes	..	..	..	3	0	0	0	0	..	..
4320 Gift taxes	..	..	..	5	0	0	0	0	..	..
4400 Taxes on financial and capital transactions	..	..	..	43	1	0	0	0	0	0
Real property transfer tax	..	..	..	30	1	0	0	0	0	0
4500 Non-recurrent taxes	..	..	..	0	0	0	0	0	0	0
4510 On net wealth	..	..	..	..	..	..	..	..	..	..
4520 Other non-recurrent taxes	..	..	..	..	..	..	..	..	..	..
4600 Other recurrent taxes on property	..	..	..	0	0	0	0	0	0	0
5000 Taxes on goods and services	..	..	..	**3 864**	**7 123**	**7 127**	**8 436**	**9 275**	**11 374**	**11 195**
5100 Taxes on production, sale, transfer, etc.	..	..	..	3 631	6 580	6 573	7 780	8 573	10 527	10 371
5110 General taxes	..	..	..	2 168	4 147	4 182	4 696	5 423	6 830	6 820
5111 Value added taxes	..	..	..	2 168	4 147	4 182	4 696	5 423	6 830	6 820
5112 Sales tax	..	..	..	0	0	0	0	0	0	0
5113 Other	..	..	..	0	0	0	0	0	0	0
5120 Taxes on specific goods and services	..	..	..	1 464	2 433	2 391	3 084	3 151	3 697	3 550

	1965	1980	1990	2000	2007	2010	2013	2015	2019	2020
5121 Excise duties	..	..	..	971	2 171	2 081	2 462	2 567	2 839	2 752
On hydrocarbon fuels and lubricants	..	..	..	617	1 118	1 032	1 045	1 139	1 289	1 196
On alcohol and liquers	..	..	..	143	201	197	201	205	218	208
On beer	..	..	..	43	66	56	56	57	59	57
On wine	..	..	..	12	4	4	4	4	5	5
On tobacco products	..	..	..	156	783	602	636	665	767	732
On electricity	..	..	..	0	0	16	17	13	12	12
On coal	..	..	..	0	0	1	1	0	0	0
On natural gas	..	..	..	0	0	24	25	23	23	24
5122 Profits of fiscal monopolies	..	..	..	0	0	0	0	0	0	0
5123 Customs and import duties	..	..	..	437	136	143	115	119	127	121
Customs duties	..	..	..	122	136	143	115	119	127	121
Import surcharges	..	..	..	315	0	0	0	0	0	0
Other customs revenues	..	..	..	0	0	0	0	0	0	0
5124 Taxes on exports	..	..	..	0	0	0	0	0	0	0
5125 Taxes on investment goods	..	..	..	0	0	0	6	2	3	3
5126 Taxes on specific services	..	..	..	55	125	167	501	462	728	674
5127 Other taxes on internat. trade and transactions	..	..	..	0	0	0	0	0	0	0
5128 Other taxes	..	..	..	0	0	0	0	0	0	0
5130 Unallocable between 5110 and 5120	..	..	..	0	0	0	0	0	0	0
5200 Taxes on use of goods and perform activities	..	..	..	231	438	421	505	549	666	620
5210 Recurrent taxes	..	..	..	219	372	384	466	470	523	453
5211 Paid by households: motor vehicles	..	..	..	0	0	0	0	0	0	0
5212 Paid by others: motor vehicles	..	..	..	93	153	153	198	204	233	200
5213 Paid in respect of other goods	..	..	..	127	219	231	268	266	290	253
5220 Non-recurrent taxes	..	..	..	12	66	37	39	79	142	167
5300 Unallocable between 5100 and 5200	..	..	..	2	105	134	151	153	181	204
6000 Other taxes	**..**	**..**	**..**	**0**	**0**	**0**	**0**	**0**	**0**	**0**
6100 Paid solely by business	..	..	..	..	..	..	..	..	..	..
6200 Other	..	..	..	..	..	..	..	..	..	..
Memorandum items										
Customs duties collected on behalf of the EU	..	..	..	..	136	143	115	119	127	121
SRF contributions collected on behalf of the EU	..	..	..	..	..	..	..	..	19	17
Non-wastable tax credits										
Non-wastable tax credits against 1110	..	..	..	..	252	276	265	261	338	368
Tax expenditure component	..	..	..	..	..	..	..	..	..	..
Transfer component	..	..	..	..	..	..	..	..	..	..
Non-wastable tax credits against 1210	..	..	..	..	0	0	0	0	0	0
Tax expenditure component	..	..	..	..	..	..	..	..	..	..
Transfer component	..	..	..	..	..	..	..	..	..	..
Total tax revenue on cash basis	**..**	**..**	**..**	**10 843**	**18 033**	**18 358**	**22 082**	**25 757**	**31 337**	**30 986**
Total tax revenue on accrual basis	**..**	**..**	**..**	**10 648**	**18 456**	**19 159**	**23 082**	**26 049**	**32 494**	**32 401**
Conciliation with National Accounts										
Additional taxes included in National Accounts	..	..	..	53	33	47	0	43	4	4
Taxes excluded from National Accounts	..	..	..	0	-103	-131	-148	-149	-178	-201
Difference in treatment of tax credits	..	..	..	0	0	0	0	0	0	0
Capital transfer for uncollected revenue	..	..	..	0	0	0	0	0	0	0
Voluntary social security contributions	..	..	..	0	22	31	17	11	11	12
Miscellaneous differences	..	..	..	0	0	0	0	0	0	0
National Accounts: Taxes and actual social contributions	..	..	..	10 702	18 409	19 106	22 951	25 953	32 332	32 216
Imputed social contributions	..	..	..	19	80	143	147	171	219	254
National Accounts: Taxes and all social contributions	..	..	..	10 721	18 488	19 250	23 098	26 124	32 550	32 470

.. Not available

Note: Year ending 31st December.

Data are on accrual basis.

Source: Ministry of Finance.

StatLink https://stat.link/bc9w3y

Table 5.32. Slovenia: Details of tax revenue, 1965-2020

Million EUR

	1965	1980	1990	2000	2007	2010	2013	2015	2019	2020
Total tax revenue	..	..	..	**7 114**	**13 377**	**13 758**	**13 578**	**14 498**	**17 981**	**17 508**
Total tax revenue exclusive of taxes collected for the EU	..	..	..	**7 114**	**13 292**	**13 698**	**13 526**	**14 430**	**17 911**	**17 437**
1000 Taxes on income, profits and capital gains	..	..	..	**1 280**	**3 041**	**2 692**	**2 285**	**2 547**	**3 505**	**3 388**
1100 Of individuals	..	..	..	1 041	1 919	2 020	1 849	1 977	2 548	2 471
1110 On income and profits	..	..	..	1 039	1 916	2 017	1 847	1 974	2 545	2 469
Personal income tax	..	..	..	1 039	1 916	2 017	1 847	1 974	2 545	2 469
Special contribution for the reconstruction of the Posocje region	..	..	..	0	0	0	0	0	0	0
1120 On capital gains	..	..	..	2	3	3	3	3	3	2
Taxes on winnings from lottery and gambling	..	..	..	2	3	3	3	3	3	2
1200 Corporate	..	..	..	216	1 116	668	433	568	954	914
1210 On profits	..	..	..	216	1 116	668	433	568	954	914
1220 On capital gains	..	..	..	0	0	0	0	0	0	0
1300 Unallocable between 1100 and 1200	..	..	..	24	5	4	3	2	3	2
Tax on income - copy rights, patents and trademarks	..	..	..	24	5	4	2	2	2	2
Tax on profits due to changes in land use	..	..	..	0	0	0	0	0	0	0
2000 Social security contributions	..	..	..	**2 820**	**5 046**	**5 761**	**5 647**	**5 983**	**7 587**	**7 908**
2100 Employees	..	..	..	1 447	2 490	2 785	2 637	2 910	4 168	3 895
2110 On a payroll basis	..	..	..	1 447	2 490	2 785	2 637	2 910	4 168	3 895
2120 On an income tax basis	..	..	..	0	0	0	0	0	0	0
2200 Employers	..	..	..	1 012	1 852	2 070	2 022	2 135	2 781	2 865
2210 On a payroll basis	..	..	..	1 012	1 852	2 070	2 022	2 135	2 781	2 865
2220 On an income tax basis	..	..	..	0	0	0	0	0	0	0
2300 Self-employed or non-employed	..	..	..	361	705	906	988	938	637	1 148
2310 On a payroll basis	..	..	..	361	705	906	988	938	637	1 148
2320 On an income tax basis	..	..	..	0	0	0	0	0	0	0
2400 Unallocable between 2100, 2200 and 2300	..	..	..	0	0	0	0	0	0	0
2410 On a payroll basis	..	..	..	..	..	..	..	..	..	..
2420 On an income tax basis	..	..	..	..	..	..	..	..	..	..
3000 Taxes on payroll and workforce	..	..	..	**289**	**418**	**28**	**23**	**20**	**23**	**22**
Payroll tax	..	..	..	272	391	0	0	0	0	0
Tax on work contracts	..	..	..	18	27	28	23	20	23	22
4000 Taxes on property	..	..	..	**120**	**206**	**222**	**232**	**241**	**299**	**295**
4100 Recurrent taxes on immovable property	..	..	..	81	140	173	199	199	235	237
4110 Households	..	..	..	17	38	46	61	56	70	72
Property tax on weekend cottages	..	..	..	1	1	1	1	1	1	1
Compensation on the use of building ground - paid by individuals	..	..	..	16	37	45	48	56	68	71
Tax on immovable property of higher value	..	..	..	0	0	0	13	0	0	0
4120 Others	..	..	..	65	102	127	138	142	165	164
Property tax on buildings	..	..	..	2	3	3	4	4	9	7
Compensation on the use of building ground - paid by legal entities	..	..	..	63	100	124	134	139	156	157
4200 Recurrent taxes on net wealth	..	..	..	4	0	0	0	0	0	0
4210 Individual	..	..	..	0	..	..	..	..	..	..
4220 Corporate	..	..	..	4	..	..	..	..	..	..
Tax on balance wealth paid by banks	..	..	..	4	..	..	..	..	..	..
4300 Estate, inheritance and gift taxes	..	..	..	2	9	14	8	8	16	10
4310 Estate and inheritance taxes	..	..	..	..	..	..	..	..	..	..
4320 Gift taxes	..	..	..	..	..	..	..	..	..	..
4400 Taxes on financial and capital transactions	..	..	..	23	57	32	23	29	44	40
Taxes on the sale of immovable property - from legal entities	..	..	..	11	19	7	5	7	9	7
Taxes on the sale of immovable property - from individuals	..	..	..	12	38	25	18	23	36	33
4500 Non-recurrent taxes	..	..	..	10	0	2	1	4	3	8
4510 On net wealth	..	..	..	0	..	0	0	0	0	0
4520 Other non-recurrent taxes	..	..	..	10	..	2	1	4	3	8
Payments for the change of use of agricultural and forest land	..	..	..	10	..	0	1	2	2	2
Granting of easements and the creation of building rights	..	..	..	0	..	2	1	3	1	6
4600 Other recurrent taxes on property	..	..	..	0	0	0	0	0	0	0
Property tax on boats	..	..	..	0	0	0	0	0	0	0
5000 Taxes on goods and services	..	..	..	**2 604**	**4 666**	**5 055**	**5 390**	**5 707**	**6 568**	**5 896**
5100 Taxes on production, sale, transfer, etc.	..	..	..	2 483	4 451	4 840	5 051	5 331	6 114	5 456
5110 General taxes	..	..	..	1 642	2 941	2 929	3 050	3 224	3 892	3 543

	1965	1980	1990	2000	2007	2010	2013	2015	2019	2020
5111 Value added taxes	..	..	..	1 611	2 941	2 929	3 050	3 224	3 892	3 543
Value added tax	..	..	..	1 599	2 923	2 926	3 046	3 220	3 889	3 542
Negative compensation of farmers in a VAT flat rate system	..	..	..	12	18	3	4	4	3	2
5112 Sales tax	..	..	..	8	0	0	0	0	0	0
Customs duties paid by individuals	..	..	..	1	..	..	..	..	..	..
Special import duties and customs charges	..	..	..	7	..	..	..	..	..	..
5113 Other	..	..	..	23	0	0	0	0	0	0
Turnover tax on goods	..	..	..	11	..	..	..	..	..	..
Turnover tax on services	..	..	..	12	..	..	..	..	..	..
Special turnover tax on alcohol	..	..	..	0	..	..	..	..	..	..
5120 Taxes on specific goods and services	..	..	..	841	1 510	1 911	2 001	2 107	2 222	1 913
5121 Excise duties	..	..	..	581	1 196	1 555	1 579	1 626	1 671	1 432
Alcohol and alcoholic drinks	..	..	..	39	71	89	96	108	122	112
Mineral oil and gas	..	..	..	405	758	1 016	998	1 033	1 053	852
Tobacco	..	..	..	97	301	391	425	419	419	404
Duty free shops - alcohol and alcoholic drinks	..	..	..	3	0	0	0	0	0	0
Duty free shops - tobacco	..	..	..	17	0	0	0	0	0	0
Electric power and coal	..	..	..	0	4	19	31	34	32	31
Tax on the sales of new motor vehicles	..	..	..	18	60	40	26	26	37	26
Tax on the sales of used motor vehicles	..	..	..	2	2	0	0	0	0	0
Additional tax on motor vehicles	..	..	..	0	0	0	3	6	8	7
5122 Profits of fiscal monopolies	..	..	..	0	0	0	0	0	0	0
5123 Customs and import duties	..	..	..	158	85	60	53	53	61	62
Import duties	..	..	..	151	0	0	0	0	0	0
Levies on imported agricultural products	..	..	..	7	0	0	0	0	0	0
Custom duties collected for the EU	..	..	..	0	85	60	53	53	61	62
5124 Taxes on exports	..	..	..	0	0	0	0	0	0	0
5125 Taxes on investment goods	..	..	..	0	0	0	0	0	0	0
5126 Taxes on specific services	..	..	..	102	230	296	369	428	490	418
Tax on special gambling (gambling in casinos)	..	..	..	25	64	53	41	48	46	26
Tax on classical gambling (lottery...)	..	..	..	1	3	3	3	3	3	3
Special tax on slot machines	..	..	..	4	0	0	0	0	0	0
Tax on insurance services	..	..	..	37	65	69	65	82	101	102
Sojourn tax	..	..	..	3	7	7	8	11	25	15
Concessions	..	..	..	1	29	40	90	79	77	64
Concessions duties on special gambling (in casinos)	..	..	..	26	55	47	38	37	39	23
Fire protection tax	..	..	..	4	6	7	8	8	9	10
Tax on lottery tickets	..	..	..	0	0	0	3	17	20	18
Tax on financial services	..	..	..	0	0	0	32	57	71	67
FIHO, FSO	..	..	..	0	0	25	26	27	26	25
SOS	..	..	..	0	0	23	10	11	12	9
Tax on balance wealth paid by banks	..	..	..	0	0	0	18	2	0	0
Commodity reserve fund	..	..	..	0	0	21	27	32	31	26
Deposit guarantee Fund, Single Resolution Fund	..	..	..	0	0	0	0	16	30	31
5127 Other taxes on internat. trade and transactions	..	..	..	0	0	0	0	0	0	0
5128 Other taxes	..	..	..	0	0	0	0	0	0	0
Sugar levy	..	..	..	..	0	..	..	..	..	..
5130 Unallocable between 5110 and 5120	..	..	..	0	0	0	0	0	0	0
5200 Taxes on use of goods and perform activities	..	..	..	121	215	215	340	377	453	440
5210 Recurrent taxes	..	..	..	121	215	215	321	353	387	375
5211 Paid by households: motor vehicles	..	..	..	49	87	86	109	118	127	128
Registration fees on motor vehicles, boats and airplanes paid by individuals	..	..	..	49	87	86	109	118	127	128
5212 Paid by others: motor vehicles	..	..	..	12	21	20	24	27	33	32
Registration fees on motor vehicles, boats and airplanes paid by legal entities	..	..	..	12	21	20	24	27	33	32
Registration fees on tractors	..	..	..	0	0	0	0	0	0	0
5213 Paid in respect of other goods	..	..	..	59	107	110	187	208	228	215
Charges on the use of water	..	..	..	4	22	23	29	32	32	32
Taxes on waste pollution	..	..	..	7	10	3	2	2	1	1
Taxes on air pollution - caused by gas and hard fuels	..	..	..	3	8	10	10	13	15	16
Cont. of nuclear power plant to finance its de-composition	..	..	..	16	8	8	8	8	6	6
Indemnity for the restricted use of area on the territory of nuclear power plant	..	..	..	0	7	10	11	12	6	6
Taxes on air pollution	..	..	..	29	21	23	98	114	145	130
Special water tax	..	..	..	0	30	33	29	27	22	24
5220 Non-recurrent taxes	..	..	..	0	0	0	19	24	66	65
Emission permits	..	..	..	..	..	..	19	24	66	65
5300 Unallocable between 5100 and 5200	..	..	..	0	0	0	0	0	0	0
6000 Other taxes	**..**	**..**	**..**	**0**	**0**	**0**	**0**	**0**	**0**	**0**
6100 Paid solely by business	..	..	..	..	..	..	..	..	..	..

	1965	1980	1990	2000	2007	2010	2013	2015	2019	2020
Memorandum items										
Customs duties collected on behalf of the EU	..	..	..	..	85	60	53	53	61	62
SRF contributions collected on behalf of the EU	..	..	..	..	..	..	..	16	9	9
Total tax revenue on cash basis	..	..	..	**7 135**	**13 140**	**13 605**	**13 485**	**14 560**	**18 118**	**17 367**
Total tax revenue on accrual basis	..	..	..	**7 114**	**13 377**	**13 758**	**13 578**	**14 498**	**17 981**	**17 508**
Conciliation with National Accounts										
Additional taxes included in National Accounts	..	..	..	..	..	87	90	94	96	96
Radio and television licence fee	..	..	..	..	..	87	90	94	96	96
Taxes excluded from National Accounts	..	..	..	..	..	..	..	..	..	..
Difference in treatment of tax credits	..	..	..	0	0	0	0	0	0	0
Capital transfer for uncollected revenue	..	..	..	-7	-35	-17	-2	-2	-2	-25
Voluntary social security contributions	..	..	..	0	0	0	0	0	0	0
Miscellaneous differences	..	..	..	0	0	0	0	0	0	0
National Accounts: Taxes and actual social contributions	..	..	..	7 107	13 342	13 828	13 667	14 590	18 075	17 580
Imputed social contributions	..	..	..	39	81	100	117	118	136	153
National Accounts: Taxes and all social contributions	..	..	..	7 146	13 423	13 928	13 784	14 708	18 211	17 733

.. Not available

Note: Year ending 31st December.

Data are on accrual basis.

Source: Statistical Office of the Republic of Slovenia.

StatLink https://stat.link/eln9aj

Table 5.33. Spain: Details of tax revenue, 1965-2020

Million EUR

	1965	1980	1990	2000	2007	2010	2013	2015	2019	2020
Total tax revenue	**1 238**	**22 002**	**103 662**	**214 114**	**391 648**	**335 563**	**337 891**	**364 683**	**431 736**	**411 973**
Total tax revenue exclusive of taxes collected for the EU	**..**	**..**	**..**	**213 067**	**389 927**	**334 019**	**336 567**	**362 175**	**429 062**	**409 471**
1000 Taxes on income, profits and capital gains	**304**	**5 714**	**31 763**	**60 145**	**130 081**	**93 798**	**97 664**	**102 645**	**123 638**	**119 785**
1100 Of individuals	177	4 481	22 527	41 248	80 719	74 118	77 230	78 896	97 956	97 770
Personal income tax	..	..	22 527	40 366	79 973	73 534	76 690	78 586	97 494	97 476
Income tax of non-residents	..	..	0	882	746	584	540	310	462	294
1110 On income and profits	..	..	..	..	..	..	..	..	..	..
1120 On capital gains	..	..	..	..	..	..	..	..	..	..
1200 Corporate	114	1 119	9 146	18 897	49 362	19 680	20 434	23 749	25 682	22 015
Corporate income tax	..	..	9 146	18 597	47 499	17 567	19 516	22 471	23 721	20 749
Income tax of non-residents (legal persons)	..	..	0	300	1 863	2 113	918	1 278	1 961	1 266
1210 On profits	..	..	..	..	..	..	..	..	..	..
Tax on commercial activity	..	..	..	..	..	..	..	..	..	..
Special tax 4 percent	..	..	..	..	..	..	..	..	..	..
Taxes on profits	..	..	..	..	..	..	..	..	..	..
1220 On capital gains	..	..	..	..	..	..	..	..	..	..
1300 Unallocable between 1100 and 1200	13	114	91	0	0	0	0	0	0	0
Local taxes	13	114	0	..	..	..	..	..	..	..
Other taxes	..	..	..	..	..	..	..	..	..	..
2000 Social security contributions	**350**	**10 682**	**36 722**	**74 683**	**127 088**	**127 235**	**116 875**	**122 835**	**152 527**	**154 276**
2100 Employees	81	2 376	5 976	11 711	19 625	19 423	16 603	18 783	23 272	22 243
2110 On a payroll basis	..	..	5 976	11 711	19 625	19 423	16 603	18 783	23 272	22 243
2120 On an income tax basis	..	..	0	..	..	..	..	..	..	..
2200 Employers	269	8 306	26 385	54 226	93 234	89 666	82 224	87 988	112 274	112 380
2210 On a payroll basis	..	..	26 385	54 226	93 234	89 666	82 224	87 988	112 274	112 380
2220 On an income tax basis	..	..	0	..	..	..	..	..	..	..
2300 Self-employed or non-employed	0	0	4 361	8 746	14 229	18 146	18 048	16 064	16 981	19 653
Self-employment	..	..	2 492	6 788	10 120	10 119	10 244	10 872	11 501	11 599
Unemployment	..	..	1 869	1 958	4 109	8 027	7 804	5 192	5 480	8 054
2310 On a payroll basis	..	..	..	..	..	..	..	..	..	..
2320 On an income tax basis	..	..	..	..	..	..	..	..	..	..
2400 Unallocable between 2100, 2200 and 2300	0	0	0	0	0	0	0	0	0	0
2410 On a payroll basis	..	..	..	..	..	..	..	..	..	..
2420 On an income tax basis	..	..	..	..	..	..	..	..	..	..
3000 Taxes on payroll and workforce	**0**	**0**	**0**	**0**	**0**	**0**	**0**	**0**	**0**	**0**
4000 Taxes on property	**79**	**1 004**	**5 718**	**13 827**	**32 133**	**22 178**	**24 250**	**27 855**	**30 567**	**27 619**
4100 Recurrent taxes on immovable property	6	41	1 478	3 988	7 281	9 666	11 829	12 623	13 488	13 161
Real State tax (IBI)/Real State tax surcharge	..	41	1 478	3 982	7 267	9 657	11 755	12 581	13 437	13 081
Special Real State tax for non-residents	..	0	0	6	6	8	8	4	2	3
Other taxes on property, land or building use	..	0	0	0	3	0	1	1	0	0
4110 Households	..	..	..	..	..	..	..	..	..	..
4120 Others	..	..	..	0	5	1	65	37	49	77
Tax on large commercial establishments	..	..	..	..	5	1	65	37	49	77
4200 Recurrent taxes on net wealth	0	107	637	1 413	2 479	688	2 049	1 904	2 240	2 297
4210 Individual	..	107	637	1 413	2 479	688	2 049	1 904	2 240	2 297
Wealth tax	..	..	637	1 199	2 054	104	1 339	1 144	1 414	1 496
Real State tax (unoccupied dwellings) and others	..	..	0	214	425	584	710	760	826	801
4220 Corporate	..	0	0	0	0	0	0	0	0	0
4300 Estate, inheritance and gift taxes	13	90	440	1 379	2 901	2 412	2 492	2 790	2 513	2 494
Inheritance and gift tax	..	..	440	1 379	2 901	2 412	2 492	2 790	2 513	2 494
4310 Estate and inheritance taxes	..	..	..	..	..	..	..	..	..	..
4320 Gift taxes	..	..	..	..	..	..	..	..	..	..
4400 Taxes on financial and capital transactions	60	767	2 478	5 939	17 025	7 603	5 301	6 984	9 329	7 535
Taxes on property transactions	60	767	2 478	5 939	17 025	7 603	5 301	6 984	9 329	7 535
Tax on financial transactions	..	..	..	..	..	..	..	..	..	..
4500 Non-recurrent taxes	0	0	646	1 108	2 447	1 809	2 579	3 554	2 997	2 132
4510 On net wealth	..	..	467	0	495	192	325	1 006	338	316
Tax on land holding gains	..	..	467	..	..	..	..	0	..	..
Urban use tax	..	..	..	..	495	192	90	73	104	82
Extraordinary resource of FGD	..	..	..	..	0	0	235	933	234	234
4520 Other non-recurrent taxes	..	..	179	1 108	1 952	1 617	2 254	2 548	2 659	1 816
Special duties	..	..	179	180	168	129	84	70	74	55
Land development contributions	..	..	0	223	368	225	71	61	66	43
Tax on the increase in value of urban terrains	..	..	0	705	1 416	1 263	1 711	2 417	2 519	1 718
Others	..	..	0	0	0	0	2	0	0	0
Levy on "Revaluation of Reserve Account"	..	..	..	0	0	0	386	0	0	0
4600 Other recurrent taxes on property	0	0	38	0	0	0	0	0	0	0
5000 Taxes on goods and services	**506**	**4 553**	**29 437**	**65 456**	**102 334**	**92 344**	**99 026**	**111 159**	**124 852**	**110 188**

	1965	1980	1990	2000	2007	2010	2013	2015	2019	2020
5100 Taxes on production, sale, transfer, etc.	503	4 552	26 732	59 383	93 814	84 985	91 122	102 912	115 125	100 936
5110 General taxes	275	2 234	16 611	37 800	62 778	55 629	60 488	69 478	81 079	70 793
5111 Value added taxes	0	0	16 304	37 785	62 743	55 318	60 314	69 294	80 889	70 616
Value added tax (VAT)	..	..	16 304	37 045	61 472	54 509	59 207	67 913	79 301	69 382
Canary Islands general indirect tax	..	..	0	740	1 271	809	1 107	1 381	1 588	1 234
5112 Sales tax	0	0	0	15	35	311	174	184	190	177
Fees for RTVE (since 2010)	..	..	..	0	0	278	174	184	190	177
Fees from Nat. Commission of Telecomms. Market	..	..	..	15	35	33	0	0	0	0
Tax on certain digital services	..	..	..	..	..	..	..	..	..	..
5113 Other	275	2 234	307	0	0	0	0	0	0	0
Cascade tax	118	1 483	197	..	..	..	..	..	..	..
Excises on luxury expenditure	96	939	15	..	..	..	..	..	..	..
Other import duties	94	832	128	..	..	..	..	..	..	..
Refund of internal taxes	-33	-1 020	-33	..	..	..	..	..	..	..
5120 Taxes on specific goods and services	228	2 317	10 120	21 583	31 036	29 356	30 634	33 434	34 046	30 143
5121 Excise duties	69	1 239	6 048	17 952	25 581	24 384	24 550	25 908	26 301	23 177
Special excises	69	1 239	10	0	0	0	0	0	0	0
On beer	0	0	87	202	307	302	302	316	352	331
On wine	0	0	0	0	0	0	0	0	0	0
On alcohol	0	0	481	785	1 008	876	775	843	874	672
On hydrocarbon	0	0	4 222	9 977	11 787	10 907	11 949	12 465	13 719	11 471
On tobacco	0	0	1 123	4 507	7 258	7 976	7 114	7 213	7 101	6 827
On electricity bills	0	0	0	703	1 153	1 483	1 558	1 458	1 460	1 309
On carbon	0	0	0	0	0	0	148	308	139	41
Tax on retail sales of specific hydrocarbons	0	0	0	0	1 356	1 238	453	7	1	0
Tax on oil derived fuels	0	0	120	237	253	220	267	314	332	254
Petrol tax	0	0	0	6	5	5	13	22	23	20
Production and storage of electricity	0	0	0	0	0	0	1 261	1 576	718	1 146
Tax Greenhouse Effect Flourinated	0	0	0	0	0	0	0	99	81	67
Other taxes	0	0	5	17	21	18	17	22	22	20
Canary Islands taxes on national products	0	0	0	51	86	71	75	85	84	86
Taxes on national products in Ceuta and Melilla	0	0	0	108	110	105	103	115	113	74
Fees from the National Energy Commission	0	0	0	13	27	35	0	0	0	0
Contribution to the National Energy Efficiency Fund	0	0	0	0	0	366	150	207	201	209
Special tax on certain means of transport	0	0	0	1 317	2 158	735	325	358	697	446
Fee for use of continental waters for electricity production	0	0	0	0	0	0	0	453	317	154
Special duties and other taxes on imported products	0	0	0	29	52	47	40	47	33	21
Other taxes on products	0	0	0	0	0	0	0	0	34	29
5122 Profits of fiscal monopolies	66	132	546	0	0	0	0	0	0	0
Tobacco	21	77	0	..	..	..	..	..	..	..
Petroleum	45	55	546	..	..	..	..	..	..	..
5123 Customs and import duties	87	561	2 078	1 044	1 816	1 593	1 401	1 899	2 063	1 739
Import duties	87	561	1 394	0	0	0	0	0	0	0
Tax on Imports of Goods in the Canary Islands	0	0	137	33	51	44	45	53	54	55
Tax on Imports in Ceuta and Melilla	0	0	36	41	42	40	39	43	43	28
Customs duties collected for the EU	..	..	511	970	1 723	1 509	1 317	1 803	1 966	1 656
5124 Taxes on exports	0	0	0	..	..	..	..	..	..	..
5125 Taxes on investment goods	0	0	0	0	0	0	0	0	0	0
5126 Taxes on specific services	7	385	1 427	2 497	3 633	3 166	4 469	5 408	5 461	5 008
Taxes on betting and gambling	0	232	1 307	1 649	2 051	1 635	1 249	1 164	1 361	820
Taxes on other specific services	6	153	120	0	0	0	0	0	0	0
Taxes on insurance premiums	0	0	0	848	1 581	1 531	1 417	1 446	1 714	1 704
Tax on deposits of credit institution	0	0	0	0	1	0	227	421	381	410
Ordinary resource DGF	0	0	0	0	0	0	1 576	1 644	1 101	1 161
Tourist tax	0	0	0	0	0	0	0	43	196	67
EU SRF contribution	..	..	..	..	..	..	..	690	708	846
5127 Other taxes on internat. trade and transactions	0	0	0	0	0	0	0	0	0	0
5128 Other taxes	0	0	22	90	6	213	214	219	221	219
EU levies	..	..	22	77	-2	35	7	15	0	0
Others	..	..	0	13	8	9	20	37	69	67
Resource CORES	..	..	0	0	0	169	187	167	152	152
5130 Unallocable between 5110 and 5120	0	0	0	0	0	0	0	0	0	0
5200 Taxes on use of goods and perform activities	3	1	2 633	6 073	8 520	7 359	7 904	8 247	9 727	9 252
5210 Recurrent taxes	3	1	1 616	4 306	5 311	5 782	6 493	6 420	6 861	6 449
Other taxes on luxury expenses	..	..	..	2	7	4	3	3	3	2
5211 Paid by households: motor vehicles	..	0	461	1 117	1 626	1 770	1 848	1 725	1 775	1 707
Car registration tax	..	..	461	1 117	1 626	1 770	1 848	1 725	1 775	1 707
5212 Paid by others: motor vehicles	..	0	117	298	502	498	503	470	491	472
Car registration tax	..	..	117	298	502	498	503	470	491	472

	1965	1980	1990	2000	2007	2010	2013	2015	2019	2020
5213 Paid in respect of other goods	..	1	1 038	2 889	3 176	3 510	4 139	4 222	4 592	4 268
Hunting and fishing taxes	..	..	0	28	28	34	34	30	27	26
Economic activity tax	..	..	925	1 934	1 633	1 785	1 701	1 794	1 890	1 838
Advertising	..	..	27	0	0	0	0	0	0	0
Taxes on environment and pollution	..	..	0	42	91	141	616	563	673	661
Tax on effluent, use of hydrocarbon and mines	..	..	0	51	83	67	158	184	194	177
Other fees paid by households for licences	..	..	0	179	264	228	206	245	328	280
Compensation for local taxes	..	..	86	140	176	165	129	118	130	125
Vehicle inspection duty	..	..	0	6	18	17	20	19	13	13
Municipal fees for private use of public space	..	..	0	509	883	1 073	1 275	1 269	1 337	1 148
5220 Non-recurrent taxes	0	0	1 017	1 767	3 209	1 577	1 411	1 827	2 866	2 803
Tax and building permits	..	..	327	1 117	2 227	859	519	575	1 108	868
Urban licenses	..	..	0	451	490	260	157	200	333	265
Greenhouse gas emission trading	..	..	0	0	0	0	138	412	1 015	1 264
Parafiscal taxes	..	..	690	199	492	458	597	640	410	406
5300 Unallocable between 5100 and 5200	0	0	72	0	0	0	0	0	0	0
6000 Other taxes	**0**	**49**	**22**	**3**	**12**	**8**	**76**	**189**	**152**	**105**
6100 Paid solely by business	..	49	0	0	0	0	0	0	0	0
6200 Other	..	0	22	3	12	8	76	189	152	105
Other taxes on production	..	..	..	3	12	8	76	189	152	105
Memorandum items										
Customs duties collected on behalf of the EU	..	..	..	970	1 723	1 509	1 317	1 803	1 966	1 656
SRF contributions collected on behalf of the EU	..	..	..	..	..	..	..	690	708	846
Non-wastable tax credits										
Non-wastable tax credits against 1110	..	..	..	..	1 323	1 897	774	1 093	2 338	2 697
Tax expenditure component	..	..	..	..	522	729	432	546	1 077	1 199
Transfer component	..	..	..	..	801	1 168	342	547	1 261	1 498
Non-wastable tax credits against 1210	..	..	..	..	0	0	0	46	177	296
Tax expenditure component	..	..	..	..	..	..	..	12	39	47
Transfer component	..	..	..	..	..	..	..	34	138	249
Total tax revenue on cash basis	**1 238**	**22 002**	**103 662**	**212 669**	**388 829**	**333 697**	**338 878**	**360 947**	**429 621**	**398 471**
Total tax revenue on accrual basis	**..**	**..**	**..**	**214 114**	**391 648**	**335 563**	**337 891**	**364 683**	**431 736**	**411 973**
Conciliation with National Accounts										
Additional taxes included in National Accounts	..	..	..	0	0	0	0	0	0	0
Taxes excluded from National Accounts	..	..	..	0	0	0	0	0	0	0
Difference in treatment of tax credits	..	..	..	0	522	729	432	558	1 116	1 246
Capital transfer for uncollected revenue	..	..	..	0	0	0	0	0	0	0
Voluntary social security contributions	..	..	..	447	937	1 155	2 209	1 170	987	891
Miscellaneous differences	..	..	..	0	0	0	0	0	0	0
National Accounts: Taxes and actual social contributions	..	..	..	214 561	393 107	337 447	340 532	366 411	433 839	414 110
Imputed social contributions	..	..	..	5 379	7 618	8 585	7 772	7 503	7 142	7 048
National Accounts: Taxes and all social contributions	..	..	..	219 940	400 725	346 032	348 304	373 914	440 981	421 158

.. Not available

Note: Year ending 31st December.

From 1995, data are on accrual basis.

Since 1995, the data are consistent with those transmitted to Eurostat in the framework of Government Finance Statistics (ESA).

From 1981 the figures take into account the classification procedures set out in the OECD Interpretative Guide. Consequently, they are not completely comparable with the figures for earlier years though the amounts involved are quite small.

Heading 2300: Contributions paid by self-employed were shown under heading 2100 until 1982.

Source: Information from the Ministry of Finance for taxes and from Social Security System for social security contributions up to 1994. Since 1995 (accrual basis), national account data (IGAE-Ministry of Finance)

StatLink https://stat.link/nb9x0u

Table 5.34. Sweden: Details of tax revenue, 1965-2020

Million SEK

	1965	1980	1990	2000	2007	2010	2013	2015	2019	2020
Total tax revenue	**40 003**	**259 216**	**755 953**	**1 204 794**	**1 491 190**	**1 532 259**	**1 624 632**	**1 816 204**	**2 162 928**	**2 132 388**
Total tax revenue exclusive of taxes collected for the EU	..	..	**755 953**	**1 200 999**	**1 485 306**	**1 526 585**	**1 619 411**	**1 809 928**	**2 156 063**	**2 126 176**
1000 Taxes on income, profits and capital gains	**21 956**	**112 730**	**314 797**	**514 729**	**580 372**	**546 696**	**566 234**	**657 539**	**772 120**	**762 656**
1100 Of individuals	19 500	106 376	291 146	426 956	464 435	430 896	466 286	533 660	620 161	613 894
1110 On income and profits	19 390	105 866	289 598	392 532	414 728	396 353	433 985	464 596	550 584	553 813
Coupon tax	9	44	233	2 040	6 306	3 047	4 108	4 615	7 216	3 551
Duties on foreign artists	4	3	3	50	86	89	-1	2	0	0
National income tax individual	8 676	31 682	70 755	66 850	44 326	42 595	44 664	52 480	57 083	52 716
Local income tax individual	9 294	78 134	220 072	336 304	479 068	522 850	581 934	635 719	748 197	766 082
Tax reduction individual	0	-3 997	-1 465	-18 872	-122 029	-179 890	-204 632	-236 613	-271 871	-278 728
Public service tax	..	..	0	5 061	6 674	6 981	7 208	7 759	9 028	9 211
Other	1 407	0	0	1 098	296	681	704	635	931	981
1120 On capital gains	110	510	1 548	34 425	49 707	34 543	32 301	69 064	69 577	60 081
Lottery prize tax	110	510	1 548	60	0	0	0	0	0	0
1200 Corporate	2 456	6 354	23 651	87 772	115 937	115 800	99 948	123 878	151 959	148 762
1210 On profits	2 456	6 354	23 651	87 772	115 937	115 800	99 948	123 878	151 959	148 762
Tax on profits not distributed	1	10	3	0	0	0	0	0	0	0
National income tax b.c. list	1 425	2 078	19 774	74 501	103 150	103 944	93 097	115 507	146 651	143 118
Local income tax b.c. list	1 030	4 266	0	0	0	0	0	0	0	0
Special tax on profits	0	0	3 874	0	0	0	0	0	0	0
Taxes on pension insurance savings	0	0	0	13 271	12 787	11 856	6 850	8 371	5 308	5 644
1220 On capital gains	0	0	0	0	0	0	0	0	0	0
1300 Unallocable between 1100 and 1200	0	0	0	0	0	0	0	0	0	0
2000 Social security contributions	**4 851**	**74 647**	**205 867**	**306 974**	**388 505**	**384 668**	**376 684**	**404 851**	**462 860**	**455 396**
2100 Employees	743	254	823	63 074	81 088	89 175	100 861	108 356	128 161	131 044
Health insurance fees	743	9	5	0	0	0	0	0	0	0
Unemployment insurance fees	0	245	818	0	0	0	0	0	0	0
Pension fees	0	0	0	63 074	81 088	89 175	100 861	108 356	128 161	131 044
2110 On a payroll basis	..	..	..	63 074	81 088	89 175	100 861	108 356	128 161	131 044
2120 On an income tax basis	..	..	..	0	0	0	0	0	0	0
2200 Employers	3 568	71 602	196 905	237 576	300 010	288 310	271 449	291 646	331 065	321 621
Survivors pension fees	0	20 343	44 181	14 847	19 611	20 362	15 693	17 305	11 159	10 493
Health insurance fees	717	26 005	58 334	74 097	100 979	71 292	58 365	64 332	66 015	62 066
Unemployment insurance fees	0	0	0	0	0	0	0	0	0	0
Labour market fees	0	982	12 516	45 975	48 471	55 443	39 007	37 926	47 682	44 078
Industrial injury insurance fees	132	1 201	4 663	12 030	7 844	8 146	4 022	4 431	3 718	3 496
Seamen's pension fees	0	10	26	30	0	0	0	0	0	0
Part pension fees	0	1 119	2 897	0	0	0	0	0	0	0
Supplementary pension fees	2 719	21 458	73 129	71 384	97 748	106 712	119 508	129 204	154 165	156 039
Parent insurance fees	0	484	1 159	19 215	25 356	26 355	34 854	38 448	48 326	45 449
2210 On a payroll basis	..	..	..	237 576	300 010	288 310	271 449	291 646	331 065	321 621
2220 On an income tax basis	..	..	..	0	0	0	0	0	0	0
2300 Self-employed or non-employed	540	2 791	8 139	5 569	8 391	7 584	5 607	5 058	4 297	4 100
Survivors pension fees	0	943	1 580	451	662	687	442	443	158	91
Health insurance fees	260	992	1 702	1 988	3 297	2 082	550	256	152	59
Industrial injury insurance fees	0	64	191	365	264	275	113	84	51	29
Parent insurance fees	0	58	106	573	856	888	960	603	518	279
Supplementary pension fees	280	734	4 560	2 192	3 312	3 652	3 542	3 672	3 420	3 641
Reduction	0	0	0	0	0	0	0	0	0	0
2310 On a payroll basis	..	..	..	5 569	8 391	7 584	5 607	5 058	4 297	4 100
2320 On an income tax basis	..	..	..	0	0	0	0	0	0	0
2400 Unallocable between 2100, 2200 and 2300	0	0	0	756	-984	-401	-1 233	-209	-662	-1 368
2410 On a payroll basis	..	..	..	756	-984	-401	-1 233	-209	-662	-1 368
2420 On an income tax basis	..	..	..	0	0	0	0	0	0	0
3000 Taxes on payroll and workforce	**13**	**6 759**	**18 686**	**50 106**	**83 279**	**107 515**	**172 170**	**194 121**	**268 832**	**255 891**
Special wage tax	0	61	0	22 391	30 225	33 090	36 832	40 283	49 367	50 836
Child care fees	0	4 740	13 080	0	0	0	0	0	0	0
Adult education fees	0	614	1 555	0	0	0	0	0	0	0
Building research fees	13	105	0	0	0	0	0	0	0	0
Labour welfare fees	0	257	2 033	0	0	0	0	0	0	0
Labour education fees	0	982	0	0	0	0	0	0	0	0
Labour market fees	0	0	0	112	156	219	7	-1	1	0
General wage fees	0	0	2 018	27 603	52 898	74 207	135 331	153 839	219 464	205 054
4000 Taxes on property	**712**	**2 424**	**26 630**	**39 890**	**36 228**	**36 509**	**41 182**	**43 852**	**47 265**	**47 885**
4100 Recurrent taxes on immovable property	10	16	8 946	23 286	25 899	26 402	31 596	32 444	34 391	34 562
4110 Households	0	0	3 877	13 321	13 474	11 666	12 936	13 320	15 387	15 966
Special tax on real estate	..	..	3 877	13 321	13 474	11 666	12 936	13 320	15 387	15 966

	1965	1980	1990	2000	2007	2010	2013	2015	2019	2020
4120 Others	10	16	5 069	9 965	12 424	14 736	18 660	19 124	19 003	18 596
Forestry levy	10	16	423	22	34	18	37	19	9	4
Special tax on real estate	0	0	4 646	9 943	12 390	14 718	18 623	19 105	18 995	18 591
4200 Recurrent taxes on net wealth	366	717	3 200	8 223	0	0	0	0	0	0
4210 Individual	361	702	3 135	8 043	..	..	..	..	..	..
4220 Corporate	5	15	65	180	..	..	..	..	..	..
4300 Estate, inheritance and gift taxes	155	545	1 433	2 549	23	9	-4	0	0	0
4310 Estate and inheritance taxes	143	495	1 118	2 088	15	9	-4	0	..	..
4320 Gift taxes	12	50	315	460	8	0	0	0	..	..
4400 Taxes on financial and capital transactions	181	1 146	13 051	5 833	10 305	10 097	9 590	11 408	12 874	13 323
Taxes on financial and capital transactions	181	1 146	6 946	4 878	9 414	8 968	8 913	10 895	12 276	12 721
Turnover tax on securities	0	0	6 105	0	0	0	0	0	0	0
Tax on life group insurances	0	0	0	955	891	1 129	678	513	598	602
4500 Non-recurrent taxes	0	0	0	0	0	0	0	0	0	0
4510 On net wealth	..	..	..	..	..	..	..	..	..	..
4520 Other non-recurrent taxes	..	..	..	..	..	..	..	..	..	..
4600 Other recurrent taxes on property	0	0	0	0	0	0	0	0	0	0
5000 Taxes on goods and services	**12 471**	**62 234**	**188 709**	**291 615**	**401 038**	**455 450**	**466 556**	**514 485**	**610 185**	**608 185**
5100 Taxes on production, sale, transfer, etc.	11 808	58 474	181 587	284 182	387 956	439 050	450 054	495 733	589 535	586 604
5110 General taxes	4 147	34 643	112 399	199 606	286 211	326 685	341 952	383 002	459 825	461 267
5111 Value added taxes	0	34 643	112 399	197 483	282 586	322 603	337 822	379 120	459 699	461 138
5112 Sales tax	4 147	0	0	0	0	0	0	0	0	0
5113 Other	0	0	0	2 123	3 625	4 082	4 130	3 882	126	129
5120 Taxes on specific goods and services	7 661	23 831	69 188	84 576	101 745	112 365	108 102	112 731	129 710	125 337
5121 Excise duties	5 953	19 941	55 332	70 313	84 873	91 470	88 168	91 572	104 451	105 144
Taxes on petrol and fuel	1 420	4 229	17 171	39 011	44 501	47 426	43 869	44 906	48 718	45 847
Special sales tax	390	585	1 098	0	0	0	0	0	0	0
Sales tax on motor vehicles	325	553	1 983	195	3	0	0	0	0	0
Tobacco tax	1 150	3 087	5 636	7 747	9 742	10 588	11 136	11 825	11 892	11 912
Tax on spirits	1 548	4 431	6 205	4 902	4 250	4 324	4 001	4 208	4 532	5 250
Tax on wine	149	930	2 922	3 567	4 001	4 589	4 887	5 654	6 143	6 552
Tax on beer and soft drinks	242	964	2 532	2 355	2 773	3 219	3 329	3 895	4 313	4 477
Tax on energy consumption	729	5 162	16 352	11 451	18 994	21 035	20 827	20 787	27 130	28 796
Taxes on electricity from certain sources	0	0	1 018	0	0	0	0	0	0	0
Tax on wastes	0	0	0	1 085	609	289	119	297	252	681
Tax on cassette tapes	0	0	194	0	0	0	0	0	0	0
Tax on video recorders	0	0	221	0	0	0	0	0	0	0
Tax on chemicals	0	0	0	0	0	0	0	0	1 469	1 629
5122 Profits of fiscal monopolies	72	204	332	3 641	3 952	5 068	5 385	5 001	1 817	2 094
Alcohol monopoly wholesale	23	116	98	0	0	0	0	0	0	0
Alcohol monopoly retailing	49	88	234	80	296	302	116	198	240	471
Gaming monopoly retailing	0	0	0	3 561	3 657	4 766	5 269	4 803	1 577	1 623
5123 Customs and import duties	1 419	2 433	8 308	3 450	5 099	5 412	4 976	6 243	6 865	6 212
Customs	1 080	1 300	3 115	3 450	5 099	5 412	4 976	6 243	6 865	6 212
Agricultural levies	339	1 133	5 193	0	0	0	0	0	0	0
5124 Taxes on exports	0	0	0	0	0	0	0	0	0	0
5125 Taxes on investment goods	0	0	40	0	0	0	0	0	0	0
Investment tax	..	..	40	..	..	..	..	..	..	..
5126 Taxes on specific services	217	1 253	5 176	5 834	3 361	4 712	6 594	7 120	13 730	10 215
Betting tax	79	223	616	0	0	0	0	0	0	0
Advertisement tax	0	202	1 073	1 116	657	335	244	200	151	114
Tax on gambling	0	69	88	1 245	1 315	1 378	1 309	1 353	3 801	3 777
Other specific services	138	656	2 938	3 473	1 388	2 999	5 041	5 567	7 993	5 829
Tax on charter travelling	0	103	461	0	0	0	0	0	0	0
Tax on air travel	..	..	0	0	0	0	0	0	1 785	495
5127 Other taxes on internat. trade and transactions	0	0	0	0	0	0	0	0	0	0
5128 Other taxes	0	0	0	1 339	4 460	5 702	2 980	2 795	2 847	1 672
5130 Unallocable between 5110 and 5120	0	0	0	0	0	0	0	0	0	0
5200 Taxes on use of goods and perform activities	663	3 760	7 122	7 433	13 083	16 400	16 502	18 752	20 650	21 581
5210 Recurrent taxes	663	3 760	7 122	7 433	13 083	16 400	16 502	18 752	20 650	21 581
5211 Paid by households: motor vehicles	336	1 241	2 003	4 969	7 414	8 550	8 275	10 897	10 067	10 347
5212 Paid by others: motor vehicles	313	2 476	5 055	2 464	5 669	7 850	8 227	7 855	10 584	11 234
5213 Paid in respect of other goods	14	43	64	0	0	0	0	0	0	0
5220 Non-recurrent taxes	0	0	0	0	0	0	0	0	0	0
5300 Unallocable between 5100 and 5200	0	0	0	0	0	0	0	0	0	0
6000 Other taxes	**0**	**422**	**1 264**	**1 479**	**1 768**	**1 421**	**1 806**	**1 356**	**1 665**	**2 374**
6100 Paid solely by business	..	0	0	0	0	0	0	0	0	0
6200 Other	..	422	1 264	1 479	1 768	1 421	1 806	1 356	1 665	2 374
Memorandum item										
Customs duties collected on behalf of the EU	..	..	..	3 450	5 099	5 412	4 976	6 243	6 865	6 212
Total tax revenue on cash basis	**40 003**	**259 216**	**755 953**	**1 144 233**	**1 465 382**	**1 496 374**	**1 611 798**	**1 762 187**	**0**	**0**
Total tax revenue on accrual basis	**..**	**..**	**..**	**1 204 794**	**1 491 190**	**1 532 259**	**1 624 632**	**1 816 204**	**2 162 928**	**2 132 388**

	1965	1980	1990	2000	2007	2010	2013	2015	2019	2020
Conciliation with National Accounts										
Additional taxes included in National Accounts	..	..	..	0	0	0	0	0	0	0
Taxes excluded from National Accounts	..	..	..	0	0	0	0	0	0	0
Difference in treatment of tax credits	..	..	..	0	0	0	0	0	0	0
Capital transfer for uncollected revenue	..	..	..	0	0	0	0	0	0	0
Voluntary social security contributions	..	..	..	7 951	12 376	13 167	15 909	16 726	24 966	24 731
Miscellaneous differences	..	..	..	0	0	0	0	0	0	0
National Accounts: Taxes and actual social contributions	..	..	..	1 212 745	1 503 566	1 545 426	1 640 541	1 832 930	2 187 894	2 157 119
Imputed social contributions	..	..	..	0	0	0	0	0	0	0
National Accounts: Taxes and all social contributions	..	..	..	1 212 745	1 503 566	1 545 426	1 640 541	1 832 930	2 187 894	2 157 119

.. Not available
Note: Year ending 31st December.
From 2000 data are on accrual basis.
Figures prior to 1970 are not strictly comparable with those of later years, though the amounts involved are insignificant.
Heading 1000: Receipts are on accrual and not on a cash basis for all years.
Source: National Financial Management Authority, Stockholm.

StatLink https://stat.link/wejqpr

Table 5.35. Switzerland: Details of tax revenue, 1965-2020

Million CHF

	1965	1980	1990	2000	2007	2010	2013	2015	2019	2020
Total tax revenue	**11 237**	**46 385**	**85 774**	**128 205**	**151 404**	**162 356**	**173 121**	**181 128**	**199 354**	**195 261**
1000 Taxes on income, profits and capital gains	**4 616**	**21 022**	**40 203**	**56 411**	**69 790**	**74 439**	**79 267**	**84 362**	**96 240**	**90 452**
1100 Of individuals	3 748	18 056	27 824	37 948	47 994	51 835	53 801	56 375	61 355	62 876
1110 On income and profits	3 547	17 622	27 824	37 948	47 994	51 835	53 801	56 375	61 355	62 876
Direct federal tax	245	2 525	4 432	5 713	8 589	9 880	9 655	10 394	11 483	12 054
Military service exemption tax	35	103	135	163	138	155	163	173	168	185
Cantonal tax individuals	1 473	7 510	12 856	17 592	23 094	24 957	26 253	27 156	29 677	30 284
Municipal tax individuals	1 322	6 235	10 402	14 481	16 174	16 844	17 731	18 651	20 026	20 353
Withholding tax	358	1 249	0	0	0	0	0	0	0	0
Coupons	114	0	0	0	0	0	0	0	0	0
1120 On capital gains	201	434	0	0	0	0	0	0	0	0
Cantonal tax individuals	84	229	..	..	..	..	..	..	..	..
Municipal tax individuals	112	190	..	..	..	..	..	..	..	..
Direct federal tax	5	15	..	..	..	..	..	..	..	..
1200 Corporate	868	2 966	6 300	11 323	16 161	16 378	17 814	19 432	22 301	21 485
1210 On profits	801	2 818	6 300	11 323	16 161	16 378	17 814	19 432	22 301	21 485
Direct federal tax	153	781	2 214	4 928	6 800	8 006	8 698	9 731	11 785	12 092
Corporate cantonal tax	363	1 230	2 576	3 989	6 098	5 445	5 985	6 294	6 900	6 127
Corporate municipal tax	285	807	1 510	2 406	3 263	2 927	3 130	3 407	3 616	3 267
Withholding tax	0	0	0	0	0	0	0	0	0	0
1220 On capital gains	67	148	..	..	..	..	..	..	..	..
Corporate tax on gains	2	7	..	..	..	..	..	..	..	..
Corporate cantonal tax	28	77	..	..	..	..	..	..	..	..
Corporate municipal tax	37	64	..	..	..	..	..	..	..	..
1300 Unallocable between 1100 and 1200	0	0	6 079	7 140	5 635	6 226	7 652	8 556	12 585	6 091
Withholding tax	..	..	4 044	6 202	4 211	4 723	5 619	6 543	9 842	3 316
Property gains tax	..	..	2 035	938	1 424	1 502	2 033	2 013	2 743	2 775
Other	..	..	..	..	..	..	..	..	..	..
2000 Social security contributions	**1 670**	**10 844**	**19 952**	**30 961**	**34 974**	**38 385**	**42 862**	**44 285**	**47 233**	**49 057**
2100 Employees	716	4 833	9 341	14 491	16 369	17 581	19 814	20 542	22 031	23 753
2110 On a payroll basis	716	4 833	9 341	14 491	16 369	17 581	19 814	20 542	22 031	23 753
2120 On an income tax basis	0	0	..	..	..	..	..	..	..	..
2200 Employers	747	4 897	9 350	14 504	16 383	17 608	19 846	20 574	22 072	22 044
2210 On a payroll basis	747	4 897	9 350	14 504	16 383	17 608	19 846	20 574	22 072	22 044
2220 On an income tax basis	0	0	..	..	..	..	..	..	..	..
2300 Self-employed or non-employed	208	1 046	1 261	1 967	2 222	3 197	3 202	3 169	3 131	3 260
2310 On a payroll basis	209	1 046	1 261	1 967	2 222	3 197	3 202	3 169	3 131	3 260
2320 On an income tax basis	0	0	..	..	..	..	..	..	..	..
2400 Unallocable between 2100, 2200 and 2300	0	68	0	0	0	0	0	0	0	0
2410 On a payroll basis	..	68	..	..	..	..	..	..	..	..
2420 On an income tax basis	..	0	..	..	..	..	..	..	..	..
3000 Taxes on payroll and workforce	**0**	**0**	**0**	**0**	**0**	**0**	**0**	**0**	**0**	**0**
4000 Taxes on property	**1 108**	**3 830**	**7 586**	**12 333**	**12 223**	**12 402**	**12 041**	**13 140**	**15 230**	**15 744**
4100 Recurrent taxes on immovable property	78	304	447	735	895	968	1 052	1 138	1 290	1 341
4110 Households	78	304	447	735	895	968	1 052	1 138	1 290	1 341
Cantonal tax on buildings	20	71	125	187	265	286	303	349	395	392
Municipal tax on buildings	58	233	322	548	630	682	748	789	895	949
4120 Others	0	0	..	..	..	..	..	..	..	..
4200 Recurrent taxes on net wealth	692	2 201	3 382	5 254	7 002	7 105	7 406	8 096	9 938	9 950
4210 Individual	420	1 383	2 194	3 972	5 309	5 576	5 787	6 606	7 932	8 246
Cantonal wealth tax	206	739	1 232	2 241	3 145	3 324	3 532	4 044	4 855	5 081
Municipal wealth tax	214	644	962	1 731	2 164	2 252	2 255	2 562	3 076	3 165
4220 Corporate	272	818	1 188	1 282	1 693	1 529	1 619	1 490	2 006	1 704
Direct federal tax on capital	21	92	0	0	0	0	0	0	0	0
Cantonal tax on capital	142	436	760	821	1 107	969	1 032	947	1 325	1 090
Municipal tax on capital	109	290	428	461	586	561	586	542	681	614
4300 Estate, inheritance and gift taxes	142	393	896	1 215	869	974	966	1 088	1 234	1 272
4310 Estate and inheritance taxes	142	393	896	1 215	869	974	966	1 088	1 234	1 272
Cantonal inheritance tax	128	361	820	1 118	774	886	854	964	1 065	1 128
Municipal inheritance tax	14	32	76	97	96	88	112	124	169	144
4320 Gift taxes	0	0	..	..	..	..	..	..	..	..
4400 Taxes on financial and capital transactions	196	932	2 245	4 342	2 562	2 428	1 671	1 902	1 701	1 992
Cantonal transfer tax	48	245	115	144	182	182	185	177	207	233
Municipal transfer tax	21	103	39	52	42	50	52	52	60	64
Securities issuance	99	175	0	0	405	779	182	360	173	179
Securities trading	19	409	0	0	1 933	1 417	1 253	1 314	1 262	1 516
Currency effects	9	0	0	0	0	0	0	0	0	0
Securities issuance and trading	0	0	2 091	4 146	0	0	0	0	0	0
4500 Non-recurrent taxes	0	0	0	0	0	0	0	0	0	0

	1965	1980	1990	2000	2007	2010	2013	2015	2019	2020
4510 On net wealth	..	..	..	..	..	..	..	..	..	..
4520 Other non-recurrent taxes	..	..	..	..	..	..	..	..	..	..
4600 Other recurrent taxes on property	0	0	616	786	895	927	946	915	1 067	1 189
5000 Taxes on goods and services	**3 843**	**10 689**	**17 894**	**28 285**	**34 168**	**36 539**	**38 287**	**38 542**	**39 636**	**38 958**
5100 Taxes on production, sale, transfer, etc.	3 582	9 863	15 975	25 302	30 669	32 264	33 861	33 771	34 327	33 544
5110 General taxes	1 191	4 772	9 871	16 917	19 962	21 035	22 870	22 791	22 915	22 435
5111 Value added taxes	0	0	9 871	16 594	19 604	20 662	22 501	22 397	22 508	22 104
5112 Sales tax	1 191	4 772	0	323	358	373	369	393	407	331
Automobile duty	..	..	..	323	358	373	369	393	407	331
Other sales taxes	..	..	..	0	0	0	0	0	0	0
5113 Other	0	0	..	..	..	..	..	..	..	..
5120 Taxes on specific goods and services	2 391	5 091	6 058	8 337	10 663	11 191	10 936	10 912	11 307	11 016
5121 Excise duties	1 016	3 427	4 604	6 810	7 805	8 295	8 099	8 056	8 353	8 049
Beer tax	26	33	0	0	107	112	113	114	117	110
Excises on tobacco	190	634	15	32	2 247	2 417	2 354	2 255	2 095	2 158
Other price supplements	104	542	1 503	1 783	3	0	0	3	3	3
Fuel tax	467	955	1 334	2 975	3 076	3 110	3 034	2 864	2 746	2 543
Additional fuel tax	229	1 263	1 753	2 020	2 071	2 082	2 025	1 905	1 821	1 683
Road tax	0	0	0	0	0	0	0	0	0	0
Mineral oil tax on combustibles	0	0	0	0	20	20	23	19	17	17
Automobile duty	0	0	0	0	0	0	0	0	0	0
Tax on distilled spirits	0	0	0	1	281	296	292	279	275	290
Electricity consumption tax	0	0	0	0	0	259	258	617	1 281	1 245
5122 Profits of fiscal monopolies	158	472	..	..	..	..	..	..	..	..
Alcohol monopoly	111	354	..	..	..	..	..	..	..	..
Salt monopoly	16	25	..	..	..	..	..	..	..	..
Water monopoly	30	90	..	..	..	..	..	..	..	..
Other	1	3	..	..	..	..	..	..	..	..
5123 Customs and import duties	1 104	953	1 201	1 096	1 040	1 079	1 059	1 056	1 143	1 187
Import duties	972	923	1 201	1 096	1 040	1 079	1 059	1 056	1 143	1 187
Tobacco duty	114	6	0	0	0	0	0	0	0	0
Additional duties	18	24	0	0	0	0	0	0	0	0
5124 Taxes on exports	0	0	..	..	..	..	..	..	..	..
5125 Taxes on investment goods	0	0	..	..	..	..	..	..	..	..
5126 Taxes on specific services	113	239	253	431	1 818	1 816	1 778	1 800	1 812	1 780
Games in B casinos Confederation	2	2	2	37	449	381	308	272	311	250
Cantonal entertainment tax	17	37	23	27	39	101	73	67	73	53
Municipal entertainment tax	11	19	46	26	18	17	15	15	15	5
Other cantonal expenditure taxes	24	63	0	0	0	0	0	0	0	0
Other municipal expenditure taxes	19	6	0	0	0	0	0	0	0	0
Premium stamp duty	40	112	0	0	645	659	700	715	717	726
Lottery taxes	0	0	181	320	474	459	466	527	493	526
Other	0	0	0	20	193	199	216	204	203	220
5127 Other taxes on internat. trade and transactions	0	0	..	..	..	..	..	..	..	..
5128 Other taxes	0	0	..	..	..	..	..	..	..	..
5130 Unallocable between 5110 and 5120	0	0	46	47	44	38	55	68	106	92
5200 Taxes on use of goods and perform activities	261	826	1 918	2 983	3 499	4 276	4 426	4 771	5 308	5 415
5210 Recurrent taxes	261	826	1 918	2 983	3 499	4 276	4 426	4 767	5 300	5 406
5211 Paid by households: motor vehicles	152	501	921	1 336	1 580	1 667	1 685	1 768	1 863	1 875
Paid by households in respect of motor vehicles	..	..	921	1 336	1 580	1 667	1 685	1 768	1 863	1 875
Paid by households in respect of motorway tax sticker	..	..	0	0	0	0	0	0	0	0
5212 Paid by others: motor vehicles	76	251	230	334	395	417	421	442	466	469
Paid by others in respect of motor vehicles	..	..	230	334	395	417	421	442	466	469
Paid by others in respect of motorway tax sticker	..	..	0	0	0	0	0	0	0	0
Paid by others in respect of heavy vehicle charge	..	..	0	0	0	0	0	0	0	0
5213 Paid in respect of other goods	33	74	768	1 314	1 524	2 192	2 319	2 556	2 971	3 062
Hunting and fishing	9	20	0	0	0	0	0	0	0	0
Cantonal dog license	3	9	6	9	8	8	10	9	11	12
Municipal dog license	2	8	14	21	25	30	33	35	43	44
Cantonal inns	12	24	0	0	0	0	0	0	0	0
Cantonal royalties	5	12	0	0	0	0	0	0	0	0
Other	2	1	0	33	33	30	31	24	12	11
Environmental incentive fees	0	0	3	73	166	755	833	1 036	1 447	1 497
Royalties and concessions	0	0	42	53	64	84	100	101	131	121
Radio and television licences	..	..	703	1 124	1 228	1 285	1 313	1 351	1 328	1 377
5220 Non-recurrent taxes	0	0	0	0	0	0	0	5	9	8
5300 Unallocable between 5100 and 5200	0	0	0	0	0	0	0	0	0	0
6000 Other taxes	**0**	**0**	**140**	**215**	**249**	**590**	**664**	**799**	**1 014**	**1 050**
6100 Paid solely by business	..	..	42	65	75	274	300	342	352	388
6200 Other	..	..	98	151	174	316	364	457	662	662
Exemption tax	..	..	98	151	174	187	191	190	197	201
Other	..	..	0	0	0	130	173	267	465	461

	1965	1980	1990	2000	2007	2010	2013	2015	2019	2020
Total tax revenue on cash basis	**11 237**	**46 385**	..	..	..	..	..	..	..	..
Total tax revenue on accrual basis	..	..	**85 774**	**128 205**	**151 404**	**162 356**	**173 121**	**181 128**	**199 354**	**195 261**
Conciliation with National Accounts										
Additional taxes included in national accounts	..	..	0	0	0	0	0	0	0	0
Tax excluded from national accounts	..	..	0	0	0	0	0	0	0	0
Difference in treatment of tax credits	..	..	0	0	0	0	0	0	0	0
Capital transfer for uncollected revenue	..	..	-242	-733	-936	-1 121	-1 309	-1 058	-1 062	-818
Voluntary social security contributions	..	..	0	0	0	0	0	0	0	0
Miscellaneous differences	..	..	0	0	0	0	0	0	0	0
National Accounts: taxes and actual social contributions	..	..	85 533	127 472	150 468	161 235	171 812	180 070	198 291	194 443
Imputed social contributions	..	..	362	502	467	454	483	337	393	785
National Accounts: taxes and all social contributions	..	..	85 895	127 974	150 935	161 689	172 295	180 407	198 684	195 228

.. Not available

Note: Calendar year ending on 31 December.

The data is on an accrual basis.

The pre-1970 figures are not strictly comparable with those from the following years which were revised.

"Parish taxes" are not reported in these statistics from 1985 onward.

In section 1100: payments made in consideration for exemption from military service could be classed under nontax receipts.

Section 2000 (Social security contributions) has been revised from 1985 onward to take account of the sectoring of government units adopted when switching to the ESA 95 system of accounts (currently ESA 2010). Consequently, health insurance contributions and those to the Swiss National Accident Insurance Fund are now excluded from section 2000.

Source: Financial Statistics, Federal Finance Administration.

StatLink https://stat.link/k03avt

Table 5.36. Türkiye: Details of tax revenue, 1965-2020

Million TRY

	1965	1980	1990	2000	2007	2010	2013	2015	2019	2020
Total tax revenue	**0**	**1**	**79**	**40 263**	**203 053**	**287 873**	**458 698**	**586 722**	**997 551**	**1 204 629**
1000 Taxes on income, profits and capital gains	**0**	**0**	**26**	**11 890**	**48 197**	**61 317**	**92 749**	**119 144**	**241 533**	**263 898**
1100 Of individuals	0	0	21	8 954	34 447	40 392	63 761	85 756	162 704	158 842
1110 On income and profits	0	0	21	8 954	34 447	40 392	63 761	85 756	162 704	158 842
Income tax	0	0	21	8 954	34 447	40 392	63 761	85 756	162 704	158 842
1120 On capital gains	0	0	0	0	0	0	0	0	0	0
1200 Corporate	0	0	5	2 935	13 751	20 925	28 988	33 388	78 829	105 057
1210 On profits	0	0	5	2 935	13 751	20 925	28 988	33 388	78 829	105 057
Corporation tax	0	0	5	2 935	13 751	20 925	28 988	33 388	78 829	105 057
1220 On capital gains	0	0	0	0	0	0	0	0	0	0
1300 Unallocable between 1100 and 1200	0	0	0	0	0	0	0	0	0	0
Fiscal balance tax	..	0	..	..	..	..	..	..	..	..
Capital gains tax on real estate sales	..	0	..	..	..	..	..	..	..	..
2000 Social security contributions	**0**	**0**	**15**	**7 543**	**44 052**	**71 696**	**125 871**	**170 282**	**312 808**	**357 677**
2100 Employees	0	0	6	2 712	17 867	26 934	49 831	64 214	120 108	137 742
2110 On a payroll basis	..	..	..	2 712	17 867	26 934	49 831	64 214	120 108	137 742
2120 On an income tax basis	..	..	..	0	0	0	0	0	0	0
2200 Employers	0	0	9	3 619	20 442	39 363	71 184	95 067	178 345	204 045
2210 On a payroll basis	..	..	..	3 619	20 442	39 363	71 184	95 067	178 345	204 045
2220 On an income tax basis	..	..	..	0	0	0	0	0	0	0
2300 Self-employed or non-employed	0	0	1	1 211	5 743	5 399	4 856	11 001	14 356	15 890
2310 On a payroll basis	..	..	..	1 211	5 743	5 399	4 856	11 001	14 356	15 890
2320 On an income tax basis	..	..	..	0	0	0	0	0	0	0
2400 Unallocable between 2100, 2200 and 2300	0	0	0	0	0	0	0	0	0	0
2410 On a payroll basis	..	..	..	..	..	..	..	..	..	..
2420 On an income tax basis	..	..	..	..	..	..	..	..	..	..
3000 Taxes on payroll and workforce	**0**	**0**	**0**	**0**	**0**	**0**	**0**	**0**	**0**	**0**
4000 Taxes on property	**0**	**0**	**2**	**1 272**	**7 621**	**11 684**	**21 280**	**28 582**	**41 721**	**53 548**
4100 Recurrent taxes on immovable property	0	0	0	191	1 464	2 669	3 847	5 882	9 681	11 204
Real estate tax	0	0	..	191	1 464	2 669	3 847	5 882	9 681	11 204
4110 Households	..	..	..	..	..	..	..	..	..	..
4120 Others	..	..	..	..	..	..	..	..	..	..
4200 Recurrent taxes on net wealth	0	0	0	0	0	0	0	0	0	0
4210 Individual	..	..	..	..	..	..	..	..	..	..
4220 Corporate	..	..	..	..	..	..	..	..	..	..
4300 Estate, inheritance and gift taxes	0	0	0	15	125	215	340	435	1 104	1 298
Gift and inheritance tax	0	0	0	15	125	215	340	435	1 104	1 298
4310 Estate and inheritance taxes	..	..	..	..	..	..	..	..	..	..
4320 Gift taxes	..	..	..	..	..	..	..	..	..	..
4400 Taxes on financial and capital transactions	0	0	2	1 065	6 032	8 800	17 093	22 265	30 937	41 045
Stamp tax	0	0	2	818	3 642	5 083	9 416	12 045	18 853	20 964
Real estate purchase tax	0	0	0	0	0	0	0	0	0	0
Title deed fees	0	0	0	207	2 000	3 329	7 072	9 530	11 213	19 001
Notary fees	0	0	0	40	389	388	606	690	872	1 081
4500 Non-recurrent taxes	0	0	0	0	0	0	0	0	0	0
4510 On net wealth	..	..	..	..	..	..	..	..	..	..
4520 Other non-recurrent taxes	..	..	..	..	..	..	..	..	..	..
4600 Other recurrent taxes on property	0	0	0	0	0	0	0	0	0	0
5000 Taxes on goods and services	**0**	**0**	**22**	**16 901**	**96 766**	**137 252**	**211 257**	**259 964**	**389 092**	**517 288**
5100 Taxes on production, sale, transfer, etc.	0	0	22	16 328	92 605	131 878	203 364	250 261	373 692	500 367
5110 General taxes	0	0	16	9 735	43 285	62 533	100 723	121 070	180 729	230 761
5111 Value added taxes	..	..	14	9 735	43 285	62 533	100 723	121 070	180 729	230 761
5112 Sales tax	..	..	0	0	0	0	0	0	0	0
5113 Other	..	..	1	0	0	0	0	0	0	0
5120 Taxes on specific goods and services	0	0	6	6 593	49 320	69 345	102 641	129 191	192 963	269 606
5121 Excise duties	0	0	1	4 718	39 111	57 285	85 462	105 922	147 131	207 273
Sales taxes	0	0	0	0	0	0	0	0	0	0
Domestic production tax	0	0	0	0	0	0	0	0	0	0
Domestic production tax on petrol	0	0	0	0	0	0	0	0	0	0
Production tax on monopoly goods	0	0	0	0	0	0	0	0	0	0
Sugar consumption taxes	0	0	0	0	0	0	0	0	0	0
Motor vehicles purchase tax (Total)	0	0	1	916	4 293	6 193	10 565	17 027	13 807	46 596
Motor vehicles purchase tax	0	0	0	498	4 293	6 193	10 565	17 027	13 807	46 596
Additional motor vehicle purchase tax	0	0	0	418	0	0	0	0	0	0
Revenue from other excises	0	0	0	533	12 765	19 395	29 739	38 066	72 328	91 667
Petroleum consumption tax	0	0	0	3 269	22 052	31 697	45 158	50 830	60 997	69 009
5122 Profits of fiscal monopolies	0	0	0	0	0	0	0	0	0	0

	1965	1980	1990	2000	2007	2010	2013	2015	2019	2020
5123 Customs and import duties	0	0	4	462	2 478	3 319	5 542	8 521	17 460	26 246
Customs duty	0	0	1	449	2 441	3 240	5 409	8 280	16 832	25 637
Customs duty on petrol	0	0	0	0	0	0	0	0	0	0
Production tax on imports	0	0	0	0	0	0	0	0	0	0
Production tax on petrol imports	0	0	0	0	0	0	0	0	0	0
Stamp duty on imports	0	0	2	0	0	0	0	0	0	0
Wharf duty	0	0	1	0	0	0	0	0	0	0
Other	0	0	0	13	37	80	133	240	628	609
5124 Taxes on exports	0	0	0	0	0	0	0	0	0	0
5125 Taxes on investment goods	0	0	0	0	0	0	0	0	0	0
5126 Taxes on specific services	0	0	1	997	7 686	4 005	6 853	10 014	24 352	30 533
Bank, insurance transaction tax	0	0	1	997	3 149	3 571	6 160	9 172	22 670	27 069
Transportation tax	0	0	0	0	0	0	0	0	0	0
PTT service tax	0	0	0	0	4 211	0	0	0	0	0
Tax on football pool	0	0	0	0	0	0	0	0	0	0
Lottery tax	0	0	0	0	327	434	692	842	1 681	3 464
5127 Other taxes on internat. trade and transactions	0	0	0	0	0	0	0	0	0	0
Foreign travel expenditures tax	0	0	..	..	..	..	..	..	..	..
5128 Other taxes	0	0	0	416	46	4 736	4 785	4 734	4 019	5 553
5130 Unallocable between 5110 and 5120	0	0	0	0	0	0	0	0	0	0
5200 Taxes on use of goods and perform activities	0	0	0	572	4 161	5 374	7 894	9 703	15 400	16 921
5210 Recurrent taxes	0	0	0	359	4 161	5 374	7 894	9 703	15 400	16 921
Motor vehicles tax	0	0	0	359	0	5 374	7 894	9 703	15 400	16 921
5211 Paid by households: motor vehicles	..	..	..	0	0	0	0	0	0	0
5212 Paid by others: motor vehicles	..	..	..	359	4 161	5 374	7 894	9 703	15 400	16 921
Motor vehicles tax	..	..	..	302	3 521	5 033	7 353	8 949	14 503	15 983
Traffic fees	..	..	..	58	640	341	540	754	897	938
5213 Paid in respect of other goods	..	..	..	0	0	0	0	0	0	0
5220 Non-recurrent taxes	0	0	0	213	0	0	0	0	0	0
Building construction tax	..	0	..	0	..	..	..	..	..	..
5300 Unallocable between 5100 and 5200	0	0	0	0	0	0	0	0	0	0
6000 Other taxes	**0**	**0**	**13**	**2 658**	**6 417**	**5 924**	**7 541**	**8 750**	**12 397**	**12 218**
6100 Paid solely by business	..	0	0	0	0	0	0	0	0	0
6200 Other	..	0	13	2 658	6 417	5 924	7 541	8 750	12 397	12 218
Funds	..	..	..	1 938	0	0	0	0	0	0
Vocatial Train Pro.F.	..	..	..	67	0	0	0	0	0	0
Tax penalties and fines	..	..	..	548	4 191	2 689	3 175	3 779	6 361	5 123
Municipalities revenue	..	..	..	106	2 227	3 235	4 366	4 971	6 035	7 095
Total tax revenue on cash basis	**0**	**1**	**79**	**40 263**	**203 053**	**287 873**	**458 698**	**586 722**	**997 551**	**1 204 629**
Total tax revenue on accrual basis	**..**	**..**	**..**	**..**	**..**	**..**	**..**	**..**	**..**	**..**
Conciliation with National Accounts										
Additional taxes included in National Accounts	..	..	..	..	..	..	..	..	..	..
Taxes excluded from National Accounts	..	..	..	..	..	..	..	..	..	..
Difference in treatment of tax credits	..	..	..	..	..	..	..	..	..	..
Capital transfer for uncollected revenue	..	..	..	..	..	..	..	..	..	..
Voluntary social security contributions	..	..	..	..	..	..	..	..	..	..
Miscellaneous differences	..	..	..	..	..	..	..	..	..	..
National Accounts: Taxes and actual social contributions	..	..	..	..	..	..	..	..	..	..
Imputed social contributions	..	..	..	..	..	..	..	..	..	..
National Accounts: Taxes and all social contributions	..	..	..	..	..	..	..	..	..	..

.. Not available

Note: From 1982 the data are based on the fiscal year ending 31st December. Before that the data are on a fiscal year basis beginning 1st March.

Revenue is reported on a cash basis except for social security contributions which are reported on an assessment basis.

The figures under the local tax collections include taxes under 'Municipalities Revenues Law' and Property tax. They also include transfers to the local authorities from central budget tax revenues under the revenue sharing system.

Heading 2000: Before 2003, contributions to some private social security schemes are included in this heading.

Source: Bulletin of national accounts and the Budget revenue Bulletin.

StatLink https://stat.link/x587fa

Table 5.37. United Kingdom: Details of tax revenue, 1965-2020

Million GBP

	1965	1980	1990	2000	2007	2010	2013	2015	2019	2020
Total tax revenue	**10 945**	**81 153**	**202 368**	**359 690**	**509 308**	**515 253**	**570 196**	**611 338**	**726 723**	**690 450**
Total tax revenue exclusive of taxes collected for the EU	..	..	**200 520**	**357 560**	**506 893**	**512 308**	**567 270**	**608 251**	**723 380**	**687 554**
1000 Taxes on income, profits and capital gains	**4 050**	**30 651**	**79 576**	**142 197**	**201 316**	**192 771**	**199 769**	**212 697**	**251 743**	**247 296**
1100 Of individuals	3 618	23 868	59 506	104 136	151 157	147 019	156 570	168 873	200 490	197 219
1110 On income and profits	3 615	23 376	57 614	101 925	147 309	144 502	152 668	163 291	191 303	186 966
Income tax	..	23 370	57 614	101 925	147 309	144 502	152 668	163 291	191 303	186 966
Surtax	..	6	0	0	0	0	0	0	0	0
1120 On capital gains	3	492	1 892	2 211	3 848	2 517	3 902	5 582	9 187	10 253
1200 Corporate	484	6 783	20 070	38 061	50 159	45 752	43 199	43 824	51 253	50 077
1210 On profits	484	6 510	18 994	35 730	46 841	44 857	42 190	42 407	49 949	49 052
Petroleum revenue tax	..	1 799	941	1 540	1 387	1 349	1 296	-552	-319	-431
Supplementary petroleum duty	..	0	0	0	0	0	0	0	0	0
Corporation tax	..	4 712	18 053	34 190	44 740	42 865	40 227	42 339	49 454	48 748
Corporation tax overspill relief	..	-1	0	0	0	0	0	0	0	0
Profits tax	..	0	0	0	0	0	0	0	0	0
Windfall tax	..	0	0	0	0	0	0	0	0	0
Betting tax	..	0	0	0	590	568	605	595	814	735
Non fossil fuel obligation levy	..	0	0	0	124	75	62	25	0	0
1220 On capital gains	0	273	1 076	2 331	3 318	895	1 009	1 417	1 304	1 025
1300 Unallocable between 1100 and 1200	-52	0	0	0	0	0	0	0	0	0
2000 Social security contributions	**1 685**	**13 531**	**34 457**	**60 252**	**93 210**	**97 346**	**106 085**	**114 173**	**143 306**	**144 990**
2100 Employees	770	5 228	13 296	24 175	36 585	38 703	41 481	44 488	56 222	56 847
2110 On a payroll basis	..	..	13 296	24 175	36 585	38 703	41 481	44 488	56 222	56 847
2120 On an income tax basis	..	..	0	0	0	0	0	0	0	0
2200 Employers	831	8 210	19 984	34 028	53 765	55 887	62 019	66 491	82 728	84 042
2210 On a payroll basis	..	..	19 984	34 028	53 765	55 887	62 019	66 491	82 728	84 042
2220 On an income tax basis	..	..	0	0	0	0	0	0	0	0
2300 Self-employed or non-employed	75	317	1 177	2 049	2 860	2 756	2 585	3 194	4 356	4 101
2310 On a payroll basis	..	..	1 177	2 049	2 860	2 756	2 585	3 194	4 356	4 101
2320 On an income tax basis	..	..	0	0	0	0	0	0	0	0
2400 Unallocable between 2100, 2200 and 2300	9	-224	0	0	0	0	0	0	0	0
2410 On a payroll basis	..	..	..	..	..	..	..	..	..	..
2420 On an income tax basis	..	..	..	..	..	..	..	..	..	..
3000 Taxes on payroll and workforce	**0**	**3 498**	**0**	**0**	**0**	**0**	**0**	**0**	**2 764**	**2 892**
Selective employment tax	..	0	..	..	..	..	..	..	0	0
National insurance surcharge	..	3 498	..	..	..	..	..	..	0	0
Apprenticeship Levy	..	0	..	..	..	..	..	..	2 764	2 892
4000 Taxes on property	**1 591**	**9 774**	**16 538**	**41 134**	**63 392**	**61 768**	**70 889**	**76 427**	**90 329**	**80 134**
4100 Recurrent taxes on immovable property	1 228	8 665	13 462	30 552	44 891	50 028	55 058	58 019	68 751	61 342
4110 Households	539	3 687	2 373	14 205	23 609	25 919	27 655	29 373	36 715	38 003
Northern Ireland rates paid to CG	..	37	113	141	265	335	346	323	416	402
Council tax	..	0	0	13 991	23 217	25 438	27 061	28 777	35 958	37 270
Rates paid to LA	..	3 650	2 260	73	127	146	248	273	341	331
4120 Others	689	4 978	11 089	16 347	21 282	24 109	27 403	28 646	32 036	23 339
National non-domestic rates	..	0	7 542	14 966	19 358	21 602	24 611	25 834	28 928	20 327
Rates paid to LA	..	4 925	2 869	149	267	497	495	480	567	542
Northern Ireland rates paid to CG	..	53	115	207	353	361	349	335	392	383
London Regional Transport levy	..	0	47	0	0	0	0	0	0	0
LA payments of NNDR	..	0	469	889	1 111	1 236	1 389	1 389	1 389	1 389
NPISH payments of NNDR	..	0	47	136	193	245	342	384	489	501
Crossrail Business rates supplement	..	0	0	0	0	168	217	224	271	197
4200 Recurrent taxes on net wealth	0	0	0	0	0	0	0	0	0	0
4210 Individual	..	..	..	..	..	..	..	..	..	..
4220 Corporate	..	..	..	..	..	..	..	..	..	..
4300 Estate, inheritance and gift taxes	287	479	1 321	2 215	3 867	2 642	4 255	4 470	5 164	5 252
Swiss Bank Tax	..	..	..	0	0	0	876	28	-1	0
4310 Estate and inheritance taxes	287	479	1 321	2 215	3 867	2 642	3 379	4 442	5 165	5 252
Death duties	..	423	1 278	2 156	3 764	2 592	3 293	4 359	5 097	5 202
Development land tax	..	42	6	0	0	0	0	0	0	0
Taxes on other capital transfers	..	14	37	59	50	50	50	50	50	50
Special tax on bank deposits	..	0	0	0	0	0	0	0	0	0
Betterment duty	..	0	0	0	0	0	0	0	0	0
Special charges	..	0	0	0	0	0	0	0	0	0
Special contribution	..	0	0	0	0	0	0	0	0	0
Equal pay on capital transfers	..	0	0	0	53	0	36	33	18	0
4320 Gift taxes	0	0	0	0	0	0	0	0	0	0
4400 Taxes on financial and capital transactions	76	630	1 755	8 367	14 634	9 098	11 540	13 791	15 962	13 187
Stamp duties	..	630	1 755	8 367	14 634	9 098	11 540	13 791	15 962	13 187

	1965	1980	1990	2000	2007	2010	2013	2015	2019	2020
4500 Non-recurrent taxes	0	0	0	0	0	0	36	147	452	353
4510 On net wealth	..	..	..	..	..	..	0	0	0	0
4520 Other non-recurrent taxes	..	..	..	..	..	..	36	147	452	353
4600 Other recurrent taxes on property	0	0	0	0	0	0	0	0	0	0
5000 Taxes on goods and services	**3 619**	**23 699**	**62 780**	**116 107**	**151 390**	**163 368**	**193 453**	**208 041**	**238 581**	**215 138**
5100 Taxes on production, sale, transfer, etc.	3 406	22 677	59 379	110 804	144 752	155 471	185 262	200 179	229 578	206 079
5110 General taxes	647	11 897	34 136	65 018	93 374	97 646	121 460	132 906	154 996	139 461
5111 Value added taxes	0	11 897	34 136	65 018	93 374	97 646	121 460	132 906	154 996	139 461
Value added tax	..	11 893	33 620	64 918	93 348	97 565	121 650	132 790	155 023	139 384
Adj. to VAT contribution	..	4	516	100	26	81	-190	116	-27	77
Purchase tax	..	0	0	0	0	0	0	0	0	0
5112 Sales tax	647	0	0	0	0	0	0	0	0	0
5113 Other	0	0	0	0	0	0	0	0	0	0
5120 Taxes on specific goods and services	2 759	10 780	25 243	45 786	51 378	57 825	63 802	67 273	74 582	66 618
5121 Excise duties	2 383	8 616	19 707	37 315	40 427	45 454	46 588	47 294	49 285	44 880
Beer	..	1 029	2 220	2 813	3 042	3 278	3 337	3 294	3 659	3 062
Wines, spirits, cider and perry	..	1 513	2 627	3 751	5 008	6 075	7 063	7 385	8 457	9 084
Tobacco	..	2 735	5 541	7 666	7 862	9 076	9 479	9 190	9 038	9 790
Hydrocarbon oil	..	3 327	9 302	23 041	24 512	27 013	26 697	27 415	27 795	22 647
Other excise duties	..	12	17	0	0	0	0	0	0	0
Sugar levy	..	12	0	44	3	12	12	10	0	0
Soft Drinks Levy	..	..	0	0	0	0	0	0	336	297
5122 Profits of fiscal monopolies	0	0	0	0	0	0	0	0	0	0
5123 Customs and import duties	343	1 109	1 837	2 086	2 522	3 058	3 042	3 219	3 516	3 385
Custom duties	..	..	..	1 800	2 074	2 933	2 914	3 077	3 343	2 896
Import duties	..	855	1 722	0	0	0	0	0	0	0
Agricultural levies	..	254	115	286	338	0	0	0	0	0
Temporary charges of import	..	0	0	0	0	0	0	0	0	0
British Transport Police	..	0	0	0	110	125	128	142	145	145
Customs Duties - UK Receipts	..	..	..	0	0	0	0	0	0	0
Digital Services Tax	..	..	..	0	0	0	0	0	28	344
5124 Taxes on exports	0	-1	36	0	0	0	0	0	0	0
Levies on exports	..	-1	36	..	..	..	..	..	..	..
5125 Taxes on investment goods	0	0	0	0	0	0	0	0	0	0
5126 Taxes on specific services	33	456	1 022	5 826	6 523	7 292	11 601	13 626	17 039	13 417
Betting and gaming	..	456	1 022	1 522	959	1 092	1 538	2 053	2 502	2 187
National Lottery contributions to fund	..	0	0	1 590	1 310	1 625	1 644	1 713	1 713	1 713
Air passenger duty	..	0	0	940	1 883	2 094	2 960	3 119	3 806	927
Insurance premium tax	..	0	0	1 707	2 306	2 401	3 018	3 294	6 417	6 306
Bank Levy - Stability Fee Scheme	..	0	0	0	0	0	2 352	3 369	2 523	2 214
Light Dues	..	0	0	67	65	80	89	78	78	70
5127 Other taxes on internat. trade and transactions	0	0	0	0	0	0	0	0	0	0
5128 Other taxes	0	600	2 641	559	1 906	2 021	2 571	3 134	4 742	4 936
Fossil fuel levy	..	0	875	56	0	0	0	0	0	0
European coal and steel levy	..	21	11	0	0	0	0	0	0	0
Gas levy	..	12	291	0	0	0	0	0	0	0
Car tax	..	83	1 464	0	0	0	0	0	0	0
Landfill tax	..	484	0	461	877	1 065	1 191	1 028	784	701
Climate change levy	..	0	0	0	690	666	1 098	1 752	2 091	1 833
Aggregates levy	..	0	0	0	339	290	282	354	396	360
Hydro benefit	..	0	0	42	0	0	0	0	0	0
Renewable energy obligations	..	0	0	0	0	0	0	0	0	0
Channel 4 advertising formula	..	0	0	0	0	0	0	0	0	0
Milk super levy	..	0	0	0	0	0	0	0	0	0
Contracts for Difference	..	0	0	0	0	0	0	0	1 471	2 042
5130 Unallocable between 5110 and 5120	0	0	0	0	0	0	0	0	0	0
5200 Taxes on use of goods and perform activities	212	1 378	3 401	5 303	6 638	7 897	8 191	7 862	9 003	9 059
5210 Recurrent taxes	212	1 378	3 401	5 303	6 638	7 897	8 191	7 862	8 848	8 905
5211 Paid by households: motor vehicles	118	729	1 841	2 996	4 146	4 618	4 377	4 021	5 048	5 089
Motor vehicle duty	..	726	1 837	2 992	4 096	4 561	4 312	3 970	4 998	5 026
Boat licences	..	3	4	4	0	0	0	0	0	0
Dartford Tolls	..	..	..	0	50	57	65	51	50	63
5212 Paid by others: motor vehicles	74	588	1 134	1 614	1 304	1 295	1 816	1 954	2 030	2 024
Motor vehicle levy	..	588	1 134	1 614	1 288	1 279	1 789	1 929	2 007	1 999
Dartford Tolls	..	..	..	0	16	16	27	25	23	25

	1965	1980	1990	2000	2007	2010	2013	2015	2019	2020
5213 Paid in respect of other goods	20	61	426	693	1 188	1 984	1 998	1 887	1 770	1 792
IBA levy	..	..	134	0	0	0	0	0	0	0
Telecommunications regulator fees	..	..	7	12	17	12	0	0	0	0
Gas regulator fees	..	..	2	0	0	0	0	0	0	0
Electricity regulator fees	..	..	5	0	0	0	0	0	0	0
Water regulator fees	..	..	6	11	11	12	24	27	36	27
Rail regulator fees	..	..	0	14	12	12	12	12	12	12
Company registration surplus fees	..	..	12	0	0	0	0	0	0	0
Consumer and credit act fees	..	..	163	119	281	480	480	480	480	480
Levy funded bodies	..	..	97	217	349	1 040	922	970	814	947
1936 Tithe Act payments	..	..	0	0	0	0	0	0	0	0
Recurrent taxes paid in respect of other goods	..	..	0	0	0	45	44	55	66	28
Land Registry - Registration Title Tax	..	..	..	285	462	331	464	285	299	234
Companies House - Registration Tax	..	..	..	35	56	52	52	58	63	64
5220 Non-recurrent taxes	0	0	0	0	0	0	0	0	155	154
Immigration Skills Charge	..	..	..	..	..	..	..	..	155	154
5300 Unallocable between 5100 and 5200	1	-356	0	0	0	0	0	0	0	0
6000 Other taxes	**0**	**0**	**9 017**	**0**	**0**	**0**	**0**	**0**	**0**	**0**
6100 Paid solely by business	..	..	0	..	..	..	..	..	..	..
6200 Other	..	..	9 017	..	..	..	..	..	..	..
Community charge	..	..	9 017	..	..	..	..	..	..	..
Memorandum item										
Customs duties collected on behalf of the EU	..	..	..	1 800	2 074	2 933	2 914	3 077	3 343	2 896
Non-wastable tax credits										
Non-wastable tax credits against 1110	..	..	7 454	4 651	20 030	28 879	29 710	28 539	18 003	15 296
Tax expenditure component	..	..	6 973	1 233	4 414	5 542	2 538	2 571	1 622	1 378
Transfer component	..	..	481	3 418	15 617	23 338	27 172	25 968	16 381	13 918
Non-wastable tax credits against 1210	..	..	0	1	918	1 313	1 156	3 273	7 254	8 590
Tax expenditure component	..	..	0	0	654	915	626	1 136	2 252	2 625
Transfer component	..	..	0	1	264	398	530	2 137	5 002	5 965
Total tax revenue on cash basis	**10 945**	**81 153**	**202 400**	**356 071**	**509 032**	**509 500**	**562 278**	**601 185**	**709 076**	**638 594**
Total tax revenue on accrual basis	**..**	**..**	**202 368**	**359 690**	**509 308**	**515 253**	**570 196**	**611 338**	**726 723**	**690 450**
Conciliation with National Accounts										
Additional taxes included in National Accounts	..	..	1 323	2 062	4 072	4 731	5 816	7 261	9 895	10 147
Taxes excluded from National Accounts	..	..	0	0	0	0	0	0	0	0
Difference in treatment of tax credits	..	..	6 973	1 233	5 068	6 457	3 164	3 707	3 874	4 003
Capital transfer for uncollected revenue	..	..	0	0	0	0	0	0	0	0
Voluntary social security contributions	..	..	3 288	8 103	18 629	21 217	22 438	25 025	33 474	38 013
Miscellaneous differences	..	..	0	0	0	0	0	0	0	0
National Accounts: Taxes and actual social contributions	..	..	213 952	371 088	537 077	547 658	601 614	647 331	773 966	742 613
Imputed social contributions	..	..	3 966	4 234	1 391	1 616	1 568	1 566	1 879	2 057
National Accounts: Taxes and all social contributions	..	..	217 918	375 322	538 468	549 274	603 182	648 897	775 845	744 670

.. Not available

Note: Year ending 31st December. From 1990 data are on accrual basis. Supranational taxes reported by the United Kingdom continue to be reported for 2020 in Revenue Statistics as in previous years. From 2021, at the end of the Brexit transition period, this will come to an end and taxes subsequently introduced by the United Kingdom will be reflected in the appropriate tax category at the national or subnational levels of government, as appropriate.

Heading 1210: The corporate tax figures include company income tax from 1990 onwards. Heading 2000: Includes some voluntary contributions which cannot be separately identified. Heading 6200: The community charge replaced domestic rates in Scotland in April 1989 and was extended to England and Wales in April 1990. This tax has been classified in heading 6200 as it is a lump-sum tax levied on each adult in a household (domestic rates are classified in heading 4100). Headings for non-wastable tax credits 1110 and 1210 are consistent with the guidelines, and the figures in the data are treated accordingly. The following method is adopted separately for Working Families 'Tax Credit and Disabled Persons Tax Credit' paid from 1999 to 2003. For each calendar year, a random sample of awards over-lapping the quarter is taken. Each recipient family's income tax liability for the fiscal year within which the quarter falls is calculated , based on the earned income reported for the award (uprated to the middle of the overlap period). And the result multiplied by the number of days in the overlap period divided by 365. The tax expenditure component is defined as the minimum of this amount and the total amount of award paid in the overlap period. The total amount of award paid and the tax expenditure component are each summed over the sample cases, and the ratio is taken as the tax expenditure ration for the quarter. From 2003, the equivalent breakdown for Child and Working tax credits is based on household survey data. Survey data is used to estimate the breakdown into the tax expenditure and the transfer components for the other smaller tax credits.

The United Kingdom Personal Tax Credit information presented in Revenue Statistics is on a cash basis (rather than an accrual basis as for the rest of the data). PTC information on a financial year basis has been used as a proxy for calendar year. Please note that since 2015-16 tax credits is no longer split into tax expenditure and transfer component. The split for years after 2014-15 is estimated by applying the 2014-15 split to total personal tax credits expenditure. The sum of tax expenditure and transfer components may not match the total due to rounding. Total values are consistent with published figures available here: https://www.gov.uk/government/statistics/hmrc-tax-and-nics-receipts-for-the-uk.

Please note that the sum of the corporate tax credit (CTC) components in the United Kingdom may not match total CTC's due to rounding. The CTC information presented in Revenue Statistics is on a cash basis (rather than an accrual basis as for the rest of the data). CTC information on a financial year basis has been used as a proxy for calendar year. Please note that the breakdown of total CTCs from 2002/03 to 2010/11 have been estimated using historic proportional splits applied to total published CTC information. Total values are consistent with published figures available here: https://www.gov.uk/government/statistics/hmrc-tax-and-nics-receipts-for-the-uk.

Source: National Income and Expenditure; Central Statistical Office; Annual reports of His Majesty's Revenue and Customs.

StatLink https://stat.link/19o8nl

Table 5.38. United States: Details of tax revenue, 1965-2020

Million USD

	1965	1980	1990	2000	2007	2010	2013	2015	2019	2020
Total tax revenue	**167 022**	**730 672**	**1 552 413**	**2 900 519**	**3 868 612**	**3 517 144**	**4 291 752**	**4 773 680**	**5 385 030**	**5 380 217**
1000 Taxes on income, profits and capital gains	**80 284**	**364 137**	**701 731**	**1 453 865**	**1 865 205**	**1 488 699**	**2 016 390**	**2 314 542**	**2 482 885**	**2 446 932**
1100 Of individuals	52 894	285 513	584 733	1 224 538	1 479 085	1 223 218	1 664 074	1 929 215	2 192 995	2 183 169
1110 On income and profits	50 401	272 879	552 859	1 088 967	1 326 736	1 163 737	1 556 113	1 753 783	2 004 445	1 967 925
Individual income tax federal	46 492	233 269	449 239	895 677	1 062 755	910 874	1 235 275	1 413 376	1 586 635	1 538 726
Individual income tax state and local govt.	3 909	39 610	103 620	193 290	263 981	252 863	320 838	340 407	417 810	429 198
1120 On capital gains	2 493	12 634	31 874	135 571	152 349	59 481	107 961	175 432	188 550	215 244
Capital gains federal	2 300	10 800	25 900	111 507	122 036	46 557	85 702	141 381	149 248	168 300
Capital gains tax state and local govt.	193	1 834	5 974	24 064	30 313	12 924	22 259	34 051	39 302	46 944
1200 Corporate	27 390	78 624	116 998	229 327	386 119	265 481	352 316	385 327	289 890	263 763
1210 On profits	26 745	73 586	106 134	170 835	330 597	240 445	313 172	337 786	242 971	227 710
Corporate income tax federal	24 861	60 525	85 736	144 590	281 040	198 698	265 274	288 486	181 893	166 401
Corporate income tax state and local govt.	1 884	13 061	20 398	26 245	49 556	41 747	47 898	49 300	61 077	61 309
1220 On capital gains	645	5 038	10 864	58 492	55 523	25 036	39 144	47 541	46 919	36 053
Capital gains tax corp. federal	600	4 143	8 776	49 506	47 200	20 689	33 157	40 602	35 125	26 346
Capital gains tax corp. state and local govt.	45	895	2 088	8 986	8 323	4 347	5 987	6 939	11 794	9 707
1300 Unallocable between 1100 and 1200	0	0	0	0	0	0	0	0	0	0
2000 Social security contributions	**22 192**	**159 763**	**396 972**	**683 104**	**907 357**	**917 409**	**1 030 099**	**1 125 493**	**1 308 696**	**1 333 998**
2100 Employees	8 459	67 022	173 860	305 555	400 941	406 404	456 777	502 103	597 633	607 264
Federal insurance contribution Act tax	8 084	66 221	..	..	..	..	..	..	..	..
Less refund federal	-192	-507	..	..	..	..	..	..	..	..
Railroad retirement taxes federal	322	590	..	..	..	..	..	..	..	..
Fed. hosp. insur. recpts from railroad retir.	0	111	..	..	..	..	..	..	..	..
Unemployment state tax federal	20	127	..	..	..	..	..	..	..	..
Temp. disability insurance state and local	225	480	..	..	..	..	..	..	..	..
2110 On a payroll basis	..	..	..	..	..	..	..	..	..	..
2120 On an income tax basis	..	..	..	..	..	..	..	..	..	..
2200 Employers	12 703	87 019	204 102	343 184	456 602	461 702	519 064	561 936	642 810	656 638
Federal insurance contributions act tax	7 802	64 768	..	..	..	..	..	..	..	..
Railroad retirement taxes federal	314	1 722	..	..	..	..	..	..	..	..
Fed. hosp. insur. recpts from railroad retir.	0	111	..	..	..	..	..	..	..	..
Military service credit federal	14	652	..	..	..	..	..	..	..	..
Old-age dis. hosp. insur. fed. Employer contr.	282	1 453	..	..	..	..	..	..	..	..
Unemployment state tax federal	3 032	11 788	..	..	..	..	..	..	..	..
Federal unemployment tax Act	615	3 246	..	..	..	..	..	..	..	..
Railroad unempl. insurance Act tax federal	152	175	..	..	..	..	..	..	..	..
Workmen's compensation state and local	484	3 039	..	..	..	..	..	..	..	..
Temp. disability insurance state and local	8	65	..	..	..	..	..	..	..	..
2210 On a payroll basis	..	..	..	..	..	..	..	..	..	..
2220 On an income tax basis	..	..	..	..	..	..	..	..	..	..
2300 Self-employed or non-employed	1 030	5 722	19 010	34 365	49 814	49 303	54 258	61 454	68 253	70 096
Federal old-age survivors trust	0	4 250	..	..	..	..	..	..	..	..
Federal disability insurance trust	1 030	733	..	..	..	..	..	..	..	..
Federal hospital insurance trust	0	739	..	..	..	..	..	..	..	..
2310 On a payroll basis	..	..	..	..	..	..	..	..	..	..
2320 On an income tax basis	..	..	..	..	..	..	..	..	..	..
2400 Unallocable between 2100, 2200 and 2300	0	0	0	0	0	0	0	0	0	0
2410 On a payroll basis	..	..	..	..	..	..	..	..	..	..
2420 On an income tax basis	..	..	..	..	..	..	..	..	..	..
3000 Taxes on payroll and workforce	**0**	**0**	**0**	**0**	**285**	**2 285**	**1 591**	**1 751**	**2 264**	**3 386**
4000 Taxes on property	**26 529**	**77 913**	**182 408**	**299 546**	**463 052**	**473 422**	**503 220**	**539 732**	**649 494**	**669 173**
4100 Recurrent taxes on immovable property	22 918	68 499	161 533	254 669	403 688	438 588	456 790	490 410	599 586	615 329
4110 Households	8 548	28 975	..	..	..	..	..	..	..	..
Property tax state and local	8 548	28 975	..	..	..	..	..	..	..	..
Other	0	0	..	..	..	..	..	..	..	..
4120 Others	14 370	39 524	..	..	..	..	..	..	..	..
Property tax state and local	14 370	39 524	..	..	..	..	..	..	..	..
Other	0	0	..	..	..	..	..	..	..	..
4200 Recurrent taxes on net wealth	0	0	0	0	0	0	0	0	0	0
4210 Individual	..	..	..	..	..	..	..	..	..	..
4220 Corporate	..	..	..	..	..	..	..	..	..	..
4300 Estate, inheritance and gift taxes	3 447	8 425	15 755	35 640	31 927	19 699	26 178	25 582	21 744	24 840
4310 Estate and inheritance taxes	3 080	8 149	..	..	..	..	..	..	..	..
Estate tax less refund federal	2 427	6 181	..	..	..	..	..	..	..	..
Estate tax state and local govt.	653	1 968	..	..	..	..	..	..	..	..
4320 Gift taxes	367	276	..	..	..	..	..	..	..	..
Gift tax less refund federal	289	209	..	..	..	..	..	..	..	..
Gift tax calculate state and local govt.	78	67	..	..	..	..	..	..	..	..

	1965	1980	1990	2000	2007	2010	2013	2015	2019	2020
4400 Taxes on financial and capital transactions	164	989	2 148	4 389	20 503	7 460	12 171	14 896	17 544	18 097
Interest equalisation tax federal	15	0	..	..	..	..	..	..	..	..
Document and stock transfer state and local	149	989	2 148	4 389	20 503	7 460	12 171	14 896	17 544	18 097
4500 Non-recurrent taxes	0	0	0	0	0	0	0	0	0	0
4510 On net wealth	..	..	..	..	..	..	..	..	0	0
4520 Other non-recurrent taxes	..	..	..	..	..	..	..	..	..	..
4600 Other recurrent taxes on property	0	0	2 972	4 848	6 934	7 675	8 081	8 844	10 621	10 907
5000 Taxes on goods and services	**38 017**	**128 844**	**271 301**	**464 004**	**632 713**	**635 329**	**740 452**	**792 162**	**941 692**	**926 730**
5100 Taxes on production, sale, transfer, etc.	33 300	111 810	235 233	404 093	540 291	546 710	640 249	695 784	823 829	809 540
5110 General taxes	8 016	51 328	125 575	221 358	301 403	295 123	343 853	374 173	443 927	448 882
5111 Value added taxes	0	0	0	0	0	0	0	0	0	0
5112 Sales tax	8 016	51 328	125 575	221 358	301 403	295 123	343 853	374 173	443 927	448 882
General sales - general receipts state and local	7 981	51 328	125 575	221 358	301 403	295 123	343 853	374 173	443 927	448 882
Other state and local	35	0	0	0	0	0	0	0	0	0
5113 Other	0	0	0	0	0	0	0	0	0	0
5120 Taxes on specific goods and services	25 284	60 482	109 658	182 735	238 888	251 587	296 396	321 611	379 902	360 658
5121 Excise duties	21 209	45 471	64 953	108 600	137 373	146 582	154 390	156 902	165 942	161 955
Alcohol taxes federal govt.	3 689	5 601	5 228	7 281	8 571	8 848	9 026	9 514	9 711	9 470
Tobacco taxes federal govt.	2 142	2 443	4 217	6 741	8 377	17 487	15 830	14 265	11 739	11 240
Airport, airway, highway federal	3 559	6 411	0	0	0	0	0	0	0	0
Manufacturer's excise taxes federal govt.	2 867	6 122	0	0	0	0	0	0	0	0
Sugar tax federal govt.	97	0	0	0	0	0	0	0	0	0
Other taxes excise federal govt.	889	2	0	0	0	0	0	0	0	0
Undistributed tax deposits federal government	-11	152	0	0	0	0	0	0	0	0
Other taxes excise and undist. fed.govt. -	0	0	13 316	32 005	31 747	26 913	33 746	35 287	36 445	34 174
Less special tax liquor occupations federal	-22	-21	0	0	0	0	0	0	0	0
Other federal (refunds)	-7	-32	0	0	0	0	0	0	0	0
Alcohol taxes state and local govt.	949	2 642	3 577	4 485	5 684	6 197	6 706	7 260	7 989	7 610
Tobacco taxes state and local govt.	1 386	3 874	6 009	8 726	16 433	18 611	18 464	18 002	18 740	18 987
Public utilities state and local govt.	871	5 888	11 814	17 989	27 879	28 892	28 544	27 834	27 414	27 167
Motor fuel taxes state and local govt.	4 331	9 822	20 792	31 373	38 682	39 634	42 074	44 740	53 904	53 307
Other state and local taxes	469	2 295	0	0	0	0	0	0	0	0
Coal tonnage tax federal govt.	0	272	0	0	0	0	0	0	0	0
Hazardous substances tax federal	0	0	0	0	0	0	0	0	0	0
Transportation fuels tax federal	0	0	0	0	0	0	0	0	0	0
Boat fuels and equipment tax federal	0	0	0	0	0	0	0	0	0	0
Waste site deposits tax federal	0	0	0	0	0	0	0	0	0	0
Leaking underground storage federal	0	0	0	0	0	0	0	0	0	0
Vaccine injury compens. federal	0	0	0	0	0	0	0	0	0	0
Ozone depletion tax federal	0	0	0	0	0	0	0	0	0	0
Oil spill liability federal	0	0	0	0	0	0	0	0	0	0
Luxury tax federal govt.	0	0	0	0	0	0	0	0	0	0
5122 Profits of fiscal monopolies	275	608	..	..	..	..	..	..	..	..
Liquor store revenue state and local govt.	1 447	3 200	..	..	..	..	..	..	..	..
Liquor store expend. state and local govt.	-1 172	-2 592	..	..	..	..	..	..	..	..
5123 Customs and import duties	1 442	7 436	17 490	21 123	28 793	28 603	35 468	38 123	77 752	68 627
Custom duties federal	1 442	7 436	17 490	21 123	28 793	28 603	35 468	38 123	77 752	68 627
Petroleum import fees federal govt.	0	0	0	0	0	0	0	0	0	0
5124 Taxes on exports	0	0	0	0	0	0	0	0	0	0
5125 Taxes on investment goods	0	0	0	0	0	0	0	0	0	0
5126 Taxes on specific services	2 358	6 967	8 895	13 857	23 639	23 642	26 899	30 153	36 446	35 914
Amusements state and local govt.	23	234	671	3 668	7 105	7 082	7 784	8 202	9 419	7 935
Parimutuels state and local govt.	386	731	659	326	328	206	193	182	196	188
Transportation of persons federal	126	1 601	0	0	0	0	0	0	0	0
Transport of property	0	92	0	0	0	0	0	0	0	0
General and toll telephone federal	1 079	1 118	0	0	0	0	0	0	0	0
Foreign insurance policies federal	0	75	0	0	0	0	0	0	0	0
Insurance state and local govt.	744	3 113	7 565	9 863	16 206	16 354	18 922	21 769	26 830	27 791
Employee pension plans federal	0	3	0	0	0	0	0	0	0	0
Inland waterway tax federal	0	0	0	0	0	0	0	0	0	0
Ship departure tax federal	0	0	0	0	0	0	0	0	0	0
5127 Other taxes on internat. trade and transactions	0	0	0	0	0	0	0	0	0	0
5128 Other taxes	0	0	18 320	39 155	49 083	52 760	79 639	96 433	99 762	94 162
5130 Unallocable between 5110 and 5120	0	0	0	0	0	0	0	0	0	0
5200 Taxes on use of goods and perform activities	4 717	17 034	36 068	59 910	92 422	88 619	100 203	96 377	117 864	117 190
5210 Recurrent taxes	3 490	9 501	21 262	37 114	68 547	66 440	70 557	74 447	88 084	89 028
5211 Paid by households: motor vehicles	1 211	3 370	8 104	11 409	14 996	16 294	17 781	18 809	21 445	21 304
Motor vehicle regis. license st. and loc.	1 056	2 981	..	..	..	..	..	..	..	..
Motor vehicle oper. license st. and loc.	152	389	..	..	..	..	..	..	..	..
Other motor vehicle	3	0	..	..	..	..	..	..	..	..

	1965	1980	1990	2000	2007	2010	2013	2015	2019	2020
5212 Paid by others: motor vehicles	937	2 343	3 564	6 688	8 484	9 108	10 071	10 702	12 300	12 259
Motor vehicle regis. license st. and loc.	937	2 343	..	..	..	..	..	..	..	..
Motor vehicle oper. license st. and loc.	0	0	..	..	..	..	..	..	..	..
5213 Paid in respect of other goods	1 342	3 788	9 594	19 017	45 067	41 038	42 705	44 936	54 339	55 464
Misc. fees permit license federal	19	0	0	0	0	0	0	0	0	0
Special tax liquor occupations federal	22	21	0	0	0	0	0	0	0	0
Use tax of certain vehicles federal	99	277	0	0	0	0	0	0	0	0
Use of internat. travel facilities federal	0	92	0	0	0	0	0	0	0	0
Use tax of aircraft federal	0	21	0	0	0	0	0	0	0	0
Corporation in general license st. and loc.	528	1 388	3 147	6 736	10 658	9 473	7 560	6 678	7 634	7 431
Alcoholic beverage license tax st. and loc.	133	179	264	308	608	596	899	824	956	983
Public utilities license tax st. and loc.	30	130	270	395	1 903	1 468	1 432	1 665	1 814	1 756
Amusements license taxes st. and loc.	7	69	202	196	966	638	604	740	750	609
Occupation and business license st. and loc.	349	1 113	3 512	7 651	16 484	17 812	19 284	20 423	23 404	24 284
Wagering occupation tax federal	7	12	0	0	0	0	0	0	0	0
Other license taxes st. and loc.	10	69	2 118	3 619	14 302	10 900	12 772	14 445	19 610	20 218
Hunting and fishing license taxes st. and loc.	138	417	82	112	146	151	155	162	171	184
Other	0	0	0	0	0	0	0	0	0	0
5220 Non-recurrent taxes	1 227	7 533	14 806	22 796	23 875	22 179	29 645	21 930	29 780	28 162
Severance state and local govt.	503	4 167	5 224	5 285	12 895	11 751	18 266	9 755	13 178	11 272
Poll taxes state and local govt.	9	0	0	0	0	0	0	0	0	0
Other taxes state and local govt.	715	3 366	9 582	17 511	10 980	10 428	11 379	12 175	16 601	16 890
5300 Unallocable between 5100 and 5200	0	0	0	0	0	0	0	0	0	0
6000 Other taxes	**0**	**15**	**0**	**0**	**0**	**0**	**0**	**0**	**0**	**0**
6100 Paid solely by business	..	0	..	..	..	..	..	..	..	..
6200 Other	..	15	..	..	..	..	..	..	..	..
Non-wastable tax credits										
Non-wastable tax credits against 1110	..	..	6 155	36 511	90 439	171 630	158 160	156 656	255 580	525 970
Tax expenditure component	..	..	1 800	9 602	35 910	69 870	41 560	42 826	102 660	92 340
Transfer component	..	..	4 355	26 909	54 529	101 760	116 600	113 830	152 920	433 630
Non-wastable tax credits against 1210	..	..	..	..	..	250	630	577	440	660
Tax expenditure component	..	..	..	..	..	240	610	527	380	630
Transfer component	..	..	..	..	..	10	20	50	60	30
Unallocable transfer component	..	..	..	..	..	2 420	4 280	4 890	4 230	2 600
Total tax revenue on cash basis	**167 022**	**730 672**	**..**	**..**	**..**	**..**	**..**	**..**	**..**	**..**
Total tax revenue on accrual basis	**..**	**..**	**..**	**..**	**..**	**..**	**..**	**..**	**..**	**..**
Conciliation with National Accounts										
Additional taxes included in National Accounts	..	..	..	..	..	..	..	..	..	..
Taxes excluded from National Accounts	..	..	..	..	..	..	..	..	..	..
Difference in treatment of tax credits	..	..	..	..	..	..	..	..	..	..
Capital transfer for uncollected revenue	..	..	..	..	..	..	..	..	..	..
Voluntary social security contributions	..	..	11 719	22 562	51 635	61 833	69 903	74 886	108 999	121 434
Miscellaneous differences	..	..	..	..	..	..	..	..	..	..
National Accounts: Taxes and actual social contributions	..	..	1 564 132	2 923 081	3 920 247	3 578 977	4 361 655	4 848 566	5 494 029	5 501 651
Imputed social contributions	..	..	3 384	3 727	7 134	9 428	9 438	9 636	8 925	9 100
National Accounts: Taxes and all social contributions	..	..	1 567 516	2 926 808	3 927 381	3 588 405	4 371 093	4 858 202	5 502 954	5 510 751

.. Not available

Note: From 1990, data are on a year ending 31st December basis. For years up to and including 1976 the dated covered fiscal years ending 30th June. Between 1977 and 1989, Federal government data covered fiscal years ending 30th September and State & Local government data covered fiscal years ending 30th June.

From 1990, data are on accrual basis. There are no separate estimates for the State and Local capital gains tax revenues.

Heading 5121: In 1994 through 1996, some Federal excise taxes formerly shown separately were included in 'Other taxes,excises and undistributed, Federal government'.

Source: Federal estimates are derived from the US Budget, the Final Monthly Treasury Statement and the Annual Report of the US Treasury Department. The State and Local estimates are derived from Government Finances, published by the Bureau of the Census.

StatLink https://stat.link/m0qrud

5.2. Memorandum tables

Table 5.39 shows different sources for financing social benefits, beyond compulsory social security contributions reported in section 5.1. In addition, this table shows data on other taxes, on voluntary contributions to government and on compulsory contributions to the private sector.

Table 5.40 shows social security contributions and payroll taxes paid by government. During the revision of the Interpretative Guide in 1984, the question arose of how to treat taxes paid by government. The two most prominent examples of such taxes are social security contributions and payroll taxes paid by government in respect of its employees. After a long discussion, it was decided that the data shown in this publication should continue to include taxes paid by government (see §7 of the Interpretative Guide in annex A).

Whilst it was recognised that for certain purposes (e.g. to show the cash flow to the government sector from the private sector) it would be appropriate to eliminate taxes paid by one sector of government to another or tax payments between different units of the same sector of government, the view was taken that to record tax flows in the context of the economy as a whole required that taxes paid by government should be included in the data. This treatment ensures that the different resource flows of an economy, including the calculation of the output of government, are measured consistently in after-tax units. Nevertheless, it was decided that data on identifiable taxes paid by government should be separately identified in a memorandum item. This is the purpose of the country tables that follow.

The data that are reproduced in the following tables refer to actual compulsory payments made by general government in respect of their employees. Fictive, voluntary and imputed contributions are excluded from these data. The definitions of social security contributions, payroll taxes and general government are those set out in §40 to §46, §47 and §3 to §4 of the Interpretative Guide. Information on the other taxes paid by government (namely property taxes and consumption taxes) is not available for most countries, although it is believed that, in all countries, taxes based upon payroll are the most important taxes paid by government. In many cases, the data are estimates and are not always constructed on a basis consistent with that used in the main tables.

Table 5.39. Financing social benefits

	1965	1980	1990	2000	2007	2010	2013	2015	2019	2020
Australia, million AUD										
Contribution under 2000 heading	..	..	..	..	..	..	..	..	..	..
Other taxes	..	..	..	..	..	..	..	..	..	..
Voluntary contributions to government	..	..	..	..	..	..	..	..	..	..
Compulsory contributions to private sector	..	..	..	..	..	..	..	..	..	..
Total	**0**	**0**	**0**	**0**	**0**	**0**	**0**	**0**	**0**	**0**
Austria, million EUR										
Contribution under 2000 heading	1 548	9 200	17 763	30 510	38 453	41 423	46 845	49 867	59 083	59 094
Other taxes	0	0	0	0	0	0	0	0	0	0
Voluntary contributions to government	32	135	141	206	256	339	299	321	336	344
Compulsory contributions to private sector	0	0	0	0	0	0	0	0	0	0
Total	**1 580**	**9 335**	**17 904**	**30 716**	**38 709**	**41 762**	**47 144**	**50 188**	**59 418**	**59 438**
Belgium, million EUR										
Contribution under 2000 heading	2 018	10 798	23 386	34 865	45 929	50 674	56 527	58 812	63 203	62 276
Other taxes	0	171	644	5 375	13 659	16 772	18 382	12 292	19 153	20 009
Voluntary contributions to government	0	41	52	58	57	59	77	70	84	82
Compulsory contributions to private sector	0	0	0	0	0	0	0	0	0	0
Total	**2 018**	**11 009**	**24 082**	**40 298**	**59 644**	**67 505**	**74 986**	**71 174**	**82 440**	**82 367**
Canada, million CAD										
Contribution under 2000 heading	854	10 649	29 653	53 109	73 722	76 787	90 394	96 371	108 366	107 866
Other taxes	1 199	0	0	0	0	0	0	0	0	0
Voluntary contributions to government	0	0	0	0	0	0	0	0	0	0
Compulsory contributions to private sector	0	0	0	0	0	0	0	0	0	0
Total	**2 053**	**10 649**	**29 653**	**53 109**	**73 722**	**76 787**	**90 394**	**96 371**	**108 366**	**107 866**
Chile, million CLP										
Contribution under 2000 heading	..	..	159 559	576 758	1 148 647	1 493 987	1 968 973	2 252 490	2 994 906	3 104 866
Other taxes	..	..	0	0	0	0	0	0	0	0
Voluntary contributions to government	..	..	0	0	0	0	0	0	0	0
Compulsory contributions to private sector	..	..	328 102	2 021 631	3 808 658	5 408 703	7 583 251	8 914 415	11 975 273	12 194 451
Total	**..**	**..**	**487 661**	**2 598 389**	**4 957 305**	**6 902 690**	**9 552 224**	**11 166 905**	**14 970 179**	**15 299 318**
Colombia, million COP										
Contribution under 2000 heading	..	..	203 596	4 989 000	9 694 000	11 478 085	16 644 445	13 585 138	19 875 398	18 615 408
Other taxes	..	..	0	0	0	0	0	0	0	0
Voluntary contributions to government	..	..	0	0	0	0	0	0	0	0
Compulsory contributions to private sector	..	..	0	0	18 667 073	27 354 493	30 808 731	31 112 566	43 732 211	40 888 910
Total	**..**	**..**	**203 596**	**4 989 000**	**28 361 073**	**38 832 579**	**47 453 177**	**44 697 703**	**63 607 609**	**59 504 318**
Costa Rica, million CRC										
Contribution under 2000 heading	..	..	33 990	297 069	885 053	1 450 531	1 928 082	2 305 133	3 026 691	2 971 589
Other taxes	..	..	..	..	..	..	..	..	..	..
Voluntary contributions to government	..	..	..	..	..	..	..	..	..	..
Compulsory contributions to private sector	..	..	..	..	..	..	..	..	..	..
Total	**..**	**..**	**33 990**	**297 069**	**885 053**	**1 450 531**	**1 928 082**	**2 305 133**	**3 026 691**	**2 971 589**
Czech Republic, million CZK										
Contribution under 2000 heading	..	..	..	341 544	573 417	576 029	603 072	659 743	889 237	901 670
Other taxes	..	..	..	0	0	0	0	0	0	0
Voluntary contributions to government	..	..	..	1 099	974	661	337	386	578	537
Compulsory contributions to private sector	..	..	..	2 837	5 757	6 094	6 424	6 741	8 921	9 048
Total	**..**	**..**	**..**	**345 480**	**580 148**	**582 784**	**609 833**	**666 871**	**898 736**	**911 255**
Denmark, million DKK										
Contribution under 2000 heading	690	710	101	8 453	1 286	1 815	1 618	1 378	991	1 359
Other taxes	0	0	0	0	0	0	0	0	0	0
Voluntary contributions to government	0	1 673	8 087	16 633	17 061	17 192	14 655	14 721	14 792	14 873
Compulsory contributions to private sector	145	554	1 278	1 445	4 526	3 847	3 068	2 964	2 828	2 875
Total	**835**	**2 937**	**9 466**	**26 531**	**22 874**	**22 854**	**19 341**	**19 063**	**18 611**	**19 107**
Estonia, million EUR										
Contribution under 2000 heading	..	..	..	674	1 683	1 879	2 077	2 300	3 256	3 331
Other taxes	..	..	..	0	0	0	0	0	0	0
Voluntary contributions to government	..	..	..	0	0	0	0	0	0	0
Compulsory contributions to private sector	..	..	..	1	341	38	268	389	299	313
Total	**..**	**..**	**..**	**674**	**2 024**	**1 918**	**2 346**	**2 689**	**3 556**	**3 644**

	1965	1980	1990	2000	2007	2010	2013	2015	2019	2020
Finland, million EUR										
Contribution under 2000 heading	93	2 776	10 012	15 756	21 384	22 648	25 632	26 639	28 295	27 326
Other taxes	47	22	0	404	0	0	0	0	0	0
Voluntary contributions to government	0	262	632	236	228	254	270	303	246	235
Compulsory contributions to private sector	0	123	431	532	653	619	694	673	655	619
Total	**140**	**3 183**	**11 075**	**16 928**	**22 265**	**23 521**	**26 596**	**27 615**	**29 196**	**28 180**
France, million EUR										
Contribution under 2000 heading	8 804	76 235	191 141	231 875	307 663	323 816	356 934	370 375	363 817	348 335
Other taxes	0	895	2 950	81 001	127 511	137 383	162 838	170 210	232 687	234 036
Voluntary contributions to government	0	0	0	0	0	0	0	0	0	0
Compulsory contributions to private sector	0	0	0	0	0	0	0	0	0	0
Total	**8 804**	**77 130**	**194 091**	**312 876**	**435 174**	**461 199**	**519 772**	**540 585**	**596 504**	**582 371**
Germany, million EUR										
Contribution under 2000 heading	19 876	98 659	170 449	299 440	320 750	354 320	392 378	424 841	508 124	512 122
Other taxes	0	0	0	0	0	0	0	0	0	0
Voluntary contributions to government	1 946	8 441	13 002	23 329	21 409	5 102	5 352	6 068	7 262	7 378
Compulsory contributions to private sector	107	690	1 462	6 120	8 243	9 386	10 444	11 202	13 780	13 860
Total	**21 929**	**107 791**	**184 914**	**328 889**	**350 402**	**368 808**	**408 174**	**442 111**	**529 166**	**533 360**
Greece, million EUR										
Contribution under 2000 heading	37	485	3 466	14 284	24 940	24 748	19 354	18 807	22 260	21 352
Other taxes	8	0	0	0	0	0	0	0	0	0
Voluntary contributions to government	0	0	0	0	0	0	0	0	0	0
Compulsory contributions to private sector	0	0	0	0	0	0	0	0	0	0
Total	**44**	**485**	**3 466**	**14 284**	**24 940**	**24 748**	**19 354**	**18 807**	**22 260**	**21 352**
Hungary, million HUF										
Contribution under 2000 heading	..	..	..	1 506 755	3 402 194	3 179 509	3 899 154	4 433 464	5 545 481	5 364 764
Other taxes	..	..	..	188 413	85 058	78 629	246 574	294 313	145 025	128 079
Voluntary contributions to government	..	..	..	1 273	1 762	1 693	1 523	1 229	983	953
Compulsory contributions to private sector	..	..	..	62 836	190 331	279 814	0	0	0	0
Total	**..**	**..**	**..**	**1 759 277**	**3 679 344**	**3 539 645**	**4 147 251**	**4 729 006**	**5 691 489**	**5 493 796**
Iceland, million ISK										
Contribution under 2000 heading	5	102	3 607	19 680	39 594	63 599	69 899	79 707	97 423	88 364
Other taxes	0	1 047	20 571	26 732	52 444	77 472	90 895	97 987	187 636	269 721
Voluntary contributions to government	0	0	0	0	0	0	0	0	0	0
Compulsory contributions to private sector	0	459	13 454	48 847	118 117	95 438	117 903	139 792	187 003	194 483
Total	**5**	**1 608**	**37 632**	**95 260**	**210 155**	**236 509**	**278 697**	**317 486**	**472 062**	**552 568**
Ireland, million EUR										
Contribution under 2000 heading	21	578	1 729	3 966	8 143	8 458	8 854	9 992	13 109	12 283
Other taxes	0	0	0	0	0	0	0	0	0	0
Voluntary contributions to government	0	0	0	0	0	0	0	0	0	0
Compulsory contributions to private sector	0	0	0	0	0	0	0	0	0	0
Total	**21**	**578**	**1 729**	**3 966**	**8 143**	**8 458**	**8 854**	**9 992**	**13 109**	**12 283**
Israel, million ILS										
Contribution under 2000 heading	..	..	..	27 565	37 909	45 343	53 364	59 561	74 420	73 031
Other taxes	..	..	..	0	0	0	0	0	0	0
Voluntary contributions to government	..	..	..	0	0	0	0	0	0	0
Compulsory contributions to private sector	..	..	..	0	0	9 100	22 400	28 700	37 700	39 200
Total	**..**	**..**	**..**	**27 565**	**37 909**	**54 443**	**75 764**	**88 261**	**112 120**	**112 231**
Italy, million EUR										
Contribution under 2000 heading	1 881	22 976	87 256	143 629	200 772	209 122	210 462	214 376	237 290	224 781
Other taxes	0	0	0	0	0	0	0	0	0	0
Voluntary contributions to government	0	0	0	464	567	561	738	750	764	724
Compulsory contributions to private sector	0	0	0	0	0	0	0	0	0	0
Total	**1 881**	**22 976**	**87 256**	**144 093**	**201 339**	**209 683**	**211 200**	**215 126**	**238 054**	**225 505**
Japan, billion JPY										
Contribution under 2000 heading	1 344	18 178	34 613	47 968	53 325	54 461	59 803	64 465	71 993	71 550
Other taxes	0	0	0	0	0	0	0	0	0	0
Voluntary contributions to government	0	0	0	0	0	0	0	0	0	0
Compulsory contributions to private sector	0	0	0	0	0	0	0	0	0	0
Total	**1 344**	**18 178**	**34 613**	**47 968**	**53 325**	**54 461**	**59 803**	**64 465**	**71 993**	**71 550**

	1965	1980	1990	2000	2007	2010	2013	2015	2019	2020
Korea, billion KRW										
Contribution under 2000 heading	..	73	3 760	22 759	53 588	69 090	91 596	104 693	140 071	150 854
Other taxes	..	0	0	0	0	0	0	0	0	0
Voluntary contributions to government	..	0	0	0	0	0	0	0	0	0
Compulsory contributions to private sector	..	0	0	0	0	0	0	0	0	0
Total	**..**	**73**	**3 760**	**22 759**	**53 588**	**69 090**	**91 596**	**104 693**	**140 071**	**150 854**
Latvia, million EUR										
Contribution under 2000 heading	..	..	..	669	1 774	1 554	1 933	2 030	2 911	2 937
Other taxes	..	..	..	12	51	36	59	80	149	128
Voluntary contributions to government	..	..	..	0	0	0	0	0	0	0
Compulsory contributions to private sector	..	..	..	0	0	0	0	0	0	0
Total	**..**	**..**	**..**	**682**	**1 825**	**1 590**	**1 992**	**2 111**	**3 060**	**3 065**
Lithuania, million EUR										
Contribution under 2000 heading	..	..	..	1 362	2 643	3 293	3 791	4 338	4 743	5 127
Other taxes	..	..	..	0	0	0	0	0	0	0
Voluntary contributions to government	..	..	..	0	2	2	3	2	2	0
Compulsory contributions to private sector	..	..	..	0	247	95	149	140	3	0
Total	**..**	**..**	**..**	**1 362**	**2 892**	**3 391**	**3 943**	**4 480**	**4 748**	**5 127**
Luxembourg, million EUR										
Contribution under 2000 heading	86	443	1 011	2 224	3 710	4 387	5 132	5 548	6 862	7 216
Other taxes	0	0	0	0	0	0	0	0	0	0
Voluntary contributions to government	0	0	4	18	18	28	33	38	48	52
Compulsory contributions to private sector	0	0	0	0	0	0	0	0	0	0
Total	**86**	**443**	**1 015**	**2 241**	**3 728**	**4 415**	**5 166**	**5 587**	**6 910**	**7 268**
Mexico, million MXN										
Contribution under 2000 heading	..	109	17 165	138 223	236 727	277 459	351 993	409 249	552 058	576 019
Other taxes	..	0	0	0	0	0	0	0	0	0
Voluntary contributions to government	..	0	0	0	0	0	0	0	0	0
Compulsory contributions to private sector	..	25	3 840	67 352	144 331	146 110	168 111	206 824	303 426	332 725
Total	**..**	**134**	**21 005**	**205 575**	**381 057**	**423 569**	**520 104**	**616 073**	**855 484**	**908 743**
Netherlands, million EUR										
Contribution under 2000 heading	3 342	26 641	39 075	64 522	77 072	82 732	97 372	96 426	109 298	108 685
Other taxes	0	0	0	0	0	0	0	0	0	0
Voluntary contributions to government	168	1 139	163	0	0	0	0	0	0	0
Compulsory contributions to private sector	1 266	7 642	5 727	37 088	..	..	..	..	..	..
Total	**4 776**	**35 422**	**44 965**	**101 610**	**77 072**	**82 732**	**97 372**	**96 426**	**109 298**	**108 685**
New Zealand, million NZD										
Contribution under 2000 heading	..	..	..	..	..	..	..	..	..	..
Other taxes	..	..	..	..	..	..	..	..	..	..
Voluntary contributions to government	..	..	..	..	..	..	..	..	..	..
Compulsory contributions to private sector	..	..	..	..	..	..	..	..	..	..
Total	**0**	**0**	**0**	**0**	**0**	**0**	**0**	**0**	**0**	**0**
Norway, million NOK										
Contribution under 2000 heading	2 009	28 205	79 362	132 170	204 473	243 002	292 461	325 130	377 057	381 838
Other taxes	1 305	4 256	0	0	0	0	0	0	0	0
Voluntary contributions to government	0	0	0	0	0	0	0	0	0	0
Compulsory contributions to private sector	0	242	339	0	0	0	0	0	0	0
Total	**3 314**	**32 703**	**79 701**	**132 170**	**204 473**	**243 002**	**292 461**	**325 130**	**377 057**	**381 838**
Poland, million PLN										
Contribution under 2000 heading	..	..	..	97 411	141 457	157 432	204 600	225 711	305 353	318 637
Other taxes	..	..	..	0	0	0	0	0	0	0
Voluntary contributions to government	..	..	..	0	0	0	34	49	46	48
Compulsory contributions to private sector	..	..	..	0	0	0	0	0	0	0
Total	**..**	**..**	**..**	**97 411**	**141 457**	**157 432**	**204 634**	**225 760**	**305 399**	**318 685**
Portugal, million EUR										
Contribution under 2000 heading	22	531	4 026	10 168	14 305	15 462	15 139	16 182	20 602	20 914
Other taxes	0	1	29	434	658	698	970	994	854	883
Voluntary contributions to government	0	0	0	0	0	0	0	0	0	0
Compulsory contributions to private sector	0	0	0	0	0	0	0	0	0	0
Total	**22**	**532**	**4 055**	**10 602**	**14 932**	**16 154**	**16 109**	**17 176**	**21 456**	**21 798**

	1965	1980	1990	2000	2007	2010	2013	2015	2019	2020
Slovak Republic, million EUR										
Contribution under 2000 heading	..	..	..	4 409	7 244	8 154	9 847	10 897	14 085	14 233
Other taxes	..	..	..	0	0	0	0	0	0	0
Voluntary contributions to government	..	..	..	0	22	31	17	11	11	12
Compulsory contributions to private sector	..	..	..	0	701	719	385	413	713	718
Total	**..**	**..**	**..**	**4 409**	**7 968**	**8 904**	**10 249**	**11 321**	**14 809**	**14 963**
Slovenia, million EUR										
Contribution under 2000 heading	..	..	..	2 824	5 046	5 761	5 647	5 983	7 587	7 908
Other taxes	..	..	..	0	0	0	0	0	0	0
Voluntary contributions to government	..	..	..	0	0	0	0	0	0	0
Compulsory contributions to private sector	..	..	..	0	0	0	0	0	0	0
Total	**..**	**..**	**..**	**2 824**	**5 046**	**5 761**	**5 647**	**5 983**	**7 587**	**7 908**
Spain, million EUR										
Contribution under 2000 heading	350	10 682	36 722	74 683	127 088	127 235	116 875	122 835	152 527	154 276
Other taxes	0	49	0	0	0	0	0	0	0	0
Voluntary contributions to government	0	0	0	447	937	1 155	2 209	1 170	987	891
Compulsory contributions to private sector	0	0	0	0	0	0	0	0	0	0
Total	**350**	**10 731**	**36 722**	**75 130**	**128 025**	**128 390**	**119 084**	**124 005**	**153 514**	**155 167**
Sweden, million SEK										
Contribution under 2000 heading	4 851	74 647	205 867	306 974	388 505	384 668	376 684	404 851	462 860	455 396
Other taxes	1 407	0	0	0	0	0	0	0	0	0
Voluntary contributions to government	0	0	0	7 951	12 376	13 167	15 909	16 726	24 966	24 731
Compulsory contributions to private sector	0	0	0	0	0	0	0	0	0	0
Total	**6 258**	**74 647**	**205 867**	**314 925**	**400 881**	**397 835**	**392 593**	**421 577**	**487 826**	**480 127**
Switzerland, million CHF										
Contribution under 2000 heading	1 670	10 844	19 952	30 961	34 974	38 385	42 862	44 285	47 233	49 057
Other taxes	336	778	1 176	4 509	6 342	6 644	7 760	7 590	6 260	3 357
Voluntary contributions to government	95	431	0	0	0	0	0	0	0	0
Compulsory contributions to private sector	2 505	9 674	20 797	29 532	42 219	45 974	49 965	52 890	59 357	60 122
Total	**4 606**	**21 727**	**41 924**	**65 002**	**83 535**	**91 004**	**100 587**	**104 765**	**112 851**	**112 536**
Türkiye, million TRY										
Contribution under 2000 heading	0	0	15	7 543	44 052	71 696	125 871	170 282	312 808	357 677
Other taxes	0	0	0	0	0	0	0	0	0	0
Voluntary contributions to government	0	0	0	0	0	0	0	0	0	0
Compulsory contributions to private sector	0	0	0	0	0	0	0	0	0	0
Total	**0**	**0**	**15**	**7 543**	**44 052**	**71 696**	**125 871**	**170 282**	**312 808**	**357 677**
United Kingdom, million GBP										
Contribution under 2000 heading	1 685	13 531	34 457	60 252	93 210	97 346	106 085	114 173	143 306	144 990
Other taxes	0	0	0	0	0	0	0	0	0	0
Voluntary contributions to government	0	11	3 288	8 103	18 629	21 217	22 438	25 025	33 474	38 013
Compulsory contributions to private sector	1 148	13 350	7 945	8 308	9 969	9 656	6 074	5 495	0	0
Total	**2 833**	**26 892**	**45 690**	**76 663**	**121 808**	**128 219**	**134 597**	**144 693**	**176 780**	**183 003**
United States, million USD										
Contribution under 2000 heading	22 192	159 763	396 972	683 104	907 357	917 409	1 030 099	1 125 493	1 308 696	1 333 998
Other taxes	0	0	0	0	0	0	0	0	0	0
Voluntary contributions to government	488	3 407	11 719	22 562	51 635	61 833	69 903	74 886	108 999	121 434
Compulsory contributions to private sector	0	0	0	0	0	0	0	0	0	0
Total	**22 680**	**163 170**	**408 691**	**705 666**	**958 992**	**979 242**	**1 100 002**	**1 200 379**	**1 417 695**	**1 455 432**

.. Not available

StatLink https://stat.link/pryvh0

Table 5.40. Social security contributions and payroll taxes paid by government, details

	1965	1980	1990	2000	2007	2010	2013	2015	2019	2020
Australia, million AUD										
2000 Social security contributions										
Federal or Central government	..	..	..	..	..	..	..	..	..	..
State/Regional	..	..	..	..	..	..	..	..	..	..
Local government	..	..	..	..	..	..	..	..	..	..
Social Security Funds	..	..	..	..	..	..	..	..	..	..
Total	**0**	**0**	**0**	**0**	**0**	**0**	**0**	**0**	**0**	**0**
3000 Taxes on payroll and workforce										
Federal or Central government	0	4	0	0	0	0	0	0	0	0
State/Regional	15	302	0	0	0	0	0	0	0	0
Local government	0	0	2	19	41	31	37	38	42	45
Social Security Funds	0	0	0	0	0	0	0	0	0	0
Multi-jurisdictional (University) sector[1]	..	..	..	..	..	..	..	..	..	..
Total	**15**	**306**	**92**	**301**	**496**	**579**	**702**	**765**	**922**	**959**
2000+3000 Total	**15**	**306**	**92**	**301**	**496**	**579**	**702**	**765**	**922**	**959**
Austria, million EUR[2]										
2000 Social security contributions										
Federal or Central government	48	230	337	620	1 244	1 532	1 664	1 825	2 209	2 261
State/Regional	13	166	337	692	988	1 179	1 255	1 376	1 702	1 800
Local government	17	145	292	699	1 036	1 277	1 379	1 515	1 815	1 906
Social Security Funds	11	79	48	176	203	226	250	264	293	303
Total	**88**	**619**	**1 015**	**2 186**	**3 471**	**4 213**	**4 547**	**4 980**	**6 018**	**6 270**
3000 Taxes on payroll and workforce										
Federal or Central government	0	49	134	186	337	533	558	624	649	658
State/Regional	0	48	74	232	351	458	485	492	507	507
Local government	1	29	79	301	262	359	396	428	455	445
Social Security Funds	0	0	39	44	51	55	61	65	71	73
Total	**1**	**125**	**326**	**763**	**1 000**	**1 405**	**1 500**	**1 609**	**1 682**	**1 682**
2000+3000 Total	**89**	**745**	**1 341**	**2 949**	**4 471**	**5 618**	**6 047**	**6 589**	**7 700**	**7 952**
Belgium, million EUR										
2000 Social security contributions										
Federal or Central government	..	536	211	259	434	493	532	859	866	908
State/Regional	..	0	614	1 218	1 600	1 873	2 089	2 440	2 756	2 771
Local government	..	434	768	1 376	2 151	2 655	3 641	3 973	4 524	4 599
Social Security Funds	..	89	176	252	308	360	416	415	411	421
Total	**..**	**1 059**	**1 769**	**3 105**	**4 493**	**5 381**	**6 678**	**7 686**	**8 557**	**8 698**
3000 Taxes on payroll and workforce										
Federal or Central government	..	..	..	..	..	..	..	..	..	..
State/Regional	..	..	..	..	..	..	..	..	..	..
Local government	..	..	..	..	..	..	..	..	..	..
Social Security Funds	..	..	..	..	..	..	..	..	..	..
Total	**..**	**0**	**0**	**0**	**0**	**0**	**0**	**0**	**0**	**0**
2000+3000 Total	**..**	**1 059**	**1 769**	**3 105**	**4 493**	**5 381**	**6 678**	**7 686**	**8 557**	**8 698**
Canada, million CAD										
2000 Social security contributions										
Federal or Central government	..	..	..	944	1 198	1 397	1 449	1 515	1 790	2 144
State/Regional	..	..	..	3 023	4 269	5 071	5 825	6 349	7 122	7 186
Local government	..	..	..	2 225	2 806	3 390	3 912	4 205	4 715	4 757
Social Security Funds	..	..	..	0	0	0	0	0	0	0
Total	**..**	**..**	**..**	**6 192**	**8 273**	**9 857**	**11 186**	**12 070**	**13 626**	**14 087**
3000 Taxes on payroll andworkforce										
Federal or Central government	..	..	..	0	0	0	0	0	0	0
State/Regional	..	..	..	173	234	328	362	362	405	412
Local government	..	..	..	0	0	0	0	0	0	0
Social Security Funds	..	..	..	0	0	0	0	0	0	0
Total	**..**	**..**	**..**	**173**	**234**	**328**	**362**	**362**	**405**	**412**
2000+3000 Total	**..**	**..**	**..**	**6 365**	**8 507**	**10 185**	**11 548**	**12 432**	**14 031**	**14 499**

	1965	1980	1990	2000	2007	2010	2013	2015	2019	2020
Chile, million CLP										
2000 Social security contributions										
Federal or Central government	..	..	..	43 210	107 911	148 006	186 652	205 125	270 571	269 335
State/Regional	..	..	..	..	..	..	..	..	..	..
Local government	..	..	..	11 317	30 218	41 518	51 114	63 603	104 484	110 058
Social Security Funds	..	..	..	106	263	449	550	600	825	872
Total	**..**	**..**	**..**	**54 633**	**138 392**	**189 974**	**238 315**	**269 328**	**375 881**	**380 265**
3000 Taxes on payroll and workforce										
Federal or Central government	..	..	..	..	..	..	..	..	..	..
State/Regional	..	..	..	..	..	..	..	..	..	..
Local government	..	..	..	..	..	..	..	..	..	..
Social Security Funds	..	..	..	..	..	..	..	..	..	..
Total	**..**	**..**	**..**	**..**	**..**	**..**	**..**	**..**	**..**	**..**
2000+3000 Total	**..**	**..**	**..**	**54 633**	**138 392**	**189 974**	**238 315**	**269 328**	**375 881**	**380 265**
Colombia, million COP										
2000 Social security contributions										
Federal or Central government	..	..	..	..	..	..	0	0	0	0
State/Regional	..	..	..	..	..	..	0	0	0	0
Local government	..	..	..	..	..	..	0	0	0	0
Social Security Funds	..	..	..	..	..	..	1 007 283	1 255 666	1 889 685	1 937 898
Total	**..**	**..**	**..**	**..**	**..**	**..**	**1 007 283**	**1 255 666**	**1 889 685**	**1 937 898**
3000 Taxes on payroll and workforce										
Federal or Central government	..	..	..	..	..	..	372 476	436 646	589 456	614 683
State/Regional	..	..	..	..	..	..	0	0	0	0
Local government	..	..	..	..	..	..	0	0	0	0
Social Security Funds	..	..	..	..	..	..	0	0	0	0
Total	**..**	**..**	**..**	**..**	**..**	**..**	**372 476**	**436 646**	**589 456**	**614 683**
2000+3000 Total	**..**	**..**	**..**	**..**	**..**	**..**	**1 379 759**	**1 692 312**	**2 479 141**	**2 552 581**
Costa Rica, million CRC										
2000 Social security contributions										
Federal or Central government	..	..	3 219	35 099	102 041	197 340	258 663	301 475	358 848	364 628
State/Regional	..	..	0	0	0	0	0	0	0	0
Local government	..	..	228	2 214	5 357	9 866	14 042	17 177	23 092	23 212
Social Security Funds	..	..	0	0	0	0	0	0	0	0
Total	**..**	**..**	**3 447**	**37 313**	**107 398**	**207 206**	**272 706**	**318 652**	**381 940**	**387 840**
3000 Taxes on payroll and workforce										
Federal or Central government	..	..	91	2 666	5 320	12 405	15 059	17 321	20 795	22 030
State/Regional	..	..	0	0	0	0	0	0	0	0
Local government	..	..	0	0	0	0	0	0	0	0
Social Security Funds	..	..	0	0	0	0	0	0	0	0
Total	**..**	**..**	**91**	**2 666**	**5 320**	**12 405**	**15 059**	**17 321**	**20 795**	**22 030**
2000+3000 Total	**..**	**..**	**3 538**	**39 979**	**112 718**	**219 611**	**287 765**	**335 973**	**402 736**	**409 870**
Czech Republic, million CZK										
2000 Social security contributions										
Federal or Central government	..	..	..	28 050	44 437	45 439	46 360	37 553	52 185	56 141
State/Regional	..	..	..	..	..	..	..	..	..	..
Local government	..	..	..	5 660	8 253	9 394	9 448	41 954	61 791	68 981
Social Security Funds	..	..	..	510	791	938	881	975	1 275	1 310
Total	**..**	**..**	**..**	**34 220**	**53 481**	**55 771**	**56 689**	**80 482**	**115 252**	**126 432**
3000 Taxes on payroll and workforce										
Federal or Central government	..	..	..	..	..	..	..	..	..	..
State/Regional	..	..	..	..	..	..	..	..	..	..
Local government	..	..	..	..	..	..	..	..	..	..
Social Security Funds	..	..	..	..	..	..	..	..	..	..
Total	**..**	**..**	**..**	**0**	**0**	**0**	**0**	**0**	**0**	**0**
2000+3000 Total	**..**	**..**	**..**	**34 220**	**53 481**	**55 771**	**56 689**	**80 482**	**115 252**	**126 432**

	1965	1980	1990	2000	2007	2010	2013	2015	2019	2020
Denmark, million DKK										
2000 Social security contributions										
Federal or Central government	..	179	..	..	..	..	..	..	..	..
State/Regional	..	..	..	..	..	..	..	..	..	..
Local government	..	0	..	..	..	..	..	..	..	..
Social Security Funds	..	0	..	..	..	..	..	..	..	..
Total	**..**	**179**	**0**	**0**	**0**	**0**	**0**	**0**	**0**	**0**
3000 Taxes on payroll and workforce										
Federal or Central government	..	..	..	..	..	..	..	..	..	..
State/Regional	..	..	..	..	..	..	..	..	..	..
Local government	..	..	..	..	..	..	..	..	..	..
Social Security Funds	..	..	..	..	..	..	..	..	..	..
Total	**..**	**0**	**0**	**0**	**0**	**0**	**0**	**0**	**0**	**0**
2000+3000 Total	**..**	**179**	**0**	**0**	**0**	**0**	**0**	**0**	**0**	**0**
Estonia, million EUR										
2000 Social security contributions										
Federal or Central government	..	..	..	115	230	258	306	359	474	514
State/Regional	..	..	..	..	..	..	..	..	..	..
Local government	..	..	..	48	155	173	203	232	335	353
Social Security Funds	..	..	..	0	1	3	4	4	8	9
Total	**..**	**..**	**..**	**163**	**386**	**434**	**513**	**596**	**817**	**876**
3000 Taxes on payroll and workforce										
Federal or Central government	..	..	..	..	..	..	..	..	..	..
State/Regional	..	..	..	..	..	..	..	..	..	..
Local government	..	..	..	..	..	..	..	..	..	..
Social Security Funds	..	..	..	..	..	..	..	..	..	..
Total	**..**	**..**	**..**	**0**	**0**	**0**	**0**	**0**	**0**	**0**
2000+3000 Total	**..**	**..**	**..**	**163**	**386**	**434**	**513**	**596**	**817**	**876**
Finland, million EUR										
2000 Social security contributions										
Federal or Central government	..	61	196	908	1 057	1 138	1 227	1 229	1 104	1 141
State/Regional	..	..	..	..	..	..	..	..	..	..
Local government	..	170	1 709	2 786	4 061	4 352	4 881	4 868	4 270	4 315
Social Security Funds	..	9	34	75	88	89	101	109	112	109
Total	**..**	**239**	**1 939**	**3 769**	**5 206**	**5 579**	**6 209**	**6 206**	**5 486**	**5 565**
3000 Taxes on payroll and workforce										
Federal or Central government	..	1	..	..	..	..	..	..	..	..
State/Regional	..	..	..	..	..	..	..	..	..	..
Local government	..	4	..	..	..	..	..	..	..	..
Social Security Funds	..	0	..	..	..	..	..	..	..	..
Total	**..**	**5**	**0**	**0**	**0**	**0**	**0**	**0**	**0**	**0**
2000+3000 Total	**..**	**245**	**1 939**	**3 769**	**5 206**	**5 579**	**6 209**	**6 206**	**5 486**	**5 565**
France, million EUR										
2000 Social security contributions										
Federal or Central government	..	3 816	8 063	10 466	12 426	12 841	12 825	12 999	14 275	14 424
State/Regional	..	..	..	..	..	..	..	..	..	..
Local government	..	2 369	5 542	10 372	15 925	18 065	20 050	21 553	22 157	22 505
Social Security Funds	..	2 594	6 940	10 827	14 035	15 427	16 614	17 399	17 548	18 178
Total	**..**	**8 779**	**20 545**	**31 665**	**42 386**	**46 333**	**49 489**	**51 951**	**53 980**	**55 107**
3000 Taxes on payroll and workforce										
Federal or Central government	..	836	494	854	1 558	1 611	1 697	1 768	1 968	2 014
State/Regional	..	..	..	..	..	..	..	..	..	..
Local government	..	27	107	324	549	698	791	852	962	992
Social Security Funds	..	629	2 234	3 413	4 531	5 028	5 374	5 522	5 782	6 047
Total	**..**	**1 492**	**2 835**	**4 591**	**6 638**	**7 337**	**7 862**	**8 142**	**8 712**	**9 053**
2000+3000 Total	**..**	**10 271**	**23 380**	**36 256**	**49 024**	**53 670**	**57 351**	**60 093**	**62 692**	**64 160**

	1965	1980	1990	2000	2007	2010	2013	2015	2019	2020
Germany, million EUR										
2000 Social security contributions										
Federal or Central government	775	1 324	2 376	1 554	1 377	1 649	1 631	1 766	2 298	2 480
State/Regional	293	2 611	4 647	5 664	6 045	6 781	7 231	7 749	9 329	9 925
Local government	325	3 140	5 791	6 920	8 296	9 499	9 967	10 767	13 768	14 464
Social Security Funds	1 495	456	767	1 806	2 131	2 446	2 614	2 840	3 333	3 584
Total	**2 887**	**7 531**	**13 581**	**15 945**	**17 849**	**20 374**	**21 443**	**23 123**	**28 728**	**30 453**
3000 Taxes on payroll and workforce										
Federal or Central government	..	..	..	..	..	..	..	..	..	..
State/Regional	..	..	..	..	..	..	..	..	..	..
Local government	..	..	..	..	..	..	..	..	..	..
Social Security Funds	..	..	..	..	..	..	..	..	..	..
Total	**0**	**0**	**0**	**0**	**0**	**0**	**0**	**0**	**0**	**0**
2000+3000 Total	**2 887**	**7 531**	**13 581**	**15 945**	**17 849**	**20 374**	**21 443**	**23 123**	**28 728**	**30 453**
Greece, million EUR										
2000 Social security contributions										
Federal or Central government	..	..	124	510	1 045	1 176	1 151	1 160	2 017	2 318
State/Regional	..	..	..	..	..	..	..	..	..	..
Local government	..	..	0	124	286	341	355	339	329	345
Social Security Funds	..	..	0	99	268	200	169	74	66	61
Total	**..**	**..**	**124**	**733**	**1 599**	**1 717**	**1 675**	**1 573**	**2 412**	**2 724**
3000 Taxes on payroll and workforce										
Federal or Central government	..	..	..	..	..	..	..	..	..	..
State/Regional	..	..	..	..	..	..	..	..	..	..
Local government	..	..	..	..	..	..	..	..	..	..
Social Security Funds	..	..	..	..	..	..	..	..	..	..
Total	**..**	**..**	**0**	**0**	**0**	**0**	**0**	**0**	**0**	**0**
2000+3000 Total	**..**	**..**	**124**	**733**	**1 599**	**1 717**	**1 675**	**1 573**	**2 412**	**2 724**
Hungary, million HUF										
2000 Social security contributions										
Federal or Central government	..	..	..	148 251	293 684	352 354	449 428	539 106	530 607	511 247
State/Regional	..	..	..	..	..	..	..	..	..	..
Local government	..	..	..	173 475	343 306	291 375	124 111	152 189	147 213	136 697
Social Security Funds	..	..	..	4 936	8 052	6 763	2 781	2 977	876	709
Total	**..**	**..**	**..**	**326 661**	**645 042**	**650 492**	**576 320**	**694 272**	**678 696**	**648 653**
3000 Taxes on payroll and workforce										
Federal or Central government	..	..	..	13 901	7 287	5 419	12 435	12 876	19 481	20 850
State/Regional	..	..	..	..	..	..	..	..	..	..
Local government	..	..	..	25 990	11 928	9 275	4 224	3 357	4 617	4 978
Social Security Funds	..	..	..	406	162	194	101	110	37	45
Total	**..**	**..**	**..**	**40 297**	**19 377**	**14 888**	**16 760**	**16 342**	**24 135**	**25 873**
2000+3000 Total	**..**	**..**	**..**	**366 958**	**664 420**	**665 380**	**593 080**	**710 614**	**702 831**	**674 526**
Iceland, million ISK										
2000 Social security contributions										
Federal or Central government	..	..	..	..	..	..	..	..	..	..
State/Regional	..	..	..	..	..	..	..	..	..	..
Local government	..	..	..	..	..	..	..	..	..	..
Social Security Funds	..	..	..	..	..	..	..	..	..	..
Total	**..**	**..**	**..**	**..**	**..**	**..**	**..**	**..**	**..**	**..**
3000 Taxes on payroll and workforce										
Federal or Central government	..	..	..	..	..	..	..	..	..	..
State/Regional	..	..	..	..	..	..	..	..	..	..
Local government	..	..	..	..	..	..	..	..	..	..
Social Security Funds	..	..	..	..	..	..	..	..	..	..
Total	**..**	**..**	**..**	**..**	**..**	**..**	**..**	**..**	**..**	**..**
2000+3000 Total	**..**	**..**	**..**	**..**	**..**	**..**	**..**	**..**	**..**	**..**

	1965	1980	1990	2000	2007	2010	2013	2015	2019	2020
Ireland, million EUR										
2000 Social security contributions										
Federal or Central government	..	21	65	166	460	395	426	497	680	629
State/Regional	..	..	..	..	..	..	..	..	..	..
Local government	..	25	83	277	862	740	799	932	1 275	1 180
Social Security Funds	..	0	1	4	6	6	6	6	6	6
Total	**..**	**46**	**149**	**447**	**1 328**	**1 140**	**1 231**	**1 435**	**1 961**	**1 816**
3000 Taxes on payroll and workforce										
Federal or Central government	..	..	..	..	..	..	..	..	..	..
State/Regional	..	..	..	..	..	..	..	..	..	..
Local government	..	..	..	..	..	..	..	..	..	..
Social Security Funds	..	..	..	..	..	..	..	..	..	..
Total	**..**	**0**	**0**	**0**	**0**	**0**	**0**	**0**	**0**	**0**
2000+3000 Total	**..**	**46**	**149**	**447**	**1 328**	**1 140**	**1 231**	**1 435**	**1 961**	**1 816**
Israel, million ILS										
2000 Social security contributions										
Federal or Central government	..	..	..	840	1 030	1 180	1 550	1 780	2 380	2 320
State/Regional	..	..	..	..	..	..	..	..	..	..
Local government	..	..	..	280	340	390	510	590	790	770
Social Security Funds	..	..	..	5	12	15	0	0	0	0
Total	**..**	**..**	**..**	**1 120**	**1 370**	**1 570**	**2 060**	**2 370**	**3 170**	**3 090**
3000 Taxes on payroll and workforce										
Federal or Central government	..	..	..	2 330	3 600	4 180	5 220	5 650	6 850	6 960
State/Regional	..	..	..	..	..	..	..	..	..	..
Local government	..	..	..	660	880	960	1 190	1 290	1 570	1 590
Social Security Funds	..	..	..	5	12	15	0	0	0	0
Total	**..**	**..**	**..**	**2 990**	**4 480**	**5 140**	**6 410**	**6 940**	**8 420**	**8 550**
2000+3000 Total	**..**	**..**	**..**	**4 110**	**5 850**	**6 710**	**8 470**	**9 310**	**11 590**	**11 640**
Italy, million EUR										
2000 Social security contributions										
Federal or Central government	..	..	..	0	0	0	0	0	0	0
State/Regional	..	..	..	..	..	..	..	..	..	..
Local government	..	..	..	0	0	0	0	0	0	0
Social Security Funds	..	..	..	36 679	47 394	50 627	49 827	49 251	52 345	52 493
Total	**..**	**..**	**..**	**36 679**	**47 394**	**50 627**	**49 827**	**49 251**	**52 345**	**52 493**
3000 Taxes on payroll and workforce										
Federal or Central government	..	..	..	..	..	..	..	..	..	..
State/Regional	..	..	..	..	..	..	..	..	..	..
Local government	..	..	..	..	..	..	..	..	..	..
Social Security Funds	..	..	..	..	..	..	..	..	..	..
Total	**..**	**..**	**..**	**0**	**0**	**0**	**0**	**0**	**0**	**0**
2000+3000 Total	**..**	**..**	**..**	**36 679**	**47 394**	**50 627**	**49 827**	**49 251**	**52 345**	**52 493**
Japan, billion JPY										
2000 Social security contributions										
Federal or Central government	..	..	507	732	766	758	810	881	932	928
State/Regional	..	..	..	..	..	..	..	..	0	0
Local government	..	..	1 510	2 168	2 216	2 223	2 392	2 524	2 615	2 608
Social Security Funds	..	..	0	0	0	0	0	0	0	0
Total	**..**	**..**	**2 017**	**2 900**	**2 982**	**2 981**	**3 202**	**3 405**	**3 547**	**3 536**
3000 Taxes on payroll and workforce										
Federal or Central government	..	..	..	..	..	..	..	..	..	..
State/Regional	..	..	..	..	..	..	..	..	..	..
Local government	..	..	..	..	..	..	..	..	..	..
Social Security Funds	..	..	..	..	..	..	..	..	..	..
Total	**..**	**..**	**0**	**0**	**0**	**0**	**0**	**0**	**0**	**0**
2000+3000 Total	**..**	**..**	**2 017**	**2 900**	**2 982**	**2 981**	**3 202**	**3 405**	**3 547**	**3 536**

	1965	1980	1990	2000	2007	2010	2013	2015	2019	2020
Korea, billion KRW										
2000 Social security contributions										
Federal or Central government	..	..	..	..	..	..	..	..	..	..
State/Regional	..	..	..	..	..	..	..	..	..	..
Local government	..	..	..	..	..	..	..	..	..	..
Social Security Funds	..	..	..	..	..	..	..	..	..	..
Total	**..**	**..**	**..**	**..**	**..**	**..**	**..**	**..**	**..**	**..**
3000 Taxes on payroll and workforce										
Federal or Central government	..	..	..	..	..	..	..	..	..	..
State/Regional	..	..	..	..	..	..	..	..	..	..
Local government	..	..	..	..	..	..	..	..	..	..
Social Security Funds	..	..	..	..	..	..	..	..	..	..
Total	**..**	**..**	**..**	**..**	**..**	**..**	**..**	**..**	**..**	**..**
2000+3000 Total	**..**	**..**	**..**	**..**	**..**	**..**	**..**	**..**	**..**	**..**
Latvia, million EUR										
2000 Social security contributions										
Federal or Central government	..	..	..	..	..	..	..	..	..	..
State/Regional	..	..	..	..	..	..	..	..	..	..
Local government	..	..	..	..	..	..	..	..	..	..
Social Security Funds	..	..	..	..	..	..	..	..	..	..
Total	**..**	**..**	**..**	**40**	**156**	**174**	**228**	**262**	**358**	**330**
3000 Taxes on payroll and workforce										
Federal or Central government	..	..	..	..	..	..	..	..	..	..
State/Regional	..	..	..	..	..	..	..	..	..	..
Local government	..	..	..	..	..	..	..	..	..	..
Social Security Funds	..	..	..	..	..	..	..	..	..	..
Total	**..**	**..**	**..**	**0**	**0**	**0**	**0**	**0**	**0**	**0**
2000+3000 Total	**..**	**..**	**..**	**40**	**156**	**174**	**228**	**262**	**358**	**330**
Lithuania, million EUR										
2000 Social security contributions										
Federal or Central government	..	..	..	179	327	335	395	426	50	50
State/Regional	..	..	..	..	..	..	..	..	..	..
Local government	..	..	..	174	294	351	348	375	40	46
Social Security Funds	..	..	..	5	14	16	15	16	1	1
Total	**..**	**..**	**..**	**358**	**635**	**701**	**758**	**818**	**91**	**98**
3000 Taxes on payroll and workforce										
Federal or Central government	..	..	..	..	..	..	..	..	..	..
State/Regional	..	..	..	..	..	..	..	..	..	..
Local government	..	..	..	..	..	..	..	..	..	..
Social Security Funds	..	..	..	..	..	..	..	..	..	..
Total	**..**	**..**	**..**	**0**	**0**	**0**	**0**	**0**	**0**	**0**
2000+3000 Total	**..**	**..**	**..**	**358**	**635**	**701**	**758**	**818**	**91**	**98**
Luxembourg, million EUR										
2000 Social security contributions										
Federal or Central government	..	..	257	273	413	488	587	648	789	828
State/Regional	..	..	..	..	..	..	..	..	..	..
Local government	..	..	2	4	4	4	4	4	4	4
Social Security Funds	..	..	7	11	12	13	14	17	22	23
Total	**..**	**..**	**267**	**288**	**429**	**505**	**605**	**669**	**814**	**855**
3000 Taxes on payroll and workforce										
Federal or Central government	..	..	..	..	..	..	..	..	..	..
State/Regional	..	..	..	..	..	..	..	..	..	..
Local government	..	..	..	..	..	..	..	..	..	..
Social Security Funds	..	..	..	..	..	..	..	..	..	..
Total	**..**	**..**	**0**	**0**	**0**	**0**	**0**	**0**	**0**	**0**
2000+3000 Total	**..**	**..**	**267**	**288**	**429**	**505**	**605**	**669**	**814**	**855**

	1965	1980	1990	2000	2007	2010	2013	2015	2019	2020
Mexico, million MXN										
2000 Social security contributions										
Federal or Central government	..	25	2 952	44 879	94 251	103 440	126 518	145 329	183 462	196 039
State/Regional	..	0	0	0	0	0	0	0	0	0
Local government	..	0	0	0	0	0	0	0	0	0
Social Security Funds	..	0	0	0	0	0	0	0	0	0
Total	**..**	**25**	**2 952**	**44 879**	**94 251**	**103 440**	**126 518**	**145 329**	**183 462**	**196 039**
3000 Taxes on payroll and workforce										
Federal or Central government	..	..	..	..	..	..	..	..	..	..
State/Regional	..	..	..	..	..	..	..	..	..	..
Local government	..	..	..	..	..	..	..	..	..	..
Social Security Funds	..	..	..	..	..	..	..	..	..	..
Total	**..**	**0**	**0**	**0**	**0**	**0**	**0**	**0**	**0**	**0**
2000+3000 Total	**..**	**25**	**2 952**	**44 879**	**94 251**	**103 440**	**126 518**	**145 329**	**183 462**	**196 039**
Netherlands, million EUR										
2000 Social security contributions										
Federal or Central government	63	1 366	286	..	..	..	..	..	..	..
State/Regional	..	..	..	..	..	..	..	..	..	..
Local government	0	0	0	..	..	..	..	..	..	..
Social Security Funds	7	91	59	..	..	..	..	..	..	..
Total	**70**	**1 457**	**345**	**2 006**	**4 310**	**..**	**..**	**..**	**..**	**..**
3000 Taxes on payroll and workforce										
Federal or Central government	..	..	..	..	..	..	..	..	..	..
State/Regional	..	..	..	..	..	..	..	..	..	..
Local government	..	..	..	..	..	..	..	..	..	..
Social Security Funds	..	..	..	..	..	..	..	..	..	..
Total	**0**	**0**	**0**	**0**	**0**	**0**	**0**	**0**	**0**	**0**
2000+3000 Total	**70**	**1 457**	**345**	**2 006**	**4 310**	**0**	**0**	**0**	**0**	**0**
New Zealand, million NZD										
2000 Social security contributions										
Federal or Central government	..	..	..	..	..	..	..	..	..	..
State/Regional	..	..	..	..	..	..	..	..	..	..
Local government	..	..	..	..	..	..	..	..	..	..
Social Security Funds	..	..	..	..	..	..	..	..	..	..
Total	**0**	**0**	**0**	**0**	**0**	**0**	**0**	**0**	**0**	**0**
3000 Taxes on payroll and workforce										
Federal or Central government	..	..	..	..	..	..	..	..	..	..
State/Regional	..	..	..	..	..	..	..	..	..	..
Local government	..	..	..	..	..	..	..	..	..	..
Social Security Funds	..	..	..	..	..	..	..	..	..	..
Total	**0**	**0**	**0**	**0**	**0**	**0**	**0**	**0**	**0**	**0**
2000+3000 Total	**0**	**0**	**0**	**0**	**0**	**0**	**0**	**0**	**0**	**0**
Norway, million NOK										
2000 Social security contributions										
Federal or Central government	..	1 242	2 859	11 895	28 233	33 746	40 145	46 487	52 458	53 465
State/Regional	..	..	..	..	..	..	..	..	..	..
Local government	..	4 538	11 964	24 831	32 110	41 024	53 123	59 556	71 600	68 072
Social Security Funds	..	1 222	3 064	0	0	0	0	0	0	0
Total	**..**	**7 002**	**17 887**	**36 726**	**60 343**	**74 770**	**93 268**	**106 043**	**124 058**	**121 537**
3000 Taxes on payroll and workforce										
Federal or Central government	..	..	..	..	..	..	..	..	..	..
State/Regional	..	..	..	..	..	..	..	..	..	..
Local government	..	..	..	..	..	..	..	..	..	..
Social Security Funds	..	..	..	..	..	..	..	..	..	..
Total	**..**	**0**	**0**	**0**	**0**	**0**	**0**	**0**	**0**	**0**
2000+3000 Total	**..**	**7 002**	**17 887**	**36 726**	**60 343**	**74 770**	**93 268**	**106 043**	**124 058**	**121 537**

	1965	1980	1990	2000	2007	2010	2013	2015	2019	2020
Poland, million PLN										
2000 Social security contributions										
Federal or Central government	..	..	..	4 566	6 023	6 643	8 145	9 840	12 801	13 908
State/Regional	..	..	..	..	..	..	..	..	..	..
Local government	..	..	..	6 756	9 856	11 411	13 702	14 796	18 859	20 175
Social Security Funds	..	..	..	279	426	499	536	518	682	736
Total	**..**	**..**	**..**	**11 601**	**16 305**	**18 553**	**22 383**	**25 154**	**32 342**	**34 819**
3000 Taxes on payroll and workforce										
Federal or Central government	..	..	..	..	..	..	..	..	..	..
State/Regional	..	..	..	..	..	..	..	..	..	..
Local government	..	..	..	..	..	..	..	..	..	..
Social Security Funds	..	..	..	..	..	..	..	..	..	..
Total	**..**	**..**	**..**	**0**	**0**	**0**	**0**	**0**	**0**	**0**
2000+3000 Total	**..**	**..**	**..**	**11 601**	**16 305**	**18 553**	**22 383**	**25 154**	**32 342**	**34 819**
Portugal, million EUR										
2000 Social security contributions										
Federal or Central government	..	0	0	0	..	..	..	..	..	..
State/Regional	..	..	..	..	..	..	..	..	..	..
Local government	..	0	33	197	..	..	..	..	..	..
Social Security Funds	..	4	0	0	..	..	..	..	..	..
Total	**..**	**4**	**33**	**197**	**0**	**0**	**0**	**0**	**0**	**0**
3000 Taxes on payroll and workforce										
Federal or Central government	..	..	..	..	..	..	..	..	..	..
State/Regional	..	..	..	..	..	..	..	..	..	..
Local government	..	..	..	..	..	..	..	..	..	..
Social Security Funds	..	..	..	..	..	..	..	..	..	..
Total	**..**	**0**	**0**	**0**	**0**	**0**	**0**	**0**	**0**	**0**
2000+3000 Total	**..**	**4**	**33**	**197**	**0**	**0**	**0**	**0**	**0**	**0**
Slovak Republic, million EUR										
2000 Social security contributions										
Federal or Central government	..	..	..	489	602	797	944	1 069	1 340	1 421
State/Regional	..	..	..	..	..	..	..	..	..	..
Local government	..	..	..	130	427	515	587	658	921	1 002
Social Security Funds	..	..	..	22	26	43	33	36	49	49
Total	**..**	**..**	**..**	**642**	**1 056**	**1 354**	**1 564**	**1 763**	**2 310**	**2 472**
3000 Taxes on payroll and workforce										
Federal or Central government	..	..	..	..	..	..	..	..	..	..
State/Regional	..	..	..	..	..	..	..	..	..	..
Local government	..	..	..	..	..	..	..	..	..	..
Social Security Funds	..	..	..	..	..	..	..	..	..	..
Total	**..**	**..**	**..**	**0**	**0**	**0**	**0**	**0**	**0**	**0**
2000+3000 Total	**..**	**..**	**..**	**642**	**1 056**	**1 354**	**1 564**	**1 763**	**2 310**	**2 472**
Slovenia, million EUR										
2000 Social security contributions										
Federal or Central government	..	..	..	178	339	409	387	375	488	539
State/Regional	..	..	..	..	..	..	..	..	..	..
Local government	..	..	..	94	175	195	187	189	243	268
Social Security Funds	..	..	..	3	7	8	7	6	8	8
Total	**..**	**..**	**..**	**275**	**521**	**612**	**582**	**571**	**739**	**815**
3000 Taxes on payroll and workforce										
Federal or Central government	..	..	..	56	77	6	7	7	8	9
State/Regional	..	..	..	..	..	..	..	..	..	..
Local government	..	..	..	29	36	3	4	4	4	4
Social Security Funds	..	..	..	1	2	0	0	0	0	0
Total	**..**	**..**	**..**	**86**	**114**	**9**	**11**	**11**	**12**	**14**
2000+3000 Total	**..**	**..**	**..**	**361**	**636**	**621**	**593**	**582**	**751**	**829**

	1965	1980	1990	2000	2007	2010	2013	2015	2019	2020
Spain, million EUR										
2000 Social security contributions										
Federal or Central government	..	387	989	1 408	1 966	2 201	2 014	2 234	2 700	2 822
State/Regional	..	2	0	4 411	9 426	10 996	10 212	11 245	14 013	15 107
Local government	..	252	1 819	2 524	4 098	4 781	4 617	4 797	5 625	5 551
Social Security Funds	..	396	1 202	1 284	484	527	498	496	517	534
Total	**..**	**1 037**	**4 010**	**9 627**	**15 974**	**18 505**	**17 341**	**18 772**	**22 855**	**24 014**
3000 Taxes on payroll and workforce										
Federal or Central government	..	..	..	..	..	..	..	..	..	..
State/Regional	..	..	..	..	..	..	..	..	..	..
Local government	..	..	..	..	..	..	..	..	..	..
Social Security Funds	..	..	..	..	..	..	..	..	..	..
Total	**..**	**0**	**0**	**0**	**0**	**0**	**0**	**0**	**0**	**0**
2000+3000 Total	**..**	**1 037**	**4 010**	**9 627**	**15 974**	**18 505**	**17 341**	**18 772**	**22 855**	**24 014**
Sweden, million SEK										
2000 Social security contributions										
Federal or Central government	..	7 543	12 430	21 153	25 164	24 729	24 595	25 707	28 554	29 222
State/Regional	..	..	..	..	..	..	..	..	..	..
Local government	..	18 149	49 298	66 215	83 877	82 141	78 774	85 373	98 072	96 956
Social Security Funds	..	0	0	0	0	0	0	0	0	0
Total	**..**	**25 692**	**61 728**	**87 367**	**109 040**	**106 870**	**103 370**	**111 079**	**126 625**	**126 178**
3000 Taxes on payroll and workforce										
Federal or Central government	..	..	1 527	3 453	5 394	6 912	11 242	12 326	16 584	16 420
State/Regional	..	..	..	..	..	..	..	..	..	..
Local government	..	..	6 060	10 808	17 980	22 958	36 005	40 935	56 961	54 480
Social Security Funds	..	..	0	0	0	0	0	0	0	0
Total	**..**	**0**	**7 587**	**14 261**	**23 374**	**29 870**	**47 247**	**53 261**	**73 545**	**70 900**
2000+3000 Total	**..**	**25 692**	**69 315**	**101 628**	**132 414**	**136 740**	**150 616**	**164 340**	**200 170**	**197 078**
Switzerland, million CHF										
2000 Social security contributions										
Federal or Central government	13	91	224	293	381	448	494	530	584	606
State/Regional	34	380	770	971	1 269	1 520	1 695	1 766	1 943	2 013
Local government	22	270	460	595	745	823	867	911	964	1 020
Social Security Funds	2	21	4	14	18	23	25	26	28	28
Total	**71**	**762**	**1 458**	**1 873**	**2 413**	**2 813**	**3 080**	**3 234**	**3 519**	**3 667**
3000 Taxes on payroll and workforce										
Federal or Central government	..	..	..	..	..	..	..	..	..	..
State/Regional	..	..	..	..	..	..	..	..	..	..
Local government	..	..	..	..	..	..	..	..	..	..
Social Security Funds	..	..	..	..	..	..	..	..	..	..
Total	**0**	**0**	**0**	**0**	**0**	**0**	**0**	**0**	**0**	**0**
2000+3000 Total	**71**	**762**	**1 458**	**1 873**	**2 413**	**2 813**	**3 080**	**3 234**	**3 519**	**3 667**
Türkiye, million TRY										
2000 Social security contributions										
Federal or Central government	..	..	9	3 619	20 442	39 363	71 184	95 067	178 345	204 045
State/Regional	..	..	..	..	..	..	..	..	..	..
Local government	..	..	0	0	0	0	0	0	0	0
Social Security Funds	..	..	0	0	0	0	0	0	0	0
Total	**..**	**..**	**9**	**3 619**	**20 442**	**39 363**	**71 184**	**95 067**	**178 345**	**204 045**
3000 Taxes on payroll and workforce										
Federal or Central government	..	..	..	..	..	..	..	..	..	..
State/Regional	..	..	..	..	..	..	..	..	..	..
Local government	..	..	..	..	..	..	..	..	..	..
Social Security Funds	..	..	..	..	..	..	..	..	..	..
Total	**..**	**..**	**0**	**0**	**0**	**0**	**0**	**0**	**0**	**0**
2000+3000 Total	**..**	**..**	**9**	**3 619**	**20 442**	**39 363**	**71 184**	**95 067**	**178 345**	**204 045**

	1965	1980	1990	2000	2007	2010	2013	2015	2019	2020
United Kingdom, million GBP										
2000 Social security contributions										
Federal or Central government	87	920	2 134	3 146	5 874	6 495	7 090	7 829	10 336	11 116
State/Regional	..	..	..	..	..	..	..	..	..	..
Local government	83	926	1 957	2 924	4 867	5 358	4 672	4 550	4 900	5 024
Social Security Funds	0	0	0	0	0	0	0	0	0	0
Total	**170**	**1 846**	**4 091**	**6 070**	**10 741**	**11 853**	**11 762**	**12 379**	**15 236**	**16 140**
3000 Taxes on payroll and workforce										
Federal or Central government	..	360	..	..	..	..	..	..	..	..
State/Regional	..	..	..	..	..	..	..	..	..	..
Local government	..	410	..	..	..	..	..	..	..	..
Social Security Funds	..	0	..	..	..	..	..	..	..	..
Total	**0**	**770**	**0**	**0**	**0**	**0**	**0**	**0**	**0**	**0**
2000+3000 Total	**170**	**2 616**	**4 091**	**6 070**	**10 741**	**11 853**	**11 762**	**12 379**	**15 236**	**16 140**
United States, million USD										
2000 Social security contributions										
Federal or Central government	301	2 053	9 059	11 323	19 628	25 434	25 938	26 803	28 485	29 202
State/Regional	699	7 585	19 802	32 814	44 061	45 936	46 832	49 105	56 812	59 775
Local government	0	0	0	0	0	0	0	0	0	0
Social Security Funds	0	0	0	0	0	0	0	0	0	0
Total	**1 000**	**9 638**	**28 861**	**44 137**	**63 689**	**71 370**	**72 770**	**75 908**	**85 297**	**88 977**
3000 Taxes on payroll and workforce										
Federal or Central government	..	..	..	..	..	..	..	..	..	..
State/Regional	..	..	..	..	..	..	..	..	..	..
Local government	..	..	..	..	..	..	..	..	..	..
Social Security Funds	..	..	..	..	..	..	..	..	..	..
Total	**0**	**0**	**0**	**0**	**0**	**0**	**0**	**0**	**0**	**0**
2000+3000 Total	**1 000**	**9 638**	**28 861**	**44 137**	**63 689**	**71 370**	**72 770**	**75 908**	**85 297**	**88 977**

.. Not available

1. The multi-jurisdictional sector contains units where jurisdiction is shared between two or more governments, or classification of a unit to a jurisdiction is otherwise unclear. The main type of units currently falling into this category is public universities.

2. There is a break in the series in 1990. The data are based on ESA 2010 from that year onwards.

StatLink https://stat.link/pizawe

6 Tax revenues by subsectors of general government

Chapter 6 provides information on tax revenues by subsectors of general government for each OECD country.

6.1. Country tables 1975, 1985, 1995, 2005 and 2020

This chapter presents detailed country information on tax revenues by level of government. The data have been attributed to the sub-sectors of general government identified in section A.12 of the Interpretative Guide (see Annex A) and the attribution criteria used are those set out in that guide.

Table 6.1. Australia, tax revenues by sub-sectors of government

Million AUD

	Federal government					State/Regional				
	1975	1995	2005	2015	2020	1975	1995	2005	2015	2020
1000 Taxes on income, profits and capital gains	**11 831**	**82 615**	**175 695**	**261 345**	**348 274**	**0**	**0**	**0**	**0**	**0**
1100 Of individuals	9 213	60 602	118 239	191 720	236 926	..	..	..	..	..
1200 Corporate	2 618	22 013	57 456	69 625	111 348	..	..	..	..	..
1300 Unallocable between 1100 and 1200	0	0	0	0	0	0	..	..	..	..
2000 Social security contributions	**0**	**0**	**0**	**0**	**0**	**0**	**0**	**0**	**0**	**0**
2100 Employees	0	0	0	0	0	0	0	0	0	0
2200 Employers	0	0	0	0	0	0	0	0	0	0
2300 Self-employed or non-employed	0	0	0	0	0	0	0	0	0	0
2400 Unallocable between 2100, 2200 and 2300	0	0	0	0	0	0	0	0	0	0
3000 Taxes on payroll and workforce	**54**	**3 065**	**369**	**670**	**1 683**	**1 171**	**7 120**	**13 095**	**22 684**	**24 700**
4000 Taxes on property	**103**	**8**	**14**	**15**	**15**	**883**	**7 988**	**16 940**	**32 533**	**39 405**
4100 Recurrent taxes on immovable property	12	0	0	0	0	217	1 840	4 559	10 029	14 382
4200 Recurrent taxes on net wealth	0	0	0	0	0	0	0	0	0	0
4300 Estate, inheritance and gift taxes	87	0	0	0	0	227	0	0	0	0
4400 Taxes on financial and capital transactions	4	8	14	15	15	439	6 148	12 381	22 504	25 023
4500 Non-recurrent taxes	0	0	0	0	0	0	0	0	0	0
4600 Other recurrent taxes on property	0	0	0	0	0	0	0	0	0	0
5000 Taxes on goods and services	**4 932**	**30 004**	**68 710**	**103 455**	**127 682**	**1 262**	**13 295**	**14 479**	**23 407**	**28 882**
5100 Taxes on production, sale, transfer, etc	4 919	29 613	67 172	97 166	120 672	532	4 923	8 188	11 884	14 428
5110 General taxes	1 408	12 970	39 436	60 680	75 298	0	0	0	0	0
5120 Taxes on specific goods and services	3 511	16 643	27 736	36 486	45 374	532	4 923	8 188	11 884	14 428
5130 Unallocable between 5110 and 5120	0	0	0	0	0	0	0	0	0	0
5200 Taxes on use of goods and perform activities	13	391	1 538	6 289	7 010	730	8 372	6 291	11 523	14 454
5300 Unallocable between 5100 and 5200	0	0	0	0	0	0	0	0	0	0
6000 Other taxes	**0**	**0**	**0**	**0**	**0**	**0**	**0**	**0**	**0**	**0**
6100 Paid solely by business	..	..	..	..	..	..	..	..	..	..
6200 Other	..	..	..	..	..	..	..	..	..	..
Total tax revenue	**16 920**	**115 692**	**244 788**	**365 485**	**477 654**	**3 316**	**28 403**	**44 514**	**78 624**	**92 987**

	Local government					Social Security Funds				
	1975	1995	2005	2015	2020	1975	1995	2005	2015	2020
1000 Taxes on income, profits and capital gains	**0**	**0**	**0**	**0**	**0**	**0**	**0**	**0**	**0**	**0**
1100 Of individuals	..	..	..	..	..	..	..	..	..	..
1200 Corporate	..	..	..	..	..	..	..	..	..	..
1300 Unallocable between 1100 and 1200	0	..	..	..	..	0	..	..	..	..
2000 Social security contributions	**0**	**0**	**0**	**0**	**0**	**0**	**0**	**0**	**0**	**0**
2100 Employees	0	0	0	0	0	0	0	0	0	0
2200 Employers	0	0	0	0	0	0	0	0	0	0
2300 Self-employed or non-employed	0	0	0	0	0	0	0	0	0	0
2400 Unallocable between 2100, 2200 and 2300	0	0	0	0	0	0	0	0	0	0
3000 Taxes on payroll and workforce	**0**	**0**	**0**	**0**	**0**	**0**	**0**	**0**	**0**	**0**
4000 Taxes on property	**883**	**5 134**	**8 726**	**16 620**	**20 089**	**0**	**0**	**0**	**0**	**0**
4100 Recurrent taxes on immovable property	883	5 134	8 726	16 620	20 089	..	..	..	..	..
4200 Recurrent taxes on net wealth	0	0	0	0	0	..	..	..	..	..
4300 Estate, inheritance and gift taxes	0	0	0	0	0	..	..	..	..	..
4400 Taxes on financial and capital transactions	0	0	0	0	0	..	..	..	..	..
4500 Non-recurrent taxes	0	0	0	0	0	..	..	..	..	..
4600 Other recurrent taxes on property	0	0	0	0	0	..	..	..	..	..
5000 Taxes on goods and services	**0**	**0**	**0**	**0**	**0**	**0**	**0**	**0**	**0**	**0**
5100 Taxes on production, sale, transfer, etc	0	0	0	0	0	0	0	0	0	0
5110 General taxes	0	0	0	0	0	0	0	0	0	0
5120 Taxes on specific goods and services	0	0	0	0	0	0	0	0	0	0
5130 Unallocable between 5110 and 5120	0	0	0	0	0	0	0	0	0	0
5200 Taxes on use of goods and perform activities	0	0	0	0	0	0	0	0	0	0
5300 Unallocable between 5100 and 5200	0	0	0	0	0	0	0	0	0	0
6000 Other taxes	**0**	**0**	**0**	**0**	**0**	**0**	**0**	**0**	**0**	**0**
6100 Paid solely by business	..	..	..	..	..	..	..	..	..	..
6200 Other	..	..	..	..	..	..	..	..	..	..
Total tax revenue	**883**	**5 134**	**8 726**	**16 620**	**20 089**	**0**	**0**	**0**	**0**	**0**

.. Not available

StatLink https://stat.link/rtkqp9

Table 6.2. Austria, tax revenues by sub-sectors of government

Million EUR

	Federal government					State/Regional				
	1975	1995	2005	2015	2020	1975	1995	2005	2015	2020
1000 Taxes on income, profits and capital gains	**3 064**	**18 452**	**28 781**	**43 714**	**43 344**	**865**	**547**	**742**	**1 081**	**1 253**
1100 Of individuals	2 381	14 649	22 126	34 901	34 467	834	459	637	941	1 129
1200 Corporate	655	2 267	5 341	7 519	8 058	31	88	104	141	125
1300 Unallocable between 1100 and 1200	27	1 536	1 313	1 295	819	0	0	0	0	0
2000 Social security contributions	**352**	**4 243**	**5 720**	**7 547**	**8 368**	**34**	**311**	**409**	**496**	**448**
2100 Employees	225	2 379	2 978	3 911	4 314	34	310	395	465	415
2200 Employers	127	1 830	2 498	3 350	3 776	0	0	0	0	0
2300 Self-employed or non-employed	0	34	243	286	278	0	1	14	31	33
2400 Unallocable between 2100, 2200 and 2300	0	0	0	0	0	0	0	0	0	0
3000 Taxes on payroll and workforce	**1 217**	**3 394**	**4 384**	**6 861**	**5 683**	**0**	**132**	**156**	**203**	**1 077**
4000 Taxes on property	**282**	**655**	**801**	**1 247**	**1 378**	**35**	**31**	**36**	**44**	**49**
4100 Recurrent taxes on immovable property	18	32	32	43	44	15	31	36	44	49
4200 Recurrent taxes on net wealth	226	58	0	0	0	10	0	0	0	0
4300 Estate, inheritance and gift taxes	24	82	140	12	0	10	0	0	0	0
4400 Taxes on financial and capital transactions	14	483	629	1 116	1 320	0	0	0	0	0
4500 Non-recurrent taxes	0	0	0	76	14	0	0	0	0	0
4600 Other recurrent taxes on property	0	0	0	0	0	0	0	0	0	0
5000 Taxes on goods and services	**4 554**	**19 894**	**29 646**	**39 720**	**42 196**	**1 013**	**222**	**234**	**362**	**424**
5100 Taxes on production, sale, transfer, etc	4 549	18 639	27 613	36 693	38 561	926	158	139	216	265
5110 General taxes	2 545	13 436	19 421	26 282	28 437	662	0	0	0	0
5120 Taxes on specific goods and services	1 991	5 159	8 148	10 408	10 122	264	158	139	216	265
5130 Unallocable between 5110 and 5120	14	44	45	4	2	0	0	0	0	0
5200 Taxes on use of goods and perform activities	5	1 255	2 033	3 027	3 635	87	64	95	146	159
5300 Unallocable between 5100 and 5200	0	0	0	0	0	0	0	0	0	0
6000 Other taxes	**52**	**486**	**699**	**517**	**526**	**8**	**50**	**61**	**91**	**90**
6100 Paid solely by business	..	..	..	..	..	..	..	..	..	..
6200 Other	..	..	..	..	..	..	..	..	..	..
Total tax revenue	**9 521**	**47 124**	**70 031**	**99 606**	**101 496**	**1 955**	**1 294**	**1 638**	**2 277**	**3 341**

	Local government					Social Security Funds				
	1975	1995	2005	2015	2020	1975	1995	2005	2015	2020
1000 Taxes on income, profits and capital gains	**887**	**46**	**0**	**0**	**0**	**0**	**0**	**0**	**0**	**0**
1100 Of individuals	771	19	0	0	..	..	..	..	..	..
1200 Corporate	115	26	0	0	..	..	..	..	..	..
1300 Unallocable between 1100 and 1200	0	0	0	0	..	..	..	..	..	..
2000 Social security contributions	**29**	**258**	**267**	**266**	**238**	**4 667**	**21 173**	**28 912**	**41 557**	**50 040**
2100 Employees	29	207	240	241	222	1 840	8 110	10 751	15 499	18 907
2200 Employers	0	50	27	26	17	2 375	10 912	14 037	19 906	23 940
2300 Self-employed or non-employed	0	0	0	0	0	453	2 151	4 125	6 153	7 193
2400 Unallocable between 2100, 2200 and 2300	0	0	0	0	0	0	0	0	0	0
3000 Taxes on payroll and workforce	**262**	**1 492**	**2 035**	**2 977**	**3 687**	**0**	**0**	**0**	**0**	**0**
4000 Taxes on property	**254**	**395**	**539**	**675**	**768**	**0**	**0**	**0**	**0**	**0**
4100 Recurrent taxes on immovable property	139	395	539	675	768	..	..	..	..	..
4200 Recurrent taxes on net wealth	35	0	0	0	0	..	..	..	..	..
4300 Estate, inheritance and gift taxes	0	0	0	0	0	..	..	..	..	..
4400 Taxes on financial and capital transactions	81	0	0	0	0	..	..	..	..	..
4500 Non-recurrent taxes	0	0	0	0	0	..	..	..	..	..
4600 Other recurrent taxes on property	0	0	0	0	0	..	..	..	..	..
5000 Taxes on goods and services	**792**	**738**	**302**	**353**	**354**	**0**	**0**	**0**	**0**	**0**
5100 Taxes on production, sale, transfer, etc	769	582	134	96	83	..	..	..	..	..
5110 General taxes	448	0	0	0	0	..	..	..	..	..
5120 Taxes on specific goods and services	321	582	134	96	83	..	..	..	..	..
5130 Unallocable between 5110 and 5120	0	0	0	0	0	..	..	..	..	..
5200 Taxes on use of goods and perform activities	24	155	168	258	271	..	..	..	..	..
5300 Unallocable between 5100 and 5200	0	0	0	0	0	..	..	..	..	..
6000 Other taxes	**55**	**60**	**103**	**129**	**71**	**0**	**0**	**0**	**0**	**0**
6100 Paid solely by business	..	..	..	..	..	..	..	..	..	..
6200 Other	..	..	..	..	..	..	..	..	..	..
Total tax revenue	**2 279**	**2 987**	**3 246**	**4 400**	**5 119**	**4 667**	**21 173**	**28 912**	**41 557**	**50 040**

.. Not available

Note: Including taxes collected on behalf of the European Union.

StatLink https://stat.link/ex4hto

Table 6.3. Belgium, tax revenues by sub-sectors of government

Million EUR

	Federal government					State/Regional				
	1975	1995	2005	2015	2020	1975	1995	2005	2015	2020
1000 Taxes on income, profits and capital gains	**8 534**	**30 905**	**45 859**	**57 131**	**53 663**	**..**	**79**	**0**	**4 283**	**10 574**
1100 Of individuals	6 929	25 997	36 007	43 436	38 654	..	79	..	4 283	10 574
1200 Corporate	1 596	4 867	9 811	13 644	14 941	..	0	..	0	0
1300 Unallocable between 1100 and 1200	10	41	42	51	68	..	0	..	0	0
2000 Social security contributions	**299**	**1 181**	**1 904**	**2 336**	**62**	**..**	**0**	**34**	**11**	**256**
2100 Employees	264	854	1 125	1 372	0	..	..	7	2	253
2200 Employers	36	228	608	715	62	..	..	27	9	3
2300 Self-employed or non-employed	0	99	171	249	0	..	..	0	0	0
2400 Unallocable between 2100, 2200 and 2300	0	0	0	0	0	..	..	0	0	0
3000 Taxes on payroll and workforce	**0**	**0**	**0**	**0**	**0**	**..**	**0**	**0**	**0**	**0**
4000 Taxes on property	**583**	**1 340**	**873**	**1 861**	**2 064**	**..**	**1 168**	**4 669**	**7 087**	**7 646**
4100 Recurrent taxes on immovable property	12	25	41	41	50	..	83	192	249	399
4200 Recurrent taxes on net wealth	0	8	189	661	984	..	0	0	0	0
4300 Estate, inheritance and gift taxes	178	42	0	0	0	..	647	1 749	2 996	2 967
4400 Taxes on financial and capital transactions	393	1 193	521	596	701	..	438	2 728	3 763	4 260
4500 Non-recurrent taxes	0	73	123	563	301	..	0	0	79	20
4600 Other recurrent taxes on property	0	0	0	0	27	..	0	0	0	0
5000 Taxes on goods and services	**5 813**	**20 951**	**29 984**	**39 004**	**41 055**	**..**	**412**	**2 044**	**2 678**	**3 000**
5100 Taxes on production, sale, transfer, etc	5 562	19 767	29 742	38 985	41 012	..	58	76	227	317
5110 General taxes	3 776	13 894	21 533	27 952	29 761	..	0	0	0	0
5120 Taxes on specific goods and services	1 785	5 872	8 208	11 034	11 250	..	58	76	227	317
5130 Unallocable between 5110 and 5120	0	0	0	0	0	..	0	0	0	0
5200 Taxes on use of goods and perform activities	249	1 178	234	10	32	..	355	1 968	2 451	2 682
5300 Unallocable between 5100 and 5200	3	6	8	9	12	..	0	0	0	0
6000 Other taxes	**0**	**0**	**0**	**0**	**0**	**..**	**0**	**68**	**40**	**0**
6100 Paid solely by business	..	..	..	..	..	..	..	0	0	..
6200 Other	..	..	..	..	..	..	..	68	40	..
Total tax revenue	**15 230**	**54 377**	**78 621**	**100 332**	**96 844**	**..**	**1 659**	**6 816**	**14 099**	**21 476**

	Local government					Social Security Funds				
	1975	1995	2005	2015	2020	1975	1995	2005	2015	2020
1000 Taxes on income, profits and capital gains	**683**	**3 058**	**2 249**	**3 052**	**3 653**	**0**	**335**	**825**	**1 106**	**1 223**
1100 Of individuals	675	3 058	2 249	3 052	3 653	..	335	825	1 106	1 223
1200 Corporate	8	0	0	0	0	..	0	0	0	0
1300 Unallocable between 1100 and 1200	0	0	0	0	0	..	0	0	0	0
2000 Social security contributions	**27**	**80**	**20**	**27**	**19**	**6 709**	**28 479**	**39 537**	**56 438**	**61 939**
2100 Employees	27	80	18	21	19	1 749	8 268	11 558	15 640	18 574
2200 Employers	0	0	3	6	0	4 347	17 746	24 613	35 510	37 261
2300 Self-employed or non-employed	0	0	0	0	0	612	2 465	3 366	5 289	6 104
2400 Unallocable between 2100, 2200 and 2300	0	0	0	0	0	0	0	0	0	0
3000 Taxes on payroll and workforce	**0**	**0**	**0**	**0**	**0**	**0**	**0**	**5**	**8**	**5**
4000 Taxes on property	**154**	**815**	**3 599**	**5 142**	**5 608**	**0**	**121**	**229**	**318**	**297**
4100 Recurrent taxes on immovable property	154	815	3 599	5 142	5 608	..	0	0	0	0
4200 Recurrent taxes on net wealth	0	0	0	0	0	..	0	0	0	0
4300 Estate, inheritance and gift taxes	0	0	0	0	0	..	0	0	0	0
4400 Taxes on financial and capital transactions	0	0	0	0	0	..	0	0	0	0
4500 Non-recurrent taxes	0	0	0	0	0	..	0	0	0	0
4600 Other recurrent taxes on property	0	0	0	0	0	..	121	229	318	297
5000 Taxes on goods and services	**166**	**332**	**523**	**715**	**639**	**14**	**330**	**1 237**	**1 520**	**1 608**
5100 Taxes on production, sale, transfer, etc	150	295	437	694	615	14	330	1 237	1 520	1 608
5110 General taxes	0	0	0	0	0	0	29	373	219	247
5120 Taxes on specific goods and services	150	295	437	694	615	14	301	865	1 302	1 361
5130 Unallocable between 5110 and 5120	0	0	0	0	0	0	0	0	0	0
5200 Taxes on use of goods and perform activities	16	37	87	22	24	0	0	0	0	0
5300 Unallocable between 5100 and 5200	0	0	0	0	0	0	0	0	0	0
6000 Other taxes	**0**	**0**	**0**	**0**	**0**	**0**	**0**	**0**	**0**	**0**
6100 Paid solely by business	..	..	..	..	..	..	..	..	..	..
6200 Other	..	..	..	..	..	..	..	..	..	..
Total tax revenue	**1 029**	**4 284**	**6 392**	**8 937**	**9 919**	**6 723**	**29 265**	**41 833**	**59 391**	**65 072**

.. Not available

Note: Including taxes collected on behalf of the European Union.

StatLink https://stat.link/sj4rl5

Table 6.4. Canada, tax revenues by sub-sectors of government

Million CAD

	Federal government					State/Regional				
	1975	1995	2005	2015	2020	1975	1995	2005	2015	2020
1000 Taxes on income, profits and capital gains	**19 047**	**82 237**	**140 013**	**191 684**	**228 269**	**8 165**	**52 373**	**78 331**	**123 157**	**148 240**
1100 Of individuals	12 822	65 384	102 366	143 315	164 902	6 074	43 428	62 435	96 989	113 953
1200 Corporate	5 741	14 739	32 197	41 726	55 216	2 091	8 944	15 896	26 168	34 287
1300 Unallocable between 1100 and 1200	484	2 114	5 450	6 643	8 151	0	0	0	0	0
2000 Social security contributions	**0**	**0**	**17 936**	**23 603**	**22 575**	**0**	**0**	**11 759**	**13 892**	**13 680**
2100 Employees	..	..	7 429	9 772	9 331	..	..	1 858	1 128	1 325
2200 Employers	..	..	10 507	13 831	13 244	..	..	9 901	12 764	12 355
2300 Self-employed or non-employed	..	..	0	0	0	..	..	0	0	0
2400 Unallocable between 2100, 2200 and 2300	..	..	0	0	0	..	..	0	0	0
3000 Taxes on payroll and workforce	**0**	**0**	**0**	**0**	**0**	**0**	**6 498**	**9 230**	**13 256**	**17 360**
4000 Taxes on property	**13**	**0**	**0**	**0**	**0**	**428**	**6 492**	**9 298**	**11 809**	**15 383**
4100 Recurrent taxes on immovable property	0	..	..	..	..	85	2 960	2 934	5 410	6 674
4200 Recurrent taxes on net wealth	0	..	..	..	..	200	2 914	3 456	372	460
4300 Estate, inheritance and gift taxes	13	..	..	..	..	143	3	0	268	339
4400 Taxes on financial and capital transactions	0	..	..	..	..	0	0	1 965	3 912	6 297
4500 Non-recurrent taxes	0	..	..	..	..	0	615	943	1 847	1 613
4600 Other recurrent taxes on property	0	..	..	..	..	0	0	0	0	0
5000 Taxes on goods and services	**8 180**	**31 160**	**48 551**	**53 837**	**60 000**	**10 128**	**42 076**	**67 537**	**95 289**	**101 559**
5100 Taxes on production, sale, transfer, etc	8 180	31 136	48 506	53 797	59 964	6 800	37 961	61 316	86 827	92 283
5110 General taxes	3 504	19 167	35 069	36 958	40 979	3 664	21 328	33 353	53 577	61 702
5120 Taxes on specific goods and services	4 676	11 969	13 437	16 839	18 985	3 136	16 633	27 963	33 250	30 582
5130 Unallocable between 5110 and 5120	0	0	0	0	0	0	0	0	0	0
5200 Taxes on use of goods and perform activities	0	24	45	40	36	3 328	4 115	6 221	8 462	9 276
5300 Unallocable between 5100 and 5200	0	0	0	0	0	0	0	0	0	0
6000 Other taxes	**198**	**0**	**0**	**0**	**0**	**0**	**0**	**0**	**0**	**0**
6100 Paid solely by business	0	..	..	..	..	..	..	..	..	..
6200 Other	198	..	..	..	..	..	..	..	..	..
Total tax revenue	**27 438**	**113 397**	**206 500**	**269 124**	**310 845**	**18 721**	**107 439**	**176 156**	**257 403**	**296 222**

	Local government					Social Security Funds				
	1975	1995	2005	2015	2020	1975	1995	2005	2015	2020
1000 Taxes on income, profits and capital gains	**0**	**0**	**0**	**0**	**0**	**0**	**0**	**0**	**0**	**0**
1100 Of individuals	..	..	..	..	..	..	..	..	..	..
1200 Corporate	..	..	..	..	..	..	..	..	..	..
1300 Unallocable between 1100 and 1200	..	..	..	..	..	..	..	..	..	..
2000 Social security contributions	**0**	**0**	**0**	**0**	**0**	**5 787**	**40 559**	**38 834**	**58 876**	**71 611**
2100 Employees	..	..	..	..	..	2 142	15 028	18 328	27 785	33 804
2200 Employers	..	..	..	..	..	3 527	24 765	18 328	27 785	33 804
2300 Self-employed or non-employed	..	..	..	..	..	118	766	2 177	3 307	4 002
2400 Unallocable between 2100, 2200 and 2300	..	..	..	..	..	0	0	0	0	0
3000 Taxes on payroll and workforce	**0**	**0**	**0**	**0**	**0**	**0**	**0**	**0**	**0**	**0**
4000 Taxes on property	**5 018**	**24 415**	**40 495**	**65 969**	**75 228**	**0**	**0**	**0**	**0**	**0**
4100 Recurrent taxes on immovable property	4 770	23 150	37 409	57 241	65 524	..	..	..	..	..
4200 Recurrent taxes on net wealth	0	0	0	0	0	..	..	..	..	..
4300 Estate, inheritance and gift taxes	0	0	0	0	0	..	..	..	..	..
4400 Taxes on financial and capital transactions	0	0	375	1 063	1 641	..	..	..	..	..
4500 Non-recurrent taxes	248	1 265	2 711	7 665	8 063	..	..	..	..	..
4600 Other recurrent taxes on property	0	0	0	0	0	..	..	..	..	..
5000 Taxes on goods and services	**142**	**406**	**833**	**1 149**	**1 221**	**0**	**0**	**0**	**0**	**0**
5100 Taxes on production, sale, transfer, etc	22	51	104	126	127	..	..	..	..	..
5110 General taxes	10	40	88	63	47	..	..	..	..	..
5120 Taxes on specific goods and services	12	11	16	63	80	..	..	..	..	..
5130 Unallocable between 5110 and 5120	0	0	0	0	0	..	..	..	..	..
5200 Taxes on use of goods and perform activities	120	355	729	1 023	1 094	..	..	..	..	..
5300 Unallocable between 5100 and 5200	0	0	0	0	0	..	..	..	..	..
6000 Other taxes	**525**	**3 662**	**1 483**	**748**	**867**	**0**	**0**	**0**	**0**	**0**
6100 Paid solely by business	437	2 946	541	0	0	..	..	..	..	..
6200 Other	88	716	942	748	867	..	..	..	..	..
Total tax revenue	**5 685**	**28 483**	**42 811**	**67 866**	**77 316**	**5 787**	**40 559**	**38 834**	**58 876**	**71 611**

.. Not available

StatLink https://stat.link/ys5xvc

Table 6.5. Chile, tax revenues by sub-sectors of government

Million CLP

	Central government					State/Regional				
	1975	1995	2005	2015	2020	1975	1995	2005	2015	2020
1000 Taxes on income, profits and capital gains	..	**1 359 694**	**5 171 293**	**11 840 521**	**12 540 342**	..	..	..	..	..
1100 Of individuals	..	281 293	738 620	3 199 876	3 976 009	..	..	..	..	..
1200 Corporate	..	836 725	3 155 480	6 839 133	9 429 787	..	..	..	..	..
1300 Unallocable between 1100 and 1200	..	241 676	1 277 193	1 801 512	-865 454	..	..	..	..	..
2000 Social security contributions	..	**155 855**	**287 422**	**434 659**	**510 829**	..	..	..	..	..
2100 Employees	..	142 001	249 526	370 745	399 998	..	..	..	..	..
2200 Employers	..	13 854	37 896	63 914	110 830	..	..	..	..	..
2300 Self-employed or non-employed	..	0	0	0	0	..	..	..	..	..
2400 Unallocable between 2100, 2200 and 2300	..	0	0	0	0	..	..	..	..	..
3000 Taxes on payroll and workforce	..	**0**	**0**	**0**	**0**	..	..	..	..	..
4000 Taxes on property	..	**181 432**	**490 120**	**379 603**	**534 971**	..	..	..	..	..
4100 Recurrent taxes on immovable property	..	13 044	4 909	15 249	25 367	..	..	..	..	..
4200 Recurrent taxes on net wealth	..	0	0	0	0	..	..	..	..	..
4300 Estate, inheritance and gift taxes	..	13 245	23 184	92 236	155 433	..	..	..	..	..
4400 Taxes on financial and capital transactions	..	155 143	462 027	272 118	354 171	..	..	..	..	..
4500 Non-recurrent taxes	..	0	0	0	0	..	..	..	..	..
4600 Other recurrent taxes on property	..	0	0	0	0	..	..	..	..	..
5000 Taxes on goods and services	..	**3 179 304**	**6 831 482**	**16 182 903**	**19 422 146**	..	..	..	..	..
5100 Taxes on production, sale, transfer, etc	..	3 169 645	6 811 389	16 131 136	19 209 620	..	..	..	..	..
5110 General taxes	..	2 187 602	5 391 285	13 273 958	15 963 032	..	..	..	..	..
5120 Taxes on specific goods and services	..	982 043	1 420 104	2 857 178	3 246 588	..	..	..	..	..
5130 Unallocable between 5110 and 5120	..	0	0	0	0	..	..	..	..	..
5200 Taxes on use of goods and perform activities	..	9 659	20 094	51 767	212 526	..	..	..	..	..
5300 Unallocable between 5100 and 5200	..	0	0	0	0	..	..	..	..	..
6000 Other taxes	..	**-29 554**	**-85 954**	**-579 303**	**-175 017**	..	..	..	..	..
6100 Paid solely by business	..	0	0	0	0	..	..	..	..	..
6200 Other	..	-29 554	-85 954	-579 303	-175 017	..	..	..	..	..
Total tax revenue	..	**4 846 730**	**12 694 362**	**28 258 382**	**32 833 271**	..	..	..	..	..

	Local government					Social Security Funds				
	1975	1995	2005	2015	2020	1975	1995	2005	2015	2020
1000 Taxes on income, profits and capital gains	..	**0**	**0**	**0**	**0**	..	**0**	**0**	**0**	**0**
1100 Of individuals	..	..	..	..	..	..	..	..	..	..
1200 Corporate	..	..	..	..	..	..	..	..	..	..
1300 Unallocable between 1100 and 1200	..	..	..	..	..	..	..	..	..	..
2000 Social security contributions	..	**0**	**0**	**0**	**0**	..	**193 269**	**644 295**	**1 817 831**	**2 594 038**
2100 Employees	..	..	..	..	..	..	193 269	644 295	1 817 831	2 594 038
2200 Employers	..	..	..	..	..	..	0	0	0	0
2300 Self-employed or non-employed	..	..	..	..	..	..	0	0	0	0
2400 Unallocable between 2100, 2200 and 2300	..	..	..	..	..	..	0	0	0	0
3000 Taxes on payroll and workforce	..	**0**	**0**	**0**	**0**	..	**0**	**0**	**0**	**0**
4000 Taxes on property	..	**157 193**	**411 656**	**1 041 671**	**1 536 950**	..	**0**	**0**	**0**	**0**
4100 Recurrent taxes on immovable property	..	157 193	411 656	1 041 671	1 536 950	..	..	..	..	..
4200 Recurrent taxes on net wealth	..	0	0	0	0	..	..	..	..	..
4300 Estate, inheritance and gift taxes	..	0	0	0	0	..	..	..	..	..
4400 Taxes on financial and capital transactions	..	0	0	0	0	..	..	..	..	..
4500 Non-recurrent taxes	..	0	0	0	0	..	..	..	..	..
4600 Other recurrent taxes on property	..	0	0	0	0	..	..	..	..	..
5000 Taxes on goods and services	..	**192 325**	**514 952**	**1 415 658**	**1 852 967**	..	**0**	**0**	**0**	**0**
5100 Taxes on production, sale, transfer, etc	..	52 690	140 703	385 532	404 630	..	..	..	..	..
5110 General taxes	..	0	0	0	0	..	..	..	..	..
5120 Taxes on specific goods and services	..	52 690	140 703	385 532	404 630	..	..	..	..	..
5130 Unallocable between 5110 and 5120	..	0	0	0	0	..	..	..	..	..
5200 Taxes on use of goods and perform activities	..	139 635	374 249	1 030 126	1 448 337	..	..	..	..	..
5300 Unallocable between 5100 and 5200	..	0	0	0	0	..	..	..	..	..
6000 Other taxes	..	**0**	**0**	**0**	**0**	..	**0**	**0**	**0**	**0**
6100 Paid solely by business	..	..	..	..	..	..	..	..	..	..
6200 Other	..	..	..	..	..	..	..	..	..	..
Total tax revenue	..	**349 518**	**926 608**	**2 457 329**	**3 389 917**	..	**193 269**	**644 295**	**1 817 831**	**2 594 038**

.. Not available

StatLink https://stat.link/isdbax

Table 6.6. Colombia, tax revenues by sub-sectors of government

Million COP

	Federal government					State/Regional				
	1975	1995	2005	2015	2020	1975	1995	2005	2015	2020
1000 Taxes on income, profits and capital gains	..	**3 393 700**	**17 348 618**	**52 656 876**	**61 812 525**	..	**0**	**0**	**0**	**0**
1100 Of individuals	..	131 405	3 594 441	9 219 350	14 469 873	..	..	..	..	..
1200 Corporate	..	988 082	13 044 361	41 409 107	43 240 197	..	..	..	..	..
1300 Unallocable between 1100 and 1200	..	2 274 213	709 816	2 028 420	4 102 455	..	..	..	..	..
2000 Social security contributions	..	**0**	**0**	**0**	**0**	..	**0**	**0**	**0**	**0**
2100 Employees	..	..	..	..	..	..	..	..	..	..
2200 Employers	..	..	..	..	..	..	..	..	..	..
2300 Self-employed or non-employed	..	..	..	..	..	..	..	..	..	..
2400 Unallocable between 2100, 2200 and 2300	..	..	..	..	..	..	..	..	..	..
3000 Taxes on payroll and workforce	..	**599 198**	**2 179 842**	**2 797 308**	**3 670 490**	..	**0**	**0**	**0**	**0**
4000 Taxes on property	..	**0**	**2 863 946**	**12 094 140**	**9 057 760**	..	**0**	**0**	**0**	**0**
4100 Recurrent taxes on immovable property	..	..	0	0	0	..	..	..	..	..
4200 Recurrent taxes on net wealth	..	..	462 720	5 352 940	957 137	..	..	..	..	..
4300 Estate, inheritance and gift taxes	..	..	0	0	0	..	..	..	..	..
4400 Taxes on financial and capital transactions	..	..	2 401 226	6 741 200	7 476 295	..	..	..	..	..
4500 Non-recurrent taxes	..	..	0	0	624 327	..	..	..	..	..
4600 Other recurrent taxes on property	..	..	0	0	0	..	..	..	..	..
5000 Taxes on goods and services	..	**4 773 500**	**21 645 318**	**51 831 190**	**60 110 745**	..	**771 560**	**2 507 423**	**4 986 314**	**6 575 397**
5100 Taxes on production, sale, transfer, etc	..	4 773 500	21 645 318	51 831 190	60 110 745	..	771 560	2 228 909	4 456 650	5 548 940
5110 General taxes	..	3 427 600	17 427 948	41 659 696	53 912 648	..	0	0	0	0
5120 Taxes on specific goods and services	..	1 345 900	4 217 370	10 171 494	6 198 096	..	771 560	2 228 909	4 456 650	5 548 940
5130 Unallocable between 5110 and 5120	..	0	0	0	0	..	0	0	0	0
5200 Taxes on use of goods and perform activities	..	0	0	0	0	..	0	278 514	529 665	1 026 457
5300 Unallocable between 5100 and 5200	..	0	0	0	0	..	0	0	0	0
6000 Other taxes	..	**17 900**	**682 084**	**419 939**	**286 914**	..	**0**	**575 919**	**2 624 769**	**2 519 571**
6100 Paid solely by business	..	0	0	0	0	..	..	0	0	0
6200 Other	..	17 900	682 084	419 939	286 914	..	..	575 919	2 624 769	2 519 571
Total tax revenue	..	**8 784 297**	**44 719 808**	**119 799 453**	**134 938 434**	..	**771 560**	**3 083 342**	**7 611 084**	**9 094 967**

	Local government					Social Security Funds				
	1975	1995	2005	2015	2020	1975	1995	2005	2015	2020
1000 Taxes on income, profits and capital gains	..	**0**	**0**	**0**	**0**	..	**0**	**0**	**0**	**0**
1100 Of individuals	..	..	..	..	..	..	..	..	..	..
1200 Corporate	..	..	..	..	..	..	..	..	..	..
1300 Unallocable between 1100 and 1200	..	..	..	..	..	..	..	..	..	..
2000 Social security contributions	..	**0**	**0**	**0**	**0**	..	**3 159 328**	**7 845 000**	**13 585 138**	**18 615 408**
2100 Employees	..	..	..	..	..	..	..	..	..	..
2200 Employers	..	..	..	..	..	..	..	..	..	..
2300 Self-employed or non-employed	..	..	..	..	..	..	..	..	..	..
2400 Unallocable between 2100, 2200 and 2300	..	..	..	..	..	..	3 159 328	7 845 000	13 585 138	18 615 408
3000 Taxes on payroll and workforce	..	**0**	**0**	**0**	**0**	..	**0**	**0**	**0**	**0**
4000 Taxes on property	..	**365 051**	**1 974 213**	**6 061 965**	**9 109 598**	..	**0**	**0**	**0**	**0**
4100 Recurrent taxes on immovable property	..	365 051	1 974 213	6 061 965	9 109 598	..	..	..	..	..
4200 Recurrent taxes on net wealth	..	0	0	0	0	..	..	..	..	..
4300 Estate, inheritance and gift taxes	..	0	0	0	0	..	..	..	..	..
4400 Taxes on financial and capital transactions	..	0	0	0	0	..	..	..	..	..
4500 Non-recurrent taxes	..	0	0	0	0	..	..	..	..	..
4600 Other recurrent taxes on property	..	0	0	0	0	..	..	..	..	..
5000 Taxes on goods and services	..	**471 710**	**3 496 411**	**8 899 062**	**11 066 402**	..	**0**	**0**	**0**	**0**
5100 Taxes on production, sale, transfer, etc	..	471 710	3 496 411	8 400 241	10 300 667	..	..	..	..	..
5110 General taxes	..	471 710	2 506 452	7 025 204	8 954 004	..	..	..	..	..
5120 Taxes on specific goods and services	..	0	989 959	1 375 037	1 346 662	..	..	..	..	..
5130 Unallocable between 5110 and 5120	..	0	0	0	0	..	..	..	..	..
5200 Taxes on use of goods and perform activities	..	0	0	498 821	765 735	..	..	..	..	..
5300 Unallocable between 5100 and 5200	..	0	0	0	0	..	..	..	..	..
6000 Other taxes	..	**355 943**	**588 614**	**4 200 992**	**4 839 779**	..	**0**	**0**	**0**	**0**
6100 Paid solely by business	..	0	0	0	0	..	..	..	..	..
6200 Other	..	355 943	588 614	4 200 992	4 839 779	..	..	..	..	..
Total tax revenue	..	**1 192 705**	**6 059 238**	**19 162 019**	**25 015 779**	..	**3 159 328**	**7 845 000**	**13 585 138**	**18 615 408**

.. Not available

StatLink https://stat.link/zovk0c

Table 6.7. Costa Rica, tax revenues by sub-sectors of government

Million CRC

	Central government					State/Regional				
	1975	1995	2005	2015	2020	1975	1995	2005	2015	2020
1000 Taxes on income, profits and capital gains	..	**47 678**	**324 224**	**1 247 308**	**1 651 249**	..	..	..	..	..
1100 Of individuals	..	..	16 438	386 241	556 084	..	..	..	..	..
1200 Corporate	..	..	288 355	659 951	692 551	..	..	..	..	..
1300 Unallocable between 1100 and 1200	..	47 678	19 430	201 116	402 613	..	..	..	..	..
2000 Social security contributions	..	**11 096**	**30 854**	**63 458**	**79 428**	..	..	..	..	..
2100 Employees	..	..	..	..	..	..	..	..	..	..
2200 Employers	..	0	0	0	0	..	..	..	..	..
2300 Self-employed or non-employed	..	..	..	..	..	..	..	..	..	..
2400 Unallocable between 2100, 2200 and 2300	..	11 096	30 854	63 458	79 428	..	..	..	..	..
3000 Taxes on payroll and workforce	..	**0**	**0**	**0**	**0**	..	..	..	..	..
4000 Taxes on property	..	**2 023**	**10 846**	**37 334**	**39 956**	..	..	..	..	..
4100 Recurrent taxes on immovable property	..	440	0	4 076	4 655	..	..	..	..	..
4200 Recurrent taxes on net wealth	..	0	0	0	0	..	..	..	..	..
4300 Estate, inheritance and gift taxes	..	0	0	0	0	..	..	..	..	..
4400 Taxes on financial and capital transactions	..	1 583	10 846	33 258	35 300	..	..	..	..	..
4500 Non-recurrent taxes	..	0	0	0	0	..	..	..	..	..
4600 Other recurrent taxes on property	..	0	0	0	0	..	..	..	..	..
5000 Taxes on goods and services	..	**185 943**	**917 118**	**2 536 562**	**2 611 481**	..	..	..	..	..
5100 Taxes on production, sale, transfer, etc	..	177 808	884 359	2 385 807	2 497 206	..	..	..	..	..
5110 General taxes	..	84 034	485 168	1 368 601	1 649 531	..	..	..	..	..
5120 Taxes on specific goods and services	..	93 774	399 192	1 017 206	847 675	..	..	..	..	..
5130 Unallocable between 5110 and 5120	..	0	0	0	0	..	..	..	..	..
5200 Taxes on use of goods and perform activities	..	8 135	32 758	150 755	114 275	..	..	..	..	..
5300 Unallocable between 5100 and 5200	..	0	0	0	0	..	..	..	..	..
6000 Other taxes	..	**11 010**	**54 338**	**162 200**	**166 912**	..	..	..	..	..
6100 Paid solely by business	..	0	0	0	0	..	..	..	..	..
6200 Other	..	11 010	54 338	162 200	166 912	..	..	..	..	..
Total tax revenue	..	**257 751**	**1 337 380**	**4 046 862**	**4 549 026**	..	..	..	..	..

	Local government					Social Security Funds				
	1975	1995	2005	2015	2020	1975	1995	2005	2015	2020
1000 Taxes on income, profits and capital gains	..	**0**	**0**	**0**	**0**	..	**0**	**0**	**0**	**0**
1100 Of individuals	..	..	..	..	..	..	..	..	..	..
1200 Corporate	..	..	..	..	..	..	..	..	..	..
1300 Unallocable between 1100 and 1200	..	..	..	..	..	..	..	..	..	..
2000 Social security contributions	..	**0**	**0**	**0**	**0**	..	**106 727**	**586 829**	**2 241 674**	**2 892 160**
2100 Employees	..	..	..	..	..	..	..	..	..	..
2200 Employers	..	..	..	..	..	..	14 654	84 988	318 652	387 840
2300 Self-employed or non-employed	..	..	..	..	..	..	..	..	..	..
2400 Unallocable between 2100, 2200 and 2300	..	..	..	..	..	..	92 073	501 841	1 923 022	2 504 321
3000 Taxes on payroll and workforce	..	**0**	**0**	**0**	**0**	..	**22 992**	**115 730**	**423 616**	**537 654**
4000 Taxes on property	..	**2 037**	**14 264**	**85 927**	**122 994**	..	**0**	**0**	**0**	**0**
4100 Recurrent taxes on immovable property	..	2 037	14 264	85 927	122 970	..	..	..	..	..
4200 Recurrent taxes on net wealth	..	0	0	0	0	..	..	..	..	..
4300 Estate, inheritance and gift taxes	..	0	0	0	0	..	..	..	..	..
4400 Taxes on financial and capital transactions	..	0	0	0	0	..	..	..	..	..
4500 Non-recurrent taxes	..	0	0	0	24	..	..	..	..	..
4600 Other recurrent taxes on property	..	0	0	0	0	..	..	..	..	..
5000 Taxes on goods and services	..	**1 214**	**27 506**	**125 341**	**133 636**	..	**0**	**0**	**0**	**0**
5100 Taxes on production, sale, transfer, etc	..	0	94	3 093	3 304	..	..	..	..	..
5110 General taxes	..	..	0	0	0	..	..	..	..	..
5120 Taxes on specific goods and services	..	..	94	3 093	3 304	..	..	..	..	..
5130 Unallocable between 5110 and 5120	..	..	0	0	0	..	..	..	..	..
5200 Taxes on use of goods and perform activities	..	1 214	27 411	122 248	130 332	..	..	..	..	..
5300 Unallocable between 5100 and 5200	..	0	0	0	0	..	..	..	..	..
6000 Other taxes	..	**2 935**	**3 207**	**155**	**58**	..	**0**	**0**	**0**	**0**
6100 Paid solely by business	..	0	0	0	0	..	..	..	..	..
6200 Other	..	2 935	3 207	155	58	..	..	..	..	..
Total tax revenue	..	**6 185**	**44 976**	**211 422**	**256 688**	..	**129 718**	**702 559**	**2 665 291**	**3 429 814**

.. Not available

StatLink https://stat.link/9y5clt

Table 6.8. Czech Republic, tax revenues by sub-sectors of government

Million CZK

	Central government[1]					State/Regional				
	1975	1995	2005	2015	2020	1975	1995	2005	2015	2020
1000 Taxes on income, profits and capital gains	..	**137 616**	**273 549**	**329 768**	**453 244**	..	..	..	..	..
1100 Of individuals	..	70 361	137 937	164 678	266 628	..	..	..	..	..
1200 Corporate	..	67 255	135 611	165 090	186 617	..	..	..	..	..
1300 Unallocable between 1100 and 1200	..	0	0	0	0	..	..	..	..	..
2000 Social security contributions	..	**0**	**0**	**0**	**0**	..	..	..	..	..
2100 Employees	..	..	..	..	..	..	..	..	..	..
2200 Employers	..	..	..	..	..	..	..	..	..	..
2300 Self-employed or non-employed	..	..	..	..	..	..	..	..	..	..
2400 Unallocable between 2100, 2200 and 2300	..	..	..	..	..	..	..	..	..	..
3000 Taxes on payroll and workforce	..	**0**	**0**	**0**	**0**	..	..	..	..	..
4000 Taxes on property	..	**3 857**	**8 050**	**11 607**	**35**	..	..	..	..	..
4100 Recurrent taxes on immovable property	..	0	5	20	26	..	..	..	..	..
4200 Recurrent taxes on net wealth	..	0	0	0	0	..	..	..	..	..
4300 Estate, inheritance and gift taxes	..	393	728	20	7	..	..	..	..	..
4400 Taxes on financial and capital transactions	..	3 464	7 317	11 566	3	..	..	..	..	..
4500 Non-recurrent taxes	..	0	0	0	0	..	..	..	..	..
4600 Other recurrent taxes on property	..	0	0	0	0	..	..	..	..	..
5000 Taxes on goods and services	..	**175 869**	**343 554**	**505 085**	**599 441**	..	..	..	..	..
5100 Taxes on production, sale, transfer, etc	..	162 913	325 662	487 086	580 114	..	..	..	..	..
5110 General taxes	..	91 673	215 118	333 274	422 479	..	..	..	..	..
5120 Taxes on specific goods and services	..	71 240	110 544	153 812	157 635	..	..	..	..	..
5130 Unallocable between 5110 and 5120	..	0	0	0	0	..	..	..	..	..
5200 Taxes on use of goods and perform activities	..	12 956	17 892	17 999	19 326	..	..	..	..	..
5300 Unallocable between 5100 and 5200	..	0	0	0	0	..	..	..	..	..
6000 Other taxes	..	**545**	**55**	**387**	**170**	..	..	..	..	..
6100 Paid solely by business	..	0	0	0	0	..	..	..	..	..
6200 Other	..	545	55	387	170	..	..	..	..	..
Total tax revenue	..	**317 887**	**625 207**	**846 847**	**1 052 890**	..	..	..	..	..

	Local government					Social Security Funds				
	1975	1995	2005	2015	2020	1975	1995	2005	2015	2020
1000 Taxes on income, profits and capital gains	..	**0**	**0**	**0**	**0**	..	**0**	**0**	**0**	**0**
1100 Of individuals	..	..	..	..	..	..	..	..	..	..
1200 Corporate	..	..	..	..	..	..	..	..	..	..
1300 Unallocable between 1100 and 1200	..	..	..	..	..	..	..	..	..	..
2000 Social security contributions	..	**0**	**0**	**0**	**0**	..	**227 871**	**481 626**	**659 743**	**901 670**
2100 Employees	..	..	..	..	..	..	54 536	108 316	133 878	187 733
2200 Employers	..	..	..	..	..	..	148 342	307 618	417 778	573 753
2300 Self-employed or non-employed	..	..	..	..	..	..	24 993	65 692	108 088	140 184
2400 Unallocable between 2100, 2200 and 2300	..	..	..	..	..	..	0	0	0	0
3000 Taxes on payroll and workforce	..	**0**	**0**	**0**	**0**	..	**0**	**0**	**0**	**0**
4000 Taxes on property	..	**3 778**	**4 987**	**10 313**	**11 580**	..	**0**	**0**	**0**	**0**
4100 Recurrent taxes on immovable property	..	3 778	4 987	10 313	11 580	..	..	..	..	..
4200 Recurrent taxes on net wealth	..	0	0	0	0	..	..	..	..	..
4300 Estate, inheritance and gift taxes	..	0	0	0	0	..	..	..	..	..
4400 Taxes on financial and capital transactions	..	0	0	0	0	..	..	..	..	..
4500 Non-recurrent taxes	..	0	0	0	0	..	..	..	..	..
4600 Other recurrent taxes on property	..	0	0	0	0	..	..	..	..	..
5000 Taxes on goods and services	..	**1 150**	**7 395**	**7 749**	**8 370**	..	**0**	**0**	**0**	**0**
5100 Taxes on production, sale, transfer, etc	..	124	199	292	151	..	..	..	..	..
5110 General taxes	..	0	0	0	0	..	..	..	..	..
5120 Taxes on specific goods and services	..	124	199	292	151	..	..	..	..	..
5130 Unallocable between 5110 and 5120	..	0	0	0	0	..	..	..	..	..
5200 Taxes on use of goods and perform activities	..	1 026	7 196	7 457	8 219	..	..	..	..	..
5300 Unallocable between 5100 and 5200	..	0	0	0	0	..	..	..	..	..
6000 Other taxes	..	**0**	**0**	**0**	**0**	..	**0**	**0**	**0**	**0**
6100 Paid solely by business	..	..	..	..	..	..	..	..	..	..
6200 Other	..	..	..	..	..	..	..	..	..	..
Total tax revenue	..	**4 928**	**12 382**	**18 063**	**19 950**	..	**227 871**	**481 626**	**659 743**	**901 670**

.. Not available

Note: Including taxes collected on behalf of the European Union.

1. Tax revenues of the regions are reported under the heading of central government up to and including 1995 and under local government thereafter.

StatLink https://stat.link/a6ykxs

Table 6.9. Denmark, tax revenues by sub-sectors of government

Million DKK

	Central government					State/Regional				
	1975	1995	2005	2015	2020	1975	1995	2005	2015	2020
1000 Taxes on income, profits and capital gains	**28 694**	**164 962**	**258 922**	**384 883**	**451 576**	**..**	**..**	**..**	**..**	**..**
1100 Of individuals	25 904	124 613	167 082	304 329	336 794	..	..	..	..	..
1200 Corporate	2 790	23 803	54 597	57 723	66 551	..	..	..	..	..
1300 Unallocable between 1100 and 1200	0	16 546	37 244	22 832	48 230	..	..	..	..	..
2000 Social security contributions	**143**	**562**	**1 180**	**836**	**758**	**..**	**..**	**..**	**..**	**..**
2100 Employees	0	559	1 177	826	751	..	..	..	..	..
2200 Employers	142	3	3	10	8	..	..	..	..	..
2300 Self-employed or non-employed	0	0	0	0	0	..	..	..	..	..
2400 Unallocable between 2100, 2200 and 2300	0	0	0	0	0	..	..	..	..	..
3000 Taxes on payroll and workforce	**0**	**2 262**	**2 907**	**5 894**	**4 203**	**..**	**..**	**..**	**..**	**..**
4000 Taxes on property	**1 779**	**7 094**	**11 801**	**11 084**	**14 048**	**..**	**..**	**..**	**..**	**..**
4100 Recurrent taxes on immovable property	16	170	0	0	0	..	..	..	..	..
4200 Recurrent taxes on net wealth	414	930	0	0	0	..	..	..	..	..
4300 Estate, inheritance and gift taxes	336	2 372	3 154	5 177	6 676	..	..	..	..	..
4400 Taxes on financial and capital transactions	936	3 584	8 613	5 907	7 372	..	..	..	..	..
4500 Non-recurrent taxes	77	38	34	0	0	..	..	..	..	..
4600 Other recurrent taxes on property	0	0	0	0	0	..	..	..	..	..
5000 Taxes on goods and services	**29 014**	**156 578**	**253 352**	**301 504**	**336 458**	**..**	**..**	**..**	**..**	**..**
5100 Taxes on production, sale, transfer, etc	27 338	149 393	239 951	277 791	311 776	..	..	..	..	..
5110 General taxes	15 117	94 368	154 654	191 479	231 628	..	..	..	..	..
5120 Taxes on specific goods and services	12 221	55 026	85 298	86 312	80 148	..	..	..	..	..
5130 Unallocable between 5110 and 5120	0	0	0	0	0	..	..	..	..	..
5200 Taxes on use of goods and perform activities	1 676	4 739	9 379	16 537	15 076	..	..	..	..	..
5300 Unallocable between 5100 and 5200	0	2 446	4 021	7 177	9 606	..	..	..	..	..
6000 Other taxes	**0**	**0**	**203**	**320**	**258**	**..**	**..**	**..**	**..**	**..**
6100 Paid solely by business	..	..	203	320	258	..	..	..	..	..
6200 Other	..	..	0	0	0	..	..	..	..	..
Total tax revenue	**59 630**	**331 457**	**528 366**	**704 520**	**807 301**	**..**	**..**	**..**	**..**	**..**
	Local government					Social Security Funds				
	1975	1995	2005	2015	2020	1975	1995	2005	2015	2020
1000 Taxes on income, profits and capital gains	**22 171**	**140 762**	**214 581**	**220 815**	**263 001**	**0**	**0**	**0**	**0**	**0**
1100 Of individuals	22 170	140 758	214 581	220 815	263 001	..	..	..	..	..
1200 Corporate	1	5	0	0	0	..	..	..	..	..
1300 Unallocable between 1100 and 1200	0	0	0	0	0	..	..	..	..	..
2000 Social security contributions	**0**	**0**	**0**	**0**	**0**	**58**	**0**	**529**	**542**	**601**
2100 Employees	..	..	..	..	..	0	..	0	0	0
2200 Employers	..	..	..	..	..	58	..	529	542	601
2300 Self-employed or non-employed	..	..	..	..	..	0	..	0	0	0
2400 Unallocable between 2100, 2200 and 2300	..	..	..	..	..	0	..	0	0	0
3000 Taxes on payroll and workforce	**0**	**0**	**0**	**0**	**0**	**0**	**0**	**0**	**0**	**0**
4000 Taxes on property	**3 518**	**10 155**	**17 466**	**28 085**	**31 581**	**0**	**0**	**0**	**0**	**0**
4100 Recurrent taxes on immovable property	3 518	10 155	17 466	28 085	31 581	..	..	..	..	..
4200 Recurrent taxes on net wealth	0	0	0	0	0	..	..	..	..	..
4300 Estate, inheritance and gift taxes	0	0	0	0	0	..	..	..	..	..
4400 Taxes on financial and capital transactions	0	0	0	0	0	..	..	..	..	..
4500 Non-recurrent taxes	0	0	0	0	0	..	..	..	..	..
4600 Other recurrent taxes on property	0	0	0	0	0	..	..	..	..	..
5000 Taxes on goods and services	**0**	**0**	**0**	**0**	**0**	**0**	**0**	**0**	**0**	**0**
5100 Taxes on production, sale, transfer, etc	0	..	..	..	..	..	..	..	..	..
5110 General taxes	0	..	..	..	..	..	..	..	..	..
5120 Taxes on specific goods and services	0	..	..	..	..	..	..	..	..	..
5130 Unallocable between 5110 and 5120	0	..	..	..	..	..	..	..	..	..
5200 Taxes on use of goods and perform activities	..	..	..	..	..	..	..	..	..	..
5300 Unallocable between 5100 and 5200	0	..	..	..	..	..	..	..	..	..
6000 Other taxes	**0**	**0**	**0**	**0**	**0**	**0**	**0**	**0**	**0**	**0**
6100 Paid solely by business	..	..	..	..	..	..	..	..	..	..
6200 Other	..	..	..	..	..	..	..	..	..	..
Total tax revenue	**25 689**	**150 918**	**232 047**	**248 900**	**294 582**	**58**	**0**	**529**	**542**	**601**

.. Not available

Note: Including taxes collected on behalf of the European Union.

StatLink https://stat.link/au27e5

Table 6.10. Estonia, tax revenues by sub-sectors of government

Million EUR

	Central government					State/Regional				
	1975	1995	2005	2015	2020	1975	1995	2005	2015	2020
1000 Taxes on income, profits and capital gains	**..**	**301**	**782**	**1 607**	**2 102**	**..**	**..**	**..**	**..**	**..**
1100 Of individuals	..	234	622	1 182	1 652	..	..	..	..	..
1200 Corporate	..	67	160	424	450	..	..	..	..	..
1300 Unallocable between 1100 and 1200	..	0	0	0	0	..	..	..	..	..
2000 Social security contributions	**..**	**191**	**636**	**1 191**	**1 744**	**..**	**..**	**..**	**..**	**..**
2100 Employees	..	0	0	0	0	..	..	..	..	..
2200 Employers	..	191	636	1 179	1 634	..	..	..	..	..
2300 Self-employed or non-employed	..	0	0	12	110	..	..	..	..	..
2400 Unallocable between 2100, 2200 and 2300	..	0	0	0	0	..	..	..	..	..
3000 Taxes on payroll and workforce	**..**	**0**	**0**	**0**	**0**	**..**	**..**	**..**	**..**	**..**
4000 Taxes on property	**..**	**3**	**0**	**0**	**0**	**..**	**..**	**..**	**..**	**..**
4100 Recurrent taxes on immovable property	..	3	..	..	..	..	..	..	..	..
4200 Recurrent taxes on net wealth	..	0	..	..	..	..	..	..	..	..
4300 Estate, inheritance and gift taxes	..	0	..	..	..	..	..	..	..	..
4400 Taxes on financial and capital transactions	..	0	..	..	..	..	..	..	..	..
4500 Non-recurrent taxes	..	0	..	..	..	..	..	..	..	..
4600 Other recurrent taxes on property	..	0	..	..	..	..	..	..	..	..
5000 Taxes on goods and services	**..**	**350**	**1 385**	**2 864**	**3 581**	**..**	**..**	**..**	**..**	**..**
5100 Taxes on production, sale, transfer, etc	..	345	1 348	2 790	3 383	..	..	..	..	..
5110 General taxes	..	266	908	1 873	2 439	..	..	..	..	..
5120 Taxes on specific goods and services	..	79	440	917	944	..	..	..	..	..
5130 Unallocable between 5110 and 5120	..	0	0	0	0	..	..	..	..	..
5200 Taxes on use of goods and perform activities	..	5	37	74	198	..	..	..	..	..
5300 Unallocable between 5100 and 5200	..	0	0	0	0	..	..	..	..	..
6000 Other taxes	**..**	**0**	**0**	**0**	**0**	**..**	**..**	**..**	**..**	**..**
6100 Paid solely by business	..	..	..	..	..	..	..	..	..	..
6200 Other	..	..	..	..	..	..	..	..	..	..
Total tax revenue	**..**	**845**	**2 803**	**5 662**	**7 427**	**..**	**..**	**..**	**..**	**..**

	Local government					Social Security Funds				
	1975	1995	2005	2015	2020	1975	1995	2005	2015	2020
1000 Taxes on income, profits and capital gains	**..**	**0**	**0**	**0**	**0**	**..**	**0**	**0**	**0**	**0**
1100 Of individuals	..	0	0	0	0	..	0	0	0	0
1200 Corporate	..	0	0	0	0	..	0	0	0	0
1300 Unallocable between 1100 and 1200	..	0	0	0	0	..	0	0	0	0
2000 Social security contributions	**..**	**0**	**0**	**0**	**0**	**..**	**149**	**511**	**1 110**	**1 587**
2100 Employees	..	..	..	..	..	..	0	31	99	139
2200 Employers	..	..	..	..	..	..	143	466	1 002	1 340
2300 Self-employed or non-employed	..	..	..	..	..	..	6	14	8	107
2400 Unallocable between 2100, 2200 and 2300	..	..	..	..	..	..	0	0	0	0
3000 Taxes on payroll and workforce	**..**	**0**	**0**	**0**	**0**	**..**	**0**	**0**	**0**	**0**
4000 Taxes on property	**..**	**7**	**32**	**58**	**58**	**..**	**0**	**0**	**0**	**0**
4100 Recurrent taxes on immovable property	..	7	32	58	58	..	..	..	..	..
4200 Recurrent taxes on net wealth	..	0	0	0	0	..	..	..	..	..
4300 Estate, inheritance and gift taxes	..	0	0	0	0	..	..	..	..	..
4400 Taxes on financial and capital transactions	..	0	0	0	0	..	..	..	..	..
4500 Non-recurrent taxes	..	0	0	0	0	..	..	..	..	..
4600 Other recurrent taxes on property	..	0	0	0	0	..	..	..	..	..
5000 Taxes on goods and services	**..**	**1**	**7**	**11**	**12**	**..**	**0**	**0**	**0**	**0**
5100 Taxes on production, sale, transfer, etc	..	0	2	4	5	..	..	..	..	..
5110 General taxes	..	0	0	0	0	..	..	..	..	..
5120 Taxes on specific goods and services	..	0	2	4	5	..	..	..	..	..
5130 Unallocable between 5110 and 5120	..	0	0	0	0	..	..	..	..	..
5200 Taxes on use of goods and perform activities	..	1	5	7	7	..	..	..	..	..
5300 Unallocable between 5100 and 5200	..	0	0	0	0	..	..	..	..	..
6000 Other taxes	**..**	**0**	**0**	**0**	**0**	**..**	**0**	**0**	**0**	**0**
6100 Paid solely by business	..	..	..	..	..	..	..	..	..	..
6200 Other	..	..	..	..	..	..	..	..	..	..
Total tax revenue	**..**	**8**	**40**	**69**	**70**	**..**	**149**	**511**	**1 110**	**1 587**

.. Not available

Note: Including taxes collected on behalf of the European Union.

StatLink https://stat.link/ou0g9p

Table 6.11. Finland, tax revenues by sub-sectors of government

Million EUR

	Central government					State/Regional				
	1975	1995	2005	2015	2020	1975	1995	2005	2015	2020
1000 Taxes on income, profits and capital gains	**1 304**	**6 538**	**12 885**	**12 127**	**12 329**	**..**	**..**	**..**	**..**	**..**
1100 Of individuals	1 146	5 320	8 791	9 248	9 396	..	..	..	..	..
1200 Corporate	157	1 218	4 094	2 879	2 933	..	..	..	..	..
1300 Unallocable between 1100 and 1200	0	0	0	0	0	..	..	..	..	..
2000 Social security contributions	**0**	**25**	**0**	**0**	**0**	**..**	**..**	**..**	**..**	**..**
2100 Employees	..	0	..	..	..	..	..	..	..	..
2200 Employers	..	25	..	..	..	..	..	..	..	..
2300 Self-employed or non-employed	..	0	..	..	..	..	..	..	..	..
2400 Unallocable between 2100, 2200 and 2300	..	0	..	..	..	..	..	..	..	..
3000 Taxes on payroll and workforce	**153**	**0**	**0**	**0**	**0**	**..**	**..**	**..**	**..**	**..**
4000 Taxes on property	**127**	**533**	**1 169**	**1 414**	**1 619**	**..**	**..**	**..**	**..**	**..**
4100 Recurrent taxes on immovable property	0	0	0	0	0	..	..	..	..	..
4200 Recurrent taxes on net wealth	33	35	129	0	0	..	..	..	..	..
4300 Estate, inheritance and gift taxes	14	167	486	631	797	..	..	..	..	..
4400 Taxes on financial and capital transactions	80	331	554	783	822	..	..	..	..	..
4500 Non-recurrent taxes	0	0	0	0	0	..	..	..	..	..
4600 Other recurrent taxes on property	0	0	0	0	0	..	..	..	..	..
5000 Taxes on goods and services	**2 099**	**13 241**	**21 768**	**29 650**	**33 270**	**..**	**..**	**..**	**..**	**..**
5100 Taxes on production, sale, transfer, etc	2 082	12 937	21 178	28 592	31 814	..	..	..	..	..
5110 General taxes	1 030	7 621	13 748	18 974	22 005	..	..	..	..	..
5120 Taxes on specific goods and services	1 052	5 316	7 430	9 618	9 809	..	..	..	..	..
5130 Unallocable between 5110 and 5120	0	0	0	0	0	..	..	..	..	..
5200 Taxes on use of goods and perform activities	16	304	590	1 058	1 456	..	..	..	..	..
5300 Unallocable between 5100 and 5200	0	0	0	0	0	..	..	..	..	..
6000 Other taxes	**10**	**90**	**68**	**81**	**73**	**..**	**..**	**..**	**..**	**..**
6100 Paid solely by business	0	0	0	0	0	..	..	..	..	..
6200 Other	10	90	68	81	73	..	..	..	..	..
Total tax revenue	**3 693**	**20 427**	**35 890**	**43 272**	**47 291**	**..**	**..**	**..**	**..**	**..**

	Local government					Social Security Funds				
	1975	1995	2005	2015	2020	1975	1995	2005	2015	2020
1000 Taxes on income, profits and capital gains	**1 547**	**9 313**	**13 574**	**20 244**	**22 633**	**0**	**0**	**0**	**0**	**0**
1100 Of individuals	1 393	8 319	12 420	18 576	20 477	..	..	..	..	..
1200 Corporate	154	994	1 154	1 668	2 156	..	..	..	..	..
1300 Unallocable between 1100 and 1200	0	0	0	0	0	..	..	..	..	..
2000 Social security contributions	**0**	**0**	**0**	**0**	**0**	**1 347**	**13 493**	**18 879**	**26 639**	**27 326**
2100 Employees	..	..	..	..	..	278	2 537	3 464	6 364	8 553
2200 Employers	..	..	..	..	..	990	9 447	14 127	18 232	16 704
2300 Self-employed or non-employed	..	..	..	..	..	79	1 509	1 288	2 043	2 069
2400 Unallocable between 2100, 2200 and 2300	..	..	..	..	..	0	0	0	0	0
3000 Taxes on payroll and workforce	**0**	**0**	**0**	**0**	**0**	**0**	**0**	**0**	**0**	**0**
4000 Taxes on property	**0**	**441**	**725**	**1 603**	**1 950**	**0**	**0**	**0**	**0**	**0**
4100 Recurrent taxes on immovable property	0	441	725	1 603	1 950	..	..	..	..	..
4200 Recurrent taxes on net wealth	0	0	0	0	0	..	..	..	..	..
4300 Estate, inheritance and gift taxes	0	0	0	0	0	..	..	..	..	..
4400 Taxes on financial and capital transactions	0	0	0	0	0	..	..	..	..	..
4500 Non-recurrent taxes	0	0	0	0	0	..	..	..	..	..
4600 Other recurrent taxes on property	0	0	0	0	0	..	..	..	..	..
5000 Taxes on goods and services	**3**	**7**	**8**	**2**	**1**	**0**	**0**	**0**	**0**	**0**
5100 Taxes on production, sale, transfer, etc	1	1	4	1	1	..	..	..	..	..
5110 General taxes	0	0	0	0	0	..	..	..	..	..
5120 Taxes on specific goods and services	1	1	4	1	1	..	..	..	..	..
5130 Unallocable between 5110 and 5120	0	0	0	0	0	..	..	..	..	..
5200 Taxes on use of goods and perform activities	2	6	4	1	0	..	..	..	..	..
5300 Unallocable between 5100 and 5200	0	0	0	0	0	..	..	..	..	..
6000 Other taxes	**0**	**0**	**0**	**0**	**0**	**0**	**0**	**0**	**0**	**0**
6100 Paid solely by business	..	..	..	..	..	..	..	..	..	..
6200 Other	..	..	..	..	..	..	..	..	..	..
Total tax revenue	**1 550**	**9 761**	**14 307**	**21 849**	**24 584**	**1 347**	**13 493**	**18 879**	**26 639**	**27 326**

.. Not available

Note: Including taxes collected on behalf of the European Union.

StatLink https://stat.link/8nxl31

Table 6.12. France, tax revenues by sub-sectors of government

Million EUR

	Central government					State/Regional				
	1975	1995	2005	2015	2020	1975	1995	2005	2015	2020
1000 Taxes on income, profits and capital gains	**13 106**	**69 134**	**98 623**	**121 529**	**140 092**	..	..	..	..	..
1100 Of individuals	8 743	43 963	56 862	75 366	87 264	..	..	..	..	..
1200 Corporate	4 282	25 172	41 761	46 163	52 828	..	..	..	..	..
1300 Unallocable between 1100 and 1200	80	0	0	0	0	..	..	..	..	..
2000 Social security contributions	**419**	**3 733**	**5 796**	**7 941**	**8 192**	..	..	..	..	..
2100 Employees	419	3 733	4 812	6 048	7 132	..	..	..	..	..
2200 Employers	0	0	984	1 893	1 060	..	..	..	..	..
2300 Self-employed or non-employed	0	0	0	0	0	..	..	..	..	..
2400 Unallocable between 2100, 2200 and 2300	0	0	0	0	0	..	..	..	..	..
3000 Taxes on payroll and workforce	**1 194**	**10 299**	**13 117**	**4 796**	**12 230**	..	..	..	..	..
4000 Taxes on property	**1 372**	**7 356**	**13 945**	**20 362**	**20 363**	..	..	..	..	..
4100 Recurrent taxes on immovable property	26	9	30	100	80	..	..	..	..	..
4200 Recurrent taxes on net wealth	0	1 309	3 053	5 224	1 999	..	..	..	..	..
4300 Estate, inheritance and gift taxes	616	4 261	9 006	12 317	15 039	..	..	..	..	..
4400 Taxes on financial and capital transactions	731	1 777	1 856	2 721	3 245	..	..	..	..	..
4500 Non-recurrent taxes	0	0	0	0	0	..	..	..	..	..
4600 Other recurrent taxes on property	0	0	0	0	0	..	..	..	..	..
5000 Taxes on goods and services	**26 154**	**129 457**	**167 750**	**178 755**	**155 485**	..	..	..	..	..
5100 Taxes on production, sale, transfer, etc	25 618	126 699	163 729	173 782	149 936	..	..	..	..	..
5110 General taxes	19 077	89 768	127 096	141 371	113 642	..	..	..	..	..
5120 Taxes on specific goods and services	6 540	36 931	36 633	32 411	36 294	..	..	..	..	..
5130 Unallocable between 5110 and 5120	0	0	0	0	0	..	..	..	..	..
5200 Taxes on use of goods and perform activities	536	2 758	4 021	4 973	5 549	..	..	..	..	..
5300 Unallocable between 5100 and 5200	..	0	0	0	0	..	..	..	..	..
6000 Other taxes	**49**	**924**	**3 522**	**1 683**	**1 068**	..	..	..	..	..
6100 Paid solely by business	32	871	3 502	1 677	1 046	..	..	..	..	..
6200 Other	17	53	21	6	22	..	..	..	..	..
Total tax revenue	**42 294**	**220 903**	**302 753**	**335 066**	**337 430**	..	..	..	..	..

	Local government					Social Security Funds				
	1975	1995	2005	2015	2020	1975	1995	2005	2015	2020
1000 Taxes on income, profits and capital gains	**0**	**0**	**0**	**20**	**25**	**0**	**14 997**	**80 173**	**112 983**	**136 601**
1100 Of individuals	0	0	0	13	13	0	14 997	80 173	112 978	135 630
1200 Corporate	0	0	0	7	12	0	0	0	5	971
1300 Unallocable between 1100 and 1200	0	0	0	0	0	0	0	0	0	0
2000 Social security contributions	**0**	**0**	**0**	**0**	**0**	**33 089**	**217 995**	**275 433**	**362 434**	**340 143**
2100 Employees	..	..	..	..	..	6 683	65 964	65 369	87 719	77 112
2200 Employers	..	..	..	..	..	24 236	135 892	190 090	246 280	235 833
2300 Self-employed or non-employed	..	..	..	..	..	2 170	16 139	19 975	28 435	27 198
2400 Unallocable between 2100, 2200 and 2300	..	..	..	..	..	0	0	0	0	0
3000 Taxes on payroll and workforce	**299**	**2 529**	**5 437**	**9 278**	**9 185**	**107**	**36**	**1 767**	**20 500**	**22 241**
4000 Taxes on property	**2 876**	**27 105**	**44 534**	**68 949**	**71 316**	**0**	**0**	**0**	**0**	**0**
4100 Recurrent taxes on immovable property	2 626	23 117	35 989	57 331	54 767	..	..	..	..	..
4200 Recurrent taxes on net wealth	..	0	0	0	0	..	..	..	..	..
4300 Estate, inheritance and gift taxes	0	0	0	0	0	..	..	..	..	..
4400 Taxes on financial and capital transactions	250	3 988	8 545	11 618	16 549	..	..	..	..	..
4500 Non-recurrent taxes	0	0	0	0	0	..	..	..	..	..
4600 Other recurrent taxes on property	..	0	0	0	0	..	..	..	..	..
5000 Taxes on goods and services	**496**	**8 056**	**14 708**	**43 987**	**50 581**	**301**	**5 708**	**12 776**	**36 159**	**74 367**
5100 Taxes on production, sale, transfer, etc	297	4 168	12 233	39 742	46 134	301	5 429	12 393	35 202	73 251
5110 General taxes	0	0	0	12 973	19 012	248	1 810	4 271	15 569	49 391
5120 Taxes on specific goods and services	297	4 168	12 233	26 769	27 122	53	3 620	8 122	19 633	23 860
5130 Unallocable between 5110 and 5120	..	0	0	0	0	..	0	0	0	0
5200 Taxes on use of goods and perform activities	198	3 888	2 475	4 245	4 447	0	279	383	957	1 116
5300 Unallocable between 5100 and 5200	..	0	0	0	0	..	0	0	0	0
6000 Other taxes	**2 577**	**18 971**	**22 334**	**9 120**	**10 618**	**0**	**0**	**0**	**568**	**827**
6100 Paid solely by business	2 577	18 970	22 334	9 120	10 618	..	..	..	568	827
6200 Other	0	1	0	0	0	..	..	..	0	0
Total tax revenue	**6 248**	**56 661**	**87 013**	**131 354**	**141 725**	**33 497**	**238 737**	**370 149**	**532 644**	**574 179**

.. Not available

Note: Including taxes collected on behalf of the European Union.

StatLink https://stat.link/w038lj

Table 6.13. Germany, tax revenues by sub-sectors of government

Million EUR

	Federal government					State/Regional				
	1975	1995	2005	2015	2020	1975	1995	2005	2015	2020
1000 Taxes on income, profits and capital gains	**26 782**	**90 688**	**89 383**	**143 652**	**168 531**	**26 428**	**77 258**	**83 503**	**133 852**	**153 279**
1100 Of individuals	23 469	83 710	77 468	129 730	152 680	23 267	71 598	70 916	118 871	138 402
1200 Corporate	3 314	6 978	11 915	13 922	15 851	3 160	5 659	12 587	14 981	14 877
1300 Unallocable between 1100 and 1200	0	0	0	0	0	0	0	0	0	0
2000 Social security contributions	**0**	**0**	**0**	**0**	**0**	**0**	**0**	**0**	**0**	**0**
2100 Employees	..	..	..	..	..	..	..	..	..	..
2200 Employers	..	..	..	..	..	..	..	..	..	..
2300 Self-employed or non-employed	..	..	..	..	..	..	..	..	..	..
2400 Unallocable between 2100, 2200 and 2300	..	..	..	..	..	..	..	..	..	..
3000 Taxes on payroll and workforce	**0**	**0**	**0**	**0**	**0**	**0**	**0**	**0**	**0**	**0**
4000 Taxes on property	**1 225**	**175**	**0**	**1 688**	**1 517**	**2 606**	**9 080**	**8 985**	**17 537**	**27 750**
4100 Recurrent taxes on immovable property	0	0	..	0	0	0	0	0	0	1 515
4200 Recurrent taxes on net wealth	920	147	..	1 688	1 517	1 993	4 163	97	-2	0
4300 Estate, inheritance and gift taxes	0	0	..	0	0	271	1 815	4 097	6 290	8 657
4400 Taxes on financial and capital transactions	305	28	..	0	0	342	3 102	4 791	11 249	17 578
4500 Non-recurrent taxes	0	0	..	0	0	0	0	0	0	0
4600 Other recurrent taxes on property	0	0	..	0	0	0	0	0	0	0
5000 Taxes on goods and services	**35 370**	**125 377**	**147 967**	**199 447**	**185 544**	**13 082**	**62 564**	**82 093**	**107 685**	**128 891**
5100 Taxes on production, sale, transfer, etc	35 370	125 377	147 967	188 870	172 933	10 371	55 506	66 406	99 805	120 876
5110 General taxes	18 458	67 178	74 361	110 451	95 124	9 194	52 783	62 851	96 751	117 563
5120 Taxes on specific goods and services	16 913	58 200	73 170	78 127	77 521	1 177	2 723	3 555	3 054	3 313
5130 Unallocable between 5110 and 5120	0	0	436	292	288	0	0	0	0	0
5200 Taxes on use of goods and perform activities	0	0	0	10 577	12 611	2 711	7 058	15 687	7 880	8 015
5300 Unallocable between 5100 and 5200	0	0	0	0	0	0	0	0	0	0
6000 Other taxes	**0**	**0**	**-1**	**0**	**0**	**0**	**0**	**0**	**0**	**0**
6100 Paid solely by business	..	..	0	..	..	..	..	..	..	..
6200 Other	..	..	-1	..	..	..	..	..	..	..
Total tax revenue	**63 378**	**216 240**	**237 349**	**344 787**	**355 592**	**42 116**	**148 902**	**174 581**	**259 074**	**309 920**

	Local government					Social Security Funds				
	1975	1995	2005	2015	2020	1975	1995	2005	2015	2020
1000 Taxes on income, profits and capital gains	**11 819**	**40 295**	**46 725**	**73 882**	**82 773**	**0**	**0**	**0**	**0**	**0**
1100 Of individuals	9 931	33 761	31 261	50 761	57 862	..	..	..	..	..
1200 Corporate	1 888	6 534	15 464	23 121	24 911	..	..	..	..	..
1300 Unallocable between 1100 and 1200	0	0	0	0	0	..	..	..	..	..
2000 Social security contributions	**0**	**0**	**0**	**0**	**0**	**64 290**	**268 052**	**311 530**	**424 841**	**512 122**
2100 Employees	..	..	..	..	..	28 106	117 916	134 939	186 305	217 235
2200 Employers	..	..	..	..	..	34 609	133 120	148 507	196 679	244 692
2300 Self-employed or non-employed	..	..	..	..	..	1 575	17 016	28 084	41 857	50 195
2400 Unallocable between 2100, 2200 and 2300	..	..	..	..	..	0	0	0	0	0
3000 Taxes on payroll and workforce	**1 533**	**0**	**0**	**0**	**0**	**0**	**0**	**0**	**0**	**0**
4000 Taxes on property	**3 461**	**9 794**	**10 247**	**13 215**	**13 160**	**0**	**0**	**0**	**0**	**0**
4100 Recurrent taxes on immovable property	2 122	7 027	10 247	13 215	13 160	..	..	..	..	..
4200 Recurrent taxes on net wealth	911	2 615	0	0	0	..	..	..	..	..
4300 Estate, inheritance and gift taxes	0	0	0	0	0	..	..	..	..	..
4400 Taxes on financial and capital transactions	428	151	0	0	0	..	..	..	..	..
4500 Non-recurrent taxes	0	0	0	0	0	..	..	..	..	..
4600 Other recurrent taxes on property	0	0	0	0	0	..	..	..	..	..
5000 Taxes on goods and services	**162**	**448**	**3 395**	**5 947**	**10 329**	**0**	**0**	**0**	**0**	**0**
5100 Taxes on production, sale, transfer, etc	94	271	3 136	5 615	9 941	..	..	..	..	..
5110 General taxes	0	0	2 909	4 734	9 195	..	..	..	..	..
5120 Taxes on specific goods and services	94	271	227	881	746	..	..	..	..	..
5130 Unallocable between 5110 and 5120	0	0	0	0	0	..	..	..	..	..
5200 Taxes on use of goods and perform activities	68	176	259	332	388	..	..	..	..	..
5300 Unallocable between 5100 and 5200	0	0	0	0	0	..	..	..	..	..
6000 Other taxes	**67**	**130**	**79**	**216**	**208**	**0**	**0**	**0**	**0**	**0**
6100 Paid solely by business	0	0	0	0	0	..	..	..	..	..
6200 Other	67	130	79	216	208	..	..	..	..	..
Total tax revenue	**17 042**	**50 666**	**60 446**	**93 260**	**106 470**	**64 290**	**268 052**	**311 530**	**424 841**	**512 122**

.. Not available

Note: Including taxes collected on behalf of the European Union.

StatLink https://stat.link/9uij2d

Table 6.14. Greece, tax revenues by sub-sectors of government

Million EUR

	Central government					State/Regional				
	1975	1995	2005	2015	2020	1975	1995	2005	2015	2020
1000 Taxes on income, profits and capital gains	**64**	**5 456**	**16 101**	**14 577**	**13 104**	..	..	..	..	..
1100 Of individuals	43	3 011	8 719	10 146	10 440	..	..	..	..	..
1200 Corporate	17	2 067	6 487	3 800	1 999	..	..	..	..	..
1300 Unallocable between 1100 and 1200	4	378	895	631	665	..	..	..	..	..
2000 Social security contributions	**0**	**380**	**1 048**	**745**	**59**	..	..	..	..	..
2100 Employees	..	380	1 031	744	59	..	..	..	..	..
2200 Employers	..	0	17	1	0	..	..	..	..	..
2300 Self-employed or non-employed	..	0	0	0	0	..	..	..	..	..
2400 Unallocable between 2100, 2200 and 2300	..	0	0	0	0	..	..	..	..	..
3000 Taxes on payroll and workforce	**1**	**0**	**0**	**0**	**0**	..	..	..	..	..
4000 Taxes on property	**47**	**1 060**	**2 263**	**3 931**	**3 483**	..	..	..	..	..
4100 Recurrent taxes on immovable property	1	0	0	3 046	2 483	..	..	..	..	..
4200 Recurrent taxes on net wealth	0	138	284	180	187	..	..	..	..	..
4300 Estate, inheritance and gift taxes	5	274	258	134	169	..	..	..	..	..
4400 Taxes on financial and capital transactions	41	641	1 469	509	630	..	..	..	..	..
4500 Non-recurrent taxes	0	0	73	0	0	..	..	..	..	..
4600 Other recurrent taxes on property	0	7	179	62	14	..	..	..	..	..
5000 Taxes on goods and services	**224**	**10 586**	**21 526**	**25 088**	**24 222**	..	..	..	..	..
5100 Taxes on production, sale, transfer, etc	205	9 953	19 454	20 899	20 629	..	..	..	..	..
5110 General taxes	90	5 504	13 605	12 904	12 929	..	..	..	..	..
5120 Taxes on specific goods and services	114	4 413	5 772	7 901	7 672	..	..	..	..	..
5130 Unallocable between 5110 and 5120	0	36	77	94	28	..	..	..	..	..
5200 Taxes on use of goods and perform activities	20	385	1 780	3 187	2 930	..	..	..	..	..
5300 Unallocable between 5100 and 5200	0	248	292	1 002	663	..	..	..	..	..
6000 Other taxes	**0**	**0**	**0**	**0**	**0**	..	..	..	..	..
6100 Paid solely by business	..	..	..	..	..	..	..	..	..	..
6200 Other	..	..	..	..	..	..	..	..	..	..
Total tax revenue	**337**	**17 482**	**40 938**	**44 341**	**40 868**	..	..	..	..	..

	Local government					Social Security Funds				
	1975	1995	2005	2015	2020	1975	1995	2005	2015	2020
1000 Taxes on income, profits and capital gains	**3**	**0**	**0**	**0**	**0**	**0**	**0**	**0**	**9**	**7**
1100 Of individuals	2	..	..	..	..	0	..	..	9	7
1200 Corporate	0	..	..	..	..	0	..	..	0	0
1300 Unallocable between 1100 and 1200	1	..	..	..	..	0	..	..	0	0
2000 Social security contributions	**0**	**0**	**0**	**0**	**0**	**148**	**7 991**	**20 288**	**18 062**	**21 293**
2100 Employees	..	..	..	..	..	62	4 181	10 206	10 351	11 563
2200 Employers	..	..	..	..	..	62	3 810	10 082	7 711	9 730
2300 Self-employed or non-employed	..	..	..	..	..	0	0	0	0	0
2400 Unallocable between 2100, 2200 and 2300	..	..	..	..	..	24	0	0	0	0
3000 Taxes on payroll and workforce	**0**	**0**	**0**	**0**	**0**	**0**	**0**	**0**	**0**	**0**
4000 Taxes on property	**1**	**447**	**1 208**	**1 449**	**1 555**	**0**	**66**	**361**	**38**	**0**
4100 Recurrent taxes on immovable property	0	180	420	546	581	..	32	83	0	..
4200 Recurrent taxes on net wealth	0	267	788	903	974	..	0	0	0	..
4300 Estate, inheritance and gift taxes	0	0	0	0	0	..	0	0	0	..
4400 Taxes on financial and capital transactions	0	0	0	0	0	..	34	278	38	..
4500 Non-recurrent taxes	0	0	0	0	0	..	0	0	0	..
4600 Other recurrent taxes on property	0	0	0	0	0	..	0	0	0	..
5000 Taxes on goods and services	**10**	**89**	**197**	**96**	**71**	**0**	**124**	**248**	**240**	**112**
5100 Taxes on production, sale, transfer, etc	7	87	185	82	59	..	102	195	224	109
5110 General taxes	2	32	26	3	1	..	86	85	170	77
5120 Taxes on specific goods and services	6	55	159	79	58	..	16	110	47	25
5130 Unallocable between 5110 and 5120	0	0	0	0	0	..	0	0	7	7
5200 Taxes on use of goods and perform activities	3	2	12	14	12	..	22	53	16	3
5300 Unallocable between 5100 and 5200	0	0	0	0	0	..	0	0	0	0
6000 Other taxes	**0**	**0**	**0**	**0**	**0**	**0**	**0**	**0**	**0**	**0**
6100 Paid solely by business	..	..	..	..	..	..	..	..	..	..
6200 Other	..	..	..	..	..	..	..	..	..	..
Total tax revenue	**17**	**536**	**1 405**	**1 545**	**1 626**	**148**	**8 181**	**20 897**	**18 349**	**21 412**

.. Not available

Note: Including taxes collected on behalf of the European Union.

StatLink https://stat.link/nr0w3q

Table 6.15. Hungary, tax revenues by sub-sectors of government

Million HUF

	Central government					State/Regional				
	1975	1995	2005	2015	2020	1975	1995	2005	2015	2020
1000 Taxes on income, profits and capital gains	**..**	**498 608**	**1 915 178**	**2 299 697**	**3 165 553**	**..**	**..**	**..**	**..**	**..**
1100 Of individuals	..	383 744	1 449 552	1 698 410	2 543 266	..	..	..	..	..
1200 Corporate	..	106 259	465 626	601 287	622 287	..	..	..	..	..
1300 Unallocable between 1100 and 1200	..	8 605	0	0	0	..	..	..	..	..
2000 Social security contributions	**..**	**69 554**	**235 148**	**148 044**	**228 636**	**..**	**..**	**..**	**..**	**..**
2100 Employees	..	18 468	53 611	144 868	227 244	..	..	..	..	..
2200 Employers	..	51 086	175 013	3 176	1 392	..	..	..	..	..
2300 Self-employed or non-employed	..	0	0	0	0	..	..	..	..	..
2400 Unallocable between 2100, 2200 and 2300	..	0	6 524	0	0	..	..	..	..	..
3000 Taxes on payroll and workforce	**..**	**5 474**	**39 459**	**231 467**	**491 781**	**..**	**..**	**..**	**..**	**..**
4000 Taxes on property	**..**	**11 463**	**63 007**	**292 329**	**335 291**	**..**	**..**	**..**	**..**	**..**
4100 Recurrent taxes on immovable property	..	0	0	55 906	52 502	..	..	..	..	..
4200 Recurrent taxes on net wealth	..	0	0	135 661	108 104	..	..	..	..	..
4300 Estate, inheritance and gift taxes	..	1 364	7 678	7 373	9 493	..	..	..	..	..
4400 Taxes on financial and capital transactions	..	10 099	55 329	93 389	165 192	..	..	..	..	..
4500 Non-recurrent taxes	..	0	0	0	0	..	..	..	..	..
4600 Other recurrent taxes on property	..	0	0	0	0	..	..	..	..	..
5000 Taxes on goods and services	**..**	**924 906**	**2 870 189**	**5 168 034**	**6 955 620**	**..**	**..**	**..**	**..**	**..**
5100 Taxes on production, sale, transfer, etc	..	919 500	2 854 738	5 060 613	6 737 830	..	..	..	..	..
5110 General taxes	..	423 954	1 972 998	3 485 479	4 846 256	..	..	..	..	..
5120 Taxes on specific goods and services	..	495 546	881 740	1 575 134	1 891 574	..	..	..	..	..
5130 Unallocable between 5110 and 5120	..	0	0	0	0	..	..	..	..	..
5200 Taxes on use of goods and perform activities	..	5 406	15 451	107 421	217 790	..	..	..	..	..
5300 Unallocable between 5100 and 5200	..	0	0	0	0	..	..	..	..	..
6000 Other taxes	**..**	**8 901**	**25 403**	**30 665**	**14 871**	**..**	**..**	**..**	**..**	**..**
6100 Paid solely by business	..	0	4 240	9 156	0	..	..	..	..	..
6200 Other	..	0	0	0	0	..	..	..	..	..
Total tax revenue	**..**	**1 518 905**	**5 148 383**	**8 170 236**	**11 191 752**	**..**	**..**	**..**	**..**	**..**

	Local government					Social Security Funds				
	1975	1995	2005	2015	2020	1975	1995	2005	2015	2020
1000 Taxes on income, profits and capital gains	**..**	**0**	**173**	**45**	**36**	**..**	**0**	**26 307**	**126 216**	**291**
1100 Of individuals	..	0	173	45	36	..	0	26 307	126 216	291
1200 Corporate	..	0	0	0	0	..	0	0	0	0
1300 Unallocable between 1100 and 1200	..	0	0	0	0	..	0	0	0	0
2000 Social security contributions	**..**	**0**	**0**	**0**	**0**	**..**	**778 467**	**2 452 562**	**4 285 420**	**5 136 128**
2100 Employees	..	..	..	..	..	..	116 824	530 098	1 626 055	2 586 522
2200 Employers	..	..	..	..	..	..	632 478	1 894 306	2 634 154	2 520 300
2300 Self-employed or non-employed	..	..	..	..	..	..	27 466	2 080	0	0
2400 Unallocable between 2100, 2200 and 2300	..	..	..	..	..	..	1 699	26 078	25 211	29 306
3000 Taxes on payroll and workforce	**..**	**1 075**	**1 153**	**0**	**0**	**..**	**0**	**44 397**	**10 283**	**9 543**
4000 Taxes on property	**..**	**17 531**	**123 929**	**145 000**	**172 088**	**..**	**0**	**0**	**0**	**0**
4100 Recurrent taxes on immovable property	..	6 068	58 836	145 000	172 088	..	..	..	..	..
4200 Recurrent taxes on net wealth	..	0	0	0	0	..	..	..	..	..
4300 Estate, inheritance and gift taxes	..	1 364	7 932	0	0	..	..	..	..	..
4400 Taxes on financial and capital transactions	..	10 099	57 162	0	0	..	..	..	..	..
4500 Non-recurrent taxes	..	0	0	0	0	..	..	..	..	..
4600 Other recurrent taxes on property	..	0	0	0	0	..	..	..	..	..
5000 Taxes on goods and services	**..**	**41 970**	**388 385**	**625 571**	**734 092**	**..**	**0**	**0**	**103 105**	**110 739**
5100 Taxes on production, sale, transfer, etc	..	39 240	337 935	594 855	732 953	..	..	..	103 105	110 739
5110 General taxes	..	38 472	334 077	584 380	729 000	..	..	..	29 882	57 685
5120 Taxes on specific goods and services	..	768	3 858	10 475	3 953	..	..	..	73 223	53 054
5130 Unallocable between 5110 and 5120	..	0	0	0	0	..	..	..	0	0
5200 Taxes on use of goods and perform activities	..	2 730	50 450	30 716	1 139	..	..	..	0	0
5300 Unallocable between 5100 and 5200	..	0	0	0	0	..	..	..	0	0
6000 Other taxes	**..**	**0**	**0**	**0**	**0**	**..**	**21 605**	**9 616**	**14 021**	**7 422**
6100 Paid solely by business	..	..	..	..	..	..	0	0	0	0
6200 Other	..	..	..	..	..	..	0	0	0	0
Total tax revenue	**..**	**60 576**	**513 641**	**770 616**	**906 216**	**..**	**800 072**	**2 532 882**	**4 539 045**	**5 264 123**

.. Not available

Note: Including taxes collected on behalf of the European Union.

StatLink https://stat.link/m7e0gt

Table 6.16. Iceland, tax revenues by sub-sectors of government

Million ISK

	Central government					State/Regional				
	1975	1995	2005	2015	2020	1975	1995	2005	2015	2020
1000 Taxes on income, profits and capital gains	**68**	**27 156**	**105 705**	**210 536**	**287 478**	..	..	..	..	..
1100 Of individuals	55	22 914	70 944	127 535	202 698	..	..	..	..	..
1200 Corporate	13	4 242	20 297	52 544	64 447	..	..	..	..	..
1300 Unallocable between 1100 and 1200	0	0	14 464	30 457	20 333	..	..	..	..	..
2000 Social security contributions	**17**	**11 452**	**32 777**	**79 707**	**88 364**	..	..	..	..	..
2100 Employees	0	460	..	..	..	..	..	..	..	..
2200 Employers	17	10 992	..	..	..	..	..	..	..	..
2300 Self-employed or non-employed	0	0	..	..	..	..	..	..	..	..
2400 Unallocable between 2100, 2200 and 2300	0	0	32 777	79 707	88 364	..	..	..	..	..
3000 Taxes on payroll and workforce	**27**	**0**	**324**	**6 638**	**9 233**	..	..	..	..	..
4000 Taxes on property	**15**	**7 198**	**4 267**	**4 459**	**10 528**	..	..	..	..	..
4100 Recurrent taxes on immovable property	0	47	0	178	256	..	..	..	..	..
4200 Recurrent taxes on net wealth	5	3 191	2 887	657	34	..	..	..	..	..
4300 Estate, inheritance and gift taxes	0	389	866	2 919	9 059	..	..	..	..	..
4400 Taxes on financial and capital transactions	9	3 571	0	0	0	..	..	..	..	..
4500 Non-recurrent taxes	0	0	248	362	612	..	..	..	..	..
4600 Other recurrent taxes on property	0	0	266	343	567	..	..	..	..	..
5000 Taxes on goods and services	**392**	**66 356**	**177 366**	**264 323**	**329 768**	..	..	..	..	..
5100 Taxes on production, sale, transfer, etc	387	62 140	167 012	254 422	312 821	..	..	..	..	..
5110 General taxes	182	42 358	122 968	188 001	239 773	..	..	..	..	..
5120 Taxes on specific goods and services	205	19 782	44 044	66 421	73 049	..	..	..	..	..
5130 Unallocable between 5110 and 5120	0	0	0	0	0	..	..	..	..	..
5200 Taxes on use of goods and perform activities	5	4 216	10 354	9 901	16 947	..	..	..	..	..
5300 Unallocable between 5100 and 5200	0	0	0	0	0	..	..	..	..	..
6000 Other taxes	**0**	**0**	**1 504**	**38 364**	**19 174**	..	..	..	..	..
6100 Paid solely by business	..	..	565	32 477	12 046	..	..	..	..	..
6200 Other	..	..	939	5 887	7 127	..	..	..	..	..
Total tax revenue	**519**	**112 162**	**321 941**	**604 026**	**744 545**	..	..	..	..	..

	Local government					Social Security Funds				
	1975	1995	2005	2015	2020	1975	1995	2005	2015	2020
1000 Taxes on income, profits and capital gains	**78**	**21 170**	**74 465**	**170 443**	**254 557**	**0**	**0**	**0**	**0**	**0**
1100 Of individuals	74	21 170	74 455	170 443	254 557	..	..	..	..	..
1200 Corporate	4	0	10	0	0	..	..	..	..	..
1300 Unallocable between 1100 and 1200	0	0	0	0	0	..	..	..	..	..
2000 Social security contributions	**0**	**0**	**0**	**0**	**0**	**0**	**0**	**0**	**0**	**0**
2100 Employees	..	..	..	..	..	..	..	..	..	..
2200 Employers	..	..	..	..	..	..	..	..	..	..
2300 Self-employed or non-employed	..	..	..	..	..	..	..	..	..	..
2400 Unallocable between 2100, 2200 and 2300	..	..	..	..	..	..	..	..	..	..
3000 Taxes on payroll and workforce	**0**	**0**	**0**	**0**	**0**	**0**	**0**	**0**	**0**	**0**
4000 Taxes on property	**18**	**5 674**	**13 931**	**34 701**	**55 784**	**0**	**0**	**0**	**0**	**0**
4100 Recurrent taxes on immovable property	18	5 674	13 931	34 701	55 784	..	..	..	..	..
4200 Recurrent taxes on net wealth	0	0	0	0	0	..	..	..	..	..
4300 Estate, inheritance and gift taxes	0	0	0	0	0	..	..	..	..	..
4400 Taxes on financial and capital transactions	0	0	0	0	0	..	..	..	..	..
4500 Non-recurrent taxes	0	0	0	0	0	..	..	..	..	..
4600 Other recurrent taxes on property	0	0	0	0	0	..	..	..	..	..
5000 Taxes on goods and services	**9**	**2 585**	**6 904**	**2 832**	**6 203**	**0**	**0**	**0**	**0**	**0**
5100 Taxes on production, sale, transfer, etc	9	2 585	0	0	0	..	..	..	..	..
5110 General taxes	0	2 585	..	..	..	..	..	..	..	..
5120 Taxes on specific goods and services	9	0	..	..	..	..	..	..	..	..
5130 Unallocable between 5110 and 5120	0	0	..	..	..	..	..	..	..	..
5200 Taxes on use of goods and perform activities	0	0	6 904	2 832	6 203	..	..	..	..	..
5300 Unallocable between 5100 and 5200	0	0	0	0	0	..	..	..	..	..
6000 Other taxes	**14**	**0**	**93**	**0**	**0**	**0**	**0**	**0**	**0**	**0**
6100 Paid solely by business	14	..	93	..	..	..	..	..	..	..
6200 Other	0	..	0	..	..	..	..	..	..	..
Total tax revenue	**119**	**29 429**	**95 393**	**207 976**	**316 544**	**0**	**0**	**0**	**0**	**0**

.. Not available

StatLink https://stat.link/t1da0z

Table 6.17. Ireland, tax revenues by sub-sectors of government

Million EUR

	Central government					State/Regional				
	1975	1995	2005	2015	2020	1975	1995	2005	2015	2020
1000 Taxes on income, profits and capital gains	**456**	**7 022**	**21 186**	**26 599**	**36 333**	..	..	..	..	..
1100 Of individuals	382	5 563	15 674	19 722	24 380	..	..	..	..	..
1200 Corporate	73	1 458	5 511	6 873	11 954	..	..	..	..	..
1300 Unallocable between 1100 and 1200	0	0	0	4	0	..	..	..	..	..
2000 Social security contributions	**11**	**87**	**217**	**1 351**	**1 406**	..	..	..	..	..
2100 Employees	10	87	217	1 351	1 406	..	..	..	..	..
2200 Employers	0	0	0	0	0	..	..	..	..	..
2300 Self-employed or non-employed	1	0	0	0	0	..	..	..	..	..
2400 Unallocable between 2100, 2200 and 2300	0	0	0	0	0	..	..	..	..	..
3000 Taxes on payroll and workforce	**0**	**209**	**332**	**357**	**717**	..	..	..	..	..
4000 Taxes on property	**37**	**370**	**2 741**	**2 530**	**2 955**	..	..	..	..	..
4100 Recurrent taxes on immovable property	0	15	0	475	482	..	..	..	..	..
4200 Recurrent taxes on net wealth	5	0	0	169	0	..	..	..	..	..
4300 Estate, inheritance and gift taxes	17	76	255	401	505	..	..	..	..	..
4400 Taxes on financial and capital transactions	15	279	2 486	1 484	1 968	..	..	..	..	..
4500 Non-recurrent taxes	0	0	0	0	0	..	..	..	..	..
4600 Other recurrent taxes on property	0	0	0	0	0	..	..	..	..	..
5000 Taxes on goods and services	**671**	**6 763**	**19 122**	**19 686**	**20 592**	..	..	..	..	..
5100 Taxes on production, sale, transfer, etc	639	6 419	18 106	17 709	18 773	..	..	..	..	..
5110 General taxes	223	3 666	12 373	11 831	12 753	..	..	..	..	..
5120 Taxes on specific goods and services	416	2 753	5 733	5 878	6 020	..	..	..	..	..
5130 Unallocable between 5110 and 5120	0	0	0	0	0	..	..	..	..	..
5200 Taxes on use of goods and perform activities	33	344	1 015	1 977	1 819	..	..	..	..	..
5300 Unallocable between 5100 and 5200	0	0	0	0	0	..	..	..	..	..
6000 Other taxes	**0**	**0**	**0**	**12**	**9**	..	..	..	..	..
6100 Paid solely by business	..	..	..	0	0	..	..	..	..	..
6200 Other	..	..	..	12	9	..	..	..	..	..
Total tax revenue	**1 175**	**14 451**	**43 598**	**50 535**	**62 012**	..	..	..	..	..

	Local government					Social Security Funds				
	1975	1995	2005	2015	2020	1975	1995	2005	2015	2020
1000 Taxes on income, profits and capital gains	**0**	**0**	**0**	**0**	**0**	**0**	**0**	**0**	**0**	**0**
1100 Of individuals	..	..	..	..	..	..	..	..	..	..
1200 Corporate	..	..	..	..	..	..	..	..	..	..
1300 Unallocable between 1100 and 1200	0	..	..	..	..	0	..	..	..	..
2000 Social security contributions	**0**	**56**	**90**	**121**	**83**	**198**	**2 215**	**6 230**	**8 527**	**10 796**
2100 Employees	..	56	90	121	83	73	576	1 415	1 856	2 295
2200 Employers	..	0	0	0	0	125	1 528	4 427	6 211	7 868
2300 Self-employed or non-employed	..	0	0	0	0	0	111	388	460	632
2400 Unallocable between 2100, 2200 and 2300	..	0	0	0	0	0	0	0	0	0
3000 Taxes on payroll and workforce	**0**	**0**	**0**	**0**	**0**	**0**	**0**	**0**	**0**	**0**
4000 Taxes on property	**110**	**408**	**1 020**	**1 389**	**733**	..	**0**	**0**	**0**	**0**
4100 Recurrent taxes on immovable property	110	408	1 020	1 389	733	..	..	..	..	..
4200 Recurrent taxes on net wealth	0	0	0	0	0	..	..	..	..	..
4300 Estate, inheritance and gift taxes	0	0	0	0	0	..	..	..	..	..
4400 Taxes on financial and capital transactions	0	0	0	0	0	..	..	..	..	..
4500 Non-recurrent taxes	0	0	0	0	0	..	..	..	..	..
4600 Other recurrent taxes on property	0	0	0	0	0	..	..	..	..	..
5000 Taxes on goods and services	**0**	**0**	**0**	**0**	**0**	**0**	**0**	**0**	**0**	**0**
5100 Taxes on production, sale, transfer, etc	..	..	..	..	..	..	..	..	..	..
5110 General taxes	..	..	..	..	..	..	..	..	..	..
5120 Taxes on specific goods and services	..	..	..	..	..	..	..	..	..	..
5130 Unallocable between 5110 and 5120	0	..	..	..	..	0	..	..	..	..
5200 Taxes on use of goods and perform activities	..	..	..	..	..	0	..	..	..	..
5300 Unallocable between 5100 and 5200	0	..	..	..	..	0	..	..	..	..
6000 Other taxes	**0**	**0**	**0**	**0**	**0**	**0**	**0**	**0**	**0**	**0**
6100 Paid solely by business	..	..	..	..	..	..	..	..	..	..
6200 Other	..	..	..	..	..	..	..	..	..	..
Total tax revenue	**110**	**464**	**1 110**	**1 510**	**816**	**198**	**2 215**	**6 230**	**8 527**	**10 796**

.. Not available

Note: Including taxes collected on behalf of the European Union. The personal income tax data shown for the country table for Ireland is different to the ESA2010 presentation as the expenditure component of the payable tax credits are excluded in accordance with the OECD Interpretative Guide.

StatLink https://stat.link/gkja2q

Table 6.18. Israel, tax revenues by sub-sectors of government

Million ILS

	Central government					State/Regional				
	1975	1995	2005	2015	2020	1975	1995	2005	2015	2020
1000 Taxes on income, profits and capital gains	..	**37 422**	**73 082**	**113 966**	**139 321**	..	..	..	..	..
1100 Of individuals	..	28 399	47 062	70 885	91 900	..	..	..	..	..
1200 Corporate	..	8 514	21 909	34 676	38 831	..	..	..	..	..
1300 Unallocable between 1100 and 1200	..	509	4 111	8 405	8 590	..	..	..	..	..
2000 Social security contributions	..	**0**	**0**	**0**	**0**	..	..	..	..	..
2100 Employees	..	..	..	..	..	..	..	..	..	..
2200 Employers	..	..	..	..	..	..	..	..	..	..
2300 Self-employed or non-employed	..	..	..	..	..	..	..	..	..	..
2400 Unallocable between 2100, 2200 and 2300	..	..	..	..	..	..	..	..	..	..
3000 Taxes on payroll and workforce	..	**5 007**	**9 920**	**13 770**	**16 191**	..	..	..	..	..
4000 Taxes on property	..	**4 122**	**5 547**	**10 593**	**11 433**	..	..	..	..	..
4100 Recurrent taxes on immovable property	..	786	322	44	10	..	..	..	..	..
4200 Recurrent taxes on net wealth	..	0	0	0	0	..	..	..	..	..
4300 Estate, inheritance and gift taxes	..	0	0	0	0	..	..	..	..	..
4400 Taxes on financial and capital transactions	..	2 049	3 591	6 732	6 864	..	..	..	..	..
4500 Non-recurrent taxes	..	1 287	1 634	3 817	4 559	..	..	..	..	..
4600 Other recurrent taxes on property	..	0	0	0	0	..	..	..	..	..
5000 Taxes on goods and services	..	**38 673**	**75 877**	**136 829**	**147 233**	..	..	..	..	..
5100 Taxes on production, sale, transfer, etc	..	36 637	70 741	128 277	138 750	..	..	..	..	..
5110 General taxes	..	31 975	59 374	107 765	118 854	..	..	..	..	..
5120 Taxes on specific goods and services	..	4 662	11 367	20 512	19 896	..	..	..	..	..
5130 Unallocable between 5110 and 5120	..	0	0	0	0	..	..	..	..	..
5200 Taxes on use of goods and perform activities	..	2 036	5 136	8 552	8 484	..	..	..	..	..
5300 Unallocable between 5100 and 5200	..	0	0	0	0	..	..	..	..	..
6000 Other taxes	..	**0**	**0**	**0**	**0**	..	..	..	..	..
6100 Paid solely by business	..	..	..	..	..	..	..	..	..	..
6200 Other	..	..	..	..	..	..	..	..	..	..
Total tax revenue	..	**85 224**	**164 425**	**275 158**	**314 177**	..	..	..	..	..

	Local government					Social Security Funds				
	1975	1995	2005	2015	2020	1975	1995	2005	2015	2020
1000 Taxes on income, profits and capital gains	..	**0**	**0**	**0**	**0**	..	**0**	**0**	**0**	**0**
1100 Of individuals	..	0	0	0	0	..	0	0	0	0
1200 Corporate	..	..	..	..	..	..	..	..	..	..
1300 Unallocable between 1100 and 1200	..	0	0	0	0	..	0	0	0	0
2000 Social security contributions	..	**0**	**0**	**0**	**0**	..	**14 958**	**34 597**	**59 561**	**73 031**
2100 Employees	..	..	..	..	..	..	7 953	19 720	34 692	40 797
2200 Employers	..	..	..	..	..	..	4 672	10 679	17 247	22 564
2300 Self-employed or non-employed	..	..	..	..	..	..	2 334	4 198	7 622	9 670
2400 Unallocable between 2100, 2200 and 2300	..	..	..	..	..	..	0	0	0	0
3000 Taxes on payroll and workforce	..	**0**	**0**	**0**	**0**	..	**0**	**0**	**0**	**0**
4000 Taxes on property	..	**7 363**	**16 435**	**30 016**	**31 976**	..	**0**	**0**	**0**	**0**
4100 Recurrent taxes on immovable property	..	5 592	13 962	23 658	25 022	..	..	..	..	..
4200 Recurrent taxes on net wealth	..	0	0	0	0	..	..	..	..	..
4300 Estate, inheritance and gift taxes	..	0	0	0	0	..	..	..	..	..
4400 Taxes on financial and capital transactions	..	0	0	0	0	..	..	..	..	..
4500 Non-recurrent taxes	..	1 771	2 473	6 358	6 955	..	..	..	..	..
4600 Other recurrent taxes on property	..	0	0	0	0	..	..	..	..	..
5000 Taxes on goods and services	..	**298**	**748**	**1 309**	**1 400**	..	**0**	**0**	**0**	**0**
5100 Taxes on production, sale, transfer, etc	..	0	0	0	0	..	..	..	..	..
5110 General taxes	..	0	0	0	0	..	..	..	..	..
5120 Taxes on specific goods and services	..	0	0	0	0	..	..	..	..	..
5130 Unallocable between 5110 and 5120	..	0	0	0	0	..	..	..	..	..
5200 Taxes on use of goods and perform activities	..	298	748	1 309	1 400	..	..	..	..	..
5300 Unallocable between 5100 and 5200	..	0	0	0	0	..	..	..	..	..
6000 Other taxes	..	**0**	**0**	**0**	**0**	..	**0**	**0**	**0**	**0**
6100 Paid solely by business	..	..	..	..	..	..	..	..	..	..
6200 Other	..	..	..	..	..	..	..	..	..	..
Total tax revenue	..	**7 661**	**17 183**	**31 325**	**33 377**	..	**14 958**	**34 597**	**59 561**	**73 031**

.. Not available

StatLink https://stat.link/gql7es

Table 6.19. Italy, tax revenues by sub-sectors of government

Million EUR

	Central government					State/Regional				
	1975	1995	2005	2015	2020	1975	1995	2005	2015	2020
1000 Taxes on income, profits and capital gains	**3 897**	**128 458**	**165 580**	**195 451**	**215 340**	..	..	..	..	..
1100 Of individuals	2 767	98 695	131 047	156 320	172 678	..	..	..	..	..
1200 Corporate	1 131	32 890	31 969	31 421	34 162	..	..	..	..	..
1300 Unallocable between 1100 and 1200	0	-3 127	2 564	7 710	8 500	..	..	..	..	..
2000 Social security contributions	**0**	**0**	**0**	**0**	**0**	..	..	..	..	..
2100 Employees	..	..	..	..	..	..	..	..	..	..
2200 Employers	..	..	..	..	..	..	..	..	..	..
2300 Self-employed or non-employed	..	..	..	..	..	..	..	..	..	..
2400 Unallocable between 2100, 2200 and 2300	..	..	..	..	..	..	..	..	..	..
3000 Taxes on payroll and workforce	**0**	**1 136**	**0**	**0**	**0**	..	..	..	..	..
4000 Taxes on property	**587**	**13 546**	**15 717**	**22 226**	**22 454**	..	..	..	..	..
4100 Recurrent taxes on immovable property	4	0	0	3 892	3 740	..	..	..	..	..
4200 Recurrent taxes on net wealth	0	4 494	0	231	427	..	..	..	..	..
4300 Estate, inheritance and gift taxes	39	587	56	638	396	..	..	..	..	..
4400 Taxes on financial and capital transactions	544	8 464	13 794	16 310	17 252	..	..	..	..	..
4500 Non-recurrent taxes	0	0	1 322	303	67	..	..	..	..	..
4600 Other recurrent taxes on property	0	0	545	852	572	..	..	..	..	..
5000 Taxes on goods and services	**5 506**	**95 323**	**123 870**	**157 330**	**163 150**	..	..	..	..	..
5100 Taxes on production, sale, transfer, etc	5 306	92 042	121 824	154 713	157 155	..	..	..	..	..
5110 General taxes	2 685	52 531	80 619	93 282	99 902	..	..	..	..	..
5120 Taxes on specific goods and services	2 621	39 245	41 205	61 431	57 253	..	..	..	..	..
5130 Unallocable between 5110 and 5120	0	323	0	0	0	..	..	..	..	..
5200 Taxes on use of goods and perform activities	200	2 802	1 535	2 191	4 555	..	..	..	..	..
5300 Unallocable between 5100 and 5200	0	479	511	426	1 440	..	..	..	..	..
6000 Other taxes	**1**	**0**	**0**	**0**	**0**	..	..	..	..	..
6100 Paid solely by business	0	..	..	..	..	..	..	..	..	..
6200 Other	1	..	..	..	..	..	..	..	..	..
Total tax revenue	**9 991**	**238 462**	**305 167**	**375 007**	**400 944**	..	..	..	..	..

	Local government					Social Security Funds				
	1975	1995	2005	2015	2020	1975	1995	2005	2015	2020
1000 Taxes on income, profits and capital gains	**134**	**5 658**	**18 494**	**30 483**	**16 528**	**0**	**0**	**0**	**0**	**0**
1100 Of individuals	81	145	16 995	28 302	16 528	..	..	..	..	..
1200 Corporate	54	97	1 491	2 109	0	..	..	..	..	..
1300 Unallocable between 1100 and 1200	0	5 416	8	72	0	..	..	..	..	..
2000 Social security contributions	**0**	**0**	**0**	**0**	**0**	**8 607**	**119 612**	**179 362**	**214 376**	**224 781**
2100 Employees	..	..	..	..	..	1 692	23 036	31 998	39 805	41 351
2200 Employers	..	..	..	..	..	6 915	79 716	125 099	143 273	149 824
2300 Self-employed or non-employed	..	..	..	..	..	0	16 860	22 265	31 298	33 606
2400 Unallocable between 2100, 2200 and 2300	..	..	..	..	..	0	0	0	0	0
3000 Taxes on payroll and workforce	**0**	**0**	**0**	**0**	**0**	**0**	**0**	**0**	**0**	**0**
4000 Taxes on property	**29**	**7 915**	**13 484**	**24 033**	**17 989**	**0**	**0**	**0**	**0**	**0**
4100 Recurrent taxes on immovable property	29	7 449	11 736	21 666	17 530	..	..	..	..	..
4200 Recurrent taxes on net wealth	0	0	0	0	0	..	..	..	..	..
4300 Estate, inheritance and gift taxes	0	0	5	36	0	..	..	..	..	..
4400 Taxes on financial and capital transactions	0	466	904	935	0	..	..	..	..	..
4500 Non-recurrent taxes	0	0	481	6	54	..	..	..	..	..
4600 Other recurrent taxes on property	0	0	358	1 390	405	..	..	..	..	..
5000 Taxes on goods and services	**4**	**6 941**	**30 231**	**34 551**	**24 146**	**0**	**0**	**0**	**0**	**0**
5100 Taxes on production, sale, transfer, etc	0	1 505	17 114	15 138	4 659	..	..	..	..	..
5110 General taxes	..	0	4 698	7 410	0	..	..	..	..	..
5120 Taxes on specific goods and services	..	1 505	12 416	7 728	4 659	..	..	..	..	..
5130 Unallocable between 5110 and 5120	..	0	0	0	0	..	..	..	..	..
5200 Taxes on use of goods and perform activities	4	2 838	7 512	8 939	8 245	..	..	..	..	..
5300 Unallocable between 5100 and 5200	0	2 597	5 605	10 474	11 242	..	..	..	..	..
6000 Other taxes	**0**	**0**	**34 690**	**28 072**	**19 403**	**0**	**0**	**0**	**0**	**0**
6100 Paid solely by business	..	..	34 690	28 072	19 403	..	..	..	..	..
6200 Other	..	..	0	0	0	..	..	..	..	..
Total tax revenue	**168**	**20 514**	**96 899**	**117 139**	**78 066**	**8 607**	**119 612**	**179 362**	**214 376**	**224 781**

.. Not available

Note: Including taxes collected on behalf of the European Union.

StatLink https://stat.link/jl3v1d

Table 6.20. Japan, tax revenues by sub-sectors of government

Billion JPY

	Central government					State/Regional				
	1975	1995	2005	2015	2020	1975	1995	2005	2015	2020
1000 Taxes on income, profits and capital gains	**9 747**	**33 255**	**29 975**	**31 607**	**33 894**	**..**	**..**	**..**	**..**	**..**
1100 Of individuals	5 482	19 515	16 702	18 178	19 591	..	..	..	..	..
1200 Corporate	4 265	13 740	13 274	13 429	14 302	..	..	..	..	..
1300 Unallocable between 1100 and 1200	0	0	0	0	0	..	..	..	..	..
2000 Social security contributions	**0**	**0**	**0**	**0**	**0**	**..**	**..**	**..**	**..**	**..**
2100 Employees	..	..	..	..	..	..	..	..	..	..
2200 Employers	..	..	..	..	..	..	..	..	..	..
2300 Self-employed or non-employed	..	..	..	..	..	..	..	..	..	..
2400 Unallocable between 2100, 2200 and 2300	..	..	..	..	..	..	..	..	..	..
3000 Taxes on payroll and workforce	**0**	**0**	**0**	**0**	**0**	**..**	**..**	**..**	**..**	**..**
4000 Taxes on property	**871**	**5 561**	**2 735**	**3 018**	**3 234**	**..**	**..**	**..**	**..**	**..**
4100 Recurrent taxes on immovable property	0	406	0	0	0	..	..	..	..	..
4200 Recurrent taxes on net wealth	0	0	0	0	0	..	..	..	..	..
4300 Estate, inheritance and gift taxes	310	2 690	1 566	1 968	2 315	..	..	..	..	..
4400 Taxes on financial and capital transactions	561	2 464	1 169	1 050	920	..	..	..	..	..
4500 Non-recurrent taxes	0	0	0	0	0	..	..	..	..	..
4600 Other recurrent taxes on property	0	0	0	0	0	..	..	..	..	..
5000 Taxes on goods and services	**3 888**	**16 147**	**19 580**	**25 345**	**27 805**	**..**	**..**	**..**	**..**	**..**
5100 Taxes on production, sale, transfer, etc	3 579	15 083	18 424	24 673	27 095	..	..	..	..	..
5110 General taxes	0	7 238	10 583	17 426	20 971	..	..	..	..	..
5120 Taxes on specific goods and services	3 579	7 845	7 840	7 247	6 124	..	..	..	..	..
5130 Unallocable between 5110 and 5120	0	0	0	0	0	..	..	..	..	..
5200 Taxes on use of goods and perform activities	309	1 065	1 157	671	710	..	..	..	..	..
5300 Unallocable between 5100 and 5200	0	0	0	0	0	..	..	..	..	..
6000 Other taxes	**0**	**0**	**0**	**0**	**0**	**..**	**..**	**..**	**..**	**..**
6100 Paid solely by business	..	..	..	..	0	..	..	..	..	..
6200 Other	..	..	..	..	0	..	..	..	..	..
Total tax revenue	**14 506**	**54 963**	**52 290**	**59 969**	**64 933**	**..**	**..**	**..**	**..**	**..**

	Local government					Social Security Funds				
	1975	1995	2005	2015	2020	1975	1995	2005	2015	2020
1000 Taxes on income, profits and capital gains	**4 472**	**17 752**	**16 655**	**19 362**	**20 040**	**0**	**0**	**0**	**0**	**0**
1100 Of individuals	2 147	10 283	8 520	12 669	13 597	..	..	..	..	..
1200 Corporate	2 325	7 470	8 135	6 693	6 443	..	..	..	..	..
1300 Unallocable between 1100 and 1200	0	0	0	0	0	..	..	..	..	..
2000 Social security contributions	**0**	**0**	**0**	**0**	**0**	**9 253**	**44 794**	**50 848**	**64 465**	**71 550**
2100 Employees	..	..	..	..	..	3 436	18 404	20 982	28 224	31 839
2200 Employers	..	..	..	..	..	4 825	21 432	23 154	29 479	33 245
2300 Self-employed or non-employed	..	..	..	..	..	992	4 958	6 712	6 763	6 465
2400 Unallocable between 2100, 2200 and 2300	..	..	..	..	..	0	0	0	0	0
3000 Taxes on payroll and workforce	**0**	**0**	**0**	**0**	**0**	**0**	**0**	**0**	**0**	**0**
4000 Taxes on property	**2 029**	**10 653**	**10 593**	**10 382**	**11 094**	**0**	**0**	**0**	**0**	**0**
4100 Recurrent taxes on immovable property	1 848	9 865	10 116	10 005	10 719	..	..	..	..	..
4200 Recurrent taxes on net wealth	0	0	0	0	0	..	..	..	..	..
4300 Estate, inheritance and gift taxes	0	0	0	0	0	..	..	..	..	..
4400 Taxes on financial and capital transactions	181	788	477	377	374	..	..	..	..	..
4500 Non-recurrent taxes	0	0	0	0	0	..	..	..	..	..
4600 Other recurrent taxes on property	0	0	0	0	0	..	..	..	..	..
5000 Taxes on goods and services	**1 636**	**4 941**	**7 206**	**8 942**	**9 248**	**0**	**0**	**0**	**0**	**0**
5100 Taxes on production, sale, transfer, etc	1 234	3 245	5 299	7 198	7 338	..	..	..	..	..
5110 General taxes	0	0	2 551	4 974	5 424	..	..	..	..	..
5120 Taxes on specific goods and services	1 234	3 245	2 747	2 223	1 914	..	..	..	..	..
5130 Unallocable between 5110 and 5120	0	0	0	0	0	..	..	..	..	..
5200 Taxes on use of goods and perform activities	402	1 697	1 907	1 744	1 910	..	..	..	..	..
5300 Unallocable between 5100 and 5200	0	0	0	0	0	..	..	..	..	..
6000 Other taxes	**20**	**329**	**351**	**413**	**444**	**0**	**0**	**0**	**0**	**0**
6100 Paid solely by business	15	307	297	361	385	..	..	..	..	..
6200 Other	5	22	54	52	60	..	..	..	..	..
Total tax revenue	**8 157**	**33 675**	**34 805**	**39 099**	**40 826**	**9 253**	**44 794**	**50 848**	**64 465**	**71 550**

.. Not available

StatLink https://stat.link/aztr0e

Table 6.21. Korea, tax revenues by sub-sectors of government

Billion KRW

	Central government					State/Regional				
	1975	1995	2005	2015	2020	1975	1995	2005	2015	2020
1000 Taxes on income, profits and capital gains	**344**	**23 000**	**55 109**	**106 162**	**149 319**	**..**	**..**	**..**	**..**	**..**
1100 Of individuals	134	13 713	24 766	60 828	93 334	..	..	..	..	..
1200 Corporate	139	8 988	30 343	45 334	55 985	..	..	..	..	..
1300 Unallocable between 1100 and 1200	71	300	0	0	0	..	..	..	..	..
2000 Social security contributions	**0**	**0**	**0**	**0**	**0**	**..**	**..**	**..**	**..**	**..**
2100 Employees	..	..	..	..	..	..	..	..	..	..
2200 Employers	..	..	..	..	..	..	..	..	..	..
2300 Self-employed or non-employed	..	..	..	..	..	..	..	..	..	..
2400 Unallocable between 2100, 2200 and 2300	..	..	..	..	..	..	..	..	..	..
3000 Taxes on payroll and workforce	**0**	**0**	**0**	**0**	**0**	**..**	**..**	**..**	**..**	**..**
4000 Taxes on property	**65**	**2 482**	**6 769**	**15 164**	**29 160**	**..**	**..**	**..**	**..**	**..**
4100 Recurrent taxes on immovable property	0	106	535	1 666	4 281	..	..	..	..	..
4200 Recurrent taxes on net wealth	0	0	0	0	0	..	..	..	..	..
4300 Estate, inheritance and gift taxes	11	1 029	1 873	5 044	10 375	..	..	..	..	..
4400 Taxes on financial and capital transactions	49	1 258	4 363	8 454	14 504	..	..	..	..	..
4500 Non-recurrent taxes	5	89	-2	0	0	..	..	..	..	..
4600 Other recurrent taxes on property	0	0	0	0	0	..	..	..	..	..
5000 Taxes on goods and services	**920**	**29 170**	**63 480**	**93 127**	**102 903**	**..**	**..**	**..**	**..**	**..**
5100 Taxes on production, sale, transfer, etc	920	29 170	63 480	93 127	102 903	..	..	..	..	..
5110 General taxes	198	14 637	36 118	54 159	64 883	..	..	..	..	..
5120 Taxes on specific goods and services	722	14 533	27 362	38 968	38 020	..	..	..	..	..
5130 Unallocable between 5110 and 5120	0	0	0	0	0	..	..	..	..	..
5200 Taxes on use of goods and perform activities	0	0	0	0	0	..	..	..	..	..
5300 Unallocable between 5100 and 5200	0	0	0	0	0	..	..	..	..	..
6000 Other taxes	**64**	**2 121**	**2 108**	**3 435**	**4 165**	**..**	**..**	**..**	**..**	**..**
6100 Paid solely by business	0	0	0	0	0	..	..	..	..	..
6200 Other	64	2 121	2 108	3 435	4 165	..	..	..	..	..
Total tax revenue	**1 393**	**56 774**	**127 466**	**217 888**	**285 547**	**..**	**..**	**..**	**..**	**..**

	Local government					Social Security Funds				
	1975	1995	2005	2015	2020	1975	1995	2005	2015	2020
1000 Taxes on income, profits and capital gains	**36**	**1 704**	**5 500**	**12 989**	**17 245**	**0**	**0**	**0**	**0**	**0**
1100 Of individuals	0	1 137	2 804	6 772	7 952	..	..	..	..	..
1200 Corporate	0	565	2 696	6 217	9 293	..	..	..	..	..
1300 Unallocable between 1100 and 1200	36	3	0	0	0	..	..	..	..	..
2000 Social security contributions	**0**	**0**	**0**	**0**	**0**	**13**	**9 913**	**43 902**	**104 693**	**150 854**
2100 Employees	..	..	..	..	..	0	4 539	17 632	44 281	65 384
2200 Employers	..	..	..	..	..	13	3 918	18 486	47 846	67 676
2300 Self-employed or non-employed	..	..	..	..	..	0	1 456	7 784	12 566	17 794
2400 Unallocable between 2100, 2200 and 2300	..	..	..	..	..	0	0	0	0	0
3000 Taxes on payroll and workforce	**0**	**237**	**514**	**1 122**	**1 607**	**0**	**0**	**0**	**0**	**0**
4000 Taxes on property	**87**	**8 960**	**17 928**	**33 461**	**47 352**	**0**	**0**	**0**	**0**	**0**
4100 Recurrent taxes on immovable property	45	2 636	4 495	10 820	15 763	..	..	..	..	..
4200 Recurrent taxes on net wealth	0	0	0	0	0	..	..	..	..	..
4300 Estate, inheritance and gift taxes	0	0	0	0	0	..	..	..	..	..
4400 Taxes on financial and capital transactions	42	6 324	13 433	22 641	31 589	..	..	..	..	..
4500 Non-recurrent taxes	0	0	0	0	0	..	..	..	..	..
4600 Other recurrent taxes on property	0	0	0	0	0	..	..	..	..	..
5000 Taxes on goods and services	**36**	**4 218**	**7 561**	**17 199**	**28 450**	**0**	**0**	**0**	**0**	**0**
5100 Taxes on production, sale, transfer, etc	19	2 464	5 589	10 127	20 316	..	..	..	..	..
5110 General taxes	0	0	0	6 003	16 569	..	..	..	..	..
5120 Taxes on specific goods and services	19	2 464	5 589	4 124	3 747	..	..	..	..	..
5130 Unallocable between 5110 and 5120	0	0	0	0	0	..	..	..	..	..
5200 Taxes on use of goods and perform activities	17	1 754	1 972	7 072	8 134	..	..	..	..	..
5300 Unallocable between 5100 and 5200	0	0	0	0	0	..	..	..	..	..
6000 Other taxes	**0**	**198**	**4 474**	**6 207**	**7 395**	**0**	**0**	**0**	**0**	**0**
6100 Paid solely by business	..	0	0	0	0	..	..	..	..	..
6200 Other	..	198	4 474	6 207	7 395	..	..	..	..	..
Total tax revenue	**159**	**15 316**	**35 977**	**70 978**	**102 049**	**13**	**9 913**	**43 902**	**104 693**	**150 854**

.. Not available

StatLink https://stat.link/fgjalt

Table 6.22. Latvia, tax revenues by sub-sectors of government

Million EUR

	Central government					State/Regional				
	1975	1995	2005	2015	2020	1975	1995	2005	2015	2020
1000 Taxes on income, profits and capital gains	**..**	**68**	**453**	**677**	**576**	**..**	**..**	**..**	**..**	**..**
1100 Of individuals	..	0	195	289	363	..	..	..	..	..
1200 Corporate	..	68	258	389	213	..	..	..	..	..
1300 Unallocable between 1100 and 1200	..	0	0	0	0	..	..	..	..	..
2000 Social security contributions	**..**	**0**	**0**	**0**	**97**	**..**	**..**	**..**	**..**	**..**
2100 Employees	..	..	..	..	97	..	..	..	..	..
2200 Employers	..	..	..	..	0	..	..	..	..	..
2300 Self-employed or non-employed	..	..	..	..	0	..	..	..	..	..
2400 Unallocable between 2100, 2200 and 2300	..	..	..	..	0	..	..	..	..	..
3000 Taxes on payroll and workforce	**..**	**0**	**4**	**3**	**3**	**..**	**..**	**..**	**..**	**..**
4000 Taxes on property	**..**	**4**	**48**	**47**	**50**	**..**	**..**	**..**	**..**	**..**
4100 Recurrent taxes on immovable property	..	0	0	0	0	..	..	..	..	..
4200 Recurrent taxes on net wealth	..	0	0	0	0	..	..	..	..	..
4300 Estate, inheritance and gift taxes	..	0	0	3	3	..	..	..	..	..
4400 Taxes on financial and capital transactions	..	4	48	42	44	..	..	..	..	..
4500 Non-recurrent taxes	..	0	0	3	3	..	..	..	..	..
4600 Other recurrent taxes on property	..	0	0	0	0	..	..	..	..	..
5000 Taxes on goods and services	**..**	**453**	**1 553**	**3 139**	**4 051**	**..**	**..**	**..**	**..**	**..**
5100 Taxes on production, sale, transfer, etc	..	453	1 510	2 997	3 841	..	..	..	..	..
5110 General taxes	..	343	1 002	2 130	2 720	..	..	..	..	..
5120 Taxes on specific goods and services	..	110	508	867	1 121	..	..	..	..	..
5130 Unallocable between 5110 and 5120	..	0	0	0	0	..	..	..	..	..
5200 Taxes on use of goods and perform activities	..	1	43	142	211	..	..	..	..	..
5300 Unallocable between 5100 and 5200	..	0	0	0	0	..	..	..	..	..
6000 Other taxes	**..**	**0**	**0**	**0**	**0**	**..**	**..**	**..**	**..**	**..**
6100 Paid solely by business	..	..	..	..	..	..	..	..	..	..
6200 Other	..	..	..	..	..	..	..	..	..	..
Total tax revenue	**..**	**525**	**2 058**	**3 867**	**4 778**	**..**	**..**	**..**	**..**	**..**

	Local government					Social Security Funds				
	1975	1995	2005	2015	2020	1975	1995	2005	2015	2020
1000 Taxes on income, profits and capital gains	**..**	**197**	**538**	**1 156**	**1 445**	**..**	**0**	**0**	**0**	**0**
1100 Of individuals	..	197	538	1 156	1 445	..	..	..	..	..
1200 Corporate	..	0	0	0	0	..	..	..	..	..
1300 Unallocable between 1100 and 1200	..	0	0	0	0	..	..	..	..	..
2000 Social security contributions	**..**	**0**	**0**	**0**	**0**	**..**	**445**	**1 079**	**2 030**	**2 840**
2100 Employees	..	..	..	..	..	..	12	292	585	744
2200 Employers	..	..	..	..	..	..	433	781	1 432	2 068
2300 Self-employed or non-employed	..	..	..	..	..	..	1	7	12	29
2400 Unallocable between 2100, 2200 and 2300	..	..	..	..	..	..	0	0	0	0
3000 Taxes on payroll and workforce	**..**	**0**	**0**	**0**	**0**	**..**	**0**	**0**	**0**	**0**
4000 Taxes on property	**..**	**37**	**88**	**197**	**222**	**..**	**0**	**0**	**4**	**9**
4100 Recurrent taxes on immovable property	..	37	88	197	222	..	..	..	..	..
4200 Recurrent taxes on net wealth	..	0	0	0	0	..	..	..	..	..
4300 Estate, inheritance and gift taxes	..	0	0	0	0	..	..	0	4	9
4400 Taxes on financial and capital transactions	..	0	0	0	0	..	..	..	..	..
4500 Non-recurrent taxes	..	0	0	0	0	..	..	..	..	..
4600 Other recurrent taxes on property	..	0	0	0	0	..	..	..	..	..
5000 Taxes on goods and services	**..**	**2**	**8**	**18**	**10**	**..**	**0**	**0**	**0**	**0**
5100 Taxes on production, sale, transfer, etc	..	0	5	7	2	..	..	..	..	..
5110 General taxes	..	0	0	0	0	..	..	..	..	..
5120 Taxes on specific goods and services	..	0	5	7	2	..	..	..	..	..
5130 Unallocable between 5110 and 5120	..	0	0	0	0	..	..	..	..	..
5200 Taxes on use of goods and perform activities	..	2	3	11	8	..	..	..	..	..
5300 Unallocable between 5100 and 5200	..	0	0	0	0	..	..	..	..	..
6000 Other taxes	**..**	**0**	**0**	**0**	**0**	**..**	**0**	**0**	**0**	**0**
6100 Paid solely by business	..	..	..	..	..	..	..	..	..	..
6200 Other	..	..	..	..	..	..	..	..	..	..
Total tax revenue	**..**	**236**	**634**	**1 371**	**1 677**	**..**	**445**	**1 079**	**2 034**	**2 849**

.. Not available

Note: Including taxes collected on behalf of the European Union.

StatLink https://stat.link/5qeyib

Table 6.23. Lithuania, tax revenues by sub-sectors of government

Million EUR

	Central government					State/Regional				
	1975	1995	2005	2015	2020	1975	1995	2005	2015	2020
1000 Taxes on income, profits and capital gains	..	**646**	**1 871**	**2 013**	**4 296**	..	..	..	..	..
1100 Of individuals	..	487	1 435	1 440	3 517	..	..	..	..	..
1200 Corporate	..	160	437	574	780	..	..	..	..	..
1300 Unallocable between 1100 and 1200	..	0	0	0	0	..	..	..	..	..
2000 Social security contributions	..	**0**	**0**	**0**	**0**	..	..	..	..	..
2100 Employees	..	..	..	..	..	..	..	..	..	..
2200 Employers	..	..	..	..	..	..	..	..	..	..
2300 Self-employed or non-employed	..	..	..	..	..	..	..	..	..	..
2400 Unallocable between 2100, 2200 and 2300	..	..	..	..	..	..	..	..	..	..
3000 Taxes on payroll and workforce	..	**0**	**0**	**0**	**0**	..	..	..	..	..
4000 Taxes on property	..	**0**	**0**	**1**	**5**	..	..	..	..	..
4100 Recurrent taxes on immovable property	..	..	..	1	5	..	..	..	..	..
4200 Recurrent taxes on net wealth	..	..	..	0	0	..	..	..	..	..
4300 Estate, inheritance and gift taxes	..	..	..	0	0	..	..	..	..	..
4400 Taxes on financial and capital transactions	..	..	..	0	0	..	..	..	..	..
4500 Non-recurrent taxes	..	..	..	0	0	..	..	..	..	..
4600 Other recurrent taxes on property	..	..	..	0	0	..	..	..	..	..
5000 Taxes on goods and services	..	**892**	**2 273**	**4 220**	**5 595**	..	..	..	..	..
5100 Taxes on production, sale, transfer, etc	..	869	2 235	4 164	5 508	..	..	..	..	..
5110 General taxes	..	635	1 584	2 913	3 931	..	..	..	..	..
5120 Taxes on specific goods and services	..	234	651	1 252	1 577	..	..	..	..	..
5130 Unallocable between 5110 and 5120	..	0	0	0	0	..	..	..	..	..
5200 Taxes on use of goods and perform activities	..	24	38	56	87	..	..	..	..	..
5300 Unallocable between 5100 and 5200	..	0	0	0	0	..	..	..	..	..
6000 Other taxes	..	**0**	**0**	**0**	**0**	..	..	..	..	..
6100 Paid solely by business	..	..	..	..	..	..	..	..	..	..
6200 Other	..	..	..	..	..	..	..	..	..	..
Total tax revenue	..	**1 539**	**4 145**	**6 235**	**9 896**	..	..	..	..	..

	Local government					Social Security Funds				
	1975	1995	2005	2015	2020	1975	1995	2005	2015	2020
1000 Taxes on income, profits and capital gains	..	**0**	**0**	**0**	**0**	..	**0**	**0**	**0**	**0**
1100 Of individuals	..	..	..	..	..	..	..	..	..	..
1200 Corporate	..	..	..	..	..	..	..	..	..	..
1300 Unallocable between 1100 and 1200	..	..	..	..	..	..	..	..	..	..
2000 Social security contributions	..	**0**	**0**	**0**	**0**	..	**559**	**1 864**	**4 338**	**5 127**
2100 Employees	..	..	..	..	..	..	17	154	873	3 872
2200 Employers	..	..	..	..	..	..	537	1 522	2 916	378
2300 Self-employed or non-employed	..	..	..	..	..	..	4	188	549	877
2400 Unallocable between 2100, 2200 and 2300	..	..	..	..	..	..	0	0	0	0
3000 Taxes on payroll and workforce	..	**0**	**0**	**0**	**0**	..	**0**	**0**	**0**	**0**
4000 Taxes on property	..	**25**	**72**	**125**	**142**	..	**0**	**0**	**0**	**0**
4100 Recurrent taxes on immovable property	..	25	71	124	140	..	..	..	..	..
4200 Recurrent taxes on net wealth	..	0	0	0	0	..	..	..	..	..
4300 Estate, inheritance and gift taxes	..	0	1	1	2	..	..	..	..	..
4400 Taxes on financial and capital transactions	..	0	0	0	0	..	..	..	..	..
4500 Non-recurrent taxes	..	0	0	0	0	..	..	..	..	..
4600 Other recurrent taxes on property	..	0	0	0	0	..	..	..	..	..
5000 Taxes on goods and services	..	**23**	**17**	**18**	**28**	..	**0**	**0**	**0**	**0**
5100 Taxes on production, sale, transfer, etc	..	0	0	0	0	..	..	..	..	..
5110 General taxes	..	..	..	..	..	..	..	..	..	..
5120 Taxes on specific goods and services	..	..	..	..	..	..	..	..	..	..
5130 Unallocable between 5110 and 5120	..	..	..	..	..	..	..	..	..	..
5200 Taxes on use of goods and perform activities	..	23	17	18	28	..	..	..	..	..
5300 Unallocable between 5100 and 5200	..	0	0	0	0	..	..	..	..	..
6000 Other taxes	..	**0**	**0**	**0**	**0**	..	**0**	**0**	**0**	**0**
6100 Paid solely by business	..	..	..	..	..	..	..	..	..	..
6200 Other	..	..	..	..	..	..	..	..	..	..
Total tax revenue	..	**48**	**89**	**143**	**170**	..	**559**	**1 864**	**4 338**	**5 127**

.. Not available

Note: Including taxes collected on behalf of the European Union.

StatLink https://stat.link/g4i9cx

Table 6.24. Luxembourg, tax revenues by sub-sectors of government

Million EUR

	Central government					State/Regional				
	1975	1995	2005	2015	2020	1975	1995	2005	2015	2020
1000 Taxes on income, profits and capital gains	**353**	**1 873**	**3 454**	**6 405**	**8 401**	..	..	..	..	..
1100 Of individuals	254	1 214	2 161	4 716	6 290	..	..	..	..	..
1200 Corporate	99	659	1 293	1 689	2 111	..	..	..	..	..
1300 Unallocable between 1100 and 1200	0	0	0	0	0	..	..	..	..	..
2000 Social security contributions	**4**	**20**	**89**	**150**	**200**	..	..	..	..	..
2100 Employees	3	15	89	150	200	..	..	..	..	..
2200 Employers	0	0	0	0	0	..	..	..	..	..
2300 Self-employed or non-employed	1	5	0	0	0	..	..	..	..	..
2400 Unallocable between 2100, 2200 and 2300	0	0	0	0	0	..	..	..	..	..
3000 Taxes on payroll and workforce	**0**	**0**	**0**	**0**	**0**	..	..	..	..	..
4000 Taxes on property	**42**	**371**	**928**	**1 661**	**2 398**	..	..	..	..	..
4100 Recurrent taxes on immovable property	0	0	0	0	0	..	..	..	..	..
4200 Recurrent taxes on net wealth	21	268	698	1 318	1 852	..	..	..	..	..
4300 Estate, inheritance and gift taxes	3	15	44	74	84	..	..	..	..	..
4400 Taxes on financial and capital transactions	18	88	186	269	462	..	..	..	..	..
4500 Non-recurrent taxes	0	0	0	0	0	..	..	..	..	..
4600 Other recurrent taxes on property	0	0	0	0	0	..	..	..	..	..
5000 Taxes on goods and services	**189**	**1 374**	**3 241**	**4 466**	**5 412**	..	..	..	..	..
5100 Taxes on production, sale, transfer, etc	182	1 350	3 202	4 381	5 316	..	..	..	..	..
5110 General taxes	112	670	1 812	2 946	3 674	..	..	..	..	..
5120 Taxes on specific goods and services	70	680	1 390	1 435	1 642	..	..	..	..	..
5130 Unallocable between 5110 and 5120	0	0	0	0	0	..	..	..	..	..
5200 Taxes on use of goods and perform activities	7	23	39	85	95	..	..	..	..	..
5300 Unallocable between 5100 and 5200	0	0	0	0	0	..	..	..	..	..
6000 Other taxes	**0**	**6**	**11**	**27**	**21**	..	..	..	..	..
6100 Paid solely by business	..	6	10	27	21	..	..	..	..	..
6200 Other	..	0	0	0	0	..	..	..	..	..
Total tax revenue	**588**	**3 644**	**7 722**	**12 708**	**16 433**	..	..	..	..	..

	Local government					Social Security Funds				
	1975	1995	2005	2015	2020	1975	1995	2005	2015	2020
1000 Taxes on income, profits and capital gains	**46**	**331**	**460**	**606**	**969**	**0**	**0**	**0**	**0**	**0**
1100 Of individuals	0	0	0	0	0	..	..	..	..	..
1200 Corporate	46	331	460	606	969	..	..	..	..	..
1300 Unallocable between 1100 and 1200	0	0	0	0	0	..	..	..	..	..
2000 Social security contributions	**0**	**0**	**0**	**0**	**0**	**268**	**1 460**	**3 086**	**5 399**	**7 015**
2100 Employees	..	..	..	..	..	102	577	1 321	2 348	3 145
2200 Employers	..	..	..	..	..	150	684	1 378	2 335	2 959
2300 Self-employed or non-employed	..	..	..	..	..	16	200	387	715	911
2400 Unallocable between 2100, 2200 and 2300	..	..	..	..	..	0	0	0	0	0
3000 Taxes on payroll and workforce	**9**	**0**	**0**	**0**	**0**	**0**	**0**	**0**	**0**	**0**
4000 Taxes on property	**6**	**21**	**35**	**54**	**64**	**0**	**0**	**0**	**0**	**0**
4100 Recurrent taxes on immovable property	6	17	26	36	39	..	..	..	..	..
4200 Recurrent taxes on net wealth	0	0	0	0	0	..	..	..	..	..
4300 Estate, inheritance and gift taxes	0	0	0	0	0	..	..	..	..	..
4400 Taxes on financial and capital transactions	0	4	10	18	25	..	..	..	..	..
4500 Non-recurrent taxes	0	0	0	0	0	..	..	..	..	..
4600 Other recurrent taxes on property	0	0	0	0	0	..	..	..	..	..
5000 Taxes on goods and services	**1**	**4**	**8**	**10**	**5**	**0**	**0**	**0**	**0**	**0**
5100 Taxes on production, sale, transfer, etc	1	3	7	8	4	..	..	..	..	..
5110 General taxes	0	0	0	0	0	..	..	..	..	..
5120 Taxes on specific goods and services	1	3	7	8	4	..	..	..	..	..
5130 Unallocable between 5110 and 5120	0	0	0	0	0	..	..	..	..	..
5200 Taxes on use of goods and perform activities	0	1	1	1	1	..	..	..	..	..
5300 Unallocable between 5100 and 5200	0	0	0	0	0	..	..	..	..	..
6000 Other taxes	**0**	**1**	**2**	**1**	**1**	**0**	**0**	**0**	**0**	**0**
6100 Paid solely by business	..	1	2	1	1	..	..	..	..	..
6200 Other	..	0	0	0	0	..	..	..	..	..
Total tax revenue	**62**	**357**	**505**	**671**	**1 039**	**268**	**1 460**	**3 086**	**5 399**	**7 015**

.. Not available

Note: Including taxes collected on behalf of the European Union.

StatLink https://stat.link/5y3afu

Table 6.25. Mexico, tax revenues by sub-sectors of government

Million MXN

	Federal government					State/Regional				
	1975	1995	2005	2015	2020	1975	1995	2005	2015	2020
1000 Taxes on income, profits and capital gains	..	**76 148**	**402 036**	**1 230 555**	**1 768 161**	..	**1**	**0**	**0**	**0**
1100 Of individuals	..	..	195 869	609 384	872 598	..	..	..	..	..
1200 Corporate	..	..	135 840	592 443	832 120	..	..	..	..	..
1300 Unallocable between 1100 and 1200	..	76 148	70 327	28 728	63 443	..	1	..	..	..
2000 Social security contributions	..	**0**	**0**	**0**	**0**	..	**0**	**0**	**0**	**0**
2100 Employees	..	..	..	..	..	..	..	..	..	..
2200 Employers	..	..	..	..	..	..	..	..	..	..
2300 Self-employed or non-employed	..	..	..	..	..	..	..	..	..	..
2400 Unallocable between 2100, 2200 and 2300	..	..	..	..	..	..	..	..	..	..
3000 Taxes on payroll and workforce	..	**0**	**0**	**0**	**0**	..	**2 976**	**20 429**	**70 221**	**105 456**
4000 Taxes on property	..	**0**	**0**	**0**	**0**	..	**2 927**	**10 905**	**22 481**	**26 447**
4100 Recurrent taxes on immovable property	..	..	..	..	..	..	2 198	6 544	14 245	17 631
4200 Recurrent taxes on net wealth	..	..	..	..	..	..	0	0	0	0
4300 Estate, inheritance and gift taxes	..	..	..	..	..	..	2	0	0	0
4400 Taxes on financial and capital transactions	..	..	..	..	..	..	727	4 361	8 235	8 816
4500 Non-recurrent taxes	..	..	..	..	..	..	0	0	0	0
4600 Other recurrent taxes on property	..	..	..	..	..	..	0	0	0	0
5000 Taxes on goods and services	..	**91 452**	**416 533**	**1 116 026**	**1 522 289**	..	**441**	**2 124**	**24 355**	**21 210**
5100 Taxes on production, sale, transfer, etc	..	88 372	401 580	1 115 525	1 521 797	..	22	1 364	4 357	5 358
5110 General taxes	..	51 785	318 432	707 213	987 525	..	0	0	0	0
5120 Taxes on specific goods and services	..	36 587	83 148	408 312	534 273	..	22	1 364	4 357	5 358
5130 Unallocable between 5110 and 5120	..	0	0	0	0	..	0	0	0	0
5200 Taxes on use of goods and perform activities	..	3 080	14 954	501	491	..	419	760	19 998	15 852
5300 Unallocable between 5100 and 5200	..	0	0	0	0	..	0	0	0	0
6000 Other taxes	..	**5 149**	**8 616**	**27 379**	**57 011**	..	**228**	**1 537**	**6 489**	**8 042**
6100 Paid solely by business	..	0	0	0	0	..	0	0	0	0
6200 Other	..	5 149	8 616	27 379	57 011	..	228	1 537	6 489	8 042
Total tax revenue (collecting government)	..	**172 749**	**827 186**	**2 373 960**	**3 347 460**	..	**6 573**	**34 995**	**123 545**	**161 155**
Adjustment[1]	..	**-49 115**	**-278 892**	**-629 130**	**0**	..	**39 225**	**218 291**	**494 239**	**635 159**
Total tax revenue (beneficiary government)	..	**123 634**	**548 294**	**1 744 830**	**3 347 460**	..	**45 798**	**253 286**	**617 784**	**796 313**

	Local government					Social Security Funds				
	1975	1995	2005	2015	2020	1975	1995	2005	2015	2020
1000 Taxes on income, profits and capital gains	..	**16**	**0**	**0**	**0**	..	**0**	**0**	**0**	**0**
1100 Of individuals	..	..	..	..	..	..	..	..	..	..
1200 Corporate	..	..	..	..	..	..	..	..	..	..
1300 Unallocable between 1100 and 1200	..	16	..	..	..	..	..	..	..	..
2000 Social security contributions	..	**0**	**0**	**0**	**0**	..	**50 871**	**206 551**	**409 249**	**576 019**
2100 Employees	..	..	..	..	..	..	..	..	..	..
2200 Employers	..	..	..	..	..	..	..	..	..	..
2300 Self-employed or non-employed	..	..	..	..	..	..	..	..	..	..
2400 Unallocable between 2100, 2200 and 2300	..	..	..	..	..	..	50 871	206 551	409 249	576 019
3000 Taxes on payroll and workforce	..	**6**	**32**	**1**	**0**	..	**0**	**0**	**0**	**0**
4000 Taxes on property	..	**2 702**	**15 891**	**35 193**	**52 790**	..	**0**	**0**	**0**	**0**
4100 Recurrent taxes on immovable property	..	1 854	10 098	23 715	35 097	..	..	..	..	..
4200 Recurrent taxes on net wealth	..	0	0	0	0	..	..	..	..	..
4300 Estate, inheritance and gift taxes	..	0	0	0	0	..	..	..	..	..
4400 Taxes on financial and capital transactions	..	848	5 793	11 477	17 694	..	..	..	..	..
4500 Non-recurrent taxes	..	0	0	0	0	..	..	..	..	..
4600 Other recurrent taxes on property	..	0	0	0	0	..	..	..	..	..
5000 Taxes on goods and services	..	**582**	**288**	**789**	**657**	..	**0**	**0**	**0**	**0**
5100 Taxes on production, sale, transfer, etc	..	575	214	728	519	..	..	..	..	..
5110 General taxes	..	0	0	0	0	..	..	..	..	..
5120 Taxes on specific goods and services	..	572	214	728	519	..	..	..	..	..
5130 Unallocable between 5110 and 5120	..	3	0	0	0	..	..	..	..	..
5200 Taxes on use of goods and perform activities	..	7	74	61	139	..	..	..	..	..
5300 Unallocable between 5100 and 5200	..	0	0	0	0	..	..	..	..	..
6000 Other taxes	..	**179**	**1 539**	**10 743**	**10 618**	..	**0**	**0**	**0**	**0**
6100 Paid solely by business	..	0	0	0	0	..	..	..	..	..
6200 Other	..	179	1 539	10 743	10 618	..	..	..	..	..
Total tax revenue (collecting government)	..	**3 485**	**17 750**	**46 726**	**64 066**	..	**50 871**	**206 551**	**409 249**	**576 019**
Adjustment[1]	..	**9 890**	**60 601**	**134 892**	**208 387**	..	**0**	**0**	**0**	**0**
Total tax revenue (beneficiary government)	..	**13 375**	**78 351**	**181 617**	**272 452**	..	**50 871**	**206 551**	**409 249**	**576 019**

.. Not available

1. This adjustment is for taxes collected by Federal government in which States and Local governments have a share. Sub-central government's shares cannot be identified by type of tax.

StatLink https://stat.link/7qjxco

Table 6.26. Netherlands, tax revenues by sub-sectors of government

Million EUR

	Central government					State/Regional				
	1975	1995	2005	2015	2020	1975	1995	2005	2015	2020
1000 Taxes on income, profits and capital gains	**15 075**	**33 520**	**52 640**	**70 849**	**97 810**	**..**	**..**	**..**	**..**	**..**
1100 Of individuals	11 713	23 557	33 905	52 405	73 116	..	..	..	..	..
1200 Corporate	3 361	9 963	18 735	18 444	24 694	..	..	..	..	..
1300 Unallocable between 1100 and 1200	0	0	0	0	0	..	..	..	..	..
2000 Social security contributions	**0**	**0**	**0**	**0**	**0**	**..**	**..**	**..**	**..**	**..**
2100 Employees	..	..	..	..	..	..	..	..	..	..
2200 Employers	..	..	..	..	..	..	..	..	..	..
2300 Self-employed or non-employed	..	..	..	..	..	..	..	..	..	..
2400 Unallocable between 2100, 2200 and 2300	..	..	..	..	..	..	..	..	..	..
3000 Taxes on payroll and workforce	**0**	**0**	**0**	**0**	**0**	**..**	**..**	**..**	**..**	**..**
4000 Taxes on property	**767**	**2 880**	**6 235**	**4 731**	**7 522**	**..**	**..**	**..**	**..**	**..**
4100 Recurrent taxes on immovable property	50	0	0	1 345	1 888	..	..	..	..	..
4200 Recurrent taxes on net wealth	231	671	60	0	0	..	..	..	..	..
4300 Estate, inheritance and gift taxes	163	773	1 709	1 614	2 081	..	..	..	..	..
4400 Taxes on financial and capital transactions	323	1 436	4 466	1 772	3 553	..	..	..	..	..
4500 Non-recurrent taxes	0	0	0	0	0	..	..	..	..	..
4600 Other recurrent taxes on property	0	0	0	0	0	..	..	..	..	..
5000 Taxes on goods and services	**9 716**	**31 892**	**57 116**	**70 161**	**88 408**	**..**	**..**	**..**	**..**	**..**
5100 Taxes on production, sale, transfer, etc	9 113	29 728	54 658	65 990	83 705	..	..	..	..	..
5110 General taxes	6 257	19 832	36 950	44 879	58 971	..	..	..	..	..
5120 Taxes on specific goods and services	2 856	9 896	17 708	21 111	24 734	..	..	..	..	..
5130 Unallocable between 5110 and 5120	0	0	0	0	0	..	..	..	..	..
5200 Taxes on use of goods and perform activities	604	2 164	2 458	4 171	4 703	..	..	..	..	..
5300 Unallocable between 5100 and 5200	0	0	0	0	0	..	..	..	..	..
6000 Other taxes	**109**	**491**	**989**	**416**	**1 529**	**..**	**..**	**..**	**..**	**..**
6100 Paid solely by business	109	448	372	0	0	..	..	..	..	..
6200 Other	0	43	617	416	1 529	..	..	..	..	..
Total tax revenue	**25 667**	**68 783**	**116 980**	**146 157**	**195 269**	**..**	**..**	**..**	**..**	**..**

	Local government					Social Security Funds				
	1975	1995	2005	2015	2020	1975	1995	2005	2015	2020
1000 Taxes on income, profits and capital gains	**77**	**0**	**0**	**0**	**0**	**0**	**0**	**0**	**0**	**0**
1100 Of individuals	77	0	0	0	0	0	0	0	0	0
1200 Corporate	0	0	0	0	0	0	0	0	0	0
1300 Unallocable between 1100 and 1200	0	0	0	0	0	0	0	0	0	0
2000 Social security contributions	**0**	**0**	**0**	**0**	**0**	**16 732**	**48 532**	**66 547**	**96 426**	**108 685**
2100 Employees	..	..	..	..	..	7 139	32 795	35 383	48 213	40 295
2200 Employers	..	..	..	..	..	7 687	5 941	20 595	34 614	44 135
2300 Self-employed or non-employed	..	..	..	..	..	1 905	9 796	10 569	13 599	24 255
2400 Unallocable between 2100, 2200 and 2300	..	..	..	..	..	0	0	0	0	0
3000 Taxes on payroll and workforce	**0**	**0**	**0**	**0**	**0**	**0**	**0**	**0**	**0**	**0**
4000 Taxes on property	**272**	**2 287**	**4 341**	**5 037**	**6 022**	**0**	**0**	**0**	**0**	**0**
4100 Recurrent taxes on immovable property	272	2 287	4 341	5 037	6 022	..	..	..	..	..
4200 Recurrent taxes on net wealth	0	0	0	0	0	..	..	..	..	..
4300 Estate, inheritance and gift taxes	0	0	0	0	0	..	..	..	..	..
4400 Taxes on financial and capital transactions	0	0	0	0	0	..	..	..	..	..
4500 Non-recurrent taxes	0	0	0	0	0	..	..	..	..	..
4600 Other recurrent taxes on property	0	0	0	0	0	..	..	..	..	..
5000 Taxes on goods and services	**153**	**1 533**	**3 330**	**4 652**	**5 101**	**0**	**0**	**0**	**0**	**0**
5100 Taxes on production, sale, transfer, etc	14	59	118	249	278	..	..	..	..	..
5110 General taxes	0	6	10	43	67	..	..	..	..	..
5120 Taxes on specific goods and services	14	53	108	206	211	..	..	..	..	..
5130 Unallocable between 5110 and 5120	0	0	0	0	0	..	..	..	..	..
5200 Taxes on use of goods and perform activities	139	1 474	3 212	4 403	4 823	..	..	..	..	..
5300 Unallocable between 5100 and 5200	0	0	0	0	0	..	..	..	..	..
6000 Other taxes	**0**	**0**	**0**	**0**	**0**	**0**	**0**	**0**	**0**	**0**
6100 Paid solely by business	..	..	..	..	..	..	..	..	..	..
6200 Other	..	..	..	..	..	..	..	..	..	..
Total tax revenue	**502**	**3 820**	**7 671**	**9 689**	**11 123**	**16 732**	**48 532**	**66 547**	**96 426**	**108 685**

.. Not available

Note: Including taxes collected on behalf of the European Union.

StatLink https://stat.link/l21xw7

Table 6.27. New Zealand, tax revenues by sub-sectors of government

Million NZD

	Central government					State/Regional				
	1975	1995	2005	2015	2020	1975	1995	2005	2015	2020
1000 Taxes on income, profits and capital gains	**2 296**	**21 253**	**37 379**	**44 723**	**65 298**	**..**	**..**	**..**	**..**	**..**
1100 Of individuals	1 874	15 626	24 373	30 297	44 494	..	..	..	..	..
1200 Corporate	407	4 122	9 957	11 407	17 819	..	..	..	..	..
1300 Unallocable between 1100 and 1200	16	1 505	3 049	3 019	2 985	..	..	..	..	..
2000 Social security contributions	**0**	**0**	**0**	**0**	**0**	**..**	**..**	**..**	**..**	**..**
2100 Employees	..	0	0	0	0	..	..	..	..	..
2200 Employers	..	0	0	0	0	..	..	..	..	..
2300 Self-employed or non-employed	..	0	0	0	0	..	..	..	..	..
2400 Unallocable between 2100, 2200 and 2300	..	0	0	0	0	..	..	..	..	..
3000 Taxes on payroll and workforce	**0**	**0**	**0**	**0**	**0**	**..**	**..**	**..**	**..**	**..**
4000 Taxes on property	**83**	**218**	**86**	**84**	**88**	**..**	**..**	**..**	**..**	**..**
4100 Recurrent taxes on immovable property	3	-1	0	0	0	..	..	..	..	..
4200 Recurrent taxes on net wealth	0	0	0	0	0	..	..	..	..	..
4300 Estate, inheritance and gift taxes	54	3	3	0	0	..	..	..	..	..
4400 Taxes on financial and capital transactions	25	216	83	84	88	..	..	..	..	..
4500 Non-recurrent taxes	0	0	0	0	0	..	..	..	..	..
4600 Other recurrent taxes on property	0	0	0	0	0	..	..	..	..	..
5000 Taxes on goods and services	**807**	**11 395**	**18 744**	**31 146**	**43 104**	**..**	**..**	**..**	**..**	**..**
5100 Taxes on production, sale, transfer, etc	770	10 833	17 792	29 551	40 943	..	..	..	..	..
5110 General taxes	311	7 895	14 133	24 587	35 397	..	..	..	..	..
5120 Taxes on specific goods and services	459	2 938	3 659	4 964	5 546	..	..	..	..	..
5130 Unallocable between 5110 and 5120	0	0	0	0	0	..	..	..	..	..
5200 Taxes on use of goods and perform activities	37	562	952	1 595	2 161	..	..	..	..	..
5300 Unallocable between 5100 and 5200	0	0	0	0	0	..	..	..	..	..
6000 Other taxes	**0**	**0**	**14**	**2**	**1**	**..**	**..**	**..**	**..**	**..**
6100 Paid solely by business	..	..	0	0	0	..	..	..	..	..
6200 Other	..	..	14	2	1	..	..	..	..	..
Total tax revenue	**3 186**	**32 866**	**56 223**	**75 955**	**108 491**	**..**	**..**	**..**	**..**	**..**

	Local government					Social Security Funds				
	1975	1995	2005	2015	2020	1975	1995	2005	2015	2020
1000 Taxes on income, profits and capital gains	**0**	**0**	**0**	**0**	**0**	**0**	**0**	**0**	**0**	**0**
1100 Of individuals	0	0	0	0	0	0	0	0	0	0
1200 Corporate	0	0	0	0	0	0	0	0	0	0
1300 Unallocable between 1100 and 1200	0	0	0	0	0	0	0	0	0	0
2000 Social security contributions	**0**	**0**	**0**	**0**	**0**	**0**	**0**	**0**	**0**	**0**
2100 Employees	..	0	0	0	0	..	0	0	0	0
2200 Employers	..	0	0	0	0	..	0	0	0	0
2300 Self-employed or non-employed	..	0	0	0	0	..	0	0	0	0
2400 Unallocable between 2100, 2200 and 2300	..	0	0	0	0	..	0	0	0	0
3000 Taxes on payroll and workforce	**0**	**0**	**0**	**0**	**0**	**0**	**0**	**0**	**0**	**0**
4000 Taxes on property	**237**	**1 646**	**2 825**	**4 962**	**6 273**	**0**	**0**	**0**	**0**	**0**
4100 Recurrent taxes on immovable property	237	1 646	2 825	4 962	6 273	..	..	..	..	..
4200 Recurrent taxes on net wealth	0	0	0	0	0	..	..	..	..	..
4300 Estate, inheritance and gift taxes	0	0	0	0	0	..	..	..	..	..
4400 Taxes on financial and capital transactions	0	0	0	0	0	..	..	..	..	..
4500 Non-recurrent taxes	0	0	0	0	0	..	..	..	..	..
4600 Other recurrent taxes on property	0	0	0	0	0	..	..	..	..	..
5000 Taxes on goods and services	**29**	**184**	**310**	**582**	**836**	**0**	**0**	**0**	**0**	**0**
5100 Taxes on production, sale, transfer, etc	18	33	30	33	179	..	..	..	..	..
5110 General taxes	0	0	0	0	0	..	..	..	..	..
5120 Taxes on specific goods and services	18	33	30	33	179	..	..	..	..	..
5130 Unallocable between 5110 and 5120	0	0	0	0	0	..	..	..	..	..
5200 Taxes on use of goods and perform activities	11	151	280	549	657	..	..	..	..	..
5300 Unallocable between 5100 and 5200	0	0	0	0	0	..	..	..	..	..
6000 Other taxes	**0**	**0**	**0**	**0**	**0**	**0**	**0**	**0**	**0**	**0**
6100 Paid solely by business	..	..	..	..	..	..	..	..	..	..
6200 Other	..	..	..	..	..	..	..	..	..	..
Total tax revenue	**266**	**1 830**	**3 135**	**5 544**	**7 109**	**0**	**0**	**0**	**0**	**0**

.. Not available

StatLink https://stat.link/z7swiq

Table 6.28. Norway, tax revenues by sub-sectors of government

Million NOK

	Central government[1]					State/Regional				
	1975	1995	2005	2015	2020	1975	1995	2005	2015	2020
1000 Taxes on income, profits and capital gains	**6 495**	**67 402**	**316 851**	**314 792**	**277 300**	**..**	**..**	**..**	**..**	**..**
1100 Of individuals	5 424	38 059	87 503	174 617	195 917	..	..	..	..	..
1200 Corporate	1 071	29 343	229 348	140 175	81 383	..	..	..	..	..
1300 Unallocable between 1100 and 1200	0	0	0	0	0	..	..	..	..	..
2000 Social security contributions	**1 341**	**6 013**	**173 151**	**325 130**	**381 838**	**..**	**..**	**..**	**..**	**..**
2100 Employees	331	1 233	58 320	112 662	134 450	..	..	..	..	..
2200 Employers	1 010	4 780	104 794	190 923	222 175	..	..	..	..	..
2300 Self-employed or non-employed	0	0	10 037	21 545	25 213	..	..	..	..	..
2400 Unallocable between 2100, 2200 and 2300	0	0	0	0	0	..	..	..	..	..
3000 Taxes on payroll and workforce	**0**	**0**	**0**	**0**	**2 065**	**..**	**..**	**..**	**..**	**..**
4000 Taxes on property	**771**	**3 497**	**11 178**	**12 209**	**16 525**	**..**	**..**	**..**	**..**	**..**
4100 Recurrent taxes on immovable property	0	0	0	0	0	..	..	..	..	..
4200 Recurrent taxes on net wealth	490	1 172	4 741	3 488	5 109	..	..	..	..	..
4300 Estate, inheritance and gift taxes	146	975	1 768	295	64	..	..	..	..	..
4400 Taxes on financial and capital transactions	135	1 350	4 669	8 426	11 352	..	..	..	..	..
4500 Non-recurrent taxes	0	0	0	0	0	..	..	..	..	..
4600 Other recurrent taxes on property	0	0	0	0	0	..	..	..	..	..
5000 Taxes on goods and services	**25 056**	**141 645**	**232 462**	**359 255**	**422 361**	**..**	**..**	**..**	**..**	**..**
5100 Taxes on production, sale, transfer, etc	24 367	134 965	220 898	342 410	403 893	..	..	..	..	..
5110 General taxes	13 670	81 772	153 820	256 029	312 936	..	..	..	..	..
5120 Taxes on specific goods and services	10 697	53 193	67 078	86 381	90 957	..	..	..	..	..
5130 Unallocable between 5110 and 5120	0	0	0	0	0	..	..	..	..	..
5200 Taxes on use of goods and perform activities	689	6 680	11 564	16 845	18 468	..	..	..	..	..
5300 Unallocable between 5100 and 5200	0	0	0	0	0	..	..	..	..	..
6000 Other taxes	**130**	**15**	**0**	**0**	**0**	**..**	**..**	**..**	**..**	**..**
6100 Paid solely by business	124	1	..	..	..	..	..	..	..	..
6200 Other	6	14	..	..	..	..	..	..	..	..
Total tax revenue	**33 793**	**218 572**	**733 642**	**1 011 386**	**1 100 089**	**..**	**..**	**..**	**..**	**..**
	Local government					Social Security Funds				
	1975	1995	2005	2015	2020	1975	1995	2005	2015	2020
1000 Taxes on income, profits and capital gains	**13 725**	**67 978**	**100 512**	**160 582**	**193 212**	**2 728**	**0**	**0**	**0**	**0**
1100 Of individuals	12 877	61 784	100 512	160 582	193 212	2 728	..	..	..	..
1200 Corporate	848	6 194	0	0	0	0	..	..	..	..
1300 Unallocable between 1100 and 1200	0	0	0	0	0	0	..	..	..	..
2000 Social security contributions	**0**	**0**	**0**	**0**	**0**	**15 224**	**84 563**	**0**	**0**	**0**
2100 Employees	..	..	..	..	..	2 949	30 417	..	..	..
2200 Employers	..	..	..	..	..	11 315	48 396	..	..	..
2300 Self-employed or non-employed	..	..	..	..	..	960	5 750	..	..	..
2400 Unallocable between 2100, 2200 and 2300	..	..	..	..	..	0	0	..	..	..
3000 Taxes on payroll and workforce	**0**	**0**	**0**	**0**	**0**	**0**	**0**	**0**	**0**	**0**
4000 Taxes on property	**772**	**7 352**	**10 283**	**21 812**	**28 168**	**0**	**0**	**0**	**0**	**0**
4100 Recurrent taxes on immovable property	278	2 792	4 324	11 177	14 818	..	..	..	..	..
4200 Recurrent taxes on net wealth	494	4 560	5 959	10 635	13 350	..	..	..	..	..
4300 Estate, inheritance and gift taxes	0	0	0	0	0	..	..	..	..	..
4400 Taxes on financial and capital transactions	0	0	0	0	0	..	..	..	..	..
4500 Non-recurrent taxes	0	0	0	0	0	..	..	..	..	..
4600 Other recurrent taxes on property	0	0	0	0	0	..	..	..	..	..
5000 Taxes on goods and services	**0**	**431**	**2 281**	**1 574**	**1 643**	**51**	**267**	**0**	**0**	**0**
5100 Taxes on production, sale, transfer, etc	0	0	0	0	0	51	267	..	..	..
5110 General taxes	0	0	0	0	0	0	0	..	..	..
5120 Taxes on specific goods and services	0	0	0	0	0	51	267	..	..	..
5130 Unallocable between 5110 and 5120	0	0	0	0	0	0	0	..	..	..
5200 Taxes on use of goods and perform activities	0	431	2 281	1 574	1 643	0	0	..	..	..
5300 Unallocable between 5100 and 5200	0	0	0	0	0	0	0	..	..	..
6000 Other taxes	**432**	**0**	**0**	**0**	**0**	**0**	**0**	**0**	**0**	**0**
6100 Paid solely by business	0	..	..	..	..	..	..	..	..	..
6200 Other	432	..	..	..	..	..	..	..	..	..
Total tax revenue	**14 929**	**75 761**	**113 076**	**183 968**	**223 023**	**18 003**	**84 830**	**0**	**0**	**0**

.. Not available

1. The Norwegian National Insurance has been integrated into the Central government sector from the year 2000 onwards.

StatLink https://stat.link/1dy6nj

Table 6.29. Poland, tax revenues by sub-sectors of government

Million PLN

	Central government					State/Regional				
	1975	1995	2005	2015	2020	1975	1995	2005	2015	2020
1000 Taxes on income, profits and capital gains	..	**32 774**	**40 398**	**71 381**	**108 211**	..	..	..	..	..
1100 Of individuals	..	23 937	24 518	45 462	66 746	..	..	..	..	..
1200 Corporate	..	8 837	15 880	25 919	41 465	..	..	..	..	..
1300 Unallocable between 1100 and 1200	..	0	0	0	0	..	..	..	..	..
2000 Social security contributions	..	**0**	**0**	**0**	**0**	..	..	..	..	..
2100 Employees	..	..	..	..	..	..	..	..	..	..
2200 Employers	..	..	..	..	..	..	..	..	..	..
2300 Self-employed or non-employed	..	..	..	..	..	..	..	..	..	..
2400 Unallocable between 2100, 2200 and 2300	..	..	..	..	..	..	..	..	..	..
3000 Taxes on payroll and workforce	..	**831**	**2 555**	**4 028**	**7 683**	..	..	..	..	..
4000 Taxes on property	..	**0**	**0**	**0**	**0**	..	..	..	..	..
4100 Recurrent taxes on immovable property	..	..	..	..	..	..	..	..	..	..
4200 Recurrent taxes on net wealth	..	..	..	..	..	..	..	..	..	..
4300 Estate, inheritance and gift taxes	..	..	..	..	..	..	..	..	..	..
4400 Taxes on financial and capital transactions	..	..	..	..	..	..	..	..	..	..
4500 Non-recurrent taxes	..	..	..	..	..	..	..	..	..	..
4600 Other recurrent taxes on property	..	..	..	..	..	..	..	..	..	..
5000 Taxes on goods and services	..	**43 483**	**120 207**	**207 129**	**292 680**	..	..	..	..	..
5100 Taxes on production, sale, transfer, etc	..	42 863	119 805	203 303	279 425	..	..	..	..	..
5110 General taxes	..	21 051	75 783	125 895	185 964	..	..	..	..	..
5120 Taxes on specific goods and services	..	21 812	44 022	77 408	93 461	..	..	..	..	..
5130 Unallocable between 5110 and 5120	..	0	0	0	0	..	..	..	..	..
5200 Taxes on use of goods and perform activities	..	620	402	3 826	13 255	..	..	..	..	..
5300 Unallocable between 5100 and 5200	..	0	0	0	0	..	..	..	..	..
6000 Other taxes	..	**99**	**18**	**0**	**0**	..	..	..	..	..
6100 Paid solely by business	..	0	0	..	..	..	..	..	..	..
6200 Other	..	99	18	..	..	..	..	..	..	..
Total tax revenue	..	**77 187**	**163 178**	**282 538**	**408 574**	..	..	..	..	..

	Local government					Social Security Funds				
	1975	1995	2005	2015	2020	1975	1995	2005	2015	2020
1000 Taxes on income, profits and capital gains	..	**4 896**	**23 093**	**45 697**	**67 634**	..	**0**	**0**	**0**	**0**
1100 Of individuals	..	4 427	17 916	38 512	56 227	..	..	..	..	..
1200 Corporate	..	469	5 177	7 185	11 407	..	..	..	..	..
1300 Unallocable between 1100 and 1200	..	0	0	0	0	..	..	..	..	..
2000 Social security contributions	..	**0**	**0**	**0**	**0**	..	**38 808**	**121 522**	**225 711**	**318 637**
2100 Employees	..	..	..	..	..	..	16 727	49 469	92 052	132 901
2200 Employers	..	..	..	..	..	..	19 364	47 753	89 570	121 101
2300 Self-employed or non-employed	..	..	..	..	..	..	2 717	24 300	44 089	64 635
2400 Unallocable between 2100, 2200 and 2300	..	..	..	..	..	..	0	0	0	0
3000 Taxes on payroll and workforce	..	**0**	**0**	**0**	**0**	..	**0**	**0**	**0**	**0**
4000 Taxes on property	..	**4 370**	**14 723**	**24 637**	**30 293**	..	**0**	**0**	**0**	**0**
4100 Recurrent taxes on immovable property	..	3 579	12 718	22 206	26 454	..	..	..	..	..
4200 Recurrent taxes on net wealth	..	0	0	0	0	..	..	..	..	..
4300 Estate, inheritance and gift taxes	..	44	242	246	313	..	..	..	..	..
4400 Taxes on financial and capital transactions	..	747	1 763	2 185	3 526	..	..	..	..	..
4500 Non-recurrent taxes	..	0	0	0	0	..	..	..	..	..
4600 Other recurrent taxes on property	..	0	0	0	0	..	..	..	..	..
5000 Taxes on goods and services	..	**1 340**	**3 492**	**4 139**	**3 958**	..	**0**	**0**	**0**	**0**
5100 Taxes on production, sale, transfer, etc	..	0	0	0	0	..	..	..	..	..
5110 General taxes	..	..	..	..	..	..	..	..	..	..
5120 Taxes on specific goods and services	..	..	..	..	..	..	..	..	..	..
5130 Unallocable between 5110 and 5120	..	..	..	..	..	..	..	..	..	..
5200 Taxes on use of goods and perform activities	..	1 340	3 492	4 139	3 958	..	..	..	..	..
5300 Unallocable between 5100 and 5200	..	0	0	0	0	..	..	..	..	..
6000 Other taxes	..	**158**	**278**	**647**	**986**	..	**0**	**0**	**0**	**0**
6100 Paid solely by business	..	0	0	0	0	..	..	..	..	..
6200 Other	..	158	278	647	986	..	..	..	..	..
Total tax revenue	..	**10 764**	**41 586**	**75 120**	**102 871**	..	**38 808**	**121 522**	**225 711**	**318 637**

.. Not available

Note: Including taxes collected on behalf of the European Union.

StatLink https://stat.link/ag8ubn

Table 6.30. Portugal, tax revenues by sub-sectors of government

Million EUR

	Central government					State/Regional				
	1975	1995	2005	2015	2020	1975	1995	2005	2015	2020
1000 Taxes on income, profits and capital gains	**81**	**6 557**	**11 576**	**17 516**	**18 197**	**..**	**..**	**..**	**..**	**..**
1100 Of individuals	..	4 691	7 694	12 316	13 123	..	..	..	..	..
1200 Corporate	..	1 866	3 761	5 199	5 074	..	..	..	..	..
1300 Unallocable between 1100 and 1200	81	0	121	0	0	..	..	..	..	..
2000 Social security contributions	**0**	**1 560**	**1 887**	**2 064**	**2 105**	**..**	**..**	**..**	**..**	**..**
2100 Employees	..	941	1 629	1 867	1 969	..	..	..	..	..
2200 Employers	..	619	259	198	136	..	..	..	..	..
2300 Self-employed or non-employed	..	0	0	0	0	..	..	..	..	..
2400 Unallocable between 2100, 2200 and 2300	..	0	0	0	0	..	..	..	..	..
3000 Taxes on payroll and workforce	**12**	**0**	**0**	**0**	**0**	**..**	**..**	**..**	**..**	**..**
4000 Taxes on property	**12**	**226**	**308**	**202**	**481**	**..**	**..**	**..**	**..**	**..**
4100 Recurrent taxes on immovable property	0	0	0	6	149	..	..	..	..	..
4200 Recurrent taxes on net wealth	0	0	0	0	0	..	..	..	..	..
4300 Estate, inheritance and gift taxes	4	57	68	0	0	..	..	..	..	..
4400 Taxes on financial and capital transactions	7	169	240	196	331	..	..	..	..	..
4500 Non-recurrent taxes	0	0	0	0	0	..	..	..	..	..
4600 Other recurrent taxes on property	0	0	0	0	0	..	..	..	..	..
5000 Taxes on goods and services	**198**	**10 402**	**19 495**	**21 488**	**23 750**	**..**	**..**	**..**	**..**	**..**
5100 Taxes on production, sale, transfer, etc	187	10 195	19 233	20 881	22 773	..	..	..	..	..
5110 General taxes	52	5 481	11 846	13 745	15 215	..	..	..	..	..
5120 Taxes on specific goods and services	135	4 714	7 387	7 136	7 558	..	..	..	..	..
5130 Unallocable between 5110 and 5120	0	0	0	0	0	..	..	..	..	..
5200 Taxes on use of goods and perform activities	12	178	235	594	970	..	..	..	..	..
5300 Unallocable between 5100 and 5200	0	30	27	13	7	..	..	..	..	..
6000 Other taxes	**2**	**98**	**431**	**570**	**682**	**..**	**..**	**..**	**..**	**..**
6100 Paid solely by business	1	18	143	333	434	..	..	..	..	..
6200 Other	0	81	288	237	248	..	..	..	..	..
Total tax revenue	**304**	**18 844**	**33 697**	**41 840**	**45 215**	**..**	**..**	**..**	**..**	**..**

	Local government					Social Security Funds				
	1975	1995	2005	2015	2020	1975	1995	2005	2015	2020
1000 Taxes on income, profits and capital gains	**0**	**307**	**725**	**1 246**	**1 351**	**0**	**0**	**0**	**0**	**0**
1100 Of individuals	..	156	298	832	886	..	..	..	..	..
1200 Corporate	..	151	427	414	466	..	..	..	..	..
1300 Unallocable between 1100 and 1200	0	0	0	0	0	..	..	..	..	..
2000 Social security contributions	**0**	**2**	**7**	**19**	**0**	**161**	**5 267**	**11 133**	**14 099**	**18 809**
2100 Employees	..	2	7	19	..	62	2 100	4 053	5 106	6 325
2200 Employers	..	0	0	0	..	97	3 167	7 080	8 993	12 484
2300 Self-employed or non-employed	..	0	0	0	..	2	0	0	0	0
2400 Unallocable between 2100, 2200 and 2300	..	0	0	0	..	0	0	0	0	0
3000 Taxes on payroll and workforce	**0**	**0**	**0**	**0**	**0**	**0**	**0**	**0**	**0**	**0**
4000 Taxes on property	**0**	**599**	**1 541**	**2 105**	**2 447**	**0**	**0**	**0**	**0**	**0**
4100 Recurrent taxes on immovable property	..	310	827	1 529	1 486	..	..	..	..	..
4200 Recurrent taxes on net wealth	..	0	0	0	0	..	..	..	..	..
4300 Estate, inheritance and gift taxes	..	0	1	0	0	..	..	..	..	..
4400 Taxes on financial and capital transactions	..	289	713	576	961	..	..	..	..	..
4500 Non-recurrent taxes	..	0	0	0	0	..	..	..	..	..
4600 Other recurrent taxes on property	..	0	0	0	0	..	..	..	..	..
5000 Taxes on goods and services	**0**	**499**	**962**	**1 132**	**1 289**	**0**	**335**	**823**	**1 179**	**1 087**
5100 Taxes on production, sale, transfer, etc	0	442	827	876	997	..	335	823	1 179	1 074
5110 General taxes	0	318	563	629	704	..	276	592	994	883
5120 Taxes on specific goods and services	0	124	264	247	293	..	59	231	184	191
5130 Unallocable between 5110 and 5120	0	0	0	0	0	..	0	0	0	0
5200 Taxes on use of goods and perform activities	0	57	133	256	292	..	0	0	0	13
5300 Unallocable between 5100 and 5200	0	0	1	0	0	..	0	0	0	0
6000 Other taxes	**0**	**3**	**28**	**10**	**10**	**0**	**1**	**0**	**0**	**0**
6100 Paid solely by business	..	0	25	8	8	..	0	..	..	..
6200 Other	..	3	3	2	2	..	1	..	..	..
Total tax revenue	**0**	**1 410**	**3 262**	**4 512**	**5 098**	**161**	**5 603**	**11 956**	**15 278**	**19 896**

.. Not available

Note: Including taxes collected on behalf of the European Union.

StatLink https://stat.link/bn497w

Table 6.31. Slovak Republic, tax revenues by sub-sectors of government

Million EUR

	Central government					State/Regional				
	1975	1995	2005	2015	2020	1975	1995	2005	2015	2020
1000 Taxes on income, profits and capital gains	..	**1 993**	**2 968**	**5 542**	**6 535**	..	..	..	..	..
1100 Of individuals	..	695	1 496	2 464	3 500	..	..	..	..	..
1200 Corporate	..	1 166	1 345	2 917	2 800	..	..	..	..	..
1300 Unallocable between 1100 and 1200	..	132	128	162	235	..	..	..	..	..
2000 Social security contributions	..	**85**	**240**	**253**	**422**	..	..	..	..	..
2100 Employees	..	10	104	58	136	..	..	..	..	..
2200 Employers	..	75	136	195	285	..	..	..	..	..
2300 Self-employed or non-employed	..	0	0	0	1	..	..	..	..	..
2400 Unallocable between 2100, 2200 and 2300	..	0	0	0	0	..	..	..	..	..
3000 Taxes on payroll and workforce	..	**0**	**0**	**0**	**0**	..	..	..	..	..
4000 Taxes on property	..	**27**	**28**	**0**	**0**	..	..	..	..	..
4100 Recurrent taxes on immovable property	..	8	9	0	0	..	..	..	..	..
4200 Recurrent taxes on net wealth	..	0	0	0	0	..	..	..	..	..
4300 Estate, inheritance and gift taxes	..	2	1	0	0	..	..	..	..	..
4400 Taxes on financial and capital transactions	..	16	18	0	0	..	..	..	..	..
4500 Non-recurrent taxes	..	0	0	0	0	..	..	..	..	..
4600 Other recurrent taxes on property	..	0	0	0	0	..	..	..	..	..
5000 Taxes on goods and services	..	**2 782**	**6 031**	**8 974**	**10 818**	..	..	..	..	..
5100 Taxes on production, sale, transfer, etc	..	2 594	5 773	8 442	10 221	..	..	..	..	..
5110 General taxes	..	1 616	3 880	5 423	6 820	..	..	..	..	..
5120 Taxes on specific goods and services	..	978	1 893	3 020	3 401	..	..	..	..	..
5130 Unallocable between 5110 and 5120	..	0	0	0	0	..	..	..	..	..
5200 Taxes on use of goods and perform activities	..	189	256	532	597	..	..	..	..	..
5300 Unallocable between 5100 and 5200	..	0	2	0	0	..	..	..	..	..
6000 Other taxes	..	**0**	**0**	**0**	**0**	..	..	..	..	..
6100 Paid solely by business	..	..	..	..	..	..	..	..	..	..
6200 Other	..	..	..	..	..	..	..	..	..	..
Total tax revenue	..	**4 887**	**9 267**	**14 770**	**17 775**	..	..	..	..	..

	Local government					Social Security Funds				
	1975	1995	2005	2015	2020	1975	1995	2005	2015	2020
1000 Taxes on income, profits and capital gains	..	**0**	**0**	**0**	**0**	..	**0**	**0**	**0**	**0**
1100 Of individuals	..	..	..	..	..	..	..	..	..	..
1200 Corporate	..	..	..	..	..	..	..	..	..	..
1300 Unallocable between 1100 and 1200	..	..	..	..	..	..	..	..	..	..
2000 Social security contributions	..	**0**	**0**	**0**	**0**	..	**2 817**	**6 037**	**10 643**	**13 811**
2100 Employees	..	..	..	0	0	..	540	1 377	2 352	3 341
2200 Employers	..	..	..	0	0	..	1 774	3 356	6 124	8 369
2300 Self-employed or non-employed	..	..	..	0	0	..	503	1 304	2 168	2 102
2400 Unallocable between 2100, 2200 and 2300	..	..	..	0	0	..	0	0	0	0
3000 Taxes on payroll and workforce	..	**0**	**0**	**0**	**0**	..	**0**	**0**	**0**	**0**
4000 Taxes on property	..	**84**	**220**	**335**	**438**	..	**0**	**0**	**0**	**0**
4100 Recurrent taxes on immovable property	..	72	220	335	438	..	..	..	..	..
4200 Recurrent taxes on net wealth	..	0	0	0	0	..	..	..	..	..
4300 Estate, inheritance and gift taxes	..	0	0	0	0	..	..	..	..	..
4400 Taxes on financial and capital transactions	..	12	0	0	0	..	..	..	..	..
4500 Non-recurrent taxes	..	0	0	0	0	..	..	..	..	..
4600 Other recurrent taxes on property	..	0	0	0	0	..	..	..	..	..
5000 Taxes on goods and services	..	**17**	**198**	**182**	**239**	..	**0**	**0**	**0**	**0**
5100 Taxes on production, sale, transfer, etc	..	10	9	12	12	..	..	..	..	..
5110 General taxes	..	0	0	0	0	..	..	..	..	..
5120 Taxes on specific goods and services	..	10	9	12	12	..	..	..	..	..
5130 Unallocable between 5110 and 5120	..	0	0	0	0	..	..	..	..	..
5200 Taxes on use of goods and perform activities	..	1	94	17	22	..	..	..	..	..
5300 Unallocable between 5100 and 5200	..	6	95	153	204	..	..	..	..	..
6000 Other taxes	..	**0**	**0**	**0**	**0**	..	**0**	**0**	**0**	**0**
6100 Paid solely by business	..	..	..	..	..	..	..	..	..	..
6200 Other	..	..	..	..	..	..	..	..	..	..
Total tax revenue	..	**101**	**418**	**517**	**676**	..	**2 817**	**6 037**	**10 643**	**13 811**

.. Not available

Note: Including taxes collected on behalf of the European Union.

StatLink https://stat.link/v7k0hd

Table 6.32. Slovenia, tax revenues by sub-sectors of government

Million EUR

	Central government					State/Regional				
	1975	1995	2005	2015	2020	1975	1995	2005	2015	2020
1000 Taxes on income, profits and capital gains	..	**479**	**1 828**	**1 528**	**2 062**	..	..	..	..	..
1100 Of individuals	..	413	1 029	958	1 145	..	..	..	..	..
1200 Corporate	..	54	795	568	914	..	..	..	..	..
1300 Unallocable between 1100 and 1200	..	12	5	2	2	..	..	..	..	..
2000 Social security contributions	..	**38**	**42**	**59**	**78**	..	..	..	..	..
2100 Employees	..	20	24	31	41	..	..	..	..	..
2200 Employers	..	17	15	23	31	..	..	..	..	..
2300 Self-employed or non-employed	..	1	3	5	6	..	..	..	..	..
2400 Unallocable between 2100, 2200 and 2300	..	0	0	0	0	..	..	..	..	..
3000 Taxes on payroll and workforce	..	**14**	**521**	**20**	**22**	..	..	..	..	..
4000 Taxes on property	..	**5**	**3**	**2**	**2**	..	..	..	..	..
4100 Recurrent taxes on immovable property	..	0	0	0	0	..	..	..	..	..
4200 Recurrent taxes on net wealth	..	0	3	0	0	..	..	..	..	..
4300 Estate, inheritance and gift taxes	..	0	0	0	0	..	..	..	..	..
4400 Taxes on financial and capital transactions	..	0	0	0	0	..	..	..	..	..
4500 Non-recurrent taxes	..	5	0	2	2	..	..	..	..	..
4600 Other recurrent taxes on property	..	0	0	0	0	..	..	..	..	..
5000 Taxes on goods and services	..	**1 554**	**3 826**	**5 543**	**5 746**	..	..	..	..	..
5100 Taxes on production, sale, transfer, etc	..	1 524	3 645	5 205	5 336	..	..	..	..	..
5110 General taxes	..	1 192	2 489	3 224	3 543	..	..	..	..	..
5120 Taxes on specific goods and services	..	332	1 156	1 981	1 792	..	..	..	..	..
5130 Unallocable between 5110 and 5120	..	0	0	0	0	..	..	..	..	..
5200 Taxes on use of goods and perform activities	..	31	181	338	410	..	..	..	..	..
5300 Unallocable between 5100 and 5200	..	0	0	0	0	..	..	..	..	..
6000 Other taxes	..	**0**	**0**	**0**	**0**	..	..	..	..	..
6100 Paid solely by business	..	..	..	..	..	..	..	..	..	..
6200 Other	..	..	..	..	..	..	..	..	..	..
Total tax revenue	..	**2 090**	**6 221**	**7 152**	**7 910**	..	..	..	..	..

	Local government					Social Security Funds				
	1975	1995	2005	2015	2020	1975	1995	2005	2015	2020
1000 Taxes on income, profits and capital gains	..	**194**	**559**	**1 019**	**1 326**	..	**0**	**0**	**0**	**0**
1100 Of individuals	..	192	556	1 019	1 326	..	..	..	..	..
1200 Corporate	..	0	0	0	0	..	..	..	..	..
1300 Unallocable between 1100 and 1200	..	2	2	0	0	..	..	..	..	..
2000 Social security contributions	..	**0**	**0**	**0**	**0**	..	**1 793**	**4 354**	**5 924**	**7 829**
2100 Employees	..	..	..	..	..	..	812	2 124	2 879	3 854
2200 Employers	..	..	..	..	..	..	806	1 579	2 112	2 834
2300 Self-employed or non-employed	..	..	..	..	..	..	175	652	933	1 142
2400 Unallocable between 2100, 2200 and 2300	..	..	..	..	..	..	0	0	0	0
3000 Taxes on payroll and workforce	..	**2**	**0**	**0**	**0**	..	**0**	**0**	**0**	**0**
4000 Taxes on property	..	**53**	**167**	**239**	**293**	..	**0**	**0**	**0**	**0**
4100 Recurrent taxes on immovable property	..	37	122	199	236	..	..	..	..	..
4200 Recurrent taxes on net wealth	..	0	0	0	0	..	..	..	..	..
4300 Estate, inheritance and gift taxes	..	1	5	8	10	..	..	..	..	..
4400 Taxes on financial and capital transactions	..	12	40	29	40	..	..	..	..	..
4500 Non-recurrent taxes	..	3	0	3	6	..	..	..	..	..
4600 Other recurrent taxes on property	..	0	0	0	0	..	..	..	..	..
5000 Taxes on goods and services	..	**7**	**91**	**96**	**78**	..	**0**	**0**	**0**	**0**
5100 Taxes on production, sale, transfer, etc	..	7	43	57	49	..	..	..	..	..
5110 General taxes	..	0	0	0	0	..	..	..	..	..
5120 Taxes on specific goods and services	..	7	43	57	49	..	..	..	..	..
5130 Unallocable between 5110 and 5120	..	0	0	0	0	..	..	..	..	..
5200 Taxes on use of goods and perform activities	..	0	48	39	30	..	..	..	..	..
5300 Unallocable between 5100 and 5200	..	0	0	0	0	..	..	..	..	..
6000 Other taxes	..	**0**	**0**	**0**	**0**	..	**0**	**0**	**0**	**0**
6100 Paid solely by business	..	..	..	..	..	..	..	..	..	..
6200 Other	..	..	..	..	..	..	..	..	..	..
Total tax revenue	..	**256**	**817**	**1 354**	**1 697**	..	**1 793**	**4 354**	**5 924**	**7 829**

.. Not available

Note: Including taxes collected on behalf of the European Union.

StatLink https://stat.link/2zp9u3

Table 6.33. Spain, tax revenues by sub-sectors of government

Million EUR

	Federal government					State/Regional				
	1975	1995	2005	2015	2020	1975	1995	2005	2015	2020
1000 Taxes on income, profits and capital gains	**1 388**	**38 846**	**71 598**	**62 198**	**60 956**	**..**	**588**	**19 503**	**34 814**	**52 062**
1100 Of individuals	897	31 789	38 219	39 659	40 290	..	457	19 104	34 600	51 797
1200 Corporate	490	7 057	33 379	22 539	20 666	..	131	399	214	265
1300 Unallocable between 1100 and 1200	1	0	0	0	0	..	0	0	0	0
2000 Social security contributions	**0**	**2 027**	**3 027**	**3 505**	**3 443**	**..**	**0**	**0**	**0**	**0**
2100 Employees	..	1 017	1 369	1 541	1 363	..	..	..	..	..
2200 Employers	..	1 010	1 658	1 964	2 080	..	..	..	..	..
2300 Self-employed or non-employed	..	0	0	0	0	..	..	..	..	..
2400 Unallocable between 2100, 2200 and 2300	..	0	0	0	0	..	..	..	..	..
3000 Taxes on payroll and workforce	**0**	**0**	**0**	**0**	**0**	**..**	**0**	**0**	**0**	**0**
4000 Taxes on property	**421**	**405**	**77**	**1 197**	**359**	**..**	**4 050**	**19 031**	**10 286**	**11 015**
4100 Recurrent taxes on immovable property	1	3	5	4	3	..	0	2	38	77
4200 Recurrent taxes on net wealth	0	166	38	32	59	..	419	1 246	961	1 270
4300 Estate, inheritance and gift taxes	56	1	24	222	57	..	835	2 315	2 454	2 315
4400 Taxes on financial and capital transactions	364	235	10	6	6	..	2 796	15 468	6 833	7 353
4500 Non-recurrent taxes	0	0	0	933	234	..	0	0	0	0
4600 Other recurrent taxes on property	0	0	0	0	0	..	0	0	0	0
5000 Taxes on goods and services	**1 609**	**32 388**	**71 536**	**89 031**	**89 142**	**..**	**2 556**	**7 956**	**6 553**	**5 271**
5100 Taxes on production, sale, transfer, etc	1 599	32 206	70 895	87 536	86 843	..	2 387	7 637	6 022	4 686
5110 General taxes	990	20 331	51 583	61 839	63 167	..	786	1 980	2 571	2 431
5120 Taxes on specific goods and services	608	11 875	19 312	25 697	23 676	..	1 601	5 657	3 451	2 255
5130 Unallocable between 5110 and 5120	0	0	0	0	0	..	0	0	0	0
5200 Taxes on use of goods and perform activities	10	182	641	1 495	2 299	..	169	319	531	585
5300 Unallocable between 5100 and 5200	0	0	0	0	0	..	0	0	0	0
6000 Other taxes	**0**	**0**	**0**	**101**	**66**	**..**	**0**	**1**	**19**	**8**
6100 Paid solely by business	0	..	..	0	0	..	..	0	0	0
6200 Other	0	..	..	101	66	..	..	1	19	8
Total tax revenue	**3 418**	**73 666**	**146 238**	**156 032**	**153 966**	**..**	**7 194**	**46 491**	**51 672**	**68 356**

	Local government					Social Security Funds				
	1975	1995	2005	2015	2020	1975	1995	2005	2015	2020
1000 Taxes on income, profits and capital gains	**175**	**2 514**	**4 892**	**5 633**	**6 767**	**0**	**0**	**0**	**0**	**0**
1100 Of individuals	131	2 137	3 426	4 637	5 683	..	..	..	..	..
1200 Corporate	0	377	1 466	996	1 084	..	..	..	..	..
1300 Unallocable between 1100 and 1200	44	0	0	0	0	..	..	..	..	..
2000 Social security contributions	**0**	**0**	**0**	**0**	**0**	**3 367**	**49 851**	**106 040**	**119 330**	**150 833**
2100 Employees	..	..	..	..	..	645	7 372	15 332	17 242	20 880
2200 Employers	..	..	..	..	..	2 722	35 137	77 989	86 024	110 300
2300 Self-employed or non-employed	..	..	..	..	..	0	7 342	12 719	16 064	19 653
2400 Unallocable between 2100, 2200 and 2300	..	..	..	..	..	0	0	0	0	0
3000 Taxes on payroll and workforce	**0**	**0**	**0**	**0**	**0**	**0**	**0**	**0**	**0**	**0**
4000 Taxes on property	**26**	**3 759**	**8 869**	**16 372**	**16 245**	**0**	**0**	**0**	**0**	**0**
4100 Recurrent taxes on immovable property	26	2 754	6 038	12 581	13 081	..	..	..	..	..
4200 Recurrent taxes on net wealth	0	177	431	911	968	..	..	..	..	..
4300 Estate, inheritance and gift taxes	0	19	79	114	122	..	..	..	..	..
4400 Taxes on financial and capital transactions	0	166	423	145	176	..	..	..	..	..
4500 Non-recurrent taxes	0	643	1 898	2 621	1 898	..	..	..	..	..
4600 Other recurrent taxes on property	0	0	0	0	0	..	..	..	..	..
5000 Taxes on goods and services	**104**	**6 072**	**12 810**	**13 067**	**13 273**	**0**	**0**	**0**	**0**	**0**
5100 Taxes on production, sale, transfer, etc	104	1 976	5 946	6 846	6 905	..	..	..	..	..
5110 General taxes	95	1 805	4 186	5 068	5 195	..	..	..	..	..
5120 Taxes on specific goods and services	10	171	1 760	1 778	1 710	..	..	..	..	..
5130 Unallocable between 5110 and 5120	0	0	0	0	0	..	..	..	..	..
5200 Taxes on use of goods and perform activities	0	4 096	6 864	6 221	6 368	..	..	..	..	..
5300 Unallocable between 5100 and 5200	0	0	0	0	0	..	..	..	..	..
6000 Other taxes	**0**	**8**	**6**	**69**	**31**	**0**	**0**	**0**	**0**	**0**
6100 Paid solely by business	..	0	0	0	0	..	..	..	..	..
6200 Other	..	8	6	69	31	..	..	..	..	..
Total tax revenue	**305**	**12 353**	**26 577**	**35 141**	**36 316**	**3 367**	**49 851**	**106 040**	**119 330**	**150 833**

.. Not available

Note: Including taxes collected on behalf of the European Union.

StatLink https://stat.link/p7kdor

Table 6.34. Sweden, tax revenues by sub-sectors of government

Million SEK

	Central government					State/Regional				
	1975	1995	2005	2015	2020	1975	1995	2005	2015	2020
1000 Taxes on income, profits and capital gains	**28 216**	**72 342**	**123 698**	**21 820**	**-3 425**	..	..	..	..	..
1100 Of individuals	25 626	22 541	21 708	-102 059	-152 187	..	..	..	..	..
1200 Corporate	2 590	49 801	101 989	123 878	148 762	..	..	..	..	..
1300 Unallocable between 1100 and 1200	0	0	0	0	0	..	..	..	..	..
2000 Social security contributions[1]	**0**	**50 560**	**212 964**	**180 723**	**186 304**	..	..	..	..	..
2100 Employees	..	0	0	0	0	..	..	..	..	..
2200 Employers	..	49 222	209 370	179 056	186 742	..	..	..	..	..
2300 Self-employed or non-employed	..	1 338	4 639	1 875	930	..	..	..	..	..
2400 Unallocable between 2100, 2200 and 2300	..	0	-1 044	-209	-1 368	..	..	..	..	..
3000 Taxes on payroll and workforce	**5 723**	**17 800**	**62 432**	**194 121**	**255 891**	..	..	..	..	..
4000 Taxes on property	**1 469**	**23 260**	**40 116**	**27 917**	**28 559**	..	..	..	..	..
4100 Recurrent taxes on immovable property	11	15 263	25 139	16 509	15 236	..	..	..	..	..
4200 Recurrent taxes on net wealth	647	3 583	4 998	0	0	..	..	..	..	..
4300 Estate, inheritance and gift taxes	335	1 388	1 092	0	0	..	..	..	..	..
4400 Taxes on financial and capital transactions	476	3 026	8 887	11 408	13 323	..	..	..	..	..
4500 Non-recurrent taxes	0	0	0	0	0	..	..	..	..	..
4600 Other recurrent taxes on property	0	0	0	0	0	..	..	..	..	..
5000 Taxes on goods and services	**31 985**	**237 720**	**354 724**	**508 210**	**601 974**	..	..	..	..	..
5100 Taxes on production, sale, transfer, etc	29 820	233 671	343 704	489 458	580 393	..	..	..	..	..
5110 General taxes	15 806	166 557	250 470	383 002	461 267	..	..	..	..	..
5120 Taxes on specific goods and services	14 014	67 114	93 234	106 456	119 125	..	..	..	..	..
5130 Unallocable between 5110 and 5120	0	0	0	0	0	..	..	..	..	..
5200 Taxes on use of goods and perform activities	2 165	4 049	11 019	18 752	21 581	..	..	..	..	..
5300 Unallocable between 5100 and 5200	0	0	0	0	0	..	..	..	..	..
6000 Other taxes	**260**	**1 438**	**1 347**	**1 356**	**2 374**	..	..	..	..	..
6100 Paid solely by business	0	0	0	0	0	..	..	..	..	..
6200 Other	260	1 438	1 347	1 356	2 374	..	..	..	..	..
Total tax revenue	**67 653**	**403 120**	**795 281**	**934 146**	**1 071 677**	..	..	..	..	..

	Local government					Social Security Funds				
	1975	1995	2005	2015	2020	1975	1995	2005	2015	2020
1000 Taxes on income, profits and capital gains	**38 415**	**265 068**	**435 577**	**635 719**	**766 082**	**0**	**0**	**0**	**0**	**0**
1100 Of individuals	35 269	265 068	435 577	635 719	766 082	..	..	..	..	..
1200 Corporate	3 146	0	0	0	0	..	..	..	..	..
1300 Unallocable between 1100 and 1200	0	0	0	0	0	..	..	..	..	..
2000 Social security contributions[1]	**0**	**0**	**0**	**0**	**0**	**25 756**	**186 992**	**151 019**	**224 129**	**269 092**
2100 Employees	..	..	..	..	..	0	28 989	74 178	108 356	131 044
2200 Employers	..	..	..	..	..	24 203	154 154	74 438	112 589	134 879
2300 Self-employed or non-employed	..	..	..	..	..	1 553	3 849	2 403	3 183	3 170
2400 Unallocable between 2100, 2200 and 2300	..	..	..	..	..	0	0	0	0	0
3000 Taxes on payroll and workforce	**0**	**0**	**0**	**0**	**0**	**0**	**0**	**0**	**0**	**0**
4000 Taxes on property	**0**	**0**	**0**	**15 935**	**19 326**	**0**	**0**	**0**	**0**	**0**
4100 Recurrent taxes on immovable property	..	..	..	15 935	19 326	..	..	..	..	..
4200 Recurrent taxes on net wealth	..	..	..	0	0	..	..	..	..	..
4300 Estate, inheritance and gift taxes	..	..	..	0	0	..	..	..	..	..
4400 Taxes on financial and capital transactions	..	..	..	0	0	..	..	..	..	..
4500 Non-recurrent taxes	..	..	..	0	0	..	..	..	..	..
4600 Other recurrent taxes on property	..	..	..	0	0	..	..	..	..	..
5000 Taxes on goods and services	**149**	**786**	**0**	**0**	**0**	**0**	**0**	**0**	**0**	**0**
5100 Taxes on production, sale, transfer, etc	119	732	0	0	0	..	..	..	..	..
5110 General taxes	0	0	0	0	0	..	..	..	..	..
5120 Taxes on specific goods and services	119	732	0	0	0	..	..	..	..	..
5130 Unallocable between 5110 and 5120	0	0	0	0	0	..	..	..	..	..
5200 Taxes on use of goods and perform activities	30	54	0	0	0	..	..	..	..	..
5300 Unallocable between 5100 and 5200	0	0	0	0	0	..	..	..	..	..
6000 Other taxes	**0**	**0**	**0**	**0**	**0**	**0**	**0**	**0**	**0**	**0**
6100 Paid solely by business	..	..	..	..	..	..	..	..	..	..
6200 Other	..	..	..	..	..	..	..	..	..	..
Total tax revenue	**38 564**	**265 854**	**435 577**	**651 654**	**785 407**	**25 756**	**186 992**	**151 019**	**224 129**	**269 092**

.. Not available

Note: Including taxes collected on behalf of the European Union.

1. From 1985, social security contributions are classified using the SNA definition of Social security Funds which means that a proportion of these payments are shown under the heading of Central Government. Prior to that year, all such payments were classified under the heading of Social Security.

StatLink https://stat.link/zqvjy1

Table 6.35. Switzerland, tax revenues by sub-sectors of government

Million CHF

	Federal government					State/Regional				
	1975	1995	2005	2015	2020	1975	1995	2005	2015	2020
1000 Taxes on income, profits and capital gains	**3 422**	**10 468**	**16 341**	**26 841**	**27 647**	**7 756**	**19 408**	**26 544**	**34 657**	**37 964**
1100 Of individuals	2 712	5 699	7 823	10 567	12 239	6 342	16 182	21 289	27 156	30 284
1200 Corporate	710	2 678	4 519	9 731	12 092	1 414	2 628	4 627	6 294	6 127
1300 Unallocable between 1100 and 1200	0	2 092	4 000	6 543	3 316	0	598	628	1 207	1 553
2000 Social security contributions	**0**	**0**	**0**	**0**	**0**	**0**	**0**	**0**	**0**	**0**
2100 Employees	..	..	..	..	..	..	..	..	..	..
2200 Employers	..	..	..	..	..	..	..	..	..	..
2300 Self-employed or non-employed	..	..	..	..	..	..	..	..	..	..
2400 Unallocable between 2100, 2200 and 2300	..	..	..	..	..	..	..	..	..	..
3000 Taxes on payroll and workforce	**0**	**0**	**0**	**0**	**0**	**0**	**0**	**0**	**0**	**0**
4000 Taxes on property	**463**	**1 703**	**2 703**	**1 674**	**1 694**	**1 428**	**4 116**	**5 523**	**7 191**	**8 857**
4100 Recurrent taxes on immovable property	0	0	0	0	0	60	162	230	349	392
4200 Recurrent taxes on net wealth	89	0	0	0	0	988	2 467	3 683	4 992	6 171
4300 Estate, inheritance and gift taxes	0	0	0	0	0	270	974	824	964	1 128
4400 Taxes on financial and capital transactions	374	1 703	2 703	1 674	1 694	110	103	157	177	233
4500 Non-recurrent taxes	0	0	0	0	0	0	0	0	0	0
4600 Other recurrent taxes on property	0	0	0	0	0	0	411	629	709	932
5000 Taxes on goods and services	**7 431**	**20 854**	**28 489**	**35 508**	**35 761**	**795**	**1 706**	**2 373**	**2 901**	**3 017**
5100 Taxes on production, sale, transfer, etc	7 431	19 763	27 114	33 093	32 867	154	266	447	615	592
5110 General taxes	3 205	12 428	18 429	22 791	22 435	0	0	0	0	0
5120 Taxes on specific goods and services	4 226	7 335	8 685	10 302	10 432	154	236	410	594	578
5130 Unallocable between 5110 and 5120	0	0	0	0	0	0	29	37	20	14
5200 Taxes on use of goods and perform activities	0	1 092	1 375	2 415	2 893	641	1 440	1 927	2 286	2 424
5300 Unallocable between 5100 and 5200	0	0	0	0	0	0	0	0	0	0
6000 Other taxes	**0**	**0**	**0**	**0**	**69**	**0**	**19**	**23**	**230**	**372**
6100 Paid solely by business	..	..	..	..	0	..	6	7	64	97
6200 Other	..	..	..	..	69	..	13	16	165	275
Total tax revenue	**11 316**	**33 026**	**47 533**	**64 023**	**65 170**	**9 979**	**25 249**	**34 462**	**44 979**	**50 210**

	Local government					Social Security Funds				
	1975	1995	2005	2015	2020	1975	1995	2005	2015	2020
1000 Taxes on income, profits and capital gains	**6 403**	**15 575**	**18 091**	**22 865**	**24 842**	**0**	**0**	**0**	**0**	**0**
1100 Of individuals	5 398	13 340	15 326	18 651	20 353	..	..	..	..	..
1200 Corporate	1 005	1 624	2 316	3 407	3 267	..	..	..	..	..
1300 Unallocable between 1100 and 1200	0	611	450	806	1 222	..	..	..	..	..
2000 Social security contributions	**0**	**0**	**0**	**0**	**0**	**8 111**	**28 019**	**32 332**	**44 285**	**49 057**
2100 Employees	..	..	..	..	..	3 589	13 115	15 133	20 542	23 753
2200 Employers	..	..	..	..	..	3 618	13 126	15 146	20 574	22 044
2300 Self-employed or non-employed	..	..	..	..	..	840	1 778	2 053	3 169	3 260
2400 Unallocable between 2100, 2200 and 2300	..	..	..	..	..	64	0	0	0	0
3000 Taxes on payroll and workforce	**0**	**0**	**0**	**0**	**0**	**0**	**0**	**0**	**0**	**0**
4000 Taxes on property	**1 068**	**2 614**	**3 251**	**4 275**	**5 193**	**0**	**0**	**0**	**0**	**0**
4100 Recurrent taxes on immovable property	182	443	588	789	949	..	..	..	..	..
4200 Recurrent taxes on net wealth	809	1 873	2 393	3 104	3 779	..	..	..	..	..
4300 Estate, inheritance and gift taxes	27	89	79	124	144	..	..	..	..	..
4400 Taxes on financial and capital transactions	50	42	38	52	64	..	..	..	..	..
4500 Non-recurrent taxes	0	0	0	0	0	..	..	..	..	..
4600 Other recurrent taxes on property	0	168	153	206	257	..	..	..	..	..
5000 Taxes on goods and services	**22**	**97**	**78**	**132**	**181**	**0**	**0**	**0**	**0**	**0**
5100 Taxes on production, sale, transfer, etc	17	55	26	63	84	..	..	..	..	..
5110 General taxes	0	0	0	0	0	..	..	..	..	..
5120 Taxes on specific goods and services	17	29	20	15	5	..	..	..	..	..
5130 Unallocable between 5110 and 5120	0	25	6	48	78	..	..	..	..	..
5200 Taxes on use of goods and perform activities	5	42	52	70	97	..	..	..	..	..
5300 Unallocable between 5100 and 5200	0	0	0	0	0	..	..	..	..	..
6000 Other taxes	**0**	**164**	**223**	**569**	**609**	**0**	**0**	**0**	**0**	**0**
6100 Paid solely by business	..	49	67	277	291	..	..	..	..	..
6200 Other	..	115	156	292	318	..	..	..	..	..
Total tax revenue	**7 493**	**18 451**	**21 643**	**27 841**	**30 824**	**8 111**	**28 019**	**32 332**	**44 285**	**49 057**

.. Not available

StatLink https://stat.link/whjka2

Table 6.36. Türkiye, tax revenues by sub-sectors of government

Million TRY

	Central government					State/Regional				
	1975	1995	2005	2015	2020	1975	1995	2005	2015	2020
1000 Taxes on income, profits and capital gains	..	**433**	**30 324**	**104 699**	**231 752**	..	..	..	..	..
1100 Of individuals	..	330	20 458	75 426	139 546	..	..	..	..	..
1200 Corporate	..	103	9 866	29 272	92 206	..	..	..	..	..
1300 Unallocable between 1100 and 1200	..	0	0	0	0	..	..	..	..	..
2000 Social security contributions	..	**0**	**0**	**0**	**0**	..	..	..	..	..
2100 Employees	..	..	..	..	..	..	..	..	..	..
2200 Employers	..	..	..	..	..	..	..	..	..	..
2300 Self-employed or non-employed	..	..	..	..	..	..	..	..	..	..
2400 Unallocable between 2100, 2200 and 2300	..	..	..	..	..	..	..	..	..	..
3000 Taxes on payroll and workforce	..	**0**	**0**	**0**	**0**	..	..	..	..	..
4000 Taxes on property	..	**49**	**3 626**	**20 211**	**37 182**	..	..	..	..	..
4100 Recurrent taxes on immovable property	..	0	0	0	0	..	..	..	..	..
4200 Recurrent taxes on net wealth	..	0	0	0	0	..	..	..	..	..
4300 Estate, inheritance and gift taxes	..	1	78	379	1 139	..	..	..	..	..
4400 Taxes on financial and capital transactions	..	29	3 548	19 832	36 044	..	..	..	..	..
4500 Non-recurrent taxes	..	19	0	0	0	..	..	..	..	..
4600 Other recurrent taxes on property	..	0	0	0	0	..	..	..	..	..
5000 Taxes on goods and services	..	**574**	**71 956**	**231 227**	**459 582**	..	..	..	..	..
5100 Taxes on production, sale, transfer, etc	..	567	69 266	222 702	444 732	..	..	..	..	..
5110 General taxes	..	475	30 343	107 451	203 411	..	..	..	..	..
5120 Taxes on specific goods and services	..	92	38 923	115 251	241 321	..	..	..	..	..
5130 Unallocable between 5110 and 5120	..	0	0	0	0	..	..	..	..	..
5200 Taxes on use of goods and perform activities	..	8	2 691	8 526	14 850	..	..	..	..	..
5300 Unallocable between 5100 and 5200	..	0	0	0	0	..	..	..	..	..
6000 Other taxes	..	**259**	**4 181**	**3 779**	**5 123**	..	..	..	..	..
6100 Paid solely by business	..	0	0	0	0	..	..	..	..	..
6200 Other	..	259	4 181	3 779	5 123	..	..	..	..	..
Total tax revenue	..	**1 316**	**110 088**	**359 915**	**733 639**	..	..	..	..	..

	Local government					Social Security Funds				
	1975	1995	2005	2015	2020	1975	1995	2005	2015	2020
1000 Taxes on income, profits and capital gains	..	**63**	**4 011**	**14 445**	**32 146**	..	**0**	**0**	**0**	**0**
1100 Of individuals	..	48	2 706	10 330	19 296	..	..	..	..	..
1200 Corporate	..	15	1 305	4 116	12 851	..	..	..	..	..
1300 Unallocable between 1100 and 1200	..	0	0	0	0	..	..	..	..	..
2000 Social security contributions	..	**0**	**0**	**0**	**0**	..	**212**	**35 321**	**170 282**	**357 677**
2100 Employees	..	..	..	..	..	..	82	12 128	64 214	137 742
2200 Employers	..	..	..	..	..	..	110	16 132	95 067	204 045
2300 Self-employed or non-employed	..	..	..	..	..	..	19	7 061	11 001	15 890
2400 Unallocable between 2100, 2200 and 2300	..	..	..	..	..	..	0	0	0	0
3000 Taxes on payroll and workforce	..	**0**	**0**	**0**	**0**	..	**0**	**0**	**0**	**0**
4000 Taxes on property	..	**4**	**1 627**	**8 371**	**16 365**	..	**0**	**0**	**0**	**0**
4100 Recurrent taxes on immovable property	..	0	1 148	5 882	11 204	..	..	..	..	..
4200 Recurrent taxes on net wealth	..	0	0	0	0	..	..	..	..	..
4300 Estate, inheritance and gift taxes	..	0	10	56	159	..	..	..	..	..
4400 Taxes on financial and capital transactions	..	4	469	2 433	5 002	..	..	..	..	..
4500 Non-recurrent taxes	..	0	0	0	0	..	..	..	..	..
4600 Other recurrent taxes on property	..	0	0	0	0	..	..	..	..	..
5000 Taxes on goods and services	..	**84**	**5 649**	**28 737**	**57 706**	..	**0**	**0**	**0**	**0**
5100 Taxes on production, sale, transfer, etc	..	82	5 295	27 560	55 635	..	..	..	..	..
5110 General taxes	..	69	4 014	13 619	27 350	..	..	..	..	..
5120 Taxes on specific goods and services	..	13	1 281	13 940	28 284	..	..	..	..	..
5130 Unallocable between 5110 and 5120	..	0	0	0	0	..	..	..	..	..
5200 Taxes on use of goods and perform activities	..	1	354	1 177	2 071	..	..	..	..	..
5300 Unallocable between 5100 and 5200	..	0	0	0	0	..	..	..	..	..
6000 Other taxes	..	**73**	**721**	**4 971**	**7 095**	..	**0**	**0**	**0**	**0**
6100 Paid solely by business	..	0	0	0	0	..	..	..	..	..
6200 Other	..	73	721	4 971	7 095	..	..	..	..	..
Total tax revenue	..	**224**	**12 008**	**56 525**	**113 312**	..	**212**	**35 321**	**170 282**	**357 677**

.. Not available

StatLink https://stat.link/9lo6v5

Table 6.37. United Kingdom, tax revenues by sub-sectors of government

Million GBP

	Central government					State/Regional				
	1975	1995	2005	2015	2020	1975	1995	2005	2015	2020
1000 Taxes on income, profits and capital gains	**16 716**	**92 147**	**177 149**	**212 697**	**247 296**	**..**	**..**	**..**	**..**	**..**
1100 Of individuals	14 936	71 973	130 135	168 873	197 219	..	..	..	..	..
1200 Corporate	2 310	20 174	47 014	43 824	50 077	..	..	..	..	..
1300 Unallocable between 1100 and 1200	-530	0	0	0	0	..	..	..	..	..
2000 Social security contributions	**0**	**0**	**0**	**0**	**0**	**..**	**..**	**..**	**..**	**..**
2100 Employees	..	..	..	..	..	..	..	..	..	..
2200 Employers	..	..	..	..	..	..	..	..	..	..
2300 Self-employed or non-employed	..	..	..	..	..	..	..	..	..	..
2400 Unallocable between 2100, 2200 and 2300	..	..	..	..	..	..	..	..	..	..
3000 Taxes on payroll and workforce	**-1**	**0**	**0**	**0**	**2 892**	**..**	**..**	**..**	**..**	**..**
4000 Taxes on property	**619**	**15 730**	**32 583**	**46 526**	**41 441**	**..**	**..**	**..**	**..**	**..**
4100 Recurrent taxes on immovable property	44	12 369	19 523	28 265	23 002	..	..	..	..	..
4200 Recurrent taxes on net wealth	0	0	0	0	0	..	..	..	..	..
4300 Estate, inheritance and gift taxes	307	1 441	3 150	4 470	5 252	..	..	..	..	..
4400 Taxes on financial and capital transactions	266	1 920	9 910	13 791	13 187	..	..	..	..	..
4500 Non-recurrent taxes	2	0	0	0	0	..	..	..	..	..
4600 Other recurrent taxes on property	0	0	0	0	0	..	..	..	..	..
5000 Taxes on goods and services	**8 982**	**85 507**	**137 262**	**204 954**	**212 242**	**..**	**..**	**..**	**..**	**..**
5100 Taxes on production, sale, transfer, etc	8 502	81 175	131 362	197 092	203 183	..	..	..	..	..
5110 General taxes	3 515	47 539	84 649	132 906	139 461	..	..	..	..	..
5120 Taxes on specific goods and services	4 987	33 636	46 713	64 186	63 722	..	..	..	..	..
5130 Unallocable between 5110 and 5120	0	0	0	0	0	..	..	..	..	..
5200 Taxes on use of goods and perform activities	698	4 332	5 900	7 862	9 059	..	..	..	..	..
5300 Unallocable between 5100 and 5200	-218	0	0	0	0	..	..	..	..	..
6000 Other taxes	**0**	**0**	**0**	**0**	**0**	**..**	**..**	**..**	**..**	**..**
6100 Paid solely by business	..	..	..	..	..	..	..	..	..	..
6200 Other	..	..	..	..	..	..	..	..	..	..
Total tax revenue	**26 316**	**193 384**	**346 994**	**464 177**	**503 871**	**..**	**..**	**..**	**..**	**..**

	Local government					Social Security Funds				
	1975	1995	2005	2015	2020	1975	1995	2005	2015	2020
1000 Taxes on income, profits and capital gains	**0**	**0**	**0**	**0**	**0**	**0**	**0**	**0**	**0**	**0**
1100 Of individuals	0	..	..	..	..	0	..	..	..	..
1200 Corporate	0	..	..	..	..	0	..	..	..	..
1300 Unallocable between 1100 and 1200	0	..	..	..	..	0	..	..	..	..
2000 Social security contributions	**0**	**0**	**0**	**0**	**0**	**6 540**	**44 397**	**84 459**	**114 173**	**144 990**
2100 Employees	..	..	..	..	..	2 562	18 646	35 159	44 488	56 847
2200 Employers	..	..	..	..	..	4 068	24 210	46 475	66 491	84 042
2300 Self-employed or non-employed	..	..	..	..	..	195	1 541	2 825	3 194	4 101
2400 Unallocable between 2100, 2200 and 2300	..	..	..	..	..	-285	0	0	0	0
3000 Taxes on payroll and workforce	**0**	**0**	**0**	**0**	**0**	**0**	**0**	**0**	**0**	**0**
4000 Taxes on property	**4 127**	**9 303**	**21 255**	**29 901**	**38 693**	**0**	**0**	**0**	**0**	**0**
4100 Recurrent taxes on immovable property	3 978	9 303	21 255	29 754	38 340	..	..	..	..	..
4200 Recurrent taxes on net wealth	0	0	0	0	0	..	..	..	..	..
4300 Estate, inheritance and gift taxes	0	0	0	0	0	..	..	..	..	..
4400 Taxes on financial and capital transactions	0	0	0	0	0	..	..	..	..	..
4500 Non-recurrent taxes	0	0	0	147	353	..	..	..	..	..
4600 Other recurrent taxes on property	149	0	0	0	0	..	..	..	..	..
5000 Taxes on goods and services	**0**	**0**	**0**	**0**	**0**	**0**	**0**	**0**	**0**	**0**
5100 Taxes on production, sale, transfer, etc	..	..	..	..	..	..	..	..	..	..
5110 General taxes	..	..	..	..	..	..	..	..	..	..
5120 Taxes on specific goods and services	..	..	..	..	..	..	..	..	..	..
5130 Unallocable between 5110 and 5120	..	..	..	..	..	..	..	..	..	..
5200 Taxes on use of goods and perform activities	..	..	..	..	..	..	..	..	..	..
5300 Unallocable between 5100 and 5200	..	..	..	..	..	..	..	..	..	..
6000 Other taxes	**0**	**0**	**0**	**0**	**0**	**0**	**0**	**0**	**0**	**0**
6100 Paid solely by business	..	..	..	..	..	..	..	..	..	..
6200 Other	..	..	..	..	..	..	..	..	..	..
Total tax revenue	**4 127**	**9 303**	**21 255**	**29 901**	**38 693**	**6 540**	**44 397**	**84 459**	**114 173**	**144 990**

.. Not available

Note: Including taxes collected on behalf of the European Union.

StatLink https://stat.link/369nxu

Table 6.38. United States, tax revenues by sub-sectors of government

Million USD

	Federal government					State/Regional				
	1975	1995	2005	2015	2020	1975	1995	2005	2015	2020
1000 Taxes on income, profits and capital gains	**163 072**	**750 144**	**1 268 412**	**1 883 845**	**1 899 773**	**25 509**	**157 598**	**275 728**	**391 166**	**498 672**
1100 Of individuals	122 386	594 213	948 921	1 554 757	1 707 026	..	128 429	226 576	343 101	436 179
1200 Corporate	40 686	155 931	319 490	329 088	192 747	..	29 169	49 152	48 065	62 493
1300 Unallocable between 1100 and 1200	0	0	0	0	0	..	0	0	0	0
2000 Social security contributions	**0**	**0**	**0**	**0**	**0**	**0**	**0**	**0**	**0**	**0**
2100 Employees	..	..	..	..	..	..	..	..	..	..
2200 Employers	..	..	..	..	..	..	..	..	..	..
2300 Self-employed or non-employed	..	..	..	..	..	..	..	..	..	..
2400 Unallocable between 2100, 2200 and 2300	..	..	..	..	..	..	..	..	..	..
3000 Taxes on payroll and workforce	**0**	**0**	**0**	**0**	**0**	**0**	**0**	**0**	**1 751**	**3 386**
4000 Taxes on property	**4 613**	**14 948**	**24 989**	**20 191**	**19 122**	**3 284**	**16 880**	**28 808**	**31 133**	**37 557**
4100 Recurrent taxes on immovable property	0	0	0	0	0	1 451	7 240	9 037	13 286	16 021
4200 Recurrent taxes on net wealth	0	0	0	0	0	0	0	0	0	0
4300 Estate, inheritance and gift taxes	4 611	14 948	24 989	20 191	19 122	1 418	5 061	5 322	5 143	5 312
4400 Taxes on financial and capital transactions	2	0	0	0	0	415	2 386	11 711	8 679	11 371
4500 Non-recurrent taxes	0	0	0	0	0	0	0	0	0	0
4600 Other recurrent taxes on property	0	0	0	0	0	0	2 193	2 738	4 025	4 853
5000 Taxes on goods and services	**20 773**	**75 553**	**99 411**	**140 319**	**158 007**	**52 032**	**232 033**	**377 795**	**502 682**	**593 481**
5100 Taxes on production, sale, transfer, etc	20 442	75 553	99 411	140 319	158 007	43 960	200 495	323 137	438 463	519 793
5110 General taxes	0	0	0	0	0	24 916	135 132	218 917	289 600	343 653
5120 Taxes on specific goods and services	20 442	75 553	99 411	140 319	158 007	19 044	65 363	104 220	148 863	176 140
5130 Unallocable between 5110 and 5120	0	0	0	0	0	0	0	0	0	0
5200 Taxes on use of goods and perform activities	331	0	0	0	0	8 072	31 538	54 658	64 219	73 687
5300 Unallocable between 5100 and 5200	0	0	0	0	0	0	0	0	0	0
6000 Other taxes	**0**	**0**	**0**	**0**	**0**	**0**	**0**	**0**	**0**	**0**
6100 Paid solely by business	..	..	..	..	..	..	..	..	..	..
6200 Other	..	..	..	..	..	..	..	..	..	..
Total tax revenue	**188 458**	**840 645**	**1 392 812**	**2 044 356**	**2 076 902**	**80 825**	**406 511**	**682 331**	**926 733**	**1 133 095**

	Local government					Social Security Funds				
	1975	1995	2005	2015	2020	1975	1995	2005	2015	2020
1000 Taxes on income, profits and capital gains	**2 635**	**15 795**	**28 272**	**39 531**	**48 486**	**0**	**0**	**0**	**0**	**0**
1100 Of individuals	..	13 308	22 481	31 357	39 963	..	..	..	..	..
1200 Corporate	..	2 487	5 791	8 174	8 523	..	..	..	..	..
1300 Unallocable between 1100 and 1200	..	0	0	0	0	..	..	..	..	..
2000 Social security contributions	**0**	**0**	**0**	**0**	**0**	**85 039**	**510 476**	**831 410**	**1 125 493**	**1 333 998**
2100 Employees	..	..	..	..	..	36 382	221 800	362 829	502 103	607 264
2200 Employers	..	..	..	..	..	45 241	261 805	423 936	561 936	656 638
2300 Self-employed or non-employed	..	..	..	..	..	3 416	26 871	44 645	61 454	70 096
2400 Unallocable between 2100, 2200 and 2300	..	..	..	..	..	0	0	0	0	0
3000 Taxes on payroll and workforce	**0**	**0**	**0**	**0**	**0**	**0**	**0**	**0**	**0**	**0**
4000 Taxes on property	**50 040**	**197 392**	**359 344**	**488 409**	**612 493**	**0**	**0**	**0**	**0**	**0**
4100 Recurrent taxes on immovable property	50 040	195 339	342 203	477 124	599 308	..	..	..	..	..
4200 Recurrent taxes on net wealth	0	0	0	0	0	..	..	..	..	..
4300 Estate, inheritance and gift taxes	0	30	114	249	406	..	..	..	..	..
4400 Taxes on financial and capital transactions	0	50	13 570	6 217	6 726	..	..	..	..	..
4500 Non-recurrent taxes	0	0	0	0	0	..	..	..	..	..
4600 Other recurrent taxes on property	0	1 973	3 457	4 819	6 054	..	..	..	..	..
5000 Taxes on goods and services	**8 389**	**57 507**	**108 696**	**149 160**	**175 242**	**0**	**0**	**0**	**0**	**0**
5100 Taxes on production, sale, transfer, etc	6 518	42 269	76 976	117 002	131 740	..	..	..	..	..
5110 General taxes	4 322	29 316	53 842	84 573	105 229	..	..	..	..	..
5120 Taxes on specific goods and services	2 196	12 953	23 134	32 429	26 511	..	..	..	..	..
5130 Unallocable between 5110 and 5120	0	0	0	0	0	..	..	..	..	..
5200 Taxes on use of goods and perform activities	1 871	15 238	31 720	32 158	43 502	..	..	..	..	..
5300 Unallocable between 5100 and 5200	0	0	0	0	0	..	..	..	..	..
6000 Other taxes	**0**	**0**	**0**	**0**	**0**	**0**	**0**	**0**	**0**	**0**
6100 Paid solely by business	..	..	..	..	..	..	..	..	..	..
6200 Other	..	..	..	..	..	..	..	..	..	..
Total tax revenue	**61 064**	**270 695**	**496 313**	**677 099**	**836 222**	**85 039**	**510 476**	**831 410**	**1 125 493**	**1 333 998**

.. Not available

StatLink https://stat.link/4cfhom

Annex A. The OECD classification of taxes and interpretative guide

Table of Contents

A.1. The OECD Classification of Taxes

A.2. Coverage

A.3. Basis of reporting

A.4. General classification criteria

A.5. Commentaries on items of the list

A.6. Conciliation with National Accounts

A.7. Memorandum item on the financing of social security benefits

A.8. Memorandum item on identifiable taxes paid by government

A.9. Relation of OECD classification of taxes to national accounting systems

A.10. Relation of OECD classification of taxes to the international monetary fund system

A.11. Comparison of the OECD classification of taxes with other international classifications

A.12. Attribution of tax revenues by subsectors of general government

A.1 The OECD Classification of Taxes

1. **1000. Taxes on income, profits and capital gains**

    1100. Taxes on income, profits and capital gains of individuals

        1110. On income and profits

        1120. On capital gains

    1200. Corporate taxes on income, profits and capital gains

        1210. On income and profits

        1220. On capital gains

    1300. Unallocable as between 1100 and 1200

2. **2000. Social security contributions**

    2100. Employees

        2110. On a payroll basis

        2120. On an income tax basis

    2200. Employers

        2210. On a payroll basis

        2220. On an income tax basis

    2300. Self-employed or non-employed

        2310. On a payroll basis

        2320. On an income tax basis

    2400 Unallocable as between 2100, 2200 and 2300

        2410. On a payroll basis

        2420. On an income tax basis

3. **3000. Taxes on payroll and workforce**

4. **4000. Taxes on property**

    4100. Recurrent taxes on immovable property

        4110. Households

        4120. Other

    4200 Recurrent taxes on net wealth

        4210. Individual

        4220. Corporate

    4300. Estate, inheritance and gift taxes

        4310. Estate and inheritance taxes

        4320. Gift taxes

    4400. Taxes on financial and capital transactions

4500. Other non-recurrent taxes on property

4510. On net wealth

4520. Other non-recurrent taxes

4600. Other recurrent taxes on property

5. **5000. Taxes on goods and services**

5100. Taxes on production, sale, transfer, leasing and delivery of goods and rendering of services

5110. General taxes

5111. Value added taxes

5112. Sales taxes

5113. Turnover and other general taxes on goods and services

5120. Taxes on specific goods and services

5121. Excises

5122. Profits of fiscal monopolies

5123. Customs and import duties

5124. Taxes on exports

5125. Taxes on investment goods

5126 . Taxes on specific services

5127. Other taxes on international trade and transactions

5128. Other taxes on specific goods and services

5130. Unallocable as between 5110 and 5120

5200. Taxes on use of goods, or on permission to use goods or perform activities

5210. Recurrent taxes

5211. Paid by households in respect of motor vehicles

5212. Paid by others in respect of motor vehicles

5213. Other recurrent taxes

5220. Non-recurrent taxes

5300. Unallocable as between 5100 and 5200

6. **6000. Other taxes**

6100. Paid solely by business

6200. Paid by other than business or unidentifiable

A.2 Coverage

General criteria

1. In the OECD classification, the term "taxes" is confined to compulsory unrequited payments to the general government or to a supranational authority. Taxes are unrequited in the sense that benefits provided by government to taxpayers are not normally in proportion to their payments.

2. The term "tax" does not include fines, penalties and compulsory loans paid to government. Borderline cases between tax and non-tax revenues in relation to certain fees and charges are discussed in §12–15.

3. General government consists of the central administration, agencies whose operations are under its effective control, state and local governments and their administrations, certain social security schemes and autonomous governmental entities, excluding public enterprises. This definition of government follows that of the 2008 *System of National Accounts* (SNA).[1] In that publication, the general government sector and its sub-sectors are defined in Chapter 4, paragraphs 4.117 to 4.165.

4. Extra-budgetary units are part of the general government system. These are general government entities with individual budgets that are not fully covered by the main or general budget. These entities operate under the authority or control of a central, state, or local government. Extra-budgetary entities may have their own revenue sources, which may be supplemented by grants (transfers) from the general budget or from other sources. Even though their budgets may be subject to approval by the legislature, similar to that of budgetary accounts, they have discretion over the volume and composition of their spending. Such entities may be established to carry out specific government functions, such as road construction, or the nonmarket production of health or education services. Budgetary arrangements vary widely across countries, and various terms are used to describe these entities, but they are often referred to as "extra-budgetary funds" or "decentralised agencies."

5. Compulsory, unrequited payments collected by national governments and paid to supranational authorities are also included as taxes under the definition in paragraph 1. Taxes that are collected by national governments and paid to a supranational authority are included as tax revenues at the level of the supranational authority in the SNA2008 (paragraphs 22.60-61, 22.88 and 22.99 refer) and the ESA2010 (paragraph 20.165 refers). In Revenue Statistics, these taxes include customs duties, contributions to the EU Single Resolution Fund, and any other taxes collected by EU member states on behalf of the European Union. They are included in the tax revenue amounts in the country tables (Chapter 5) of the country in which they are collected and are attributed to the supranational level of government (see §102).

6. In countries where the church forms part of general government, church taxes are included, provided they meet the criteria set out in §1 above. As the data refer to receipts of general government and to supranational authorities, levies paid to non-government bodies, welfare agencies or social insurance schemes outside general government, trade unions or trade associations, even where such levies are compulsory, are excluded. Compulsory payments to general government earmarked for such bodies are, however, included, provided that the government is not simply acting in an agency capacity.[2] Profits from fiscal monopolies are distinguished from those of other public enterprises and are treated as taxes because they reflect the exercise of the taxing power of the state by the use of monopoly powers (see §66–68), as are profits received by the government from the purchase and sale of foreign exchange at different rates (see §76).

7. Taxes paid by governments (e.g., social security contributions and payroll taxes paid by governments in their capacity as an employer, consumption taxes on their purchases or taxes on their property) are not excluded from the data provided. However, where it is possible to identify the amounts of revenue involved,[3] they are shown in Table 5.40 of this Report.

8. The relationship between this classification and that of the System of National Accounts (SNA) is set out in Sections A.9 and A.11 below. Because of the differences between the two classifications, the data shown in national accounts are sometimes calculated or classified differently from the practice set out in this guide. These and other differences are mentioned where appropriate (e.g., in §31 below) but it is not possible to refer to all of them. There may also be some differences between this classification and that employed domestically by certain national administrations (e.g., see §13 below), so that OECD and national statistics data may not always be consistent: any such differences, however, are likely to be very slight in terms of amounts of revenues involved.

Social security contributions

9. Compulsory social security contributions, as defined in §40, and paid to general government, are treated here as tax revenues. They may, however, differ from other taxes in that the receipt of social security benefits depends, in most countries, upon appropriate contributions having been made, although the size of the benefits is not necessarily related to the amount of the contributions. Better comparability between countries is obtained by treating social security contributions as taxes, but they are listed under a separate heading so that they can be distinguished in any analysis.

10. The strict dividing line between tax revenues (compulsory unrequited payments to general government or a supranational authority) and non-tax compulsory payments (NTCPs) (payments that are either requited or made to other institutions) is clearly defined. However, within the range of different compulsory payments to governments existing across countries, it is not always straightforward in practice to decide whether specific payments are either taxes or NTCPs. For example, compulsory pension savings that are controlled by general government and that accumulate on an individual account earning a market return or a rate that compensates for inflation would at first sight be categorised as NTCPs as opposed to taxes. However, even these payments might still be 'unrequited' and therefore classify as taxes instead of NTCPs (for example if these pension savings are not paid out when the taxpayer dies before reaching the pension age and the funds are then used to provide a minimum pension to all taxpayers that are insured). These issues result in the social security revenue figures reported for most countries being based on the premise that all types of compulsory payments to general government are judged to some extent to have a re-distributional element. It should be noted that this conclusion is based on a typically broad interpretation of the term 'unrequited' in the tax definition.

11. Social security contributions which are either voluntary or not payable to general government (see §1) are not treated as taxes, though in some countries, as indicated in the country footnotes, there are difficulties in completely eliminating voluntary contributions and certain compulsory payments to the private sector from the revenue figures. Imputed social security contributions are also not treated as taxes.

Fees, user charges and licence fees

12. Apart from vehicle licence fees, which are universally regarded as taxes, it is not easy to distinguish between those fees and user charges which are to be treated as taxes and those which are not, since, whilst a fee or charge is levied in connection with a specific service or activity, the strength of the link between the fee and the service provided may vary considerably, as may the relation between the amount of the fee and the cost of providing the service. Where the recipient of a service pays a fee clearly related to the cost of providing the service, the levy may be regarded as requited and under the definition of §1 would not be considered as a tax. In the following cases, however, a levy could be considered as 'unrequited':

- *a)* where the charge greatly exceeds the cost of providing the service;
- *b)* where the payer of the levy is not the receiver of the benefit (e.g., a fee collected from slaughterhouses to finance a service which is provided to farmers);

c) where government is not providing a specific service in return for the levy which it receives even though a licence may be issued to the payer (e.g., where the government grants a hunting, fishing or shooting licence which is not accompanied by the right to use a specific area of government land);

d) where benefits are received only by those paying the levy but the benefits received by each individual are not necessarily in proportion to his payments (e.g., a milk marketing levy paid by dairy farmers and used to promote the consumption of milk).

13. In marginal cases, however, the application of the criteria set out in §1 can be particularly difficult. The solution adopted — given the desirability of international uniformity and the relatively small amounts of revenue usually involved — is to follow the predominant practice among tax administrations rather than to allow each country to adopt its own view as to whether such levies are regarded as taxes or as non-tax revenue.[4]

14. A list of the main fees and charges in question and their normal[5] treatment in this publication is as follows:

Non-tax revenues:	court fees; driving licence fees; harbour fees; passport fees; radio and television licence fees where public authorities provide the service
Taxes within heading 5200	permission to perform such activities as distributing films; hunting, fishing and shooting; providing entertainment or gambling facilities; selling alcohol or tobacco; permission to own dogs or to use or own motor vehicles or guns; severance taxes

15. In practice, it may not always be possible to isolate tax receipts from non-tax revenue receipts when they are recorded together. If it is estimated that the bulk of the receipts derive from non-tax revenues, the whole amount involved is treated as a non-tax revenue; otherwise, such government receipts are included and classified according to the rules provided in §33 below.

Royalties

16. The ownership of subsoil assets in the form of deposits of minerals or fossil fuels (coal, oil, or natural gas) depends upon the way in which property rights are defined by law and also on international agreements in the case of deposits below international waters. In some cases, either the ground below which the mineral deposits are located, the deposits themselves or both may belong to a local or central government unit.

17. In such cases, these general government units may grant leases to other institutional units that permit them to extract these deposits over a specified period of time in return for a payment or series of payments. These payments are often described as 'royalties' but they are essentially rent that accrues to owners of natural resources in return for putting these assets at the disposal of other units for specified periods of time. The rent may take the form of periodic payments of fixed amounts, irrespective of the rate of extraction, or, more commonly, they may be a function of the quantity, volume, or value of the asset extracted. Enterprises engaged in exploration on government land may make payments to general government units in exchange for the right to undertake test drilling or otherwise investigate the existence and location of subsoil assets. Such payments are also recorded as rents even though no extraction may take place. These payments are therefore classified as non-tax revenues.

18. The same principles apply when other institutional units are granted leases that permit them to fell timber in natural forests on land owned by general government units. These payments are also classified as non-tax revenues.

19. These rents or royalties paid to general government should not be confused with taxes on income and profits, severance taxes, business licenses, or other taxes. If the payments are levied on the profits from the extraction activity, then they should be classified as taxes on incomes, profits and gains (1000).

In addition, any severance payments that are imposed on the extraction of minerals and fossil fuels from reserves owned privately or by another government should be classified as taxes. Payments related to the gross value of production should be classified as other taxes on goods and services (5128). Payments for a license or permit to conduct extraction operations should be classified as taxes on use of goods and on permission to use goods or perform activities (5213).

Fines and penalties

20. In principle, fines and penalties charged on overdue taxes or penalties imposed for the attempted evasion of taxes should not be recorded as tax revenues. However, it may not be possible to separate payments of fines or other penalties from the revenues from the taxes to which they relate. In this case, the fines and penalties relating to a particular tax are recorded together with the revenues from that tax and fines and penalties paid with revenue from unidentifiable taxes are classified as other taxes in Category 6000. Fines not relating to tax offences (e.g., for parking offences), or not identifiable as relating to tax offences, are also not treated as tax revenues.

A.3 Basis of reporting

Accrual or cash reporting

21. The data reported in the *Revenue Statistics* publications for recent years are predominantly recorded on an accrual basis for OECD countries, i.e. recorded at the time that the tax liability was created. Further information is provided in the footnotes to the country table in Chapter 5 of the Report.

22. However, data for earlier years and for non-OECD countries are still predominantly recorded on a cash basis, i.e. at the time at which the payment was received by government. Thus, for example, taxes withheld by employers in one year but paid to the government in the following year and taxes due in one year but actually paid in the following year are both included in the receipts of the second year. Corrective transactions, such as refunds, repayments and drawbacks, are deducted from gross revenues of the period in which they are made.

23. Data on tax revenues are recorded without offsets for the administrative expenses connected with tax collection. Similarly, where the proceeds of tax are used to subsidise particular members of the community, the subsidy is not deducted from the yield of the tax, though the tax may be shown net of subsidies in the national records of some countries.

24. As regards fiscal monopolies (heading 5122), only the amount actually transferred to the government is included in government revenues. However, if any expenditures of fiscal monopolies are considered to be government expenditures (e.g., social expenditures undertaken by fiscal monopolies at the direction of the government) they are added back for the purpose of arriving at tax revenue figures (see §66 below).

The distinction between tax and expenditure provisions[6]

25. Because this publication is concerned only with the revenue side of government operations, no account being taken of the expenditure side, a distinction has to be made between tax and expenditure provisions. Normally there is no difficulty in making this distinction as expenditures are made outside the tax system and the tax accounts and under legislation separate from the tax legislation. In borderline cases, cash flow is used to distinguish between tax provisions and expenditure provisions. Insofar as a provision affects the flow of tax payments from the taxpayer to the government, it is regarded as a tax provision and is taken into account in the data shown in this publication. A provision which does not affect this flow is seen as an expenditure provision and is disregarded in the data recorded in this publication.

26. Tax allowances, exemptions and deductions against the tax base clearly affect the amount of tax paid to the government and are therefore considered as tax provisions. At the other extreme, those subsidies which cannot be offset against tax liability and which are clearly not connected with the assessment process, do not reduce tax revenues as recorded in this publication. Tax credits are amounts deductible from tax payable (as distinct from deductions from the tax base). Two types of tax credits are distinguished, those (referred to here as wastable tax credits) which are limited to the amount of the tax liability and therefore cannot give rise to a payment by the authorities to the taxpayer, and those (referred to as non-wastable tax credits) which are not so limited, so that the excess of the credit over the tax liability can be paid to the taxpayer.[7] A wastable tax credit, like a tax allowance, clearly affects the amount of tax paid to the government, and is therefore considered as a tax provision. The practice followed for non-wastable tax credits[8] is to distinguish between the 'tax expenditure component',[9] which is that portion of the credit that is used to reduce or eliminate a taxpayer's liability, and the 'transfer component', which is the portion that exceeds the taxpayer's liability and is paid to that taxpayer. Reported tax revenues should be reduced by the amount of the tax expenditure component but not by the amount of the transfer component. In addition, the amounts of the tax expenditure and transfer components should be reported as memorandum items in the country tables. Countries that are unable to distinguish between the tax expenditure and transfer components should indicate whether or not the tax revenues have been reduced by the total of these components, and provide any available estimates of the amounts of the two components. Further information is given in Chapter 1 of the Report, which illustrates the effect of alternative treatments of non-wastable tax credits on tax to GDP.

Calendar and fiscal years

27. National authorities whose fiscal years do not correspond to the calendar year show data, where possible, on a calendar year basis to permit maximum comparability with the data of other countries. There remain a few countries where data refer to fiscal years. For these the GDP data used in the comparative tables also correspond to the fiscal years.

A.4 General classification criteria

The main classification criteria

28. The classification of receipts among the main headings (1000, 2000, 3000, 4000, 5000 and 6000) is generally governed by the base on which the tax is levied: 1000 income, profits and capital gains; 2000 and 3000 earnings, payroll or number of employees; 4000 property; 5000 goods and services; 6000 multiple bases, other bases or unidentifiable bases. Where a tax is calculated on more than one base, the receipts are, where possible, split among the various headings (see §33 and §84). The headings 4000 and 5000 cover not only taxes where the tax base is the property, goods or services themselves but also certain related taxes. Thus, taxes on the transfer of property are included in 4400[10] and taxes on the use of goods or on permission to perform activities in 5200. In headings 4000 and 5000 a distinction is made in certain sub-headings between recurrent and non-recurrent taxes: recurrent taxes are defined as those levied at regular intervals (usually annually) and non-recurrent taxes are levied once and for all (see also §48 to §51, §54, §55 and §81 for particular applications of this distinction).

29. Earmarking of a tax for specific purposes does not affect the classification of tax receipts. However, as explained in §40 on the classification of social security contributions, the conferment of an entitlement to social benefits is crucial to the definition of the 2000 main heading.

30. The way that a tax is levied or collected (e.g., by use of stamps) does not affect classification.

Classification of taxpayers

31. In certain sub-headings, distinctions are made between different categories of taxpayers. These distinctions vary from tax to tax:

a) *Between individuals and corporations in relation to income and net wealth taxes*

The basic distinction is that corporation income taxes, as distinct from individual income taxes, are levied on the corporation as an entity, not on the individuals who own it, and without regard to the personal circumstances of these individuals. The same distinction applies to net wealth taxes on corporations and those on individuals. Taxes paid on the profits of partnerships and the income of institutions, such as life insurance or pension funds, are classified according to the same rule. They are classified as corporate taxes (1200) if they are charged on the partnership or institution as an entity without regard to the personal circumstances of the owners. Otherwise, they are treated as individual taxes (1100). Usually, there is different legislation for the corporation taxes and for the individual taxes.[11] The distinction made here between individuals and corporations does not follow the sector classification between households, enterprises, and so on of the System of National Accounts for income and outlay accounts. The SNA classification requires certain unincorporated businesses[12] to be excluded from the household sector and included with non-financial enterprises and financial institutions. The tax on the profits of these businesses, however, cannot always be separated from the tax on the other income of their owners, or can be separated only on an arbitrary basis. No attempt at this separation is made here and the whole of the individual income tax is shown together without regard to the nature of the income chargeable.

b) *Between households and others in relation to taxes on immovable property*

Here the distinction is that adopted by the SNA for the production and consumption expenditure accounts. The distinction is between households as consumers (i.e. excluding non-incorporated business) on the one hand and producers on the other hand. However, taxes on dwellings occupied by households, whether paid by owner-occupiers, tenants or landlords, are classified under households. This follows the common distinction made between taxes on domestic property versus taxes on business property. Some countries are not, however, in a position to make this distinction.

c) *Between households and others in relation to motor vehicle licences*

Here the distinction is between households as consumers on the one hand and producers on the other, as in the production and consumption expenditure accounts of the SNA.

d) *Between business and others in relation to the residual taxes (6000)*

The distinction is the same as in c) above between producers on the one hand and households as consumers on the other hand. Taxes which are included under the heading 6000 because they involve more than one tax base or because the tax base does not fall within any of the previous categories but which are identifiable as levyable only on producers and not on households are included under 'business'. The rest of the taxes which are included under the heading 6000 are shown as 'other' or non-identified.

Surcharges

32. Receipts from surcharges in respect of particular taxes are usually classified with the receipts from the relevant tax whether or not the surcharge is temporary. If, however, the surcharge has a characteristic which would render it classifiable in a different heading of the OECD list, receipts from the surcharge are classified under that heading separately from the relevant tax.

Unidentifiable tax receipts and residual sub-headings

33. A number of cases arise where taxes cannot be identified as belonging entirely to a heading or sub-heading of the OECD classification and the following practices are applied in such cases:

a) The heading is known, but it is not known how receipts should be allocated between sub-headings: receipts are classified in the appropriate residual sub-heading (1300, 2400, 4520, 4600, 5128, 5130, 5300 or 6200).

b) It is known that the bulk of receipts from a group of taxes (usually local taxes) is derived from taxes within a particular heading or sub-heading, but some of the taxes in the group whose amount cannot be precisely ascertained may be classifiable in other headings or sub-headings: receipts are shown in the heading or sub-heading under which most of the receipts fall.

c) Neither the heading nor sub-heading of a tax (usually local) can be identified: the tax is classified in 6200 unless it is known that it is a tax on business in which case it is classified in 6100.

A.5 Commentaries on items of the list

1000 — Taxes on income, profits and capital gains

34. This heading covers taxes levied on the net income or profits (i.e. gross income minus allowable tax reliefs) of individuals and enterprises. Also covered are taxes levied on the capital gains of individuals and enterprises, and gains from gambling.

35. Included in the heading are:

a) taxes levied predominantly on income or profits, though partially on other bases. Taxes on various bases which are not predominantly income or profits are classified according to the principles laid down in §33 and §84;

b) taxes on property, which are levied on a presumed or estimated income as part of an income tax (see also §48(a), (c) and (d));

c) compulsory payments to social security fund contributions that are levied on income but do not confer an entitlement to social benefits. When such contributions do confer an entitlement to social benefits, they are included in heading 2000 (see §40);

d) receipts from integrated scheduler income tax systems are classified as a whole in this heading, even though certain of the scheduler taxes may be based upon gross income and may not take into account the personal circumstances of the taxpayer.

36. The main subdivision of this heading is between levies on individuals (1100) and those on corporate enterprises (1200). Under each subdivision a distinction is made between taxes on income and profits (1110 and 1210), and taxes on capital gains (1120 and 1220). If certain receipts cannot be identified as appropriate to either 1100 or 1200, or if in practice this distinction cannot be made (e.g., because there are no reliable data on the recipients of payments from which withholding taxes are deducted) they are classified in 1300 as not-allocable.

Treatment of credits under imputation systems

37. Under imputation systems of corporate income tax, a company's shareholders are wholly or partly relieved of their liability to income tax on dividends paid by the company out of income or profits liable to corporate income tax. In countries with such systems,[13] part of the tax on the company's profits is available

to provide relief against the shareholders' own tax liability. The relief to the shareholder takes the form of a tax credit, the amount of which may be less than, equal to, or more than the shareholder's overall tax liability. If the tax credit exceeds this tax liability the excess may be payable to the shareholder. As this type of tax credit is an integral part of the imputation system of corporate income tax, any payment to the shareholders is treated as a repayment of tax and not as expenditure (compare the treatment of other tax credits described in §26).

38. As the tax credit under imputation systems (even when exceeding tax liability) is to be regarded as a tax provision, the question arises whether it should be deducted from individual income tax receipts (1110) or corporate income tax receipts (1210). In this Report, the full amount of corporate income tax paid is shown under 1210 and no imputed tax is included under 1110. Thus, the full amount of the credit reduces the amount of 1110 whether the credit results in a reduction of personal income tax liability or whether an actual refund is made because the credit exceeds the income tax liability. (Where, however, such tax credits are deducted from corporation tax in respect of dividends paid to corporations the amounts are deducted from the receipts of 1210).

1120 and 1220 — Taxes on capital gains

39. These sub-headings comprise taxes imposed on capital gains, 1120 covering those levied on the gains of individuals and 1220 those levied on the gains of corporate enterprises, where receipts from such taxes can be separately identified. In many countries, this is not the case and the receipts from such taxes are then classified with those from the income tax. Heading 1120 also includes taxes on gains from gambling.

2000 — Social security contributions

40. Classified here are all compulsory payments to general government that confer an entitlement to receive a (contingent) future social benefit. Such payments are usually earmarked to finance social benefits and are often paid to institutions of general government that provide such benefits. However, such earmarking is not part of the definition of social security contributions and is not required for a tax to be classified here. However, conferment of an entitlement is required for a tax to be classified under this heading. So, levies on income or payroll that are earmarked for social security funds but do not confer an entitlement to benefit are excluded from this heading and shown under personal income taxes (1100) or taxes on payroll and workforce (3000). Taxes on other bases, such as goods and services, which are earmarked for social security benefits are not shown here but are classified according to their respective bases because they generally confer no entitlement to social security benefits.

41. Contributions for the following types of social security benefits would, *inter alia*, be included: unemployment insurance benefits and supplements, accident, injury and sickness benefits, old-age, disability and survivors' pensions, family allowances, reimbursements for medical and hospital expenses or provision of hospital or medical services. Contributions may be levied on both employees and employers.

42. Contributions may be based on earnings or payroll ('on a payroll basis') or on net income after deductions and exemptions for personal circumstances ('on an income tax basis'), and the revenues from the two bases should be separately identified if possible. However, where contributions to a general social security scheme are on a payroll basis, but the contributions of particular groups (such as the self-employed) cannot be assessed on this basis and net income is used as a proxy for gross earnings, the receipts may still be classified as being on a payroll basis. In principle, this heading excludes voluntary contributions paid to social security schemes. When separately identifiable these are shown in the memorandum item on the financing of social security benefits. In practice, however, they cannot always be separately identified from compulsory contributions, in which case they are included in this heading.

43. Contributions to social insurance schemes which are not institutions of general government and to other types of insurance schemes, provident funds, pension funds, friendly societies or other saving schemes are not considered as social security contributions. Provident funds are arrangements under which the contributions of each employee and of the corresponding employer on his/her behalf are kept in a separate account earning interest and withdrawable under specific circumstances. Pension funds are separately organised schemes negotiated between employees and employers and carry provisions for different contributions and benefits, sometimes more directly tied to salary levels and length of service than under social security schemes. When contributions to these schemes are compulsory or quasi-compulsory (e.g., by virtue of agreement with professional and union organisations) they are shown in the memorandum item (refer to Table 5.39 of the Report).

44. Contributions by government employees and by governments in respect of their employees, to social security schemes classified within general government are included in this heading. Contributions to separate schemes for government employees, which can be regarded as replacing general social security schemes, are also regarded as taxes.[14] Where, however, a separate scheme is not seen as replacing a general scheme and has been negotiated between the government, in its role as an employer, and its employees, it is not regarded as social security and contributions to it are not regarded as taxes, even though the scheme may have been established by legislation.

45. This heading excludes 'imputed' contributions, which correspond to social benefits paid directly by employers to their employees or former employees or to their representatives (e.g., when employers are legally obliged to pay sickness benefits for a certain period).

46. Contributions are divided into those of employees (2100), employers (2200), and self-employed or non-employed (2300), and then further sub-divided according to the basis on which they are levied. Employees are defined for this purpose as all persons engaged in activities of business units, government bodies, private non-profit institutions, or other paid employment, except the proprietors and their unpaid family members in the case of unincorporated businesses. Members of the armed forces are included, irrespective of the duration and type of their service, if they contribute to social security schemes. The contributions of employers are defined as their payments on account of their employees to social security schemes. Where employees or employers are required to continue the payment of social security contributions when the employee becomes unemployed these contributions, data permitting, are shown in 2100 and 2200 respectively. Accordingly, the sub-heading 2300 is confined to contributions paid by the self-employed and by those outside of the labour force (e.g., disabled or retired individuals).

3000 — Taxes on payroll and workforce

47. These consist of taxes payable by enterprises assessed either as a proportion of the wages or salaries paid or as a fixed amount per person employed. They do not include compulsory social security contributions paid by employers or any taxes paid by employees themselves out of their wages or salaries

4000 — Taxes on property

48. This heading covers recurrent and non-recurrent taxes on the use, ownership or transfer of property. These include taxes on immovable property or net wealth, taxes on the change of ownership of property through inheritance or gift and taxes on financial and capital transactions. The following kinds of tax are excluded from this heading:

- *a)* taxes on capital gains resulting from the sale of a property (1120 or 1220);
- *b)* taxes on the use of goods or on permission to use goods or perform activities (5200); see §78;

c) taxes on immovable property levied on the basis of a presumed net income which take into account the personal circumstances of the taxpayer. They are classified as income taxes along with taxes on income and capital gains derived from property (1100);

d) taxes on the use of property for residence, where the tax is payable by either proprietor or tenant and the amount payable is a function of the user's personal circumstances (pay, dependants, and so on). They are classified as taxes on income (1100);

e) taxes on building in excess of permitted maximum density, taxes on the enlargement, construction or alteration of certain buildings beyond a permitted value and taxes on building construction. They are classified as taxes on permission to perform activities (5200);

f) taxes on the use of one's own property for special trading purposes like selling alcohol, tobacco, meat or for exploitation of land resources (e.g., United States severance taxes). They are classified as taxes on permission to perform activities (5200).

4100 — Recurrent taxes on immovable property

49. This sub-heading covers taxes levied regularly in respect of the use or ownership of immovable property.

- these taxes are levied on land and buildings;
- they can be in the form of a percentage of an assessed property value based on a national rental income, sales price, or capitalised yield; or in terms of other characteristics of real property, (for example size or location) from which a presumed rent or capital value can be derived.
- such taxes can be levied on proprietors, tenants, or both. They can also be paid by one level of government to another level of government in respect of property under the jurisdiction of the latter.
- debts are not taken into account in the assessment of these taxes, and they differ from taxes on net wealth in this respect.

50. Taxes on immovable property are further sub-divided into those paid by households (4110) and those paid by other entities (4120), according to the criteria set out in §31(*b*) above.

4200 — Recurrent taxes on net wealth

51. This sub-heading covers taxes levied regularly (in most cases annually) on net wealth, i.e. taxes on a wide range of movable and immovable property, net of debt. It is sub-divided into taxes paid by individuals (4210) and taxes paid by corporate enterprises (4220) according to the criteria set out in §31(*a*) above. If separate figures exist for receipts paid by institutions, the tax payments involved are added to those paid by corporations.

4300 — Estate, inheritance and gift taxes

52. This sub-heading is divided into taxes on estates and inheritances (4310) and taxes on gifts (4320).[15] Estate taxes are charged on the amount of the total estate whereas inheritance taxes are charged on the shares of the individual recipients; in addition the latter may take into account the relationship of the individual recipients to the deceased.

4400 — Taxes on financial and capital transactions

53. This sub-heading comprises, *inter alia*, taxes on the issue, transfer, purchase and sale of non-financial and financial assets (including foreign exchange or securities), taxes on cheques and other forms of payment, and taxes levied on specific legal transactions such as validation of contracts and the sale of immovable property. The heading does not include:

a) taxes on the use of goods or property or permission to perform certain activities (5200);

b) fees paid to cover court charges, charges for birth, marriage or death certificates, which are normally regarded as non-tax revenues (see §12);

c) taxes on capital gains (1000);

d) recurrent taxes on immovable property (4100);

e) recurrent taxes on net wealth (4200);

f) once-and-for-all levies on property or wealth (4500);

g) stamp taxes not related to financial and capital transactions

   i. Stamp taxes on the sale of specific products, such as alcoholic beverages or tobacco (5121);

   ii. Stamp taxes restricted by law to imported products (5123) or to exported products (5124); or

   iii. Stamp taxes not falling exclusively on a single category of transaction (6000).

4500 — Other non-recurrent taxes on property

54. This sub-heading covers once-and-for-all, as distinct from recurrent, levies on property. It is divided into taxes on net wealth (4510) and other non-recurrent taxes on property (4520). Heading 4510 would include taxes levied to meet emergency expenditures, or for redistribution purposes. Heading 4520 would cover taxes levied to take account of increases in land value due to permission given to develop or provision of additional local facilities by general government, any taxes on the revaluation of capital and once-and-for-all taxes on particular items of property.

4600 — Other recurrent taxes on property

55. These rarely exist in OECD member countries, but the heading would include taxes on goods such as cattle, jewellery, windows, and other external signs of wealth.

5000 — Taxes on goods and services

56. All taxes and duties levied on the production, extraction, sale, transfer, leasing or delivery of goods, and the rendering of services (5100), or in respect of the use of goods or permission to use goods or to perform activities (5200) are included here. The heading thus covers:

a) multi-stage cumulative taxes;

b) general sales taxes — whether levied at manufacture/production, wholesale or retail level;

c) value-added taxes;

d) excises;

e) taxes levied on the import and export of goods;

f) taxes levied in respect of the use of goods and taxes on permission to use goods, or perform certain activities;

g) taxes on the extraction, processing or production of minerals and other products.

57. Borderline cases between this heading and heading 4000 (taxes on property) and 6100 (other taxes on business) are referred to in §48, §53 and §80. Residual sub-headings (5300) and (5130) cover tax receipts which cannot be allocated between 5100 and 5200 and between 5110 and 5120, respectively; see §33.

5100 — Taxes on the production, sale, transfer, leasing and delivery of goods and rendering of services

58. This sub-heading consists of all taxes, levied on transactions in goods and services on the basis of their intrinsic characteristics (e.g., value, weight of tobacco, strength of alcohol, and so on) as distinct from taxes imposed on the use of goods, or permission to use goods or perform activities, which fall under 5200.

5110 — General taxes on goods and services

59. This sub-heading includes all taxes, other than import and export duties (5123 and 5124), levied on the production, leasing, transfer, delivery or sales of a wide range of goods and/or the rendering of a wide range of services, irrespective of whether they are domestically produced or imported and irrespective of the stage of production or distribution at which they are levied. It thus covers value-added taxes, sales taxes and multi-stage cumulative taxes. Receipts from border adjustments in respect of such taxes when goods are imported are added to gross receipts for this category, and repayments of such taxes when goods are exported are deducted. These taxes are subdivided into 5111 value-added taxes, 5112 sales taxes, 5113 turnover and other general taxes on goods and services.

60. Borderline cases arise between this heading and taxes on specific goods (5120) when taxes are levied on a large number of goods, for example, the United Kingdom purchase tax (repealed in 1973) and the Japanese commodity tax (repealed in 1988). In conformity with national views, the former United Kingdom purchase tax is classified as a general tax (5112) and the former Japanese commodity tax as excises (5121).

5111 — Value-added taxes

61. All general consumption taxes charged on value-added are classified in this sub-heading, irrespective of the method of deduction and the stages at which the taxes are levied. In practice, all OECD countries with value-added taxes normally allow immediate deduction of taxes on purchases by all but the final consumer and impose tax at all stages. In some countries the heading may include certain taxes, such as those on financial and insurance activities, either because receipts from them cannot be identified separately from those from the value-added tax, or because they are regarded as an integral part of the value-added tax, even though similar taxes in other countries might be classified elsewhere (e.g., 5126 as taxes on services or 4400 as taxes on financial and capital transactions).

5112 — Sales taxes

62. All general taxes levied at one stage only, whether at manufacturing or production, wholesale or retail stage are classified here.

5113 — Turnover and other general taxes on goods and services

63. These are multi-stage cumulative taxes and taxes where elements of consumption taxes are combined with multistage taxes. These taxes are levied each time a transaction takes place without deduction for taxes paid on inputs. Multi-stage taxes can be combined with elements of value-added or sales taxes.

5120 — Taxes on specific goods and services

64. Excises, profits generated and transferred from fiscal monopolies, and customs and imports duties as well as taxes on exports, foreign exchange transactions, investment goods and betting stakes and special taxes on services, which do not form part of a general tax of 5110, are included in this category.

5121 — Excises

65. Excises are taxes levied as a product specific unit tax on a predefined limited range of goods. Excises are usually levied at differentiated rates on nonessential or luxury goods, alcoholic beverages, tobacco, and energy. Excises may be imposed at any stage of production or distribution and are usually assessed as a specific charge per unit based on characteristics by reference to the value, weight, strength, or quantity of the product. Included are special taxes on individual products such as sugar, sugar beets, matches, and chocolates; taxes levied at varying rates on a certain range of goods; and taxes levied on tobacco goods, alcoholic drinks, motor fuels, and hydrocarbon oils. If a tax collected principally on imported goods also applies, or would apply, under the same law to comparable domestically produced goods, then the revenue from this tax is classified as arising from excises rather than from import duties. This principle applies even if there is no comparable domestic production or no possibility of such production. Taxes on the use of utilities such as water, electricity, gas, and energy are regarded as excises rather than taxes on specific services (5126). Excises exclude those taxes that are levied as general taxes on goods and services (5110); profits of fiscal monopolies (5122); customs and other import duties (5123); or taxes on exports (5124).

5122 — Profits of fiscal monopolies

66. This sub-heading covers that part of the profits of fiscal monopolies which is transferred to general government or which is used to finance any expenditures considered to be government expenditures (see §24). Amounts are shown when they are transferred to general government or used to make expenditures considered to be government expenditures.

67. Fiscal monopolies reflect the exercise of the taxing power of government by the use of monopoly powers. Fiscal monopolies are non-financial public enterprises exercising a monopoly in most cases over the production or distribution of tobacco, alcoholic beverages, salt, matches, playing cards and petroleum or agricultural products (i.e. on the kind of products which are likely to be, alternatively or additionally, subject to the excises of 5121), to raise the government revenues which in other countries are gathered through taxes on dealings in such commodities by private business units. The government monopoly may be at the production stage or, as in the case of government-owned and controlled liquor stores, at the distribution stage.

68. Fiscal monopolies are distinguished from public utilities such as rail transport, electricity, post offices, and other communications, which may enjoy a monopoly or quasi-monopoly position but where the primary purpose is normally to provide basic services rather than to raise revenue for government. Transfers from such other public enterprises to the government are considered as non-tax revenues. The traditional concept of fiscal monopoly is not generally extended to include state lotteries, the profits of which are usually accordingly regarded as non-tax revenues. However, they can be included as tax revenues if the prime reason for their operation is to raise revenues to finance government expenditure. Fiscal monopoly profits are distinguished from export and import monopoly profits (5127) transferred from marketing boards or other enterprises dealing with international trade.

5123 — Customs and other import duties

69. Taxes, stamp duties and surcharges restricted by law to imported products are included here. Also included are levies on imported agricultural products which are imposed in member countries of the European Union and amounts paid by certain of these countries under the Monetary Compensation Accounts (MCA) system.[16] Customs duties collected by European Union member states on behalf of the European Union are reported under this heading at the supranational level of government in the country tables (in Chapter 5 of the Report). Excluded here are taxes collected on imports as part of a general tax on goods and services, or an excise applicable to both imported and domestically produced goods.

5124 — Taxes on exports

70. In the 1970s, export duties were levied in Australia, Canada and Portugal as a regular measure and they have been used in Finland for counter-cyclical purposes. Some member countries of the European Union pay, as part of the MCA system, a levy on exports (see note 16 to §69). Where these amounts are identifiable, they are shown in this heading. This heading does not include repayments of general consumption taxes or excises or customs duties on exported goods, which should be deducted from the gross receipts under 5110, 5121 or 5123, as appropriate.

5125 — Taxes on investment goods

71. This sub-heading covers taxes on investment goods, such as machinery. These taxes may be imposed for a number of years or temporarily for counter-cyclical purposes. Taxes on industrial inputs which are also levied on consumers [e.g., the Swedish energy tax which is classified under (5121)] are not included here.

5126 — Taxes on specific services

72. All taxes assessed on the payment for specific services, such as taxes on insurance premiums, banking services, gambling and betting stakes (e.g., from horse races, football pools, lottery tickets), transport, entertainment, restaurant and advertising charges, fall into this category. Taxes on entry to casinos, races, other similar events or venues as well as stamp taxes on specific services are also classified under this heading. Taxes levied on the gross income of companies providing a specific service (e.g. transportation [including airport and other passenger taxes] insurance, banking, entertainment, restaurants, and advertising) are also classified under this heading.

73. Tax revenues from bank levies and payments to deposit insurance and financial stability schemes are also included here:

- Compulsory payments of stability fees, bank levies and deposit insurance should generally be treated as tax revenues where the payments are made to general government or supranational authorities and are allocated to the governments' consolidated or general funds so that the government is free to make immediate use of the money for the purposes that it chooses. This principle would apply regardless of whether the government is promising to make payments to guarantee the banks' customer deposits in some future contingency.
- If the compulsory payments are made to general government and placed in funds that are earmarked to be entirely channelled back to the sector of the economy that comprises the companies that are subject to the payment, they would still generally be treated as tax revenues on the grounds that the funds would be available for the government and would reduce its budget deficit, the fee is unrequited for an individual entity and the amounts raised could be unrelated to any eventual pay out to depositors or expenditure on wider support for the financial sector.

- Payments to made to the smaller long-standing schemes for insuring 'retail' deposits, where the payment levels are consistent with the costs of insurance should be classified as fee for service.
- Any payments which involve governments realising the assets of a failed institution or receiving a priority claim on its assets in liquidation in order to fund payments of compensation to customers for their lost deposits would be treated as a fee for a service as opposed to tax revenues.
- Compulsory payments that are made to funds operated outside the government sector and non-state institutions backed by the deposit takers and all payments to voluntary schemes should not be treated as tax revenues.
- Contributions made to the EU Single Resolution Fund are also included here and recorded under the supranational level of government in the country tables.

74. Excluded from this sub-heading are:

a) taxes on services forming part of a general tax on goods and services (5110);

b) taxes on electricity, gas and energy (5121 as excises);

c) taxes on individual gains from gambling (1120 as taxes on capital gains of individuals and non-corporate enterprises) and lump-sum taxes on the transfer of private lotteries or on the permission to set up lotteries (5200);[17]

d) taxes on cheques and on the issue, transfer or redemption of securities (4400 as taxes on financial and capital transactions);

e) general taxes on turnover (5113).

5127 — Other taxes on international trade and transactions

75. This sub-heading covers revenue received by the government from the purchase and sale of foreign exchange at different rates. When the government exercises monopoly powers to extract a margin between the purchase and sales price of foreign exchange, other than to cover administrative costs, the revenue derived constitutes a compulsory levy exacted in indeterminate proportions from both purchaser and seller of foreign exchange. It is the common equivalent of an import duty and export duty levied in a single exchange rate system or of a tax on the sale or purchase of foreign exchange. Like the profits of fiscal monopolies and import or export monopolies transferred to government, it represents the exercise of monopoly powers for tax purposes and is included in tax revenues.

76. The sub-heading covers also the profits of export or import monopolies, which do not however exist in OECD countries, taxes on purchase or sale of foreign exchange, and any other taxes levied specifically on international trade or transactions.

5128 — Other taxes on specific goods and services

77. This item includes taxes on the extraction of minerals, fossil fuels and other exhaustible resources from deposits owned privately or by another government together with any other unallocable receipts from taxes on specific goods and services. Taxes on the extraction of exhaustible resources are usually a fixed amount per unit of quality or weight, but can be a percentage of value. The taxes are recorded when the resources are extracted. Payments from the extraction of exhaustible resources from deposits owned by the government unit receiving the payment are classified as rent.

5200 — Taxes on use of goods or on permission to use goods or perform activities

78. This sub-heading covers taxes which are levied in respect of the use of goods as distinct from taxes on the goods themselves. Unlike the latter taxes – reported under 5100 –, they are not assessed on the value of the goods but usually as fixed amounts. Taxes on permission to use goods or to perform activities are also included here, as are pollution taxes not based upon the value of particular goods. It is

sometimes difficult to distinguish between compulsory user charges and licence fees which are regarded as taxes and those which are excluded as non-tax revenues. The criteria which are employed are noted in §12–13.

79. Although the sub-heading refers to the 'use' of goods, registration of ownership rather than use may be what generates liability to tax, so that the taxes of this heading may apply to the ownership of animals or goods rather than their use (e.g., race horses, dogs and motor vehicles) and may apply even to unusable goods (e.g., unusable motor vehicles or guns).

80. Borderline cases arise with:

a) taxes on the permission to perform business activities which are levied on a combined income, payroll or turnover base and, accordingly, are classified following the rules in §84;

b) taxes on the ownership or use of property of headings 4100, 4200 and 4600. The heading 4100 is confined to taxes on the ownership or tenancy of immovable property and – unlike the taxes of 5200 – they are related to the value of the property. The net wealth taxes and taxes on chattels of 4200 and 4600 respectively are confined to the ownership rather than the use of assets, apply to groups of assets rather than particular goods and again are related to the value of the assets,

5210 — Recurrent taxes on use of goods and on permission to use goods or perform activities

81. The principal characteristic of taxes classified here is that they are levied at regular intervals and that they are usually fixed amounts. The most important item in terms of revenue receipts is vehicle licence taxes. This sub-heading also covers taxes on permission to hunt, shoot, fish or to sell certain products and taxes on the ownership of dogs and on the performance of certain services, provided that they meet the criteria set out in §12–13. The sub-divisions of 5210 are:

- user taxes on motor vehicles paid by households (5211);
- taxes on motor vehicles paid by others (5212); and
- other recurrent taxes (5213). This sub-heading covers business and professional licences paid by enterprises in order to obtain a licence to carry on a particular kind of business or profession when the levies are on a recurring basis. Licences such as taxi and casino licences are included. Dog licences and recurrent general licences for hunting, shooting and fishing where the right to carry out these activities is not granted as part of a normal commercial transaction are also included under this heading.

82. Excluded from sub-heading 5213 are:

a) licences where the right to carry out such activities is granted as part of a normal commercial transaction (e.g., the granting of the licence is accompanied by the right to use a specific area which is owned by government);

b) payments relating to the checks carried out by the government on the suitability and or safety of the business premises or equipment, or on the quality or standard of goods or services produced as a condition for granting such a licence. These payments are not unrequited and should be treated as payments for services rendered, unless the amounts charged for the licences are out of all proportion to the costs of the checks carried out by governments.

5220 — Non-recurrent taxes on use of goods and on permission to use goods or perform activities

83. This section covers non-recurrent taxes levied on the use of goods or on permission to use goods or perform activities and taxes levied each time goods are used. It includes taxes levied on the emission or discharge into the environment of noxious gases, liquids or other harmful substances.

- Payments for tradable emission permits issued by governments under cap and trade schemes should be recorded here at the time the emissions occur. No revenue should be recorded for permits that governments issue free of charge. The accrual basis of recording means that there can be a timing difference between the cash being received by government for the permits and the time the emission occurs. In the national accounts, this timing gives rise to a financial liability for government during the period.
- Payments made for the collection and disposal of waste or noxious substances by public authorities should be excluded as they constitute a sale of services to enterprises.

84. Other taxes falling under heading 5200 that are not levied recurrently are also included here. Thus, once-and-for-all payments for permission to sell liquor or tobacco or to set up betting shops are included provided they meet the criteria set out in §12–13.

6000 — Other taxes

85. Taxes levied on a base, or bases, other than those described under headings 1000, 3000, 4000 and 5000, or on bases of which cannot be considered to be related to any one of these headings, are included here. Where taxes are levied on a multiple base and it is possible to estimate the receipts related to each base the separate amounts are included under the appropriate headings. If separate amounts cannot be estimated and it is known that most of the receipts are derived from one base, the whole of the receipts are classified according to that base. Otherwise, they are classified here. Other revenues included here are presumptive taxes not included elsewhere in the classification system, taxes on individuals in the form of a poll tax or capitation tax, stamp taxes not related to financial and capital transactions nor falling exclusively on a single category of transaction, expenditure taxes where personal deductions or exemptions are applied and unidentifiable tax receipts. A subdivision is made between taxes levied wholly or predominantly on business (6100) and those levied on others (6200).

A.6 Conciliation with National Accounts

86. This section of the tables provides a re-conciliation between the OECD calculation of total tax revenues and the total of all taxes and social contributions paid to general government as recorded in the country's National Accounts. Where the country is a member of the European Union (EU), the comparison is between the OECD calculation of total tax revenues and the sum of tax revenues and social contributions recorded in the combination of the general government and the institutions of the EU sectors of the National Accounts.

A.7 Memorandum item on the financing of social security benefits

87. In view of the varying relationship between taxation and social security contributions and the cases referred to in §40 to §46, a memorandum item collects together all payments earmarked for social security-type benefits, other than voluntary payments to the private sector. Data are presented as follows (refer Table 5.39 of the Report):

a) Taxes of 2000 series.

b) Taxes earmarked for social security benefits.

c) Voluntary contributions to the government.

d) Compulsory contributions to the private sector.

Guidance on the breakdown of (a) to (d) above is provided in §40 to §46.

A.8 Memorandum item on identifiable taxes paid by government

88. Identifiable taxes actually paid by government are presented in a memorandum item classified by the main headings of the OECD classification of taxes. In the vast majority of countries, only social security contributions and payroll taxes paid by government can be identified. These are, however, usually the most important taxes paid by governments (refer to Table 5.40 of the Report).

A.9 Relation of OECD classification of taxes to national accounting systems

89. A system of national accounts (SNA) seeks to provide a coherent framework for recording and presenting the main flows relating respectively to production, consumption, accumulation and external transactions of a given economic area, usually a country or a major region within a country. Government revenues are an important part of the transactions recorded in SNA. The final version of the 2008 SNA was jointly published by five international organisations: the United Nations, the International Monetary Fund, the European Union, the Organisation for Economic Co-operation and Development, and the World Bank in August 2009. The *System* is a comprehensive, consistent and flexible set of macroeconomic accounts. It is designed for use in countries with market economies, whatever their stage of economic development, and also in countries in transition to market economies. The important parts of the SNA's conceptual framework and its definitions of the various sectors of the economy have been reflected in the OECD's classification of taxes.

90. There are, however, some differences between the OECD classification of taxes and SNA concepts that are listed below. They arise because the aim of the former is to provide the maximum disaggregation of statistical data on what are generally regarded as taxes by tax administrations.

a) OECD includes compulsory social security contributions paid to general government in total tax revenues. Imputed and voluntary contributions plus those paid to private funds are not treated as taxes (§9 and §11 above);

b) there are different points of view on whether or not some levies and fees are classified as taxes (§12 and §13 above);

c) OECD excludes imputed taxes or subsidies resulting from the operation of official multiple exchange rates or from the central bank paying a rate of interest on required reserves that is different from other market rates;

d) there are differences in the treatment of non-wastable tax credits

91. As noted in §1 and §2, headings 1000 to 6000 of the OECD list of taxes cover all unrequited payments to general government or to a supranational authority, other than compulsory loans and fines. Such unrequited payments including fines, but excluding compulsory loans can be obtained from adding together the following figures in the 2008 SNA

- value-added type taxes (D.211);
- taxes and duties on imports, excluding VAT (D.212);
- export taxes (D.213);
- taxes on products, excluding VAT, import and export taxes (D.214);

- other taxes on production (D.29);
- taxes on income (D.51);
- other current taxes (D.59);
- actual social contributions (D.611 and D613), excluding voluntary contributions and payments to employment-related schemes that are not social security schemes
- capital taxes (D.91).

A.10 The OECD classification of taxes and the International Monetary Fund (GFS) system

92. The coverage and valuation of tax revenues in the GFS system and the 2008 SNA are very similar. Therefore, the differences between the OECD classification and that of the 2008 SNA (see §90 above) also apply to the GFS. In addition, the International Monetary Fund subdivides the OECD 5000 heading into section IV (Domestic Taxes on Goods and Services) and section V (Taxes on International Trade and Transactions). This reflects the fact that while the latter usually yield insignificant amounts of revenue in OECD countries, this is not the case in many non-OECD countries.

A.11 Comparison of the OECD classification of taxes with other international classifications

93. The table below describes an item by item comparison of the OECD classification of taxes and the classifications used in the following:

a) System of National Accounts (2008 SNA);

b) European System of Accounts (2010 ESA);

c) IMF Government Finance Statistics Manual (GFSM2014).

94. These comparisons represent those that would be expected to apply in the majority of cases. However in practice some flexibility should be used in their application. This is because in particular cases, countries can adopt varying approaches to the classification of revenues in National Accounts.

OECD Classification				2008 SNA	2010 ESA	GFSM2014
1000			Taxes on income, profits and capital gains			
	1100		Individuals			
		1110	Income and profits	D51-8.61a	D51A	1111
		1120	Capital gains	D51-8.61c, d	D51C, D	1111
	1200		Corporations			
		1210	Income and profits	D51-8.61b	D51B	1112
		1220	Capital gains	D51-8.61c	D51C	1112
	1300		Unallocable as between 1100 and 1200			1113
2000			Social security contributions			
	2100		Employees	D613-8.85	D613	1211
	2200		Employers	D611-8.83	D611	1212
	2300		Self-employed, non-employed	D613-8.85	D613	1213
	2400		Unallocable as between 2100, 2200 and 2300			1214
3000			Taxes on payroll and workforce	D29-7.97a	D29C	112
4000			Taxes on property			
	4100		Recurrent taxes on immovable property			

		4110		Households	D59-8.63a	D59A	1131
		4120		Other	D29-7.97b	D29A	1131
	4200			Recurrent net wealth taxes			
		4210		Individual	D59-8.63b	D59A	1132
		4220		Corporations	D59-8.63b	D59A	1132
	4300			Estate, inheritance and gift taxes			
		4310		Estate and inheritance taxes	D91-10.207b	D91A	1133
		4320		Gift taxes	D91-10.207b	D91A	1133
	4400			Taxes on financial and capital transactions	D59-7.96d; D29-7.97e	D214B, C	114114; 1161
	4500			Other non-recurrent taxes on property	D91-10.207a	D91B	1135
	4600			Other recurrent taxes on property	D59-8.63c	D59A	1136
5000				Taxes on goods and services			
	5100			Taxes on production, sale and transfer of goods and services			
		5110		General taxes on goods and services			
			5111	Value-added taxes	D211-7.89	D211; D29G	11411
			5112	Sales taxes	D2122-7.94a; D214-7.96a	D21224; D214I	11412
			5113	Turnover and other general taxes on goods and services	D214-7.96a	D214I	11413
		5120		Taxes on specific goods and services			
			5121	Excises	D2122-7.94b; D214-7.96b	D21223; D214A, B, D	1142
			5122	Profits of fiscal monopolies	D214-7.96e	D214J	1143
			5123	Customs and other import duties	D2121-7.93	D2121; D21221, 2	1151
			5124	On exports	D213-7.95a	D214K	1152-4
			5125	On investment goods			
			5126	On specific services	D2122-7.94c; D214-7.96c	D21225; D214E, F, G, H; D29F	1144; 1156
			5127	Other taxes on international trade and transactions	D2122-7.94d D29-7.95b D29-7.97g D59-8.64d	D21226; D29D; D59E	1153; 1155-6
			5128	Other taxes on specific goods and services			1146
		5130		Unallocable between 5110 and 5120			
	5200			Taxes on use of goods and on permission to use goods or perform activities			
		5210		Recurrent taxes on use of goods and on permission to use goods or perform activities			
			5211	Motor vehicle taxes households	D59-8.64c	D59D	11451
			5212	Motor vehicles taxes others	D29-7.97d	D214D; D29B	11451
			5213	Other recurrent taxes on use of goods and on permission to use goods or perform activities	D29-7.97c, d, f D59-8.64c	D29B, E, F; D59D	11452
		5220		Non-recurrent taxes on permission to use goods or perform activities			11452
	5300			Unallocable as between 5100 and 5200			
6000				Other taxes			
	6100			Payable solely by business			1161
	6200			Payable by other than business, or unidentifiable	D59-8.64a, b	D59B, C	1162

A.12 Attribution of tax revenues by sub-sectors of general government

95. The OECD classification requires a breakdown of tax revenues by sub-sectors of government. The definition of each sub-sector and the criteria to be used to attribute tax revenues between these sub-sectors are set out below. They follow the guidance of the 2008 SNA and GFSM 2014.

Sub-sectors of general government to be identified

a) Central government

96. The central government sub-sector includes all governmental departments, offices, establishments and other bodies which are agencies or instruments of the central authority whose competence extends over the whole territory, with the exception of the administration of social security funds. Central government therefore has the authority to impose taxes on all resident and non-resident units engaged in economic activities within the country.

b) State, provincial or regional government

97. This sub-sector consists of intermediate units of government exercising a competence at a level below that of central government. It includes all such units operating independently of central government in a part of a country's territory encompassing a number of smaller localities, with the exception of the administration of social security funds. In unitary countries, regional governments may be considered to have a separate existence where they have substantial autonomy to raise a significant proportion of their revenues from sources within their control and their officers are independent of external administrative control in the actual operation of the unit's activities.

98. At present, federal countries comprise the majority of cases where revenues attributed to intermediate units of government are identified separately. Colombia and Spain are the only two unitary countries in this position. In the remaining unitary countries, regional revenues are included with those of local governments.

c) *Local* government

99. This sub-sector includes all other units of government exercising an independent competence in part of the territory of a country, with the exception of the administration of social security funds. It encompasses various urban and/or rural jurisdictions (e.g., local authorities, municipalities, cities, boroughs, districts).

d) Social security funds

100. Social security funds form a separate sub-sector of general government. The social security sub-sector is defined in the 2008 SNA by the following extracts from paragraphs 4.124 to 4.126 and 4.147:

"Social security schemes are social insurance schemes covering the community as a whole or large section of the community that are imposed and controlled by government units. The schemes cover a wide variety of programmes, providing benefits in cash or in kind for old age, invalidity or death, survivors, sickness and maternity, work injury, unemployment, family allowance, health care, etc. There is not necessarily a direct link between the amount of the contribution paid by an individual and the benefits he or she may receive." (Paragraph 4.124).

"When social security schemes are separately organised from the other activities of government units and hold their assets and liabilities separately from the latter and engage in financial transactions on their own account they qualify as institutional units that are described as social security funds." (Paragraph 4.125).

"The amounts raised, and paid out, in social security contributions and benefits may be deliberately varied in order to achieve objectives of government policy that have no direct connection with the concept of social security as a scheme to provide social benefits to members of the community. They may be raised or lowered in order to influence the level of aggregate demand in the economy, for example. Nevertheless, so long as they remain separately constituted funds, they must be treated as separate institutional units in the SNA. (Paragraph 4.126).

"The social security funds sub-sector (of general government) consists of the social security funds operating at all levels of government. Such funds are social insurance schemes covering the community as a whole or large section of the community that are imposed by government units." (Paragraph 4.147).

101. This definition of social security funds is followed in the OECD classification with the two following exceptions which are excluded

- Schemes imposed by government and operated by bodies outside the general government sector, as defined in §3 of this manual; and
- Schemes to which all contributions are voluntary.

Supranational Authorities

102. This sub-sector covers the revenue-raising operations of supra-national authorities within a country. In practice, the only relevant supranational authority in the OECD area is that of the institutions of the European Union (EU). Tax revenues collected by member countries and paid to the EU are included in the *Revenue Statistics* at the supranational level of government. Income taxes and social security contributions collected by European Institutions and paid by European civil servants who are resident of EU member countries should not be included.

Criteria to be used for the attribution of tax revenues

103. When a government collects taxes and pays them over in whole or in part to other governments, it is necessary to determine whether the revenues should be considered to be those of the collecting government which it distributes to others as grants, or those of the beneficiary governments which the collecting government receives and passes on only as their agent. The criteria to be used in the attribution of revenues are set out in §104 to §107 which replicate paragraphs 3.70 to 3.73 from the 2008 SNA.

104. In general, a tax is attributed to the government unit that

a) exercises the authority to impose the tax (either as a principal or through the delegated authority of the principal),

b) has final discretion to set and vary the rate of the tax

105. Where an amount is collected by one government for and on behalf of another government, and the latter government has the authority to impose the tax, and set and vary its rate, then the former is acting as an agent for the latter and the tax is reassigned. Any amount retained by the collecting government as a collection charge should be treated as a payment for a service. Any other amount retained by the collecting government, such as under a tax-sharing arrangement, should be treated as a current grant. If the collecting government was delegated the authority to set and vary the rate, then the amount collected should be treated as tax revenue of this government.

106. Where different governments jointly and equally set the rate of a tax and jointly and equally decide on the distribution of the proceeds, with no individual government having ultimate overriding authority, then the tax revenues are attributed to each government according to its respective share of the proceeds. If an arrangement allows one government unit to exercise ultimate overriding authority, then all of the tax revenue is attributed to that unit.

107. There may also be the circumstance where a tax is imposed under the constitutional or other authority of one government, but other governments individually set the tax rate in their jurisdictions. The proceeds of the tax generated in each respective government's jurisdiction are attributed as tax revenues of that government.

108. The levies paid by the member states of the EU take the form specific levies which include

a) custom duties and levies on agricultural goods (5123),

b) gross monetary compensation accounts (5123 if relating to imports and 5124 if relating to exports);

c) contributions to the Single Resolution Fund (5126); and

d) Steel, coal, sugar and milk levies (5128).

109. The custom duties collected by member states on behalf of the EU are recorded

- on a gross of collection fee basis;
- using figures adjusted so that duties are shown on a 'final destination' as opposed to a 'country of first entry' basis where such adjustments can be made. These adjustments concern in particular duties collected at important (sea) ports. Although the EU duties are collected by the authorities of the country of first entry, when possible these duties should be excluded from the revenue of the collecting country and be included in the revenue of the country of final destination

110. These are the specific EU levies that most clearly conform to the attribution criterion described in §102 above. Consequently, these amounts are footnoted as a memorandum item to the EU member state country tables (in Chapter 5) and are shown as supranational revenues against each of the tax headings identified in §108.

1. All references to SNA are to the 2008 edition.

2. See section A.12 of this guide for a discussion of the concept of agency capacity.

3. It is usually possible to identify amounts of social security contributions and payroll taxes, but not other taxes paid by government.

4. If, however, a levy which is considered as non-tax revenue by most countries is regarded as a tax — or raises substantial revenue — in one or more countries, the amounts collected are footnoted at the end of the relevant country tables, even though the amounts are not included in total tax revenues.

5. Names, however, can frequently be misleading. For example, though a passport fee would normally be considered a non-tax revenue, if a supplementary levy on passports (as is the case in Portugal) were imposed in order to raise substantial amounts of revenue relative to the cost of providing the passport, the levy would be regarded as a tax under 5200.

6. A more detailed explanation of this distinction can be found in the special feature, 'Current issues in reporting tax revenues', in the 2001 edition of *Revenue Statistics*.

7. Sometimes the terms 'non-refundable' and 'refundable' are used, but it may be considered illogical to talk of 'refundable' when nothing has been paid.

8. A different treatment, however, is accorded to non-wastable tax credits under imputation systems of corporate income tax (§37–39).

9. This is not strictly a true tax expenditure in the formal sense. Such tax expenditures require identification of a benchmark tax system for each country or, preferably, a common international benchmark. In practice it has not been possible to reach agreement on a common international benchmark.

10. Unless based on the profit made on a sale, in which case they would be classified as capital gains taxes under 1120 or 1220.

11. In some countries the same legislation applies to both individual and corporate enterprises for particular taxes on income. However, the receipts from such taxes are usually allocable between individuals and enterprises and can therefore be shown in the appropriate sub-heading.

12. For example, "... sufficiently self-contained and independent that they behave in the same way as corporations... (including) keeping a complete set of accounts" (2008 SNA, section 4.44).

13. In Canada — a country also referred to as having an imputation system — the (wastable) tax credit for the shareholder is in respect of domestic corporation tax deemed to have been paid whether or not a corporation tax liability has arisen. As there is no integral connection between the corporation tax liability and the credit given against income tax under such systems, these credits for dividends are treated, along with other tax credits, on the lines described in §26.

14. This may also apply where a scheme for government employees existed prior to the introduction of a general social security scheme.

15. In the 2008 SNA, these are regarded as capital transfers and not as taxes (see section A.8).

16. This is the system by which the European Union adjusts for differences between the exchange rates used to determine prices under the Common Market Agricultural Policy and actual exchange rates. Payments under the system may relate to imports or exports and where these amounts are separately identifiable they are shown under the appropriate heading (5123 or 5124). In this Report, these amounts are shown gross (i.e. without deducting any subsidies paid out under the MCA system).

17. Transfers of profits of State lotteries are regarded as non-tax revenues (see also §68).

ww.ingramcontent.com/pod-product-compliance
tning Source LLC
hersburg PA
61158240926
B00006B/1049